Nova Scotia Immigrants

NOVA SCOTIA
IMMIGRANTS

to
1867

Compiled by
Col. Leonard H. Smith Jr.
(A.U.S. Retired)
M.A. (Genealogy), Certified Genealogist
and
Norma H. Smith

VOLUME II

From Non-Nova Scotia Periodicals and
from Published Diaries and Journals

CLEARFIELD

Reprinted for
Clearfield Company by
Genealogical Publishing Co.
Baltimore, Maryland
2008

ISBN-13: 978-0-8063-0845-6
ISBN-10: 0-8063-0845-1

Made in the United States of America

CONTENTS

	Page
Abbreviations	vi
Preface	vii
Introduction	1
Key	15

Part 1

Immigrants	19
Appendix	
Immigrant Vessels	255
Bibliography	
Publications Screened	257
Articles Abstracted	257

Part 2

Immigrants	263
Appendices	
Immigrant Vessels	293
Other Vessels Named	293
Bibliography	
Diaries and Journals Screened	295

ABBREVIATIONS

Adj.- Adjutant
app. - approximately
b. - born
bap. - baptized
Bn. - Battalion
Brig. - Brigade
ca. - circa (about)
Capt. - Captain
ch. - children
C. of E. - Church of England
Co. - County, Company
Col./Colo. - Colonel
Corp. - Corporal
d. - died
dau. - daughter
Dr. - Doctor
Esq. - Esquire
f. - female
fam. - family
Gen. - General
Gov. - Governor
Jr. - Junior (the younger of two of same name; no necessary relationship)
Lt./Lieut. - Lieutenant
m. - male

Maj. - Major
marr. - married or marriage
Mr. - Mister (title of respect)
Mrs. - Mistress (title of respect, not necessarily a married woman)
N. Britain - North Britain (Scotland)
N.B. - New Brunswick
N.E. - New England
N.S. - Nova Scotia or New Style (calendar)
O.S. - Old Style (calendar)
P.E.I. - Prince Edward Island
Pvt. - Private
R.C. - Roman Catholic
R.N. - Royal Navy
Rev. - Reverend
s. - son(s)
Serj. - Serjeant
Sgt. - Sergeant
Sr. - Senior (the older of two of same name; no necessary relationship)
w. - woman
y. - young
(1st, 2nd, etc.) - Identifiers for persons of same name

PREFACE

This volume is the second in a series designed
to help searchers for Nova Scotia genealogical data,
and results from my own ancestry problems. I am sure
its users will be well aware of the problems in tracing Nova Scotia ancestors, and hope these volumes are
of genuine assistance.

It deals with information abstracted from periodicals published outside Nova Scotia. "We Lived,"
perhaps unfamiliar, is from New Brunswick. Its pagination was somewhat irregular; the page numbers shown
are those resulting from a sequential reassignment of
page numbers. The number of pages published is not
great; it is hoped the pagination will not interfere
with the use of the data.

In the first volume of this series I gave some
detail of the problems I encountered tracing my father's family; he came to the United States in 1883.
His mother, Mary Ann Doyle, who came a few years
later, and whom I knew, was the daughter of Joseph
Doyle and Elizabeth Dousset, both Roman Catholics, but
who were married in the Anglican Church at Digby - for
what reason remains as yet unexplained. Elizabeth
Dousset's mother was Anne Lanoue, the daughter of
Pierre Lanoue and Mary Doane, as is recorded in the
Township Book at Liverpool. It is not clear how they
first met, but Pierre had been a victim of the depor-
tation of the Acadians in 1755. Mary Doane was from
Chatham, Mass., and went to Nova Scotia with her
mother and stepfather in 1760 or 1761. Like many of
the Chatham people, her roots trace to the MAYFLOWER.

Joseph Doyle died a widower in 1851 or 1852,
leaving his daughter Mary Anne, then 15, to the care
of Timothy Deveau and having deeded his property to
that neighbor in return for maintenance until his
death. He left one son, who made his way to San

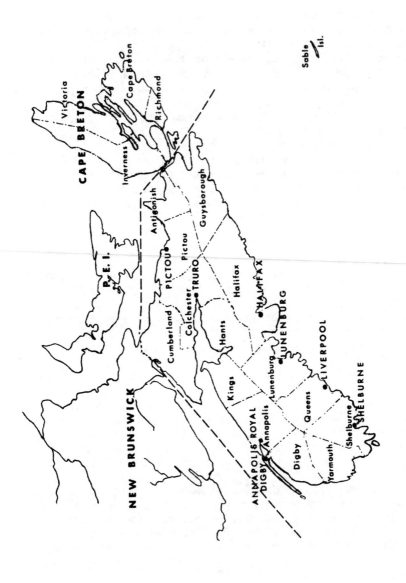

PENINSULAR NOVA SCOTIA

Francisco, where he married, had a child, and died. A potential father could be Edward Doyle, who was present at Sissiboo (now Weymouth) at the proper time, according to Isaiah W. Wilson's *Digby County*. As you might guess, that work is unindexed and there is only one mention of him, which says he came from New Brunswick. No success has been found there, either.

This volume is limited to persons who entered British controlled Nova Scotia prior to the Confederation of Canada in 1867. The geographical area with which it deals is shown on the map opposite this page; it will be noted that the Island of Cape Breton is not included.

Modern computer technologies control the division of words, perhaps rather differently than usually expected. Revision of a line-by-line basis would have involved an inordinate amount of time and effort and greatly delayed this publication. It is therefore hoped that this anomaly will be pardoned.

I trust the inevitable errors will be few in number and not serious.

INTRODUCTION

This volume continues the presentation of finding aids for immigrants to Nova Scotia which began with Volume I in 1992. The first volume identified immigrants reported in selected manuscripts (Part 1) and Nova Scotia periodicals (Part 2). The current volume identifies immigrants reported in selected periodicals published outside Nova Scotia (Part 1) and selected published diaries and journals.

Like the first volume, this continuation makes no pretense of absolute total coverage of the field. It is always possible that additional names may be found in works which are not named in the Appendices listing the sources screened.

The abstracted data are those sufficient to indicate that the named individual did immigrate to Nova Scotia in the time period with which the volume deals; additional data of genealogical interest is frequently to be found in the source.

No one who has worked with the United States censuses of New England can have failed to notice the frequency with which the words "Nova Scotia" appear in the columns headed "Birthplace of Father" and "Birthplace of Mother." It is clear that thousands of the persons enumerated trace their ancestry through that province.

Tracing that ancestry, however, is often no small problem. While no records have been made for the purposes of genealogy, there are many types which can provide bits of information leading to the eventual solution of the identity of an unknown ancestor. Vital records (birth, death, and marriage), land records, probate records, passenger lists, town records, church records are, among others, of help to a person trying to trace a family.

Tracing and documenting the origin of the immigrant who came to Nova Scotia before 1867 is almost always a major task. With the exception of passenger

1

lists and town records, however, the usual sources only rarely offer information as to the former home of an immigrant. The scarcity of those records in early Nova Scotia magnifies the problem.

VITAL RECORDS

The present provincial records of birth, death, and marriage only commenced in 1908. In the negotiations for the confederation of the Canadian provinces, which became effective in 1867, Nova Scotia undertook the maintenance of registers of birth, death, and marriage. The registers start with 1864, but do not approach full coverage until 1867. For a decade more the records are fairly complete, but then, when the federal government failed to take over the program, the province ended it. The registers for that period are accessible on microfilm at the Public Archives of Nova Scotia (P.A.N.S.) at Halifax. Marriage licenses from 1849 to the early 20th Century and surviving marriage bonds back to 1763 are, likewise, there.

LAND RECORDS

Indexes of persons who have received land grants are held by P.A.N.S.; the grant register itself, from which copies may be secured, is located at the Nova Scotia Department of Lands and Forests. These sources may be helpful in identifying the origin of an immigrant, but cannot be depended on to do so. They can be helpful in determining the composition of a grantee's family. Deeds evidencing private transfers of property occasionally identify the origin of the grantee.

PROBATE RECORDS

Probate-court records may possibly offer some help. However, wills and estate administrations rarely disclose the origin of the decedent. Such records are held by County Clerks; some are at P.A.N.S.

TOWNSHIP BOOKS

Those Nova Scotia townships which were established by New Englanders kept records similar to those of New England towns. Early in the life of the township the families were recorded, with birth dates of all children being shown, normally together with the record of the parents' marriage. Once this record was established a chronological record of deaths, births, and marriages followed. These records often show the origin of the immigrant. They should be sought at P.A.N.S.

CHURCH RECORDS

The principal non-governmental record is the parish register kept by the churches. Baptisms, marriages, and burials are recorded there. The availability of the registers to the researcher varies widely. Many have been deposited at P.A.N.S.; most of these are open to the public, but some require written consent of the church authorities. Others are held tightly by church authorities and are found in all sorts of locations. A major difficulty is loss of the records due to fire.

While these registers (other than those of the Baptists, who do not practise infant baptism) supply valid data as to parentage, they rarely offer much in the nature of identifying an immigrant's origin. The registers of the Roman Catholic churches are an exception. Marriage entries in these registers are often endorsed to show the parish in which a contracting party was baptized and a record of the marriage is sent to that parish. Thus, if the marriage entry can be located, the origin may be found.

PASSENGER LISTS

It will be realized that identifying the origin of an immigrant to Nova Scotia can be more of a problem than it might at first seem. Obviously, the apparent solution to the problem of fixing the origin of an immigrant to Nova Scotia is to consult a passenger list; however, such lists were not required until

1865. Some do exist, having been made for other purposes and having escaped destruction or loss. Some,
but not all, of these data have been published. No-
where are the lists assembled in one place. They are
found only with lengthy and often unrewarding search
through literally hundreds of disparate, unalpha-
betized, unindexed, and widely spread sources.

HISTORY

A basic comprehension of the flow of Nova Scotian history is essential to an understanding of the
immigration of people into the region. During long and
bitter rivalries between France and England, this
American territory was an inevitable pawn. A look at
some of the highlights of its turbulent history will
show how its immigration reflects that history. The
list is, of course, far from complete.

Wrested from France, which had established a
temporary settlement in the region as early as 1598
and called the area Acadia, Nova Scotia came into
existence with the granting of the Royal Charter of
September 1621 to Sir William Alexander by James VI of
Scotland, who had become James I of England in 1603.[1]
That charter is written in Latin, which presumably
accounts for the name of the colony and its successor
province taking the Latin, rather than the more pro-
saic English, form: New Scotland. The region covered
by the original grant included the Nova Scotia peninsula, Cape Breton, Price Edward Island, the Magdelen
Islands, present New Brunswick, and the Gaspé peninsula. Contemporary French claims excluded the northern
shore of the Gaspé peninsula from the surrendered
lands.[2] In July 1625 the charter was confirmed to
Alexander by another patent from Charles I of
England.[3]

In 1632 Acadia was restored to France by the
Treaty of St. Germain. Four years later the first
French families arrived at Port Royal on the SAINT
JEHAN. Alexander's colonists were evacuated.[4]

4

FIRST PERMANENT ENGLISH

Port Royal was again taken by the English in 1654. In 1656 Oliver Cromwell granted the portion of Nova Scotia which was then under British control to Charles de St. Etienne, sieur de Latour, Thomas Temple, and William Crowne, and appointed Temple governor.[5] In 1657 Colonel Sir Thomas Temple arrived at Boston on board the SATISFACTION and proceeded on to St. John (now New Brunswick). On board were Pierre Laverdure, his wife Priscilla Mellanson, and their three sons, John, Charles, and Pierre. Twenty years later Laverdure's widow petitioned the Massachusetts General Court for the remission of a bond which she had posted to insure her son John's appearance at a trial for participation in an alleged kidnapping of Indians and their sale as slaves, which bond John had jumped. In the petition she describes herself as an Englishwoman and her late husband as a French Protestant. She, her husband, and her son John had fled to Massachusetts. Charles and Pierre had moved into Port Royal, assumed the surname of Melanson (perhaps to escape religious persecution), and married Catholic girls. They appear to have been the first permanent Nova Scotian settlers of British origin.[6] The French had regained control of the area by the terms of the Treaty of Breda in 1667, which may well have triggered the move of the Laverdures to Boston.[7]

ENGLISH TAKE ACADIA

In September 1710 an expedition of thirty-six vessels left Nantasket, in Boston harbor, with the intent of capturing Port Royal. The French garrison surrendered on October 16; twelve days later the expedition returned to Boston, leaving two hundred marines and two hundred and fifty New England volunteers at Port Royal, then renamed Annapolis Royal.[8] In 1713 Acadia was confirmed to the British by the Treaty of Utrecht. A governing council was formed.[9] English troops took Cape Breton in 1745, but French claims to it were not resolved until it was ceded to France by the Treaty of Aix-la-Chapelle in 1748.[10] It is outside the limits of this study.

FOUNDING OF HALIFAX

France was, of course, concerned about retaining protection for the mouth of the St. Lawrence River, her only access to Quebec and New France. She at once commenced to fortify Louisbourg, posing a threat to Nova Scotia to which the British responded by settling and fortifying Halifax in 1749. Thirteen vessels, with 2,576 passengers, were sent out from England to populate that city.[11] Of these, six hundred and fifty seven families, a total of 1,185 persons, fail to appear on any subsequent list other than the mess list and must be deemed to have moved on, probably to New England.[12]

THE "FOREIGN PROTESTANTS"

In its effort to populate Nova Scotia with non-Catholics, Britain turned an open ear to a proposal to solicit Protestant immigrants from the European continent. In 1752 and 1753 some 2,500 persons, usually called "Foreign Protestants," were sent (in family groups), principally out of Rotterdam, to Halifax. Largely from the many German states, the group included, however, immigrants from France, Switzerland, Holland, Denmark, the Countship of Montbéliard (not yet then a part of France), and perhaps other sovereignties as well. These immigrants were expected to remain in Halifax, but soon found themselves dissatisfied there, and 1,500 of them were relocated at Lunenburg in the spring of 1753.[13]

EXPULSION OF THE ACADIANS

The Acadians were naturally unwilling to take up arms against France. England feared their lack of loyalty might lead to disaster in a conflict with France. Who was responsible for the decision has never been clearly determined, but in 1755 an order was issued for the mass expulsion of the Acadians. Of the estimated 8,000 Acadians on the Nova Scotia peninsula, approximately 3,000 were deported or driven into exile. At least two-thirds of the exiles eventually returned.[14]

CAPITULATION OF LOUISBOURG

In July, 1758, the French garrison at Louisbourg capitulated. With the signing of the Treat of Paris on February 10, 1763, Nova Scotia was ceded to the British. The Louisbourg inhabitants were returned to France; the garrison, numbering 5,637 men, were sent to England.[15]

THE "PRE-LOYALISTS"

In October, 1758, and January, 1759, proclamations were issued offering the lands vacated by the exiled Acadians to New Englanders and in 1760 and 1761 a group often called the Pre-Loyalists took up lands at Liverpool, Annapolis, Minas, Pisiquid (now Windsor), Horton, Cornwallis, and Falmouth. This immigration totaled approximately 4,500 persons.[16]

In July, 1759, a grant was approved to a group of New Englanders for the Township of Onslow. These commenced a permanent settlement in the spring of 1760.[17]

McNUTT'S IRISH

On October 9, 1761, Alexander McNutt, an agent of the British government, arrived at Halifax with some 300 settlers from the north of Ireland. They settled in Onslow, Truro, and other locations. Other Scots-Irish followed, some by way of New Hampshire.[18]

THE SCOTS

In 1765 a grant of land in the Pictou area was made to fourteen persons from Philadelphia, who were required to provide settlers. They sent six families in 1767. They then agreed with one John Ross to furnish land to such settlers as he might enlist from Scotland. The first contingent of these settlers arrived at Pictou on the HECTOR on September 15, 1773. Extensive immigration of both Highland and Lowland Scots followed over the next eighty years.[19]

THE YORKSHIREMEN

In the early 1770s about 2,000 immigrants arrived from the British Isles, including about 1,000 Yorkshiremen who settled at the Isthmus of Chignecto.[20]

THE LOYALISTS

The American Revolution was responsible for two migrations to Nova Scotia of persons sympathetic to the British side of the conflict. The evacuation of the British Army from Boston in 1776 brought the first group of these Loyalists (said to have numbered about 1,500) to Nova Scotia.[21] The surrender of the British forces in 1783 was followed by the exodus of another 40,000 to Nova Scotia. Many of the latter group were at once taken to that portion of Nova Scotia which became the new province of New Brunswick. Others settled on the southeast coast, including Shelburne, and at Weymouth in Annapolis (now Digby) County.[22]

Those immigrants include discharged British soldiers, as well as so-called Hessians, some of whom had been held as prisoners-of-war by the American forces. These mercenary troops came from the German states of Hesse, Ansbach, and Brunswick.

Also included were 3,000 blacks, many of whom were former slaves who had cast their lot with the British Army in their effort to gain their freedom.[23]

THE BOTSFORD AND HATFIELD GRANTS

In 1765 a grant of 125,000 acres, called Conway (now Digby), was made to McNutt and others, including Sebastian Zouberbuhler, the only grantee to make any improvements. That grant was never registered. In 1784 it was escheated and the land granted to Loyalists. A new grant was made to Amos Botsford in 1801 to quiet title to the lands.[24] On January 29, 1801, a grant of 91,732 acres in the township of Digby was made to Isaac Hatfield and 275 others.[25]

8

THE MAROONS

In July, 1796, about five hundred "Maroons" arrived in Halifax from Jamaica. The Maroons were the descendants of former slaves who had fled their Spanish masters when England captured Jamaica in 1655. When they rebelled in 1795 the English threatened to chase them down with dogs and under this threat negotiated a peace, following which, in violation of the peace terms, they were deported to Halifax. They were removed to Sierra Leone in August, 1800.[26]

THE WAR OF 1812

As is commonly the case with any country at the end of a war, Britain at the end of the War of 1812 faced the problem of demobilization. And as had been the earlier solution, the disbanded soldiers were offered land grants at Sherbrooke (later called New Ross), Dalhousie, and Wellington. The first to arrive at Halifax were the Royal Newfoundland Fencibles; ninety-nine officers and men agreed to stay in the province. They were followed by pensioners from Chelsea. The pensioners were doubtless physically, and the disbanded soldiers psychologically, unsuited to the hardships of settlement. Within a few years many of these settlers had drifted away. Many slaves in the Chesapeake Bay region took refuge on British ships. Several hundred of them arrived at Halifax on September 1, 1814, from where they were resettled.[27]

1817-1862

In 1817 more than 300 persons fled to Halifax, refugees from November fires at St. Johns, Newfoundland; they were resettled throughout the province.[28] A number of Welsh immigrants arrived in 1818 and were granted land at Shelburne.[29] Numerous Irish immigrants settled throughout the province. One researcher has detailed the ancestry of twenty-five families and identified sixty-eight others in Halifax alone.[30] A substantial movement from Liverpool occurred in 1862.

INDIVIDUALS OF INTEREST

The immigrants so far mentioned include a number of origins: French (Acadians), English, Scottish, Irish, Ulstermen, Welsh, American Pre-Loyalists, American Loyalists, the "Foreign Protestants," Newfoundlanders, the "Maroons," discharged soldiers and pensioners, and blacks.

There were others. Several persons who arrived in Nova Scotia individually are not without interest. One is Cécile Murat, whose father's brother was the King of Naples. Her father was lost at sea while she was visiting at Church Point, Digby County, in 1795, and she was then "adopted" by her Acadian hosts.[31]

Another, who was called Jerome in the absence of any way to determine his true name, was found on the shore at St. Mary's Bay (now in Digby County) in 1864, with both legs recently professionally amputated at the knees. He was found to apparently understand both French and Italian, but would never speak, although he apparently could. He died in Clare.[32]

In July 1863, "Miss Lewly" registered at the Halifax Hotel; she remained in Halifax until 1872. Adèle, the youngest daughter of Victor Hugo, was pursuing a lost love.[33]

Several writers have spoken of the arrival of the Marquis de Conte "and other foreign settlers" in 1750 from the Azores. The Marquis was a Sicilian soldier of fortune; the others in fact English. All had sailed on board the NANCY but had been stranded in the Azores and arrived on a later ship.[34]

MAGNITUDE OF IMMIGRATION 1817-1838

A study of Nova Scotian immigration between 1817 and 1838, made under the direction of the Archivist of Nova Scotia, concluded that there is no way of determining how many immigrants arrived during that period, but that there were at least 40,000. "Scots predominated, the Irish were a fair second, and the English a poor third."[35] Half of these immigrants arrived at

Halifax. The population of Pictou rose from 8,737 in 1817 to 13,949 in 1827 and to 21,449 in 1838.

While natural population growth certainly made a substantial contribution to the totals, some conception of the magnitude of the immigration may be obtained from the following table. The historian's figures, however, do not appear to be consistent with the number of Loyalists who arrived in 1784.

PROVINCIAL POPULATION

Year	Families	Individuals
1763	1,797	
1766	2,575	9,789
1801		8,532
1817		86,668
1827		141,544

Source: Murdoch, 2:435, 467, 3:215, 590-591.

HETEROGENEITY

When one considers the origins of the major groups of immigrants, the indigenous Indians, and the inevitable variety of nationalities arriving by means of shipwreck (one even from the Cape of Good Hope) there emerges a picture of a population far less homogeneous than might be expected. Obviously, that heterogeneity has been greatly increased since Nova Scotia became a part of Canada in 1867.

It is inherent in the wide variety of sources from which the immigrants came that the identification of the origin of a particular individual is a major problem, one to which allusion was made in the opening paragraphs of this introduction and to which no easy answer exists.

NOTES

(1) Quoted in Latin and in Elglish translation in *Nova Scotia: The Royal Charter of 1621 to Sir Villiam Alexander: Address by Col. Alexander Fraser, L.L.D.*, 24-51; Beanish Murdoch, *History of Nova Scotia*, hereinafter Murdoch, 1:65, as corrected on 1:543; for reign of James see M. E. Hudson and

Mary Clark, *Crown of a Thousand Years*, revised edition (Sherborne, Dorset, England: Alphabet and Image, 1978), 94.

(2) *The Royal Charter (vide Note 1)*, 20-21.

(3) Murdoch, 1:66.

(4) Robert R. McLeod, *Markland or Nova Scotia* (Toronto?: Markland Publishing Co., Ltd., 1903), 19; Murdoch, 1:84-85; Archange Godbout, "The Passenger List of the Ship SAINT JEHAN and the Acadian Origins," *French Canadian and Acadian Genealogical Review*, hereinafter F.C.A.G.R., 1(1968):53.

(5) Murdoch, 1:127, 138.

(6) Murdoch, 1:138-139; Rev. Clarence J. d'Entremont, "New Findins on the Melansons," *F.C.A.G.R.* 2(1969):219-239, and "The Melansons of Acadia Had a French Father and an English Mother," *ibid.* 6(1978):53-55.

(7) Murdoch, 1:133.

(8) Murdoch, 1:310-316.

(9) Murdoch, 1:340.

(10) Murdoch, 2:123.

(11) Thomas B. Akins, *History of Halifax City* (Belleville, Ontario: Mika Publishing, 1973), 5; Thomas C. Halliburton, *History of Nova Scotia* (Belleville, Ontario: Mika Publishing, 1973), herinafter Halliburton, 1:137, claims 3,760 were sent.

(12) George T. Bates, "The Great Exodus of 1749, or the Cornwallis Settlers Who Didn't," *Collections of the Nova Scotia Historical Society*, hereinafter *Coll. N.S.H.S.*, 38(1973):31.

(13) Winthrop Pickard Bell, *The "Foreign Protestants" and the Settlement of Nova Scotia*, 95; Murdoch, 2:210; Duncan Campbell, *Nova Scotia in Its Historical, Mercantile and Industrial Relations* (Montreal: John Lovell, 1873), 112.

(14) James Hannay, *The Hisory of Acadia* (St. John, N.B.: J. & A. McMillan, 1879), pp. 408-409; *cf.* figures given by Charles Bruce Fergusson, "Pre-Revolutionary Settlements in Nova Scotia," *Coll. N.S.H.S.* 37(1970):10, 14; for Governor Lawrence's recommendation for this action, see Murdoch, 2:299-301.

(15) Halliburton, 1:205-213.

(16) Murdoch, 2:365, 387-388; Halliburton, 1:220-223; Fergusson, 17.

(17) Thomas Miller, *Historical and Genealogical Record of the First Settlers of Colchester County*, 14; Israel Longworth, "A Chapter in the History of the Township of Onslow, Nova Scotia," *Coll. N.S.H.S.* 9(1895):39-42.

(18) Murdoch, 2:407; Miller (*vide* Note 17), 15.

(19) J. M. Bumstead, *The People's Clearance, 1770-1815*, 63; Murdoch, 2:513, erroneously says 1772; for a detailed analysis of this movement see Donald MacKay, *Scotland Farewell*; for a listing of the Scottish immigrant vessels between 1773 and 1853 see Colin S. MacDonald, "Early Highland Immigration to Nova Scotia and Prince Edward Island," *Coll. N.S.H.S.* 23(1936):41-48.

(20) Fergusson, 20.

(21) Murdoch, 2:568-569.

(22) For a breakdown see Murdoch, 3:17-24.

(23) "Book of Negroes," manuscript at Public Record Office, Kew, Surrey, England.

(24) Murdoch, 2:528; Isaiah W. Wilson, *A Geography and History of the County of Digby, Nova Scotia*, 78.

(25) Murdoch, 3:204.

(26) Campbell, 197-205; Murdoch, 3:147-148, 155-157, 165.

(27) J. S. Martell, "Military Settlements in Nova Scotia After the War of 1812," *Coll. N.S.H.S.* 24(1938):75-105.

(28) Murdoch, 3:416-417.

(29) Halliburton, 1:300.

(30) Terrence M. Punch, "Irish Miscellany: Some Have Gone from Us," *Nova Scotia Historical Quarterly*, herinafter *N.S.H.Q.*, 10(1980):89-109.

(31) J.-Alphonse Deveau, *Le Journal de Cécile Murat*.

(32) Lila Smith Bird, "The Mystery Man of Clare," *N.S.H.Q.* 9(1979):313-317.

(33) Robert Paton Harvey, "When Victor Hugo's Daughter Was a Haligonian," *N.S.H.Q.* 7(1977):243-256.

(34) Winthrop Bell, "The Settlers from the Azores, 1750," *Coll. N.S.H.S.* 31(1957):19-20.

(35) J. S. Martell, *Immigration to and Emigration from Nova Scotia 1815-1838*, 8; the work is a detailed analysis of the subject.

KEY

This volume presents abstracts of the important data found in sources of varying quality. It should be considered only as a guide to those sources and not as a valid source for citations. Full information should be secured by consulting the cited sources, together with all others listed for the immigrant in this or the preceding volume.

Each entry cites the source of the data in parentheses at the end of the entry. It may be merely the number assigned to the article or published diary or journal in the bibliography of sources abtracted, *e.g.* (27), that number followed by a page number, *e.g.* (34:259), or that number followed by an issue number and a page number, *e.g.* (3:2:27). Reference to the bibliography will identify the source.

Entries will be found which complement (or may duplicate) data taken from another source for the same person. Apparent duplicate entries may be found where two or more persons share the same citation. It should be remembered that more than one person may conform to any entry and the source should be consulted to insure that possibility is not overlooked.

Names including the prefixes Mac (Mc, M') or Van may also appear without the prefix. Original spellings have been retained; a careful check of variant spellings is urged.

A listing such as: "Plus wife/2 ch. 10+/3 ch.-10/3 svts" means that the named individual was accompanied by his wife, 2 children over 10 years old, 3 children under 10 years old, and 3 servants. Ages reported for children as "over 10" (or 8) are shown as 10+ (or 8+). Ages reported as "under 10" (or 8) are shown as -10 (or -8). The description "spinster" may mean either unmarried woman or an occupation.

The periodical articles are frequently vague as to whether an individual actually came to Nova Scotia or to Cape Breton, which has at times been part of Nova Scotia and at other times a separate province. As a result doubtless some entries which ought to have been included were omitted and some listed which should have been left out.

Names of vessels are shown in capital letters.

NOVA SCOTIA IMMIGRANTS

to

1867

Part 1 – From Non-Nova Scotia Periodicals

Compiled by

Col. Leonard H. Smith Jr.
(A.U.S. Retired)
M.A. (Genealogy), Certified Genealogist

Note: Listings in Part 1 may refer to multiple identical entries.

- A -

Abba, Elizabeth. 20; servant; Hull, Yorkshire, to Nova Scotia; on TWO FRIENDS 28 Feb.-7 Mar. 1774 (25:30).

Abbesté, Jno. C. Capt.; plus 2 svts; Hessian Service; mustered at Digby 19 May 1784 (39:118).

Abbot, Samel. Arr. Annapolis from New York 19 Oct. 1782 (37:126).

Absalom. Negro slave to Capt. Y.; mustered at Digby 19 May 1784 (39:118).

Achton, Samuel. Loyalist; mustered at Digby 19 May 1784 (39:118).

Ackland, Philip. Plus 1 f./1 ch./1 svt.; mariner; Port Roseway Associate (6:13).

Aclenburg, William. Loyalist; plus 1 f.; mustered at Digby 19 May 1784 (39:118).

Adams, Samuel Charles. Son of Charles/ Rosana (Balentine) of Stranrowr, Scotland; marr. Halifax 10 Apr. 1834 Marianne Spence (q.v.) (33:54).

Addington, William. Grantee "Digby New Grant" 29 Jan. 1801 (5:81).

Aheran, Ann. Dau. of Thomas/Ellen (Ryan) of Clonmel, Co. Tipperary, Ireland; marr. Halifax 16 Apr. 1845 Thomas Walsh (q.v.) (35:145).

Aheran, Elizabeth. Dau. of Edmund/ Catherine (Twohig) of Co. Cork, Ireland; marr. Halifax 15 Apr. 1833 Peter Dawson (q.v.) (33:56).

Aheran, Michael. S. of Edward/Johanna (Mahony) of Co. Waterford, Ireland; marr. Halifax 17 May 1842 Ann Aheron (35:134).

Aheron, Catherine. Dau. of Edmund/ Catherine (Frahy) of Co. Cork, Ireland; widow of John Flinn; marr. Halifax 30 May 1829 Denis Cronin (q.v.) (32:108).

Aheron, Edward. S. of John/Catherine (O'Brien) of Co. Cork, Ireland; marr. Halifax 3 Nov 1829 Mary Cashman (q.v.) (32:105).

Aheron, Ellen. Dau. of Maurice/Mary of Castlemartyr, Co. Cork, Ireland; marr. Halifax 7 Feb 1829 James O'Brien (q.v.) (32:116).

Aheron, Joanna. Dau. of John/Mary (Mahony) of Nfld.; marr. Halifax 1 July 1832 Michael Prendergast (q.v.) (33:66).

Aheron, Mary Ann. Dau. of John/Mary (Mahony) of St. John's. Nfld.; marr. Halifax 12 Jan 1829 William Doyle (q.v.) (32:109).

Aheron, Timothy. Laborer; of Cove, Co. Cork, Ireland; marr. Halifax 6 Sep. 1831 Mary McDonald (33:54).

Aikens, James. Loyalist; mustered at Digby 19 May 1784 (39:118).

Aikins, John. Grantee "Digby New Grant" 29 Jan. 1801 (5:81).

Aikins, John. Loyalist; plus 1 f.; mustered at Digby 19 May 1784 (39:118).

Aikins, Samuel. Plus 1 f./4 ch./1 svt.; carpenter; Port Roseway Associate (6:13).

Ailward, Mary. Dau. of John/Mary (Magrath) of Co. Kilkenny, Ireland; marr. Halifax 25 Aug. 1831 Richard Connelly (q.v.) (33:55).

Ainson, Mary. 1, daughter of Miles; Hull to Fort Cumberland on ALBION 7-14 March 1774 (21:139).

Ainson, Mary. 30, wife of Miles; Hull to Fort Cumberland on ALBION 7-14

March 1774 (21:139).

Ainson, Miles. 42, blacksmith; Hull
to Fort Cumberland on ALBION 7-14
March 1774 (21:139).

Ainson, Miles. 6, son of Miles; Hull
to Fort Cumberland on ALBION 7-14
March 1774 (21:139).

Ainson, Thomas. 3, son of Miles; Hull
to Fort Cumberland on ALBION 7-14
March 1774 (21:139).

Albe, Gideon. New England to Annapolis on CHARMING MOLLY May 1760
(18:271).

Albee, Benjamin. S. of Obadiah/Jane;
to Liverpool ca. 1760 (47:126:96).

Albree, Obediah. Liverpool proprietor
(19:102).

Aldworth, Samuel. Plus 1 f./1 ch.;
gunsmith; Port Roseway Associate
(6:13).

Alexander, Patrick. Son of John/
Catherine (Dier) of Co. Sligo,
Ireland; marr. Halifax 28 Jan.
1834 Margaret Nagle (q.v.)
(33:54).

Aleyter, Enoch. Liverpool proprietor
(19:102).

Allaine, Ann Barba. Dau. of Lewis/
Jane; to (or b.?) Liverpool by
1802 (47:127:274).

Allaine, Lewis. S. of William/Ann
(Barbee); to Liverpool by 1782
(47:126:282).

Allan, Patrick. S. of Thomas/Johanna
(Inglish) of Co. Waterford, Ire-
land; marr. Halifax 24 May 1837
Elizabeth Cahill (q.v.) (34:125).

Allen, James. Plus 1 f./2 ch.; carpenter; Port Roseway Associate
(6:13).

Allen, Mary. Dau. of Edward/Mary
(Fanning) of Glenroach, Co. Wexford, Ireland; marr. Halifax 14
Dec. 1802 Patrick Christopher
(q.v.) (30:103).

Allen, Patrick. S. of Lawrence/
Catherine (Kearney) of Co. Cork,
Ireland; marr. Halifax 17 May
1814 Barbara Hawes (30:102).

Almon, William James. Surgeon in
Royal Artillery; New York to N.S.
at end of Revolutionary War;
settled in Halifax (8:39).

Amberman, Paul. Grantee "Digby New
Grant" 29 Jan. 1801 (5:81).

Anderson, Arthur. S. of Bartholomew/
Elenor (Flinn) of Co. Kerry,
Ireland; marr. Halifax 7 Jul 1816
Margaret Ast (q.v.) (30:102).

Anderson, Eliza. Dau. of Lewis/Ann
(Berrigan) of Kilkenny, Ireland;
marr. Halifax 6 Jan. 1834 Robert
McNelly (q.v.) (33:63).

Anderson, Eliza. See Carr, Eliza.

Anderson, Elizabeth. 36; to join
husband; Hull, Yorkshire, to
Halifax; on JENNY 3-10 April 1775
(22:124).

Anderson, Jane. 7; dau.of Elizabeth;
Hull, Yorkshire, to Halifax; on
JENNY 3-10 April 1775 (22:124).

Anderson, John. 1; s. of Elizabeth;
Hull, Yorkshire, to Halifax; on
JENNY 3-10 April 1775 (22:124).

Anderson, John. Plus 1 f./2 ch./3
svts.; farmer; Port Roseway Associate (6:13).

Anderson, Margaret. Dau. of William/
Isabella (Newlan) of Elgin, Scot-
and; marr. Halifax 3 Aug. 1836
Jeremiah Ryan (q.v.) (34:137).

Anderson, Mary. 9; dau.of Elizabeth;
Hull, Yorkshire, to Halifax; on
JENNY 3-10 April 1775 (22:124).

Anderson, Moses. 5; s. of Elizabeth;
Hull, Yorkshire, to Halifax; on
JENNY 3-10 April 1775 (22:124).

Anderson, Peter. Mariner; Port Roseway Associate (6:13).

Anderson, Walter. Plus 1 f.; arr.

Annapolis from New York 19 Oct. 1782 (37:125).

Anderson, William. Plus 1 f./2 ch./2 svts.; farmer; Port Roseway Associate (6:13).

Anderson, William. 4; s. of Elizabeth; Hull, Yorkshire, to Halifax; on JENNY 3-10 April 1775 (22:124).

Andrews, Hannah. 1; dau. of Thomas; Hull, Yorkshire, to Nova Scotia; on TWO FRIENDS 28 Feb.-7 Mar. 1774 (25:31).

Andrews, John. 5; s. of Thomas; Hull, Yorkshire, to Nova Scotia; on TWO FRIENDS 28 Feb.-7 Mar. 1774 (25:31).

Andrews, Lilley. 37; wife of Thomas; Hull, Yorkshire, to Nova Scotia; on TWO FRIENDS 28 Feb.-7 Mar. 1774 (25:31).

Andrews, Mary. 3; dau.of Thomas; Hull, Yorkshire, to Nova Scotia; on TWO FRIENDS 28 Feb.-7 Mar. 1774 (25:31).

Andrews, Mary. 7; dau.of Thomas; Hull, Yorkshire, to Nova Scotia; on TWO FRIENDS 28 Feb.-7 Mar. 1774 (25:31).

Andrews, Thomas. 37; husband [sic]; Hull, Yorkshire, to Nova Scotia; on TWO FRIENDS 28 Feb.-7 Mar. 1774 (25:31).

Annis, James. S. of Thomas/Lydia; Barnstable, Mass., to Liverpool by 1789 (47:127:121).

Annis, Lydia. Wife or widow of -----; to Liverpool by 1770 (47:126:282).

Antha, William H. Laborer; 20; English; Liverpool to Nova Scotia May 1864 on EUROCLYDON (45:181).

Appleby, Robert. 21; husbandman; Hull, Yorkshire, to Nova Scotia; on TWO FRIENDS 28 Feb.-7 Mar. 1774 (25:28).

Appleton, Robert. 24, husbandman;

Hull to Fort Cumberland on ALBION 7-14 March 1774 (21:137).

Apsley, Thomas. English; 11; Liverpool to Nova Scotia May 1864 on EUROCLYDON (45:181).

Archer, Ellen. Dau. of Michael/ Catherine (Carey) of Thomastown, Co. Kilkenny, Ireland; marr. Halifax 19 Feb. 1844 Michael Howley (q.v.) (35:139).

Archer, James. S. of Edmond/Eleanor (Carroll) of Cahir, Co. Tipperary, Ireland; widower of Eleanor; marr. Halifax 28 Apr 1826 Sarah Burns (q.v.) (32:105).

Archibald, Ann. Dau. of William/Jane (Stewart) of Scotland; widow of James Torrens; marr. Halifax 16 Jun 1830 John Jones (q.v.) (32:113).

Archibald, David 2nd. From N.H.; effective land grant at Truro 31 Oct. 1765 (4:245).

Archibald, David 3rd. From N.H.; effective land grant at Truro 31 Oct. 1765 (4:245).

Archibald, David. From N.H.; effective land grant at Truro 31 Oct. 1765 (4:245).

Archibald, James. From N.H.; effective land grant at Truro 31 Oct. 1765 (4:245).

Archibald, John Jr. Grantee 'Digby New Grant' 29 Jan. 1801 (5:81).

Archibald, John. From N.H.; effective land grant at Truro 31 Oct. 1765 (4:245).

Archibald, John. Grantee 'Digby New Grant' 29 Jan. 1801 (5:81).

Archibald, Matthew. From N.H.; effective land grant at Truro 31 Oct. 1765 (4:245).

Archibald, Robert. From Ireland; land grant at Londonderry 6 Mar. 1775 (4:258).

Archibald, Samuel. From N.H.; effective land grant at Truro 31 Oct. 1765 (4:245).

Archibald, Samuel. From Ireland; land grant at Londonderry 6 Mar. 1775 (4:258).

Archibald, Thomas Jr. From N.H.; effective land grant at Truro 31 Oct. 1765 (4:245).

Archibald, Thomas. From N.H.; effective land grant at Truro 31 Oct. 1765 (4:245).

Arents, Stephen. Plus 1 f./4 ch.; bricklayer; Port Roseway Associate (6:13).

Armon, Catherine. Dau. of Maurice/Janet (Conors) of Co. Waterford, Ireland; marr. Halifax 16 June 1835 Redmond Lynch (q.v.) (34:133).

Armstrong, Francis. Grantee "Digby New Grant" 29 Jan. 1801 (5:81).

Armstrong, Francis. Loyalist; plus 1 f./2 ch.; mustered at Digby 19 May 1784 (39:118).

Armstrong, Thomas. Plus wife/4 ch.; Casco Bay, Mass. (now Me.), to Chester with first settlers (16:45).

Armstrong, William. Grantee "Digby New Grant" 29 Jan. 1801 (5:81).

Armstrong, William. Loyalist; mustered at Digby 19 May 1784 (39:118).

Arndell, Wm. H. Laborer; 27; English; Liverpool to Nova Scotia May 1864 on EUROCLYDON (45:181).

Arnold, Benjamin. To Liverpool by 1771 (47:126:164).

Arnold, Luther. Liverpool proprietor (19:102).

Arnold, Luther. To Liverpool ca. 1760 (47:126:96).

Arnold, Phineas. Loyalist; from Port Mouton; mustered at Digby 19 May

1784 (39:118).

Arnold, Stephen. Grantee "Digby New Grant" 29 Jan. 1801 (5:81).

Arrigan, Eleanor. Dau. of Patrick/Mary (Gorman) of Parish Portlaw, Co. Waterford, Ireland; marr. Halifax 27 Jul 1827 Michael Tinan (q.v.) (32:119).

Asbel, Bridget. See Mackey, Bridget.

Ash, Patrick. S. of Richard/Margaret (Barry) of Co. Cork, Ireland; marr. Halifax 22 Jun 1813 Elenor Thibaut (q.v.) (30:102).

Ast, Ann. See Morrice, Ann.

Ast, John. S. of Robert/Margaret (Watson) of Clonmel, Co. Tipperary, Ireland; marr. Halifax 9 May 1822 Bridget Kehoe (q.v.) (31:40).

Ast, John. S. of Robert/Margaret (Watson) of Clonmel, Co. Tipperary, Ireland; widower of Bridget Kehoe; marr. Halifax 29 June 1834 Catherine McKenna (q.v.) (33:54).

Ast, Margaret. Dau. of Robert/Margaret (Watson) of Clonmel, Tipperary, Ireland; marr. Halifax 7 Jul 1816 Arthur Anderson (q.v.) (30:102).

Ast, Robert. S. of Robert/Margaret (Watson) of Clonmel, Co. Tipperary, Ireland; marr. Halifax 21 Apr 1822 Mary Hunt (q.v.) (31:40).

Atkins, Elizabeth. Dau. of Joseph/Wate; to (or b.?) Liverpool by 1802 (47:127:278).

Atkins, Hannah. See Deane, Hannah.

Atkins, Joseph Jr. S. of Joseph/Wate; to (or b.?) Liverpool by 1801 (47:127:273).

Atkins, Robert. S. of Thomas/Ruth; to (or b.?) Liverpool by 1775 (47:127:49).

Atkins, Ruth. Dau. of Joseph/Wate; to (or b.?) Liverpool by 1797 (47:127:270).

Atkins, Wate. Dau. of Joseph/Wate; to
(or b.?) Liverpool by 1802
(47:127:273).

Atkinson, Ann. 19, servant; Hull to
Fort Cumberland on ALBION 7-14
March 1774 (21:134).

Atkinson, Ann. 21, wife of Robert;
Hull to Fort Cumberland on ALBION
7-14 March 1774 (21:139).

Atkinson, Charles. 6, s. of John;
Hull to Fort Cumberland on ALBION
7-14 March 1774 (21:136).

Atkinson, Frances. 30, wife of John;
Hull to Fort Cumberland on ALBION
7-14 March 1774 (21:136).

Atkinson, John. 1, s. of John; Hull
to Fort Cumberland on ALBION 7-14
March 1774 (21:136).

Atkinson, John. 45, laborer; Hull to
Fort Cumberland on ALBION 7-14
March 1774 (21:136).

Atkinson, Martha. 4, dau. of John;
Hull to Fort Cumberland on ALBION
7-14 March 1774 (21:136).

Atkinson, Michael. 3, s. of John;
Hull to Fort Cumberland on ALBION
7-14 March 1774 (21:136).

Atkinson, Robert. 28, farmer; Hull to
Fort Cumberland on ALBION 7-14
March 1774 (21:139).

Atkinson, William. 16, tanner; Hull
to Fort Cumberland on ALBION 7-14
March 1774 (21:138).

Attwood, Joshua. Barrington petitioner 19 Oct. 1776 (1:365).

Atwood, Joseph. Barrington petitioner
19 Oct. 1776 (1:365).

Atword, John. Capt.; plus wife/1 ch.;
Mass., to Chester with first
settlers (16:45).

Auld, George. Baker; Port Roseway
Associate (6:13).

Austen, Stephen. Loyalist; mustered
at Digby 19 May 1784 (39:118).

Austin, James. Disbanded soldier 1st
N.J. Vols; mustered at Digby 19
May 1784 (39:118).

Austin, John. Loyalist; mustered at
Digby 19 May 1784 (39:118).

Avery, James. Lieut.; Conn. to N.S.;
to U.S. 1776; lived 1785 at Machias, Me. (36:65).

Ayer, Elijah Jr. Conn. to N.S.; to
U.S. 1776; lived 1785 at Mass.
[which then incl. Me.] (36:65).

Ayer, Obadiah. Conn. to N.S.; to U.S.
1776; dead by 1785 (36:65).

Aylward, Bridget. Dau. of John/Mary
(McGrath) of Co. Kilkenny, Ireland; widow of John Walsh; marr.
Halifax 19 Feb 1829 John Connelly
(q.v.) (32:107).

Ayres, Elijah. Conn. to N.S.; to U.S.
1776; lived 1785 at Edmunds, Me.,
and N.S. (36:65).

- B -

Babcock, Benjn. Arr. Annapolis from
New York 19 Oct. 1782 (37:125).

Bacon, John. New England to Annapolis
on CHARMING MOLLY May 1760
(18:271).

Bailey, Jacob. Born 1731 at Rowley,
Mass. (26:44).

Bailey, Jacob. Pownalborough, Me., to
Halifax June 1779 (26:45).

Bailey, Jacob. Rev.; Pownalborough,
Me., to Boston, Mass., Oct. 1777;
later to Halifax (41:14).

Baine, George. Grantee "Digby New
Grant" 29 Jan. 1801 (5:81).

Baird, Thomas. From Ireland; land
grant at Londonderry 6 Mar. 1775
(4:258).

Baizeley, William. A sailor; mustered
at Digby 19 May 1784 (39:119).

Baizely, James. Master of the PEGGY;
mustered at Digby 19 May 1784
(39:119).

Baker, Barnabas. S. of Judah; b. Yarmouth, Mass., 23 Feb. 1734; Chatham, Mass., to Barrington by 1763 (50:98).

Baker, Elizabeth. Dau. of Barnabas; to Barrington by 1763 (50:98).

Baker, John. New England to Annapolis 1760 (18:271).

Baker, John. Rev.; s. of Nicholas/Mary; Bedeford (sic, for Bideford?), Devonsh., England; to Liverpool by 1823 (47:128:114).

Baker, John. S. of Barnabas; to Barrington by 1763 (50:98).

Baker, Judah. S. of Barnabas; to Barrington by 1763 (50:98).

Baker, Mehitable Smith. Wife of Barnabas; b. Chatham, Mass., 30 Oct. 1735; to Barrington by 1763 (50:98).

Ball, James. S. of James/Phoebe; to (or b.?) Liverpool by 1784 (47:126:284).

Ballad, Joseph. See Ballard, Joseph.

Ballard, Charles. S. of George/Mary (Flinn) of Nfld.; marr. Halifax 24 Feb. 1840 Mary Ann Murphy (q.v.) (34:125).

Ballard, Joseph. From Mass.; land grant at Truro 1759 (4:242).

Balsor, Israel. Loyalist from Port Mouton; plus 1 f.; mustered at Digby 19 May 1784 (39:119).

Bambrick, Elenor. Dau. of Hugh/Sarah (Knox) of Louisbourg, Cape Breton; marr. Halifax 22 Apr. 1805 John Phelan (q.v.) (30:109).

Bane, George. Loyalist; plus 1 f./2 ch.; mustered at Digby 19 May 1784 (39:118).

Bangs, Joseph. B. Hardwick, Mass., 22 Apr. 1743; s. of Joseph/Thankfull; to Liverpool by 1764 (47:126:164).

Bangs, Sarah. Dau. of Joseph/Mary; to (or b.?) Liverpool by 1788 (47:127:56).

Bannister, Thomas. Loyalist; plus 1 svt.; mustered at Gulliver's Hole/St. Mary's Bay/Sissiboo 1/6 June 1784; settled at Sisiboo (now Weymouth) (40:261).

Barclay, Andrew. Plus 1 f./7 ch./5 svts.; stationer; Port Roseway Associate (6:13).

Barclay, John. S. of John/Grace of Co. Donegal, Ireland; marr. Halifax 21 May 1813 Lydia Makaisie (q.v.) (30:102).

Bare, Richard. 26; butcher; Hull, Yorkshire, to Nova Scotia; on TWO FRIENDS 28 Feb.-7 Mar. 1774 (25:29).

Barlow, Joseph. Carpenter; Port Roseway Associate (6:13).

Barlow, Joseph. Laborer; 26; English; Liverpool to Nova Scotia May 1864 on EUROCLYDON (45:181).

Barlow, Thomas. Plus 1 f./3 ch.; carpenter; Port Roseway Associate (6:13).

Barnhill, John. From Mass.; land grant at Onslow 21 Feb. 1769 (4:225).

Barnhill, John. From Ireland; land grant at Londonderry 6 Mar. 1775 (4:258).

Barnhill, Robert. From Ireland; land grant (to heirs) at Londonderry 6 Mar. 1775 (4:258).

Barret, -----. Widow; Loyalist; mustered at Digby 19 May 1784 (39:118).

Barret, James. Loyalist; mustered at Digby 19 May 1784 (39:119).

Barrett, Bridget. Of Parish Stradbally, Co. Waterford, Ireland; marr. Halifax 14 Jan. 1836 Nicholas Power (q.v.) (34:137).

Barrett, Elizabeth. See Fitzgerald, Elizabeth.

Barrett, James. S. of Thomas/Eliza-
beth (Fennell) of Co. Tipperary,
Ireland; marr. Halifax 16 July
1822 Honora Hennessy (31:40).
Barrett, James. S. of John/Mary
(O'Brien) of Kilkenny City, Ire-
land; marr. Halifax 6 Nov. 1834
Mary Leahy widow of John Ross
(q.v.) (34:125).
Barrett, John. S. of Timothy/Cather-
ine (Hanifan) of Co. Cork, Ire-
land; widower of Margaret Ryan;
marr. Halifax 24 Oct. 1831 Honora
Connors (q.v.) (33:54).
Barrett, Thomas. S. of John/Eleanor
(Rourke) of Parish Reary, Leix,
Ireland; marr. Halifax 11 June
1828 Margaret Murphy (q.v.)
(32:105).
Barretts. See Barret.
Barron, Bridget. Dau. of Patrick/
Catherine (Tate) of Parish Skel-
lins, Co. Wexford, Ireland; marr.
Halifax 15 July 1821 Philip Mc-
Gragh (q.v.) (31:46).
Barron, Catherine. Dau. of Michael/
arbara (Skerry) of Wexford, Ire-
land; marr. Halifax 19 Feb. 1843
Pvt. Bernard Connors (q.v.)
(35:136).
Barron, Elizabeth. Dau. of Peter/
argaret (Tobin) of Co. Kilkenny,
Ireland; marr. Halifax 7 Aug. 1838
John Barron (q.v.) (34:125).
Barron, John. S. of Lawrence/Cather-
ine of Waterford City, Ireland;
marr. Halifax 4 July 1818 Bridget
Ryan (q.v.) (31:40).
Barron, John. S. of Martin/Alice
(Cody) of Co. Kilkenny, Ireland;
marr. Halifax 7 Aug. 1838 Eliza-
beth Barron (q.v.) (34:125).
Barron, John. S. of Peter/Ellen
(Tobin) of Co. Kilkenny, Ireland;
marr. Halifax 17/30 July 1841

Ellen Croke (q.v.) (35:134).
Barron, Mary. Dau. of Edmond/Mary
(Roach) of Tintern, Co. Wexford,
Ireland; marr. Halifax 15 Apr.
1822 John Blanch (q.v.) (31:41).
Barron, Peter. S. of Patrick/Cather-
ine (Murphy) of Parish St. James,
Wexford, Ireland; marr. Halifax 1
June 1828 Elizabeth McGrath
(32:105).
Barron, Robert. S. of Edward/Bridget
(Kehoe) of Burris (sic for Bor-
ris), Co. Carlow, Ireland; marr.
Halifax 21 Aug. 1820 Sarah Grant
(q.v.) (31:40).
Barron, Robert. S. of Edward/Bridget
(Kehoe) of Borris, Co. Carlow,
Ireland; widower of Sarah Grant;
marr. Halifax 4 July 1840 Eliza-
beth White (34:125).
Barron, Robert. Widower; s. of Ed-
ward/Bridget (Kehoe) of Borris,
Co. Carlow, Ireland; marr. Halifax
11 May 1823 Margaret Helpert (31:
40).
Barron, William. Grocer; s. of Walt-
er/Margaret (Walsh) of Innistioge,
Kilkenny, Ireland; marr. Halifax
17 May 1832 Ellen Power (q.v.)
(33:54).
Barron, William. S. of William/Mary
(Rutledge) of Co. Waterford, Ire-
land; marr. Halifax 23 Nov. 1831
Joanna Haley (q.v.) (33:54).
Barron, William. S. of Walter/Marga-
ret (Walsh) of Innistioge, Co.
Kilkenny, Ireland; widower of
Ellen Power of Waterford, Ireland;
marr. Halifax 12 June 1840 Alice
Morrisy (q.v.) (34:125).
Barrs, Sarah. 21, servant; Hull to
Fort Cumberland on ALBION 7-14
March 1774 (21:137).
Barry, David A. S. of James/Mary
(Flinn) of Co. Cork, Ireland;

marr. Halifax 12 Sep. 1843 Mary
Ann Casey (35:134).

Barry, Joanna. Dau. of David/Mary
(Kehoe) of Co. Cork, Ireland;
marr. Halifax 16 Sep. 1841 John
Smyth (q.v.) (35:144).

Barry, John St. Lawrence. S. of
Lawrence/Mary (Guess) of Cove of
Cork, Ireland; marr. Halifax 27
May 1827 Anne Rooney (q.v.) (32:
105).

Barry, Joseph. S. of John/Bridget
(Finessey) of Co. Tipperary, Ire-
land; marr. Halifax 26 Nov. 1832
Judith Dwyer (q.v.) (33:54).

Barry, Mary. Dau. of Robert/Eleanor
(Coleman) of Co. Cork, Ireland;
marr. Halifax 16 Dec. 1829 Edward
Collins (q.v.) (32:107).

Barry, Mary. Dau. of John/Bridget
(Power) of Co. Waterford, Ireland;
marr. Halifax 7 Aug. 1832 Timothy
Grady (q.v.) (33:59).

Barry, Mary. Dau. of Garrett/Ellen
(Molshough) of Co. Cork, Ireland;
marr. Halifax 8 Jan. 1833 William
Keating (q.v.) (33:60).

Barry, Mary. See Flinn, Mary.

Bars, Ruth. Dau. of Jonathan/Ruth; to
(or b.?) Liverpool by 1783 (47:
126:288).

Barss, Benjamin. S. of Jonathan/Ruth;
to (or b.?) Liverpool by 1791 (47:
127:203).

Barss, David. S. of Benjamin/Jane; to
Liverpool by 1771 (47:127:52).

Barss, David. S. of David/Rebeckah;
to (or b.?) Liverpool by 1799 (47:
127:272).

Barss, Hannah. Dau. of David/Rebecca;
to (or b.?) Liverpool by 1792 (47:
127:204).

Barss, John. S. of Joseph/Elizabeth;
to (or b.?) Liverpool by 1802 (47:
128:28).

Barss, Jonathan. To Liverpool ca.
1760 (47:126:98).

Barss, Joseph. Capt.; s. of Joseph/
Lydia (Deane); b. Hyannis or Chatham, Mass.; d. Liverpool 11 Aug.
1826 ae 76 (49:138).

Barss, Joseph. S. of Joseph/Lydia; to
Liverpool by 1773 (47:126:168).

Barss, Lydia. Dau. of Joseph/Eliza-
beth; to (or b.?) Liverpool by
1794 (47:127:212).

Barss, Rebeca. Dau. of Jonathan/Ruth;
to Liverpool by 1784 (47:127:56).

Barss, Ruth. Wife of Jonathan; to
Liverpool ca. 1760 (47:126:98).

Bartlet, Joseph. To Liverpool ca.
1760 (47:126:98).

Bartlet, Lidia. Wife of Joseph; to
Liverpool ca. 1760 (47:126:98).

Bartlet, Richard. From Ireland; land
grant at Londonderry 6 Mar. 1775
(4:258).

Bartlet, William. S. of Uriah/Lois;
to (or b.?) Liverpool by 1790 (47:
127:276).

Bartlett, Joseph. Liverpool proprietor (19:102).

Barton, James. Col.; disbanded officer; plus 2 svts.; mustered at Digby 19 May 1784 (39:118).

Barton, John. Mason; of Co. Kilkenny,
Ireland; widower of Mary Barry;
marr. Halifax 29 Jan. 1845 Catherine Wallace (q.v.) (35:134).

Barton, Joseph. (Heirs) grantee
"Digby New Grant" 29 Jan. 1801
(5:81).

Barton, Michael. S. of John/Mary
(Barry) of Co. Kilkenny, Ireland;
marr. Halifax 1 May 1834 Margaret
McGinty (q.v.) (33:54).

Bary, Mary. Of Cove, Co. Cork, Ireland; marr. Halifax 16 Sep. 1817
Richard Cody (q.v.) (30:103).

Bassett, Ebenezer. From Mass.; land

grant at Truro 1759 (4:242).

Bates, Eleanor. Dau. of Edmund/Margaret (Brown) of Co. Tipperary, Ireland; marr. Halifax 14 Sep. 1816 Michael Grantfield (q.v.) (30:105).

Bates, Nathaniel. Loyalist; plus 1 ch.; mustered at Digby 19 May 1784 (39:118).

Bates, William. Widower of Ann Whelan; of Clonmel, Co. Tipperary, Ireland; marr. Halifax 22 June 1829 Elizabeth Manning (q.v.) (32:105).

Bath, John. 23; servant; Hull, Yorkshire, to Annapolis on JENNY 3-10 April 1775 (22:124).

Batman, Samuel. Barrington petitioner 19 Oct. 1776 (1:365).

Battle, Samuel. Liverpool proprietor (19:102).

Battman, Joseph. Or Peter; arrived on Transport JOSEPH; mustered at Digby 19 May 1784 (39:119).

Battman, Peter. See Battman, Joseph.

Baucher, John. Loyalist; mustered at Digby 19 May 1784 (39:119).

Baxter, James. Grantee "Digby New Grant" 29 Jan. 1801 (5:81).

Baxter, James. Loyalist; plus 1 f./3 ch.; mustered at Digby 19 May 1784 (39:119).

Baxter, Jonathan. Carpenter; Port Roseway Associate (6:13).

Baxter, Samuel. Plus 1 f./2 ch./5 svts.; mariner; Port Roseway Associate (6:13).

Baxter, Simon. Loyalist; New Hampshire to New York; to N.S. March 1782 (41:13).

Baxter, William. (Heirs) grantee "Digby New Grant" 29 Jan. 1801 (5:81).

Bayard, Robert. M.D.; England to Windsor; to N.Y.; Portland, Me.,

to St. John May 1813; died St. John June 1868 ae 81 (9:133).

Bayeau, Thomas. Grantee "Digby New Grant" 29 Jan. 1801 (5:81).

Bayeaux, Thomas. Loyalist; plus 1 f./7 ch.; mustered at Digby 19 May 1784 (39:119).

Beacon, William. S. of John/Ellen (Gobrick) of Co. Fermanagh, Ireland; marr. Halifax 1 Aug. 1837 Louisa Corbett (34:125).

Beal, James. From Mass.; land grant at Truro 1759 (4:242).

Beal, John. From Mass.; land grant at Truro 1759 (4:242).

Beardman, Andrew. Loyalist; mustered at Digby 19 May 1784 (39:119).

Bearse, Jonathan. S. of Benjamin; b. Chatham, Mass.; to Liverpool by Jan. 1762 (50:98).

Bearse, Mercy/"Massa". Wife of Benjamin; to Barrington betw. Nov. 1764 and 1770 (50:98).

Bearse, Ruth Eldredge. Wife of Jonathan; to Liverpool by Jan. 1762 (50:99).

Beartse, Benjamin. S. of Benjamin; b. Chatham, Mass.; to Barrington bet. Nov. 1764 and 1770 (50:98).

Beattie, George. Plus 1 f./5 ch./3 svts.; Port Roseway Associate (6:13).

Beaver, Elizabeth. 30; housekeeper; Hull, Yorkshire, to Fort Cumberland on JENNY 3-10 April 1775 (22:123).

Bee, Martha. Dau. Thomas/Sarah; to Liverpool by 3 Oct. 1785 (return dated 1784) (47:126:286).

Bee, Sarah. Dau. of Thomas/Sarah; to Liverpool by 1775 (47:127:57).

Bee, Thomas. Liverpool proprietor (19:102).

Bee, Thomas. S. of John; b. Chatham, Mass., ca. 1730; d. Liverpool 16

June 1769 (50:99).

Beeman, -----. Widow; grantee "Digby New Grant" 29 Jan. 1801 (5:81).

Beeman, Joseph. Grantee "Digby New Grant" 29 Jan. 1801 (5:81).

Belcher, Adam. Arr. Annapolis from New York 19 Oct. 1782 (37:126).

Bell, Elizabeth. From N.H.; effective land grant at Truro 31 Oct. 1765 (4:245).

Bell, Jane. See Snowden, Jane.

Bell, Jeremiah. Loyalist; mustered at Digby 19 May 1784 (39:119).

Bell, Rachel. Loyalist; plus 2 ch.; mustered at Digby 19 May 1784 (39:119).

Belling, John. Plus 1 f.; arrived on Transport JOSEPH; mustered at Digby 19 May 1784 (39:119).

Beman, Ebenezer. Loyalist; mustered at Digby 19 May 1784 (39:119).

Beman, Elizabeth. Loyalist; plus 2 ch.; mustered at Digby 19 May 1784 (39:119).

Beman, Thomas. Loyalist; mustered at Digby 19 May 1784 (39:119).

Bencraft, Samuel. From Mass.; land grant at Onslow 21 Feb. 1769 (4:225).

Bennett, David. 30, farmer; Hull to Fort Cumberland on ALBION 7-14 Mar. 1774 (21:139).

Bennett, David. Plus 1 f./1 ch./1 svt.; bricklayer; Port Roseway Associate (6:13).

Bennett, Ellen. Dau. of Francis/atherine (Cannell) of Quebec; marr. Halifax 16 Nov. 1829 John Clifford (q.v.) (32:107).

Bennett, James. 37th Regt.; s. of Jeremiah/Eliza (Walsh) of Waterford, Ireland; marr. Halifax 23 Dec. 1839 Catherine Lynch (q.v.) (34:125).

Bennett, James. S. of John/Catherine

(Murphy) of Co. Wexford, Ireland; marr. Halifax 10 Nov. 1830 Bridget Ronan (q.v.) (32:105).

Bennett, Mary Anne. Dau. of Michael/nne of Ardfinnen, Co. Tipperary, Ireland; marr. Halifax 24 Sep. 1810 Dr. Thomas Keegan Jr. (q.v.) (30:106).

Bennett, Mary. 30, wife of David; Hull to Fort Cumberland on ALBION 7-14 March 1774 (21:139).

Benson, Joseph. Late of N.S. Regt.; s. of James/Elizabeth (Sullivan) of Nfld.; marr. Halifax 24 June 1823 Mary Kenedy (q.v.) (31:40).

Bent, Samuel. New England to Annapolis on CHARMING MOLLY May 1760 (18:271).

Berdsall, Jeremiah. Loyalist; plus 1 f./1 ch.; mustered at Digby 19 May 1784 (39:119).

Berigan, Honora. Dau. of William/Catherine (Nowlan) of Co. Kilkenny, Ireland; marr. Halifax 3 Nov. 1829 James Duggan (q.v.) (32:109).

Berningham, Michael. S. of Richard/Catherine (Rourke) of Waterford, Ireland; marr. Halifax 27 Oct. 1827 Celina Night (32:105).

Bernard, Margaret. Dau. of Philip/Mary (Egan) of Carlow, Ireland; marr. Halifax 9 Sep. 1803 Gerard Howes (q.v.) (30:106).

Berrigan, David. S. of Thomas/Mary (Waters) of Co. Kilkenny, Ireland; marr. Halifax 22 Apr. 1833 Elizabeth Deniffe (q.v.) (33:54).

Berrigan, Peter. S. of John/Margaret (Dunn) of Co. Kilkenny, Ireland; marr. Halifax 11 Sep. 1842 Margery Cullin (q.v.) (35:135).

Berth, A.J. German Service (Anspach); mustered at Bear River 11/25 June 1784 (38:259).

Bertrim, Mary Elizabeth. Dau. of

Thomas/Margaret (Maurice) of
Prince Edward Isl.; marr. Halifax
23 July 1831 Thomas Magher (q.v.)
(33:63).

Betts, Hiram. Grantee "Digby New
Grant" 29 Jan. 1801 (5:81).

Beusefield, Adam. Laborer; 23, Irish;
Liverpool to Nova Scotia May 1864
on EUROCLYDON (45:181).

Bevin, Mary. Of Ireland; marr. Halifax 24 Sep. 1819 Daniel Price
(q.v.) (31:52).

Beys, John. 24, husbandman; Hull to
Fort Cumberland on ALBION 7-14
March 1774 (21:137).

Bice, John. Loyalist; mustered at
Digby 19 May 1784 (39:119).

Bickell, Caspar. Disbanded soldier,
Waldeck Regt.; mustered at Bear
River 11/25 June 1784 (38:259).

Bicker, Caspar. Disbanded soldier,
Waldeck Regt.; mustered at Bear
River 11/25 June 1784 (38:259).

Biehler, -----. Disbanded soldier,
German Service; mustered at Bear
River 11/25 June 1784 (38:259).

Bierman, Andrew. Plus 1 f.; baker;
Port Roseway Associate (6:13).

Bignall, Robert. Loyalist; plus 1
f./1 ch.; mustered at Digby 19 May
1784 (39:119).

Bignell, George. Corp. 37th Regt.; of
Devonsh., England; marr. Halifax
27 May 1841 Mary Croughan (q.v.)
(35:135).

Bishop, Daniel Lathrop. S. of Samuel;
Lisbon, Conn., to Liverpool by
1805 (47:127:273).

Bishop, Jonathan. Loyalist; mustered
at Digby 19 May 1784 (39:118).

Bishop, Leveritt. Grantee "Digby New
Grant" 29 Jan. 1801 (5:81).

Black, Elizabeth. 36; wife of William; Hull, Yorkshire, to Fort
Cumberland on JENNY 3-10 April

1775 (22:123).

Black, George. Grantee "Digby New
Grant" 29 Jan. 1801 (5:81).

Black, John. 15, s. of William; Hull,
Yorkshire, to Fort Cumberland on
JENNY 3-10 April 1775 (22:123).

Black, Joseph. Plus 2 ch; Port Roseway Associate (6:13).

Black, Richard. 11; s. of William;
Hull, Yorkshire, to Fort Cumberland on JENNY 3-10 April 1775
(22:123).

Black, Sarah. 7, dau.of William;
Hull, Yorkshire, to Fort Cumberland on JENNY 3-10 April 1775
(22:123).

Black, Sarah. Widow of John Smyth, of
Harpswell Isl., N.B.; marr. Halifax 16 Sep. 1823 James Dorcey
(q.v.) (31:44).

Black, Thomas. 9, s. of William;
Hull, Yorkshire, to Fort Cumberland on JENNY 3-10 April 1775
(22:123).

Black, William. 14; s. of William;
Hull, Yorkshire, to Fort Cumberland on JENNY 3-10 April 1775
(22:123).

Black, William. 43; linen draper;
Hull, Yorkshire, to Fort Cumberland on JENNY 3-10 April 1775
(22:123).

Black, William. Plus 1 f./1 ch./1
svt.; cabinet maker; Port Roseway
Associate (6:13).

Blackburn, Jacob. 27, servant; Hull
to Fort Cumberland on ALBION 7-14
March 1774 (21:140).

Blackden, Ann. B. 21 Mar. 1742 at
London, England; d. (as wife of
Dr. Jonathan Prescott) Feb. 1810
at Halifax (14:8).

Blackford, Martin. Grantee "Digby New
Grant" 29 Jan. 1801 (5:81).

Blackford, Martin. Loyalist; mustered

at Digby 19 May 1784 (39:118).

Blackmar, David. From Mass.; land grant at Truro 1759 (4:242).

Blackmar, Simeon. From Mass.; land grant at Truro 1759 (4:242).

Blackmar, Solomon. From Mass.; land grant at Truro 1759 (4:242).

Blackmar, William. From Mass.; land grant at Truro 1759 (4:242).

Blackmore, David. From Mass.; land grant at Onslow 21 Feb. 1769 (4:224).

Blackmore, Elizabeth. From Mass.; land grant at Onslow 21 Feb. 1769 (4:225).

Blackwell, John. Plus 1 f./3 ch.; farmer; Port Roseway Associate (6:13).

Blair, Frances. From Mass.; land grant at Onslow 21 Feb. 1769 (4:224).

Blair, Jane. Wife of William; dau. of ----- Barnes; to N.S. with husband (4:229).

Blair, John. From Mass.; land grant at Onslow 21 Feb. 1769 (4:225).

Blair, William Jr. From Mass.; land grant at Onslow 21 Feb. 1769 (4:225).

Blair, William. From Mass.; land grant at Onslow 21 Feb. 1769 (4:224).

Blair, William. S. of Robert/Isabella (Rankin), Ulster Scot descent, (from County Antrim, Ireland, to Worcester County, Mass., by 1720); plus wife Jane (Barnes); to Colchester 1759; Onslow proprietor (4:229).

Blaisdell, Moses. From N.H.; effective land grant at Truro 31 Oct. 1765 (4:245).

Blake, Frances. Dau. of James/Bridget (Gounan) of Co. Donegal, Ireland; marr. Halifax 15 Nov. 1842 John

Blake (q.v.) (35:135).

Blake, John. Pvt. 64th Regt.; of Co. Donegal, Ireland; marr. Halifax 15 Nov. 1842 Frances Blake (q.v.) (35:135).

Blanch, Catherine. Dau. of James/ Catherine (Buckly) of Thomastown, Co. Kilkenny, Ireland; marr. Halifax 14 May 1833 Richard O'Neill (q.v.) (33:65).

Blanch, James. Loyalist; plus 1 f.; mustered at Digby 19 May 1784 (39:118).

Blanch, John. S. of James/Mary (Dunne) of Davidstown, Co. Wexford, Ireland; marr. Halifax 15 Apr. 1822 Mary Barron (q.v.) (31:41).

Blanchard, Nicholas. From Mass.; land grant at Onslow 21 Feb. 1769 (4:225).

Blinkey, Charles. 33, farmer; Hull to Fort Cumberland on ALBION 7-14 Mar. 1774 (21:138).

Blinkey, Jane. 6, daughter of Charles; Hull to Fort Cumberland on ALBION 7-14 March 1774 (21:138).

Blinkey, Mary. 1, daughter of Charles; Hull to Fort Cumberland on ALBION March 1774 (21:138).

Blinkey, Sarah. 33, wife of Charles; Hull to Fort Cumberland on ALBION 7-14 March 1774 (21:138).

Blinkhorn, Ann. 29; wife of William; Hull, Yorkshire, to Nova Scotia; on TWO FRIENDS 28 Feb.-7 Mar. 1774 (25:29).

Blinkhorn, Ann. 3; dau.of William; Hull, Yorkshire, to Nova Scotia; on TWO FRIENDS 28 Feb.-7 Mar. 1774 (25:29).

Blinkhorn, Eleanor. 1; dau. of William; Hull, Yorkshire, to Nova Scotia; on TWO FRIENDS 28 Feb.-7 Mar. 1774 (25:29).

Blinkhorn, John. 4; s. of William;
Hull, Yorkshire, to Nova Scotia;
on TWO FRIENDS 28 Feb.-7 Mar. 1774
(25:29).

Blinkhorn, William. 33; farmer; Hull,
Yorkshire, to Nova Scotia; on TWO
FRIENDS 28 Feb.-7 Mar. 1774 (25:
29).

Blinkhorn, William. 7; s. of William;
Hull, Yorkshire, to Nova Scotia;
on TWO FRIENDS 28 Feb.-7 Mar. 1774
(25:29).

Blocker, Jacob. Disbanded soldier,
38th Regt.; plus 1 f./1 ch.; mustered at Digby 19 May 1784
(39:119).

Blowers, George. S. of George/Eliza-
beth; Sax Mundum, England, to Liverpool by 1793 (47:127:124).

Boehme, -----. Surgeon, Waldeck
Regt.; mustered at Bear River
11/25 June 1784 (38:259).

Boggy, Mary. Dau. of John/Mary
(Canvel) of Castlecomer. Co.
Kilkenny, Ireland; marr. Halifax 1
Dec. 1826 Pierce Ryan (q.v.)
(32:118).

Boice, Jacob. Grantee "Digby New
Grant" 29 Jan. 1801 (5:81).

Boland, James. S. of William/Cather-
ine (Ward) of Co. Wexford, Ireland; marr. Halifax 23 Jan. 1835
Mary Jordan (q.v.) (34:126).

Bollinger, Eva. Wife of Hans Jakob
Roost; Beringen, Canton Schaffhausen, [Switzerland,] to Halifax
1742 (44:193).

Bolton, Henry. Plus 1 f./7 ch./1
svt.; Port Roseway Associate (6:
13).

Boncha, Malachi. Disbanded soldier,
1st N.J. Vols.; mustered at Digby
19 May 1784 (39:118).

Bonhann. See Boncha.

Bonnell, Isaac. Grantee "Digby New

Grant" 29 Jan. 1801 (5:81).

Bonnell, Isaac. Loyalist; plus 1
svt.; mustered at Digby 19 May
1784 (39:119).

Bonnet, Robert. Of Kilmurray, Co.
Wicklow, Ireland; marr. Halifax
28 Aug. 1817 Mary Doul (q.v.)
(30:102).

Booadstreet, James. Loyalist; mustered at Digby 19 May 1784
(39:118).

Boomer, Elizabeth. Wife of Job; dau.
of Benjamin and Bethiah Godfrey of
Chatham, Mass.; d. 5 Mar. 1813 ae.
45th (49:121).

Boomer, Job. S. of Joshua; Freetown,
Mass., to Liverpool by 1789 (47:
127:121).

Booth, Elizabeth. Dau. of Jesse/Ann
(O'Brien) of Co. Tyrone, Ireland;
marr. Halifax 30 Jan. 1815 Michael
Burn (q.v.) (30:103).

Botner, Elias Loyalist; plus 1 f./7
ch.; mustered at Digby 19 May 1784
(39:118).

Botsford, Amos. Esq.; plus 1 f./4 ch.
8+/1 ch. -8; arr. Annapolis from
New York 19 Oct. 1782 (37:126).

Botsford, Amos. Loyalist; plus 1 f./3
ch./2 svts.; mustered at Digby 19
May 1784 (39:119).

Botsford, Amos. Loyalist; New York to
N.S. 1782 (41:14).

Bouchan, Alexr. Plus 1 f./2 ch. -8;
arr. Annapolis from New York 19
Oct. 1782 (37:125).

Bourgar, Alexr. Plus 1 f./3 ch. 8+/1
ch. -8; arr. Annapolis from New
York 19 Oct. 1782 (37:125).

Bourk, Walter. Ireland; Boston,
Mass., to Chester 30 July 1759
(16:46).

Bow, John. S. of Maurice/Mary (Quirk)
of Co. Kilkenny, Ireland; marr.
Halifax 16 June 1833 Margaret

Carroll (q.v.) (33:54).

Bow, Michael. S. of Michael/Margaret (Power) of Kilmadenogue, Co. Kilkenny, Ireland; marr. Halifax 23 June 1823 Elener Sullivan (q.v.) (31:41).

Bowes, Catherine. Dau. of Pierce/Catherine (Burke) of Co. Waterford, Ireland; marr. Halifax 23 July 1835 William Triby (q.v.) (34:139).

Bowes, John. S. of Pierce/Catherine (Burke) of Co. Waterford, Ireland; marr. Halifax 15 Feb. 1831 Mary Ann Murry (33:54).

Bowes, Margaret. Dau. of Pierce/Catherine (Burke) of Co. Waterford, Ireland; marr. Halifax 15 May 1832 Edward Morissey (q.v.) (33:64).

Bowes, Robert. Laborer; 25; English; Liverpool to Nova Scotia May 1864 on EUROCLYDON (45:181).

Bowes, Thomas. S. of Pierce/Catherine (Burke) of Co. Waterford, Ireland; marr. Halifax 19 Feb. 1833 Rose Kearney (q.v.) (33:54).

Bowldby, Charles. Plus 1 f./2 ch.; farmer; Port Roseway Associate (6:13).

Bowldby, Edward. Farmer; Port Roseway Associate (6:13).

Bowles, William. New England to Annapolis 1760 (18:271).

Bowlsby, Abraham. Grantee "Digby New Grant" 29 Jan. 1801 (5:81).

Bowlsby, Richard. Esq.; grantee "Digby New Grant" 29 Jan. 1801 (5:81).

Bowser, Ann. 26; servant; Hull, Yorkshire, to Nova Scotia; on TWO FRIENDS 28 Feb.-7 Mar. 1774 (25:30).

Bowser, Ann. 60; shopkeeper; Hull, Yorkshire, to Nova Scotia; on TWO FRIENDS 28 Feb.-7 Mar. 1774 (25:30).

Bowser, John. Plus 1 f./3 ch./1 svt.; Port Roseway Associate (6:13).

Bowser, Richard. 29; farmer; Hull, Yorkshire, to Nova Scotia; on TWO FRIENDS 28 Feb.-7 Mar. 1774 (25:30).

Boyce, William. Clerk; plus wife/3 ch.; b. Co. Antrim, Ireland, ca. 1769; Belfast or Greenock to Halifax on POLLY, spring 1799 (29:83).

Boyd, Adam. From N.H.; effective land grant at Truro 31 Oct. 1765 (4:245).

Boylan, James. S. of Martin/Mary (White) of Co. Leix, Ireland; marr. Halifax 5 Feb. 1837 Margaret Doyle (q.v.) (34:126).

Boyle, Anne. Dau. of John/Martha of Co. Antrim, Ireland; marr. Halifax 3 Oct. 1818 John Baptist Deeder (q.v.) (31:44).

Boyle, Elener. Dau. of John/Mary (Brown) of Co. Waterford, Ireland; marr. Halifax 21 May 1812 James Walsh (q.v.) (30:111).

Boyle, John. S. of Henry/Joanna (Keefe) of Co. Kilkenny, Ireland; marr. Halifax 4 Oct. 1832 Eleanor Murphy (q.v.) (33:54).

Bradbyrne, Alexander. Plus 1 f./2 ch.; Port Roseway Associate (6:13).

Bradden, Mary. Dau. of Thomas/Rose (Reynolds) of Co. Longford, Ireland; widow of John Flinn; marr. Halifax 16 Nov. 1840 Thomas Condon (q.v.) (34:127).

Bradford, Bartlet. S. of Peleg/Lydia; Kingston, Mass., to Liverpool by 1775 (47:127:56).

Bradford, Bartlett. S. Peleg/Lydia; b. New England; d. at sea 10 Aug. 1801 ae 51st; bur. Liverpool (49:

132).

Bradford, Carpenter. From Mass.; land grant at Onslow 21 Feb. 1769 (4: 224).

Bradford, Hannah. See Deane, Hannah.

Bradley, Mary. Dau. of William/Susana (Deganzy) of Falmouth, England; marr. Halifax 23 June 1823 (q.v.) (31:43).

Bradley, Susannah. Dau. of John/Ann (Ryan) of Co. Derry, Ireland; marr. Halifax 21 May 1836 David Morris (q.v.) (34:135).

Bradly, Margaret. Dau. of Andrew/Catherine (McGinty) of Co. Donegal, Ireland; marr. Halifax 8 Dec. 1837 William Grannan (q.v.) (34:130).

Bradshaw, Abraham. Plus wife/5 ch.; Lexington, Mass., to Chester with first settlers (16:45).

Bradstreet. See Broadstreet.

Brady, Arthur. S. of Michael/Ellinor (Carey) of Parish Rakeany, Co. Meath, Ireland; marr. Halifax 20 Apr. 1836 Catherine Carney (q.v.) (34:126).

Brady, Thomas. S. of John/Mary (Connan) of Carrick, Co. Tipperary, Ireland; marr. Halifax 19 Sep. 1829 Mary Ann Rudolf widow of Frederick Silver (32:105).

Bragg, John. Loyalist; plus 1 f.; mustered at Digby 19 May 1784 (39:118).

Bragg, John. Plus 1 f.; arr. Annapolis from New York 19 Oct. 1782 (37:125).

Brandan, Conrad. Disbanded soldier, German Service; mustered at Bear River 11/25 June 1784 (38:259).

Brandon, John. Plus 1 f./1 ch. -8; arr. Annapolis from New York 19 Oct. 1782 (37:125).

Brannagan, Thomas. Laborer not set-

tled; mustered at Digby 19 May 1784 (39:119).

Branthwaite, William. Plus 1 f./2 ch./1 svt.; merchant; Port Roseway Associate (6:13).

Braton, Mary. Dau. of Thomas/Rose (Reynolds) of Co. Longford, Ireland; marr. Halifax 1 July 1830 John Flinn (q.v.) (32:111).

Brawderick, Catherine. Dau. of John/Joanna (Nolan) of Co. Kilkenny, Ireland; marr. Halifax 30 Apr. 1833 John Dooley (q.v.) (33:56).

Brawderick, Lawrence. S. of Michael/Margaret (O'Brien) of Co. Kilkenny, Ireland; marr. Halifax 28 May 1831 Ellen Butler (q.v.) (33:54).

Brawderick, Mary. Dau. of John/Judith (Nolan) of Co. Kilkenny, Ireland; marr. Halifax 8 Aug. 1839 Patrick Connelly (q.v.) (34:127).

Brawderick, Michael. S. of John/Joanna (Mahony) of Co. Waterford, Ireland; marr. Halifax 10 Dec. 1840 Ann Harry widow of Thomas Kelly (34:126).

Brawders, Mary. Dau. of William/Bridget (Gaul) of Co. Kilkenny, Ireland; marr. Halifax 12 Sep. 1828 Brien McDonald (q.v.) (32:115).

Brawders, Mary. Dau. of Richard/Eleanor (Fogarty) of Co. Kilkenny, Ireland; marr. Halifax 4 Feb. 1829 Richard Walsh (q.v.) (32:119).

Brazel, Richard. Plus 1 f./1 ch./1 svt.; merchant; Port Roseway Associate (6:13).

Breen, James. S. of Edward/Ellen (Ryan) of Co. Wicklow, Ireland; marr. Halifax 26 June 1842 Ann Harrington (q.v.) (35:135).

Brehant, Thomas. Liverpool proprietor (19:102).

Brehaut, Lydia. Dau. of Thomas/

Rachel; to (or b.?) Liverpool by
178- (47:126:282).

Brehaut, Thomas. Guernsey to Liverpool by 1770 (47:126:287).

Brenan, Alice. Dau. of John/Mary
(Shortis) of Carrick-on-Suir, Co.
Tipperary, Ireland; m,. Halifax 6
Nov. 1830 Peter Brenan (q.v.)
(32:105).

Brenan, Alice. Dau. of John/Mary
(Shortis) of Carrick-on-Suir, Co.
Tipperary, Ireland; marr. Halifax
6 Nov. 1830 Peter Brenan (q.v.)
(33:54).

Brenan, Bridget. Dau. of John/Cather-
ine (Griffin) of Co. Carlow, Ireland; marr. Halifax 14 Oct. 1830
Adam Grace (q.v.) (32:112).

Brenan, Edmund. S. of Mathew/Mary
(Kirwan) of Co. Kilkenny, Ireland;
marr. Halifax 15 Dec. 1829 Catherine Brown (q.v.) (32:106).

Brenan, Eleanor. Dau. of Thomas/Ann
(Gorman) of Parish Newbawn, Co.
Wexford, Ireland; marr. Halifax 9
May 1828 John Flinn (q.v.)
(32:111).

Brenan, Mary. Dau. of Edmund/Johanna
(MacDonnell) of Co. Kilkenny, Ire-
land; marr. Halifax 23 Oct. 1831
Edmund Phelan (q.v.) (33:65).

Brenan, Owen. S. of Owen/Juliana of
Co. Kerry, Ireland; marr. Halifax
11 Nov. 1818 Catherine Granville
(q.v.) (31:41).

Brenan, Patrick. S. of John/Catherine
(Griffin) of Co. Carlow, Ireland;
marr. Halifax 3 Mar. 1829 Margaret
Dunn (q.v.) (32:106).

Brenan, Patrick. S. of Peter/Mary
(Murphy) of Co. Wexford, Ireland;
marr. Halifax 24 May 1836 Mary
Tyrrell (q.v.) (34:126).

Brenan, Peter. S. of Mathias/Mary
(Long) of Co. Kilkenny, Ireland;

marr. Halifax 6 Nov. 1830 Alice
Brenan (q.v.) (32:105).

Brenan, Peter. S. of Mathias/Mary
(Long) of Co. Kilkenny, Ireland;
marr. Halifax 6 Nov. 1830 Alice
Brenan (q.v.) (33:54).

Brennan, Alice. Dau. of John/Alice
(Londrigan) of Parish Mullinahone,
Co. Tipperary, Ireland; marr.
Halifax 11 Aug. 1836 John Mullumby
(q.v.) (34:135).

Brennan, Bernard. S. of Hugh/Honora
(Quilty) of Co. Mayo, Ireland;
marr. Halifax 3 June 1813 Mary
Jennings (q.v.) (30:102).

Brennan, Caroline. Dau. of Daniel/
Maria (Fegan) of Castlepollard,
Co. Westmeath, Ireland; marr.
Halifax 22 Aug. 1836 John Rourk
(q.v.) (34:137).

Brennan, Edward. S. of John/Mary
(Delapp) of Arklow, Co. Wicklow,
Ireland; marr. Halifax 28 Jan.
1816 Ann Scanlan widow of John
Boarows (30:102).

Brennan, George. S. of Michael/Ann
(Dwire) of Co. Donegal, Ireland;
marr. Halifax 29 Oct. 1831 Judith
Power (q.v.) (33:54).

Brennan, Patrick. S. of Patrick/
Margaret (Noonan) of Co. Waterford, Ireland; marr. Halifax 23
July 1821 Margaret Power (q.v.)
(31:41).

Brennan, Patrick. S. of John/Mary
(Byrne) of Gowran, Co. Kilkenny;
marr. Halifax 1 May 1823 Elenor
Patton (q.v.) (31:41).

Brennan, Solomon. S. of Solomon/
Elizabeth (Roney) of Co. Down,
Ireland; marr. Halifax 29 Feb.
1840 Joanna Shortt (q.v.)
(34:126).

Brerer, Jonathan. Liverpool proprietor (19:101).

Brewer, Christian. Loyalist; plus 1
f./2 ch.; Loyalist; mustered at
Digby 19 May 1784 (39:118).

Brewer, Jacob. Grantee "Digby New
Grant" 29 Jan. 1801 (5:81).

Brewer, Jacob. Loyalist; mustered at
Digby 19 May 1784 (39:118).

Brewer, John. From Mass.; land grant
at Truro 1759 (4:242).

Brian, John. S. of Martin/Johanna
(Whelan) of Parish Kill, Co. Waterford, Ireland; marr. Halifax 30
Oct. 1827 Mary Toppin (q.v.)
(32:106).

Bride, Bachelor. Loyalist; mustered
at Digby 19 May 1784 (39:118).

Bride, Mary. Dau. of Thomas/Margaret
(Doherty) of Co. Cork, Ireland;
marr. Halifax 20 Apr. 1841 Patrick
McCarthy (q.v.) (35:140).

Bride, Maurice. S. of John/Mary
(Hodnett) of Killeagh, Co. Cork,
Ireland; marr. Halifax 24 Oct.
1842 Mary Sinclair (q.v.)
(35:135).

Bridge, Benjamin. Plus wife/3 ch.;
Mass. to Chester with first settlers (16:45).

Bridgman, John. Plus 1 f./5 ch.;
farmer; Port Roseway Associate
(6:13).

Brien, Ann. Dau. of Catherine; 5;
Irish; Liverpool to Nova Scotia
May 1864 on EUROCLYDON (45:181).

Brien, Catherine (Mrs.). Irish; 40;
Liverpool to Nova Scotia May 1864
on EUROCLYDON (45:181).

Brien, Fanny. Dau. of Catherine; 11;
Irish; Liverpool to Nova Scotia
May 1864 on EUROCLYDON (45:181).

Brien, Jane. Dau. of Catherine; 7;
Irish; Liverpool to Nova Scotia
May 1864 on EUROCLYDON (45:181).

Brien, John. S. of Catherine; 3;
Irish; Liverpool to Nova Scotia

May 1864 on EUROCLYDON (45:181).

Brien, Mary. Dau. of David/Bridget
(Burns) of Parish Ballkinan, Tip-
perary, Ireland; marr. Halifax 15
Sep. 1826 John Collins (32:107).

Briere, Johnsidere. Loyalist; mustered at Digby 19 May 1784 (39:
118).

Briggs, Gabriel. Loyalist; plus 1
f./2 ch.; mustered at Digby 19 May
1784 (39:118).

Briggs, George. Liverpool proprietor
(19:102).

Briggs, George. S. of James/Betsey;
to Liverpool by 1762 (47:126:288).

Briggs, Lucy. Dau. of James; to (or
b.?) Liverpool by 1783 (47:127:
51).

Briggs, Wate. Dau. of James; to (or
b.?) Liverpool by 1785 (47:127:
52).

Brigs, Thomas. 28; blacksmith; Hull,
Yorkshire, to Nova Scotia; on TWO
FRIENDS 28 Feb.-7 Mar. 1774 (25:
29).

Brill, -----. Widow; plus 1 svt.;
Loyalist; mustered at Digby 19 May
1784 (39:118).

Brinley, Sarah. New Rutland, Mass.,
to Chester 30 July 1759 (16:46).

Briscoe, Mary. Dau. of Henry/Mary
(Headon) of Co. Tipperary, Ire-
land; marr. Halifax 21 Oct. 1834
William Keating (q.v.) (34:132).

Broderick, James. S. of Edmund/Marga-
ret (Shea) of Co. Kilkenny, Ireland; marr. Halifax 12 Oct. 1842
Ellen McDonnell (q.v.) (35:135).

Broderick, Thomas. S. of John/Judith
(Nolan) of Co. Kilkenny, Ireland;
marr. Halifax 2 June 1836 Ellen
Ryan (q.v.) (34:126).

Brooks, Abner. From Mass.; land grant
at Onslow 21 Feb. 1769 (4:224).

Brooks, Abner. From Mass.; land grant

at Truro 1759 (4:242).

Brooks, Abraham. Grantee "Digby New Grant" 29 Jan. 1801 (5:81).

Brooks, Benjamin. From Mass.; land grant (to heirs) at Onslow 21 Feb. 1769 (4:225).

Brooks, Benjamin. From Mass.; land grant at Truro 1759 (4:242).

Brooks, Edward Jr. From Mass.; land grant at Onslow 21 Feb. 1769 (4:225).

Brooks, Edward. From Mass.; land grant at Onslow 21 Feb. 1769 (4:224).

Brooks, Edward. From Mass.; land grant at Truro 1759 (4:242).

Brooks, Martin. From Mass.; land grant at Onslow 21 Feb. 1769 (4:224).

Brooks, Martin. From Mass.; land grant at Truro 1759 (4:242).

Brooks, Mercy. From Mass.; land grant at Onslow 21 Feb. 1769 (4:225).

Brooks, Phineas. From Mass.; land grant at Truro 1759 (4:242).

Brooks, Silvanus. From Mass.; land grant at Onslow 21 Feb. 1769 (4:225).

Brophy, Anastasia. Dau. of John/Judy (Keating) of Co. Carlow, Ireland; marr. Halifax 7 June 1843 Thomas Kennedy (q.v.) (35:140).

Brophy, Ellen. Dau. of Michael/Ellen (McSweeny) of Co. Carlow, Ireland; marr. Halifax 18 June 1834 Patrick Nolan (q.v.) (33:64).

Brophy, Margaret. Dau. of Thomas/Margaret (Dunn) of Co. Kilkenny, Ireland; marr. Halifax 14 Feb. 1831 Thomas Ready (q.v.) (33:66).

Brophy, Mary. Dau. of John/Bridget (Ryan) of Co. Tipperary, Ireland; marr. Halifax 5 Feb. 1831 William Fogarty (q.v.) (33:58).

Brophy, Mary. Dau. of James/Anastasia

(O'Brien) of Co. Carlow, Ireland; marr. Halifax 23 Oct. 1831 Martin Smith (q.v.) (33:67).

Brothes, Catherine. See Henebery, Catherine.

Brown, Bridget. Dau. of Francis/Anastasia (Clowney) of Parish Innistioge, Kilkenny, Ireland; marr. Halifax 11 July 1824 Cornelius O'Solovan (q.v.) (31:54).

Brown, Catherine. Dau. of Francis/Anastasia (Cloney) of Co. Kilkenny; Ireland; marr. Halifax 15 Dec. 1829 Edmund Brenan (q.v.) (32:106).

Brown, Eleanor. Grantee "Digby New Grant" 29 Jan. 1801 (5:81).

Brown, Jacob. S. of Thomas; to Liverpool by 1787 (47:128:30).

Brown, James. 17; husbandman; Hull, Yorkshire, to Nova Scotia; on TWO FRIENDS 28 Feb.-7 Mar. 1774 (25:29).

Brown, James. From Mass.; land grant at Onslow 21 Feb. 1769 (4:225).

Brown, Jane. 1; dau.of William; Hull, Yorkshire, to Nova Scotia; on TWO FRIENDS 28 Feb.-7 Mar. 1774 (25:29).

Brown, Jane. 21; wife of William; Hull, Yorkshire, to Nova Scotia; on TWO FRIENDS 28 Feb.-7 Mar. 1774 (25:28).

Brown, Joanna. Dau. of Francis/Anastaasia (Lowery) of Innistioque, Co. Kilkenny, Ireland; marr. Halifax 16 Aug. 1829 James Herbert (q.v.) (32:112).

Brown, Johanna. Widow of Timothy O'Brien of Youghal, Co. Cork, Ireland; marr. Halifax 19 Feb. 1833 John O'Brien (q.v.) (33:65).

Brown, John. Loyalist; plus 1 f./3 ch.; mustered at Digby 19 May 1784 (39:119).

Brown, Joseph. From Mass.; land grant at Truro 1759 (4:242).

Brown, Mary. 26; servant; Hull, Yorkshire, to Nova Scotia; on TWO FRIENDS 28 Feb.-7 Mar. 1774 (25: 29).

Brown, Mary. Dau. of Michael/Mary (Murphy) of Co. Wexford, Ireland; marr. Halifax 3 Sep. 1835 Thomas Tracy (q.v.) (34:139).

Brown, Mary. Widow of Hugh, of Dublin, Ireland; marr. Halifax 5 Aug. 1823 Patrick Cowney widower of Mary Ruddy (31:43).

Brown, Michael. Of Donaghedy, Co. Tyrone, Ireland; marr. Halifax 15 Sep. 1817 Honora Daily (q.v.) (30:102).

Brown, Michael. Of Parish Donaghedy, Co. Tyrone, Ireland; marr. Halifax 15 Sep. 1817 Honora Daily (q.v.) (31:41).

Brown, Patrick. S. of James/Margaret (Roche) of Co. Waterford, Ireland; marr. Halifax 5 May 1811 Elizabeth Peterkin (q.v.) (30:102).

Brown, Peter. Loyalist; mustered at Digby 19 May 1784 (39:119).

Brown, Rose. Dau. of Henry/Mary (MacNamee) of Co. Tyrone, Ireland; marr. Halifax 6 Oct. 1832 Charles Rodden (q.v.) (33:66).

Brown, Samuel. From Mass.; land grant at Truro 1759 (4:242).

Brown, Stephen. S. of Michael/Mary (Murphy) of Co. Wexford, Ireland; marr. Halifax 7 July 1839 Mary Londrigan (q.v.) (34:126).

Brown, Thomas. Liverpool proprietor (19:101).

Brown, Thomas. S. of Thomas/Catherine (Landrigan) of Co. Tipperary, Ireland; marr. Halifax 25 Nov. 1834 Elizabeth Mathews (q.v.) (34:126).

Brown, William. 22; carpenter; Hull, Yorkshire, to Nova Scotia; on TWO FRIENDS 28 Feb.-7 Mar. 1774 (25:28).

Browne, Charlotte Elizabeth. Dau. of Rev. Michael Browne; b. 1 Oct. 1790 at Norwich, England; to Annapolis Royal (27:229).

Browne, Daniel. Plus 1 f./2 ch.; Port Roseway Associate (6:13).

Browne, James. A sailor; plus 1 svt.; mustered at Digby 19 May 1784 (39: 119).

Browne, Nicholas. Plus 1 f./7 ch./2 svts.; planter; Port Roseway Associate (6:13).

Browne, Samuel. Plus 1 svt.; blacksmith; Port Roseway Associate (6: 13).

Browner, Thomas. S. of William/Sarah (Martin) of Templelanigan. Co. Wexford, Ireland; marr. Halifax 18 Nov. 1829 Catherine Hewson (q.v.) (32:106).

Brownler, William. Laborer; 21; Irish; Liverpool to Nova Scotia May 1864 on EUROCLYDON (45:181).

Brude. See Bride.

Bruff, Charles Oliver. Plus 1 f./5 ch./8 svts.; cutler; Port Roseway Associate (6:13)n

Brundige, Abraham. Loyalist; mustered at Digby 19 May 1784 (39:119).

Bryan, Ellen. Of Mullinahone, Co. Tipperary, Ireland; widow of John Grady; marr. Halifax 21 May 1838 Thomas Connolly (q.v.) (34:127).

Bryden, William E. S. of James/Mary (Hogg); b. Dornach Parish, Co. Dumfries, Scotland; to Brookfield; to Liverpool; d. 24 Sep. 1864 ae. 77 yrs. 6 mos. (49:133).

Bryden, William. S. of James/Mary; Annan, Dumfriesh., Scotland, to Liverpool by 1827 (47:128:115-116).

Buck, John Ames. S. of Jacob/Hannah; to (or b.?) Liverpool by 1789 (47: 127:208).

Buckley, Daniel. B. Co. Cork, Ireland; resident Windsor; marr. Halifax 19 Sep. 1819 Eleanor Power (q.v.) (31:41).

Buckley, Daniel. S. of Patrick/Mary (Flynn) of Parish Ardnageehy, Co. Cork, Ireland; marr. Halifax 15 June 1836 Mary Tooney (q.v.) (34:126).

Buckley, Elizabeth. Wife of Simon Kearney; bur. Halifax 30 Nov. 1836 ae. 28 (34:125).

Buckley, Elizabeth. Dau. of Daniel/Catherine (Linehan) of Co. Cork, Ireland; marr. Halifax 23 Oct. 1834 Simon Karney (q.v.) (34:132).

Buckley, Ellen. See Power, Ellen.

Buckley, Thomas. S. of Patrick/Mary (Casy) of Co. Tipperary, Ireland; marr. Halifax 21 Nov. 1839 Joanna Flanery (q.v.) (34:126).

Buckley, William. S. of James/Margaret (Barry) of Co. Cork, Ireland; marr. Halifax 24 May 1833 Bridget Kavanagh (q.v.) (33:54).

Buckwall, Hannah. Loyalist; plus 4 ch.; mustered at Digby 19 May 1784 (39:119).

Budd, Betsey. Grantee "Digby New Grant" 29 Jan. 1801 (5:81).

Budd, Elisha. Grantee "Digby New Grant" 29 Jan. 1801 (5:81).

Budd, Tamar. Grantee "Digby New Grant" 29 Jan. 1801 (5:81).

Buggy, Mary. See Mary Crowley.

Buhler, A. Disbanded soldier, German Service; plus 1 f./3 ch.; mustered at Bear River 11/25 June 1784 (38:259).

Bulger, Anastasia. Dau. of Patrick/Johanna (Hamilton) of Gowran, Co. Kilkenny, Ireland; marr. Halifax 7 Feb. 1827 Patrick Murphy (q.v.) (32:116).

Bulger, Edward. S. of Thomas/Ann (McDonohoe) of Co. Wexford, Ireland; marr. Halifax 14 Nov. 1830 Mary Neiff (q.v.) (32:106).

Bulger, Richard. S. of Philip/Mary (Condon) of Ireland; marr. Halifax 19 July 1817 Bridget Ryan (q.v.) (30:103).

Bull, Elizabeth. Grantee "Digby New Grant" 29 Jan. 1801 (5:81).

Bull, William Robert. Loyalist; mustered at Digby 19 May 1784 (39:119).

Bulmer, George. 14; s. of John; Hull, Yorkshire, to Nova Scotia; on TWO FRIENDS 28 Feb.-7 Mar. 1774 (25:30).

Bulmer, Grace. 46; wife of John; Hull, Yorkshire, to Nova Scotia; on TWO FRIENDS 28 Feb.-7 Mar. 1774 (25:30).

Bulmer, James. 20; s. of John; Hull, Yorkshire, to Nova Scotia; on TWO FRIENDS 28 Feb.-7 Mar. 1774 (25:30).

Bulmer, John. 45; farmer; Hull, Yorkshire, to Nova Scotia; on TWO FRIENDS 28 Feb.-7 Mar. 1774 (25:30).

Bulmer, Joseph. 10; s. of John; Hull, Yorkshire, to Nova Scotia; on TWO FRIENDS 28 Feb.-7 Mar. 1774 (25:30).

Bunnel, Solomon. Plus 1 f./4 ch. 8+/1 ch. -8; arr. Annapolis from New York 19 Oct. 1782 (37:126).

Bunnell, Solomon. Loyalist; plus 1 f./5 ch.; mustered at Gulliver's Hole/St. Mary's Bay/Sissiboo 1/6 June 1784; settled at Sissiboo (now Weymouth) (40:261).

Burbank, Elizabeth. Dau. of Timothy/Betty; to Liverpool by 1779 (47:

128:29).

Burbank, Mary. Dau. of Timothy/Lydia; to Liverpool by 1787 (47:127:56).

Burbank, Timothy. Liverpool proprietor (19:102).

Burbanks, Timothy. S. of Timo./Mary; to Liverpool ca. 1760 (47:126:96).

Burbanks, Timothy. To Liverpool ca. 1760 (47:126:99).

Burbanks, William. Loyalist; mustered at Digby 19 May 1784 (39:119).

Burdette, Anne. Dau. of Henry/Anne (Burridge) of Plymouth, England; marr. Halifax 30 Jan. 1830 John Smith (q.v.) (32:118).

Burk, Anthony. Mass. to N.S.; to U.S. 1776; lived 1785 at Mass. [which then incl. Me.] (36:64).

Burk, Ellen. Dau. of Patrick/Ellen (Corcoran) of Co. Cork, Ireland; marr. Halifax 15 Feb. 1833 Timothy O'Brien (q.v.) (33:65).

Burk, Marianne. Dau. of Patrick/Mary (O'Brien) of Co. Tipperary, Ireland; marr. Halifax 11 Aug. 1833 Michael Hogan (q.v.) (33:59).

Burk, William. S. of Watt/Nancy; to (or b.?) Liverpool by 1786 (47:127:52).

Burke, Bridget. Dau. of Michael/Catherine (Magrath) of Co. Waterford, Ireland; marr. Halifax 26 Nov. 1836 Michael Cody (q.v.) (34:127).

Burke, Bridget. Spinster; 22; Irish; Liverpool to Nova Scotia May 1864 on EUROCLYDON (45:181).

Burke, Catherine. Irish; 11; Liverpool to Nova Scotia May 1864 on INDIAN QUEEN (45:181).

Burke, David. S. of David/Anne (Lee) of Mainadieu, Cape Breton; marr. Halifax 7 May 1839 Eliza Talant (q.v.) (34:126).

Burke, Edward. S. of John/Mary of

Parish Thomastown, Co. Waterford, Ireland; marr. Halifax 23 Oct. 1825 Catherine Larrassy (q.v.) (31:41).

Burke, Elener. Dau. of Edmund/Margaret (Cody), widow of Peter Kelly of Nfld.; marr. Halifax 9 June 1811 Jeremiah English (q.v.) (30:105).

Burke, Honora. Dau. of Richard/Barbara (Kean) of Co. Mayo, Ireland; marr. Halifax 18 Dec. 1832 Mathew Nolan (q.v.) (33:64).

Burke, John. Pvt. 30th Regt.; s. of Thomas/Mary (Hogan) of Co. Galway, Ireland; marr. Halifax 28 Apr. 1842 Martha Kinsela (q.v.) (35:135).

Burke, John. S. of William/Margaret (Heany) of Parish Stradbally, Co. Waterford, Ireland; marr. Halifax 7 June 1836 Mary Threighe (q.v.) (34:126).

Burke, Mary. Dau. of Michael/Elenor (Curry) of Parish Adare, Co. Limerick, Ireland; marr. Halifax 29 July 1821 John Russell (q.v.) (31:53).

Burke, Patrick. Of Co. Kilkenny, Ireland; widower of Bridget Murphy; marr. Halifax 20 May 1844 Bridget Dunn (q.v.) (35:135).

Burke, Thomas. Laborer; 20; Irish; Liverpool to Nova Scotia May 1864 on EUROCLYDON (45:181).

Burke, Thomas. Late of N.S. Regt.; s. of Thomas/Alice (Karney) of Cashel, Co. Tipperary, Ireland; marr. Halifax 9 Apr. 1823 Mary Kelly widow of George McAndrew (31:41).

Burke, Thomas. S. of Thomas/Jane (Martell) of Mainadieu, Cape Breton; marr. Halifax 10 Nov. 1836 Anne Kennedy (q.v.) (34:126).

Burke, Thomas. S. of Walter/Margaret

(O'Neal) of Mainadieu, Cape Breton; m,. Halifax 9 Jan. 1835 Catherine McGowen (q.v.) (34:126).

Burke, William. Plus 1 f./4 ch.; fisherman; Port Roseway Associate (6:13).

Burke, William. S. of John/Ann (Ronan) of Co. Tipperary, Ireland; marr. Halifax 31 May 1832 Ann Clary (q.v.) (33:54).

Burkett, James. Laborer not settled; mustered at Digby 19 May 1784 (39:119).

Burkett, John. Loyalist; plus 1 f./4 ch./6 svts.; mustered at Digby 19 May 1784 (39:118).

Burkett, John. Grantee "Digby New Grant" 29 Jan. 1801 (5:81).

Burkett. See Bull.

Burn, Mary. Dau. of John/Catherine (Rannels) of Co. Kilkenny, Ireland; marr. Halifax 7 Apr. 1818 Richard Haberlin (q.v.) (31:46).

Burn, Michael. S. of Moses/Mary of Co. Wexford, Ireland; marr. Halifax 30 Jan. 1815 Elizabeth Booth (q.v.) (30:103).

Burnaby, Joseph. B. Provincetown, Mass., 14 July 1736 O.S.; s. of Joseph/Lydia; to Liverpool by 1771 (47:126:167).

Burnaby, Joseph. Liverpool proprietor (19:102).

Burnaby, Thomas. Liverpool proprietor (19:102).

Burnaby, Thomas. S. of Joseph/Mercy; to (or b.?) Liverpool by 1792 (47:127:210).

Burnall, Katharine. To (or b.?) Liverpool by 1784 (47:127:51).

Burne, Joanna. Dau. of Michael/Sara (Neil) of St. John's, Nfld.; marr. Halifax 17 Nov. 1818 John Cahill (q.v.) (31:42).

Burne, Martin. S. of Michael/Rosana

(Murphy) of Co. Kilkenny, Ireland; marr. Halifax 6 June 1838 Bridget Murphy (q.v.) (34:127).

Burnet, Daniel. Mustered at Digby 19 May 1784 (39:119).

Burnet, William. Arr. Annapolis from New York 19 Oct. 1782 (37:125).

Burns, Bridget (Mrs.). Irish; 30; Liverpool to Nova Scotia June 1864 on INDIAN QUEEN (45:181).

Burns, Catherine. Dau. of Thomas/Margaret (Murray) of Co. Fermanagh, Ireland; marr. Halifax 24 Sep. 1806 John Scanlon (q.v.) (30:110).

Burns, George. Disbanded soldier, King's American Regt.; mustered at Gulliver's Hole/St. Mary's Bay/Sissiboo 1/6 June 1784; settled at Sissiboo (now Weymouth) (40:261).

Burns, Honora. Dau. of Bridget; 6; Irish; Liverpool to Nova Scotia June 1864 on INDIAN QUEEN (45:181).

Burns, James. S. of Patrick/Jane (Walsh) of Parish Thomastown, Co. Kilkenny, Ireland; marr. Halifax 11 June 1828 Catherine Murphy (q.v.) (32:106).

Burns, Michael. Loyalist; plus 1 f./8 ch.; mustered at Digby 19 May 1784 (39:119).

Burns, Richard. S. of Daniel/Catherine (O'Donnell) of Clogheen, Tipperary, Ireland; marr. Halifax 22 Dec. 1828 Bridget Fagan (q.v.) (32:106).

Burns, Sarah. Dau. of James/Mary (Drew) of Myshall, Co. Carlow, Ireland; marr. Halifax 28 Apr. 1826 James Archer (q.v.) (32:105).

Burns, William. Grantee "Digby New Grant" 29 Jan. 1801 (5:81).

Burns, William. Loyalist; plus 1 f./7 ch.; mustered at Digby 19 May 1784

(39:119).

Burrell, Josiah. Disbanded soldier Loyal American Regt.; plus 1 f./5 ch.; mustered at Digby 19 May 1784 (39:118).

Burrowes, James. Deserted 7 Mar. 1806 from the Corps of Royal Military Artificers; 5'7", fair complexion, light brown hair, grey eyes, has a cut near the bottom of his nose, 36, b. Ireland; advertised *The Weekly Chronicle*, 29 Mar. 1806 (28:34).

Burton, William. Plus 1 f./3 ch./2 svts.; pumpmaker; Port Roseway Associate (6:13).

Burtrict, Donald. Loyalist; mustered at Digby 19 May 1784 (39:118).

Busfield, John. 30; farmer; Hull, Yorkshire, to Nova Scotia; on TWO FRIENDS 28 Feb.-7 Mar. 1774 (25: 28).

Butler, Alice Elizabeth. Dau. of Michael/Eleanor of Co. Kilkenny; marr. Halifax 18 Oct. 1810 Patrick Keating *(q.v.)* (30:106).

Butler, Catherine. Dau. of Walter/ Eleanor (Doil) of Glamore, Mullinavat, Kilkenny, Ireland; marr. Halifax 6 Apr. 1818 Daniel McLaughlin *(q.v.)* (31:49).

Butler, Eleanor. Dau. of Thomas/ Catherine of Cashel, Co. Tipperary, Ireland; widow of Michael Ryan; marr. Halifax 13 Jan. 1830 William Cummins *(q.v.)* (32:108).

Butler, Eleanor. Dau. of Thomas/ Catherine of Cashel, Co. Tipperary, Ireland; widow of Michael Ryan; marr. Halifax 13 Jan. 1830 (sic) William Cummins *(q.v.)* (33:56).

Butler, Elisabeth Alice. Dau. of Michael/Eleanor of Co. Kilkenny, Ireland; widow of Patrick Keating;

marr. Halifax 17 Sep. 1818 Henry O'Neill (q.v.) (31:51).

Butler, Ellen. Dau. of Martin/Teresa (Scoli) of Co. Kilkenny, Ireland; marr. Halifax 28 May 1831 Lawrence Brawderick *(q.v.)* (33:54).

Butler, James. S. of Richard/Margaret (N---) of Parish Pollrone, Co. Kilkenny, Ireland; marr. Halifax 12 Apr. 1825 Mary Holly (31:41).

Butler, James. S. of Thomas/Elizabeth (Lewis) of Co. Kilkenny, Ireland; marr. Halifax 30 Sep. 1833 Mary Ann Quinan (33:54).

Butler, James. S. of Philip/Catherine (Whelan) of Rossmore, Co. Kilkenny, Ireland; marr. Halifax 15 June 1842 Sarah Doherty *(q.v.)* (35: 135).

Butler, James. Widower of Mary Ann Quinan; s. of Thomas/Elizabeth (Lewis) of Co. Kilkenny, Ireland; marr. Halifax 20 June 1835 Mary Carey *(q.v.)* (34:126).

Butler, Joanna. Dau. of James/Mary (Ready) of Co. Kilkenny, Ireland; marr. Halifax 21 Jan. 1834 John Doyle *(q.v.)* (33:57).

Butler, John. S. of Richard/Margaret (McCarthy) of Co. Tipperary, Ireland; marr. Halifax 8 Nov. 1841 Margaret Dorney *(q.v.)* (35:135).

Butler, Maria. Dau. of John/Ellen (Kelly) of Co. Tipperary, Ireland; marr. Halifax 27 Apr. 1842 Robert Kinsela *(q.v.)* (35:140).

Butler, Martin. S. of William/Mary (Goodman) of Co. Kilkenny, Ireland; marr. Halifax 28 July 1840 Catherine Downy *(q.v.)* (34:126).

Butler, Mary. Dau. of John/Mary (Tavish) of Co. Cork, Ireland; marr. Halifax 18 Jan. 1838 John Dimssy *(q.v.)* (34:128).

Butler, Michael. S. of John/Elener

(Hearn) of Parish Cloyne, Cork, Ireland; marr. Halifax 2 July 1824 Anne Fitzmorris (31:41).

Butler, Patrick. S. of Thomas/Mary (Nory) of Co. Kilkenny, Ireland; marr. Halifax 10 Oct. 1830 Judith Lahey (q.v.) (32:106).

Butler, Patrick. S. of Thomas/Elizabeth (Lewis) of Co. Kilkenny, Ireland; marr. Halifax 11 Apr. 1831 Joanna Holden (q.v.) (33:54).

Butler, Patrick. S. of William/Mary (Goodman) of Co. Kilkenny, Ireland; marr. Halifax 28 July 1840 Catherine Downy widow of William Hanigan (34:126).

Butler, Patrick. S. of John/Bridget (Burke) of Co. Wexford, Ireland; marr. Halifax 28 July 1840 Mary Ryan (q.v.) (34:126).

Butler, Samuel Jr. Carpenter; Port Roseway Associate (6:13).

Butterfield, Nathaniel. Loyalist; mustered at Digby 19 May 1784 (39:118).

Byrn, Denis. S. of Denis/Catherine (Devine) of Dunkeef (sic for Drumcliff), Sligo, Ireland) marr. Halifax 4 Aug. 1825 Mary MacLaughlan (31:42).

Byrne, Bridget. Dau. of Michael/Margaret (Egan) of Machel, Co. Carlow, Ireland; marr. Halifax 28 Oct. 1827 Patrick McGennis (q.v.) (32:115).

Byrne, Bridget. Dau. of James/Margaret (Murphy) of Co. Carlow, Ireland; marr. Halifax 12 May 1841 John Power (q.v.) (35:143).

Byrne, Catherine. Dau. of Walter/Mary (Deloughrey) of Co. Kilkenny, Ireland; marr. Halifax 8 Jan. 1826 John Finlon (q.v.) (31:45).

Byrne, Catherine. Dau. of Walter/Mary (Deloughrey) of Co. Kilkenny, Ireland; marr. Halifax 8 Jan. 1826 John Finlon (q.v.) (32:110).

Byrne, James. S. of Andrew/Elizabeth (McEvoy) of Parish Dunleckney, Co. Carlow, Ireland; marr. Halifax 24 June 1825 Mary Anne McCarthy (q.v.) (31:42).

Byrne, Michael. Widower of Margaret Eagan; of Parish Balinkiln, Co. Carlow, Ireland; marr. Halifax 18 Sep. 1823 Lucy Donnars, widow of William Burnett (31:42).

Byrne, Thomas. S. of Patrick of Co. Wexford, Ireland; marr. Halifax 10 Dec. 1821 Anne Henlon widow of Thomas Mara (31:41).

Byrnes, Ann. Dau. of Michael/Mary (McAvoy) of Queen's Co. Ireland; marr. Halifax 12 Feb. 1800 (sic for 1830?) John Curramore (q.v.) (32:108).

Byrnes, Catherine. Dau. of James/ Honora (Hawes) of Co. Kilkenny, Ireland; marr. Halifax 4 June 1837 Richard McEvoy (q.v.) (34:133).

Byrnes, Edmund. S. of Martin/Mary (Hinessy) of Co. Kilkenny, Ireland; marr. Halifax 30 Oct. 1832 Honora Magher (q.v.) (33:55).

Byrnes, Edward. S. of Patrick/Mary (Brophy) of Co. Kildare, Ireland; marr. Halifax 28 Oct. 1839 Mary Devenay (34:126).

Byrnes, Ellen. Dau. of Thomas/Mary (O'Brien) of Co. Waterford, Ireland; marr. Halifax 19 Feb. 1844 Richard Keefe (q.v.) (35:139).

Byrnes, James. S. of John/Elizabeth (Cody) of Co. Wexford, Ireland; marr. Halifax 16 Oct. 1831 Letitia Carew (q.v.) (33:55).

Byrnes, James. S. of Michael/Margaret (Egan) of Co. Carlow, Ireland; marr. Halifax 15 Sep. 1841 Mary Hunt (35:135).

Byrnes, Mary. Dau. of Michael/Mary
(McAvoy) of Queen's Co., Ireland;
marr. Halifax 6 Feb. 1830 Thomas
Walsh (q.v.) (32:120).

Byrnes, Mary. Dau. of Andrew/Mary
(Casey) of Co. Longford, Ireland;
marr. Halifax 28 Apr. 1835 Patrick
Curran (q.v.) (34:128).

Byrnes, Michael. S. of John/Joanna
(Whelan) of Carrick-on-Suir, Tipperary, Ireland; marr. Halifax 3
Oct. 1829 Margaret Rice (q.v.)
(32:106).

Byrnes, Michael. S. of John/Catherine
(Keefe) of Co. Kilkenny, Ireland;
marr. Halifax 1 Oct. 1833 Bridget
Sexton (q.v.) (33:55).

Byrnes, Richard. S. of Sandy/Eliza-
beth (Connors) of Co. Tipperary,
Ireland; marr. Halifax 10 June
1833 Mary Magher (q.v.) (33:55).

Byrnes, Sarah. Dau. of James/Mary
(Drew) of Myshall, Co. Carlow,
Ireland; widow of James Archer;
marr. Halifax 27 May 1834 Lawrence
Clarey (q.v.) (33:55).

Byrnes, William. S. of Martin/Marga-
ret (Kearney) of Co. Kilkenny,
Ireland; marr. Halifax 13 June
1838 Ann Hobin (q.v.) (34:126).

Byrnes, William. S. of Thomas/Mary
(O'Brien) of Co. Waterford, Ire-
land; marr. Halifax 18 Feb. 1841
Joanna Sullivan (q.v.) (35:135).

Byrns, Ann. Dau. of Patrick/Ann
(Murphy) of Co. Waterford, Ire-
land; marr. Halifax 25 Apr. 1831
Capt. John Gibbons (q.v.) (33:58).

Byron, Michael. S. of Richard/Ann of
Dublin; marr. Halifax 15 Feb. 1810
Anne Cousins (q.v.) (30:103).

- C -

Caddigan, Ellen. Dau. of Denis/Honora

(McCarthy) of Co. Cork, Ireland;
marr. Halifax 31 Jan. 1833 John
Mahony (q.v.) (33:63).

Cadigan, Patrick. S. of John/Cather-
ine (Lowney) of Parish St. Multis,
Kinsale, Co. Cork, Ireland; marr.
Halifax 6 Dec. 1825 Jane Newcum
(31:42).

Cahill, Elizabeth. Dau. of Michael/
Joanna (Manning) of Co. Kerry,
Ireland; marr. Halifax 27 Oct.
1830 John Harrington (q.v.)
(32:112).

Cahill, Elizabeth. Dau. of Darby/
Anastas (Donnelly) of Co. Waterford, Ireland; marr. Halifax 24
May 1837 Patrick Allan (q.v.)
(34:125).

Cahill, John. Of Co. Kilkenny, Ireland; widower of Mary Meagher;
marr. Halifax 21 Nov. 1835 Catherine Londrigan (q.v.) (34:127).

Cahill, John. S. of James of Co.
Tipperary, Ireland; marr. Halifax
17 Nov. 1818 Joanna Burne (q.v.)
(31:42).

Cahill, Margaret. Dau. of John/Marga-
ret (Bain) of Co. Waterford,
Ireland; marr. Halifax 2 Oct. 1831
James O'Donnell (q.v.) (33:65).

Cahoon, Charles. S. of William/Eliza-
beth; to (or b.?) Liverpool by
1796 (47:127:212).

Cahoon, Desire. Dau. of William/
Elisabeth; to Liverpool ca. 1760
(47:126:160).

Cahoon, Elisabeth. Wife of William;
to Liverpool ca. 1760 (47:126:
160).

Cahoon, Elisabeth. B. 11 July 1727;
wife of William; to Liverpool ca.
1760 (47:126:163).

Cahoon, Elisabeth. B. 3 June 1759;
dau. of William/Elisabeth; to Liverpool ca. 1760 (47:126:163).

Cahoon, Elizabeth. Dau. of Nathaniel/
Thankfull; to (or b.?) Liverpool
by 1791 (47:127:117).

Cahoon, Elizabeth. Dau. of Downing/
Elizabeth; to (or b.?) Liverpool
by 1796 (47:127:212).

Cahoon, Nathaniel Jr. S. of Natha-
niel/Thankful; to (or b.?) Liverpool by 1783 (47:126:288).

Cahoon, Sarah. Dau. of William/Ta-
batha; to (or b.?) Liverpool by
1801 (47:127:273).

Cahoon, Waitstill. B. 10 Feb. 1755;
dau. of William/Elisabeth; to
Liverpool ca. 1760 (47:126:163).

Cahoon, Wate. Dau. of William/Eliza-
beth; to (or b.?) Liverpool by
1775 (47:127:49).

Cahoon, William Jr. B. 20 Sep. 1752;
s. of William/Elisabeth; to Liverpool ca. 1760 (47:126:163).

Cahoon, William Jr. S. of William/
Elisabeth; to Liverpool by 1774
(47:127:53).

Cahoon, William K. Liverpool proprietor (19:101).

Cahoon, William. B. New England 23
June 1724; to Liverpool ca. 1760
(47:126:163).

Cahoon, William. To Liverpool ca.
1760 (47:126:160).

Cain, Ellen. Dau. of Patrick/Joanna
(Shea) of Co. Tipperary, Ireland;
marr. Halifax 21 Feb. 1835 John
Tinehan (q.v.) (34:138).

Cain, Peter. S. of John/Mary (Ryan)
of Parish St. John, Kilkenny, Ireland; marr. Halifax 25 June 1825
Johanna Prendergast (q.v.) (31:
42).

Calaghan, Edmund. S. of Edmund/Joanna
(Toomy) of Co. Cork, Ireland;
marr. Halifax 8 Jan. 1843 Margaret
Ronan (q.v.) (35:135).

Calaghan, Martin. S. of Michael/Mary
(Wall) of Co. Waterford, Ireland;
marr. Halifax 22 Sep. 1842 Ann
Landrigan (q.v.) (35:135).

Calanan, Michael. S. of Michael/Susan
(Lynch) of Cloyne, Co. Cork, Ire-
land; marr. Halifax 1 Feb. 1821
Catherine Glavin (31:42).

Calderwood, Robert. From Ireland;
land grant at Londonderry 6 Mar.
1775 (4:258).

Caldwell, John. From N.H.; effective
land grant at Truro 31 Oct. 1765
(4:245).

Caldwell, John. Plus 3 ch.; in JOSEPH
from Bermuda; mustered at Digby 19
May 1785 (39:120).

Caldwell, Mary. Dau. of James/Mary
(Magrath) of Harbour Grace, Nfld.;
marr. Halifax 19 Oct. 1808 Patrick Donnelly (q.v.) (30:104).

Cale, William. Loyalist; mustered at
Digby 19 May 1784 (39:119).

Calf, Daniel. From Mass.; land grant
at Onslow 21 Feb. 1769 (4:225).

Calihan, John. S. of Cornelius/Marga-
ret (Harrigan) of Co. Cork, Ireland; marr. Halifax 12 Jan. 1830
Catherine Sweeney (q.v.) (32:106).

Callaghan, Martin. S. of John/Eleanor
(Dunn) of Co. Cork, Ireland; marr.
Halifax 20 May 1816 Mary Anne
Mooney (q.v.) (30:103).

Callaghan, Michael. S. of Edward/
Margaret (Frahill) of Co. Donegal,
Ireland; marr. Halifax 3 May 1832
Joanna Power (q.v.) (33:55).

Callahan, Robert. To Liverpool by
1782 (47:126:287).

Callahan, William. S. of James/Mary
(McGrath) of Callan, Co. Kilkenny,
Ireland; marr. Halifax 8 Feb. 1827
Elizabeth Ann Marshall (32:106).

Callanan, Nicholas. S. of John/Mary

44

(Foley) of Co. Cork, Ireland;
widow Sarah Johnson remarried
Halifax 10 Jan. 1842 Philip Elward
(q.v.) (35:137).

Callanan, William. S. of Patrick/Mary
(Corrigan) of Co. Kilkenny, Ire-
land; marr. Halifax 24 Nov. 1839
Alice Deereen (q.v.) (34:127).

Callinan, Bridget. Dau. of John/Mary
(Foley) of Co. Cork, Ireland;
marr. Halifax 24 Oct. 1833 Michael
Murphy (q.v.) (33:64).

Calnan, Joanna. Dau. of John/Mary
(Foley) of Co. Cork, Ireland;
marr. Halifax 27 Sep. 1841 Michael
O'Brien (q.v.) (35:142).

Calnek, Jacob. B. 1745 Saxe-Coburg-
Gotha of Jewish parents; d. Cen-
tral Granville 1831 aged 86 (12:
84-85).

Calnek, Jacob. Quartermaster, Anspach
Service; plus 2 svts.; mustered at
Bear River 11/25 June 1784 (38:
259).

Calwell, William. Port Roseway Associate (6:13).

Cameron, Anne. Dau. of Duncan/Eliza-
beth of Fortunegall, Perth, Scotland; marr. Halifax 17 Sep. 1803
Michael Mara (q.v.) (30:108).

Cameron, Evan. Plus 1 f./6 ch.;
merchant; Port Roseway Associate
(6:14).

Cameron, John. Disbanded soldier,
King's American Dragoons; mustered
at Gulliver's Hole/St. Mary's Bay/
Sissiboo 1/6 June 1784; settled at
Sissiboo (now Weymouth) (40:262).

Cameron, John. Disbanded soldier,
42nd Regt.; laborer; mustered at
Gulliver's Hole/St. Mary's Bay/
Sissiboo 1/6 June 1784 (40:262).

Cameron, William. Port Roseway Associate (6:14).

Camp, Joel. From Mass.; land grant

(to heirs) at Onslow 21 Feb. 1769
(4:225).

Camp, Joel. From Mass.; land grant at
Truro 1759 (4:242).

Campbel, Archibald. Plus 1 f./1 ch./2
svts.; cooper; Port Roseway Associate (6:14).

Campbell, Alexander. Plus 2 svts.;
tailor; Port Roseway Associate
(6:14).

Campbell, Archibald. Loyalist; plus 1
ch.; mustered at Digby 19 May 1784
(39:120).

Campbell, Bridget. See Kirwan,
Bridget.

Campbell, Dougal. Plus 3 svts.; carpenter; Port Roseway Associate (6:
13).

Campbell, George. Plus 1 f./3 ch./4
svts.; Port Roseway Associate
(6:14).

Campbell, John. Loyalist; plus 1 f./3
ch.; mustered at Digby 19 May 1784
(39:120).

Campbell, Mungo. Grantee "Digby New
Grant" 29 Jan. 1801 (5:81).

Campbell, Robert. Loyalist; plus 1
ch.; mustered at Digby 19 May 1784
(39:119).

Campbell, Susannah. Of Newry, Co.
Down, Ireland; widow John McIn-
tire; marr. Halifax 31 Aug. 1840
James Connelly (q.v.) (34:127).

Can, Joshua. Laborer; 30; English;
Liverpool to Nova Scotia May 1864
on EUROCLYDON (45:181).

Canada, John. Widower of Hali Hayes,
of Co. Tipperary, Ireland; marr.
Halifax 16 Sep. 1818 Catherine
Hannery widow of Nicholas Howlet
(q.v.) (31:48).

Caniff, Daniel. Loyalist; plus 1 f./2
ch.; mustered at Gulliver's Hole/
St. Mary's Bay/Sissiboo 1/6 June
1784; settled at Sissiboo (now

Weymouth) (40:261).

Cannell, Robert. Plus 1 f.; tailor;
Port Roseway Associate (6:14).

Cantfield, Mary. Dau. of Denis/
Catherine (Ryan) of Co. Kilkenny,
Ireland; marr. Halifax 29 Nov.
1839 Richard Dunphy (q.v.)
(34:129).

Cantfield, Mary. Dau. of Thomas/Mary
(Duffy) of Co. Kilkenny, Ireland;
marr. Halifax 21 July 1836 Michael
Holden (q.v.) (34:131).

Cantfill, Patrick. S. of John/Johanna
of Parish Callan, Co. Kilkenny,
Ireland; marr. Halifax 5 Feb. 1829
Catherine O'Brien (q.v.) (32:106).

Cantwell, Jeffery. S. of William/Mary
(Pender) of Co. Kilkenny, Ireland;
marr. Halifax 16 Apr. 1833 Mary
Dowling (q.v.) (33:55).

Canty, Timothy. Of Co. Cork, Ireland;
marr. Halifax 8 June 1842 Martha
McClaherty (35:135).

Carbery, Thomas. S. of Thomas/Cather-
ine (Quinlan) of Carrick-on-Suir,
Co. Tipperary, Ireland; marr. Halifax 18 May 1843 Harriet Gordon
(35:135).

Carder, Richard. Mass., to Liverpool
by 1793 (47:127:201).

Carew, Letitia. Dau. of Robert/Ann
(Connell) of Co. Waterford, Ire-
land; marr. Halifax 16 Oct. 1831
James Byrnes (q.v.) (33:55).

Carew, Margaret. Of Mastermarch, Co.
Kilkenny, Ireland; marr. Halifax 5
Sep. 1824 John Lawricey; earlier
marr. by magistrate Cumberland
Co., N.S. (31:49).

Carew, Nicholas. S. of Patrick/Johan-
na (Brennan) of Parish Ballyhoe,
Kilkenny, Ireland; marr. Halifax 3
Feb. 1818 Elizabeth Nowlan (q.v.)
(31:42).

Carey, Ellen. Dau. of Michael/Ellen

(Timmen) of Old Leighlin, Co. Carlow, Ireland; marr. Halifax 20
Aug. 1833 James William Kihoe
(q.v.) (33:61).

Carey, Mary. Dau. of Edmund/Mary
(Cantfield, of Co. Kilkenny, Ire-
land; marr. Halifax 10 Oct. 1831
Edmund Kavanah (q.v.) (33:60).

Carey, Mary. Dau. of Pierce/Catherine
(Lart) of Co. Tipperary, Ireland;
marr. Halifax 20 June 1835 James
Butler (q.v.) (34:126).

Carey, Thomas. Of Co. Dublin, Ireland; "carpenter in Halifax for
ten years;" marr. Halifax 11 Jan.
1837 Ellen Finan (q.v.) (34:127).

Carey, William. From Mass.; land
grant at Truro 1759 (4:242).

Carey, William. S. of John/Mary
(Hullihan) of Co. Kilkenny, Ire-
land; marr. Halifax 2 Feb. 1829
Joanna Power (q.v.) (32:106).

Carlan, Mary. Dau. of Owen/Jane
(Birch) of Co. Meath, Ireland;
marr. Halifax 8 Sep. 1831 Owen
Gibny (q.v.) (33:58).

Carleton, Ellen. Of Co. Longford,
Ireland; widow of Philip Martin;
marr. Halifax 16 Jan. 1841 Roger
Sullivan (35:145).

Carleton, Osgood. To Liverpool by
1763 (47:126:101).

Carley, Joseph. From Mass.; land
grant at Truro 1759 (4:242).

Carney, Catherine. Dau. of Patrick/
Catherine (Power) of Parish Bally-
han, Co. Waterford, Ireland; widow
of Thomas Hannigan; marr. Halifax
20 Apr. 1836 Arthur Brady (q.v.)
(34:126).

Carney, Denis. Shoemaker; s. John/
Johanna (Laudey) of Cashel, Tipperary, Ireland; marr. Halifax 12
Nov. 1826 Margaret Sullivan (q.v.)
(32:106).

Carpenter, Bradford. Lieut.; Mass. to
N.S.; to U.S. 1776; lived 1785 at
Mass. [which then incl. Me.] (36:
64).

Carpenter, Isaiah. From Mass.; land
grant at Truro 1759 (4:242).

Carr, Bridget. Dau. of Cormick/Eliza-
beth (Hunt) of Parish Neigh, Co.
Fermanagh, Ireland; marr. Halifax
9 June 1823 Pvt. Brien Hanagan
(q.v.) (31:47).

Carr, Eliza. Dau. of John/Eliza
(Austin) of Co. Tipperary, Ireland; widow of William Anderson;
marr. Halifax 15 Apr. 1833 Michael
Curran (q.v.) (33:56).

Carrier, Green. Plus 1 f./1(?) ch.
8+/2 ch. -8; arr. Annapolis from
New York 19 Oct. 1782 (37:126).

Carroll, Daniel. Plus 1 f./3 ch./1
svt.; merchant; Port Roseway Associate (6:14).

Carroll, Ellen. Dau. of James/Cather-
ine (MacDonnell) of Co. Kilkenny,
Ireland; marr. Halifax 27 Oct.
1831 Martin Walsh (q.v.) (33:68).

Carroll, James. Pvt. 64th Regt.; of
Co. Monaghan, Ireland; marr. Halifax 15 May 1841 Ann McInnis widow
of Benjamin Murtough (35:135).

Carroll, Johanna. Dau. of William/
Bridget (Cleary) of Parish Mullinavat, Co. Kilkenny, Ireland;
marr. Halifax 25 Oct. 1843 Patrick
Weston (q.v.) (35:145).

Carroll, John. S. of James/Mary (Haberlin) of Parish Skarte (sic),
Co. Kilkenny, Ireland; marr. Halifax 1 Feb. 1818 Elizabeth Watson
(q.v.) (31:42).

Carroll, Margaret. Dau. of Richard/
Bridget (Butler) of Co. Kilkenny,
Ireland; marr. Halifax 16 June
1833 John Bow (q.v.) (33:54).

Carroll, Michael. S. of James/Cather-

ine of Co. Kilkenny, Ireland;
marr. Halifax 2 June 1840 Rebecca
Murphy (34:127).

Carroll, Peter. S. of Thomas/Bridget
(White) of Clara, King's Co., Ire-
land; marr. Halifax 8 July 1827
Anne Devany (q.v.) (32:106).

Carroll, Thomas. 37th Regt.; s. of
Michael/ Jane (Karney) of Co.
Mayo, Ireland; marr. Halifax 13
Nov. 1840 Isabella Homan (34:127).

Carroll, Thomas. S. of Michael/Win-
ifred (Shaughnessy) of Banagher,
Co. Offaly, Ireland; marr. Halifax
22 June 1840 Esther Mulligan
(q.v.) (34:127).

Carron, James. Arr. Annapolis from
New York 19 Oct. 1782 (37:125).

Carson, William. Plus 1 f./3 ch./1
svt.; planter; Port Roseway Associate (6:14).

Carten, John. S. of Cormac/Margaret;
Newtown Limarady, Co. Londonderry,
Ulster, Ireland, to Liverpool by
1833 (47:128:115).

Carten, Samuel. See Curten, Samuel.

Carter, John. From Mass.; land grant
at Onslow 21 Feb. 1769 (4:224).

Carter, Richard. 27, farmer; Hull to
Fort Cumberland on ALBION 7-14
Mar. 1774 (21:139).

Carton, Philip. S. of Cormick/Marga-
ret (Carig) of Newtown Limavidy,
Co. Derry, Ireland; marr. Halifax
16 Feb. 1830 Frances Magrath (32:
106).

Cary, Mary. Dau. of Michael/Ellen
(Timons) of Old Leighlin, Co. Carlow, Ireland; marr. Halifax 22
Nov. 1838 William Kehoe (q.v.)
(34:132).

Casey, Ellen. Dau. of John/Catherine
(Donihue) of Nfld.; marr. Halifax
22 Apr. 1829 Benjamin Summers
(q.v.) (32:119).

Casey, Mary. Of Parish Newtown Forbes, Co. Longford, Ireland; marr. Halifax 3 Oct. 1834 Thomas Tigh (34:138).

Casey, Michael. S. of Michael/Margaret (Costello) of Co. Waterford, Ireland; marr. Halifax 15 May 1842 Mary Lyons (q.v.) (35:135).

Casey, Thomas. S. of Patrick/Bridget (Fling) of Dungarvan, Co. Waterford, Ireland; marr. Halifax 21 May 1839 Eliza Quirk (q.v.) (34:127).

Casey, William. S. of Patrick/Bridget (Flinn) of Dungarvan, Co. Waterford, Ireland; marr. Halifax 21 Jan. 1842 Johanna Elward (q.v.) (35:135).

Cashin, John. S. of Pierce/Catherine (Skerry) of Co. Kilkenny, Ireland; marr. Halifax 29 Apr. 1842 Sophia Catherine Richards (35:135).

Cashin, Michael. S. of Patrick/Margaret (Barnevile) of Ballingarry, Tipperary, Ireland; marr. Halifax 22 Feb. 1830 Bridget Doyle (q.v.) (32:106).

Cashin, William. S. of William/Elenor (Alwart) of Co. Waterford, Ireland; marr. Halifax 27 Nov. 1819 Mary Fleming (31:42).

Cashman, Bridget. Dau. of Patrick/Bridget (Walsh) of Co. Cork, Ireland; marr. Halifax 30 May 1833 James O'Brien (q.v.) (33:65).

Cashman, Johanna. Dau. of Patrick/Honora (Many) of Co. Cork, Ireland; marr. Halifax 11 Feb. 1834 Roger Lahy (q.v.) (33:61).

Cashman, Margaret. Dau. of Patrick/Honora (Mainy) of Co. Waterford, Ireland; marr. Halifax 28 Jan. 1838 Patrick Magher (q.v.) (34:134).

Cashman, Mary. Dau. of Thomas/Mary (Savage) Of Co. Cork, Ireland; marr. Halifax 3 Nov. 1829 Edward Aheron (q.v.) (32:105).

Cashman, Mary. Dau. of Patrick/Honora (Maney) of Co. Waterford, Ireland; marr. Halifax 15 Jan. 1833 John Manning (q.v.) (33:63).

Cashman, William. S. of Patrick/Bridget (Walsh) of Co. Cork, Ireland; marr. Halifax 8 July 1835 Mary Hewson (q.v.) (34:127).

Cassidy, Hugh. S. of Dominic/Mary (Riley) of Co. Fermanagh, Ireland; marr. Halifax 26 Aug. 1813 Margaret Crooks (q.v.) (30:103).

Cassidy, James. S. of James/Dorothy (Burn) of Co. Kildare, Ireland; marr. Halifax 12 May 1809 Mary Downs (q.v.) (30:103).

Cassidy, Margaret. Dau. of Peter/Margaret (Kennedy) of Co. Wicklow, Ireland; marr. Halifax 22 Aug. 1812 Lawrence Redmond (q.v.) (30:110).

Cassidy, Thomas. S. of Thomas/Mary of Co. Wicklow, Ireland; marr. Halifax 16 June 1805 Anne Power (q.v.) (30:103).

Cassin, Pierce. Widower of Catherine Skerry, of Co. Kilkenny, Ireland; marr. Halifax 27 Mar. 1819 Johanna Downs widow of Michael Higgins (31:42).

Cassles, Mary. Dau. of Maurice/Catherine (O'Brien) of Co. Waterford, Ireland; marr. Halifax 4 June 1837 Edmond Handcox (q.v.) (34:131).

Casson, William. S. of Patrick/Mary (Walsh) of Waterford, Ireland; marr. Halifax 27 Oct. 1807 Elener Madox (q.v.) (30:103).

Castle, William. Port Roseway Associate (6:14).

Caton, James. S. of Parick/Anne

(Doyle) of St. Mullins, Carlow, Ireland; marr. Halifax 26 June 1818 Mary Anne Reaney (31:48).

Cavanagh, Elizabeth. Dau. of Denis/ Mary of Myshall, Co. Carlow, Ireland; widow of Bernard Nolan; marr. Halifax 15 Feb. 1844 Michael Kerns (q.v.) (35:140).

Cayford. See Crayford.

Ceary, John. S. of Laughlin/Margaret (Walsh) of New Ross, Co. Wexford, Ireland; marr. Halifax 15 Feb. 1825 Elenor Donovan (q.v.) (31:42).

Ceary, Timothy. S. of Richard/Johanna (Dewire) of Parish Loughmoe?, Co. Tipperary, Ireland; marr. Halifax 27 Mar. 1824 Anne Eliza Ironsides (31:42).

Ceerce, Henry. King's Orange Rangers to Liverpool by 1784 (47:126:281).

Chaddock, Isaiah. From Mass.; land grant at Truro 1759 (4:242).

Chadsey, Abel. S. of William/Lucy; No. Kingstown, R. I., to Liverpool by 1778 (47:126:289).

Chandler, Samel. Arr. Annapolis from New York 19 Oct. 1782 (37:126).

Chandler, William. Loyalist; mustered at Digby 19 May 1784 (39:120).

Chapman, Ann. 1, dau. of William; Hull to Fort Cumberland on ALBION 7-14 March 1774 (21:138).

Chapman, Ann. 8, dau. of Lancelot; Hull to Fort Cumberland on ALBION 7-14 March 1774 (21:136).

Chapman, Frances. 12, dau. of Lancelot; Hull to Fort Cumberland on ALBION 7-14 March 1774 (21:136).

Chapman, Frances. 42, wife of Lancelot; Hull to Fort Cumberland on ALBION 7-14 March 1774 (21:136).

Chapman, Hannah. 4, dau. of Lancelot; Hull to Fort Cumberland on ALBION 7-14 March 1774 (21:136).

Chapman, Henry. 7, s.of William; Hull to Fort Cumberland on ALBION 7-14 March 1774 (21:138).

Chapman, Jane. 15, dau. of William; Hull to Fort Cumberland on ALBION 7-14 March 1774 (21:138).

Chapman, John. 13, s.of William; Hull to Fort Cumberland on ALBION 7-14 March 1774 (21:138).

Chapman, Jonathan. 5, s.of William; Hull to Fort Cumberland on ALBION 7-14 March 1774 (21:138).

Chapman, Lancelot. 49, farmer; Hull to Fort Cumberland on ALBION 7-14 March 1774 (21:136).

Chapman, Lancelot. 6, s.of Lancelot; Hull to Fort Cumberland on ALBION 7-14 March 1774 (21:136).

Chapman, Martin. 10, s.of Lancelot; Hull to Fort Cumberland on ALBION 7-14 March 1774 (21:136).

Chapman, Mary. 42, wife of William; Hull to Fort Cumberland on ALBION 7-14 March 1774 (21:138).

Chapman, Mary. 9, dau. of William; Hull to Fort Cumberland on ALBION 7-14 March 1774 (21:138).

Chapman, Rachael. 14, dau. of Lancelot; Hull to Fort Cumberland on ALBION 7-14 March 1774 (21:136).

Chapman, Sarah. 3, dau. of William; Hull to Fort Cumberland on ALBION 7-14 March 1774 (21:138).

Chapman, Thomas. 17, s.of William; Hull to Fort Cumberland on ALBION 7-14 March 1774 (21:138).

Chapman, Thomas. 18, s.of Lancelot; Hull to Fort Cumberland on ALBION 7-14 March 1774 (21:136).

Chapman, William. 19, s.of William; Hull to Fort Cumberland on ALBION 7-14 March 1774 (21:138).

Chapman, William. 44, farmer; Hull to Fort Cumberland on ALBION 7-14 Mar. 1774 (21:138).

Charles. Negro slave of Capt. Young; mustered at Digby 19 May 1784 (39:120).

Charlocke, Andrew. S. of Robert of Co. Meath, Ireland; marr. Halifax 6 July 1818 Sara Witham widow of John Story (q.v.) (31:53).

Charlton, Robert. 17, husbandman; Hull to Port Cumberland on ALBION 7-14 March 1774 (21:136).

Charmick, Henry. 31, chandler; Hull to Port Cumberland on ALBION 7-14 March 1774 (21:139).

Chase, Amni. Plus 1 svt.; carpenter; Port Roseway Associate (6:13).

Cheever, Bethiah. B. Dartmouth, Mass., 31 Jan. 17--; dau. of Rev. Israel/Esther; to Liverpool ca. 1760 (47:126:99).

Cheever, Esther Torrey. Dau. of Rev. Israel/Esther; to Liverpool by 1775 (47:126:166).

Cheever, Esther. B. Dartmouth, Mass., 16 June 17--; dau. of Rev. Israel/Esther; to Liverpool ca. 1760 (47:126:99).

Cheever, Israel. Rev.; Dartmouth, Mass., to Liverpool ca. 1760 (47:126:99).

Cheever, Joseph Mann. B. Dartmouth, Mass., 11 Oct. 17--; s. of Rev. Israel/Esther; to Liverpool ca. 1760 (47:126:99).

Cheever, Molly. B. Dartmouth, Mass., 11 Apr. 17--; dau. of Rev. Israel/Esther; to Liverpool ca. 1760 (47:126:99).

Cheever, Ruth. Dau. of Rev. Israel/Esther; to Liverpool by 1771 (47:126:166).

Cheever, Ruthey. B. Dartmouth, Mass., 7 Mar. 17--; dau. of Rev. Israel/Esther; to Liverpool ca. 1760 (47:126:99).

Cheever, William. B. Dartmouth,

Mass., 18 Oct. 17--; s. of Rev. Israel/Esther; to Liverpool ca. 1760 (47:126:99).

Cheever, William. S. of Rev. Israel/Esther; to Liverpool by 1775 (47:126:285).

Chester, Simeon. Deacon; Conn. to N.S.; to U.S. 1776; lived 1785 at Conn. (36:65).

Chetwynde, Thomas. Plus 1 f./2 ch./2 svts.; merchant; Port Roseway Associate (6:14).

Child, Ebenezer. From Mass.; land grant at Truro 1759 (4:242).

Chisholm, Angus. B. Scotland; to Liverpool by 1770 (47:127:53).

Chisholm, Anna. Dau. of Angus/Mary; to (or b.?) Liverpool by 1793 (47:127:117).

Chisholm, George. Plus 1 f./1 ch./1 svt.; merchant; Port Roseway Associate (6:13).

Chives, Thomas. S. of Thomas/Elizabeth (Reede) of Co. Cork, Ireland; marr. Halifax 30 Oct. 1828 Catherine Pride (32:107).

Christ, Jacob. Loyalist; plus 1 f.; mustered at Digby 19 May 1784 (39:120).

Christopher, Patrick. S. of John/Honor (Magrah) of Ballinsentien, Waterford, Ireland; marr. Halifax 14 Dec. 1802 Mary Allen (q.v.) (30:103).

Christopher, Thomas. S. of William/Susannah; to (or b.?) Liverpool by 1786 (47:127:54).

Chryst, Jacob. Grantee "Digby New Grant" 29 Jan. 1801 (5:81).

Church, Jonathan. From Mass.; land grant at Onslow 18 Oct. 1759 (4:223).

Church, Jonathan. New England to Annapolis on CHARMING MOLLY May 1760 (18:271).

Clancy, Joanna. Dau. of James/Catherine (Murphy) of Co. Cork, Ireland; marr. Halifax 24 Apr. 1843 Malachy Gerarty (q.v.) (35:138).

Clancy, Michael. S. of Thomas/Alice (Grady) of Co. Waterford, Ireland; marr. Halifax 11 Sep. 1830 Elizabeth McLaughlin (32:107).

Clancy, William. S. of James/Ellen (Scott) of Co. Kilkenny, Ireland; widower of Margaret Hanly; marr. Halifax 28 Jan. 1831 Catherine Whelan (q.v.) (33:55).

Clarck, John. S. of John/Mary (McCallon) of Co. Kilkenny, Ireland; marr. Halifax 3 Feb. 1817 Elizabeth Murphy (30:103).

Clarey, Lawrence. S. of Patrick/Joanna (Burke) of Thurles, Co. Tipperary, Ireland; marr. Halifax 27 May 1834 Sarah Byrnes (q.v.) (33:55).

Clark, Mary. 13; dau.of William; Hull, Yorkshire, to Annapolis on JENNY 3-10 April 1775 (22:123).

Clark, Parker. Dr.; Mass. to N.S.; to U.S. 1776; lived 1785 at Machias, Me. (36:65).

Clark, Rachael. 3; dau.of William; Hull, Yorkshire, to Annapolis on JENNY 3-10 April 1775 (22:123).

Clark, Richard. 9; s. of William; Hull, Yorkshire, to Annapolis on JENNY 3-10 April 1775 (22:123).

Clark, William Jr. Grantee "Digby New Grant" 29 Jan. 1801 (5:81).

Clark, William. 10; s. of William; Hull, Yorkshire, to Annapolis on JENNY 3-10 April 1775 (22:123).

Clark, William. 42, farmer; Hull, Yorkshire, to Annapolis on JENNY 3-10 April 1775 (22:123).

Clark, William. Belfast or Greenock to Halifax on POLLY, spring 1799 (29:83).

Clarke, Archi'd. Plus 1 f./3 ch.; merchant; Port Roseway Associate (6:14).

Clarke, John. From Ireland; land grant at Londonderry 6 Mar. 1775 (4:258).

Clarke, Margaret. See Kavanagh, Margaret.

Clarke, Patrick. S. of John/Jane (Horan) of Co. Galway, Ireland; marr. Halifax 22 Aug. 1812 Anne Fulmer (30:103).

Clarke, Robert. Loyalist; plus 1 f.; mustered at Digby 19 May 1784 (39:120).

Clarke, Uriah. New England to Annapolis on CHARMING MOLLY May 1760 (18:271).

Clarkson, Charles. 19, husbandman; Hull to Fort Cumberland on ALBION 7-14 March 1774 (21:139).

Clary, Ann. Dau. of Rodger/Mary (Ryan) of Co. Tipperary, Ireland; marr. Halifax 31 May 1832 William Burke (q.v.) (33:54).

Clary, Honora. Dau. of Michael/Ann (Magher) of Co. Tipperary, Ireland; marr. Halifax 27 Aug. 1832 James Whelan (q.v.) (33:68).

Clary, Mary. Dau. of Michael/Mary (Whelan) of Co. Kilkenny, Ireland; marr. Halifax 25 Nov. 1832 David Cuddy (q.v.) (33:55).

Clary, Michael. S. of Michael/Mary (Whelan) of Co. Kilkenny, Ireland; marr. Halifax 1 Nov. 1838 Elizabeth Doyle (34:127).

Clayton, John. Sgt. 37th Regt.; of Co. Tipperary, Ireland; marr. Halifax 22 Feb. 1841 Joanna Julian (35:136).

Clayton, Robert. S. of Edward/Eleanor (Murphy) of Co. Cork, Ireland; marr. Halifax 30 Nov. 1816 Sarah Gerard widow of Maurice Reaney

(30:103).

Cleary, James. S. of Timothy/Catherine (Coglan) of Kilrush, Waterford, Ireland; marr. Halifax 24 Apr. 1822 Rosina Lyons (31:42).

Clifford, John. S. of Edward/Mary (Fowler) of Dungarvan, Co. Waterford, Ireland; marr. Halifax 16 Nov. 1829 Ellen Bennett (q.v.) (32:107).

Clifford, John. Shoemaker; widower of Ellen Bennett; of Dungarvon, Waterford, Ireland; marr. Halifax 14 Sep. 1832 Honora Scanlon (q.v.) (33:55).

Cline, Peter, Loyalist; mustered at Digby 19 May 1784 (39:119).

Clinton, Brien. S. of Michael/Catherine (Mulloy) of Co. Louth, Ireland; marr. Halifax 27 Oct. 1830 Bridget Cummings (q.v.) (32:107).

Clisby, John. Plus 1 f./2 ch./2 svts.; farmer; Port Roseway Associate (6:13).

Clossan, Anthony. Loyalist; plus 1 f./1 ch.; mustered at Digby 19 May 1784 (39:120).

Clossan, Jonathan. Loyalist; plus 1 f./2 ch./3 svts.; mustered at Digby 19 May 1784 (39:119).

Clossan, Reuben. Loyalist; plus 1 f./2 svts.; mustered at Digby 19 May 1784 (39:119).

Cloutier, Madeleine. Dau. of Pierre/ Madeleine (Tessier) of Lorette, Quebec; marr. Halifax 8 Nov. 1814 John Manning (q.v.) (30:108).

Clubb, James. Loyalist; plus 1 f./1 ch.; mustered at Digby 19 May 1784 (39:119).

Coatnam, Thomas. Loyalist; mustered at Digby 19 May 1784 (39:120).

Coattam. See Coatnam.

Cobb, Hannah. Dau. of Jabez/Sarah; to (or b.?) Liverpool by 1795

(47:127:206).

Cobb, Jabez. Plymouth, Mass., to Liverpool ca. 1760 (47:126:98).

Cobb, Jabish. Liverpool proprietor (19:101).

Cobb, John. B. Plymouth, Mass., 29 Jan. 1752; s. of Jabez; to Liverpool ca. 1760 (47:126:98).

Cobb, John. S. of Jabez/Sarah; to Liverpool by 1773 (47:126:165).

Cobb, Martha. Dau. of Jabez/Sarah; to (or b.?) Liverpool by 1794 (47: 127:203).

Cobb, Mary. Dau. of Capt. Silvanus; to Liverpool by 1763 (47:126:162).

Cobb, Mary. Dau. of Jabez/Sarah; to (or b.?) Liverpool by 1780 (47: 128:35).

Cobb, Nicholas. Loyalist; plus 1 ch.; mustered at Digby 19 May 1784 (39: 119).

Cobb, Sarah. B. Plymouth, Mass., 8 Dec. 1757; dau. of Jabez; to Liverpool ca. 1760 (47:126:98).

Cobb, Sarah. Dau. of John/Mary; to (or b.?) Liverpool by 1795 (47: 127:276).

Cobb, Sarah. Wife of Jabez; Plymouth, Mass., to Liverpool ca. 1760 (47:126:98).

Cobb, Silvanus. B. Plymouth, Mass., 2 Apr. 1754; s. of Jabez; to Liverpool ca. 1760 (47:126:98).

Cobb, Silvanus. S. of Jabez/Sarah; to (or b.?) Liverpool by 1785 (47: 127:125).

Cobb, Sylvanus. Liverpool proprietor (19:101).

Cochran, Catherine. See Donohoe, Catherine.

Cockene, Alexander. Plus 1 f./3 svts.; mariner; Port Roseway Associate (6:14).

Coddigan, Catherine. Widow of Daniel O'Brien of Co. Cork, Ireland;

marr. Halifax 28 Nov. 1835 Hugh
Connors *(q.v.)* (34:128).

Code, Nicholas. S. of Nicholas/
Eleanor (Kehoe) of Co. Wexford,
Ireland; marr. Halifax 29 Aug.
1810 Elizabeth Cox (30:103).

Cody, Michael. Of Thomastown, Co.
Kilkenny, Ireland; widower of
Abigail Drewhan; marr. Halifax 26
Nov. 1836 Bridget Burke *(q.v.)*
(34:127).

Cody, Michael. S. of Edmund/Mary
(Mulloy) of Co. Kilkenny, Ireland;
marr. Halifax 23 Nov. 1830 Alice
O'Brien *(q.v.)* (32:107).

Cody, Richard. Of Owning, Co. Kilkenny, Ireland; marr. Halifax 16 Sep.
1817 Mary Bary *(q.v.)* (30:103).

Cody, William. Of Co. Carlow, Ireland; widower of Mary McDonald;
marr. Halifax 27 Nov. 1834 Margaret Dunphy *(q.v.)* (34:127).

Coffee, Bridget. Dau. of Cornelius/
Ellen (Mulcahy) of Co. Waterford,
Ireland; marr. Halifax 11 Nov.
1834 William Oldfield *(q.v.)*
(34:136).

Coffee, Michael. S. of Patrick/Ann
(Donovan) of Co. Cavan, Ireland;
marr. Halifax 9 Oct. 1841 Catherine Magrath *(q.v.)* (35:136).

Coffee, Patrick. S. of James/Cather-
ine (Foley) of Youghal, Co. Cork,
Ireland; marr. Halifax 16 Apr.
1842 Mary Mihan *(q.v.)* (35:136).

Coffil, John. S. of Patrick/Bridget
(Murray) of Clonmacnoon, Co.
Galway, Ireland; marr. Halifax 27
Aug. 1836 Mary Walsh *(q.v.)* (34:
127).

Coffin, Judith. To Liverpool *ca.* 1760
(47:126:97).

Coffin, Peter. Liverpool proprietor
(19:101).

Coghlan, Catherine. See Donohoe,
Catherine.

Cohoon, Reuben. Barrington petitioner
19 Oct. 1776 (1:365).

Coile, Elleanor. Dau. of John/Cather-
ine (Riley) of Co. Cavan, Ireland;
marr. Halifax 2 June 1829 Philip
Lynch *(q.v.)* (32:114).

Coine, Catherine. Dau. of Maurice/
Anastasia (Danihy) of Co. Waterford, Ireland; marr. Halifax 16
Dec. 1832 Patrick Hollorn *(q.v.)*
(33:60).

Colbourne, Charles. Grantee "Digby
New Grant" 29 Jan. 1801 (5:81).

Colclough, Samuel. 52nd Regt.; s. of
John/Mary of Co. Clare, Ireland;
marr. Halifax 10 July 1828 Marian
Power (32:107).

Cole, Ambrose. Mass. to N.S.; to U.S.
1776; lived 1785 at Mass. [which
then incl. Me.] (36:65).

Cole, Benjamin Jr. S. of Benjamin/
Desire; to Liverpool by 1774 (47:
126:167).

Cole, Benjamin. Liverpool proprietor
(19:101).

Cole, Benjamin. To Liverpool *ca.* 1760
(47:126:95).

Cole, Desire. To Liverpool *ca.* 1760
(47:126:161).

Cole, Desire. Wife of Benjamin; to
Liverpool *ca.* 1760 (47:126:95).

Cole, Edward. Mass. to N.S.; to U.S.
1776; dead by 1785 (36:65).

Cole, Israel. S. of Benjamin/Desire;
to (or b.?) Liverpool by 1789 (47:
127:120).

Cole, Rebekah. Dau. of Benjamin/De-
sire; to Liverpool by 1772 (47:
126:290).

Coleman, Andrew. S. of Patrick/Ellen
of Youghal, Co. Cork, Ireland;
marr. Halifax 6 Feb. 1806 Mary
McManus *(q.v.)* (30:103).

Coleman, Elline. Dau. of John/Julia

(Harney) of Parish Moathill, Co. Waterford, Ireland; marr. Halifax 13 June 1836 Patrick Flynn *(q.v.)* (34:130).

Coleman, Joanna. Dau. of John/Honora (Buckley) of Co. Cork, Ireland; marr. Halifax 19 Feb. 1833 Maurice Heffernan *(q.v.)* (33:59).

Coleman, Mary. Dau. of John/Ann (Mallen) of Sligo, Ireland; marr. Halifax 11 Jan. 1843 Pvt. James Cook *(q.v.)* (35:136).

Coleman, Patrick. S. of John/Johana (White) of Co. Waterford, Ireland; marr. Halifax 3 July 1818 Elizabeth Grant (31:43).

Coleman, Patrick. S. of Michael/Mary (Dore) of Youghal, Co. Cork, Ireland; marr. Halifax 5 Aug. 1843 Catherine Connaughton *(q.v.)* (35:136).

Colens, John. Loyalist; mustered at Digby 19 May 1784 (39:120).

Coley, Benjamin Jr. From Mass.; land grant at Truro 1759 (4:242).

Coley, Gedeon. From Mass.; land grant at Truro 1759 (4:242).

Colford, Jane. See O'Neal, Jane.

Colford, Mary. Dau. of Philip/Mary (Murphy) of Co. Wexford, Ireland; marr. Halifax 26 Sep. 1818 John Leonard Compton (31:43).

Colford, Thomas. S. of Philip/Mary (Murphy) of Co. Wexford, Ireland; marr. Halifax 22 Jan. 1818 Jane O'Neal (31:43).

Collicut, George. Plus wife/1 ch.; Halifax, Mass., to Chester with first settlers (16:45).

Collings, Benajah. East Haddam, Conn., to Liverpool ca. 1771 (47:126:165).

Collings, Deborah. B. East Haddam, Conn., 17 Jan. 1771; dau. of Benajah/Susanna; to Liverpool ca. 1771

(47:126:165).

Collings, Stephen. S. of Joseph/Abigail; to Liverpool by 1771 (47:126:166).

Collings, Susanna. Wife of Benajah; East Haddam, Conn., to Liverpool ca. 1771 (47:126:165).

Collins, Abigail Crowell. Wife of Joseph; b. Yarmouth, Mass., 13 Sep. 1715; Chatham, Mass., to Liverpool after 1756 (50:99).

Collins, Abigail. B. ca. 1716; d. Liverpool 1788 (47:127:56).

Collins, Abigail. Dau. of Hallet/Rhoda; to (or b.?) Liverpool by 1793 (47:127:123).

Collins, Benjamin. S. of Joseph/Desire; to (or b.?) Liverpool by 1801 (47:127:274).

Collins, Betsy. Dau. of Joseph/Desiah; to (or b.?) Liverpool by 1799 (47:127:269).

Collins, Bridget. Dau. of Patrick/Mary (Williams) of Co. Carlow, Ireland; marr. Halifax 13 Aug. 1843 John Neill (35:142).

Collins, Catherine. Dau. of Thomas/Mary (Butler) of Co. Kilkenny, Ireland; marr. Halifax 9 Oct. 1830 John Connell *(q.v.)* (32:107).

Collins, Cyrenius. Liverpool proprietor (19:102).

Collins, Cyrenius. To Liverpool ca. 1760 (47:126:98).

Collins, Cyrenus. S. of Solomon; b. Chatham, Mass., 26 June 1735; to Liverpool bef. July 1760 (50:99).

Collins, David. S. of John/Elenor (Fitzgerald) of Dungarvan, Co. Waterford, Ireland; marr. Halifax 21 Apr. 1825 Mary Rattigan *(q.v.)* (31:43).

Collins, Edward. S. of Denis/Honora (Cronin) of Co. Cork, Ireland; marr. Halifax 16 Dec. 1829 Mary

Barry (*q.v.*) (32:107).

Collins, Esther. Dau. of Stephen/
Ruth; to (or b.?) Liverpool by
1797 (47:127:209).

Collins, George. S. of Benajah/Susan-
na; to (or b.?) Liverpool by 1794
(47:127:212).

Collins, Hallet. Esq.; s. of Joseph
and Abigail; b. 1749 Mass.; to
N.S. 1758; d. Liverpool 3 June
1831 (49:131).

Collins, Hallet. S. of Joseph/Abi-
gail; to Liverpool by 1771 (47:
126:167).

Collins, Hallet. S. of Joseph; b.
Chatham, Mass., 1749; to Liverpool
after 1756 (50:99).

Collins, Hallet. To (or b.?) Liverpool by 1789 (47:127:125).

Collins, Hannah. Dau. of Stephen/
Ruth; to (or b.?) Liverpool by
1801 (47:127:273).

Collins, Jarusha. Dau. of Peter/Mary;
to (or b.?) Liverpool by 1796 (47:
127:271).

Collins, Jeremiah. S. of William/
Eleanor (Connell) of Kilbolane,
Co. Cork, Ireland; marr. Halifax
12 Nov. 1829 Juliana Lane (*q.v.*)
(32:107).

Collins, Joseph Jr. Liverpool proprietor (19:102).

Collins, Joseph Jr. To Liverpool ca.
1760 (47:126:161).

Collins, Joseph. B. ca. 1715;
Chatham, Mass., to Liverpool; d.
1771 (47:127:56).

Collins, Joseph. Brother of Anna
(wife of Jonathan, s. of Paul); to
Liverpool bef. 1762 (50:99).

Collins, Joseph. Liverpool proprietor
(19:101).

Collins, Joseph. One of earliest
settlers of Liverpool; d. 12 Jan.
1771 ae 57th (49:131).

Collins, Joseph. S. of Joseph/Desier;
to (or b.?) Liverpool by 1794 (47:
127:209).

Collins, Joseph. S. of John; b. Eastham, Mass., 14 Aug. 1713; Chatham,
Mass., to Liverpool after 1756
(50:99).

Collins, Joseph. S. of Joseph; b.
Chatham, Mass., 5 Nov. 1741; to
Liverpool after 1756 (50:99).

Collins, Lucy. Dau. of Hallet/Rhoda;
to (or b.?) Liverpool by 1804 (47:
127:277).

Collins, Mathew. Of Co. Cork, Ireland; widower of Elizabeth Fling;
marr. Halifax 24 July 1843 Sarah
Moser widow of John Ross (35:136).

Collins, Paul. S. of Joseph/Abigail;
to (or b.?) Liverpool by 1778 (47:
126:290).

Collins, Peter. S. of Joseph; b.
Chatham, Mass., 1756; to Liverpool
after 1756 (50:99).

Collins, Rebecca Eldredge. Wife of
Cyrenus; b. Chatham, Mass., 16
Nov. 1735; to Liverpool bef. July
1760 (2371:99).

Collins, Rebeckah. Wife of Cyrenius;
to Liverpool ca. 1760 (47:126:98).

Collins, Rhoda. Dau. of Hallet/Rhoda;
to (or b.?) Liverpool by 1795 (47:
127:210).

Collins, Ruthy. Dau. of Stephen/Ruth;
to Liverpool by 1801 (47:128:29).

Collins, Sarah. Dau. of Halet/Rhoda;
to (or b.?) Liverpool by 1802
(47:128:28).

Collins, Stephen. S. of Stephen/Ruth;
to (or b.?) Liverpool by 1801 (47:
127:273).

Collins, Stephen. S. of Joseph; b.
Chatham, Mass., 31 Oct. 1745; to
Liverpool after 1756 (50:99).

Collins, Susannah. Dau. of Benajah/
Susannah; to (or b.?) Liverpool by

1793 (47:127:123).

Collins, Thomas. S. of Thomas/Mary
(Cunnard) of Co. Waterford, Ireland; marr. Halifax 16 May 1830
Catherine Matthews (q.v.)
(32:107).

Collins, William. Loyalist; mustered
at Gulliver's Hole/St. Mary's Bay/
Sissiboo 1/6 June 1784; settled at
Wilmot (40:261).

Collis, Mary Ann. Dau. of William/
Rose (Pidigran) of Co. Kilkenny,
Ireland; marr. Halifax 28 July
1835 Joseph Homes (q.v.) (34:131).

Colpits, Robert. 28, farmer; Hull,
Yorkshire, to Fort Cumberland on
JENNY 3-10 April 1775 (22:123).

Colton, Daniel Jr. From Mass.; land
grant at Truro 1759 (4:242).

Colton, Isaac. From Mass.; land grant
at Truro 1759 (4:242).

Colville, John. Grantee "Digby New
Grant" 29 Jan. 1801 (5:81).

Comfort, John. Loyalist; plus 1 f./1
ch.; mustered at Digby 19 May 1784
(39:120).

Comings, Bruen Vomkes. Plus wife/2
ch.; Mass. to Chester with first
settlers (16:45).

Compton, John. Plus 1 f./5 ch./1
svt.; farmer; Port Roseway Associate (6:14).

Condon, David. S. of John/Bridget
(Cleary) of Co. Tipperary, Ire-
land; marr. Halifax 2 Nov. 1820
Bridget Mulcahy (q.v.) (31:43).

Condon, John. Deserted 14 Apr. 1805
from H.M. Corps of Royal Military
Artificers, stationed at Halifax;
5'8", fair complexion, sandy hair,
blue eyes, speaks thick, is a
carpenter, 29, b. Parish of Kilworth, Co. Cork, Ireland; advertised The Weekly Chronicle, 20
Apr. 1805 (28:35).

Condon, John. Husband of Mary Sinclair; bur. Halifax 8 Dec. 1840
ae. 28 (34:125).

Condon, John. Mariner; s. of Maurice/
Mary (O'Hara) of Waterford, Ire-
land; marr. Halifax 12 Nov. 1828
Bridget Power (q.v.) (32:107).

Condon, John. S. of James/Mary
(Keefe) of Co. Cork, Ireland;
marr. Halifax 8 May 1813 Elizabeth Hurley (30:103).

Condon, Margaret. Dau. of Patrick/
Catherine (Broders) of Co. Waterford, Ireland; marr. Halifax 28
June 1814 James Fleming (q.v.)
(30:105).

Condon, Margaret. Dau. of John/
Bridget (Clery) of Co. Tipperary,
Ireland; marr. Halifax 27 July
1820 Michael Leonard (q.v.)
(31:49).

Condon, Margaret. Dau. of late John/
Bridget (Clery) of Co. Tipperary.
Ireland; widow of Michael Leonard;
marr. Halifax 25 Jan. 1826 Hugh
McDead (32:115).

Condon, Margaret. Dau. of John/Ellen
(Sullivan) of Co. Cork, Ireland;
marr. Halifax 26 July 1834 John
McGrath (33:62).

Condon, Mary. See Sinclair, Mary.

Condon, Michael. Of Parish Poorstown,
Tipperary, Ireland; marr. Halifax
26 June 1822 Mary Kelly (q.v.)
(31:43).

Condon, Thomas. S. of Edward/Mary
(Connors) of Co. Tipperary, Ire-
land; marr. Halifax 16 Nov. 1840
Mary Bradden (q.v.) (34:127).

Condon, William. S. of John/Margaret
(Duling) of Youghal, Co. Cork,
Ireland; marr. Halifax 9 Nov. 1829
Ann Ryan widow of William Condon
(sic) (32:107).

Condon, William. S. of Thomas/Mary

(Hacket) of Thurles, Co. Tipperary, Ireland; marr. Halifax 27 Nov. 1835 Catherine Power (q.v.) (34:127).

Congrove, Eliza. Dau. of Ambrose/Joanna (Horan) of Co. Waterford, Ireland; marr. Halifax 8 June 1829 John Lawler (q.v.) (32:114).

Conna, Joseph. Laborer; 19; Irish; Liverpool to Nova Scotia May 1864 on EUROCLYDON (45:181).

Connaughton, Catherine. Dau. of James/Bridget (Kelly) of St. John, N.B.; marr. Halifax 5 Aug. 1843 Patrick Coleman (q.v.) (35:136).

Connel, Patrick. S. of Morris/Catherine; Lismore, Co. Waterford, Ireland, to Liverpool by 1796 (47:127:209).

Connell, Anne. Dau. of Matthew; of Queen's Co., Ireland; marr. Halifax 3 June 1820 Patrick Mahony (q.v.) (31:50).

Connell, Edward. S. of James/Margaret (Connary) of Co. Cork, Ireland; marr. Halifax 20 Aug. 1840 Bridget Landrigan (q.v.) (34:127).

Connell, John. S. of Maurice/Judith (Callaghan) of Co. Cork, Ireland; marr. Halifax 9 Oct. 1830 Catherine Collins (q.v.) (32:107).

Connell, Margaret. Dau. of John/Honora (Collins) of Mallow, Co. Cork, Ireland; marr. Halifax 7 Oct. 1837 Patrick Murphy (q.v.) (34:135).

Connell, Patrick. To Cornwallis by 1793 (47:128:29).

Connell, Rachel. Wife of Patrick; to Cornwallis by 1793 (47:128:29).

Connelly, Anne. See Phelan, Anne.

Connelly, Anthony. Of Parish Kilcash, Co. Tipperary, Ireland; widower of Mary Whelan; marr. Halifax 21 Jan. 1840 Mary Grant (q.v.) (34:127).

Connelly, Catherine. Dau. of John/Mary (Quinlan) of Co. Tipperary, Ireland; marr. Halifax 7 June 1839 Thomas Lynch (q.v.) (34:133).

Connelly, David. S. of David/Joanna (Moore) of Midleton, Co. Cork, Ireland; marr. Halifax 20 Aug. 1829 Joanna Hurly (q.v.) (32:107).

Connelly, James. Late 52nd Regt.; of Borris, Co. Carlow, Ireland; widower of Charlotte Richards; marr. Halifax 31 Aug. 1840 Susannah Campbell (q.v.) (34:127).

Connelly, John. S. of Edmund/Mary (Dullehanty) of Co. Kilkenny, Ireland; marr. Halifax 19 Feb. 1829 Bridget Aylward widow of John Walsh (q.v.) (32:107).

Connelly, Lawrence. S. of Michael/Bridget (Walsh) of Co. Kilkenny, Ireland; marr. Halifax 23 Oct. 1831 Bridget Ryan (q.v.) (33:55).

Connelly, Patrick. S. of John/Mary (Quinlan) of Mullinahone, Co. Tipperary, Ireland; marr. Halifax 8 Aug. 1839 Mary Brawderick (q.v.) (34:127).

Connelly, Richard. S. of Edmund/Mary (Dulhanty) of Co. Kilkenny, Ireland; marr. Halifax 25 Aug. 1831 Mary Ailward (q.v.) (33:55).

Connelly, Susannah. Dau. of James/Catherine (Phelan) of Price Edward Isl.; marr. Halifax 26 Nov. 1831 George Mulloy (q.v.) (33:64).

Connely, Michael. Disbanded soldier, 40th Regt.; mustered at Digby 19 May 1784; settled at Annapolis (39:120).

Conner, Bartholomew. S. of Jeremiah/Elinor (Keeff) of Midleton, Co. Cork, Ireland; marr. Halifax 7 June 1803 Margaret Connor (q.v.) (30:103).

Conner, John. S. of Patrick/Elizabeth

(Hart) of Co. Sligo, Ireland; marr. Halifax 12 Sep. 1832 Mary Keefe (q.v.) (33:55).

Conners, Catherine. Dau. of Hugh/ Bridget of Co. Kerry, Ireland; marr. Halifax 17 July 1838 Patrick Conners (q.v.) (34:128).

Conners, Catherine. See Magrath, Catherine.

Conners, Patrick. S. of John/Joanna (Cavanah) of Milltown, Co. Kerry, Ireland; marr. Halifax 17 July 1838 Catherine Conners (q.v.) (34:128).

Connolly, Edward. 27th Regt.; s. of Edward/ Margaret (Maganalty) of Co. Tyrone, Ireland; marr. Halifax 20 Nov. 1814 Elizabeth Waymouth (q.v.) (30:103).

Connolly, Joseph. Grantee "Digby New Grant" 29 Jan. 1801 (5:81).

Connolly, Thomas. S. of John/Mary (Quinlan) of Mullinahone, Co. Tipperary, Ireland; marr. Halifax 21 May 1838 Ellen Bryan (q.v.) (34:127).

Connor, Christ'r. Plus 1 f./1 ch./2 svts.; farmer; Port Roseway Associate (6:14).

Connor, Margaret. Dau. of Cornelius/ Catherine (Fitzmaurice) of Cork, Ireland; marr. 7 June 1803 Bartholomew Conner (q.v.) (30:103).

Connor, Patrick. Of Co. Carlow, Ireland; marr. Halifax 11 Nov. 1819 Judith Reily (q.v.) (31:43).

Connor, Samuel. Conn. to N.S.; to U.S. 1776; dead by 1785 (36:65).

Connors, Andrew. S. of John/Margaret (Carroll) of Co. Waterford, Ireland; marr. Halifax 10 Sep. 1842 Hannah Quirk (q.v.) (35:136).

Connors, Bernard. Pvt. 64th Regt.; s. of Peter/Mary (Frail) of Co. Offaly, Ireland; marr. Halifax 19 Feb.

1843 Catherine Barron (q.v.) (35:136).

Connors, Bridget. Dau. of Michael/ Bridget (McAulan) of Co. Kilkenny, Ireland; marr. Halifax 27 Feb. 1843 William O'Brien (q.v.) (35:142).

Connors, Elizabeth. See Hartery, Elizabeth.

Connors, George. S. of Patrick/Ann (Campbell) of Co. Donegal, Ireland; marr. Halifax 24 Aug. 1816 Elizabeth G., widow of Edward Evans (30:104).

Connors, Honora. Dau. of James/Margaret (Lahy) of Co. Cork, Ireland; marr. Halifax 24 Oct. 1831 John Barrett (q.v.) (33:54).

Connors, Hugh. S. of Maurice/Catherine (Conroy) of Co. Kerry, Ireland; marr. Halifax 28 Nov. 1835 Catherine Coddigan (q.v.) (34:128).

Connors, John. S. of James/Catherine (Hand) of Davidstown, Co. Wexford, Ireland; marr. Halifax 23 June 1823 Mary Bradley (q.v.) (31:43).

Connors, Margaret. Dau. of John/ Catherine (Bolan) of Co. Tipperary, Ireland; marr. Halifax 12 July 1828 Martin Shine (q.v.) (32:118).

Connors, Mary. Dau. of Jeremiah/ Eleanor (Keefe) of Midleton, Co. Cork, Ireland; marr. Halifax 12 June 1810 Henry Green (q.v.) (30:105).

Connors, Michael. Of Parish Callan, Co. Kilkenny, Ireland; marr. Halifax 26 Jan. 1836 Catherine Donohoe alias Coghlan (q.v.) (34:128).

Connors, Michael. S. of Michael/ Catherine (Brophy) of Co. Kilkenny, Ireland; marr. Halifax 9 Nov. 1838 Joanna Nugent (q.v.)

(34:128).

Connors, Robert. S. of Edward/Elenor (Lambert) of Parish Duncormuck, Wexford, Ireland; marr. Halifax 27 Dec. 1825 Anne Martin (31:43).

Connors, William. S. of John/Elenor (Crolly) of Parish Affane, Co. Waterford, Ireland; marr. Halifax 20 June 1836 Elizabeth Kelly (q.v.) (34:128).

Connover, Samuel. See Connor, Samuel.

Conrick, Edmund. S. of Edmund/Mary (Londrigan) of Co. Tipperary, Ireland; marr. Halifax 8 Feb. 1831 Ellen Sullivan (q.v.) (33:55).

Conroy, William. S. of Bryan/Eleanor (Farrell) of Co. Cork, Ireland; marr. Halifax July 1816 Margaret Doyle (q.v.) (30:104).

Conty, Comer. Laborer; 20; Irish; Liverpool to Nova Scotia May 1864 on EUROCLYDON (45:181).

Conway, Ellen. Dau. of Thomas/Elenor (Lanegan) of Co. Tipperary, Ireland; marr. Halifax 28 May 1835 Richard Walsh (q.v.) (34:139).

Conway, Jeremiah. S. of Patrick/Mary (Cahill) of Golden, Co. Tipperary, Ireland; marr. Halifax 5 Oct. 1831 Susannah Webb (q.v.) (33:55).

Cook, Elizabeth. Dau. of Robert/Mary (Knox) of Co. Armagh, Ireland; marr. Halifax 9 May 1844 Bernard Divine (q.v.) (35:137).

Cook, James. From Ireland; land grant at Londonderry 6 Mar. 1775 (4:258).

Cook, James. Pvt. 64th Regt.; s. of James/ Ellen (Brown) of Arkin Parish of Kilursa, Co. Galway, Ireland; marr. Halifax 11 Jan. 1843 Mary Coleman (q.v.) (35:136).

Cook, William. From Ireland; land grant (to heirs) at Londonderry 6 Mar. 1775 (4:258).

Cooke, John. Port Roseway Associate (6:14).

Coombs, Ebenezer Hill. S. of Joshua/ Margaret; Bath, Mass. (now Me.), to Liverpool by 1807 (47:128:32).

Coop, John. To (or b.?) Liverpool by 1787 (47:127:211).

Cooper, Henry. S. of Thomas/Mary (Cormack) of Co. Wexford, Ireland; marr. Halifax 16 June 1838 Margaret Whelan (q.v.) (34:128).

Copeland, Abraham. Liverpool proprietor (19:102).

Copeland, Abraham. To Liverpool ca. 1760 (47:126:97).

Corbet, Patrick. S. of James/Elizabeth (Curry) of Newmarket, Co. Tipperary, Ireland; marr. Halifax 6 May 1830 Margaret Kavanagh (sic) (q.v.) (32:107).

Corbet, Patrick. S. of James/Elizabeth (Curry) of Newmarket, Co. Tipperary, Ireland; marr. Halifax 6 May 1830 Jane Kenedy (sic) (q.v.) (32:107).

Corbitt, William Jr. From N.H.; effective land grant at Truro 31 Oct. 1765 (4:244).

Corbitt, William. From N.H.; effective land grant at Truro 31 Oct. 1765 (4:244).

Corcoran, Edward. S. of Patrick/Mary (Walsh) of Parish Killea, Co. Waterford, Ireland; marr. Halifax 11 Apr. 1825 Catherine Farrell widow of James Terry (31:43).

Corcoran, James. S. of Timothy/Margaret (Flood) of Granard, Co. Longford, Ireland; marr. Halifax 28 Sep. 1829 Catherine Walsh (q.v.) (32:107).

Corcoran, Margaret. Dau. of Martin/ Mary (Walsh) of Ballyhail, Co. Kilkenny, Ireland; marr. Halifax 23 Aug. 1829 Edward Walsh (q.v.)

(32:120).

Corcoran, Michael. S. of James/Marga-
ret (Morissy) of Co. Tipperary,
Ireland; marr. Halifax 10 Jan.
1839 Margaret Dwyer (q.v.)
(34:128).

Corcoran, Patrick. S. of James/Elenor
(Dermody) of Co. Kilkenny, Ire-
land; marr. Halifax 24 Apr. 1842
Bridget Dunn (q.v.) (35:136).

Cord, Elisha. Plus 1 svt.; Port Roseway Associate (6:14).

Corell, Timothy. Barrington petitioner 19 Oct. 1776 (1:365).

Corney, John. Of Co. Tipperary, Ireland; marr. Halifax 10 July 1841
Ellen Harney (35:136).

Corney, Nicholas. Casco Bay, Mass.
(now Me.), to Chester with first
settlers (16:45).

Cornforth, Elizabeth. 4, dau. of
William; Hull to Fort Cumberland
on ALBION 7-14 March 1774 (21:
136).

Cornforth, Mary. 1, dau. of William;
Hull to Fort Cumberland on ALBION
7-14 March 1774 (21:136).

Cornforth, Mary. 26, wife of William;
Hull to Fort Cumberland on ALBION
7-14 March 1774 (21:136).

Cornforth, Paul. 70, farmer; Hull to
Fort Cumberland on ALBION 7-14
Mar. 1774 (21:136).

Cornforth, Phillis. 68, wife of Paul;
Hull to Fort Cumberland on ALBION
7-14 March 1774 (21:136).

Cornforth, William. 34, farmer; Hull
to Fort Cumberland on ALBION 7-14
Mar. 1774 (21:136).

Cornwall, Jacob. Grantee "Digby New
Grant" 29 Jan. 1801 (5:81).

Cornwall, Thomas. Grantee "Digby New
Grant" 29 Jan. 1801 (5:81).

Cornwell, Benjamin. Loyalist; plus 1
f./1 ch./1 svt.; mustered at

Gulliver's Hole/St. Mary's Bay/
Sissiboo 1/6 June 1784; settled at
Sissiboo (now Weymouth) (40:261).

Corrall, Lawrence. Port Roseway
Associate (6:14).

Corrigan, Mary. See Mary Deniffe.

Corrigan, Patrick. S. of Michael/
Elenor (Cahill) of Callan, Co.
Kilkenny, Ireland; marr. Halifax
14 Aug. 1830 Mary Denniff (q.v.)
(32:107).

Cosgrove, Catherine. Dau. of Francis/
Mary (Cooper) of Dublin, Ireland;
marr. Halifax 19 Jan. 1813 Lawrence O'Melia (q.v.) (30:109).

Cosman, James. Grantee "Digby New
Grant" 29 Jan. 1801 (5:81).

Cosman, John. Grantee "Digby New
Grant" 29 Jan. 1801 (5:81).

Cossaboom, David. Grantee "Digby New
Grant" 29 Jan. 1801 (5:81).

Cossaboom, James. Grantee "Digby New
Grant" 29 Jan. 1801 (5:81).

Cossaboom, Samuel. Grantee "Digby New
Grant" 29 Jan. 1801 (5:81).

Cossaboom, William. Loyalist; plus 1
f./4 ch.; mustered at Digby 19 May
1784 (39:120).

Cossaboom. See Cassaboom.

Cossins, Thomas. Grantee "Digby New
Grant" 29 Jan. 1801 (5:81).

Cossman, John. Loyalist; mustered at
Gulliver's Hole/St. Mary's Bay/
Sissiboo 1/6 June 1784; settled at
Sissiboo (now Weymouth) (40:261).

Costello, Anastasia. Dau. of John/
Catherine (Maxwell) of Co. Kilkenny, Ireland; marr. Halifax 5 July
1831 Timothy Crummin (q.v.)
(33:55).

Costin, Patrick. S. of Michael/Mary
(Daley) of Co. Waterford, Ireland;
marr. Halifax 12 June 1837 Frances
Ryer (34:128).

Costin, Thomas. S. of Thomas/Cather-

60

ine (Carroll) of Parish Clonfert, Co. Galway, Ireland; marr. Halifax 23 Sep. 1823 Bridget Grady widow of Michael English (31:43).

Costin, William. S. of John/Catherine (Power) of Prince Edward Isl.; marr. Halifax 8 Sep. 1816 Marjorie Matthews (q.v.) (30:104).

Cotman, Christopher. B. England; to Liverpool by 1780 (47:127:267).

Cotter, Catherine. Dau. of William/Honora (Calaghan) of Co. Cork, Ireland; marr. Halifax 4 Oct. 1842 John Lewis Hutt (35:139).

Cotter, Juliana. Dau. of William/Honora (Callaghan) of Co. Cork, Ireland; marr. Halifax 27 Oct. 1830 Patrick Quinn (q.v.) (32:117).

Cotter, Mary. Dau. of William/Honora (Calaghan) of Co. Cork, Ireland; marr. Halifax 28 Nov. 1833 Paul Kingston (q.v.) (33:61).

Cotton, Catherine. See Mullowney, Catherine.

Cotton, Michael. S. of William/Mary (Magher) of Co. Kilkenny, Ireland; marr. Halifax 8 Feb. 1842 Julian Gerarty (q.v.) (35:136).

Coughlan, Richard. S. of James/Eleanor (Scully) of Co. Cork, Ireland; marr. Halifax 23 Dec. 1833 Catherine O'Neal (q.v.) (33:55).

Coughlin, John. S. of Jeremiah/Joanna (MacCauliff) of Co. Cork, Ireland; marr. Halifax 14 Aug. 1831 Mary Wallace (q.v.) (33:55).

Coulson, John. 20, farmer; Hull to Fort Cumberland on ALBION 7-14 March 1774 (21:134).

Coulson, Mary. 20, wife of John; Hull to Fort Cumberland on ALBION 7-14 March 1774 (21:134).

Courtney, James. Plus 1 f./1 ch./7 svts.; merchant tailor; Port Roseway Associate (6:14).

Courtney, Richard. Plus 1 f./2 ch./4 svts.; merchant tailor; Port Roseway Associate (6:13).

Courtney, Thomas. Plus 1 f./2 ch./5 svts.; merchant tailor; Port Roseway (6:13).

Cousins, Anne. Dau. of John/Catherine (Simmonds) of England; marr. Halifax 15 Feb. 1810 Michael Byron (q.v.) (30:103).

Cousins, Thomas. Loyalist; mustered at Digby 19 May 1784 (39:120).

Covert, John Jr. Grantee "Digby New Grant" 29 Jan. 1801 (5:81).

Covert, John. Grantee "Digby New Grant" 29 Jan. 1801 (5:81).

Cox, Charles. From N.H.; effective land grant at Truro 31 Oct. 1765 (4:245).

Craig, James. Grantee "Digby New Grant" 29 Jan. 1801 (5:81).

Craig, James. Loyalist; plus 1 f./2 ch./1 svt.; mustered at Digby 19 May 1784 (39:119).

Craig, John. Grantee "Digby New Grant" 29 Jan. 1801 (5:81).

Craiges, James. Plus 1 f./1 ch. 8+; arr. Annapolis from New York 19 Oct. 1782 (37:126).

Crain, John. S. of John/Jane; Charles Co., Md., to Liverpool by 1773 (47:127:54).

Crain, Thos. Arr. Annapolis from New York 19 Oct. 1782 (37:126).

Crane, Thomas. Loyalist; mustered at Digby 19 May 1784 (39:119).

Cranke, Joseph. Loyalist; plus 1 f./7 ch.; mustered at Digby 19 May 1784 (39:119).

Crawford, Andrew. 28; husbandman; Hull, Yorkshire, to Nova Scotia; on TWO FRIENDS 28 Feb.-7 Mar. 1774 (25:30).

Crawford, Gideon. 39, master mariner;
Poole to Nova Scotia on SQUIRREL
Nov. 1775 (24:45).

Crawford, John. From Mass.; land
grant at Truro 1759 (4:242).

Crawford, John. From N.H.; effective
land grant at Truro 31 Oct. 1765
(4:245).

Crawley, Abraham. From Mass.; land
grant at Truro 1759 (4:242).

Crawley, Charles. S. of Timothy/Mary
(Sullivan) of Co. Cork, Ireland;
marr. Halifax 15 Jan. 1845 Margaret Dunigan (q.v.) (35:136).

Crawley, John. From Mass.; land grant
at Truro 1759 (4:242).

Crawley, Martin. S. of Patrick/Anas-
tatia (Brith) of Leighlinbridge,
Co. Carlow, Ireland; marr. Halifax
5 July 1836 Elline O'Donnell
(q.v.) (34:128).

Crayford, Jane. Loyalist; mustered at
Digby 19 May 1784 (39:119).

Crayford, Sarah. Loyalist; mustered
at Digby 19 May 1784 (39:119).

Creamer, Daniel. S. of William/Mary
(Collins) of Parish Clonmeen, Co.
Cork, Ireland; marr. Halifax 14
Apr. 1825 Mary Harvey widow of
William Ridgeway (31:43).

Creamer, Michael. Widower of Mary
Turner; of Co. Cork, Ireland;
marr. Halifax 5 Sep, 1831 Rebecca
Peters widow of John Foley (33:
55).

Creavan, Bridger. Dau. of John/Mary
(White) of Co. Roscommon, Ireland;
marr. Halifax 21 Feb. 1838 George
Johnston (q.v.) (34:132).

Creaven, Bridget. Dau. of John/Mary
(White) of Co. Roscommon, Ireland;
widow of George Johnston, mariner;
marr. Halifax 10 Feb. 1841 Maurice
Nihily (q.v.) (35:142).

Creed, Mary. Dau. of James/Margaret
(Daune) of Cashel, Co. Tipperary,
Ireland; marr. Halifax 21 Jan.
1845 Joseph Doyle (q.v.) (35:137).

Creedon, Alice. Dau. of Alexander/
Margaret (Hennessey) of Lismore,
Co. Waterford, Ireland; marr.
Halifax 13 June 1828 David Ronan
(q.v.) (32:118).

Creighton, James. Loyalist; mustered
at Digby 19 May 1784 (39:119).

Croak, Mary. See Shortell, Mary.

Crofford, Margaret. Of Dundalk, Co.
Louth, Ireland; marr. Halifax 16
Nov. 1819 James Sullivan (q.v.)
(31:54).

Croke, Ann. Dau. of Thomas/Mary
(Shortle) of Co. Tipperary, Ire-
land; marr. Halifax 2 July 1833
William Wise (q.v.) (33:69).

Croke, Ellen. Dau. of Patrick/Mary
(Canavan) of Co. Kilkenny, Ireland; marr. Halifax 17/30 July
1841 John Barron (q.v.) (35:134).

Cronan, Margaret. Dau. of Patrick/
Joanna (Girvan) of Knockmanagh,
Co. Kerry, Ireland; marr. Halifax
6 May 1838 Timothy Driscoll (q.v.)
(34:129).

Cronin, Denis. S. of Michael/Cather-
ine (Crowly) of Kinsale, Co. Cork,
Ireland; marr. Halifax 30 May 1829
Catherine Aheron widow of John
Flinn (q.v.) (32:108).

Cronk, Joseph. Grantee "Digby New
Grant" 29 Jan. 1801 (5:81).

Crook, Anne. Dau. of William/Judith
(Conoly) of Ballingarry, Co.
Tipperary, Ireland; marr. Halifax
8 July 1830 Thomas Walsh (q.v.)
(32:120).

Crook, John. Plus wife/2 ch.; Lunenburg, Mass., to Chester with first
settlers (16:45).

Crook, Joseph. Plus 1 f./4 ch. 8+; 2
ch. -8; arr. Annapolis from New

York 19 Oct. 1782 (37:125).

Crooks, Margaret. Dau. of Thomas/
Elizabeth (Cahoon) of Northumberland, England; marr. Halifax 26
Aug. 1813 Hugh Cassidy (q.v.)
(30:103).

Crosby, John. Plus 2 f.; arr. Annapolis from New York 19 Oct. 1782
(37:125).

Cross, William. Grantee 'Digby New
Grant' 29 Jan. 1801 (5:81).

Cross, William. Loyalist; plus 1 f./2
ch./1 svt.; mustered at Digby 19
May 1784 (39:119).

Croughan, Mary. Of Strokestown, Co.
Roscommon, Ireland; widow of
Thomas Riley; marr. Halifax 27 May
1841 Corp. George Bignell (q.v.)
(35:135).

Crow, John. S. of David/Joanna of Co.
Tipperary, Ireland; marr. Halifax
19 Oct. 1812 Anne Williams (q.v.)
(30:104).

Crowel, Alice. To Liverpool ca. 1760
(47:126:96).

Crowel, Betty. Dau. of Paul; to Liverpool ca. 1760 (47:126:96).

Crowel, Betty. To Liverpool ca. 1760
(47:126:99).

Crowell, Abigail. Dau. of Jonathan/
Anna; to (or b.?) Liverpool by
1788 (47:127:125).

Crowell, Abigail. Sister of Jonathan
(s. of Paul); to Liverpool bef.
1762 (50:99).

Crowell, Achsah. Dau. of Jonathan/
Ann; to Liverpool by 1771
(47:127:50).

Crowell, Ann. Wife of Jonathan; dau.
of ----- Nickerson; to Liverpool
with husband (49:127).

Crowell, Anna Collins. Wife of Jonathan (s. of Paul); to Liverpool
bef. 1762 (50:99).

Crowell, Anne. Dau. of Jonathan/Anne;

to Liverpool by 1768 (47:126:165).

Crowell, David. Barrington petitioner
19 Oct. 1776 (1:365).

Crowell, David. S. of Jonathan (s. of
Isaac); b. Chatham, Mass.; to Barrington by 1762 (50:100).

Crowell, Elizabeth. Dau. of Jonathan/
Anne; to Liverpool by 1773 (47:
126:168).

Crowell, Elizabeth. Dau. of Archelaus; to (or b.?) Liverpool by
1791 (47:127:203).

Crowell, Elizabeth. Wife of John;
dau. of Alexander/Jannet More;
Roxbury, N. Y., to Liverpool ca.
1811 (47:128:33).

Crowell, Hannah. Dau. of Jonathan/
Joanna; to (or b.?) Liverpool by
1791 (47:127:118).

Crowell, Hannah. Dau. of Archibald/
Mary; to (or b.?) Liverpool by
1796 (47:127:211).

Crowell, Jannet. B. Roxbury, N. Y.,
11 Oct. 1807; dau. of John/Eliza-
beth; to Liverpool ca. 1811
(47:128:33).

Crowell, Joanna. Dau. of Jonathan/
Joana; to (or b.?) Liverpool by
1796 (47:127:271).

Crowell, John. B. Roxbury, N. Y., 18
Nov. 1805; s. of John/Elizabeth;
to Liverpool ca. 1811 (47:128:33).

Crowell, Jonathan Jr. S. of Jonathan/
Anne; to Liverpool by 1772
(47:126:165).

Crowell, Jonathan Jr. S. of Jonathan
(s. of Isaac); b. Chatham, Mass.;
to Barrington by 1762 (50:100).

Crowell, Jonathan. Liverpool proprietor (19:101).

Crowell, Jonathan. S. of Paul; Yarmouth Mass., to Liverpool; d. 17
Feb. 1776 ae 57th (49:127).

Crowell, Jonathan. S. of Paul; b.
Chatham, Mass., 25 Feb. 1718; to

Liverpool bef. 1762 (50:99).

Crowell, Jonathan. S. of Jonathan (s. of Paul); b. Chatham, Mass., 1745; to Liverpool bef. 1762 (50:99).

Crowell, Jonathan. S. of Isaac; b. Chatham, Mass., ca. 1718; to Barrington by 1762 (50:100).

Crowell, Judah. S. of Thomas; b. Chatham, Mass., ca. 1705; to Barrington by 1770? (50:100).

Crowell, Judah. S. of Judah; b. prob. Chatham, Mass., ca. 1734; to Barrington by 1770? (50:100).

Crowell, Mary. Dau. of Jonathan (s. of Isaac); b. Chatham, Mass.; to Barrington by 1762 (50:100).

Crowell, Robert. From Mass.; land grant at Onslow 21 Feb. 1769 (4: 224).

Crowell, Samuel. B. Roxbury, N. Y., 6 June 1810; s. of John/Elizabeth; to Liverpool ca. 1811 (47:128:33).

Crowell, Samuel. Liverpool proprietor (19:102).

Crowell, Samuel. S. of Jonathan (s. of Paul); b. Chatham, Mass., 16 Mar. 1742/3; to Liverpool bef. 1762 (50:99).

Crowell, Sarah Kenney. Wife of Thomas; to Barrington ca. 1760 (50:100).

Crowell, Tabitha Nickerson. Wife of Judah; b. Chatham, Mass., 15 June 1713; to Barrington by 1770? (50:100).

Crowell, Thomas "Sr." S. of Judah; b. prob. Chatham, Mass., ca. 1735; to Barrington by 1770? (50:100).

Crowell, Thomas. Barrington petitioner 19 Oct. 1776 (1:365).

Crowell, Thomas. S. of Paul; b. Chatham, Mass., 27 Oct. 1739; to Barrington ca. 1760 (50:100).

Crowell, William. From Mass.; land grant at Onslow 21 Feb. 1769 (4:

225).

Crowley, Daniel. S. of Daniel/Mary (Barry) of Bandon, Co. Cork, Ireland; marr. Halifax 25 June 1836 Mary Sullivan (q.v.) (34:128).

Crowley, Ellen. Of Co. Cork, Ireland; widow of John Walsh; marr. Halifax 19 Sep. 1838 Patrick Rafter (q.v.) (34:137).

Crowley, Mary. Widow of John Buggy; of Co. Leix, Ireland; marr. Halifax 11 Jan. 1831 Thomas Walsh (q.v.) (33:68).

Crowly, Catherine. Dau. of Timothy/ Mary (Sullivan) of Co. Cork, Ireland; marr. Halifax 18 Apr. 1839 James Walsh (q.v.) (34:139).

Crummin, Timothy. S. of Timothy/Ellen (Cronin) of Co. Kerry, Ireland; marr. Halifax 5 July 1831 Anastasia Costello (q.v.) (33:55).

Cubberly, Stephen. Loyalist; mustered at Digby 19 May 1784 (39:120).

Cuddihy, James. S. of James/Mary (Mokler) of Co. Tipperary, Ireland; marr. Halifax 25 Nov. 1837 Ellen Downey (q.v.) (34:128).

Cuddy, David. S. of David/Judith (Murphy) of Co. Kilkenny, Ireland; marr. Halifax 25 Nov. 1832 Mary Clary (q.v.) (33:55).

Cudmore, William. Loyalist; mustered at Digby 19 May 1784 (39:119).

Cuffy, Barbara. Liverpool proprietor (19:101).

Culbert, Mary Anne. See Williams, Mary Anne.

Cullen, John. S. of Patrick/Bridget (Lahy) of St. Johns, Nfld.; marr. Halifax 25 Aug. 1812 Ellen Dulhanty (q.v.) (30:104).

Cullen, Mary. Dau. of James/Bridget of Carlow Town, Ireland; marr. Halifax 9 Feb. 1823 Pierce Ryan (q.v.) (31:53).

Cullerton, Bridget. Dau. of James/
Bridget (Costly) of Co. Wexford,
Ireland; marr. Halifax 6 June 1834
Edward Redmond (q.v.) (33:66).

Cullerton, Margaret. See Walsh,
Margaret.

Cullerton, Thomas. S. of Patrick/
Joanna (Cummins) of Co. Wexford,
Ireland; marr. Halifax 27 Oct.
1831 Mary Murphy (q.v.) (33:55).

Cullin, Catherine. Dau. of Martin/
Mary (Breen) of Co. Wexford, Ire-
land; marr. Halifax 24 Apr. 1834
John Duffield (q.v.) (33:57).

Cullin, James. S. of George/Mary
(Casey) of Co. Limerick, Ireland;
marr. Halifax 27 Aug. 1839 Lydia
Mitchell (q.v.) (34:128).

Cullin, John. S. of Michael/Honora
(Power) of Waterford, Ireland;
marr. Halifax 24 Aug. 1831 Eliza
King (33:55).

Cullin, Margery. Dau. of Paul/Mary
(Walsh) of Millpath, Myshall, Co.
Carlow, Ireland; marr. Halifax 11
Sep. 1842 Peter Berrigan (q.v.)
(35:135).

Cullum, Arthur. Plus 1 f./5 ch.; Port
Roseway Associate (6:14).

Cummerford, Bridget. See Purcell,
Bridget.

Cummings, Bridget. Dau. of William/
Judith (Byrnes) of Co. Longford,
Ireland; marr. Halifax 27 Oct.
1830 Brien Clinton (q.v.)
(32:107).

Cummings, Samel. Esq.; plus 1 f./4
ch. 8+/1 ch. -8; arr. Annapolis
from New York 19 Oct. 1782 (37:
126).

Cummings, Samuel. Esq.; Loyalist;
from Hollis, N.H.; New York to
N.S. 1782 (41:14).

Cummings, Thomas. Loyalist; from New
Hampshire; petitioner at Digby 20

Feb. 1784 (41:18).

Cummings, Thos. Plus 1 f./1 ch. 8+/1
ch. -8; arr. Annapolis from New
York 19 Oct. 1782 (37:126).

Cummings, William. Disbanded soldier,
King's American Dragoons; mustered
at Gulliver's Hole/St. Mary's Bay/
Sissiboo 1/6 June 1784; settled at
Sissiboo (now Weymouth) (40:262).

Cummins, Andrew. S. of Stephen/Mary
(Ryan) of Co. Carlow, Ireland;
marr. Halifax 11 Jan. 1825 Anne
Phelan (q.v.) (31:43).

Cummins, Benjamin. From Mass.; land
grant at Truro 1759 (4:242).

Cummins, Ellen. Dau. of John/Mary
(Daly) of Co. Wexford, Ireland;
marr. Halifax 4 July 1830 Robert
Curry (q.v.) (32:108).

Cummins, Frances. Dau. of Michael/
Maria (MacLaughlan) of Co. Fermanagh, Ireland; marr. Halifax 9
Nov. 1833 Henry Haney (q.v.)
(33:59).

Cummins, James. S. of Mathew/Ann of
Co. Wexford, Ireland; marr. Halifax 1 Dec. 1838 Bridget McLean
widow of Walter Spruhan (34:128).

Cummins, Mary. Dau. of John/Mary
(Finn) of Co. Tipperary, Ireland;
marr. Halifax 30 Nov. 1816 William
Rafter (q.v.) (30:110).

Cummins, Mary. Dau. of Alexander/Jane
(MacQuine) of Scotland; marr. Halifax 1 Nov. 1825 Owen O'Neil
(q.v.) (31:51).

Cummins, William. Disbanded soldier,
42nd Regt.; laborer; mustered at
Gulliver's Hole/St. Mary's Bay/
Sissiboo 1/6 June 1784 (40:262).

Cummins, William. S. of Nicholas/
Elenor (McCarthy) of Waterford
City, Ireland; marr. Halifax 13
Jan. 1830 Eleanor Butler (q.v.)
(32:108).

Cummins, William. S. of Nicholas/
Elenor (McCarthy) of Waterford
City, Ireland; widower of Elizabeth Power; marr. Halifax 13 Jan.
1830 (sic) Eleanor Butler (q.v.)
(33:56).

Cunard, Robert. Carpenter; Port
Roseway Associate (6:14).

Cunningham, David. Loyalist; plus 1
f./4 ch.; mustered at Digby 19 May
1784 (39:120).

Cunningham, Elizabeth. Grantee "Digby
New Grant" 29 Jan. 1801 (5:81).

Cunningham, James. Of Co. Monaghan,
Ireland; widower of Mary Darcy;
marr. Halifax 7 Jan. 1844 Ann
Fitzgerald (q.v.) (35:136).

Cunningham, Michael. S. of John/Mary
(Woods) of Co. Waterford, Ireland;
marr. Halifax 18 Dec. 1832 Mary
Kelly (q.v.) (33:56).

Cunningham, Richard. Disbanded soldier, 3rd N.J. Vols.; mustered at
Digby 19 May 1784 (39:120).

Curramore, John. S. of Daniel/Mary
(Keefe) of Parish Ballylough, Co.
Cork, Ireland; marr. Halifax 12
Feb. 1800 (sic for 1830?) Ann
Byrnes (q.v.) (32:108).

Curran, Mary. Dau. of Thomas/Judith
(Burnes) of Co. Kildare, Ireland;
marr. Halifax 11 May 1834 William
Tierney (q.v.) (33:67).

Curran, Michael. S. of Thomas/Judith
(Berrans) of Co. Kildare, Ireland;
marr. Halifax 15 Apr. 1833 Eliza
Carr (q.v.) (33:56).

Curran, Patrick. S. of Henry of Co.
Carlow; Ireland; marr. Halifax 28
Apr. 1835 Mary Byrnes (q.v.)
(34:128).

Curren, James. S. of David/Catherine
(Murphy) of Co. Carlow, Ireland;
marr. Halifax 29 May 1821 Catherine Duncanson (q.v.) (31:43).

Curren, Thomas. Plus 1 f./3 ch./1
svt.; tailor; Port Roseway Associate (6:13).

Curren, Thomas. S. of Bartholomew/
Norry (Barron) of Thomastown,
Waterford, Ireland; marr. Halifax
7 Feb. 1826 Elizabeth Harney
(q.v.) (32:108).

Currey, Alexander. Plus 1 f.; Port
Roseway Associate (6:14).

Curry, Robert. S. of John/Elizabeth
(Phronfrey) of St. John. N.B.;
marr. Halifax 4 July 1830 Ellen
Cummins (q.v.) (32:108).

Curten, Samuel. S. of Neal/Sally
(Conan) of Co. Derry, Ireland;
marr. Halifax 4 May 1822 Catherine
Hughes (31:44).

Curtin, Susanna. Dau. of James/Susan-
na (O'Brien) of St. John's. Nfld.;
marr. Halifax 16 Apr. 1822 Thomas
Lawlor (q.v.) (31:49).

Curtin, Thomas. S. of James/Mary
(Nagle) of Co. Cork, Ireland;
marr. Halifax 4 Aug. 1831 Joanna
Walsh (q.v.) (33:56).

Curtis, Elenor. See Flinn, Elenor.

Curtis, William. Plus wife; New
England to Annapolis on CHARMING
MOLLY May 1760 (18:271).

Curtis, William. S. of William/Mary
(Aheran) of Co. Cork, Ireland;
marr. Halifax 16 Oct. 1840 Catherine O'Donnell (q.v.) (34:128).

Curtiss, Fear. To Liverpool ca. 1760
(47:126:96).

Cushan, Thomas. S. of James/Elenor
(Pursel) of Co. Tipperary, Ire-
land; marr. Halifax 15 Sep. 1835
Ann Riley (q.v.) (34:128).

Cushen, John. S. of Patrick/Mary
(Houghney) of Graignamanagh, Co.
Kilkenny, Ireland; marr. Halifax
11 Feb. 1822 Sally Kenny (q.v.)
(31:44).

Cushin, David. S. of John/Catherine
(O'Neal) of Cove, Co. Cork, Ire-
land; marr. Halifax 9 Jan. 1836
Catherine Martin (34:128).

Cushing, Job. New England to Annapolis 1760 (18:271).

Cushion, Mary. Dau. of John/Catherine
(Neill) of Cove of Cork, Ireland;
marr. Halifax 31 Jan. 1829 Daniel
Millerick *(q.v.)* (32:116).

Cutler, Ebenezer. Grantee "Digby New
Grant" 29 Jan. 1801 (5:81).

Cutler, Ebenezer. Sutler, Halifax,
Mass., to Chester 30 July 1759
(16:46).

Cutler, Jonas. Sutler, Halifax,
Mass., to Chester 30 July 1759
(16:46).

Cutt, Mary. Dau. of Thomas/Margaret
(Power) of Co. Waterford, Ireland;
marr. Halifax 20 Apr. 1830 John
Henissey (q.v.) (32:112).

Cutten, David. See Cutting.

Cutting, David. From Mass.; land
grant at Onslow 21 Feb. 1769
(4:224).

Cutting, David. From Dudley/Oxford,
Mass. to Onslow; returned to Dud-
ley by 1770 (4:230).

Cutting, John. From Mass.; land grant
at Onslow 21 Feb. 1769 (4:225).

Cutting, John. S. of David and Sarah
(Edmunds); to Onslow with parents
(4:230).

Cutting, Mary. Dau. of David and
Sarah (Edmunds); to Onslow with
parents (4:230).

Cutting, Sarah. Dau. of David and
Sarah (Edmunds); to Onslow with
parents (4:230).

Cutting, Sarah. Wife of David; dau.
of ----- Edmunds; to N.S. with
husband (4:230).

Cutting, William. S. of David and
Sarah (Edmunds); to Onslow with

parents (4:230).

Cypher, Jacob. Loyalist; plus 1 f./2
ch.; mustered at Digby 19 May 1784
(39:119).

- D -

Dady, Michael. S. of Patrick/Mary
(McDonnell) of Co. Waterford, Ireland; widower of Judith Monaghan;
marr. Halifax 4 Mar. 1832 Anastasia Foley *(q.v.)* (33:56).

Dahler, -----. Disbanded soldier,
German Service; mustered at Bear
River 11/25 June 1784 (38:259).

Daily, Ellen. Of Cork City, Ireland;
widow of John Walsh; marr. Halifax
29 Sep. 1836 Patrick Headon *(q.v.)*
(34:131).

Daily, Honora. Of Donaghedy, Co. Tyrone, Ireland; marr. Halifax 15
Sep. 1817 Michael Brown *(q.v.)*
(30:102).

Daily, Honora. Of Parish Donaghedy,
Co. Tyrone, Ireland; marr. Halifax
15 Sep. 1817 Michael Brown *(q.v.)*
(31:41).

Dakin, Thomas. Grantee "Digby New
Grant" 29 Jan. 1801 (5:82).

Daley, Anastasia. Dau. of Edmund/
Anastasia (Fitzgerald) of Co. Kilkenny, Ireland; marr. Halifax 27
June 1831 Patrick Hogan *(q.v.)*
(33:59).

Daley, Mary. Dau. of Anthony/Eliza-
beth (Downy) of Co. Longford, Ireland; marr. Halifax 3 July 1835
John Laurence *(q.v.)* (34:133).

Daley, Michael. S. of James/Catherine
(Donovan) of Watergrasshill, Co.
Cork, Ireland; marr. Halifax 14
Nov. 1828 Margaret Shortel *(q.v.)*
(32:108).

Dalton, Catherine. Dau. of Michael/
Mary (Wall) of Co. Kilkenny, Ire-

land; marr. Halifax 26 July 1811
Michael Kerwick *(q.v.)* (30: 107).

Dalton, Daniel. Grantee "Digby New
Grant" 29 Jan. 1801 (5:82).

Dalton, Ellen. Dau. of Thomas/Mary
(Ryan) of Co. Kilkenny, Ireland;
marr. Halifax 9 Jan. 1835 Pvt.
Michael McCarthy *(q.v.)* (34:133).

Dalton, Margaret. Dau. of Redmond/
Alice (Whelan) of Co. Waterford,
Ireland; marr. Halifax 4 Oct. 1839
John Lynch *(q.v.)* (34:133).

Dalton, Richard. S. of James/Joanna
(Walsh) of Co. Kilkenny, Ireland;
marr. Halifax 28 Oct. 1834 Catherine Neagle *(q.v.)* (34:128).

Daly, John. S. of Daniel/Bridget
(Cashman) of Co. Waterford, Ire-
land; marr. Halifax 23 Sep. 1813
Charlotte White (30:104).

Daly, Mary. Dau. of John/Honora
(Sweeny) of Co. Cork, Ireland;
marr. Halifax 14 Nov. 1841 Daniel
Derine *(q.v.)* (35:136).

Daly, Patrick. S. of Hugh/Mary
(Macabot) of Co. Monaghan, Ire-
land; marr. Halifax 20 July 1838
Bridget Logan *(q.v.)* (34:128).

Damon, Edmund. New England to Annapolis on CHARMING MOLLY May 1760
(18:271).

Damon, Edward Jr. From Mass.; land
grant at Truro 1759 (4:242).

Damon, Edward. From Mass.; land grant
at Truro 1759 (4:242).

Damon, John. From Mass.; land grant
at Truro 1759 (4:242).

Damon, John. New England to Annapolis
on CHARMING MOLLY May 1760 (18:
271).

Damon, Thomas. New England to Annapolis on CHARMING MOLLY May 1760
(18:271).

Daniell, James. S. of Edmund/Anasta-
sia (Walsh) of Co. Kilkenny, Ire-

land; marr. Halifax 21 July 1838
Ann Jones *(q.v.)* (34:128).

Daniels, Joseph. New England to Annapolis 1760 (18:271).

Darcy, Edward. 96th Regt.; s. of
Thomas/Mary (Marshall) of Co.
Leix, Ireland; marr. Halifax 31
Dec. 1831 Jean Constable (33:56).

Darcy, Honora. Dau. of Andrew/Mary
(Cottelon) of Co. Carlow, Ireland;
marr. Halifax 1 May 1832 Edward
Eustace *(q.v.)* (33:57).

Darge, James. Loyalist; mustered at
Digby 19 May 1784 (39:120).

Darge, Jane. Loyalist; mustered at
Digby 19 May 1784 (39:120).

Darling, Jonathan Liverpool proprietor (19:102).

Darmody, Bridget. Dau. of James/
Honora (Condon) of Co. Tipperary,
Ireland; marr. Halifax 7 Jan. 1834
Richard Wallace *(q.v.)* (33:68).

Darmody, Patrick. S. of William/Mary
(Reily) of Mullinavat, Co. Kilkenny, Ireland; marr. Halifax 27 Apr.
1827 Lavinia Masters Boyd (32:
108).

Darrow, Edmund. S. of Jonathan/A----
of New London, Conn.; d. Liverpool
24 Nov. 1784 (47:126:285).

Darrow, Ichabod. S. of Jonathan/A----
of New London, Conn.; to Liverpool
by 20 Oct. 1784 (47:126:285).

Darrow, Ichabod. S. of Jonathan of
New London, Conn.; d. Liverpool ae
50 (49:130).

Davenport, Thomas. Loyalist; plus 1
f./3 ch.; mustered at Digby 19 May
1784 (39:120).

Davenport, William. Loyalist; mustered at Digby 19 May 1784 (39:
120).

Daveran, John. S. of Michael/Bridget
(Burke) of Thurles, Co. Tipperary,
Ireland; marr. Halifax 29 Aug.

1831 Dorothy Hansimer widow of
William Charlton (33:56).

Davidson, John. Plus 1 f./1 svt.;
carpenter; Port Roseway Associate
(6:14).

Davine, Mary. Dau. of James/Ann
(Gelery) of Co. Leitrim, Ireland;
marr. Halifax 8 Sep. 1822 Patrick
Martin (q.v.) (31:50).

Davis, James. Laborer; 24; English;
24; Liverpool to Nova Scotia June
1864 on INDIAN QUEEN (45:181).

Davis, Sarah. Wife of James; 22;
English; Liverpool to Nova Scotia
June 1864 on INDIAN QUEEN (45:
181).

Davis, Simon. From Mass.; land grant
at Truro 1759 (4:242).

Davis, Sophia. Dau. of James; infant;
English; Liverpool to Nova Scotia
June 1864 on INDIAN QUEEN (45:
181).

Davis, Stephen. From Mass.; land
grant at Truro 1759 (4:242).

Davison, Joseph. Mariner; s. James/
Mary (Walker) of Workington, Cumberland, England; marr. Halifax 20
July 1829 Mary Foy (q.v.) (32:
108).

Davison, William. From Ireland; land
grant at Londonderry 6 Mar. 1775
(4:258).

Dawkins, Edward. Plus 1 f.; mustered
at Digby 19 May 1784; from Bermuda
on JOSEPH (39:120).

Dawson, Catherine. Dau. of William/
Catherine (Mahoney) of Inishannon,
Co. Cork, Ireland; marr. Halifax 6
June 1826 Darby Minahan (q.v.)
(32:116).

Dawson, Mary. Of Laughlin, Co. Kilkenny, Ireland; marr. Halifax 5
June 1832 Martin Murphy (q.v.)
(33:64).

Dawson, Peter. S. of William/Cather-

ine (Mahony) of Co. Cork, Ireland;
marr. Halifax 15 Apr. 1833 Elizabeth Aheran (q.v.) (33:56).

Dawson, Richard. S. of Patrick/Joanna
(Larissy) of Co. Kilkenny, Ire-
land; marr. Halifax 19 May 1841
Bridget Kirwan (q.v.) (35:136).

Day, John. Mass. to N.S.; to U.S.
1776; lived 1785 at Mass. [which
then included Me.] (36:65).

Day, John. S. of -----/Martha; to (or
b.?) Liverpool by 1785 (47:127:
277).

Day, Luke. S. of Richard/Catherine
(Kinsella) of Co. Wexford, Ire-
land; marr. Halifax 4 Aug. 1814
Susanna Ballentry (30:104).

Dayley, James. To Shelburne by 1789
(47:126:286).

Deady, James. S. of James/Mary
(Murphy) of Co. Kilkenny, Ireland;
marr. Halifax 9 June 1831 Judith
Foley (q.v.) (33:56).

Dean, Atwood. S. of Ephrain/Martha;
to (or b.?) Liverpool by 1801 (47:
127:273).

Dean, Ephraim. S. of Ephraim/Martha;
to (or b.?) Liverpool by 1787 (47:
127:212).

Dean, Ephraim. To Liverpool ca. 1761
(47:126:163).

Dean, Hannah. B. New England 14 July?
17--; dau. of James/Hannah; to
Liverpool ca. 1760 (47:126:100).

Dean, Hannah. Dau. of James/Hannah;
to (or b.?) Liverpool by 1779 (47:
126:284).

Dean, Hannah. Wife of James; to Liverpool ca. 1760 (47:126:100).

Dean, Isaac. B. Eastham, Mass., 15
Jan. 1761; to Liverpool ca. 1761
(47:126:163).

Dean, Isaac. S. of Ephraim/Martha; to
(or b.?) Liverpool by 1780 (47:
128:35).

Dean, James. To Liverpool ca. 1760 (47:126:100).

Dean, Lydia. B. New England 10 Sep. 17--; dau. of James/Hannah; to Liverpool ca. 1760 (47:126:100).

Dean, Lydia. Dau. of James/Hannah; to (or b.?) Liverpool by 1778 (47:126:284).

Dean, Martha. Wife of Ephraim; to Liverpool ca. 1761 (47:126:163).

Deane, Hannah. Widow of Capt. James; dau. of Joseph Atkins; b. Scarboro, Me.; d. (as wife of Capt. Bartlett Bradford) Liverpool 2 Mar. 1828 ae 86 (49:136).

Deane, James. Capt.; s. Thomas and Lydia (Cole) of Scarborough, Me.; d. Liverpool 11 Dec. 1771 ae 32nd (49:136).

DeCoudres, -----. Lieut., Anspach Service; plus 1 f./2 ch./1 svt.; mustered at Bear River 11/25 June 1784 (38:259).

DeCourcy, Garrett. Widower of Mary Crowly; of Co. Cork, Ireland; marr. Halifax 15 Feb. 1831 Mary Mullany (q.v.) (33:56).

DeCoursey, Mary. See Mullany, Mary.

Dee, James. S. of John/Mary (McLoughlan) of Co. Tipperary, Ireland; marr. Halifax 1 May 1845 Wilhelmina Ainslie (35:136).

Dee, Margaret. Dau. of Thomas/Bridget (Whelan) of Co. Waterford, Ireland; marr. Halifax 22 Nov. 1833 Patrick Lahy (q.v.) (33:61).

Dee, Margaret. Of Co. Waterford, Ireland; widow of Edward Kelly; marr. Halifax 4 June 1834 James Walsh (q.v.) (33:68).

Dee, Mary. Dau. of Thomas/Bridget (Power), of Co. Waterford, Ireland; marr. Halifax 24 Apr. 1834 (q.v.) (33:58).

Dee, Mary. Dau. of Daniel/Margaret

(Lowry) of Co. Limerick, Ireland; marr. Halifax 6 Oct. 1842 Richard Kehoe (35:139).

Deeder, John Baptist. S. of Francis/Catherine of Antwerp, Brabant; marr. Halifax 3 Oct. 1818 Anne Boyle (q.v.) (31:44).

Deegan, Patrick. S. of John/Alice (Brophy) of Co. Leix, Ireland; marr. Halifax 19 Nov. 1832 Bridget Tallant (q.v.) (33:56).

Deegan, William. S. of Patrick/Elizabeth (Dempsy) of Co. Kilkenny, Ireland; marr. Halifax 4 Feb. 1820 Mary Fitzgerald (q.v.) (31:44).

Deer, Ann. Dau. of Peter/Ann (Ward) of Co. Longford, Ireland; marr. Halifax 13 June 1832 John Nugent (q.v.) (33:64).

Deer, Catherine. Dau. of Peter/Ann (Ward) of Co. Longford, Ireland; marr. 24 Oct. 1830 Ezechiel Shaddock (q.v.) (32:118).

Deereen, Alice, Dau. of Richard/Catherine (Hacket) of Callan, Co. Kilkenny, Ireland; marr. Halifax 24 Nov. 1839 William Callanan (q.v.) (34:127).

Degan, William. Loyalist; mustered at Digby 19 May 1784 (39:120).

DeLancey, Stephen. Grantee "Digby New Grant" 29 Jan. 1801 (5:82).

Delaney, Elener. Dau. of Daniel/Margaret (Conners) of Placentia, Nfld.; marr. Halifax 21 Nov. 1808 David Rourk (q.v.) (30:110).

Delany, Catherine. See Magher, Catherine.

Delany, William. S. of James/Catherine (Pendergast) of Co. Kilkenny, Ireland; marr. Halifax 9 Feb. 1834 Catherine Magher; Halifax-Co. Kilkenny, Ireland-Halifax ca. 1845 (33:56).

Delany, William. S. of Simon/Margaret

(Cuddihy) of Kilconnel, Co. Tipperary, Ireland; marr. Halifax 27 Aug. 1837 Honora Foley *(q.v.)* (34:128).

Delory, David. Pvt. 64th Regt.; s. of John/Joanna (Calahan) of Co. Cork, Ireland; marr. Halifax 25 Jan. 1843 Catherine Kerenegh *(q.v.)* (35:136).

Deloughrey, Michael. S. of James/Catherine (Cassin) of Co. Kilkenny, Ireland; marr. Halifax 17 Nov. 1806 Mary Smyth *(q.v.)* (30:104).

Demill, John. Plus 1 f.; carpenter; Port Roseway Associate (6:14).

Demolitor, -----. Capt., Anspach Service; plus 1 f./4 svts.; mustered at Bear River 11/25 June 1784 (38:259).

Demolitor, S. Lieut., German Service; plus 1 f./1 ch.; mustered at Bear River 11/25 June 1784 (38:259).

Dempsey, Roger. Port Roseway Associate (6:14).

Dempsey, William. S. of. Patrick/Mary (Connor) of Parish Ballanamodagh, Co. Wexford, Ireland; marr. Halifax 4 July 1820 Margaret Sullivan *q.v.)* (31:44).

Denham, Thomas. Plus 1 f./1 ch./2 svts.; Port Roseway Associate (6:14).

Deniffe, Elizabeth. Dau. of Richard/Mary (Blanchfill) of Thomastown, Co. Kilkenny, Ireland; marr. Halifax 22 Apr. 1833 David Berrigan *(q.v.)* (33:54).

Deniffe, Mary. Widow of Patrick Corrigan; dau. Richard/Mary (Blanchfield) of Thomastown, Co. Kilkenny, Ireland; marr. Halifax 24 Oct. 1833 Richard Waid *(q.v.)* (33:67).

Dennan, Michael. S. of Owen/Margaret (Kelly) of Currykedmon?, Co. Longford, Ireland; marr. Halifax 27 Apr. 1827 Mary McGee *(q.v.)* (32:108).

Dennief, Mary. Dau. of Richard/Mary (Blanchfield) of Thomastown, Co. Kilkenny, Ireland; marr. Halifax 14 Aug. 1830 Patrick Corrigan *(q.v.)* (32:107).

Dennison, Edward. Loyalist; from Port Mouton; mustered at Digby 19 May 1784 (39:120).

Dennison, Patrick. Loyalist; plus 1 f./1 ch.; from Port Mouton; mustered at Digby 19 May 1784 (39:120).

Denniston, Patrick. Grantee "Digby New Grant" 29 Jan. 1801 (5:82).

Denny, Jane. See Dill, Jane.

Denny, John. From Ireland; land grant at Londonderry 6 Mar. 1775 (4:258).

Denton, Joseph. Grantee "Digby New Grant" 29 Jan. 1801 (5:82).

Denton, Joseph. Loyalist; plus 1 f./3 ch.; mustered at Digby 19 May 1784 (39:120).

Denton, Stephen. Loyalist; plus 1 f./3 ch.; mustered at Digby 19 May 1784 (39:120).

Derine, Daniel. S. of Daniel/Ellen (Donovan) of Co. Cork, Ireland; marr. Halifax 14 Nov. 1841 Mary Daly *(q.v.)* (35:136).

DesCoudres, Louis. (Heirs) grantee "Digby New Grant" 29 Jan. 1801 (5:82).

Desmond, Cornelius. S. of William/Ellen (Mahony) of Kinsale, Co. Cork, Ireland; marr. Halifax 22 Aug. 1829 Margaret Mahony *(q.v.)* (32:108).

Desmond, Ellen. Dau. of Daniel/Ellen (Crowley) of Co. Cork, Ireland; marr. Halifax 16 Jan. 1830 Thomas

Mahony (q.v.) (32:115).

Devanny, Michael. S. of Darby/Margaret (Gillan) of Co. Sligo, Ireland; marr. Halifax 24 Nov. 1831 Ann Magowen (q.v.) (33:56).

Devany, Anne. Dau. of Henry/Mary (Cambell) of Noghaville, Co. Westmeath, Ireland; marr. Halifax 8 July 1827 Peter Carroll (q.v.) (32:106).

Deveraux, Nicholas. S. of Patrick/Eliza (Rosider) of Co. Wexford, Ireland; marr. Halifax 26 May 1834 Ellen Walsh (q.v.) (33:56).

Deveraux, Patrick. S. of Patrick/Catherine (Mary) of Co. Wexford, Ireland; marr. Halifax 9 Jan. 1833 Joanna Ryan (q.v.) (33:56).

Devett, Rose. See Giron, Rose.

Devlin, James. S. of Farrell/Mary (Gormany) of Co. Tyrone, Ireland; marr. Halifax 26 Sep. 1843 Elizabeth Morrisy (q.v.) (35:136).

Dewaal, John Henry. S. of John/Patronella; Cape of Good Hope to Liverpool by 1809 (47:128:31).

Dexter, Anna. Dau. of Isaac/Anna; to (or b.?) Liverpool by 1802 (47:127:272).

Dexter, Azubah Collins Godfrey. Wife of Joseph; b. Chatham, Mass., 10 June 1734; to Liverpool 1760 (50:101).

Dexter, Benjamin. B. Rochester, Mass., 23 Mar. 1758; s. of Ebenezer/Lydia; to Liverpool ca. 1760 (47:126:101).

Dexter, Ebenezer. Liverpool proprietor (19:102).

Dexter, Ebenezer. To Liverpool ca. 1760 (47:126:101).

Dexter, Hannah. B. Dartmouth, Mass., 5 Sep. 1750; dau. of Ebenezer/Lydia; to Liverpool ca. 1760 (47:126:101).

Dexter, Hannah. Dau. of Ebenezer/Lydia; to Liverpool by 1776 (47:126:287).

Dexter, Isaac. B. Dartmouth, Mass., 15 Oct. 1751; s. of John; to Liverpool by 1776 (47:126:290).

Dexter, Jesse. B. Rochester, Mass., 10 July 1747; s. of Peleg; to Liverpool ca. 1760 (47:126:95).

Dexter, John. B. Rochester, Mass., 27 June 1745; s. of Peleg; to Liverpool ca. 1760 (47:126:95).

Dexter, John. S. of Isaac/Anna; to (or b.?) Liverpool by 1802 (47:127:273).

Dexter, Joseph. B. 27 Feb. 1732; s. of Benjamin/Hannah; to Liverpool ca. 1760 (47:126:163).

Dexter, Joseph. S. of Benjamin; b. Rochester, Mass., 27 Feb. 1732; to Liverpool 1760 (50:101).

Dexter, Katherine. Wife of Peleg; Rochester, Mass., to Liverpool ca. 1760 (47:126:95).

Dexter, Lydia. Wife of Ebenezer; to Liverpool ca. 1760 (47:126:101).

Dexter, Peleg. Liverpool proprietor (19:101).

Dexter, Peleg. Rochester, Mass., to Liverpool ca. 1760 (47:126:95).

Dexter, Rachael. Wife or widow of Reubin; to (or b.?) Liverpool by 1783 (47:126:287).

Dexter, Rebeccah. B. Rochester, Mass., 10 May 1760; dau. of Ebenezer/Lydia; to Liverpool ca. 1760 (47:126:101).

Dexter, Rebeckah. Dau. of Ebenezer/Lydia; to Liverpool by 1776 (47:126:285).

Dexter, Samuel. S. of Ebenezer/Lydia; to (or b.?) Liverpool by 1799 (47:127:276).

Dibble, Tyler (Fyler). Plus 1 f./5 ch./2 svts.; farmer; Port Roseway

Associate (6:14).

Dickie, Adam. From N.H.; effective
land grant at Truro 31 Oct. 1765
(4:245).

Dickie, David. From N.H.; effective
land grant at Truro 31 Oct. 1765
(4:245).

Dickie, Robert. From N.H.; effective
land grant at Truro 31 Oct. 1765
(4:245).

Dickinson, ----- (Mrs.). From London;
50; Liverpool to Nova Scotia April
1864 on EUROPA (45:181).

Dickinson, Johathan. From Mass.; land
grant at Truro 1759 (4:242).

Dickinson, Nath'l. Plus 1 f./3 svts.;
planter; Port Roseway Associate
(6:14).

Dickinson, Nehemiah. From Mass.; land
grant at Truro 1759 (4:242).

Dickson, Robert. Grantee "Digby New
Grant" 29 Jan. 1801 (5:82).

Dickson, Robert. Loyalist; plus 4
ch.; mustered at Digby 19 May 1784
(39:120).

Dickson, Robert. S. of Robert/Eliza-
beth; Markethill, Armah, Ireland,
to Liverpool by 1779 (47:127:121).

Die, David. Laborer; 22; Irish; Liverpool to Nova Scotia June 1864 on
INDIAN QUEEN (45:181).

Digey, Arthur. Loyalist; mustered at
Digby 19 May 1784 (39:120).

Dill, Jane. Wife of Robert; dau. of
----- Denny; born 1753 at Donegal,
Ireland; buried at Folly Village,
Londonderry (4:262).

Dill, Robert. Born 1740 at Donegal,
Ireland; buried at Folly Village,
Londonderry (4:262).

Dill, Robert. From Ireland; land
grant at Londonderry 6 Mar. 1775
(4:258).

Dillon, Amos. Grantee "Digby New
Grant" 29 Jan. 1801 (5:82).

Dillon, Daniel. S. of John/Mary
(Doyle) of New Ross, Co. Wexford,
Ireland; marr. Halifax 14 Jan.
1831 Mary Potter widow of Patrick
Newnan (33:56).

Dillon, Edward. S. of Philip/Ellen
Quann of Co. Tipperary, Ireland;
marr. Halifax 28 Aug. 1831 Ellen
Green (q.v.) (33:56).

Dillon, Ellen. Dau. of William/Ellen
(Doran) of Co. Tipperary, Ireland;
marr. Halifax 13 Nov. 1841 William
Scully (q.v.) (35:144).

Dillon, John. S. of William/Ellen
(Doran) of Co. Tipperary, Ireland;
marr. Halifax 19 Feb. 1843 Mary
McDonald (q.v.) (35:136).

Dillon, Margaret. Dau. of Matthew/
Mary (Tankard) of Dublin, Ireland;
marr. Halifax 15 Apr. 1822 Edward
Kelly (q.v.) (31:48).

Dillon, Mary. Dau. of Patrick/Ann
(Thompson) of Coloughmore, Co.
Waterford, Ireland; marr. (R.C.)
Halifax 25 June 1834 (also married
(C. of E.) Halifax 28 May 1835)
Manus Flanelly (q.v.) (33:58).

Dillon, Michael. S. of William/Ellen
(Doran) of Co. Tipperary, Ireland;
marr. Halifax 29 Sep. 1842 Joanna
Tobin (q.v.) (35:136).

Dillon, Patrick. S. of Charles/Anne
(Wardick) of Co. Tipperary, Ire-
land; marr. Halifax 5 Oct. 1825
Eliza McGarrett (31:44).

Dillon, Thomas. Of Co. Tipperary,
Ireland; widower of Bridget Hynes;
marr. Halifax 5 Feb. 1844 Margaret
Shiels (q.v.) (35:136).

Dillon, William. S. of Patrick/Anne
(Thompson) of Coloughmore, Co.
Waterford, Ireland; marr. Halifax
6 Feb. 1826 Hannah Dealy (32:108).

Dimond, Alice. 24, servant; Hull to
Fort Cumberland on ALBION 7-14

March 1774 (21:139).

Dimssy, John. Of Co. Cork, Ireland; widower of Anne Walsh; marr. Halifax 18 Jan. 1838 Mary Butler (q.v.) (34:128).

Dinan, Elenor. Of Ireland; marr. Halifax 30 Sep. 1819 Michael Ronan (q.v.) (31:52).

Direns, Mary. Dau. of Conner/Ann (Heffernan) of Kilmore, Co. Mayo, Ireland; marr. Halifax 10 Jan. 1843 James Lally (q.v.) (35:140).

Ditmars, John. Grantee "Digby New Grant" 29 Jan. 1801 (5:82).

Divine, Bernard. S. of Bernard/Sarah (Boyle) of Co. Derry, Ireland; marr. Halifax 9 May 1844 Elizabeth Cook (q.v.) (35:137).

Divine, Martin. S. of Austen/Catherine (Carmon) of Co. Mayo, Ireland; marr. Halifax 20 Jan. 1834 Eliza Martin (q.v.) (33:56).

Divine, Mary. Dau. of Thomas/Catherine (Wall) of Co. Longford, Ireland; marr. Halifax 19 Feb. 1833 Denis Ryan (q.v.) (33:66).

Doane, Edmund. Barrington petitioner 19 Oct. 1776 (1:365).

Doane, Lettice Eldridge. Wife of Thomas; b. prob. Chatham, Mass., ca. 1740; d. Barrington 26 July 1766 (50:101).

Doane, Mary. B. Chatham, Mass., 15 Mar. 1750; dau. Joseph/Mary; to Liverpool by 1767 (47:126:288).

Doane, Thomas. S. of Thomas; b. Chatham, Mass., Mar. 1737; at Barrington 26 July 1766 (50:101).

Doane, Ths. Barrington petitioner 19 Oct. 1776 (1:365).

Doanes, Saml. Osborne. Barrington petitioner 19 Oct. 1776 (1:365).

Dobbin, Johannah. Dau. of James/ Honora (Power) of Co. Waterford, Ireland; marr. Halifax 14 June

1820 Thomas Smith (q.v.) (31:53).

Dobbin, Michael. S. of John/Catherine (Butler) of Waterford, Ireland; marr. Halifax 10 July 1805 Johanna Martin (30:104).

Dobbin, William. S. of Edmund/Johanna (David) of Co. Tipperary, Ireland; marr. Halifax 2 Oct. 1805 Mary Murphy (q.v.) (30:104).

Dobson, Richard. 72, gentleman; Hull to Fort Cumberland on ALBION 7-14 March 1774 (21:137).

Dogget, Abigail. Dau. of John/Abigail; to Liverpool by 1779 (47:126:286).

Dogget, Elizabeth. Dau. of Samuel/ Deborah; to (or b.?) Liverpool by 1789 (47:127:122).

Dogget, Lois. Dau. of Samuel/Deborah; to (or b.?) Liverpool by 1789 (47:127:120).

Doggett, Abigal. B. New England Sat. 4 June 175- (i.e. 1757); dau. of John/Abigail; to Liverpool ca. 1760 (47:126:100).

Doggett, Abigal. Dau. of Howe?; to Liverpool ca. 1760 (47:126:100).

Doggett, Abner. B. New England 16 Aug. 1749; s. of John/Abigal; to Liverpool ca. 1760 (47:126:100).

Doggett, Deborah. Wife of Samuel; Plymouth, Mass., to Liverpool ca. 1760 (47:126:161).

Doggett, Deborah. B. Plymouth, Mass., 8 Aug. 1758; dau. of Samuel/Deborah; to Liverpool ca. 1760 (47:126:161).

Doggett, Ebenezer. Liverpool proprietor (19:101).

Doggett, Ebenezer. B. New England 9 July 1752; s. of John/Abigal; to Liverpool ca. 1760 (47:126:100).

Doggett, Ebenezer. Boston, Mass., to Liverpool ca. 1760 (47:126:161).

Doggett, Ebenezer. B. Plymouth,

Mass., 24 Aug. 1754; s. Ebenezer/
Elisabeth; to Liverpool ca. 1760
(47:126:161).

Doggett, Elisabeth. Wife of Ebenezer;
Boston, Mass., to Liverpool ca.
1760 (47:126:161).

Doggett, Elizabeth. B. Plymouth,
Mass., 9 Nov. 1749; dau. Ebenezer/
Elisabeth; to Liverpool ca. 1760
(47:126:161).

Doggett, Ichabod. B. Scituate, Mass.,
14 Nov. 1770; s. of John/Abigal;
to Liverpool ca. 1760 (47:
126:100).

Doggett, John Liverpool proprietor
(19:101).

Doggett, John. B. New England 13 Sep.
1754; s. of John/Abigal; to Liverpool ca. 1760 (47:126:100).

Doggett, John. Esq.; to Liverpool ca.
1760 (47:126:100).

Doggett, Katharine. B. Plymouth,
Mass., 7 Apr. 1760; dau. of Sa-
muel/Deborah; to Liverpool ca.
1760 (47:126:161).

Doggett, Samuel. B. New England Sat.
16 Sep. 175- (i.e. 1758); s. of
John/Abigal; to Liverpool ca. 1760
(47:126:100).

Doggett, Samuel. Liverpool proprietor
(19:101).

Doggett, Samuel. Plymouth, Mass., to
Liverpool ca. 1760 (47:126:161).

Doggett, Thomas. B. Boston, Mass., 19
Dec. 1756; s. Ebenezer/Elisabeth;
to Liverpool ca. 1760 (47:126:
161).

Doggett, William. B. Boston, Mass., 3
Aug. 1759; s. Ebenezer/Elisabeth;
to Liverpool ca. 1760 (47:126:
161).

Doherty, Patrick. S. of George/Marga-
ret (Robinson) of Derry, Ireland;
marr. Halifax 9 May 1820 Mary
Murphy (31:44).

Doherty, Sarah. Dau. of William/
Sophia (McNanniny) of Mullinahone,
Co. Tipperary, Ireland; marr.
Halifax 15 June 1842 James Butler
(q.v.) (35:135).

Dolan, Hannah. Dau. of Matthew/Johan-
na (Noonan) of Co. Kilkenny, Ireland; marr. Halifax 25 Oct. 1812
David Moore (q.v.) (30:108).

Dolany, Mary. Dau. of John/Mary
(Mulrony) of Co. Kilkenny, Ire-
land; marr. Halifax 17 Aug. 1835
John Gibbons (q.v.) (34:130).

Dolby, Sarah. Dau. of William/Sarah
(Cheesman) of Boston, Mass.; marr.
Halifax 23 Feb. 1808 Edmund Leary
(q.v.) (30:107).

Dole, James. Plus 1 f./5 ch./6 svts.;
merchant; Port Roseway Associate
(6:14).

Doliver, Elizebeth. Dau. of Samuel/
Mary; to Liverpool by 1762 (47:
126:288).

Doliver, Gamaliel. S. of Samuel/Mary;
to (or b.?) Liverpool by 1783 (47:
127:51).

Doliver, Hannah. Dau. of Samuel/
Hannah; to (or b.?) Liverpool by
1793 (47:127:124).

Doliver, James. S. of John/Thankful;
to (or b.?) Liverpool by 1787 (47:
127:55).

Doliver, Mary. Dau. of Samuel/Mary;
to Liverpool by 1770 (47:127:53).

Dolliver, John. Liverpool proprietor
(19:102).

Dolliver, Robert Mayo. S. of Robert/
Sarah; to (or b.?) Liverpool by
1797 (47:127:270).

Dolliver, Robert. S. of William/
Sarah; Penobscot, Mass. (now Me.),
to Liverpool by 1776 (47:127:270-
271).

Dolliver, Samuel. Liverpool proprietor (19:101).

Dolliver, Sarah. Dau. of Samuel/Mary; to Liverpool by 1766 (47:127:205).

Dolliver, William. S. of Gamaliel/Lucy; to (or b.?) Liverpool by 1802 (47:127:278).

Dollover, Deborah. Dau. of Samuel/Mary; to Liverpool by 1773 (47:127:202).

Dollover, Elisha. B. Casco Bay; s. of John/Thankful; to Liverpool by 1773 (47:127:202).

Dominei, Francis. Grantee "Digby New Grant" 29 Jan. 1801 (5:82).

Donagan, Mary. Dau. of Matherew/Margaret (Hurley) of Co. Cork, Ireland; marr. Halifax 4 Oct. 1828 John Mahony (q.v.) (32:115).

Donahue, Edmond. S. of Edmond/Sally of Clonmel, Co. Tipperary, Ireland; marr. Halifax 15 July 1821 Catherine Doyle (q.v.) (31:44).

Donaldson, Alexander. Plus 1 f.; Port Roseway Associate (6:14).

Donelly, Patrick. S. of John/Catherine (Butler) of Co. Kilkenny, Ireland; marr. Halifax 15 Sep. 1828 Joanna Kinan (q.v.) (32:108).

Donnelly, Bridget. Dau. of John/Honora (Morissy) of Co. Kilkenny, Ireland; marr. Halifax 25 Feb. 1838 Andrew Dullhanty (q.v.) (34:129).

Donnelly, Jane. Widow of John May; of Co. Longford, Ireland; marr. Halifax 26 Oct. 1837 Patrick Ryan (q.v.) (34:137).

Donnelly, John. Loyalist; mustered at Digby 19 May 1784 (39:120).

Donnelly, Mary. Dau. of John/Honora (Morrisy) of Co. Kilkenny, Ireland; marr. Halifax 2 Mar. 1840 Michael McMahan (q.v.) (34:134).

Donnelly, Patrick. Surgeon, R.N.; s. of Felix/Mary (Quinn) of Co. Tyrone, Ireland; marr. Halifax 19

Oct. 1808 Mary Caldwell (q.v.) (30:104).

Donnelly, Stephen. S. of John/Mary (Murphy) of Co. Kilkenny, Ireland; marr. Halifax 2 Mar. 1835 Ellen Magee (q.v.) (34:129).

Donohoe, Catherine. Alias Coghlan; widow of Daniel Cochran; of Parish Rahoon, Co. Kerry, Ireland; marr. Halifax 26 Jan. 1836 Michael Connors (q.v.) (34:128).

Donohoe, James. Sgt. 81st Regt.; s. of Patrick/Bridget (Murphy) of Drumcullin, King's Co., Ireland; marr. Halifax 4 Feb. 1822 Elizabeth Tuttle (q.v.) (31:44).

Donohoe, John. 60th Regt.; s. of John/Mary (Ryan) of Co. Limerick, Ireland; marr. Halifax 30 Apr. 1823 Mary Keating (q.v.) (31:44).

Donohoe, Mary. Dau. of Jeremiah/Bridget (Ryan) of Co. Carlow, Ireland; marr. Halifax 27 Nov. 1841 George Smyth (q.v.) (35:144).

Donohue, Jeremiah. S. of Cornelius/Julian (Kean) of Co. Kerry, Ireland; marr. Halifax 4 May 1843 Anastasia Magher (q.v.) (35:137).

Donoly, James. S. of James/Catherine (Shay) of Parish Moore, Co. Roscommon, Ireland; marr. Halifax 10 June 1836 Mary Pender (q.v.) (34:129).

Donovan, Elenor. Widow of John Hamilton; d. Michael/Bridget (Keefe); of New Ross, Co. Wexford, Ireland; marr. Halifax 15 Feb. 1825 John Ceary (q.v.) (31:42).

Donovan, Ellen. Dau. of Timothy/Catherine (Hawks) of Kinsale, Co. Cork, Ireland; marr. Halifax 23 May 1838 James Fawson (34:129).

Donovan, Ellen. Dau. of Timothy/Catherine (Sullivan) of Co. Cork, Ireland; marr. Halifax 24 May 1838

John Hurly (q.v.) (34:131).

Donovan, Frances Agnes. Dau. of Simon/Jane (Gallway) of Cork City, Ireland; marr. Halifax 5 Sep. 1833 Thomas Stephen Tobin (33:67).

Donovan, Frances. See Hennessy, Frances.

Donovan, Jeremiah. S. of Patrick/Margaret (Savage) of Parish Clonfert, Co. Cork, Ireland; marr. Halifax 31 Oct. 1826 Mary Rearden (q.v.) (32:108).

Donovan, Margaret. Dau. of Michael/Elizabeth (Kenny) of Co. Kilkenny, Ireland; marr. Halifax 16 Nov. 1830 Patrick Martin (q.v.) (32:116).

Donovan, Simon. S. of Simon/Jane (Gallwey) of Cork, Ireland; marr. Halifax 6 Nov. 1827 Anastasia Heffernan (32:108).

Donovan, Thomas. S. of Patrick/Ellen (Ormond) of Co. Kilkenny, Ireland; marr. Halifax 2 Apr. 1845 Bridget Keating (q.v.) (35:137).

Donovan, William. S. of Thomas/Margaret (Maher) of Co. Tipperary, Ireland; marr. Halifax 6 Feb. 1812 Johanna Heffernan (q.v.) (30:104).

Donovan, William. S. of Michael/Elizabeth (Kenny) of Co. Kilkenny, Ireland; marr. Halifax 24 July 1830 Catherine Griffin (q.v.) (32:108).

Donovan, William. S. of Randal/Margaret (Walsh) of Co. Cork, Ireland; marr. Halifax 13 May 1839 Mary Sullivan (34:129).

Doolan, Bridget. Dau. of Thomas/Margaret (McCarthy) of Co. Kilkenny, Ireland; marr. Halifax 12 May 1834 Kieran Dunn (q.v.) (33:57).

Dooley, John. S. of John/Margaret (Coogan) of Co. Kilkenny, Ireland;

marr. Halifax 30 Apr. 1833 Catherine Brawderick (q.v.) (33:56).

Dooley, Michael. S. of Patrick/Eleanor (Whelan) of Rahens, Co. Waterford, Ireland; marr. Halifax 27 Jan. 1829 Joanna Tobin (q.v.) (32:108).

Dooly, Ellen. Dau. of Patrick/Ellen (Whelan) of Ballyduff, Co. Waterford, Ireland; marr. Halifax 3 Sep. 1829 Edward Haden (q.v.) (32:112).

Doran, Elizabeth. Of Co. Wexford, Ireland; marr. Halifax 6 July 1833 Brien Smith (q.v.) (33:67).

Doran, John. S. of James/Bridget (Follis) of Co. Kilkenny, Ireland; marr. Halifax 21 June 1832 Margaret O'Brien (q.v.) (33:56).

Doran, John. S. of Patrick/Eleanor (Cormack) of Co. Kilkenny, Ireland; marr. Halifax 1 Oct. 1831 Catherine Power (33:57).

Doran, John. S. of James/Ellen (Griffin) of Co. Kilkenny, Ireland; marr. Halifax 7 Aug. 1841 Mary Hanigan (q.v.) (35:137).

Doran, Margaret. Dau. of James/Mary (Dorcey) of Castlecomer, Co. Kilkenny, Ireland; marr. Halifax 10 June 1824 James Quigley (q.v.) (31:52).

Doran, Patrick. S. of Patrick/Eloner; Waterford, Ireland, to Liverpool before 19 Jan. 1785 (47:126:160).

Doran, Thomas. S. of James/Ellen (Griffin) of Co. Kilkenny, Ireland; marr. Halifax 17 Apr. 1842 Catherine Jones (q.v.) (35:137).

Doran, William. S. of Michael/Bridget (Neill) of Co. Carlow, Ireland; marr. Halifax 4 Feb. 1833 Mary Doyle (q.v.) (33:57).

Dorcey, James. S. of John/Margaret (Headen) of Ross, Co. Wexford,

Ireland; marr. Halifax 16 Sep.
1823 Sarah Black (q.v.) (31:44).

Dormy, Luke. Plus 1 f./1 ch.; farmer;
Port Roseway Associate (6:14).

Dorney, Margaret. Of Co. Cork, Ireland; widow of David Hasey; marr.
Halifax 8 Nov. 1841 John Butler
(q.v.) (35:135).

Doten, Abner. Liverpool proprietor
(19:102).

Doten, Edward. B. Plymouth, Mass., 24
Oct. 1745; s. of Edward; to Liverpool ca. 1768 (47:126:95).

Doten, Edward. Plymouth, Mass., to
Liverpool ca. 1760 (47:126:95).

Doten, Elisha. B. Plymouth, Mass., 2
Dec. 1743; s. of Edward; to Liverpool ca. 1760 (47:126:95).

Doten, John. B. Plymouth, Mass., 7
Aug. 1751; s. of Edward; to Liverpool ca. 1760 (47:126:95).

Doten, Lemuel. B. Plymouth, Mass., 9
Aug. 1754; s. of Edward; to Liverpool ca. 1760 (47:126:95).

Doten, Phebe. Wife of Edward; Plymouth, Mass., to Liverpool ca.
1760 (47:126:95).

Doten, Thomas. B. Plymouth, Mass., 18
Mar. 1748; s. of Edward; to Liverpool ca. 1760 (47:126:95).

Dotey, Edward. Liverpool proprietor
(19:101).

Doucett, Peter. (Heirs) grantee
"Digby New Grant" 29 Jan. 1801
(5:82).

Dougherty, Michael. Deserted 28 Feb.
1806 from Royal Newfoundland
Regiment, stationed at Annapolis;
5'11", fair complexion, sandy
hair, hazel eyes, 28, b. Ireland;
advertised The Weekly Chronicle,
15 Mar. 1806 (28:34).

Doughton, Paul. Liverpool proprietor
(19:101).

Doughty, Samuel [2nd of name]. Marin-

er; mustered at Gulliver's Hole/
St. Mary's Bay/Sissiboo 1/6 June
1784; not settled (40:262).

Douglas, Mary. D. Josiah Godfrey; d.
Liverpool 4 Jan. 1816 ae 47 (49:
122).

Douglas, Russel. S. of Nathan and
Ann; b. New London, Conn.; to
Liverpool; d. 17 Aug. 1849 ae 82
(49:122).

Douglas, Russell. S. of Nathan/Anna;
New London, Conn., to Liverpool by
1793 (47:127:124).

Doul, Mary. Of Rossbercon, Co. Kilkenny, Ireland; marr. Halifax 28
Aug. 1817 Robert Bonnet (q.v.)
(30:102).

Dove, Alexander. Bookbinder; Port
Roseway Associate (6:14).

Dowd, Nancy. Widow of George of Co.
Donegal, Ireland; marr. Halifax 3
June 1822 Thomas Maher (q.v.)
(31:50).

Dowlan, Mary. See Kelly, Mary.

Dowlin, Dennis. Arr. Annapolis from
New York 19 Oct. 1782 (37:126).

Dowling, -----. Loyalist; plus 1 ch.;
mustered at Digby 19 May 1784
(39:120).

Dowling, Ann. Dau. of James/Elenor
(Mulhawl) of Kilkenny, Ireland;
marr. Halifax 19 Mar. 1838 Lawrence O'Connor (q.v.) (34:136).

Dowling, Denis. S. of Stephen/Anasta-
sina (Ruell) of Loughmore, Co.
Tipperary, Ireland; marr. Halifax
17 Sep. 1826 Mary Fannon (q.v.)
(32:108).

Dowling, Dennis. Grantee "Digby New
Grant" 29 Jan. 1801 (5:82).

Dowling, George. Widower of Sophia
Cole; of Cork City, Ireland; marr.
Halifax 2 Mar. 1829 Ellen Richard-
son (q.v.) (32:109).

Dowling, James. S. of Michael/Winnifred (Phelan) of Co. Carlow, Ireland; marr. Halifax 18 Apr. 1833 Margaret McDonald (q.v.) (33:57).

Dowling, Mary. Dau. of Thomas/Margaret (McCarthy) of Co. Kilkenny, Ireland; marr. Halifax 16 Apr. 1833 Jeffery Cantwell (q.v.) (33:55).

Dowling, Patrick. S. of Thomas/Ann (Murphy) of Co. Wexford, Ireland; marr. Halifax 25 Sep. 1816 Margaret Kennedy (30:104).

Dowly, William. S. of John/Bridget (Whelan) of Co. Waterford, Ireland; marr. Halifax 9 May 1834 Joanna Quinlan (q.v.) (33:57).

Downey, Ellen. Dau. of Robert/Elizabeth (Sullivan) of Co. Cork, Ireland; marr. Halifax 25 Nov. 1837 James Cuddihy (q.v.) (34:128).

Downey, Judith. Dau. of Patrick/Elenor (Costovan) of King's Co., Ireland; marr. Halifax 2 Dec. 1820 Cornelius Murphy (q.v.) (31:51).

Downing, James. From N.H.; effective land grant at Truro 31 Oct. 1765 (4:244).

Downing, William. From N.H.; effective land grant at Truro 31 Oct. 1765 (4:244).

Downs, Mary. Dau. of Cornelius/Margaret (Connel) of Co. Waterford, Ireland; marr. Halifax 12 May 1809 James Cassidy (q.v.) (30:103).

Downy, Catherine. Of Co. Waterford, Ireland; widow of William Hanigan; marr. Halifax 26 Oct. 1839 Martin Butler (q.v.) (34:126).

Downy, John. S. of James/Elizabeth (Henessy) of Co. Kilkenny, Ireland; marr. Halifax 11 Sep. 1831 Honora Fenton (q.v.) (33:57).

Doyle, Ann. Dau. of John/Bridget (Brenan) of Co. Carlow, Ireland; marr. Halifax 25 June 1844 John Kline (35:140).

Doyle, Bridget. Dau. of Lawrence/Bridget (Connor) of Co. Carlow, Ireland; widow of Edmond Doyle; marr. Halifax 22 Feb. 1830 Michael Cashin (q.v.) (32:106).

Doyle, Bridget. Dau. of Patrick/Catherine (Doran) of Co. Carlow, Ireland; marr. Halifax 9 Sep. 1833 Thomas Farrell (q.v.) (33:57).

Doyle, Catherine. Dau. of Garret/Elener (Burke) of Clonmel, Co. Tipperary, Ireland; marr. Halifax 15 July 1821 Edmond Donahue (q.v.) (31:44).

Doyle, Catherine. Dau. of Patrick/Elizabeth (Skelton) of Parish Machel, Co. Carlow, Ireland; marr. Halifax 7 Jan. 1828 Michael McLean (q.v.) (32:115).

Doyle, Denis. S. of Bryan/Mary (Byrne) of Parish Camm, Co. Wicklow, Ireland; marr. Halifax 4 June 1828 Mary Martin widow of James Connell (32:109).

Doyle, Eleanor. Dau. of Patrick/Honora (Holden) of Co. Carlow, Ireland; marr. Halifax 4 Feb. 1829 Patrick Kenny (q.v.) (32:114).

Doyle, James. Of Parish Borris, Co. Carlow, Ireland; marr. Halifax 10 Feb. 1835 Janet Fraser (q.v.) (34:129).

Doyle, Joanna. Dau. of James/Catherine (Gorman) of Dunleckney, Co. Carlow, Ireland; widow of Valentine Flinn of Carlow, Ireland; marr. Halifax 15 Jan. 1836 John Hayden (q.v.) (34:131).

Doyle, Joanna. See O'Brien, Joanna.

Doyle, Johanna. Dau. of James/Catherine (Walsh) of Co. Kilkenny,

Ireland; marr. Halifax 5 Oct.
1807 John Walsh *(q.v.)* (30:111).

Doyle, John. S. of Michael/Alice
(Maloney) of Newmarket-in-Ossory,
Kilkenny, Ireland; marr. Halifax
15 Oct. 1801 Elizabeth Smith (30:
104).

Doyle, John. S. of Walter/Catherine
(Gorman) of Co. Waterford, Ire-
land; marr. Halifax 21 Jan. 1834
Joanna Butler *(q.v.)* (33:57).

Doyle, Joseph. S. of John/Mary
(Ailworth) of Cashel, Co. Tipperary, Ireland; marr. Halifax 21
Jan. 1845 Mary Creed *(q.v.)* (35:
137).

Doyle, Judy. Dau. of James/Catherine
(Gorman) of Dunleckney, Co. Carlow, Ireland; marr. Halifax 15
July 1823 Valentine Flinn *(q.v.)*
(31:45).

Doyle, Lawrence. S. of James/Cather-
ine (Cavanah) of Ross, Co. Wexford, Ireland; marr. Halifax 30
May 1803 Bridget O'Connor *(q.v.)*
(30:104).

Doyle, Margaret. Dau. of John/Mary
(Kiely) of Bristol, England; marr.
Halifax July 1816 William Conroy
(q.v.) (30:104).

Doyle, Margaret. Dau. of John/Joanna
(Walsh) of Co. Tipperary, Ireland;
marr. Halifax 5 Feb. 1837 James
Boylan *(q.v.)* (34:126).

Doyle, Martin. S. of Peter/Margaret
(Cleary) of Co. Wexford, Ireland;
marr. Halifax 7 Jan. 1820 Catherine O'Sullivan (31:44).

Doyle, Mary. Dau. of John/Mary
(Daily) of Bristol, England; marr.
Halifax 3 Feb. 1810 Patrick Ryan
(q.v.) (30:110).

Doyle, Mary. Dau. of Patrick/Eliza-
beth (Skellan) of Co. Carlow,
Ireland; marr. Halifax 4 Feb. 1833

William Doran *(q.v.)* (33:57).

Doyle, Mary. See Ryan, Mary.

Doyle, Michael. S. of Owen/Bridget
(Byrne) of Parish Kilrush, Co.
Wexford, Ireland; marr. Halifax 2
Mar. 1821 Honour Kenedy *(q.v.)*
(31:44).

Doyle, Michael. S. of Andrew/Mary
(Adams) of Co. Carlow, Ireland;
marr. Halifax 25 Aug. 1828 Mary
Kenedy *(q.v.)* (32:109).

Doyle, Michael. S. of Daniel/Mary
(Murphy) of Co. Kerry, Ireland;
marr. Halifax 9 Oct. 1842 Catherine Sullivan *(q.v.)* (35:137).

Doyle, Richard. S. of William/Bridget
(Dunn) of Enniscorthy, Co. Wexford, Ireland; marr. Halifax 7
Nov. 1835 Mary Fitzpatrick *(q.v.)*
(34:129).

Doyle, Thomas. S. of John/Catherine
of Co. Wexford, Ireland; marr.
Halifax 26 Nov. 1831 Joanna O'Bri-
en *(q.v.)* (33:57).

Doyle, William. Mariner; s. Philip/
Mary (Murphy) of Wexford, Ireland;
marr. Halifax 12 Jan. 1829 Mary
Ann Aheron *(q.v.)* (32:109).

Doyle, William. S. of Patrick/Mary
(Martin) of Co. Wexford, Ireland;
marr. Halifax 5 Feb. 1843 Mary
Pringle (35:137).

Drady, Anastatia. Dau. of William/
Mary (Brennan) of Co. Tipperary,
Ireland; marr. Halifax 3 Apr. 1820
Malachy O'Brien *(q.v.)* (31:41).

Drake, Benjamin. Loyalist; mustered
at Digby 19 May 1784 (39:120).

Drake, William. Grantee "Digby New
Grant" 29 Jan. 1801 (5:82).

Drake, William. Loyalist; mustered at
Digby 19 May 1784 (39:120).

Draper, James. S. of William/Bridget
(Mahony) of Co. Kerry, Ireland;
marr. Halifax 28 Apr. 1839 Mary

Ann Gough (q.v.) (34:129).

Drea, Bridget. Dau. of Patrick/Frances (Richard) of Co. Kilkenny, Ireland; marr. Halifax 25 Oct. 1832 Patrick Mahony (q.v.) (33:63).

Drea, Daniel. S. of Daniel/Margaret (Corcoran) of Co. Kilkenny, Ireland; marr. Halifax 7 May 1831 Bridget Murphy (q.v.) (33:57).

Drea, Joanna. Dau. of Edwartd/Catherine (Dennis) of Co. Kilkennny, Ireland; marr. Halifax 23 May 1830 Patrick Hart (q.v.) (32:112).

Drew, Drusilla. Dau. of Lemuel/Mary; to (or b.?) Liverpool by 1786 (47:127:51).

Drew, Lemuel Jr. S. of Seth/Desire; to (or b.?) Liverpool by 1791 (47:127:117).

Drew, Lemuel. Liverpool proprietor (19:102).

Drew, Margaret. Dau. of Seth/Desire; to (or b.?) Liverpool by 1791 (47:127:57).

Drew, Mary. Dau. of Lemuel/Mary; to (or b.?) Liverpool by 1794 (47:127:209).

Drew, Seth. Liverpool proprietor (19:102).

Drew, Seth. To Liverpool ca. 1760 (47:126:161).

Driscoll, Catherine. Dau. of Lawrence/Mary (Grady) of Nfld.; marr. Halifax 8 Oct. 1828 Patrick Dunn (q.v.) (32:109).

Driscoll, John. S. of William/Elenor (O'Brien) of Clonmult, Cork, Ireland; marr. Halifax 8 Sep. 1802 Anne Fitzmaurice (q.v.) (30:104).

Driscoll, Timothy. S. of James/Catherine (O'Brien) of Roscarbery, Co. Cork, Ireland; marr. Halifax 6 May 1838 Margaret Cronan (q.v.) (34:129).

Drohan, John. Of Carrick-on-Suir, Co. Tipperary, Ireland; marr. Halifax 19 Feb. 1833 Sarah MacFarlan widow of Capt. John Nolan (33:57).

Drowhan, Catherine. Dau. of John/Catherine (Mansfield) of Co. Waterford, Ireland; marr. Halifax 25 Nov. 1837 Jeremiah O'Connell (q.v.) (34:136).

Drummond, Jane. Dau. of David/Bridget (MacOwen) of Co. Leitrim, Ireland; marr. Halifax 22 Nov. 1844 James Leddy (q.v.) (35:140).

Drummond, William. S. of David/Bridget (McKan) of Co. Leitrim, Ireland; marr. Halifax 17 June 1841 Esther Carter (35:137).

Dryter, Joseph. Liverpool proprietor (19:101).

Duchscher, George. Waldeck Regt.; mustered at Bear River 11/25 June 1784 (38:259).

Duck, Peter. Grantee "Digby New Grant" 29 Jan. 1801 (5:82).

Dudly, Ellen. Dau. of Christopher/Margartet (Walsh) of Co. Cork, Ireland; marr. Halifax 29 Apr. 1843 John Magher (q.v.) (35:141).

Duffield, John. S. of Michael/Bridget (Dyier) of Parish Tintern, Co. Wexford, Ireland; marr. Halifax 30 Sep. 1829 Margaret Kenedy widow of Patrick Dowling (32:109).

Duffield, John. Widower of Margaret Kenedy; of Co. Wexford, Ireland; marr. Halifax 24 Apr. 1834 Catherine Cullin (q.v.) (33:57).

Duffy, John. S. of James/Ellen (Doyle) of Co. Louth, Ireland; marr. Halifax 8 Sep. 1842 Rosanne Maguire (q.v.) (35:137).

Duffy, Mary. Dau. of Patrick/Margaret (Carter) of Elphin, Roscommon, Ireland; marr. Halifax 18 Apr. 1828 Daniel Sullivan (q.v.)

Duffy, Mary. Dau. of Terrence/Ann
(MacEvoy) of Co. Monaghan, Ire-
land; marr. Halifax 26 June 1832
Thomas Lemasny (q.v.) (33:62).

Duffy, Peter. S. of Owen/Margaret
(Cullins) of Co. Cavan, Ireland;
marr. Halifax 23 May 1842 Elizabeth Dunn (q.v.) (35:137).

Duggan, James. S. of James/Ann
(Broderick) of Co. Kilkenny,
Ireland; marr. Halifax 3 Nov. 1829
Honora Berigan (q.v.) (32:109).

Duggan, John. S. of James/Mary
(Fallon/Dalton?) of Iniskillen,
Fermanagh, Ireland; marr. Halifax
3 Mar. 1810 Mary Anne Mahar (30:
104).

Duggan, John. S. of Michael/Mary
(Ward) of Dungarvan, Co. Waterford, Ireland; marr. Halifax 29
June 1840 Joanna Magher (q.v.)
(34:129).

Duggan, Patrick. S. of Maurice/Anne
(Quillian) of Kilkenny City,
Ireland; marr. Halifax 21 July
1821 Lydia Harriss (31:44).

Duggan, Philip. S. of Philip/Cather-
ine (Neal) of Mullinahone, Co.
Tipperary, Ireland; marr. Halifax
13 June 1803 Mary McNamara widow
of George Scott (30:104).

Duggan, Sarah. Dau. of Paul/Cecila
(Burke) of Co. Tipperary, Ireland;
marr. Halifax 26 Apr. 1843 John
Sullivan (q.v.) (35:145).

Duggan, Timothy. S. of Denis/Eleanor
(Mahony) of Enniskeen, Co. Cork,
Ireland; marr. Halifax 6 Feb. 1826
Margaret Forrestall widow of John
Hassey and James Venable (32:109).

Dulhanty, Catherine. Dau. of William/
Elizabeth (Bulger) of Co. Kilken-
ny; marr. Halifax 5 Feb. 1820
Edward Power (q.v.) (31:52).

Dulhanty, Ellen. Dau. of Thomas/
Catherine (Grace) of Co. Kilkenny,
Ireland; marr. 25 Aug. 1812 John
Cullen (q.v.) (30:104).

Dulhanty, Ellen. Dau. of Thomas/Ellen
(Walsh) of Co. Kilkenny, Ireland;
marr. Halifax 20 Nov. 1834 John
Stephen (q.v.) (34:138).

Dulhanty, James. S. of Thomas/Elenor
(Flinn) of Co. Kilkenny, Ireland;
marr. Halifax 16 Sep. 1805 Ellen
O'Brien (q.v.) (30:105).

Dulhanty, Mary. Dau. of Thomas/
Catherine (Grace) of Knocktopher,
Kilkenny, Ireland; marr. Halifax
28 Jan. 1813 Edward Upton (q.v.)
(30:111).

Dullehanty, Catherine. Dau. of Tho-
mas/Margaret (Tobin) of Co. Kilkenny, Ireland; marr. Halifax 2
Oct. 1829 James Kelly (q.v.) (32:
113).

Dullehanty, Mary. Dau. of Edward/
Ellen of Knocktopher, Co. Kilkenny, Ireland; marr. Halifax 11 July
1842 Martin O'Brien (q.v.) (35:
142).

Dullhanty, Andrew. S. of Richard/
Ellen (Houlihan) of Knocktopher,
Co. Kilkenny, Ireland; marr.
Halifax 25 Feb. 1838 Bridget
Donnelly (q.v.) (34:129).

Dunbar, Joseph. Grantee "Digby New
Grant" 29 Jan. 1801 (5:82).

Duncan, Charlotte. Dau. of Alexander/
Jane (Duffus) of Prince Edward
Isl.; marr. Halifax 18 July 1835
Andrew Hogan (q.v.) (34:131).

Duncanson, Catherine. Dau. of Pa-
trick/Mary (Doyle) of Co. Wexford,
Ireland; marr. Halifax 29 May 1821
(q.v.) (31:43).

Dunford, John. S. of Maurice/Bridget
(Beresford) of Co. Waterford,
Ireland; marr. Halifax 7 Oct. 1841

Mary Fitzgerald (35:137).

Dunigan, Margaret. Dau. of Daniel/
Catherine (Hollihan) of Co. Cork,
Ireland; marr. Halifax 15 Jan.
1845 Charles Crawley *(q.v.)* (35:
136).

Dunlap, James. From N.H.; effective
land grant at Truro 31 Oct. 1765
(4:245).

Dunlap, Thomas. From N.H.; effective
land grant at Truro 31 Oct. 1765
(4:245).

Dunlop, ----- (Mrs.). Plus 8 ch.;
Liverpool to Nova Scotia April
1864 on KEDAR (45:181).

Dunlop, Hannah. Dau. of William/Mary;
to (or b.?) Liverpool by 1799 (47:
127:276).

Dunn, Bridget. Dau. of Arthur/Eleanor
(Miles) of Co. Wexford, Ireland;
marr. Halifax 14 June 1833 Edward
Whebby *(q.v.)* (33:68).

Dunn, Bridget. Dau. of John/Mary
(Cleer) of Co. Kilkenny, Ireland;
marr. Halifax 20 May 1844 Patrick
Burke *(q.v.)* (35:135).

Dunn, Bridget. Dau. of Patrick/Marga-
ret (Butler) of Co. Tipperary,
Ireland; marr. Halifax 24 Apr.
1842 Patrick Corcoran *(q.v.)* (35:
136).

Dunn, Denis. S. of Timothy/Bridget
(Colgan) of Kildare, Co. Kildare,
Ireland; marr. Halifax 1 Nov. 1842
Julian Ryan *(q.v.)* (35:137).

Dunn, Elizabeth. Dau. of John/Mary
(Duggan) of St. John's, Nfld.;
marr. Halifax 23 May 1842 Peter
Duffy *(q.v.)* (35:137).

Dunn, Ellen. See Sheehan, Ellen.

Dunn, James. S. of James/Catherine
(Doyle) of Parish Ballyanne, Co.
Wexford, Ireland; marr. Halifax 21
Aug. 1830 Matilda Londergan (32:
109).

Dunn, James. S. of Walter/Elenor
(Phelan) of Parish Butts?, Co.
Kilkenny, Ireland; marr. Halifax 7
Jan. 1827 Nancy McDonald *(q.v.)*
(32:109).

Dunn, Joanna. Dau. of Michael/Ann
(Hannon) of Co. Kilkenny, Ireland;
marr. Halifax 14 Feb. 1831 Michael
Hayes *(q.v.)* (33:59).

Dunn, John. S. of Michael/Ann (Hannon) of Gowran, Co. Kilkenny,
Ireland; marr. Halifax 10 July
1834 Martha Kelly *(q.v.)* (33:57).

Dunn, John. S. of Richard/Frances
(Power) of Co. Waterford, Ireland;
marr. Halifax 3 Mar. 1840 Mary
Whelan *(q.v.)* (34:129).

Dunn, Kieran. S. of Walter/Catherine
(Butler) of Co. Kilkenny, Ireland;
marr. Halifax 12 May 1834 Bridget
Doolan *(q.v.)* (33:57).

Dunn, Margaret. Dau. of Thomas/
Catherine (Kelly) of Co. Wexford,
Ireland; marr. Halifax 3 Mar. 1829
Patrick Brenan *(q.v.)* (32:106).

Dunn, Margaret. Dau. of Michael/Ann
(Hannon) of Parish Gowran, Co.
Kilkenny, Ireland; marr. Halifax
22 Jan. 1829 Edward Spruhan *(q.v.)*
(32:118).

Dunn, Mary. Dau. of Edward/Ellen
(Munrony) of Co. Kilkenny, Ire-
land; marr. Halifax 26 Nov. 1833
Edward McNamara *(q.v.)* (33:63).

Dunn, Mary. Dau. of John/Mary (Christopher) of Parish Newtown, Co.
Waterford, Ireland; marr. Halifax
15 Sep. 1835 John O'Gealy *(q.v.)*
(34:136).

Dunn, Michael. Pvt., Rifles; s.
Patrick/Margaret of Kilkank?,
Kildare, Ireland; marr. Halifax 30
May 1828 Harriet Dunn (32:109).

Dunn, Michael. S. of Richard/Mary
(Sutton) of Parish Ballyanne, Co.

Wexford, Ireland; marr. Halifax 3 Sep. 1829 Catherine Finn (q.v.) (32:109).

Dunn, Patrick. S. of James/Mary (Chapman) of Co. Wexford, Ireland; marr. Halifax 8 Oct. 1828 Catherine Driscoll (q.v.) (32:109).

Dunn, Thomas. Of Parish Tallaght, Co. Dublin, Ireland; marr. Halifax 19 Apr. 1822 Isabella widow of Andrew McDonald (31:44).

Dunn, Walter. Of Gowran, Co. Kilkenny, Ireland; widower of Ann Magrath; marr. Halifax 15 Apr. 1844 Bridget Purcell (q.v.) (35:137).

Dunnavan, William. S. of James/Catherine (Colbert) of Parish Cloyne, Co. Cork, Ireland; marr. Halifax 19 Oct. 1826 Johana Harrington (q.v.) (32:108).

Dunning, John. 24, farmer; Hull to Fort Cumberland on ALBION 7-14 March 1774 (21:137).

Dunphy, Alice. Dau. of William/Joanna (Henebery) of Co. Waterford, Ireland; marr. Halifax 25 Jan. 1830 Christopher Reynolds (q.v.) (32:117).

Dunphy, Alice. Dau. of William/Joanna (Henebery) of Co. Waterford, Ireland; widow of Christopher Reynolds of Co. Sligo, Ireland; marr. Halifax 22 Feb. 1835 Maurice Kiley (q.v.) (34:132).

Dunphy, Catherine. Dau. of William/Joanna (Henibery) of Co. Waterford, Ireland; marr. Halifax 2 Nov. 1828 Michael Tinan (q.v.) (32:119).

Dunphy, Catherine. Of Parish Fethard, Co. Tipperary, Ireland; marr. Halifax 10 Sep. 1834 Cornelius Toohill (q.v.) (34:138).

Dunphy, Francis. S. of Edward/Mary (Power) of Parish Passage, Co.

Waterford, Ireland; marr. Halifax 13 Sep. 1823 Margaret Moore (q.v.) (31:44).

Dunphy, James. S. of Edward/Mary (Power) of Parish Passage, Co. Waterford, Ireland; marr. Halifax 19 Sep. 1823 Anne Sheehan (q.v.) (31:44).

Dunphy, Margaret. Of Co. Waterford, Ireland; widow of Thomas Power; marr. Halifax 27 Nov. 1834 William Cody (q.v.) (34:127).

Dunphy, Richard. S. of Patrick/Mary (Moran) of Co. Kilkenny, Ireland; marr. Halifax 29 Nov. 1839 Mary Cantfield (q.v.) (34:129).

Dunphy, Sarah. Of Callours, Co. Kilkenny, Ireland; marr. Halifax 31 May 1835 James Walker (34:139).

Dunphy, William. S. of James/Catherine (Scully) of Co. Tipperary, Ireland; marr. Halifax 17 Sep. 1837 Margaret Walsh (q.v.) (34:129).

Durfee, Joseph. Plus 1 f./6 ch./6 svts.; farmer; Port Roseway Associate (6:14).

Durfee, Robert. Plus 1 svt.; farmer; Port Roseway Associate (6:14).

Durling, Daniel. Grantee "Digby New Grant" 29 Jan. 1801 (5:82).

Durney, Joanna. Dau. of Richard/Mary (Smullen) from Co. Wicklow, Ireland; marr. Halifax 9 May 1827 Timothy Healy (q.v.) (32:112).

Durny, Mary. See Smellon, Mary.

Duval, Peter. S. of John of Granville, France; marr. Halifax 10 Oct. 1829 Margaret Moony (q.v.) (32:109).

Dwire, William. S. of John/Johana (Mullowney) of Co. Tipperary, Ireland; marr. Halifax 14 May 1822 Johana Power (31:45).

Dwyer, James. Widower of Joanna Poore

of Co. Tipperary, Ireland; marr.
Halifax 21 Nov 1837 Mary Shortell
(q.v.) (34:129).

Dwyer, Judith. Dau. of William/Mary
(Slinsby) of Co. Tipperary, Ireland; widow of Patrick Morrissy;
marr. Halifax 26 Nov. 1832 Joseph
Barry (q.v.) (33:54).

Dwyer, Malachy. S. of James/Joanna
(Power) of Co. Tipperary, Ireland;
marr. Halifax 17 Sep. 1839 Barbary
Isner (34:129).

Dwyer, Margaret. Dau. of Martin/
Joanna (Markley) of Co. Tipperary,
Ireland; marr. Halifax 18 June
1832 Michael Heffernan (q.v.)
(33:59).

Dwyer, Margaret. Dau. of Michael/
Margaret (Mihan) of Co. Tipperary,
Ireland; marr. Halifax 10 Jan.
1839 Michael Corcoran (q.v.)
(34:128).

Dwyer, Martin. S. of Michael/Eliza-
beth of Co. Kilkenny, Ireland;
marr. Halifax 6 June 1836 Anastasia Keefe (q.v.) (34:129).

Dwyer, Mary. Dau. of James/Judith
(Cummins) of Co. Tipperary, Ire-
land; marr. Halifax 22 Aug. 1834
Patrick Henissey (q.v.) (33:59).

Dwyer, Mary. Dau. of James/Judith
(Cummings) of Co. Tipperary,
Ireland; widow of Patrick Hinessy;
marr. Halifax 12 Dec. 1837 John
Power (q.v.) (34:137).

Dwyer, Mary. See Tracy, Mary.

Dwyer, Mary. Wife of John Power; bur.
Halifax 13 Jan. 1840 ae. 30 (34:
125).

Dynore, Thomas. Late 81st Regt.; of
Co. Kerry, Ireland; marr. Halifax
10 May 1839 Christiana McDonald
(q.v.) (34:129).

- E -

Eagan, Edward. S. of John/Emilia (St.
Leger) of Loughrey, Co. Galway,
Ireland; m. Halifax 14 Sep. 1807
Elizabeth Gillman (q.v.) (30:105).

Earle, Daniel. N.Y. to N.S.; to U.S.
1776; lived 1785 at N.Y. (36:65).

Earle, Jonas Jr. N.Y. to N.S.; to
U.S. 1776; lived 1785 at N.Y. (36:
65).

Earle, Jonas. N.Y. to N.S.; to U.S.
1776; lived 1785 at N.Y. (36:65).

Earle, Nath. N.Y. to N.S.; to U.S.
1776; lived 1785 at N.Y. (36:65).

Earle, Robert. N.Y. to N.S.; to U.S.
1776; lived 1785 at N.Y. (36:65).

Early, John. S. of Peter/Eleanor
(Daily) of Co. Longford, Ireland;
marr. Halifax 3 Sep. 1814 Anne
Hartwood (30:105).

Easton, Peter. Loyalist; mustered at
Digby 19 May 1784 (39:120).

Easton, Robert. Plus 5 svts.; Port
Roseway Associate (6:14).

Eaton, Benjamin. New England to
Annapolis 1760 (18:271).

Ebenhardt, C. German Service; mustered at Bear River 11/25 June 1784
(38:259).

Ebenhardt, Christian. German Service;
mustered at Bear River 11/25 June
1784 (38:259).

Eckhardt, George. German Service;
mustered at Bear River 11/25 June
1784 (38:259).

Eckley, John. Pa. to N.S.; to U.S.
1776; lived 1785 at Mass. [which
then incl. Me.] (36:65).

Eddy, Elias. Mass. to N.S.; to U.S.
1776; lived 1785 at Eddington, Me.
(36:64).

Eddy, Ibrook. Mass. to N.S.; to U.S.
1776; lived 1785 at Eddington, Me.
(36:64).

Eddy, Jonathan Jr. Mass. to N.S.; to

U.S. 1776; lived 1785 at Mass.
[which then incl. Me.] (36:64).

Eddy, Jonathan. Born at Norton,
Mass.; to N.S.; to U.S. 1776;
lived 1785 at Eddington, Me. (36:
63-64).

Eddy, William. Mass. to N.S.; to U.S.
1776; died 1778 (36:64).

Edgar, James. Arr. Annapolis from New
York 19 Oct. 1782 (37:125).

Edgar, James. Loyalist; mustered at
Digby 19 May 1784 (39:120).

Edison, John. Grantee "Digby New
Grant" 29 Jan. 1801 (5:82).

Edison, John. Loyalist; plus 1 f./7
ch.; mustered at Digby 19 May 1784
(39:120).

Edison, Marshall. Loyalist; mustered
at Digby 19 May 1784 (39:120).

Edmonds, John. Port Roseway Associate
(6:14).

Edwards, John. Loyalist; mustered at
Digby 19 May 1784 (39:120).

Egan, Catherine. Dau. of James/Mary
(Mullally) of Co. Tipperary, Ire-
land; marr. Halifax 3 Mar. 1835
William Flinn (q.v.) (34:130).

Egan, Catherine. See Scott, Catherine.

Egan, Daniel. S. of Anthony/Mary
(Allen) of Athlone, Co. Westmeath,
Ireland; m. Halifax 28 May 1811
Catherine Macculan (q.v.) (30:
105).

Egan, Margaret. Dau. of James/Mary
(Mullally) of Co. Tipperary,
Ireland; marr. Halifax 19 Feb.
1843 John Flinn (q.v.) (35:138).

Egan, Michael. S. of James/Mary
(Mullally) of Co. Tipperary, Ire-
land; marr. Halifax 5 Mar. 1832
Mary O'Donnell (q.v.) (33:57).

Egar, Catherine. Of Co. Kerry, Ireland; widow of Timothy Kenedy;
marr. Halifax 24 Apr. 1844 Thomas

Sullivan (q.v.) (35:145).

Egerton, Hezekiah. From N.H.; effective land grant at Truro 31 Oct.
1765 (4:244).

Elderidge, Zephaniah. Liverpool
proprietor (19:101).

Eldredge, Abner. S. of James; b.
Chatham, Mass., 11 Oct. 1738; to
Liverpool by 1766 (50:102).

Eldredge, Phoebe Eldredge. Wife of
Zephania; to Liverpool by 1766
(50:102).

Eldredge, Ruth Higgins. Widow of
James; to Liverpool by 1766 (50:
102).

Eldredge, Sarah Eldredge. Wife of
Abner; to Liverpool by 1766 (50:
102).

Eldredge, Zephania. S. of James; b.
Chatham, Mass., 2 Dec. 1733; to
Liverpool by 1766 (50:102).

Eldridge, Abner. Liverpool proprietor
(19:102).

Eldridge, Mahetable. See Smith,
Mahetable.

Eldridge, Samuel. Liverpool proprietor (19:102).

Eldward, Mary. Dau. of Martin/Joanna
(Cummings) of Glamore, Co. Kilkenny, Ireland; marr. Halifax 9 July
1825 Patrick Gorman (q.v.) (31:
46).

Ellenwood, Benjamin. S. of Nathaniel/
Margaret; to (or b.?) Liverpool by
1803 (47:127:271).

Ellenwood, Nathaniel. S. of Benjamin/
Susannah; to (or b.?) Liverpool by
1781 (47:126:288).

Elliott, Anthony. From Mass.; land
grant at Onslow 21 Feb. 1769 (4:
224).

Elliott, Edward. Laborer; English;
31; Liverpool to Nova Scotia May
1864 on EUROCLYDON (45:181).

Ellis, Ephraim. Loyalist; plus 1 f./3

ch.; mustered at Digby 19 May 1784 (39:120).

Ellis, James. Plus 1 svt.; carpenter; Port Roseway Associate (6:14).

Ellis, Michael. S. of Peter/Margaret (Dignem) of Co. Cavan, Ireland; marr. Halifax 25 Jan. 1834 Margaret Walsh (q.v.) (33:57).

Elsner, -----. German Service; mustered at Bear River 11/25 June 1784 (38:259).

Elvins, Henry. Plus 1 f./2 svts.; farmer; Port Roseway Associate (6:14).

Elward, Johanna. Dau. of James/Anastasia (Shea) of Ferrah, Co. Tipperary, Ireland; marr. Halifax 21 Jan. 1842 William Casey (q.v.) (35:135).

Elward, Michael. S. of Martin/Mary (Drea) of Co. Kilkenny, Ireland; marr. Halifax 18 June 1838 Margaret Dunn widow of Edward Spruhan (34:129).

Elward, Philip. S. of John/Margaret (Magrath) of Co. Kilkenny, Ireland; marr. Halifax 10 Jan. 1842 Sarah Johnson (q.v.) (35:137).

Elvart, Anastasia. Dau. of John/Mary (Magrath) of Co. Kilkenny, Ireland; marr. Halifax 19 Sep. 1829 John Ryan (q.v.) (32:118).

English, James. S. of John/Ann (Mackey) of Clonmel, Co. Tipperary, Ireland; marr. Halifax 30 Nov. 1837 Annabella Livers (34:129).

English, Jeremiah. S. of Patrick/Elenor (Sullivan) of Clonmel, Tipperary, Ireland; m. Halifax 9 June 1811 Elener Burke (q.v.) (30:105).

English, Joseph. Plus 1 f./1 ch./2 svts.; carpenter; Port Roseway Associate (6:14).

English, Mary. D, Edmund/Bridget (O'Donnell) of Co. Tipperary, Ireland; marr. Halifax 21 May 1833 Mathew Morissy (q.v.) (33:64).

Ennis, Nicholas. S. of John/Mary (Walsh) of Clearystown, Co. Wexford, Ireland; marr. Halifax 24 Feb. 1824 Mary Collins (31:45).

Enright, Dennis. S. of Timothy/Elenor (Donahoe) of Neladerry, Limerick, Ireland; m. Halifax 4 Feb. 1804 Mary Edwards (30:105).

Enright. See Inright,

Ensenburg, F. German Service; plus 1 f.; mustered at Bear River 11/25 June 1784 (38:259).

Enslow, Isaac. Plus 1 f./2 ch./3 svts.; Port Roseway Associate (6: 14).

Euler, Conrad. German Service; plus 1 f.; mustered at Bear River 11/25 June 1784 (38:259).

Eustace, Edward. S. of Alexander/Catherine (Kavanah) of Myshall, Co. Carlow, Ireland; marr. Halifax 1 May 1832 Honora Darcy (q.v.) (33:57).

Eustace, Roland. S. of Roland/Joanna (Roche) of Co. Kilkenny, Ireland; marr. Halifax 2 June 1840 Elizabeth Doneck (34:129).

Evans, Ann. English; 9; Liverpool to Nova Scotia May 1864 on EUROCLYDON (45:181).

Evans, Ann. Wife of William; English; 35; Liverpool to Nova Scotia May 1864 on EUROCLYDON (45:181).

Evans, James. Laborer; English; 16; Liverpool to Nova Scotia May 1864 on EUROCLYDON (45:181).

Evans, Lemuel. Grantee "Digby New Grant" 29 Jan. 1801 (5:82).

Evans, Lemuel. Loyalist; plus 1 f./1 svt.; mustered at Digby 19 May 1784 (39:120).

Evans, Thomas. Laborer; English; 18;
Liverpool to Nova Scotia May 1864
on EUROCLYDON (45:181).

Evans, William. English; 11; Liverpool to Nova Scotia May 1864 on
EUROCLYDON (45:181).

Evans, William. Farmer; English; 40;
Liverpool to Nova Scotia May 1864
on EUROCLYDON (45:181).

Everitt, Catherine. Grantee "Digby
New Grant" 29 Jan. 1801 (5:82).

Everitt, James. Grantee "Digby New
Grant" 29 Jan. 1801 (5:82).

Ezra, Ann. Wife of Jonah; English;
28; Liverpool to Nova Scotia June
1864 on INDIAN QUEEN (45:181).

Ezra, David. Laborer; English; 18;
Liverpool to Nova Scotia June 1864
on INDIAN QUEEN (45:181).

Ezra, Jonah. Laborer; English; 29;
Liverpool to Nova Scotia June 1864
on INDIAN QUEEN (45:181).

Ezra, Mary Ann. English; 3; Liverpool
to Nova Scotia June 1864 on INDIAN
QUEEN (45:181).

- F -

Fairbanks, Joseph. Conn. to Onslow
before 19 Oct. 1759 (4:223).

Fallon, Margaret. Dau. of James/
Catherine (Meley) of London,
England; marr. Halifax 2 May 1820
David O'Neil (q.v.) (31:51).

Fallydown, Patience. 22; servant;
Hull, Yorkshire, to Halifax; on
JENNY 3-10 April 1775 (22:124).

Fancy, George. Liverpool proprietor
(19:101).

Fanning, Alice. See Walsh, Alice.

Fanning, John. S. of William/Mary
(Wall) of Callan, Co. Kilkenny,
Ireland; marr. 18 Apr. 1803 Elener
Forrestal (q.v.) (30:105).

Farlin, Alex'r. Plus 1 f./6 ch.;
sawyer; Port Roseway Associate (6:
14).

Farrell, Daniel John. S. of Daniel/
Catherine (Wall) of Co. Waterford,
Ireland; marr. Halifax 18 July
1807 Mary Holleran (q.v.) (30:
105).

Farrell, John. S. of Walter/Mary
(Quinn) of Co. Wexford, Ireland;
marr. Halifax 29 July 1810 Anne
Grandy (30:105).

Farrell, Mary. See Holleran, Mary.

Farrell, William. S. of Patrick/
Eleanor (Keating) of Waterford,
Ireland; marr. Halifax 10 Feb.
1823 Elenor Flinn (q.v.) (31:45).

Faulkner, James. From N.H.; effective
land grant at Truro 31 Oct. 1765
(4:244).

Faulkner, John. Grantee "Digby New
Grant" 29 Jan. 1801 (5:82).

Faulkner, Robert. B. 1733; bur. Folly
Village, Londondery (4: 262).

Faulkner, Robert. From Ireland; land
grant at Londonderry 6 Mar. 1775
(4:258).

Fawceit, Jane. 28; wife of John;
Hull, Yorkshire, to Nova Scotia;
on TWO FRIENDS 28 Feb.-7 Mar. 1774
(25:31).

Fawceit, John. 29; farmer; Hull,
Yorkshire, to Nova Scotia; on TWO
FRIENDS 28 Feb.-7 Mar. 1774 (25:
31).

Fawceit, Mary. 4; dau.of John; Hull,
Yorkshire, to Nova Scotia; on TWO
FRIENDS 28 Feb.-7 Mar. 1774 (25:
31).

Fawceit, Robert. 30; sail cloth
maker; Hull, Yorkshire, to Nova
Scotia; on TWO FRIENDS 28 Feb.-7
Mar. 1774 (25:28).

Feehan, Jeremiah. S. of Henry/Ellen

(Tool) of Co. Tipperary, Ireland;
marr. Halifax 19 May 1805 Mary
Stone (30:105).

Feelk, Joseph. Liverpool proprietor
(19:101).

Felch, Daniel. New England to Annapolis on CHARMING MOLLY May 1760
(18:271).

Felch, Ebenezer. New England to
Annapolis on CHARMING MOLLY May
1760 (18:271).

Fenby, Robert. 26; husbandman; Hull,
Yorkshire, to Nova Scotia; on TWO
FRIENDS 28 Feb.-7 Mar. 1774 (25:
30).

Fennell, Thomas. S. of Thomas/Eliza-
beth (Butler) of Co. Tipperary,
Ireland; marr. Halifax 21 Apr.
1814 Elenor Fleming (30:105).

Fenton, John. S. of Patrick of Parish
Magils (sic), Co. Cork, Ireland;
marr. Halifax 8 Feb. 1823 Sarah
Eacre (31:45).

Fenton, Mary. 9; to join father;
Hull, Yorkshire, to Halifax; on
JENNY 3-10 April 1775 (22:125).

Fenton, Sarah. 15; to join father;
Hull, Yorkshire, to Halifax; on
JENNY 3-10 April 1775 (22:125).

Fenwick, Edward. 28, labourer; Hull
to Fort Cumberland on ALBION 7-14
March 1774 (21:137).

Fenwick, Mathew. 16, servant; Hull to
Fort Cumberland on ALBION 7-14
March 1774 (21:140).

Fenwick, William. Grantee 'Digby New
Grant' 29 Jan. 1801 (5:82).

Feray, Mark. From Mass.; land grant
at Truro 1759 (4:242).

Feray, Noah. From Mass.; land grant
at Truro 1759 (4:242).

Ferguson, Charles. Grantee 'Digby New
Grant' 29 Jan. 1801 (5:82).

Ferguson, James. Carpenter; Port
Roseway Associate (6:14).

Ferguson, James. Plus 1 f./4 ch./2
svts.; farmer; Port Roseway Associate (6:14).

Ferguson, John. Plus 1 f./2 ch.; Port
Roseway Associate (6:14).

Ferrell, Isaac. From Mass.; land
grant at Onslow 21 Feb. 1769 (4:
224).

Fielding, Armistead. 42; farmer;
Hull, Yorkshire, to Nova Scotia;
on TWO FRIENDS 28 Feb.-7 Mar. 1774
(25:29).

Fielding, Elizabeth. 40; wife of
Armistead; Hull, Yorkshire, to
Nova Scotia; on TWO FRIENDS 28
Feb.-7 Mar. 1774 (25:29).

Fielding, Esther. 5; dau.of Armis-
tead; Hull, Yorkshire, to Nova
Scotia; on TWO FRIENDS 28 Feb.-7
Mar. 1774 (25:29).

Fielding, Hannah. 8; dau.of Armis-
tead; Hull, Yorkshire, to Nova
Scotia; on TWO FRIENDS 28 Feb.-7
Mar. 1774 (25:29).

Fielding, John. 15; s. of Armistead;
Hull, Yorkshire, to Nova Scotia;
on TWO FRIENDS 28 Feb.-7 Mar. 1774
(25:29).

Fielding, Joseph. 2; s. of Armistead;
Hull, Yorkshire, to Nova Scotia;
on TWO FRIENDS 28 Feb.-7 Mar. 1774
(25:29).

Fielding, Nicholas. 12; s. of Armis-
tead; Hull, Yorkshire, to Nova
Scotia; on TWO FRIENDS 28 Feb.-7
Mar. 1774 (25:29).

Fielding, William. 14; s. of Armis-
tead; Hull, Yorkshire, to Nova
Scotia; on TWO FRIENDS 28 Feb.-7
Mar. 1774 (25:29).

Finley, Jonathan. Plus 1 f./7 ch.;
tallow chandler; Port Roseway
Associate (6:14).

Finlon, John. S. of Anthony/Honora
(Ryan) of Parish St. Mullin, Co.

Carlow, Ireland; marr. Halifax 8
Jan. 1826 Catherine Byrne (q.v.)
(31:45).

Finn, Jeremiah. See Feehan, Jeremiah.

Firth, George. 30; farmer; Hull,
Yorkshire, to Nova Scotia; on TWO
FRIENDS 28 Feb.-7 Mar. 1774 (25:
29).

Fisher, David. From N.H.; effective
land grant at Truro 31 Oct. 1765
(4:245).

Fisher, James. From N.H.; effective
land grant at Truro 31 Oct. 1765
(4:245).

Fisher, John. From N.H.; effective
land grant at Truro 31 Oct. 1765
(4:245).

Fisher, Samuel. From N.H.; effective
land grant at Truro 31 Oct. 1765
(4:245).

Fisher, William Jr. From N.H.; effective land grant at Truro 31 Oct.
1765 (4:245).

Fisher, William. From N.H.; effective
land grant at Truro 31 Oct. 1765
(4:245).

Fisher, William. From Ireland; land
grant at Londonderry 6 Mar. 1775
(4:258).

Fitch, William. Liverpool proprietor
(19:102).

Fitzgerald, Daniel. Grantee "Digby
New Grant" 29 Jan. 1801 (5:82).

FitzGerald, Edward. B. Ireland ca.
1777; Belfast or Greenock to
Halifax on POLLY, spring 1799 (29:
83).

Fitzgerald, James. Grantee "Digby New
Grant" 29 Jan. 1801 (5:82).

Fitzgerald, James. S. of John/Mary
(O'Brien) of Youghal, Co. Cork,
Ireland; marr. Halifax 27 Jan.
1825 Elizabeth Rutledge (31:45).

Fitzgerald, John. S. of David/Marga-
ret (Carroll) of Kilnamagoully,

Wexford, Ireland; marr. Halifax 23
Aug. 1821 Mary Shea (q.v.) (31:
45).

Fitzgerald, Mary. Dau. of Patrick/
Elenor (Breen) of Co. Carlow,
Ireland; marr. Halifax 23 Feb.
1811 William Wise (q.v.) (30:112).

Fitzgerald, Mary. Dau. of Terence/
Bridget (Butler) of Co. Waterford,
Ireland; marr. Halifax 4 Feb. 1820
William Deegan (q.v.) (31:44).

Fitzgerald, William. Grantee "Digby
New Grant" 29 Jan. 1801 (5:82).

Fitzgibbons, Mary. Dau. of Edmund/
Sarah (Baldwin) of Co. Cork,
Ireland; marr. Halifax 14 Nov.
1814 Jeremiah Roache (q.v.)
(30:110).

Fitzmaurice, Anne. Dau. of John/Mary
(O'Keeff) of Temanagh, Limerick,
Ireland; marr. Halifax 8 Sep. 1802
John Driscoll (q.v.) (30:104).

Fitzmaurice, Julia Ann. Dau. of John/
Elizabeth (Merry) of Prince Edward
Isl.; marr. Halifax 20 June 1824
Stephen Scanlan (q.v.) (31:53).

Fitzpatrick, Daniel. S. of William/
Margaret (Barry) of Glountain, Co.
Cork, Ireland; marr. Halifax 12
Dec. 1820 Mary Ann McCarthy (q.v.)
(31:45).

Fitzpatrick, John. 60th Regt., s. of
William/Bridget (MacGowan) of
Parish St. Mary, Athlone, West-
meath, Ireland; marr. Halifax 2
July 1822 Susanna Wilkins (31:45).

Fitzrandolph, Robert. Grantee "Digby
New Grant" 29 Jan. 1801 (5:82).

Flager, Thomas. From Ireland; land
grant at Londonderry 6 Mar. 1775
(4:258).

Flager, William. From Ireland; land
grant at Londonderry 6 Mar. 1775
(4:258).

Flaharty, Edmond. S. of Thomas/Hanna

(Hollehan) of Gammansfield, Co. Tipperary, Ireland; marr. Halifax 24 Apr. 1824 Jane Manthorn (31: 45).

Flahive, John. S. of John/Elizabeth (Kenny) of Manhead, Co. Kerry, Ireland; marr. Halifax 12 Jan. 1825 Mary Houghton (31:45).

Flanagan, Bridget. Dau. of Michael/ Mary (Scanttons), of Parish Con- nogh, Co. Cork, Ireland; marr. Halifax 5 Oct. 1825 Mark Tape (q.v.) (31:54).

Flemer, Mary. Dau. of Michael/Mary (Burns) of Co. Wexford, Ireland; marr. Halifax 20 Aug. 1813 John McGovern (q.v.) (30:107).

Fleming, James. S. of Edmund/Margaret (Maguire) of Co. Tipperary, Ire- land; marr. Halifax 28 June 1814 Margaret Condon (q.v.) (30:105).

Fleming, Mary. See Flemer, Mary.

Flemming, Isabella. Wife of James; b. 1750; bur. Folly Village, London- derry (4:262).

Flemming, James. Born 1741 at London- derry, Ireland; bur. Folly Vill- age, Londonderry (4:262).

Flemming, Michael. S. of Simon/Mary (Mahar) of Parish Lislee, Co. Cork, Ireland; marr. Halifax 14 June 1825 Mary Ryan (q.v.) (31: 45).

Fletcher, Elenor. Probably wife of William; b. 1740; bur. Folly Vil- lage, Londonderry (4:262).

Fletcher, Jane. Wife of Thomas; dau. of ----- Vance; b. 1753 Ireland; bur. Folly Village, Londonderry (4:262).

Fletcher, Thomas. B. 1738 Ireland; bur. Folly Village, Londonderry (4:262).

Fletcher, William. B. 1725; bur. Fol- ly Village, Londonderry (4:262).

Flinn, Elenor. Dau. of Patrick/Mary, widow of Thomas Curtis of Harbour Grace. Nfld.; marr. Halifax 10 Feb. 1823 William Farrell (q.v.) (31:45).

Flinn, Valentine. S. of Arthur/ Bridget (Troy) of Parish Machel, Co. Carlow, Ireland; marr. Halifax 15 July 1823 Judy Doyle (q.v.) (31:45).

Florantine, Thomas. See Thomas Flor- rinane.

Florrinane, Thomas. Farmer; Port Roseway Associate (6:14).

Floyd, Simon. Halifax, Mass., to Chester with first settlers (16: 45).

Floyd, Thomas. Halifax, Mass., to Chester with first settlers (16: 45).

Fogarty, James. Of Templeinch, Co. Tipperary, Ireland; marr. Halifax 27 Apr. 1822 Johanna Dogan (31: 45).

Fogarty, Thomas. S. of David/Mary (Murphy) of Newtown Bryniton near Clonmel, Ireland; marr. Halifax 26 Oct. 1825 Hanna Connors widow of Matthew Maguire (31:46).

Foley, James. S. of John/Mary Nowlan of Co. Waterford; marr. Halifax 4 Mar. 1810 Frances Lewis (30:105).

Folley, Patrick. S. of John/Mary (Sweeney) of Co. Cork, Ireland; marr. Halifax 28 Nov. 1815 Louisa Cornwall (30:105).

Forbes, James Fraser. New York to Yarmouth; to Liverpool 1842 (19: 116).

Forbes, Robert. From Ireland; land grant at Londonderry 6 Mar. 1775 (4:258).

Forbes, William. From Ireland; land grant at Londonderry 6 Mar. 1775 (4:258).

Ford, Theodosius, Liverpool proprietor (19:101).

Forrestal, Elener. Dau. of Thomas/Mary (Doyle) of Kilmacow, Co. Kilkenny, Ireland; marr. Halifax 18 Apr. 1803 John Fanning *(q.v.)* (30:105).

Foster, John. Liverpool proprietor (19:102).

Foster, Sarah. Dau. of Thomas/Mary (Escott) of Trinity, Nfld.; marr. Halifax 10 Nov. 1802 Michael Kavanah *(q.v.)* (30:106).

Foster, Thomas. Liverpool proprietor (19:102).

Foster, William. Liverpool proprietor (19:102).

Fowler, Jonathan. Grantee "Digby New Grant" 29 Jan. 1801 (5:82).

Fowler, Matthew. From N.H.; effective land grant at Truro 31 Oct. 1765 (4:244).

Fox, Robert. Plus 1 f./2 ch./2 svts.; farmer; Port Roseway Associate (6:14).

Francis, James. S. of Richard/Mary (Murcha) of Cork, Ireland; marr. Halifax 4 Feb. 1821 Mary Ryan *(q.v.)* (31:46).

Franklin, James Botineau. Grantee "Digby New Grant" 29 Jan. 1801 (5:82).

Fraser, Alexander. Plus 1 f./2 svts.; farmer; Port Roseway Associate (6:14).

Fraser, James. B. Inverness, Scotland; to N.S. 1781 (14:8).

Frazer, Alex'r. Plus 2 svts.; Port Roseway Associate (6:14).

Frazer, Daniel. Plus 1 f./1 ch./1 svt.; Port Roseway Associate (6:14).

Frazer, Hugh. Plus 1 f./1 svt.; farmer; Port Roseway Associate (6:14).

Frazer, James. Plus 1 f./2 ch./1 svt.; shoemaker; Port Roseway Associate (6:14).

Frazer, Simon. Plus 1 svt.; Port Roseway Associate (6:14).

Freeman, Barnabas. Liverpool proprietor (19:102).

Freeman, Elisha. Liverpool proprietor (19:101).

Freeman, Hesekiah. Liverpool proprietor (19:102).

Freeman, Samuel. Liverpool proprietor (19:101).

Freeman, Simeon. Liverpool proprietor (19:102).

Freeman, Smith. Liverpool proprietor (19:102).

Fulton, James. From Ireland; land grant at Londonderry 6 Mar. 1775 (4:258).

Fulton, John. From N.H.; effective land grant at Truro 31 Oct. 1765 (4:245).

Fulton, Samuel. From Ireland; land grant at Londonderry 6 Mar. 1775 (4:258).

Fulton, Thomas. From Ireland; land grant at Londonderry 6 Mar. 1775 (4:258).

- G -

Gafney, Andrew. B. Ireland ca. 1778; Belfast or Greenock to Halifax on POLLY, spring 1799 (29:83).

Gahen, John. S. of Patrick/Francis (Stapleton) of Parish Borris, Co. Carlow, Ireland; marr. Halifax 12 Feb. 1822 Catherine Murphy *(q.v.)* (31:46).

Galagher, Daniel. S. of Daniel/Elizabeth of Co. Tyrone, Ireland; marr. Halifax 3 Jan. 1815 Helena Hacket (30:105).

Gallaghar, James. S. of William/Jane

(Doherty) of Derry, Ireland; marr. Halifax 6 July 1829 Margaret Haney (q.v.) (32:111).

Gallivan, Thomas. S. of Patrick/ Joanna (Tool) of Co. Waterford, Ireland; marr. Halifax 13 Oct. 1831 Anne Ross (q.v.) (33:58).

Gallop, Nathaniel. From Mass.; land grant at Onslow 21 Feb. 1769 (4: 224).

Galway, Elizabeth. Dau. of John/ Anastasia (Cullin) of Co. Kilkenny, Ireland; marr. Halifax 3 Sep. 1832 Thomas Wallace (q.v.) (33: 67).

Galway, Michael. S. of John/Anastasia (Cullin) of Co. Kilkenny, Ireland; marr. Halifax 25 Oct. 1832 Catherine Walsh (q.v.) (33:58).

Gamage, James. Plus 1 f./1 ch./4 svts.; Port Roseway Associate (6: 15).

Gamble, Andrew. From N.H.; effective land grant at Truro 31 Oct. 1765 (4:244).

Gamble, Catherine. Dau. of George/ Henrietta (Howard) of Dublin, Ireland; marr. Halifax 14 Feb. 1825 John Heacey (q.v.) (31:47).

Gamble, James. Corp. 64th Regt.; of Co. Westmeath, Ireland; marr. Halifax 15 Aug. 1841 Henrietta McKinnon (35:138).

Gamble, John. S. of George/Henrietta (Howard) of Co. Dublin, Ireland; marr. Halifax 25 July 1833 Rose Mellin (q.v.) (33:58).

Gamble John. From N.H.; effective land grant at Truro 31 Oct. 1765 (4:244).

Gammell, Thomas. Loyalist; plus 1 f./2 ch.; mustered at Digby 19 May 1784 (39:121).

Gammon, William. Liverpool proprietor (19:102).

Gammons, Fear. Wife of William; to Liverpool ca. 1760 (47:126:101).

Gammons, Rebecca. B. Plymouth, Mass., 26 Mar. 1753; dau. of William/ Fear; to Liverpool ca. 1760 (47: 126:101).

Gammons, William. To Liverpool ca. 1760 (47:126:101).

Gamon, Rebeccah. Dau. of William/ Fear; to Liverpool by 1771 (47: 127:52).

Gannon, Catherine. Dau. of John/Jane (Wheally) of Dublin, Ireland; marr. Halifax 17 Apr. 1811 Michael Russell (q.v.) (30:110).

Ganong, Marcus. Legion soldier; to Liverpool by 1784 (47:127:51).

Gardiner, Thomas. Liverpool proprietor (19:102).

Gardner, Abigail. Dau. of Thomas/ Sarah; to (or b.?) Liverpool by 1797 (47:127:207).

Gardner, Ebenezer. Mass. to N.S.; to U.S. 1776; lived 1785 at Machiasport, . Me. (36:64).

Gardner, John Jr. S. of Stephen/ Rebeckah; to (or b.?) Liverpool by 1803 (47:127:276).

Gardner, John. Plus 1 f./1 ch./2 svts.; mariner; Port Roseway Associate (6:14).

Gardner, Stephen. S. of Thomas/Sarah; to Liverpool by 1776 (47:126:285).

Garner, Mary Ann. Dau. of James/ Elizabeth (Walsh) of St. John's, Nfld.; marr. Halifax 28 Jan. 1835 Thomas Pierce (q.v.) (34:137).

Gaul, Ellen. Dau. of John/Catherine (Heron) of Kilmacthomas, Co. Waterford, Ireland; marr. Halifax 10 Oct. 1840 Patrick Power (q.v.) (34:137).

Gautier, James. Plus 1 f./2 svts.; Port Roseway Associate (6:15).

Gay, David. From Mass.; land grant at

Onslow 21 Feb. 1769 (4:224).

Geary, Catherine. Dau. of Denis/Mary (King) of Co. Kilkenny, Ireland; marr. Halifax 30 Aug. 1831 John McDonald (q.v.) (33:62).

Geary, Joanna. Dau. of David/Margaret (Murphy) of Co. Cork, Ireland; marr. Halifax 11 Feb. 1836 John McCauliff (q.v.) (34:133).

Geary, Margaret. Dau. of David/Margaret (Murphy) of Co. Cork, Ireland; marr. Halifax 15 Sep.1830 John Fitzgerald (q.v.) (32:110).

Gee, Judith. See Foley, Judith.

Gelliland, Joseph. Grantee "Digby New Grant" 29 Jan. 1801 (5:82).

Gemmill, Matthew. Plus 1 f./3 svts.; tobacco maker; Port Roseway Associate (6:14).

Geoffrey, William. Disbanded soldier, N.J. Vols.; mustered at Digby 19 May 1784 (39:121).

Gerarty, Julian. Dau. of Malachy/ Margaret (Melia) of Co. Mayo, Ireland; marr. Halifax 8 Feb. 1842 Michael Cotton (q.v.) (35:136).

Gerarty, Malachy. S. of Malachy/Mary (Melia) of Co. Mayo, Ireland; marr. Halifax 24 Apr. 1843 Joanna Clancy (q.v.) (35:138).

Germain, Hugh. Grantee "Digby New Grant" 29 Jan. 1801 (5:82).

Gibbons, John. Capt. brig MARIANNE; s. of Mathew/Sarah (Harroll) of Newcastle, England; marr. Halifax 25 Apr. 1831 Ann Byrns (q.v.) (33: 58).

Gibbons, John. S. of Michael/Ellen (Aheran) of Co. Tipperary, Ireland; marr. Halifax 17 Aug. 1835 Mary Dolany (q.v.) (34:130).

Gibbs, John. From Mass.; land grant at Truro 1759 (4:242).

Gibney, James. Loyalist; mustered at Gulliver's Hole/St. Mary's Bay/

Sissiboo 1/6 June 1784; settled at Wilmot (40:262).

Gibny, Owen. S. of Thomas/Mary (Riley) of Co. Meath, Ireland; marr. Halifax 8 Sep. 1831 Mary Carlan (q.v.) (33:58).

Gibson, George. 36, miller; Hull to Fort Cumberland on ALBION 7-14 March 1774 (21:140).

Gibson, William. Plus 1 f./2 ch./2 svts.; Port Roseway Associate (6:15).

Gidney, John. Grantee "Digby New Grant" 29 Jan. 1801 (5:82).

Gidney, Joseph. Grantee "Digby New Grant" 29 Jan. 1801 (5:82).

Giffin, Persis. Wife or widow of George; dau. of Thomas/Amey Peirce; to (or b.?) Liverpool by 1779 (47:127:121).

Gilbert, John. English; 33; Liverpool to Nova Scotia May 1864 on EURO- CLYDON (45:181).

Gilbert, Pearce. Loyalist; mustered at Gulliver's Hole/St. Mary's Bay/ Sissiboo 1/6 June 1784; settled at St. Mary's Bay (Plympton, Barton, Brighton) (40:262).

Gilbert, Perez. Grantee "Digby New Grant" 29 Jan. 1801 (5:82).

Gilbert, Thomas 3rd. Loyalist; must- ered at Gulliver's Hole/St. Mary's Bay/Sissiboo 1/6 June 1784; set- tled at St. Mary's Bay (Plympton, Barton, Brighton) (40:262).

Gilbert, Thomas Jr. Loyalist; plus 1 f./4 ch./1 svt.; mustered at Gulliver's Hole/St. Mary's Bay/ Sissiboo 1/6 June 1784; settled at St. Mary's Bay (Plympton, Barton, Brighton) (40:262).

Gilbert, Thomas. Col.; (heirs) gran- tee "Digby New Grant" 29 Jan. 1801 (5:82).

Gilbert, Thomas. Loyalist; plus 2 f.;

mustered at Gulliver's Hole/St.
Mary's Bay/Sissiboo 1/6 June 1784;
settled at St. Mary's Bay (Plympton, Barton, Brighton) (40:262).

Gilbert, Thomas. Maj.; grantee 'Digby
New Grant' 29 Jan. 1801 (5:82).

Gildart, John. 19, husbandman; Hull
to Fort Cumberland on ALBION 7-14
March 1774 (21:139).

Gildart, Joshua. 48, husbandman; Hull
to Fort Cumberland on ALBION 7-14
March 1774 (21:139).

Gilfoil, John. S. of Thomas/Judith
(Purcell) of Castledrum, Co.
Kilkenny, Ireland; marr. Halifax
24 Apr. 1834 Mary Dee (q.v.)
(33:58).

Gilfoil, Sarah. Dau. of Thomas/Joanna
(Egan) of Co. Kilkenny, Ireland;
marr. Halifax 14 Sep. 1833 Patrick
Lahy (q.v.) (33:61).

Gilfoil, William. S. of Thomas/Joanna
(Purcell) of Castledrum, Co.
Kilkenny, Ireland; marr. Halifax
10 May 1838 Margaret MacDodwell
(q.v.) (34:130).

Gilfoy, Alice. Dau. of Thomas/Judith
(Egan) of Co. Kilkenny, Ireland;
marr. Halifax 28 Nov. 1829 William
Moolds (q.v.) (32:116).

Gilfoy, Patrick. S. of Thomas/Judith
(Egan) of Co. Kilkenny, Ireland;
marr. Halifax 18 Aug. 1828 Judith
Tobin (q.v.) (32:111).

Gilfoyle, Bridget. Dau. of Edmund/
Catherine (Cullen) of Co. Leix,
Ireland; marr. Halifax 30 July
1835 Patrick Magher (q.v.)
(34:134).

Gilleland, William. Loyalist; mustered at Digby 19 May 1784 (39:
121).

Gillman, Elizabeth. Dau. of Daniel/
Elizabeth (Creighton) of Gibral-
tar; marr. Halifax 14 Sep.1807

Edward Eagan (q.v.) (30:105).

Gillmore, William. From N.H.; effective land grant at Truro 31 Oct.
1765 (4:244).

Gillon, William. S. of Hugh/Ann
(Murtoch) of Co. Sligo, Ireland;
marr. Halifax 14 Sep.1828 Mary
Magown (q.v.) (32:111).

Gilmore, Robert. Loyalist; mustered
at Digby 19 May 1784 (39:121).

Gimble, Henry. German Service; mustered at Bear River 11/25 June 1784
(38:259).

Girdley, Salome. Wife or widow of
Jonas; dau. of Jeremiah/Rebecca
Nickerson; to (or b.?) Liverpool
by 1787 (47:127:122).

Giron, Rose. Widow of Peter Devett;
d. John/Rose (Byrnes) of Co.
Westmeath, Ireland; marr. Halifax
9 Sep. 1833 Pvt. John Yeomans
(q.v.) (33:69).

Gisleas, Jacob. Loyalist; plus 1 f./2
svts.; mustered at Digby 19 May
1784 (39:121).

Gisler, Joseph. German Service; plus
1 f./2 ch.; mustered at Bear River
11/25 June 1784 (38:259).

Gislow, W. German Service; mustered
at Bear River 11/25 June 1784 (38:
259).

Glasford, James. From Mass.; land
grant at Truro 1759 (4:242).

Gleary, Johanna. Spinster; Irish; 20;
Liverpool to Nova Scotia May 1864
on EUROCLYDON (45:181).

Gleeson, Patrick. S. of William/Mary
(Fanning) of Co. Tipperary, Ire-
land; marr. Halifax 7 Feb. 1807
Jane Maher (q.v.) (30:105).

Glendon, Edward. S. of Thomas/Bridget
Murphy of Co. Kilkenny, Ireland;
marr. Halifax 2 Oct. 1832 Catherine MacAvoy (q.v.) (33:58).

Glinn, Hugh. Plus 1 f.; carpenter;

Port Roseway Associate (6:15).

Goddard, Jobe. Mariner; Port Roseway Associate (6:14).

Goddard, John. Carpenter; Port Roseway Associate (6:14).

Godfree, Mehetabel. To Liverpool ca. 1760 (47:126:96).

Godfrey, Alexander. S. of Josiah/ Eunice; to (or b.?) Liverpool by 1791 (47:127:122).

Godfrey, Azubah. B. 10 June 1734; wife or widow of Richard; dau. of Solomon/Eunice Collins; to Liverpool ca. 1760 (47:126:163).

Godfrey, Benjamin. Liverpool proprietor (19:102).

Godfrey, Benjamin. To Liverpool 1763-1765 (47:126:101).

Godfrey, Benjamin. B. Chatham, Mass., ca. 1739; to Liverpool by 1766; to Chatham, Mass., 1790; to Guysborough 1803 (50:102).

Godfrey, Bethia Atwood. Wife of Benjamin; b. Chatham, Mass., 3 Feb. 1743/4; to Liverpool by 1766 (50:102).

Godfrey, Bethiah. Wife of Benjamin; to Liverpool 1763-1765 (47:126:101).

Godfrey, Elizabeth. Dau. of Josiah/ Eunice; to (or b.?) Liverpool by 1787 (47:127:55).

Godfrey, Elizabeth. Dau. of Benjamin; to (or b.?) Liverpool by 1789 (47:127:121).

Godfrey, Enoch. Stepson of Joseph Dexter; b. Chatham, Mass., 20 April 1752; to Liverpool 1760 (50:101).

Godfrey, Eunice. Wife of Josiah; b. Chatham, Mass., 24 Feb. 1731; to Yarmouth by 1767 (50: 103).

Godfrey, Hannah. Dau. of Enoch/Mary; to (or b.?) Liverpool by 1799 (47: 127:276).

Godfrey, John. S. of Moses; b. Chatham, Mass., 31 May 1743; at Liverpool by 29 Nov. 1764 (50: 103).

Godfrey, Jonathan. Liverpool proprietor (19:102).

Godfrey, Jonathan. S. of Jonathan; b. Chatham, Mass., ca. 1728; at Liverpool by 20 Nov. 1764 (50: 103).

Godfrey, Joseph. S. of Benjamin/ Bethiah; to (or b.?) Liverpool by 1795 (47:127:268).

Godfrey, Joseph. S. of Moses; b. Chatham, Mass., 7 Dec. 1733; to Liverpool 1759 (50:103).

Godfrey, Josiah. S. of Samuel; b. Chatham, Mass., 1728; grant at Dartmouth recorded 1767 (50:103).

Godfrey, Josiah. S. of Josiah; b. Chatham, Mass., ca. 1749; to Yarmouth by 1767 (50:104).

Godfrey, Lucy. B. Chatham, Mass., 1 Jan. 1763; dau. of Benjamin/ Bethiah; to Liverpool 1763-1765 (47:126:101).

Godfrey, Lucy. Dau. of Benjamin; b. Chatham, Mass., 1 Jan. 1764; to Liverpool by 1766 (50:102).

Godfrey, Martha. Dau. of Josiah; b. Chatham, Mass., ca. 1751; to Yarmouth by 1767 (50:104).

Godfrey, Mary. Dau. of Josiah/Eunice; to (or b.?) Liverpool by 1793 (47: 127:124).

Godfrey, Mehitable Hamilton. Wife of Joseph; b. Chatham, Mass., ca. 1735; to Liverpool 1759 (50:103).

Godfrey, Moses. S. of Josiah/Unice; to (or b.?) Liverpool by 1799 (47: 127:267).

Godfrey, Moses. S. of Moses; b. Chatham, Mass., ca. 1705; at Barrington 16 Feb. 1773 (50:104).

Godfrey, Nathaniel. Liverpool proprietor (19:101).

Godfrey, Nathaniel. S. of Thomas; b. Chatham, Mass., ca. 1734; at Liverpool by 1765 (50:104).

Godfrey, Prince. S. of Samuel; b. Chatham, Mass., ca. 1734; at Yarmouth 1773 census (50:105).

Godfrey, Ruth. Dau. of Josiah/Eunice; to (or b.?) Liverpool by 1785 (47:127:125).

Godfrey, Samuel. S. of Moses; b. Chatham, Mass., ca. 1703; at Yarmouth June 1764 (50:104).

Godfrey, Sarah. B. New England 9 May 1757; dau. of Joseph/Mehitabel; to Liverpool ca. 1760 (47:126:97).

Godfrey, Sarah. Dau. of Joseph; b. Chatham, Mass., 9 May 1757; to Liverpool 1759 (50:103).

Godfrey, Susannah. Dau. of Josiah/Eunice; to Liverpool by 1772 (47:126:287).

Godfrey, Susannah. Dau. of Josiah; b. Chatham, Mass., ca. 1753; to Yarmouth by 1767 (50:104).

Godfrey, Thankful (Knowles?). Wife of Samuel (50:104).

Godfrey, Warren. S. of Richard/Azubah; to (or b.?) Liverpool by 1797 (47:127:207).

Godfrey, Warren. Stepson of Joseph Dexter; b. Chatham, Mass., 6 April 1757; to Liverpool 1760 (50:101).

Goffe, Margaret. Dau. of Arthur/Alice (Hickey) of Co. Waterford, Ireland; marr. Halifax 10 Nov. 1838 Patrick Sarsfield (q.v.) (34:138).

Goggan, Ann. Dau. of Denis/Mary (Roseman) of Co. Dublin, Ireland; marr. Halifax 28 June 1832 David Murphy (q.v.) (33:64).

Goggan, Kenny. S. of James/Mary (Dillon) of Co. Longford, Ireland; marr. Halifax 4 Nov. 1829 Catherine MacCormack (q.v.) (32:111).

Goggan, Mary. Dau. of John/Elizabeth (Sullivan) of Co. Cork, Ireland; marr. Halifax 3 Aug. 1831 Patrick Fitzgerald (q.v.) (33:57).

Goggin, Patrick. S. of James/Mary (Dillon) of Co. Longford, Ireland; marr. Halifax 9 Jan. 1831 Catherine May (q.v.) (33:58).

Going, Patrick. S. of James/Catherine (Henessy) of Co. Tipperary, Ireland; marr. Halifax 21 Oct. 1828 Eleanor Meagher (q.v.) (32:111).

Gold, Thomas. Plus 2 svts.; farmer; Port Roseway Associate (6:15).

Goldsbury, Samuel. Grantee "Digby New Grant" 29 Jan. 1801 (5:82).

Goldsmith, Stephen. Arr. Annapolis from New York 19 Oct. 1782 (37:126).

Goldsmith, Stephen. Loyalist; mustered at Digby 19 May 1784 (39:121).

Goodman, Isaac. Plus 1 f./2 ch./2 svts.; merchant; Port Roseway Associate (6:14).

Goodman, Mary. Dau. of John/Ann (Hadon) of Co. Kilkenny, Ireland; marr. Halifax 29 Sep. 1841 Edward Kirwin (q.v.) (35:140).

Gordon, Catherine. See Nowlan, Catherine.

Gordon, Catherine. Dau. of Michael/Charlotte (Wilson) of Co. Donegal, Ireland; marr. Halifax 4 Feb. 1845 John Joseph June? (35:139).

Gordon, Jane. Dau. of Thomas/Jane; marr. (1) Liverpool 29 Mar. 1775; marr. (2) as widow 6 Oct. 1774 (sic) (47:126:286-287).

Gordon, Richd. Plus 1 f./1 ch. -8; arr. Annapolis from New York 19 Oct. 1782 (37:126).

Gordon, Thomas. Liverpool proprietor (19:102).

Gorham, -----. Liverpool proprietor

(19:102).

Gorham, Abigail. Wife of David; Plymouth, Mass., to Liverpool ca.
1760 (47:126:97).

Gorham, David. Plymouth, Mass., to
Liverpool ca. 1760 (47:126:97).

Gorham, Hannah. B. Plymouth, Mass.,
14 Feb. 1759; dau. Jabez/Mary; to
Liverpool ca. 1760 (47:126:169).

Gorham, Hannah. Dau. of Jabez; b. 14
Feb. 1759 at Plymouth, Mass.,;
marr. 4 Mar. 1787 at Liverpool
John Coop (15:165).

Gorham, Hannah. Dau. of Jabez/Mary;
to (or b.?) Liverpool by 1787 (47:
127:211).

Gorham, Isaac. S. of Jabez/Mary; to
(or b.?) Liverpool by 1794 (47:
127:123).

Gorham, Jabez. B. Plymouth, Mass., 14
May 1757; s. Jabez/Mary; to Liverpool ca. 1760 (47:126:169).

Gorham, Jabez. Plymouth, Mass., to
Liverpool ca. 1760 (47:126:169).

Gorham, Jabez. Plymouth, Mass., to
Liverpool as a first settler; d.
13 Dec. 1806 ae 80th (49:122).

Gorham, Jabish. Liverpool proprietor
(19:101).

Gorham, James. B. Plymouth, Mass., 7
Sep. 1760; s. Jabez/Mary; to
Liverpool ca. 1760 (47:126:169).

Gorham, James. S. of Jabez/Mary; to
(or b.?) Liverpool by 1787 (47:
127:55).

Gorham, John. S. of Jabez/Mary; to
(or b.?) Liverpool by 1795 (47:
127:204).

Gorham, Lucy. Dau. of Jabez/Mary; to
(or b.?) Liverpool by 1784 (47:
126:283).

Gorham, Mary. B. Plymouth, Mass., 23
July 1755; dau. Jabez/Mary; to
Liverpool ca. 1760 (47:126:169).

Gorham, Mary. Plymouth, Mass., to

Liverpool ca. 1760 (47:126:169).

Gorham, Penallopy. B. Plymouth,
Mass., 20 Feb. 1752 O.S.; dau. of
David; to Liverpool ca. 1760 (47:
126:97).

Gorham, Prince. S. of Jabez/Mary; to
(or b.?) Liverpool by 1796 (47:
127:209).

Gorman, Daniel. S. of Mathew/Mary
(Bane) of Co. Carlow, Ireland;
marr. Halifax 20 Sep.1821 Anne
Higgins (31:46).

Gorman, Elizabeth. Dau. of John/Mary
(Burke); widow of Thomas Herron of
Cove, Cork, Ireland; marr. Halifax
22 Nov. 1821 Richard Handley
(q.v.) (31:47).

Gorman, Honora. Dau. of John/Mary
(Burke) of Cove of Cork, Ireland;
marr. Halifax 28 Nov. 1828 Daniel
Ryan (q.v.) (32:118).

Gorman, Margaret. Dau. of Michael/
Johana (Magher) of Co. Tipperary,
Ireland; marr. Halifax 24 Nov.
1841 William Kenedy (q.v.) (35:
140).

Gorman, Patrick. S. of Lawrence/
Anastasia (Hylands) of Callan, Co.
Kilkenny, Ireland; marr. Halifax 9
July 1825 Mary Eldward (q.v.) (31:
46).

Gorman, Thomas. S. of John/Mary
(Prendergast) of Parish Clonea,
Co. Waterford, Ireland; marr.
Halifax 24 Apr. 1821 Bridget
Summers (q.v.) (31:46).

Gorman, Thomas. S. of Denis/Margaret
(Warren) of Waterford, Ireland;
marr. Halifax 23 Apr. 1831 Ellen
Murphy (q.v.) (33:58).

Goslin, James. Loyalist; mustered at
Digby 19 May 1784 (39:121).

Goswell, George. Plus 1 f./4 ch.;
mariner; Port Roseway Associate
(6:15).

Goucher, Edward. Disbanded soldier, N.J. Vols.; plus 2 f./2 ch.; mustered at Digby 19 May 1784 (39: 121).

Gouger. See Goucher.

Gough, Mary Ann. Dau. of George/Mary Ann (Brown) of Co. Wexford, Ireland; marr. Halifax 28 Apr. 1839 James Draper (q.v.) (34:129).

Gough, Philip. S. of Edmund/Margaret (Ryan) of Co. Waterford, Ireland; marr. Halifax 22 Apr. 1833 Catherine Maxner (33:58).

Gourly, James. From N.H.; effective land grant at Truro 31 Oct. 1765 (4:244).

Gourly, John. From N.H.; effective land grant at Truro 31 Oct. 1765 (4:244).

Gourly, Thomas. From N.H.; effective land grant at Truro 31 Oct. 1765 (4:244).

Grace, Adam. S. of Pierce/Bridget (Kiely) of Co. Carlow, Ireland; marr. Halifax 14 Oct. 1830 Bridget Brenan (q.v.) (32:112).

Grace, Mark. S. of Patrick/Mary (Jackson) of Co. Kilkenny, Ireland; marr. Halifax 25 Sep. 1842 Ellen Malcom (35:138).

Grace, Robert. S. of Pierce/Bridget (Kiely) of Parish St. Mullins, Co. Carlow, Ireland; marr. Halifax 17 Feb. 1828 Mary Donelly widow of John Bennett (32:112).

Grady, Catherine. Dau. of Patrick/Mary (Walsh) of Co. Waterford, Ireland; marr. Halifax 17 Jan. 1843 Michael Ryan (q.v.) (35:144).

Grady, Ellen. See Bryan, Ellen.

Grady, Maurice. 37th Regt.; of Co. Tipperary, Ireland; marr. Halifax 28 Jan. 1840 Maria Magrath (q.v.) (34:130).

Grady, Norris. Loyalist; mustered at

Digby 19 May 1784 (39:121).

Grady, Timothy. S. of James/Mary (Sheehan) of Co. Tipperary, Ireland; marr. Halifax 10 May 1835 Mary Tracy (q.v.) (34:130).

Grady, Timothy. Widower of Margaret Kidney; of Co. Tipperary, Ireland; marr. Halifax 7 Aug. 1832 Mary Barry (q.v.) (33:59).

Grafton, John. S. of Thomas/Margaret (Higgins) of Co. Tipperary, Ireland; marr. Halifax 9 Jan. 1844 Matilda Haverstock (35:138).

Graham, Alexander. Loyalist; plus 1 f.; mustered at Digby 19 May 1784 (39:121).

Graham, Alexr. Plus 1 f.; arr. Annapolis from New York 19 Oct. 1782 (37:125).

Graham, David. From Ireland; land grant at Londonderry 6 Mar. 1775 (4:258).

Graham, Elizabeth. Dau. of Joseph/Helena (Yeats) of Lancashire, England; marr. Halifax 20 June 1814 Robert Thompson (q.v.) (30:111).

Graham, Elizabeth. Dau. of William/Mary (Johnston) of Co. Donegal, Ireland; marr. Halifax 1 June 1821 Matthew Hughes (q.v.) (31:47).

Graham, John. Plus 1 f./3 ch./2 svts.; planter; Port Roseway Associate (6:14).

Graham, Muir. Arr. Annapolis from New York 19 Oct. 1782 (37:126).

Graham, Patrick. Plus 1 ch. 8+; arr. Annapolis from New York 19 Oct. 1782 (37:126).

Graham, William. Plus 1 f.; Port Roseway Associate (6:15).

Grandin, Daniel. Plus 2 svts.; farmer; Port Roseway Associate (6:15).

Grannan, William. S. of Patrick/Catherine (Ronan) of Co. Kildare,

Ireland; marr. Halifax 8 Dec. 1837
Margaret Bradly (q.v.) (34:130).

Grant, David. Grantee "Digby New
Grant" 29 Jan. 1801 (5:82).

Grant, John. Grantee "Digby New
Grant" 29 Jan. 1801 (5:82).

Grant, John. Loyalist; Scot; plus
wife/7 ch.; New York to Halifax 26
Aug. 1783 on STAFFORD (43:17).

Grant, Mary. Dau. of John/Mary
(Lavin) of Co. Kilkenny, Ireland;
marr. Halifax 21 Jan. 1840 Anthony
Connelly (q.v.) (34:127).

Grant, Michael. Loyalist; mustered at
Digby 19 May 1784 (39:121).

Grant, Peter. Plus 1 f./1 ch.; Port
Roseway Associate (6:15).

Grant, Peter. Plus 1 f./3 ch./2
svts.; Port Roseway Associate (6:
15).

Grant, Sarah. (Heirs) grantee "Digby
New Grant" 29 Jan. 1801 (5:82).

Grant, Sarah. Dau. of John/Isabella
(Colden) of Scotland; marr. Halifax 21 Aug. 1820 Robert Barron
(q.v.) (31:40).

Grant, Thomas. Plus wife/3 ch.;
Lancaster, Mass., to Chester with
first settlers (16:45).

Grant, Thomas. S. of Thomas/Mary
(Gleeson) of Co. Kilkenny, Ire-
land; marr. Halifax 11 July 1842
Margaret Walsh (35:138).

Grant, William. Loyalist; mustered at
Digby 19 May 1784 (39:121).

Grantfield, Michael. S. of William/
Honora (Lahee) of Co. Kerry,
Ireland; marr. Halifax 14 Sep.1816
Eleanor Bates (q.v.) (30:105).

Granville, Catherine. Dau. of Thomas/
Juliana (Karney) of Co. Kerry,
Ireland; marr. Halifax 11 Nov.
1818 Owen Brenan (q.v.) (31:41).

Granwood, William. Barrington petitioner 19 Oct. 1776 (1:365).

Grasman, Casper. Plus 1 f./1 ch.;
farmer; Port Roseway Associate (6:
15).

Grass, Michael. Plus 1 f./7 ch.;
sadler; Port Roseway Associate (6:
15).

Gray, Elizabeth. Dau. of Henry/Marga-
ret (Lawler) of Co. Leix, Ireland;
marr. Halifax 6 June 1833 David
Hayes (q.v.) (33:59).

Gray, Henry. Loyalist; mustered at
Digby 19 May 1784 (39:121).

Gray, Isaac. Farmer; Port Roseway
Associate (6:15).

Gray, Peter. Plus 1 f.; Port Roseway
Associate (6:15).

Greaves, Thomas. Plus 1 f./1 ch.;
farmer; Port Roseway Associate (6:
14).

Greben, -----. Lieut. Anspach Service; plus 2 f.; mustered at Bear
River 11/25 June 1784 (38:259).

Green, Ellen. Dau. of Mathew/Anne
(Boland) of Co. Tipperary, Ire-
land; marr. Halifax 28 Aug. 1831
Edward Dillon (q.v.) (33:56).

Green, Henry. S. of Robert/Anne of
Peebles, Scotland; marr. Halifax
12 June 1810 Mary Connors (q.v.)
(30:105).

Green, James. Loyalist; plus 1 f./2
ch.; mustered at Digby 19 May 1784
(39:121).

Green, Reuben. Arr. Annapolis from
New York 19 Oct. 1782 (37:126).

Green, Thomas. Loyalist; plus 1 svt.;
mustered at Digby 19 May 1784 (39:
121).

Green, William. Loyalist; mustered at
Digby 19 May 1784 (39:121).

Green, William. Loyalist; plus 1 f./2
ch.; mustered at Digby 19 May 1784
(39:121).

Greenfield, Edward. Disbanded soldier, 57th Regt.; laborer; not

settled; mustered at Digby 19 May 1784 (39:121).

Greenleaf, Stephen. Bolton, Mass., to Chester 30 July 1759 (16:46).

Grennan, John. S. of James/Anne (Kelly) of Durrow, Co. Westmeath, Ireland; marr. Halifax 23 Jan. 1823 Catherine Anders (31:46).

Gress, Henry. German Service; mustered at Bear River 11/25 June 1784 (38:259).

Griessor, August. Lieut.; Waldeck Service; plus 1 f.; mustered at Bear River 11/25 June 1784 (38: 259).

Grieve, David. Dr.; s. of Thomas/Mary; Glasgow, Scotland, to Liverpool by 1821 (47:128:114).

Griffin, Catherine. Dau. of James/Ann (Purcel) of Gaulstown, Co. Kilkenny, Ireland; marr, Halifax 24 July 1830 William Donovan (q.v.) (32: 108).

Griffin, Edward. Loyalist; plus 1 f.; mustered at Digby 19 May 1784 (39: 121).

Griffin, Ellen. Dau. of James/Margaret (Walsh) of Co. Kilkenny, Ireland; marr. Halifax 30 July 1833 Patrick Morissy (q.v.) (33: 64).

Griffin, James. Farmer; Port Roseway Associate (6:15).

Griffin, James. S. of James/Ann (Purcell) of Gaulstown, Co. Kilkenny, Ireland; marr. Halifax 22 Aug. 1841 Mary Walsh (q.v.) (35: 138).

Griffin, John. Deserted 15 Aug. 1808 from a Detachment, 1st Bn., 23rd Regt. of Foot or Royal Welsh Fusiliers; 5'6", swarthy complexion, brown hair, hazel eyes, 27, b. Ireland; advertised The Weekly Chronicle, 26 Aug. 1808 (28:34).

Griffin, John. Liverpool proprietor (19:102).

Griffin, John. S. of Michael/Mary (Burn) of Ireland; marr. Halifax 11 May 1815 Ann Anderson (30:105).

Griffin, Margaret. Dau. of Walter/Elenor (Rorke) of Co. Carlow, Ireland; marr. Halifax 2 Sep. 1834 Edmund Hynes (q.v.) (33:60).

Griffin, Obadiah Jr. Grantee 'Digby Me Grant' 29 Jan. 1801 (5:82).

Griffin, Obadiah. Grantee 'Digby New Grant' 29 Jan. 1801 (5:82).

Griffin, Obadiah. Loyalist; plus 1 f.; mustered at Digby 19 May 1784 (39:121).

Griffin, William. Grantee 'Digby New Grant' 29 Jan. 1801 (5:82).

Griffith, Margaret. Dau. of Benjamin/Eleanor (Pane) of Co. Carlow, Ireland; marr. Halifax 15 Apr. 1831 Maurice Magrath (q.v.) (33: 62).

Griffiths, Mary. Dau. of Thomas/Jane (Dollard) of Dublin, Ireland; marr. Halifax 23 June 1814 George Wolffenzer (30:112).

Grigg, John. Grantee 'Digby New Grant' 29 Jan. 1801 (5:82).

Grigg, Thomas. Loyalist; plus 2 f./2 ch./2 svts.; mustered at Digby 19 May 1784 (39:121).

Griggerson, Sarah. To (or b.?) Liverpool by 1791 (47:127:117).

Griggs, John. Loyalist; plus 1 f./1 ch.; mustered at Digby 19 May 1784 (39:121).

Grogan, Richard. Loyalist; plus 1 f./1 ch.; mustered at Digby 19 May 1784 (39:121).

Grogan, Richard. Plus 1 f.; arr. Annapolis from New York 19 Oct. 1782 (37:126).

Grosvenor, Benjamin. See Benjamin Grovenor.

Grovenor, Benjamin. Plus 1 f./3 ch./2
svts.; farmer; Port Roseway Associate (6:15).

Guess, Richard, S. of Edmund/Ellen
(Walsh) of Co. Cork, Ireland;
marr. Halifax 10 Nov. 1839 Margaret Bairds (34:130).

Guilfoil, Richard John. S. of Wil-
liam/Elizabeth (English) of Co.
Kilkenny, Ireland; marr. Halifax
28 Sep.1817 Elizabeth Bartling
(30:106).

Guinan, Patrick. S. of Nicholas/
Anastasia (Londrigan) of Co.
Kilkenny, Ireland; marr. Halifax
27 Oct. 1831 Elizabeth Dearan (33:
59).

Guinan, Philip. S. of Timothy/Marga-
ret (O'Brien) of Cashel, Co.
Tipperary, Ireland; marr. Halifax
16 April 1825 Margaret Quillinan
(31:46).

Gullison, Stephen. Liverpool proprietor (19:102).

Gully, Ellen. See Magher, Ellen.

Gully, Thomas. Widower of Mary Power
of Co. Waterford, Ireland; marr.
Halifax 9 Apr. 1839 Ellen Magher
(q.v.) (34:131).

Gunn, George. Asst. Quartermaster,
Hessian Ser.; plus 1 f./3 svts.;
mustered at Digby 19 May 1784 (39:
12q).

Gunning, John. Plus 1 f.; arr. Annapolis from New York 19 Oct. 1782
(37:126).

Gunning, Thomas. S. of James/Mary
(Brady) of Co. Longford, Ireland;
marr. Halifax 6 Jan. 1834 Judith
Rogers (q.v.) (33:59).

Guy, Hannah. Dau. of James of Somer-
setshire, England; marr. Halifax
20 Apr. 1822 James Walsh (q.v.)
(31:54).

Gydon, Mary. See Holy, Mary.

Gyhan, Eleanor. Dau. of Lawrence/Mary
(Doyle) of Co. Carlow, Ireland;
marr. Halifax 13 Nov. 1828 Michael
Hogan (q.v.) (32:112).

- H -

Haberlin, Richard. S. of Richard/
Catherine (Lalor) of Co. Kilkenny,
Ireland; marr. Halifax 9 June 1808
Mary Lalor (30:106).

Haberlin, Richard. S. of Richard/
Catherine (Lawler) of Glamore, Co.
Kilkenny, Ireland; marr. Halifax 7
Apr. 1818 Mary Burn (q.v.) (31:
46).

Haberlin, Richard. S. of Thomas/Mary
(Grant) of Glancoin, Co. Kilkenny,
Ireland; marr. Halifax 14 May 1820
Anne Stephans (q.v.) (31:46).

Hackett, Alexander. S. of Edward/
Elenor (Perry) of Cloyne, Co.
Cork, Ireland; marr. Halifax 9
Aug. 1823 Mary Hollandsworth (31:
46).

Haden, Edward. S. of Mathew/Mary
(O'Brien) of Ballingarry, Co.
Tipperary, Ireland; marr. Halifax
3 Sep. 1829 Ellen Dooly (q.v.)
(32:112).

Hagan, Timothy. Laborer; Irish; 20;
Liverpool to Nova Scotia May 1864
on EUROCLYDON (45:181).

Hagarty, Elizabeth. See Turish,
Elizabeth.

Hagarty, Thomas. See Turish, Elizabeth.

Haggerty, Patrick. Loyalist; plus 1
f./3 ch./2 svts.; mustered at
Digby 19 May 1784 (39:121).

Haiden, Ann. Of Co. Tipperary, Ireland; widow of Timothy Sullivan,
57th Regt.; marr. Halifax 17 May
1842 Daniel Quinn (q.v.) (35:143).

Haily, Patrick. S. of James/Judith

(Hartigan) of Parish Tipperary,
Ireland; marr. Halifax 21 Sep.
1824 Mary Walsh (q.v.) (31:46).

Haines, Alexander. Grantee 'Digby New
Grant' 29 Jan. 1801 (5:82).

Hains, Alexander. Loyalist; plus 1
f./5 ch.; mustered at Gulliver's
Hole/St. Mary's Bay/Sissiboo 1/6
June 1784; settled at Sissiboo
(now Weymouth) (40:262).

Hair, Patrick P. Of Dennishmore, Co.
Down, Ireland; marr. Halifax 26
Aug. 1826 Bridget Wall widow of
Daniel Huse (32:112).

Hale, William. Plus 3 svts.; Port
Roseway Associate (6:15).

Hales, James. Loyalist; mustered at
Digby 19 May 1784 (39:122).

Haley, Joanna. Dau. of John/Mary
(Redmond) of Co. Waterford, Ire-
land; marr. Halifax 23 Nov. 1831
William Barron (q.v.) (33:54).

Haley, Timothy. S. of Patrick/Elenor
(Buckley) of Co. Tipperary, Ire-
land; marr. Halifax 18 Feb. 1833
Margaret Karney (q.v.) (33:59).

Hall, Abner. S. of John/Margaret; to
(or b.?) Liverpool by 1804 (47:
127:278).

Hall, Bridget. Dau. of Nicholas/Mary
(English) of St. John's, Nfld.;
widow of Richard Heaney of Co.
Waterford, Ireland; marr. Halifax
7 Oct. 1824 (q.v.) (31:53).

Hall, Cornelius. Plus 1 f./2 ch. -8;
arr. Annapolis from New York 19
Oct. 1782 (37:125).

Hall, Isaac. Plus 1 f./5 ch./3 svts.;
carpenter; Port Roseway Associate
(6:15).

Hall, Jacob. Loyalist; plus 1 f./1
ch.; mustered at Digby 19 May 1784
(39:122).

Hall, Jeremiah. B. Ireland; Belfast
or Greenock to Halifax on POLLY,

spring 1799 (29:83).

Hall, Luke. Loyalist; mustered at
Digby 19 May 1784 (39:122).

Hallaghan, Daniel. S. of Cormick/
Susan (Collins) of Parish Kilke-
vin, Roscommon, Ireland; marr.
Halifax 25 May 1823 Sarah Whelan
(q.v.) (31:46).

Haller, Wagner. German Service; mustered at Bear River 11/25 June
1784 (38:260).

Halliburton, Brenton. Sir; s. of Dr,
John and Susannah (Brenton); b. 3
Dec. 1775 at Newport, R.I; to Hal-
ifax with parents 1782 (3:191).

Halliburton, John. Dr.; Newport,
R.I., to Halifax 1782 (3:191).

Halliburton, John. S. of Dr, John and
Susannah (Brenton); to Halifax
with parents 1782 (3:191).

Halliburton, Susannah. Wife of Dr.
John; daughter of ----- Brenton;
to Halifax with husband (3:191).

Halstead, Lydia. Loyalist; mustered
at Digby 19 May 1784 (39:122).

Ham, Peter. See Hulme, Peter.

Hamilton, Abigail. Dau. of Samuel; b.
Chatham, Mass. (50:105).

Hamilton, Archibald. Grantee 'Digby
New Grant' 29 Jan. 1801 (5:82).

Hamilton, Archibald. (Heirs) grantee
'Digby New Grant' 29 Jan. 1801 (5:
82).

Hamilton, Daniel. S. of Samuel; b.
Chatham, Mass. (50:105).

Hamilton, Elenor. See Donovan,
Elenor.

Hamilton, Henry. Grantee 'Digby New
Grant' 29 Jan. 1801 (5:82).

Hamilton, John. Grantee 'Digby New
Grant' 29 Jan. 1801 (5:82).

Hamilton, Miriam Kenney. Wife of
Samuel (50:105).

Hamilton, Samuel. S. of Daniel; b.
Chatham, Mass., 29 Mar. 1738; at

Barrington 1770 census (50:105).

Hamilton, Thomas. S. of Patrick/Anne (Quigley) of Parish Pantsealy, Wexford, Ireland; marr. Halifax 12 Jan. 1825 Bridget Houghton (31: 46).

Hamilton, William. From Mass.; land grant at Onslow 21 Feb. 1769 (4: 224).

Hamilton, William. S. of Samuel; b. Chatham, Mass. (50:105).

Hammett, George. Culpepper Co., Va., to Liverpool by 1798 (47:127:269).

Hammond, Edmister. Rochester, Mass., to Chester with first settlers (16:45).

Hammond, Henry. 31, farmer; Hull to Fort Cumberland on ALBION 7-14 March 1774 (21:139).

Hammond, Henry. 5, s. of Henry; Hull to Fort Cumberland on ALBION 7-14 March 1774 (21:139).

Hammond, Jane. Daughter of Henry; Hull to Fort Cumberland on ALBION 7-14 March 1774 (21:139).

Hammond, Margaret. 27, wife of Henry; Hull to Fort Cumberland on ALBION 7-14 March 1774 (21:139).

Hammond, Margaret. 1, daughter of Henry; Hull to Fort Cumberland on ALBION 7-14 March 1774 (21:139).

Hanagan, Brien. Pvt. 81st Regt.; s. of James/Catherine (Carroll) of Parish Kilnebride, Galway, Ireland; marr. Halifax 9 June 1823 Bridget Carr (q.v.) (31:46).

Hand, Samuel. Loyalist; mustered at Digby 19 May 1784 (39:122).

Handcox, Edmond. S. of Edmond/Eliza (Flemming) of Co. Waterford, Ireland; marr. Halifax 4 June 1837 Mary Cassles (q.v.) (34:131).

Handlan, Patrick. S. of William/ Margaret (Brenan) of Shreen, Ardagh, Ireland; marr. Halifax 27

July 1826 Bridget Farrell (q.v.) (32:112).

Handley, Richard. S. of James/Mary (Hackett) of Douglas nr Cork City, Ireland; marr. Halifax 22 Nov. 1821 Elizabeth Gorman (q.v.) (31: 47).

Handselpiker, Conrad. Disbanded soldier, 2nd Bn., N.J. Vols.; plus 1 f./3 ch.; mustered at Digby 19 May 1784 (39:121).

Handwick, Elizabeth. 24, wife of James; Hull to Fort Cumberland on ALBION 7-14 March 1774 (21:137).

Handwick, James. 34, maltster; Hull to Fort Cumberland on ALBION 7-14 March 1774 (21:137).

Handy, Rufus Jr. Mariner; Port Roseway Associate (6:15).

Handy, Rufus. Plus 1 f./7 ch.; Port Roseway Associate (6:15).

Haney, Edward. S. of Thomas/Margaret (Gorman) of Co. Tipperary, Ireland; marr. Halifax 15 Apr. 1833 Mary Scott (q.v.) (33:59).

Haney, Henry. S. of Meredith/Mary (Herson) of Belfast, Co. Antrim, Ireland; marr. Halifax 9 Nov. 1833 Frances Cummins (q.v.) (33:59).

Haney, Margaret. Dau. of Patrick/Mary (Russell) of Drogheda, Ireland; marr. Halifax 6 July 1829 James Gallaghar (q.v.) (32:111).

Hanifan, Catherine. Dau. of William/ Mary (Granvill) of Co. Kerry, Ireland; marr. Halifax 7 Aug. 1830 James Fitzgerald (q.v.) (32:110).

Hanigan, Catherine. See Downy, Catherine; see Butler, Catherine.

Hanigan, James. S. of Edward/Catherine (Egan) of Co. Longford, Ireland; marr. Halifax 19 June 1829 Elizabeth Kelly (q.v.) (32:112).

Hanigan, Mary. Dau. of William/ Catherine (Downy) of Ireland;

marr. Halifax 7 Aug. 1841 John
Doran (q.v.) (35:137).

Hanigan, Thomas. S. of Timothy/Mary
(Walsh) of Co. Waterford, Ireland;
marr. Halifax 28 Feb. 1843 Mary
Terry (q.v.) (35:138).

Hanigan, William. S. of Timothy/Mary
(Walsh) of Co. Waterford, Ireland;
marr. Halifax 14 Sep. 1841 Honora
Walsh (q.v.) (35:138).

Hankinson, Reuben. Grantee "Digby New
Grant" 29 Jan. 1801 (5:82).

Hanlon, John. Pvt. 81st Regt.; of
Parish Donagh, Co. Monaghan,
Ireland; marr. clandestine Innis-
killen, Ireland, 1821, marr.
Halifax 2 Aug. 1824 Catherine
Rogers (q.v.) (31:47).

Hanna, Nath'l. Plus 1 f./3 ch./1
svt.; millwright; Port Roseway
Associate (6:15).

Hannery, Catherine. Widow of Nicholas
Howlet, of Co. Wexford, Ireland;
marr. Halifax 16 Sep. 1818 John
Canada (q.v.) (31:48).

Hanney, Edward. Plus 1 f./3 ch.;
tailor; Port Roseway Associate (6:
15).

Hanney, William. Plus 1 f./2 ch./3
svts.; carpenter; Port Roseway
Associate (6:15).

Hannigan, Catherine. See Carney,
Catherine.

Hannigan, Thomas. S. of Thomas/Mary
(Magrath) of Co. Waterford, Ire-
land; marr. Halifax 5 Nov. 1833
Catherine Karney (q.v.) (33:59).

Hanrihan, John. S, James/Bridget
(Lawrence) of Parish Innistioge,
Co. Kilkenny, Ireland; marr.
Halifax 30 Jan. 1837 Margaret
Heneberry (34:131).

Hanselpiker, William. Grantee "Digby
New Grant" 29 Jan. 1801 (5:82).

Hanway, Hugh. 52nd Regt.; s. of

Daniel/Catherine (Gribbon) of Co.
Armagh, Ireland; marr. Halifax 17
Sep. 1831 Joanna Fowler (q.v.)
(33:59).

Harden, Robert. Plus 1 f./1 svt.;
Port Roseway Associate (6:15).

Harding, Chloe. Dau. of Theodore; b.
Chatham, Mass. (50:105).

Harding, George Jr. Arr. Annapolis
from New York 19 Oct. 1782 (37:
125).

Harding, Jasper. Plus 1 f./3 ch.;
taylor; Port Roseway Associate (6:
15).

Harding, Joshua. B. Eastham, Mass.;
d. Liverpool 15 Mar. 1761 (50:
105).

Harding, Josiah. S. of Theodore; b.
Chatham, Mass., 1761 (50:105).

Harding, Martha Sears. Wife of Theodore; b. Eastham, Mass., 23 Aug.
1737 (50:105).

Harding, Paul. S. of Paul/Elizabeth;
Chatham, Mass., to Liverpool by
1792 (47:127:122).

Harding, Richard. See Richard Hardy.

Harding, Robert. See Robert Harden.

Harding, Sarah. Dau. of Theodore; b.
Chatham, Mass., 1756 (50:105).

Harding, Theodore. S. of Theodore; b.
Eastham, Mass.; Chatham, Mass., to
Barrington 1762 (50:105).

Harding, William. Plus 1 f./3 ch.
8+/4 ch. -8; arr. Annapolis from
New York 19 Oct. 1782 (37:125).

Harding, William. Plus 1 f./3 ch.
8+/1 ch. -8; arr. Annapolis from
New York 19 Oct. 1782 (37:126).

Harding, Zerviah. Wife or widow of
Joshua; to Liverpool ca. 1760
(47:126:96).

Hardy, Aaron. New England to Annapolis 1760 (18:271).

Hardy, Anne. Dau. of Joseph/Margaret
(Smyth) of St. John's, Nfld.;

marr. Halifax 12 Dec. 1807 Michael Harrison (q.v.) (30:106).

Hardy, Richard. Plus 1 f./2 ch.; Port Roseway Associate (6:15).

Hare, Thomas. Loyalist; plus 1 f.; mustered at Digby 19 May 1784 (39: 122).

Harison, Ann. See Haron, Ann.

Harkin, Jacob. Loyalist; mustered at Digby 19 May 1784 (39:122).

Harland, William. 23, farmer; Hull to Fort Cumberland on ALBION 7-14 March 1774 (21:134).

Harlow, Abner. S. of Robert/Jane; to (or b.?) Liverpool by 1796 (47: 127:211).

Harlow, Bradford. S. of Josiah/Olive; to (or b.?) Liverpool by 1796 (47: 127:271).

Harlow, James. S. of Robert/Jane; to (or b.?) Liverpool by 1795 (47: 127:205).

Harlow, Jane. Dau. of Robert/Jane; to Liverpool by 1774 (47:126:283).

Harlow, Jane. Wife of Robert; to Liverpool ca. 1760 (47:126:95).

Harlow, Josiah. S. of Samuel/Mary; Wareham, Mass., to Liverpool by 1785 (47:126:285).

Harlow, Olive. Wife of Josiah; dau. of Daniel/Mary Hunt; Wareham, Mass., to Liverpool by 1785 (47: 126:285).

Harlow, Rebecca. Dau. of Robert/Jane; to (or b.?) Liverpool by 1793 (47: 127:202).

Harlow, Rebecca. Dau. of Robert/Jane; to (or b.?) Liverpool by 1793 (47: 127:204).

Harlow, Robert Jr. S. of Robert/Jane; to Liverpool by 1779 (47:126:282).

Harlow, Robert. Liverpool proprietor (19:102).

Harlow, Robert. To Liverpool ca. 1760 (47:126:95).

Harlow, Susanah. Dau. of Robert/Jane; to (or b.?) Liverpool by 1788 (47: 127:56).

Harlow, Zoheth. S. of Robert/Jane; to (or b.?) Liverpool by 1801 (47: 128:28).

Harney, Elizabeth. Dau. of Patrick/ Margaret (Kilfoil) of Parish Rahine, Queen's Co., Ireland; marr. Halifax 7 Feb. 1826 Thomas Curren (q.v.) (32:108).

Harney, John. S. of Richard/Jane (Magragh) of St. Lawrence, Nfld.; marr. Halifax 11 Apr. 1820 Mary Lonergan (q.v.) (31:47).

Harney, John. S. of Michael/Ellean (Geary), of Parish Rawgen?, Co. Waterford, Ireland; marr. Halifax 7 Aug. 1832 Margaret Loyd (q.v.) (33:59).

Harney, Michael. S. of Michael/ Eleanor (Geary) of Parish Rawgan, Waterford, Ireland; marr. Halifax 2 Nov. 1823 Anne Haverstock (31: 47).

Harney, Richard. S. of Richard/ Catherine (Murray) of Clonmel, Co. Tipperary, Ireland; marr. Halifax 17 May 1814 Anne Allen (30:106).

Haron, Ann. Of St. John's, Nfld.; widow of Michael Harison; marr. Halifax 11 Aug. 1840 Thomas Moran (q.v.) (34:135).

Harper, Catharine. 7; dau. of Christopher; Hull, Yorkshire, to Fort Cumberland on JENNY 3-10 April 1775 (22:123).

Harper, Charlotte. 6; dau. of Christopher; Hull, Yorkshire, to Fort Cumberland on JENNY 3-10 April 1775 (22:123).

Harper, Christopher. 45, farmer; Hull, Yorkshire, to Fort Cumberland on JENNY 3-10 April 1775 (22: 123).

Harper, Christopher. 40; farmer; Hull, Yorkshire, to Nova Scotia; on TWO FRIENDS 28 Feb.-7 Mar. 1774 (25:30).

Harper, Elizabeth. 40; wife of Christopher; Hull, Yorkshire, to Port Cumberland on JENNY 3-10 April 1775 (22:123).

Harper, Elizabeth. 14; dau. of Christopher; Hull, Yorkshire, to Port Cumberland on JENNY 3-10 April 1775 (22:123).

Harper, Hannah. 15; dau. of Christopher; Hull, Yorkshire, to Port Cumberland on JENNY 3-10 April 1775 (22:123).

Harper, John. 13; s. of Christopher; Hull, Yorkshire, to Port Cumberland on JENNY 3-10 April 1775 (22:123).

Harper, Thomas. 12; s. of Christopher; Hull, Yorkshire, to Port Cumberland on JENNY 3-10 April 1775 (22:123).

Harper, William. 4; s. of Christopher; Hull, Yorkshire, to Port Cumberland on JENNY 3-10 April 1775 (22:123).

Harper, William. Plus 1 f./3 ch./2 svts.; Port Roseway Associate (6: 15).

Harrigan, David. S. of Andrew/Elline (Harrigan) of Parish Magill (Mogeely?), Co. Cork, Ireland; marr. Halifax 17 June 1836 Elline Linerd (q.v.) (34:131).

Harrigan, Margaret. Dau. of Andrew/ Ellen (Barry) of Co. Cork, Ireland; marr. Halifax 24 Nov. 1835 William O'Brien (q.v.) (34:136).

Harrington, Ann. Dau. of John/Ellen (Power) of Co. Tipperary, Ireland; marr. Halifax 26 June 1842 James Breen (q.v.) (35:135).

Harrington, Bethyah. Dau. of Benja-

min/Bethyah; to (or b.?) Liverpool by 1792 (47:127:210).

Harrington, Catherine. Dau. of Patrick/Catherine (Downes) of Co. Kerry, Ireland; marr. Halifax 14 July 1838 Eugene Sullivan (q.v.) (34:138).

Harrington, Ebenezer Jr. S. of Ebenezer/Rebeckah; to Liverpool by 1778 (47:126:288).

Harrington, Elizabeth. Dau. of James/ Jane (Walsh) of Boston, Mass.; marr. Halifax 20 July 1824 Michael Shea (q.v.) (31:53).

Harrington, Elizabeth. Dau. of Ebenezer/Rebeckah; to Liverpool by 1771 (47:126:289).

Harrington, Honora. Dau. of Jeremiah/ Catherine (Shea) of Co. Cork, Ireland; marr. Halifax 8 Oct. 1828 Patrick Sullivan (q.v.) (32:119).

Harrington, Jeremiah. Of Bantry, Co. Cork, Ireland; marr. Halifax 5 Apr. 1842 Ellen Coleman (35:138).

Harrington, Job. S. of Benjamin/ Bethyah; to (or b.?) Liverpool by 1795 (47:127:276).

Harrington, Johanna. Dau. of Timothy/ Mory (Murphy) of Berehaven, Co. Cork, Ireland; marr. Halifax 19 Oct. 1826 William Dunnavan (q.v.) (32:108).

Harrington, John. S. of Denis/Honora (Fitzgerald) of Co. Kerry, Ireland; marr. Halifax 27 Oct. 1830 Elizabeth Cahill (q.v.) (32:112).

Harrington, Lodowick. S. of Benjamin/ Bethiah; to (or b.?) Liverpool by 1796 (47:127:57).

Harrington, Thomas Jr. S. of Thomas/ Mary; to Liverpool by 178- (47: 126:282).

Harris, Francis. From Mass.; land grant at Onslow 21 Feb. 1769 (4: 225).

Harris, Francis. Grantee 'Digby New
Grant' 29 Jan. 1801 (5:82).
Harris, Francis. Loyalist; plus 1
f./3 ch.; mustered at Digby 19 May
1784 (39:122).
Harris, Peter. Loyalist; mustered at
Digby 19 May 1784 (39:122).
Harris, Samuel. Grantee 'Digby New
Grant' 29 Jan. 1801 (5:82).
Harrison, Christopher. Loyalist; plus
1 f./3 ch.; mustered at Digby 19
May 1784 (39:122).
Harrison, Eleanor. 48, widow; Hull to
Fort Cumberland on ALBION 7-14
March 1774 (21:139).
Harrison, Jane. 20; maid servant;
Hull, Yorkshire, to Nova Scotia;
on TWO FRIENDS 28 Feb.-7 Mar. 1774
(25:29).
Harrison, Mary. 17, maid servant;
Hull to Fort Cumberland on ALBION
7-14 March 1774 (21:136).
Harrison, Michael. S. of Charles/
Catherine (Esmond) of New Ross,
Wexford, Ireland; marr. Halifax 12
Dec. 1807 Anne Hardy (q.v.) (30:
106).
Harrison, Samuel. Plus 1 f./7 ch.;
farmer; Port Roseway Associate (6:
15).
Harrison, Thomas. 28; husbandman;
Hull, Yorkshire, to Nova Scotia;
on TWO FRIENDS 28 Feb.-7 Mar. 1774
(25:30).
Harrison, Thomas. Loyalist; mustered
at Digby 19 May 1784 (39:122).
Harrison, Thomas. Plus 1 f./3 ch./1
svt.; taylor; Port Roseway Asso-
ciate (6:15).
Harrison, Thomas. Taylor; Hull to
Fort Cumberland on ALBION 7-14
March 1774 (21:137).
Hart, Charles. Plus 1 f./1 ch./3
svts.; Port Roseway Associate (6:
15).

Hart, Elizabeth. Dau. of Andrew/Anne
of Germany; marr. Halifax 10 Feb.
1819 John Queeny (q.v.) (31:52).
Hart, John. 25, master mariner; Poole
to Nova Scotia on SQUIRREL Nov.
1775 (24:45).
Hart, Patrick. S. of William/Mary
(Murphy) Co. Kilkenny, Ireland;
marr. Halifax 23 May 1830 Joanna
Drea (q.v.) (32:112).
Hartenburg, Dennick. Loyalist; mustered at Digby 19 May 1784 (39:
122).
Hartery, Elizabeth. Of Harbour Grace,
Nfld.; widow of Michael Connors;
marr. Halifax 8 Feb. 1843 Nicholas
Morrissy (q.v.) (35:141).
Hartewick, Lawrence. Loyalist; plus 1
f./1 ch./2 svts.; mustered at
Digby 19 May 1784 (39:122).
Hartlemandt, A. Waldeck Service;
mustered at Bear River 11/25 June
1784 (38:260).
Hartley, Thomas. Plus 1 f./3 svts.;
farmer; Port Roseway Associate (6:
15).
Hartnett, Margaret. Dau. of Timothy/
Mary (Savage) of Co. Cork, Ire-
land; marr. Halifax 17 June 1821
James Kinsella (q.v.) (31:49).
Hartwell, James. From Mass.; land
grant at Truro 1759 (4:242).
Hartwell, William. From Mass.; land
grant at Truro 1759 (4:242).
Harvey, Elizabeth. Lady; wife of Sir
John; 3rd dau. of 1st Viscount
Lake; b. 6 Oct. 1777; d. 10 Apr.
1851 at Halifax (13:63).
Harvey, John. Loyalist; plus 1 svt.;
mustered at Digby 19 May 1784 (39:
122).
Harvey, John. Sir; Lt.Gov.; d. 22
Mar. 1852 at Halifax ae 74 (13:62-
63).
Harwood, Thomas. 34; farmer; Hull,

Yorkshire, to Nova Scotia; on TWO FRIENDS 28 Feb.-7 Mar. 1774 (25: 29).

Hasey, Margaret. See Dorney, Margaret.

Haskin, John. Plus 1 f./2 svts.; bricklayer; Port Roseway Associate (6:15).

Hastings, Joseph Stacey. Loyalist; Boston to Halifax (41:5).

Hatch, John. Plus 1 f.; arr. Annapolis from New York 19 Oct. 1782 (37:125).

Hatfield, Isaac. Grantee "Digby New Grant" 29 Jan. 1801 (5:82).

Hatfield, Isaac. Loyalist; plus 2 f./3 svts.; mustered at Digby 19 May 1784 (39:122).

Hatkes, John. Loyalist; mustered at Digby 19 May 1784 (39:121).

Hatt, Adam. Plus wife; Hemmenthal, Canton Schaffhausen, to Halifax 1751 (44:190).

Hatt, Jakob. Plus wife; Hemmenthal, Canton Schaffhausen, to Halifax 1751 (44:190).

Hatt, Konrad. Plus wife/ch.; Hemmenthal, Canton Schaffhausen, to Halifax 1751 (44:191).

Haughton, Nahum. Plus 1 f./1 ch. -8; arr. Annapolis from New York 19 Oct. 1782 (37:126).

Hauser, Frederick. Loyalist; New York to Halifax 1782 (41:15).

Hauser, Fredk. Capt.; plus 1 f./3 ch. 8+; arr. Annapolis from New York 19 Oct. 1782 (37:126).

Havens, William. Loyalist; mustered at Digby 19 May 1784 (39:122).

Hawkesworth, Samuel. S. of Samuel/ Bridget (Clansey) of Co. Limerick, Ireland; marr. Halifax 29 Jan. 1822 Bridget Nowlan (q.v.) (31: 47).

Hayden, Bridget. Dau. of Patrick/

Anastasia (Needam) of Co. Tipperary, Ireland; marr. Halifax 18 July 1842 Michael Power (q.v.) (35:143).

Hayden, John. S. of William/Bridget (Milet) of Co. Kilkenny, Ireland; marr. Halifax 15 Jan. 1836 Joanna Doyle (q.v.) (34:131).

Hayden, Thomas. Liverpool proprietor (19:102).

Hayes, Catherine. See O'Brien, Catherine.

Hayes, David. S. of William/Catherine (Stanton) of Dangan, Co. Cork, Ireland; marr. Halifax 6 June 1833 Elizabeth Gray (q.v.) (33:59).

Hayes, David. Widower of Elizabeth Gray; s. of William/Catherine (Stanton) of Dangan, Co. Cork, Ireland; marr. Halifax 4 Apr. 1837 Mary Farrell (q.v.) (34:131).

Hayes, James. S. of Thomas/Ellen (Duggan) of Buttevant, Co. Cork, Ireland; marr. Halifax 3 June 1834 Mary Walsh (q.v.) (33:59).

Hayes, Michael. S. of Richard/Anastasia (Butler) of Co. Kilkenny, Ireland; marr. Halifax 14 Feb. 1831 Joanna Dunn (q.v.) (33:59).

Hayton, George. 32; farmer; Hull, Yorkshire, to Nova Scotia; on TWO FRIENDS 28 Feb.-7 Mar. 1774 (25: 28).

Hayward, George. From Mass.; land grant at Truro 1759 (4:242).

Haywood, Deborah. Widow; land grant at Truro 1759 (4:242).

Haywood, Ephraim. From Mass.; land grant at Truro 1759 (4:242).

Haywood, John. From Mass.; land grant at Truro 1759 (4:242).

Hazard, Thomas. Plus 1 f./7 ch./4 svts.; farmer; Port Roseway Associate (6:15).

Hazeltine, Paul. New England to

Annapolis 1760 (18:271).

Heacey, John. S. of Brien/Mary (Lowhen) of Parish Kilnlakin, Co. Galway, Ireland; marr. Halifax 14 Feb. 1825 Catherine Gamble (q.v.) (31:47).

Headley, John. S. of Joseph/Ruth; to Liverpool by 1762 (47:126:163).

Headley, Ruth. Dau. of John/Elizabeth; to (or b.?) Liverpool by 1784 (47:127:270).

Headley, William. S. of Joseph/Ruth; to Liverpool by 1775 (47:126:286).

Headlock, John. From N.H.; effective land grant at Truro 31 Oct. 1765 (4:245).

Headly, Joseph. Liverpool proprietor (19:101).

Headon, Patrick. Of Co. Wexford, Ireland; widower of Elizabeth Leary; marr. Halifax 29 Sep. 1836 Ellen Daily (q.v.) (34:131).

Healy, Patrick. S. of James/Mary (Sullivan) of Castlemaine, Kilorglin, Co. Kerry, Ireland; marr. Halifax 26 Nov. 1822 Anne Frasier (31:47).

Healy, Timothy. S. of Denis/Eleanor (Murphy) of Lismore, Co. Waterford, Ireland; marr. Halifax 9 May 1827 Joanna Durney (q.v.) (32:112).

Heaney, Bridget. See Hall, Bridget.

Heary, Mary. Dau. of Patrick/Margaret (Carpenter) of Co. Carlow, Ireland; marr. Halifax 14 June 1830 James Murray (q.v.) (32:116).

Heater, John. B. Plymouth, Mass., ca. Oct. 1756; Pool, England, to Argyle by 1784 (47:127:268).

Heater, John. B. Plymouth, Mass.; to Liverpool (49:125).

Heatly, Nathan. Liverpool proprietor (19:102).

Heaton, Peter. Loyalist; plus 1 f./1 ch.; mustered at Digby 19 May 1784 (39:122).

Hebest, Robert. Liverpool proprietor (19:102).

Hecht, Frederick William. Grantee "Digby New Grant" 29 Jan. 1801 (5:82).

Heenan, John. S. of Michael/Mary (Murphy) of Co. Armagh, Ireland; marr. Halifax 19 Jan. 1845 Mary Kelly (35:138).

Heffernan, Johanna. Dau. of Patrick/Anastas (Dulhanty) of Glenmore, Kilkenny, Ireland; marr. Halifax 6 Feb. 1812 William Donovan (q.v.) (30:104).

Heffernan, Johanna. Dau. of Patrick/Anastasia (Dulhanty) of Glenmore, Co. Kilkenny, Ireland; marr. Halifax 12 Jan. 1826 John Keily (q.v.) (32:113).

Heffernan, John. Plus 1 f./1 ch./1 svt.; farmer; Port Roseway Associate (6:15).

Heffernan, Lawrence. S. of John/Mary (Williams) of Clonmel, Co. Tipperary, Ireland; marr. Halifax 13 July 1843 Ellen Woods (q.v.) (35:138).

Heffernan, Maurice. S. of John/Alice (Barton) of Co. Kerry, Ireland; marr. Halifax 19 Feb. 1833 Joanna Coleman (q.v.) (33:59).

Heffernan, Michael. S. of Thomas/Mary (Londrigan) of Co. Tipperary, Ireland; marr. Halifax 18 June 1832 Margaret Dwyer (q.v.) (33:59).

Heffernan, Timothy. S. of Patrick/Anastasia Mary (Dulhanty) of Glenmore, Kilkenny, Ireland; marr. Halifax 22 June 1805 Margaret Londergan (q.v.) (30:106).

Hein, Benjamin, Loyalist; mustered at Digby 19 May 1784 (39:122).

Henderson, Joseph. Grantee "Digby New
Grant" 29 Jan. 1801 (5:82).

Hendorff, Fred. Ensign; disbanded
officer, Hessian; plus 1 f./2
ch./2 svts.; mustered at Digby 19
May 1784 (39:121).

Henebery, Catherine. Of Co. Kilkenny,
Ireland; widow of William Broth-
ers; marr. Halifax 27 Apr. 1843
Patrick Whelan (q.v.) (35:146).

Henegan, Michael Edmund. S. of John/
Grace (Power) of Midleton, Co.
Cork, Ireland; marr. Halifax 22
Apr. 1822 Sarah Megre widow of
Douty/Reily (31:50).

Henessy, Honora. Dau. of John/Eleanor
(Prentergast) of Co. Tipperary,
Ireland; marr. Halifax 7 Oct. 1829
Jeremiah Finn (q.v.) (32:110).

Henessy, Richard. S. of Sylvester/
Elizabeth (Kelly) of Co. Kilkenny,
Ireland; marr. Halifax 17 Nov.
1830 Joanna O'Brien (q.v.) (32:
112).

Henissey, John. S. of Thomas/Bridget
(Morissy) of Co. Kilkenny, Ireland; widower of Catherine Byrns;
marr. Halifax 20 Apr. 1830 Mary
Cutt q.v.) (32:112).

Henissey, Patrick. S. of Patrick/
Bridget (O'Brien) of Co. Tipperary, Ireland; marr. Halifax 22
Aug. 1834 Mary Dwyer (q.v.) (33:
59).

Henissy, John. S. of Richard/Honora
(Hanly) of Co. Kilkenny, Ireland;
marr. Halifax 12 Jan. 1842 Mary
Murphy (q.v.) (35:138).

Henissy, John. Widower of Margaret
Murphy; of Cloyne,. Co. Cork,
Ireland; marr. Halifax 8 Feb. 1829
Ann Walsh (q.v.) (32:112).

Hennessy, Frances. Dau. of David/Mary
(Laughlan) of Co. Cork, Ireland;
widow of John Donovan; marr.

Halifax 8 Oct. 1830 Michael Hogan
(q.v.) (32:112).

Hennessy, John. S. of Maurice/Julia
(Keeff) of Parish Cloyne, Co.
Cork, Ireland; marr. Halifax 21
Aug. 1822 Margaret Murphy, widow
of Humphrey Kearns (31:47).

Herbert, James. S. of Michael/Mary
(Hodd) of St. John's, Nfld.; marr.
Halifax 16 Aug. 1829 Joanna Brown
(q.v.) (32:112).

Herbert, Margaret. See Marks, Margaret.

Herbert, Michael. 73, s. of James/
Catherine (Conelly) of Fedamore,
Limerick, Ireland.; marr. Halifax
30 Oct. 1817 Mary Mickown widow
Morrison (30:106).

Herdrick, John C. German Service;
plus 1 f./1 ch.; mustered at Bear
River 11/25 June 1784 (38:260).

Heritage, Mary. See Houlihan, Mary.

Heron, James. Mariner; s. Mathew/
Joanna (Shanahan) of Co. Waterford, Ireland; marr. Halifax 31
July 1837 Margaret Power (q.v.)
(34:131).

Herricke, C. F. German Service;
mustered at Bear River 11/25 June
1784 (38:260).

Herrington, John. S. of Jacob/Hannah;
to Liverpool by 1771 (47:126:164).

Herron, Elizabeth. See Gorman, Elizabeth.

Hespeden, -----. Cpl.; German Service; mustered at Bear River 11/25
June 1784 (38:260).

Hewett, John. From Mass.; land grant
at Onslow 21 Feb. 1769 (4:225).

Hewett, John. Grantee "Digby New
Grant" 29 Jan. 1801 (5:82).

Hewson, Catherine. Dau. of George/
Elizabeth (Drew) Limerick City,
Ireland; marr. Halifax 18 Nov.
1829 Thomas Browner (q.v.) (32:

106).
Hewson, George. Of Co. Limerick,
Ireland; bur. Halifax 18 Feb. 1840
ae. 61 (34:125).
Hewson, Mary. Dau. of George/Eliza-
beth (Drew) of Limerick, Ireland;
marr. Halifax 8 July 1835 William
Cashman (q.v.) (34:127).
Hewson. See Huson.
Hewton, Mathew; 30, yeoman; passenger
Newcastle to Nova Scotia on PROVI-
DENCE 24 April 1775 (23:15).
Hibbet, Patrick. S. of Patrick/
Bridget (Key) of Co. Leix, Ire-
land; marr. Halifax 19 Nov. 1844
Ellen Joice (q.v.) (35:138).
Hibbets, John. S. of Patrick/Bridget
(Keys) of Queen's Co., Ireland;
marr. Halifax 18 July 1828 Mary
Lonergan (32:112).
Hickey, Bridget. Dau. of Michael/
Ellen (Quirk) of Co. Kilkenny,
Ireland; marr. Halifax 27 Jan.
1834 Hugh McNamara (q.v.) (33:63).
Hickey, Ellen. Dau. of James/Mary
(Phelan) of Co. Kilkenny, Ireland;
marr. Halifax 27 Nov. 1830 Lot
Finley (q.v.) (32:110).
Hickey, John. Disbanded soldier, 2nd
Bn., N.J. Vols.; plus 1 ch.; must-
ered at Digby 19 May 1784 (39:
121).
Hickey, John. S. of John/Sarah
(Magher) of Parish Kilmantty?, Co.
Tipperary, Ireland; marr. Halifax
14 Jan. 1834 Mary Laffan (33:59).
Hickey, Lawrence. S. of Michael/
Honora (Gynan) of Co. Waterford,
Ireland; marr. Halifax 18 Feb.
1833 Catherine Faulkner (q.v.)
(33:59).
Hickey, Lawrence. S. of James/Mary
(Whelan) of Co. Kilkenny, Ireland;
marr. Halifax 27 Nov. 1835 Jennett
Lawson (q.v.) (34:131).

Hickey, Mary. Dau. of Richard/Eliza-
beth (Fitzpatrick) of Co. Kilkenny, Ireland; marr. Halifax 17 Feb.
1829 Patrick Ward; entire entry
ruled out in register (q.v.) (32:
120).
Hickey, Michael. S. of Patrick/Joanna
(?Reshan) of Limerick, Ireland;
marr. Halifax 15 Feb. 1806 Cather-
ine Lanigan (q.v.) (30:106).
Hickey, Patrick. S. of Patrick/Ellen
(Flinn) of Co. Waterford, Ireland;
marr. Halifax 23 Sep. 1831 Ellen
Tynan (q.v.) (33:59).
Hicks, Oliver. Loyalist; plus 1 f./1
ch./1 svt.; mustered at Digby 19
May 1784 (39:122).
Higgins, Bridget. Dau. of Thomas/Mary
(Cunningham) of Co. Sligo, Ire-
land; marr. Halifax 20 Feb. 1844
James Maguire (q.v.) (35:141).
Higgins, John. S. of Patrick/Bridget
(Naughen) of Co. Roscommon, Ire-
land; marr. Halifax 3 Feb. 1843
Mary Keily (35:138).
Higgins, Jonathan Jr. From Mass.;
land grant at Onslow 21 Feb. 1769
(4:225).
Higgins, Jonathan. From Mass.; land
grant at Onslow 21 Feb. 1769 (4:
224).
Higgins, Michael. S. of Michael/Mary
(Cunningham) of Co. Cork, Ireland;
marr. Halifax 4 Nov. 1830 Mary
Rogers (q.v.) (32:112).
Hill, Anthony. 57; farmer; Hull,
Yorkshire, to Nova Scotia; on TWO
FRIENDS 28 Feb.-7 Mar. 1774 (25:
28).
Hill, Elizabeth. 2, daughter of John;
Hull to Fort Cumberland on ALBION
7-14 March 1774 (21:137).
Hill, Elizabeth. Dau. of Thomas/
Elizabeth (Cogshall) of Bir-
mingham, England; marr. Halifax 12

Apr. 1806 *(q.v.)* (30:109).

Hill, Jane. 28, wife of John; Hull to Port Cumberland on ALBION 7-14 March 1774 (21:137).

Hill, Jane. See Vance, Jane.

Hill, John. 25, farmer; Hull to Port Cumberland on ALBION 7-14 March 1774 (21:137).

Hill, John. Grantee 'Digby New Grant' 29 Jan. 1801 (5:82).

Hill, John. Loyalist; plus 1 f./1 ch./3 svts.; mustered at Digby 19 May 1784 (39:121).

Hill, John. New England to Annapolis on CHARMING MOLLY May 1760 (18:271).

Hill, Joshua. Plus 1 f./6 ch./2 svts.; farmer.; Port Roseway Associate (6:15).

Hill, Mary. 1, daughter of John; Hull to Port Cumberland on ALBION 7-14 March 1774 (21:137).

Hill, Richard. Capt.; Loyalist; plus 3 f./4 ch.; mustered at Digby 19 May 1784 (39:121).

Hill, Richard. Grantee 'Digby New Grant' 29 Jan. 1801 (5:82).

Hill, Robert. Grantee 'Digby New Grant' 29 Jan. 1801 (5:82).

Hill, Thomas 2. s. of John; Hull to Port Cumberland on ALBION 7-14 March 1774 (21:137).

Hill, Thomas. Loyalist; plus 1 f./3 ch.; mustered at Digby 19 May 1784 (39:122).

Hill, William. Plus 1 f./8 ch./6 svts.; baker; Port Roseway Associate (6:15).

Hill, Zachariah. Loyalist; plus 1 f./5 ch.; mustered at Digby 19 May 1784 (39:122).

Hilliard, Gershom. Loyalist; plus 1 f./1 ch.; mustered at Digby 19 May 1784 (39:122).

Hilton, Osgood. Liverpool proprietor

(19:102).

Hincksman. See Hinxman.

Hinden, Charles. English; Liverpool to Nova Scotia April 1864 on KEDAR (45:181).

Hines, Richard. Grantee 'Digby New Grant' 29 Jan. 1801 (5:82).

Hinessy, Ellen. Dau. of Michael/Mary (Egan) of Co. Tipperary, Ireland; marr. Halifax 2 June 1831 James Lahey *(q.v.)* (33:61).

Hinessy, Ellen. Dau. of Michael/Mary (Egan) of Co. Tipperary, Ireland; marr. Halifax 2 Mar. 1834 William McGrath *(q.v.)* (33:62).

Hinessy, Jeremiah. S. of Martin/ Honora (Donovan) of Cork, Ireland; marr. Halifax 22 Aug. 1835 Mary Granfield (34:131).

Hinessy, Mary. See Dwyer, Mary.

Hinessy, Thomas. S. of John/Ellen (Pendergast) of Co. Tipperary, Ireland; marr. Halifax 5 Feb. 1831 Ellen MacCulla *(q.v.)* (33:59).

Hingley. See Hinglin.

Hinglin, John. From N.H.; effective land grant at Truro 31 Oct. 1765 (4:245).

Hinissy, David. S. of Patrick/Mary (Callaghan) of Co. Cork, Ireland; marr. Halifax 25 Apr. 1834 Bridget Mackey *(q.v.)* (33:59).

Hinnissy, Joanna. See O'Brien, Joanna.

Hinxman, Charles. Grantee 'Digby New Grant' 29 Jan. 1801 (5:82).

Hinxman, Charles. Loyalist; plus 1 f./1 ch.; mustered at Digby 19 May 1784 (39:122).

Hislop, John. Plus 1 f./ 1 ch.; carpenter; Port Roseway Associate (6:15).

Hitchcock, John. Loyalist; mustered at Digby 19 May 1784 (39:122).

Hitchcock, Samuel. Loyalist; plus 1

f./3 ch./2 svts.; mustered at
Digby 19 May 1784 (39:122).

Hoar, David. From Mass.; land grant
at Onslow 21 Feb. 1769 (4:224).

Hoar, Ebenezer. From Mass.; land
grant at Onslow 21 Feb. 1769 (4:
225).

Hoar, Solomon. From Mass.; land grant
at Onslow 21 Feb. 1769 (4:225).

Hobin, Ann. Dau. of Lawrence/Elizab-
neth (Delaney) of Parish Gordon,
Co. Kilkenny, Ireland; marr.
Halifax 13 June 1838 William
Byrnes (q.v.) (34:126).

Hobin, Jeremiah. S. of Murtagh/Ann
(Hanlon) of Parish of Gordon, Co.
Kilkenny, Ireland; widower of
Catherine Handian; marr. Halifax
21 Aug. 1842 Anastasia MacIvoy
(q.v.) (35:138).

Hobin, Richard. S. of Murtha/Ann
(Hanlon) of Co. Kilkenny, Ireland;
marr. Halifax 13 Sep. 1829 Margaret Kilfoil (q.v.) (32:112).

Hobin, Robert. S. of Thomas/Catherine
(Fribs) of Co. Kilkenny, Ireland;
marr. Halifax 17 Oct. 1838 Catherine Flood (34:131).

Hockinhull, John. Grantee "Digby New
Grant" 29 Jan. 1801 (5:82).

Hodgkinson, Henry. Plus 1 f./1 svt.;
Port Roseway Associate (6:15).

Hodgson, William. 22; husbandman;
Hull, Yorkshire, to Nova Scotia;
on TWO FRIENDS 28 Feb.-7 Mar. 1774
(25:28).

Hodson, Thomas. Plus 1 f./1 ch./1
svt.; carpenter; Port Roseway
Associate (6:15).

Hoer, Daniel. From Mass.; land grant
at Truro 1759 (4:242).

Hoer, Francis. From Mass.; land grant
at Truro 1759 (4:242).

Hoer, Leonard. From Mass.; land grant
at Truro 1759 (4:242).

Hoer, Nathan. From Mass.; land grant
at Truro 1759 (4:242).

Hogan, Andrew. S. of William/Ann
(Farrell) of Co. Carlow, Ireland;
marr. Halifax 18 July 1835 Charlotte Duncan (q.v.) (34:131).

Hogan, Ellen. Dau. of Edward/Ellen
(Ryan) of Co. Carlow, Ireland;
marr. Halifax 28 Oct. 1830 Thomas
Murphy (q.v.) (32:116).

Hogan, Joanna. Dau. of Philip/Cather-
ine (Kearns) of Ballyhail, Co.
Kilkenny, Ireland; marr. Halifax
16 Aug. 1842 Edward Power (q.v.)
(35:143).

Hogan, Mary. Dau. of Philip/Catherine
(Kearns) of Ballyhail, Co. Kilkenny, Ireland; marr. Halifax 7 Feb.
1825 Thomas Holden (q.v.) (31:47).

Hogan, Mary. Dau. of John/Mary of Co.
Waterford, Ireland; marr. Halifax
14 June 1818 (q.v.) (31:54).

Hogan, Michael. S. of Michael/Eleanor
(Brien) of Callan, Co. Kilkenny,
Ireland; marr. Halifax 13 Nov.
1828 Eleanor Gyban (q.v.) (32:
112).

Hogan, Michael. S. of Thomas/Ellen
(O'Brine) of Co. Cork, Ireland;
marr. Halifax 8 Oct. 1830 Frances
Hennessy (q.v.) (32:112).

Hogan, Michael. S. of Philip/Cather-
ine (Kearns) of Hugganstown, Co.
Kilkenny, Ireland; marr. Halifax 7
Sep. 1829 Mary Walsh (q.v.) (32:
112).

Hogan, Michael. Sgt., the Rifle
Brig., Co. Limerick, Ireland;
marr. Halifax 11 Aug. 1833 Marianne Burk (q.v.) (33:59).

Hogan, Patrick. S. of John/Catherine
(Henessey) of Co. Kilkenny, Ire-
land; marr. Halifax 27 June 1831
Anastasia Daley (q.v.) (33:59).

Hogan, Thomas. S. of Thomas/Ann

(Roche) of Co. Wexford, Ireland; marr. Halifax 27 Nov. 1841 Ann Nugent (35:139).

Hogan, William. S. of Philip/Catherine (Keans) of Ballyhail, Co. Kilkenny, Ireland; marr. Halifax 28 Oct. 1839 Ann Murphy *(q.v.)* (34:131).

Hogarty, Catherine. Dau. of Patrick/Mary (Munnehan) of Co. Cork, Ireland; marr. Halifax 14 Dec. 1830 John McCarthy *(q.v.)* (32:114).

Hoit, Jesse Jr. Arr. Annapolis from New York 19 Oct. 1782 (37:126).

Holden, Joanna. Dau. of Michael/Margaret (Conway) of Co. Kilkenny, Ireland; marr. Halifax 11 Apr. 1831 Patrick Butler *(q.v.)* (33:54).

Holden, Michael. S. of James/Elizabeth (Morris) of Co. Kilkenny, Ireland; marr. Halifax 21 July 1836 Mary Cantfield *(q.v.)* (34:131).

Holden, Patrick. S. of Michael/Mary (Darmody) of Co. Kilkenny, Ireland; marr. Halifax 12 Sep. 1843 Mary Fox (35:139).

Holden, Philip. S. of James/Elinor (O'Brien) of Templeowens, Co. Kilkenny, Ireland; widower of Mary Dunphy; marr. Halifax 16 Jan. 1826 Mary Murphy *(q.v.)* (32:113).

Holden, Thomas. S. of William/Catherine (Connors) of Mullinavat, Co. Kilkenny, Ireland; marr. Halifax 7 Feb. 1825 Mary Hogan *(q.v.)* (31:47).

Holdstock, Joseph. Laborer; not settled; mustered at Digby 19 May 1784 (39:122).

Holdsworth, James A. Grantee "Digby New Grant" 29 Jan. 1801 (5:82).

Holdsworth, James. Loyalist; plus 1 f.; mustered at Digby 19 May 1784 (39:121).

Holdsworth, John. Grantee "Digby New Grant" 29 Jan. 1801 (5:82).

Holdsworth, John. Loyalist; mustered at Digby 19 May 1784 (39:121).

Holdsworth, Thomas. Loyalist; mustered at Digby 19 May 1784 (39:121).

Holeran, Maurice. S. of Jeremiah/Margaret (Casy) of Co. Kilkenny, Ireland; marr. Halifax 8 Apr. 1842 Elizabeth Daly (35:139).

Holihan, Mary. Dau. of Thomas/Joanna (Kenedy) of Co. Kerry, Ireland; marr. Halifax 9 Nov. 1839 John Moriarty *(q.v.)* (34:135).

Holl, Patrick. (Perhaps Hall?) Town Sgt. Dublin City, Ireland; widower of Sarah Ford; marr. Halifax 24 Sep. 1828 Margaret O'Neill *(q.v.)* (32:113).

Holland, James. Corp., 65th Regt.; of Co. Tyrone, Ireland; marr. Halifax 21 Jan. 1838 Mary Houlihan *(q.v.)* (34:131).

Holland, Michael. S. of Daniel/Mary (Walsh) of Co. Tipperary, Ireland; marr. Halifax 28 Feb. 1835 Catherine Nolan *(q.v.)* (34:131).

Holland, Rebecca. Dau. of William/Sarah (Kirkwood) of Co. Tyrone, Ireland; marr. Halifax 1 Feb. 1831 Patrick O'Neill *(q.v.)* (33:65).

Holland, William. Widower of Margaret McLaughlin; of Co. Armagh, Ireland; marr. Halifax 16 June 1834 Hannah Margery Wilson (33:60).

Holleban, Michael. S. of David/Honora (Helly) of Co. Cork, Ireland; marr. Halifax 8 Sep. 1828 Margaret Sullivan *(q.v.)* (32:113).

Holleran, Mary. Dau. of Andrew/Mary (Looby) of Co. Tipperary, Ireland; marr. Halifax 18 July 1807 Daniel John Farrell *(q.v.)* (30:105).

Holleran, Mary. Dau . of Andrew/Mary
(Looby), widow of John Farrell, of
Co. Tipperary; marr. Halifax 7
Aug. 1817 Patrick Hacket (30:106).

Hollingshead, Anthony. Loyalist; plus
1 f./4 ch.; mustered at Digby 19
May 1784 (39:121).

Hollingshead, George. Grantee "Digby
New Grant" 29 Jan. 1801 (5:82).

Hollingshead, George. Loyalist;
mustered at Digby 19 May 1784 (39:
121).

Hollorn, Patrick. S. of John/Joanna
(Kiley) of Clonmel, Co. Tipperary,
Ireland; marr. Halifax 16 Dec.
1832 Catherine Coine (q.v.) (33:
60).

Holly, Mary. Dau. of John/Mary (Redmond) of Waterford, Ireland; marr.
Halifax 26 Nov. 1831 Thomas Osborn
(q.v.) (33:65).

Holmes, Benjamin. Liverpool proprietor (19:101).

Holmes, Benjamin. Plymouth, Mass., to
Liverpool ca. 1760 (47:126:95).

Holmes, Lydia. Dau. of Benjamin/
Rebeckah; to (or b.?) Liverpool by
1789 (47:127:121).

Holmes, Rebecka. Dau. of Benjamin/
Rebecka; to Liverpool by 1775
(47:126:285).

Holmes, Rebekah. Wife of Benjamin;
Plymouth, Mass., to Liverpool ca.
1760 (47:126:95).

Holton, Israel. From Mass.; land
grant at Truro 1759 (4:242).

Holton, James. From Mass.; land grant
at Truro 1759 (4:242).

Holton, Peter. Loyalist; plus 1 f.;
mustered at Digby 19 May 1784 (39:
122).

Holy, Mary. Widow of James Gydon; of
Fethard, Co. Tipperary, Ireland;
marr. Halifax 14 May 1828 John
Walsh (q.v.) (32:120).

Homes, Joel. Loyalist; plus 1 f./1
svt.; mustered at Digby 19 May
1784 (39:122).

Homes, Joseph. S. of Joseph/Mary
(Taylor) of Twyford, Derbsh. Eng-
land; marr. Halifax 28 July 1835
Mary Ann Collis (q.v.) (34:131).

Honery, Janet. See O'Neal, Jane.

Hooper, Thomas. Plus wife/sons/3
daus.; New England to Annapolis on
CHARMING MOLLY May 1760 (18:271).

Hooten, John. Capt.; disbanded officer; Loyalist; plus 1 f./1 ch./2
svts.; mustered at Digby 19 May
1784 (39:122).

Hope, John. S. of John/Elizabeth
(Hertford) of Co. Longford, Ireland; marr. Halifax 10 Sep. 1828
Catherine McCarthy (q.v.) (32:
113).

Hopkins, Elisha. S. of John/Rebeccah;
to Liverpool by 1766 (47:127:205).

Hopkins, Elisha. S. of Elisha; b.
Chatham, Mass., ca. 1730; to
Barrington by June 1765 (50:105).

Hopkins, Elisha. S. old John; b. 26
Oct. 1743; marr. at Liverpool Nov.
1766 (50:106).

Hopkins, Elizabeth. Dau. of Elisha;
to Barrington (50:105).

Hopkins, Experience. Dau. of John
Jr./Susanna; to (or b.?) Liverpool
by 1801 (47:128:28).

Hopkins, Hannah Wing. Wife of Elisha;
b. Harwich, Mass., 15 Feb. 1733/4
(50:105).

Hopkins, John Jr. S. of John/Rebeck-
ah; to Liverpool by 1773 (47:127:
277).

Hopkins, John. Liverpool proprietor
(19:101).

Hopkins, John. S. of Elisha; erst-
while resident Dartmouth, Mass..;
Chatham, Mass., to Liverpool 1759-
1769 (50:105).

Hopkins, John. S. of old John; b. 5
Sep. 1750; marr. at Liverpool Aug.
1773 (50:106).

Hopkins, Rebecca Nickerson. Wife of
John; b. Chatham, Mass., ca. 1721
(50:105).

Hopkins, Rebeccah. Dau. of Elisha/
Sarah; to (or b.?) Liverpool by
1795 (47:127:206).

Hopkins, Sally. Dau. of Elisha/Sarah;
to (or b.?) Liverpool by 1799 (47:
127:276).

Hopkins, Samuel. S. of Elisha; b.
Chatham, Mass., 1757; to Cape
Sable (50:105).

Hopkins, Seth. S. of John; b. ca.
1754; drowned at Liverpool 14 Oct.
1790 (50:106).

Hopkins, Silvanus. S. of John (50:
106).

Hopley, Frances. Dau. of Joseph of
Ireland; marr. Halifax 7 Oct. 1819
Pierce Murphy (q.v.) (31:51).

Hopman, Michael. S. of Michael/Marga-
ret; to (or b.?) Liverpool by 1792
(47:127:120).

Horan, William. S. of William/Mary
(Keefe) of Co. Kilkenny, Ireland;
marr. Halifax 13 July 1840 Margaret Mortuagh (q.v.) (34:131).

Horen, Ellen. Dau. of Patrick/Ellen
(Curren) of Co. Kerry, Ireland;
marr. Halifax 3 Feb. 1841 Daniel
McKenna (q.v.) (35:141).

Horen, Joanna. Dau. of Patrick/Ellen
(Curran) of Co. Kerry, Ireland;
marr. Halifax 30 July 1839 Joseph
McKenna (q.v.) (34:134).

Horsman, Christopher. 27, farmer;
Hull, Yorkshire, to Fort Cumberland on JENNY 3-10 April 1775 (22:
123).

Houghney, Patrick. Of Parish Gowran,
Deoune, Co. Kilkenny, Ireland;
marr. Halifax 15 Oct. 1825 Phoebe

Breen widow of Thomas Mahony (31:
47).

Houghton, John. Bolton, Mass., to
Chester with first settlers
(16:45).

Houghton, John. Bolton, Mass., to
Chester 30 July 1759 (16:46).

Houghton, Timothy. From Mass.; land
grant at Onslow 18 Oct. 1759 (4:
223).

Houghton, Timothy. Plus wife/3 ch.;
Bolton, Mass., to Chester with
first settlers (16:45).

Houghton, Timothy. Capt.; plus wife/3
ch.; Mass.,to Chester 30 July 1759
(16:46).

Houlihan, Mary. Of Co. Wicklow,
Ireland; widow of John Heritage
65th Regt.; marr. Halifax 21 Jan.
1838 Corp. James Holland (q.v.)
(34:131).

Houston, James Jr. Arr. Annapolis
from New York 19 Oct. 1782 (37:
126).

Houston, James. Plus 1 f./3 ch. 8+/2
ch. -8; arr. Annapolis from New
York 19 Oct. 1782 (37:126).

Houston, John. Plus 1 f./2 ch./1
svt.; Port Roseway Associate (6:
15).

Howard, Ephraim Jr. From Mass.; land
grant at Onslow 21 Feb. 1769
(4:224).

Howard, Ephraim. From Mass.; land
grant at Onslow 21 Feb. 1769 (4:
224).

Howard, George. From 'Mass.; land
grant at Onslow 21 Feb. 1769 (4:
224).

Howard, James. S. of James/Bridget
(Ahern) of Co. Cork, Ireland;
marr. Halifax 7 July 1834 Mary
King (33:60).

Howard, John. From Mass.; land grant
at Onslow 21 Feb. 1769 (4:225).

Howard, Mary. Dau. of James/Margaret
(Mathews) of Howth, Co. Dublin,
Ireland; marr. Halifax 1 Dec. 1819
Thomas Keating (31:48).

Howard, Pat. Deserted 15 June 1806
from H.M. 98th Regt. of Foot,
stationed at Halifax; 4'6" [sic],
fresh complexion, brown hair, grey
eyes, ca. 30, b. Ireland; marked
with India ink on hand and arm;
advertised *The Weekly Chronicle*,
21 June 1806 (28:34).

Howard, Samuel. Loyalist; plus 1 f./1
ch.; mustered at Digby 19 May 1784
(39:121).

Howard, Sarah. Dau. of Francis/Eliza-
beth; to Liverpool by 1776 (47:
126:289).

Howard, Sarah. See Magory, Sarah.

Howard, William. Loyalist; mustered
at Digby 19 May 1784 (39:122).

Howe, Abishai. Loyalist; mustered at
Digby 19 May 1784 (39:122).

Howe, William. Mass. to N.S.; to U.S.
1776; lived 1785 at Mass. [which
then incl. Me.] (36:64).

Howe, William. Plus 1 f./2 ch. 8+/2
ch. -8; arr. Annapolis from New
York 19 Oct. 1782 (37:126).

Howell, John Drole?. S. of Thomas;
London, England, to Liverpool by
1788 (47:127:274).

Howes, Gerard. S. of Patrick/Margaret
(Mark) of Kilkenny, Ireland; marr.
Halifax 9 Sep. 1803 Margaret Ber-
nard (q.v.) (30:106).

Howlet, Catherine. See Hannery,
Catherine.

Howley, Michael. S. of Matthias/Honor
(Brawders) of Mooncoine, Co. Kilkenny, Ireland; marr. Halifax 19
Feb. 1844 Ellen Archer (q.v.) (35:
139).

Howley, Thomas. S. of Michael/Cather-
ine (Foley) of Mooncoyne, of Par-

ish Kilmacow, Co. Kilkenny, Ireland; marr. Halifax 3 May 1836
Joanna Foley (q.v.) (34:131).

Hows, George. From N.H.; effective
land grant at Truro 31 Oct. 1765
(4:245).

Hoxnoeffer, Andrew. German Service;
mustered at Bear River 11/25 June
1784 (38:260).

Hoyt, Jesse. Grantee 'Digby New
Grant' 29 Jan. 1801 (5:82).

Hoyt, Jesse. Loyalist; plus 1 f./4
ch.; mustered at Gulliver's Hole/
St. Mary's Bay/Sissiboo 1/6 June
1784; settled at Sissiboo (now
Weymouth) (40:262).

Hoyt, Jesse. Plus 1 f./3 ch. 8+; 1
ch. -8; arr. Annapolis from New
York 19 Oct. 1782 (37:126).

Hubbs, Hannah. Loyalist; mustered at
Digby 19 May 1784 (39:122).

Huggerford, Thomas. Grantee 'Digby
New Grant' 29 Jan. 1801 (5:82).

Hughes, Matthew. S. of James/Ann
(Barry) of Co. Wexford, Ireland;
marr. Halifax 1 June 1821 Elizabeth Graham (q.v.) (31:47).

Hughes, Owen. Carpenter; Port Roseway
Associate (6:15).

Hughes, William. Plus 1 f./3 ch.;
Port Roseway Associate (6:15).

Hugheston, James. Loyalist; plus 1
f./6 ch./6 svts.; mustered at
Digby 19 May 1784 (39:121).

Hughs, Bridget. Dau. of Henry/Eleanor
(Donovan) of Ross, Co. Wexford,
Ireland; marr. Halifax 28 Apr.
1829 Michael Kelly (q.v.) (32:
113).

Hughston, James. Grantee 'Digby New
Grant' 29 Jan. 1801 (5:82).

Hugs, Sarah. Widow of Francis Kelly;
of Co. Longford, Ireland; marr.
Halifax 5 Oct. 1828 John O'Connor
(q.v.) (32:117).

Huit, John. From Ireland; land grant
at Londonderry 6 Mar. 1775 (4:
258).

Hulione, Jeremiah. Loyalist; plus 1
f./1 ch.; mustered at Digby 19 May
1784 (39:122).

Hulme, Peter. Waldeck Service; mustered at Bear River 11/25 June 1784
(38:260).

Humbertone, Samuel. Plus 1 f./2 ch./4
svts.; Port Roseway Associate (6:
15).

Hunenger, Henry. Loyalist; mustered
at Digby 19 May 1784 (39:122).

Hunt, Enoch. Plus 1 f./4 svts.:
"Mr."; Port Roseway Associate (6:
15).

Hunt, Ephraim. B. Martha's Vineyard,
Mass., 5 Oct. 1751; s. of Samuel/
Lois; to Liverpool May 1762 (47:
126:99).

Hunt, Ephraim. S. of Samuel/Lois; to
(or b.?) Liverpool by 1785 (47:
127:53).

Hunt, Frederic. Loyalist; plus 1 f./4
ch.; mustered at Digby 19 May 1784
(39:122).

Hunt, Lois. B. Martha's Vineyard,
Mass., 5 Oct. 1751; dau. of Sa-
muel/Lois; to Liverpool May 1762
(47:126:99).

Hunt, Lois. Wife of Samuel; Martha's
Vineyard, Mass., to Liverpool ca.
1760 (47:126:98).

Hunt, Martin. S. of Nicholas/Cather-
ine (Carbery) of Mothell, Co.
Waterford, Ireland; marr. Halifax
30 Jan. 1808 Elener Downey widow
of John Mort (30:106).

Hunt, Mary. Dau. of John/Eleanor
(Flinn) of Co. Waterford, Ireland;
marr. Halifax 21 Apr. 1822 Robert
Ast (q.v.) (31:40).

Hunt, Oliver. B. Martha's Vineyard,
Mass., 6 Feb. 1749/50; s. of

Samuel/Lois; to Liverpool May 1762
(47:126:98).

Hunt, Patrick. S. of Nicholas/Cather-
ine (Carbery) of Mothell, Co. Waterford, Ireland; marr. Halifax 21
July 1803 Mary Power (q.v.) (30:
106).

Hunt, Samuel Jr. B. Martha's Vineyard, Mass., 5 Oct. 1751; s. of
Samuel/Lois; to Liverpool May 1762
(47:126:99).

Hunt, Samuel. Liverpool proprietor
(19:101).

Hunt, Samuel. Liverpool proprietor
(19:102).

Hunt, Samuel. Martha's Vineyard,
Mass., to Liverpool ca. 1760 (47:
126:98).

Hunt, Theodis. Loyalist; plus 1 f.;
mustered at Digby 19 May 1784 (39:
122).

Hunt, Thomas. Loyalist; mustered at
Digby 19 May 1784 (39:122).

Hunt, William. B. Martha's Vineyard,
Mass., 29 Nov. 1748; s. of Samuel/
Lois; to Liverpool May 1762 (47:
126:98).

Hunter, David. From Ireland; land
grant at Londonderry 6 Mar. 1775
(4:258).

Hunter, George. 40, farmer; Hull to
Fort Cumberland on ALBION 7-14
March 1774 (21:138).

Hunter, Robert. From N.H.; effective
land grant at Truro 31 Oct. 1765
(4:245).

Huppert, Leonard. S. of Henry/Judith
(Nibbits) of Lower Germany; marr.
Halifax 23 June 1825 Mary Anne
Williams (q.v.) (31:47).

Hurdy, Jane. 16, servant; Hull,
Yorkshire, to Fort Cumberland on
JENNY 3-10 April 1775 (22:123).

Hurley, Eleanor. See McSweeny,
Eleanor.

Hurley, Patrick. S. of Thomas/Mary (Tynan) of Co. Kilkenny, Ireland; marr. Halifax 14 Apr. 1839 Anne Kline (34:132).

Hurly, Joanna. Dau. of John/Dorothy (Donovan) of Co. Cork, Ireland; marr. Halifax 20 Aug. 1829 David Connelly (q.v.) (32:107).

Hurly, John. S. of Denis/Margaret (Cronan) of Ballingarry, Co. Cork, Ireland; marr. Halifax 24 May 1838 Ellen Donovan (q.v.) (34:131).

Huskin, Seth. S. of John/Ann; to Liverpool by 1801 (47:128:29).

Huson, Catherine. See Wallace, Catherine.

Huson, George. Widower of Elizabeth Drew of Co. Limerick, Ireland; marr. Halifax 16 July 1837 Catherine Wallace (q.v.) (34:132).

Hussy, Garrett. Of Co. Cork, Ireland; widower of Ann Handrick; marr. Halifax 4 Mar. 1842 Bridget Flood (q.v.) (35:139).

Hutchinson, Thomas. Grantee 'Digby New Grant' 29 Jan. 1801 (5:82).

Hutchinson, Thos. Arr. Annapolis from New York 19 Oct. 1782 (37:125).

Hutton, Harriet. Dau. of Robert/Bridget (McGrath) of St. John's, Nfdld.; marr. Halifax 27 Oct. 1836 Patrick Foley (q.v.) (34:130).

Hutton, James. 15; apprentice; Hull, Yorkshire, to Halifax; on JENNY 3-10 April 1775 (22:124).

Hyde, John. S. of John/Mary (Kean) of Co. Cork, Ireland; marr. Halifax 9 Jan. 1833 Ellen Franey (q.v.) (33:60).

Hyde, John. S. of Robert/Mary (O'Brien) of Co. Waterford, Ireland; marr. Halifax 16 July 1828 Eleanor McSweeny (q.v.) (32:113).

Hynes, Edmund. S. of Cornelius/Ann (Burns) of Co. Kilkenny, Ireland;
marr. Halifax 2 Sep. 1834 Margaret Griffin (q.v.) (33:60).

Hynes, Edward. S. of Edward/Sarah (Rice) of Kilkenny, Ireland; marr. Halifax 26 Nov. 1840 Eliza Campion (34:132).

Hynes, John. S. of Andrew/Mary (Cumerford) of Co. Kilkenny, Ireland; marr. Halifax 16 June 1842 Bridget Shea (q.v.) (35:139).

Hynes, Mary. Dau. of Kieran/Catherine (Kenedy) of Parish Eustace, Co. Kilkenny, Ireland; marr. Halifax 24 Oct. 1838 Michael Scallion (q.v.) (34:138).

- I -

Inglis, Anne. Dau. of Rt.Rev. Charles; b. 1776 at New York; d. 4 July 1827 at Halifax ae 51st (3:194).

Inglis, Catherine. Dau. of John/Margaret (Kenedy) of Co. Kilkenny, Ireland; marr. Halifax 27 Apr. 1820 Garrett Moore (q.v.) (31:50).

Inglis, Charles. Rt.Rev.; s. of Rev. Archibald; b. 1734 at Ireland; to Lancaster, Pa., ca. 1756; to New York Dec. 1765; to England; to Halifax Oct. 1787 (3:183).

Inglis, John. Rt.Rev.; s. of Rt.Rev. Charles; b. 1777 New York; ordained at Aylesford 1801 (3: 195).

Inglis, Margaret. Dau. of Rt.Rev. Charles; b. 1775 New York; to N.S. (3:191).

Inloes, Aquila. S. of William/Aberilla; Baltimore, Md., to Liverpool by 1790 (47:127:120).

Inright, Denis. S. of Thomas/Bridget (McNamar) of Co. Limerick, Ireland; marr. Halifax 13 July 1818 Anne Morgan (q.v.) (31:47).

Irvin, Mary. Dau. of William/Mary of England; marr. Halifax 19 Aug.

1837 James Magrath (q.v.) (34: 134).

Irvin, Mary. Dau. of Joseph/Ann (Johnston) of Co. Tyrone, Ireland; marr. Halifax 22 Nov. 1844 William Cooney (35:136).

Irwin, James. Loyalist; plus 1 f./1 svt.; mustered at Digby 19 May 1784 (39:122).

Irwin, Thomas. Pvt. 74th Regt.; s. of Samuel/Anne (Hunter) of Legataele, Tyrone, Ireland; marr. Halifax 17 June 1827 Mary Power (q.v.) (32: 113).

Isaacs, Samel. Plus 4 ch. 8+: arr. Annapolis from New York 19 Oct. 1782 (37:125).

Israel, Irad. Loyalist; plus 1 f.; mustered at Digby 19 May 1784 (39:122).

Ivory, John. S. of Nicholas/Ellen (Cullerton) of Co. Kilkenny, Ireland; marr. Halifax 13 Apr. 1820 Eleanora Ryan (q.v.) (31:48).

- J -

Jack, Samuel. Shoemaker; b. Ireland ca. 1780; Belfast or Greenock to Halifax on POLLY, spring 1799 (29: 83).

Jackman, Anne. See Murphy, Anne.

Jackman, Anne. See Whelan, Anne.

Jackson, John. Loyalist; mustered at Digby 19 May 1784 (39:123).

Jackson, William. Merchant; Port Roseway Associate (6:15).

Jackson, William. To (or b.?) Liverpool by 1791 (47:127:117).

Jacques, Elenor. 28, wife of Joseph; Hull to Fort Cumberland on ALBION 7-14 March 1774 (21:139).

Jacques, Joseph. 28, farmer; Hull to Fort Cumberland on ALBION 7-14

March 1774 (21:139).

Jakways?, John. See John Takways.

James, Thomas. S. of Thomas/Mary Ann (George) of Milford, Wales; marr. Halifax 24 May 1842 Anne McDonald (q.v.) (35:139).

Janes, Anne. Dau. of Daniel/Catherine (Smart) of Liverpool, England, marr. Halifax 5 Sep. 1827 William Sheehan (q.v.) (32:118).

Jaroleman, Jacob. Loyalist; plus 1 f./4 ch./1 svt.; mustered at Digby 19 May 1784 (39:123).

Jarvis, Ichabod. Loyalist; plus 1 f./2 ch.; mustered at Digby 19 May 1784 (39:123).

Jeanes, Jenkinson. Plus 1 f./4 ch./1 svt; Port Roseway Associate (6: 15).

Jeffery, Thomas Nickleson. Esq.; eldest s. of John Jeffery Esq. of Sans Souci, M.P. for Poole, Dorset, England; d. Halifax 21 Oct. 1847 ae 65th (13:76).

Jefferys, John. From N.H.; effective land grant at Truro 31 Oct. 1765 (4:244).

Jenkins, David. Loyalist; mustered at Digby 19 May 1784 (39:123).

Jenkins, Griffiths. Loyalist; plus 1 f./5 ch.; mustered at Digby 19 May 1784 (39:122).

Jenkins, John. Arr. Annapolis from New York 19 Oct. 1782 (37:125).

Jenkins, Richard. S. of Richard/Eliza (Connors) of Co. Tipperary, Ireland; marr. Halifax 9 Dec. 1835 Eliza McKean (q.v.) (34:132).

Jenkins, William. Plus 2 f./4 ch. 8+; arr. Annapolis from New York 19 Oct. 1782 (37:125).

Jenks, David. R.I. to N.S.; to U.S. 1776; lived 1785 at Thomaston, Me. (36:65).

Jennings, Mary. Dau. of James/Catherine (Monaghan) of Co. Galway, Ireland; marr. Halifax 3 June 1813 Bernard Brennan (q.v.) (30:102).

Jennison, Samuel. Plus wife/1 ch.; Littleton, Mass., to Chester with first settlers (16:45).

Jennison, William. New England to Annapolis 1760 (18:271).

Jiggets, Joseph. Loyalist; mustered at Digby 19 May 1784 (39:123).

Job, Jemima. Wife or widow; to (or b.?) Liverpool by 1784 (47:127: 51).

John, Peter. Grantee "Digby New Grant" 29 Jan. 1801 (5:82).

John, Peter. Loyalist; plus 1 f./4 ch.; mustered at Gulliver's Hole/ St. Mary's Bay/Sissiboo 1/6 June 1784; settled at Sissiboo (now Weymouth) (40:262).

Johnson, -----. Widow; plus 2 ch. 8+/1 ch. -8; arr. Annapolis from New York 19 Oct. 1782 (37:125).

Johnson, Adam Jr. From N.H.; effective land grant at Truro 31 Oct. 1765 (4:244).

Johnson, Adam. From N.H.; effective land grant at Truro 31 Oct. 1765 (4:244).

Johnson, Emanuel. 16; Hull, Yorkshire, to Halifax; on JENNY 3-10 April 1775 (22:124).

Johnson, George. 26; servant/carpenter; Hull, Yorkshire, to Halifax; on JENNY 3-10 April 1775 (22:124).

Johnson, George. Plus 1 f.; arr. Annapolis from New York 19 Oct. 1782 (37:125).

Johnson, Henry. Loyalist; mustered at Digby 19 May 1784 (39:122).

Johnson, Henry. Plus 1 f.; arr. Annapolis from New York 19 Oct. 1782 (37:126).

Johnson, James Jr. From N.H.; effec-

tive land grant at Truro 31 Oct. 1765 (4:244).

Johnson, James. Arr. Annapolis from New York 19 Oct. 1782 (37:125).

Johnson, James. From N.H.; effective land grant at Truro 31 Oct. 1765 (4:244).

Johnson, John Jr. From N.H.; effective land grant at Truro 31 Oct. 1765 (4:244).

Johnson, John. 27, tanner; Hull to Fort Cumberland on ALBION 7-14 March 1774 (21:138).

Johnson, John. From N.H.; effective land grant at Truro 31 Oct. 1765 (4:244).

Johnson, Joseph. 14; Hull, Yorkshire, to Halifax; on JENNY 3-10 April 1775 (22:124).

Johnson, Joseph. Loyalist; plus 1 f./1 ch.; 19 May 1784 (39:123).

Johnson, Lawrence. Loyalist; plus 1 f./5 ch.; mustered at Digby 19 May 1784 (39:122).

Johnson, Margaret. 48; Hull, Yorkshire, to Halifax; on JENNY 3-10 April 1775 (22:124).

Johnson, Martha. Wife of John; Hull to Fort Cumberland on ALBION 7-14 March 1774 (21:138).

Johnson, Martin. Grantee "Digby New Grant" 29 Jan. 1801 (5:82).

Johnson, Martin. Loyalist; plus 1 f./4 ch.; mustered at Digby 19 May 1784 (39:122).

Johnson, Martin. Plus 1 f./4 ch, 8+/1 ch. -8; arr. Annapolis from New York 19 Oct. 1782 (37:126).

Johnson, Sarah. See Elward, Philip; see Callanan, Nicholas.

Johnson, William. 1, s. of John; Hull to Fort Cumberland on ALBION 7-14 March 1774 (21:138).

Johnson, William. 28; gentleman; Hull, Yorkshire, to Fort Cumberland on JENNY 3-10 April 1775 (22: 123).

Johnson, William. 23; s. of William; Hull, Yorkshire, to Halifax; on JENNY 3-10 April 1775 (22:124).

Johnson, William. 49; farmer; Hull, Yorkshire, to Halifax; on JENNY 3-10 April 1775 (22:124).

Johnson, William. Loyalist; plus 2 f./1 ch.; mustered at Gulliver's Hole/St. Mary's Bay/Sissiboo 1/6 June 1784; settled at St. Mary's Bay (Plympton, Barton, Brighton) (40:262).

Johnson, William. Plus 2 f./1 ch. 8+; arr. Annapolis from New York 19 Oct. 1782 (37:125).

Johnston, Anne. Dau. of Loyd/Catherine (Golden) of Co. Mayo, Ireland; marr. Halifax 27 Nov. 1833 Lawrence Whelan (q.v.) (33:69).

Johnston, Bridget. See Creaven, Bridget.

Johnston, George. Loyalist; plus 1 f./1 ch.; mustered at Digby 19 May 1784 (39:122).

Johnston, George. Mariner; S. of John/Sarah (Bullen) of Cornwall, England; marr. Halifax 21 Feb. 1838 Bridger Creavan (q.v.) (34:132).

Johnston, James Wm. B. Kingston, Jamaica; Scotland to N.S. before 1815; to France 1872; d. 21 Nov. 1873 at Cheltenham, Eng., ae 81 (9:131).

Johnston, John. Plus 3 svts.; grocer; Port Roseway Associate (6:15).

Johnston, Joseph. Disbanded soldier, N.Y. Vols.; mustered at Digby 19 May 1784 (39:123).

Johnston, William. Grantee 'Digby New Grant' 29 Jan. 1801 (5:82).

Johnston, William. Plus 1 f./2 ch.; mariner; Port Roseway Associate (6:15).

Johnston, William. S. of William/ Margarett; Aberdeensh., Scotland, to Liverpool by 1817 (47:128:36).

Johnstone, Nicholas. Loyalist; plus 1 f./3 ch.; mustered at Digby 19 May 1784 (39:123).

Johnstone, William. Esq.; b. North Britain ca. 1720; d. Liverpool 1800 (47:127:52).

Joice, Catherine. Dau. of Maurice/Ann (Herrolan) of Co. Kerry, Ireland; marr. Halifax 30 Sep. 1831 Patrick Farrell (q.v.) (33:57).

Joice, Ellen. Dau. of Bartholomew/ Ellen (Brian) of Kilworth, Co. Cork, Ireland; marr. Halifax 19 Nov. 1844 Patrick Hibbet (q.v.) (35:138).

Joice, Francis. S. of Thomas/Winefred (Hanly) of Tuam, Galway, Ireland; marr. Halifax 27 June 1842 Margaret Pedan (q.v.) (35:139).

Jones, -----. Widow; Loyalist; plus 1 m./2 ch./2 svts.; mustered at Gulliver's Hole/St. Mary's Bay/ Sissiboo 1/6 June 1784; settled at Sissiboo (now Weymouth) (40:262).

Jones, Ann. Dau. of Patrick/Catherine (Kelly) of Co. Kilkenny, Ireland; marr. Halifax 21 July 1838 James Daniell (q.v.) (34:128).

Jones, Benjamin. Grantee 'Digby New Grant' 29 Jan. 1801 (5:82).

Jones, Benjamin. Loyalist; plus 1 f./3 ch.; mustered at Digby 19 May 1784 (39:122).

Jones, Catherine. Dau. of Patrick/ Catherine (Kelly) of Co. Kilkenny, Ireland; marr. Halifax 17 Apr. 1842 Thomas Doran (q.v.) (35:137).

Jones, Cereno Upham. Grantee 'Digby New Grant' 29 Jan. 1801 (5:82).

Jones, Elijah. Disbanded soldier, N.Y. Vols.; mustered at Digby 19

May 1784 (39:123).

Jones, Elisha. Disbanded soldier, N.Y. Vols.; plus 1 f./1 ch.; mustered at Digby 19 May 1784; returned to Mass., leaving s. in N.S. (39:123).

Jones, Elisha. Plus 1 f./6 ch. 8+/1 ch. -8; arr. Annapolis from New York 19 Oct. 1782 (37:126).

Jones, Elizabeth. Dau. of James/ Susanna; to (or b.?) Liverpool by 1784 (47:126:284).

Jones, Elizabeth. Loyalist; mustered at Digby 19 May 1784 (39:123).

Jones, George T. S. of J. William/ Ellen (Kent) of Mallow, Co. Cork, Ireland; marr. Halifax 8 June 1834 Joanna Stapleton (q.v.) (33:60).

Jones, Hannah. Dau. of William/Anne (Joint) of Westport, Co. Mayo, Ireland; marr. Halifax 30 June 1840 Michael McDuff (q.v.) (34:133).

Jones, Jacob. S. of James/Susanah; to Liverpool by 1772 (47:126:290).

Jones, James. Grantee "Digby New Grant" 29 Jan. 1801 (5:82).

Jones, James. Loyalist; plus 1 f./1 svt.; mustered at Digby 19 May 1784 (39:123).

Jones, John. Arr. Annapolis from New York 19 Oct. 1782 (37:125).

Jones, John. Loyalist; plus 1 f.; mustered at Digby 19 May 1784 (39:123).

Jones, John. S. of Christopher/Mary (Martin) of Co. Mayo, Ireland; marr. Halifax 16 June 1830 Ann Archibald (q.v.) (32:113).

Jones, Josiah. Grantee "Digby New Grant" 29 Jan. 1801 (5:82).

Jones, Josiah. Loyalist; plus 1 f./4 ch.; mustered at Gulliver's Hole/ St. Mary's Bay/Sissiboo 1/6 June 1784; settled at Sissiboo (now

Weymouth) (40:262).

Jones, Josiah. Loyalist; from New Hampshire; petitioner at Digby 20 Feb. 1784 (41:18).

Jones, Josiah. Plus 1 f./1 ch. 8+/2 ch. -8; arr. Annapolis from New York 19 Oct. 1782 (37:126).

Jones, Mary. Dau. of Patrick/Catherine (Kelly) of Co. Kilkenny, Ireland; marr. Halifax 2 May 1830 Thomas Smith (q.v.) (32:118).

Jones, Mary. Loyalist; mustered at Digby 19 May 1784 (39:122).

Jones, Mehitabel. Dau. of Jacob/ Rebekah; to Liverpool by 1799 (47:127:267).

Jones, Nathaniel. Grantee "Digby New Grant" 29 Jan. 1801 (5:82).

Jones, Nathaniel. Loyalist; mustered at Digby 19 May 1784 (39:123).

Jones, S. Cornet; disbanded officer, King's American Regt.; plus 1 svt.; mustered at Gulliver's Hole/ St. Mary's Bay/Sissiboo 1/6 June 1784; settled at Sissiboo (now Weymouth) (40:262).

Jones, Simeon. Grantee "Digby New Grant" 29 Jan. 1801 (5:82).

Jones, Stephen 2nd. Grantee "Digby New Grant" 29 Jan. 1801 (5:82).

Jones, Stephen. Esq.; grantee "Digby New Grant" 29 Jan. 1801 (5:82).

Jones, Stephen. Loyalist; mustered at Digby 19 May 1784 (39:123).

Jones, Susanna. Dau. of James/Susana; to Liverpool by 1773 (47:127:277).

Jones, William. Shoemaker; s. of John/Ellen (Kent) of Mallow, Co. Cork, Ireland; marr. Halifax (R.C.) 2 Apr. 1839 Catherine Jordan (34:132).

Jones, William. Shoemaker; s. of John/Ellen (Kent) of Mallow, Co. Cork, Ireland; marr. Halifax (C.of E.) 29 Mar. 1835 Catherine Jordan

(34:132).

Jordan, Martin. S. of Hugh/Mary (Mullony) of Co. Wexford, Ireland; marr. Halifax 8 Jan. 1844 Jane Black (35:139).

Jordan, Mary. Dau. of Patrick/Mary (Doyle) of Co. Wexford, Ireland; marr. Halifax 23 Jan. 1835 James Boland (q.v.) (34:126).

Jornea, William. Loyalist; mustered at Digby 19 May 1784 (39:123).

Joynt, Christopher. S. of Robert/ Hannah (Ferris) of Westport, Co. Mayo, Ireland; marr. Halifax 24 May 1841 Catherine Ferguson (q.v.) (35:139).

Judd, James. S. of Samuel/Mary (Coffee) of Co. Wicklow, Ireland; marr. Halifax 19 Oct. 1834 Margaret Wall (q.v.) (34:132).

Justicon, Isaac. Loyalist; mustered at Digby 19 May 1784 (39:123).

- K -

Kalin, Thomas. 24; servant; Hull, Yorkshire, to Halifax; on JENNY 3-10 April 1775 (22:124).

Kamlen, Eleaser. Plus wife/3 ch.; Pembroke, Mass., to Chester with first settlers (16:45).

Kane, George. Arr. Annapolis from New York 19 Oct. 1782 (37:126).

Kanna, John. S. of John/Margaret (Brown) of Co. Cork, Ireland; marr. Halifax 31 Oct. 1833 Mary Mulcahy (q.v.) (33:60).

Karigan, Honora. Dau. of Denis/Honora (McCarthy) of Co. Cork, Ireland; marr. Halifax 6 May 1841 Thomas Nevill (q.v.) (35:14%).

Karney, Catherine. Dau. of Patrick/ Catherine (Power) of Parish Bally-han, Co. Waterford, Ireland; marr. Halifax 5 Nov. 1833 Thomas Hanni-

gan (q.v.) (33:59).

Karney, James. S. of Patrick/Catherine (McDonnell) of Co. Cavan, Ireland; marr. Halifax 15 July 1836 Mary Saunders (q.v.) (34:132).

Karney, Margaret. Dau. of John/Judith (Landy) of Co. Tipperary, Ireland; marr. Halifax 18 Feb. 1833 Timothy Haley (q.v.) (33:59).

Karney, Margaret. See Sullivan, Margaret.

Karney, Simon. S. of James/Anne (Roache) of Co. Carlow, Ireland; marr. Halifax 23 Oct. 1834 Elizabeth Buckley (q.v.) (34:132).

Karr, Archibald. From Ireland; land grant at Londonderry 6 Mar. 1775 (4:258).

Kavanagh, Bridget. Dau. of Jeremiah/ Judith (Karney) of Co. Leix, Ireland; marr. Halifax 24 May 1833 William Buckley (q.v.) (33:54).

Kavanagh, Edward. S. of Morgan/Margaret (Dulhanty) of Co. Kilkenny, Ireland; widower of Mary Carey; marr. Halifax 10 May 1841 Margaret Walsh (q.v.) (35:139).

Kavanagh, James. S. of Patrick/Mary of Drumcliff, Co. Sligo, Ireland; marr. Halifax 14 Jan. 1826 Marrion Lidbetter (32:113).

Kavanagh, Margaret. Dau. of John/ Anastasia (Rochford) of Co. Wexford, Ireland; widow of Stephen Clarke; marr. Halifax 6 May 1830 Patrick Corbet (sic) (q.v.) (32:107).

Kavanagh, Patrick. Deserted 14 Apr. 1805 from H.M. Corps of Royal Military Artificers, stationed at Halifax; 5'8", fair complexion, brown hair, blue eyes, is a sawyer, 28, b. Parish of Ballyan, Co. Wexford, Ireland; advertised The Weekly Chronicle, 20 Apr. 1805

(28:35).

Kavanah, Edmund. S. of Morgan/Margaret (Dulhanty) of Co. Kilkenny, Ireland; marr. Halifax 10 Oct. 1831 Mary Carey (q.v.) (33:60).

Kavanah, Elizabeth. Dau. of Denis/ Mary of Co. Carlow, Ireland; marr. Halifax 12 Oct. 1828 Bernard Nolan (q.v.) (32:116).

Kavanah, Michael. S. of Joseph/Mary (Dowling) of Graiguenamanagh, Kilkenny, Ireland; marr. Halifax 10 Nov. 1802 Sarah Foster (q.v.) (30:106).

Kay, Ann. 9, daughter of Bryan; Hull to Fort Cumberland on ALBION 7-14 March 1774 (21:134).

Kay, Brian. 20, husbandman; Hull to Fort Cumberland on ALBION 7-14 March 1774 (21:137).

Kay, Bryan. 28, farmer; Hull to Fort Cumberland on ALBION 7-14 March 1774 (21:134).

Kay, Dorothy. 42, wife of Bryan; Hull to Fort Cumberland on ALBION 7-14 March 1774 (21:134).

Kay, Elizabeth. 16, daughter of Bryan; Hull to Fort Cumberland on ALBION 7-14 March 1774 (21:134).

Kay, Hannah. 14, daughter of Bryan; Hull to Fort Cumberland on ALBION 7-14 March 1774 (21:134).

Kay, Jane. 7, daughter of Bryan; Hull to Fort Cumberland on ALBION 7-14 March 1774 (21:134).

Kay, Robert. 42, brother of Bryan; Hull to Fort Cumberland on ALBION 7-14 March 1774 (21:134).

Kay, Sarah. 12, daughter of Bryan; Hull to Fort Cumberland on ALBION 7-14 March 1774 (21:134).

Kay, William. 20, sailor; Hull to Fort Cumberland on ALBION 7-14 March 1774 (21:135).

Kealy, Mary. Dau. of James/Ann

(Doran) of Co. Carlow, Ireland; marr. Halifax 13 Oct. 1829 John Mackesy (q.v.) (32:115).

Kean, Bridget. Dau. of Declan/Elizabeth (McCarthy) of Co. Waterford, Ireland; marr. Halifax 5 Sep. 1840 Matthew Fahy (q.v.) (34:129).

Kean, John. S. of Thomas/Mary (Graham) of Co. Tipperary, Ireland; marr. Halifax 29 Apr. 1835 Ellen Weston (q.v.) (34:132).

Kean, Mary. See Skerry, Mary.

Kean, Michael. S. of John/Mary (Farrell) of Youghal, Co. Cork, Ireland; marr. Halifax 26 Nov. 1829 Ellen Sullivan (q.v.) (32:113).

Kean, Roger. S. of Roger/Mary (Conway) of Co. Waterford, Ireland; marr. Halifax 23 July 1832 Mary Laughlin (q.v.) (33:60).

Keane, Cornelius. S. of Alexander/ Margaret (Nugent) of Co. Waterford, Ireland; marr. Halifax 17 Sep. 1841 Mary Walsh (35:139).

Keane, Mary. Dau. of Thomas of Co. Antrim, Ireland; marr. Halifax 16 June 1836 William Murphy (q.v.) (34:136).

Kearney, Elizabeth. See Buckley, Elizabeth.

Kearney, Rose. Dau. of Patrick/ Catherine (Flinn) of Co. Waterford, Ireland; marr. Halifax 19 Feb. 1833 Thomas Bowes (q.v.) (33:54).

Kearney, Thomas. S. of John/Catherine (Barry) of Co. Kilkenny, Ireland; marr. Halifax 16 Oct. 1832 Elizabeth Lewis (q.v.) (33:60).

Kearns, Catherine. Dau. of Thomas/ Mary (Toskin) of Waterford City, Ireland; marr. Halifax 14 Feb. 1830 Patrick Tobin (q.v.) (32:119).

Keating, Bridget. Dau. of Michael/

Mary (Power) of Borris, Co. Carlow, Ireland; marr. Halifax 2 Apr.
1845 Thomas Donovan *(q.v.)*
(35:137).

Keating, Edward. S. of Thomas/Julia
(Heffernan) of Co. Tipperary,
Ireland; marr. Halifax 14 Jan.
1820 Ellen Doyle (31:48).

Keating, Elizabeth Alice. See Butler,
Elizabeth Alice.

Keating, James. See Caton, James.

Keating, John. S. of Maurice/Mary
(Dealy) of Kilnehyan, Co. West-
meath, Ireland; marr. Halifax 10
Sep. 1825 Miriam Duggan (31:48).

Keating, Mary. Dau. of Richard/Marga-
ret (Hartnett) of Rathkeale, Co.
Limerick, Ireland; marr. Halifax
30 Apr. 1823 John Donohoe *(q.v.)*
(31:44).

Keating, Mary. Spinster; Irish; 20;
Liverpool to Nova Scotia May 1864
on EUROCLYDON (45:181).

Keating, Maurice. S. of Maurice/Mary
(Dealy) of Kilnbeggin, Co. Meath,
Ireland; marr. Halifax 21 Apr.
1829 Anne Thomas (32:113).

Keating, Patrick. S. of Thomas/Mary
(Walsh) of Co. Wexford; marr.
Halifax 18 Oct. 1810 Alice Eliza-
beth Butler *(q.v.)* (30:106).

Keating, Sylvester. S. of Michael/
Mary (Power) of Co. Carlow, Ireland; marr. Halifax (R.C.) 6 June
1834 (also marr. Parish of St.
Paul's, Halifax (C.of E.) 11 Oct.
1833) Margaret MacAnelly *(q.v.)*
(33:60).

Keating, William. S. of Michael/Mary
(Power) of Co. Carlow, Ireland;
marr. Halifax 21 Oct. 1834 Mary
Briscoe *(q.v.)* (34:132).

Keating, William. S. of Patrick/
Bridget (Brophy) of Co. Carlow,
Ireland; marr. Halifax 8 Jan. 1833

Mary Barry *(q.v.)* (33:60).

Keefe, Anastasia. Dau. of John/Marga-
ret (Murphy) of Co. Kilkenny,
Ireland; marr. Halifax 6 June 1836
Martin Dwyer *(q.v.)* (34:129).

Keefe, Ellen. Dau. of Thomas/Mary
(Scannel) of Castlelyons, Co.
Cork, Ireland; marr. Halifax 2
June 1813 James Stack *(q.v.)* (30:
111).

Keefe, James. S. of Thomas/Mary
(Carthy) of Co. Waterford, Ire-
land; marr. Halifax 1 Aug. 1832
Joanna Keefe *(q.v.)* (33:60).

Keefe, Joanna. Dau. of Denis/Mary
(Kiley) of Co. Waterford, Ireland;
marr. Halifax 1 Aug. 1832 James
Keefe *(q.v.)* (33:60).

Keefe, Mary. Dau. of James/Marcella
(Ryan) of Co. Kilkenny, Ireland;
marr. Halifax 2 Nov. 1830 John
Walsh *(q.v.)* (32:120).

Keefe, Richard. S. of John/Abigail
(Ronan) of Ballyspillane, Co.
Cork, Ireland; marr. Halifax 27
Oct. 1829 Mary Sullivan *(q.v.)*
(32:113).

Keefe, Richard. S. of John/Abigail
(Ronan) of Ballyspillane, Co.
Cork, Ireland; widower of Mary
Sullivan; marr. Halifax 19 Feb.
1844 Ellen Byrnes *(q.v.)* (35:139).

Keefe, Timothy. S. of John/Margaret
(Linehan) of Co. Cork, Ireland;
marr. Halifax 17 Oct. 1832 Judith
Foley *(q.v.)* (33:60).

Keefe. Mary. Dau. of Martin/Mary
(Aheran) of Fermoy, Co. Cork,
Ireland; marr. Halifax 12 Sep.
1832 John Conner *(q.v.)* (33:55).

Keeffe, Edmund. S. of John/Abigail
(Ronan) of Midleton, Co. Cork,
Ireland; marr. Halifax 15 May 1833
Abigail Linehan *(q.v.)* (33:60).

Keeffe, Edward. S. of John/Margaret

{Corcoran} of Co. Cork, Ireland; marr. Halifax 16 Apr. 1831 Sarah Coborn (33:60).

Keeffe, Edward. S. of Michael/Ellen (O'Neal) of Co. Kilkenny, Ireland; marr. Halifax 18 May 1834 Mary Flinn (q.v.) (33:60).

Keeffe, Mary. Dau. of Thomas/Mary (Poissy) of Co. Waterford, Ireland; marr. Halifax 3 Oct. 1841 Thomas Morris (q.v.) (35:141).

Keegan, Thomas Jr. Dr. s. of Patrick/Bridget of Kilmallock, Limerick, Ireland; marr. Halifax 24 Sep. 1810 Mary Anne Bennett (q.v.) (30:106).

Keeling, Bithiah. Widow; dau. of Israel Cheever; to (or b.?) Liverpool by 1784 (47:126:281).

Keen. See Kein.

Keene, Jesse. Grantee "Digby New Grant" 29 Jan. 1801 (5:82).

Kehan, James. S. of Richard/Anne (Marshall) of Co. Derry, Ireland; marr. Halifax 18 Oct. 1840 Rosanna Johnston (34:132).

Kehoe, Bridget. Dau. of John/Bridget (Keating) of Tintern, Co. Wexford, Ireland; marr. Halifax 9 May 1822 John Ast (q.v.) (31:40).

Kehoe, James. Of Co. Tipperary, Ireland; widower of Mary Condon; marr. Halifax 26 Apr. 1843 Elizabeth McDonald (35:139).

Kehoe, Sally. Dau. of Denis/Patricia (Ruban) of Cape Breton Isl.; marr. Halifax 21 May 1820 Mathew McKabyley (q.v.) (31:48).

Kehoe, William. S. of John/Catherine (Blanchfield) of Co. Carlow, Ireland; marr. Halifax 22 Nov. 1838 Mary Cary (q.v.) (34:132).

Keily, John. S. of Cornelius/Johanna (Mulcahy) of Ballynahan, Waterford, Ireland; marr. Halifax 12

Jan. 1826 Johana Heffernan (q.v.) (32:113).

Kein, Jesse. Loyalist; plus 1 f.; mustered at Digby 19 May 1784 (39:123).

Keliher, Maurice. Widower of Mary Hogan; of Killarney, Co. Kerry, Ireland; marr. Halifax 12 Apr. 1834 Ann Farrell (q.v.) (33:60).

Kelley, Matthew. Loyalist; plus 1 f.; mustered at Digby 19 May 1784 (39:123).

Kellhew, Amasa. Capt.; R.I. to N.S.; to U.S. 1776; dead by 1785 (36:65).

Kellhew, John. R.I. to N.S.; to U.S. 1776; dead by 1785 (36:65).

Kelly, Catherine. Dau. of James/Margaret (Wilson) of Derry, Ireland; marr. Halifax 6 Nov. 1804 James Noonan (q.v.) (30:109).

Kelly, Denis. S. of Daniel/Mary (Connors) of Innishannon, Co. Cork, Ireland; marr. Halifax 8 Sep. 1841 Mary Smith (35:139).

Kelly, Edward. S. of Thomas/Bridget (Doherty) of Parish Kilafree, Co. Sligo, Ireland; marr. Halifax 15 Apr. 1822 Margaret Dillon (q.v.) (31:48).

Kelly, Edward. S. of Edward/Eliza (Rylands) of Clonmel, Tipperary, Ireland; marr. Halifax 5 Aug. 1826 Bridget Laffin (32:113).

Kelly, Edward. S. of William/Ann (Connell) of Lismore, Co. Waterford, Ireland; marr. Halifax 4 Feb. 1845 Margaret MacNaughton (35:140).

Kelly, Eleanor. Dau. of Michael/Margaret (Walsh) of Waterford, Ireland; marr. Halifax 31 May 1829 John Fitzgerald (q.v.) (32:110).

Kelly, Elener. See Burke, Elener.

Kelly, Elenor. See Burke, Elenor.

Kelly, Eliza. Dau. of Owen/Ann
(Quinn) of Co. Sligo, Ireland;
marr. Halifax 18 May 1833 John
McDonagh (q.v.) (33:62).

Kelly, Elizabeth. Dau. of Thomas/Mary
(Kean) of Co. Longford, Ireland;
marr. Halifax 19 June 1829 James
Hanigan (q.v.) (32:112).

Kelly, Elizabeth. Dau. of James/Mary
(Walsh) of Burin, Nfld.; widow of
----- Lanigan; marr. Halifax 20
June 1836 William Connors (q.v.)
(34:128).

Kelly, James. S. of Richard/Mary Anne
(Doyle) of Co. Wexford, Ireland;
marr. Halifax 10 Aug. 1814 Ann
MacFarlane (q.v.) (30:106).

Kelly, James. S. of Peter/Julia
(Trainer) of Co. Kildare, Ireland;
marr. Halifax 2 Oct. 1829 Catherine Dullehanty (q.v.) (32:113).

Kelly, James. S. of Edward/Catherine
(White) of Co. Kilkenny, Ireland;
marr. Halifax 18 Feb. 1833 Joanna
DeYoung (33:60).

Kelly, James. S. of David/Eleanor
(McCarthy) of Co. Wexford, Ire-
land; marr. Halifax 1 Oct. 1831
Bridget Molony (q.v.) (33:60).

Kelly, John. Deserted 28 Feb. 1806
from Royal Newfoundland Regiment,
stationed at Annapolis; 5'4",
black complexion, black hair, grey
eyes, 27, b. Ireland; advertised
The Weekly Chronicle, 15 Mar. 1806
(28:34).

Kelly, John. Liverpool to Nova Scotia
April 1864 on KEDAR (45:181).

Kelly, John. S. of James/Anne (Stephens) of Dunmore, Co. Galway,
Ireland; marr. Halifax 28 Oct.
1821 Margaret Anne Reilly (31:48).

Kelly, John. S. of Patrick/Catherine
(Boggs) of Limerick City, Ireland;
marr. Halifax 14 May 1823 Cather-

ine Dunphy widow of Michael Mac-
Donald (31:48).

Kelly, Joseph. S. of Patrick/Cather-
ine (Walsh) of Parish St. Mary,
New Ross, Co. Wexford, Ireland;
marr. Halifax 14 May 1822 Mary
Glover (31:48).

Kelly, Margaret. Dau. Michael/Cather-
ine (Magrath) of Co. Waterford,
Ireland; marr. Halifax 22 June
1810 John Pike (q.v.) (30:109).

Kelly, Margaret. See Dee, Margaret.

Kelly, Martha. Dau. of James/Mary
(Walsh) of Burin, Nfld.; marr.
Halifax 10 July 1834 John Dunn
(q.v.) (33:57).

Kelly, Mary. Dau. of Daniel/Mary
(Walsh) of Co. Cork, Ireland;
marr. Halifax 19 Aug. 1830 James
Fogarty (q.v.) (32:111).

Kelly, Mary. Dau. of Patrick/Jean
(MacCullihan) of Co. Antrim,
Ireland; marr. Halifax 18 Dec.
1832 Michael Cunningham (q.v.)
(33:56).

Kelly, Mary. Widow of Michael Dowlan
of Nfld.; marr. Halifax 26 June
1822 Michael Condon (q.v.) (31:
43).

Kelly, Mathew. S. of William/Sarah
(Tierney) of Co. Kildare, Ireland;
marr. Halifax 4 Feb. 1834 Mary
McCarthy (q.v.) (33:60).

Kelly, Mathias. Grantee "Digby New
Grant" 29 Jan. 1801 (5:82).

Kelly, Michael. S. of Peter/Bridget
(Carrigan) of Co. Roscommon,
Ireland; marr. Halifax 11 July
1820 Anne Rodney (q.v.) (31:48).

Kelly, Michael. S. of John/Mary
(Driscoll) of Waterford, Ireland;
marr. Halifax 28 Apr. 1829 Bridget
Hughs (q.v.) (32:113).

Kelly, Owen. Of Co. Roscommon, Ireland; widower of Ann Quinn; marr.

Halifax 10 Nov. 1841 Ann Morrice (q.v.) (35:139).

Kelly, Patrick. Of Co. Wicklow, Ireland; marr. Halifax 6 June 1819 Margaret Kiely (q.v.) (31:48).

Kelly, Patrick. S. of Patrick/Mary (Brien) of Cam, Roscommon, Ireland; marr. Halifax 30 Sep. 1802 Mary Peters (30:106).

Kelly, Peter. S. of Peter/Judith (Treaner) of Co. Kildare, Ireland; marr. Halifax 16 Feb. 1832 Mary Smith (q.v.) (33:61).

Kelly, Peter. S. of James/Mary (Walsh) of Burin, Nfld.; marr. Halifax 15 Sep. 1831 Mary O'Brien (q.v.) (33:60).

Kelly, Sarah. See Hugs, Sarah.

Kelly, Terence. Tailor; s. of Richard/Mary (MacGougan) of Dromore, Co. Tyrone, Ireland; marr. Halifax 28 Nov. 1829 Susannah Murry (32:113).

Kelly, Thomas. Laborer; Irish; 25; Liverpool to Nova Scotia May 1864 on EUROCLYDON (45:182).

Kelly, Thomas. S. of Richard/Mary (Maguigan) of Dromore, Co. Tyrone, Ireland; marr. Halifax 26 Nov. 1826 Margaret Dredy (32:113).

Kelly, Walter. Deserted 28 Feb. 1806 from Royal Newfoundland Regiment, stationed at Annapolis; 6'2", ruddy complexion, black hair, blue eyes, ca. 21, b. Ireland; advertised The Weekly Chronicle, 15 Mar. 1806 (28:33).

Kelly, William. S. of Andrew/Mary (Dee) of Ballinderry, Co. Wexford, Ireland; marr. Halifax 1 June 1821 Catherine Jackson (31:48).

Kempton, Francis. S. of Richard/Fear; to (or b.?) Liverpool by 1800 (47:127:276).

Kempton, Jacob Curtis. S. of Richard/

Fear; to (or b.?) Liverpool by 1796 (47:127:271).

Kempton, John. S. of Richard/Fear; to (or b.?) Liverpool by 1794 (47:127:208).

Kempton, Mary. Dau. of Richard/Fear; to (or b.?) Liverpool by 1785 (47:127:53).

Kempton, Rebeckah. Dau. of Richard/Fear; to (or b.?) Liverpool by 1790 (47:127:268).

Kempton, Richard. B. New England; d. Liverpool 11 May 1809 ae. 69 yrs. 6 mo. 22 days (49:135).

Kempton, Richard. Liverpool proprietor (19:102).

Kempton, Richard. To Liverpool ca. 1760 (47:126:96).

Kempton, Thomas. S. of Richard/Fear; to (or b.?) Liverpool by 1789 (47:127:122).

Kenedy, Catherine. Dau. of David/Mary (Gilligy) of Co. Waterford, Ireland; marr. Halifax 4 June 1833 Thomas Spence (q.v.) (33:67).

Kenedy, Catherine. See Egar, Catherine.

Kenedy, Elenor. Dau. of John/Mary (O'Donnell) of Co. Kerry, Ireland; marr. Halifax 6 June 1835 Timothy Shea (q.v.) (34:138).

Kenedy, Eliza. Dau. of John/Sarah (McNeill) of Co. Derry, Ireland; marr. Halifax 1 Jan. 1840 Patrick Mulholland (q.v.) (34:135).

Kenedy, Elizabeth. Dau. of John/Catherine of Co. Kerry, Ireland; marr. Halifax 24 Nov. 1838 Patrick Moriarty (q.v.) (34:135).

Kenedy, Honour. Dau. of Philip/Mary (Piers) of Parish Ferns, Co. Wexford, Ireland; marr. Halifax 2 Mar. 1821 Michael Doyle (q.v.) (31:44).

Kenedy, James. S. of Philip/Mary

(Piers) of Parish Ferns, Co.
Wexford, Ireland; marr. Halifax 23
June 1821 Elizabeth Ross (31:48).

Kenedy, Jane. Dau. of John/Jane
(Fountain) of Quebec, Lower Canada; marr. Halifax 6 May 1830 Patrick Corbet (sic) (q.v.) (32:107).

Kenedy, Joanna. Dau. of Thomas/Mary
(Carrigan) of Co. Tipperary,
Ireland; marr. Halifax 8 May 1843
Andrew Saul (q.v.) (35:144).

Kenedy, John. See Canada, John.

Kenedy, Margaret. Dau. of Thomas/Mary
(Power) of Kilmacthomas, Co. Wat-
erford, Ireland; marr. Halifax 25
Sep. 1841 Zadock Bridgo (35:135).

Kenedy, Mary. Dau. of Daniel/Mary
(Murphy) of Co. Kerry, Ireland;
marr. Halifax 25 Aug. 1828 Michael
Doyle (q.v.) (32:109).

Kenedy, Mary. Dau. of John/Hannah
(Brown) McDonnell of Waterford;
widow of Denis Kenedy; marr.
Halifax 24 June 1823 Joseph Benson
(q.v.) (31:40).

Kenedy, Michael. S. of James/Mary
(Grace) of Patrick Street, Kilkenny, Ireland; marr. Halifax 10 Nov.
1824 Mary Mulcahy (31:48).

Kenedy, Patrick. S. of Patrick/Honora
(Mannix) of Co. Carlow, Ireland;
marr. Halifax 1 Oct. 1828 Joanna
Londergan (q.v.) (32:113).

Kenedy, Patrick. S. of James/Eliza-
beth (Brown) of Dingle, Co. Kerry,
Ireland; marr. Halifax 9 Nov. 1839
Joanna Moriarty (q.v.) (34:132).

Kenedy, William. S. of Thomas/Mary
(Power) of Kilmacthomas, Co. Waterford, Ireland; marr. Halifax 15
Nov. 1834 Ann O'Brien (q.v.)
(34:132).

Kenedy, William. S. of William/Honora
(Bratchy) of Co. Tipperary, Ireland; marr. Halifax 24 Nov. 1841

Margaret Gorman (q.v.) (35:140).

Kennedy, Anne. Dau. of Thomas/Mary
(Power) of Kilmacthomas, Co. Waterford, Ireland; marr. Halifax 10
Nov. 1836 Thomas Burke (q.v.)
(34:126).

Kennedy, Dennis. Plus 1 f./2 ch./1
svt.; Port Roseway Associate
(6:15).

Kennedy, Ellen. Dau. of John/Honora
(Bulger) of Co. Kilkenny, Ireland;
marr. Halifax 14 Jan. 1833 Patrick
Walsh (q.v.) (33:68).

Kennedy, Patrick. S. of Thomas/Mary
(Power) of Co. Waterford, Ireland;
marr. Halifax 7 Aug. 1843 Margaret
Burke (35:140).

Kennedy, Thomas. Disbanded solider,
82nd Regt.; plus 1 f./1 ch.; mustered at Digby 19 May 1784 (39:
123).

Kennedy, Thomas. S. of Hugh/Bridget
(Finlen) of Co. Carlow, Ireland;
marr. Halifax 7 June 1843 Anastasia Brophy (q.v.) (35:140).

Kennedy, William. From N.H.; effective land grant at Truro 31 Oct.
1765 (4:245).

Kenney, Elisha. Liverpool proprietor
(19:101).

Kenney, Gamaliel. Barrington petitioner 19 Oct. 1776 (1:365).

Kenney, Heman. S. of Nathan; b. Chatham, Mass., 1732; to Barrington by
1761/2 (50:106).

Kenney, Heman. S. of Heman; b. Chatham, Mass., 27 June 1753 (50:106).

Kenney, Isaac. Barrington petitioner
19 Oct. 1776 (1:365).

Kenney, Isaac. S. of Heman; b. Chatham, Mass., 1765 (50:106).

Kenney, John. Plus 1 f./4 ch.; farmer; Port Roseway Associate (6:15).

Kenney, Marcy. Barrington petitioner
19 Oct. 1776 (1:365).

Kenney, Mercy Nickerson. Wife of
Henan (50:106).

Kenney, Nathan. S. of Nathan; b.
Chatham, Mass., 1741; marr. Barrington June 1764 (50:107).

Kenny, Bernard. S. of Hugh/Catherine
(Doyle) of Co. Wexford, Ireland;
marr. Halifax 26 Sep. 1837 Joanna
O'Brien (q.v.) (34:132).

Kenny, Edward. S. of Jeremiah/Joanna
(Crean) of Parish Kilmoily, Co.
Kerry, Ireland; marr. Halifax 16
Oct. 1832 Anne Forrestall; later
Sir Edward, a Senator for Canada
(33:61).

Kenny, Elisha. B. Sheepscot, Me., 8
Jan. 1758; s. of Elisha/Jean; to
Liverpool ca. 1761 (47:126:101).

Kenny, Elisha. To Liverpool ca. 1761
(47:126:101).

Kenny, Hugh. 15th Regt.; s. of Hugh/
Mary (Spence) of Dublin, Ireland;
marr. Halifax 25 Aug. 1820 Bridget
Phelan (q.v.) (31:48).

Kenny, Jean. B. Sheepscot, Me., 23
Jan. 1756; dau. of Elisha/Jean; to
Liverpool ca. 1761 (47:126:101).

Kenny, Jean. Wife of Elisha; to
Liverpool ca. 1761 (47:126:101).

Kenny, John. B. Sheepscot, Me., 10
Apr. 1761; s. of Elisha/Jean; to
Liverpool ca. 1761 (47:126:101).

Kenny, Margaret. Dau. of Michael/Mary
(Dunn) of Myshall, Co. Carlow,
Ireland; marr. Halifax 11 June
1842 Maurice Power (q.v.) (35:
143).

Kenny, Michael. S. of James/Bridget
(Reddy) of Parish Suttons, Co.
Wexford, Ireland; marr. Halifax 25
Sep. 1824 Elenor Falvey (31:48).

Kenny, Obadiah. B. Sheepscot, Me., 31
Dec. 1754; s. of Elisha/Jean; to
Liverpool ca. 1761 (47:126:101).

Kenny, Patrick. S. of Andrew/Mary of

Co. Wexford, Ireland; marr. Halifax 4 Feb. 1829 Eleanor Doyle
(q.v.) (32:114).

Kenny, Peter. S. of Nicholas/Maria
(McLaughlan) of Co. Longford, Ireland; marr. Halifax 24 May 1838
Catherine Robbinson (q.v.) (34:
132).

Kenny, Rachal. B. Sheepscot, Me., 11
Aug. 1752; dau. of Elisha/Jean; to
Liverpool ca. 1761 (47:126:101).

Kenny, Sally. Dau. of Moses/Anastatia
(Redmond) of Ferns, Co. Wexford,
Ireland; marr. Halifax 11 Feb.
1822 (q.v.) (31:44).

Kenny, Samuel. B. Sheepscot, Me., 22
Mar. 1751; s. of Elisha/Jean; to
Liverpool ca. 1761 (47:126:101).

Kent, Isaac. New England to Annapolis
on CHARMING MOLLY May 1760 (18:
271).

Kent, Patrick. Husband of Sophia
Anderson; bur. Halifax 16 July
1841 ae. 32 (34:125).

Kent, Patrick. S. of Mark/Margaret
(Miler) of Co. Wexford, Ireland;
marr. Halifax 24 Apr. 1836 Sophia
Anderson (34:132).

Kenwrick, Joseph. Barrington petitioner 19 Oct. 1776 (1:365).

Kenwrick, Solomon Jr. Barrington
petitioner 19 Oct. 1776 (1:365).

Kerenegh, Catherine. Dau. of Owen/
Bridget (Ronohen?) of Co. Leitrim,
Ireland; marr. Halifax 25 Jan.
1843 Pvt. David Delory (q.v.) (35:
136).

Kern, Nicholas. German Service; plus
1 svt.; mustered at Bear River
11/25 June 1784 (38:260).

Kerns, Catherine. Dau. of Edmund/
Catherine (Troy) of Killeagh,
Cork, Ireland; marr. Halifax 11
Feb. 1822 John Flinn (31:45).

Kerns, John. 64th Regt.; of Co. Gal-

way, Ireland; marr. Halifax 22
July 1842 Margaret Murphy (q.v.)
(35:140).

Kerns, Michael. S. of John/Ellen
(Murphy) of Carrigtwohill, Co.
Cork, Ireland; marr. Halifax 15
Feb. 1844 Elizabeth Cavanagh
(q.v.) (35:140).

Kerr, William. Grantee 'Digby New
Grant' 29 Jan. 1801 (5:82).

Kervick, James. S. of James/Mary
(Durnfort) of Parish Mullinavat,
Co. Kilkenny, Ireland; marr.
Halifax 10 Nov. 1828 Mary Power
(32:114).

Kerwan, Catherine. Dau. of John/
Margaret (Walsh) of Co. Kilkenny,
Ireland; marr. Halifax 3 Nov. 1828
(q.v.) (32:118).

Kerwan, Catherine. Dau. of John/
Margaret (Daly) of Co. Waterford,
Ireland; marr. Halifax 3 Feb. 1831
Richard Thomas Flinn (q.v.) (33:
58).

Kerwick, Michael. S. of James/Cather-
ine (Whalen) of Co. Kilkenny, Ireland; marr. Halifax 26 July 1811
Catherine Dalton (q.v.) (30:107).

Ketchum, Jehiel. Grantee 'Digby New
Grant' 29 Jan. 1801 (5:82).

Ketchum, Jehiel. Loyalist; plus 1
f./3 ch.; mustered at Digby 19 May
1784 (39:123).

Kewan, John. S. of John/Eleanor
(Looby) of Clanum?, Co. Tipperary,
Ireland; marr. Halifax 15 Oct.
1832 Eleanor Keating widow of
James Fox (33:61).

Keys, John. S. of Timothy/Bridget
(Wall) of Kilteery, Loughill, Co.
Limerick, Ireland; marr. Halifax 4
May 1837 Martha Murphy (q.v.) (34:
132).

Keys, William. From Mass.; land grant
at Onslow 24 July 1759 (4:222).

Kid, Emilia. Dau. of John/Ann (Lawlor) of Co. Leix, Ireland; marr.
Halifax 22 June 1842 Edward Nolan
(q.v.) (35:142).

Kiely, Margaret. Of Nfld.; marr.
Halifax 6 June 1819 Patrick Kelly
(q.v.) (31:48).

Kiho, John. S. of Patrick/Mary
(Morphy) of Co. Kilkenny, Ireland;
marr. Halifax 15 Oct. 1817 Margaret Groves (30:107).

Kihoe, James William. S. of John/
Catherine (Blanchfield) of Co.
Carlow, Ireland; marr. Halifax 20
Aug. 1833 Ellen Carey (q.v.) (33:
61).

Kihoe, John. S. of Michael/Bridget
(Slow) of Kilnamin, Co. Wexford,
Ireland; marr. Halifax 26 Apr.
1828 Maria Greenwood (32:114).

Kihoe, Mary. Dau. of Philip/Margaret
(Parl) of Co. Wexford, Ireland;
marr. Halifax 28 Sep. 1841 Martin
Madigan (q.v.) (35:141).

Kihough, Martin. S. of James/Mary
(Power) of Ross, Co. Wexford,
Ireland; marr. Halifax 21 Oct.
1833 Honora Lahy (q.v.) (33:61).

Kiley, James. 8th Regt.; s. of Ed-
ward/Catherine (Cull) of Limerick,
Ireland; marr. Halifax 31 Oct.
1841 Ann Levenson (q.v.) (35:140).

Kiley, Maurice. S. of Thomas/Mary
(Heney) of Co. Waterford, Ireland;
marr. Halifax 22 Feb. 1835 Alice
Dunphy (q.v.) (34:132).

Kiley, Thomas. S. of John/Catherine
(Coveny) of Co. Waterford, Ire-
land; marr. Halifax 24 Aug. 1834
Honora Power (q.v.) (33:61).

Kilfoil, Honora. Dau. of Patrick/
Catherine (Mullally) of Co. Tipperary, Ireland; marr. Halifax 17
Sep. 1833 James Foley (q.v.)
(33:58).

Kilfoil, John. S. of Thomas/Joanna
(Egan) of Co. Kilkenny, Ireland;
marr. Halifax 16 July 1836 Catherine Fowler (q.v.) (34:133).

Kilfoil, Margaret. Dau. of Thomas/
Judith (Egan) of Co. Kilkenny,
Ireland; marr. Halifax 13 Sep.
1829 Richard Hobin (q.v.) (32:
112).

Kilfoil, Michael. S. of Timothy/
Winefred (Burke) of Birr, Kings
Co., Ireland; marr. Halifax 28
Sep. 1813 Catherine Gladel (30:
107).

Kilfoile, Joanna. See Tobin, Joanna.

Killeen, John. S. of Cornelius/Anas-
tasia (Elward) of Co. Cork, Ireland; marr. Halifax 29 Jan. 1844
Margaret Keating (35:140).

Killeen, Mary. Dau. of Cornelius/
Anastasia (Elliard) of Co. Cork,
Ireland; marr. Halifax 18 Nov.
1828 Redmond Fitzgerald (q.v.)
(32:110).

Killeen, Thomas. S. of Cornelius/
Anastasia (Elliard) of Co. Cork,
Ireland; marr. Halifax 10 Sep.
1834 Bridget Ryan (q.v.) (34:133).

Killeen, Timothy. S. of Cornelius/
Anastas (Elliard) of Co. Cork,
Ireland; marr. Halifax 19 May 1831
Honora Sullivan (q.v.) (33:61).

Kily, Christiana. See McDonald,
Christiana.

Kinan, Joanna. Dau. of Owen/Mary
(Egan) of Co. Longford, Ireland;
marr. Halifax 15 Sep. 1828 Patrick
Donelly (q.v.) (32:108).

King, Harmonious. Loyalist; mustered
at Digby 19 May 1784 (39:123).

King, Isaac Jr. Barrington petitioner
19 Oct. 1776 (1:365).

King, Isaac. Barrington petitioner 19
Oct. 1776 (1:365).

King, Margaret. Dau. of Christopher/

Mary (Mullen) of Co. Meath, Ireland; marr. Halifax 2 Apr. 1820
Henry McHenry (q.v.) (31:47).

King, Thomas. 21; blacksmith; Hull,
Yorkshire, to Fort Cumberland on
JENNY 3-10 April 1775 (22:123).

Kingland, William. Loyalist; mustered
at Digby 19 May 1784 (39:123).

Kingston, Elizabeth. Dau. of William/
Mary (Leary) of Drumbeg, Co. Cork,
Ireland; marr. Halifax 10 Dec.
1832 Michael Wall (q.v.) (33:67).

Kingston, John. Plus 1 f./1 ch.;
goldsmith; Port Roseway Associate
(6:15).

Kingston, John. S. of William/Mary
(Leary) of Drumbeg, Co. Cork,
Ireland; marr. Halifax 6 Oct. 1831
Juliana Murphy (q.v.) (33:61).

Kingston, Paul. S. of William/Mary
(Leary) of Drumbeg,. Co. Cork,
Ireland; marr. Halifax 28 Nov.
1833 Mary Cotter (q.v.) (33:61).

Kinna, Thomas. Of Co. Tipperary,
Ireland; widower of Bridget Sulli-
van; marr. Halifax 10 July 1838
Mary Walsh (q.v.) (34:133).

Kinney, Abiel. Dau. of Elisha/Jain;
to (or b.?) Liverpool by 1792 (47:
127:125).

Kinney, Jane. Dau. of Elisha/Jane; to
Liverpool by 1773 (47:127:54).

Kinney, Rachel. Dau. of Elisha/Jane;
to Liverpool by 1770 (47:126:287).

Kinney, Samuel Jr. S. of Samuel/
Sarah; to (or b.?) Liverpool by
1799 (47:127:276).

Kinney, Samuel. S. of Elisha/Jane; to
Liverpool by 1776 (47:126:289).

Kinsela, James. Widower of Mary Ryan;
of Co. Waterford, Ireland; marr.
Halifax 21 Aug. 1832 Mary Terry
(q.v.) (33:61).

Kinsela, Margaret. Dau. of Thomas/
Mary (Byrne) of Parish Ballmikiln,

Kildare, Ireland; marr. Halifax 29
May 1825 John Ryan (q.v.) (31:53).

Kinsela, Martha. Dau. of Michael/
Elizabeth (Whitny) of Co. Wexford,
Ireland; marr. Halifax 28 Apr.
1842 Pvt. John Burke (q.v.) (35:
135).

Kinsela, Robert. S. of Robert/Cather-
ine (Ketther) of Co. Kilkenny,
Ireland; marr. Halifax 27 Apr.
1842 Maria Butler (q.v.) (35:140).

Kinselie, Joseph. S. of Darby/Agnes
(Combs) Parish Kilnyross, Co.
Cork, Ireland; widower of Margaret
Belew; marr. Halifax 9 Feb. 1828
Mary Rourke (q.v.) (32:114).

Kinsella, James. S. of Edward/Cather-
ine (Kelly) of Co. Carlow, Ireland; marr. Halifax 17 June 1821
Margaret Hartnett (q.v.) (31:49).

Kipp, Samuel. Loyalist; mustered at
Digby 19 May 1784 (39:123).

Kipp, Thomas. Loyalist; plus 1 f./2
ch.; mustered at Digby 19 May 1784
(39:123).

Kirby, Benjamin. Barrington petitioner 19 Oct. 1776 (1:365).

Kirby, Thomas. S. of John/Hannah
(Breen) of Co. Waterford. Ireland;
marr. Halifax 13 Sep. 1814 Sophia
Nolty (30:107).

Kirwan,, Joanna. See Flemming, Joanna.

Kirwan, Bridget. Of Co. Wicklow,
Ireland; widow of Michael Campbell
of Co. Kilkenny, Ireland; marr.
Halifax 19 May 1841 Richard Dawson
(q.v.) (35:136).

Kirwan, Ellen. See Walsh, Patrick.

Kirwan, Margaret. Dau. of Patrick/
Mary (Power) of Co. Waterford,
Ireland; marr. Halifax 26 Apr.
1838 Roger Feeny (q.v.) (34:130).

Kirwan, Margaret. Dau. of Michael/
Catherine (Sheehy) of Co. Water-

ford, Ireland; marr. Halifax 3
Mar. 1840 Patrick Flinn (q.v.)
(34:130).

Kirwen, Ellen. Dau. of Edmond/Bridget
(Malony) of Co. Waterford, Ire-
land; marr. Halifax 22 Jan. 1831
Patrick Walsh (q.v.) (33:68).

Kirwen, Patrick. S. of William/Joanna
(Sheehy) of Co. Waterford, Ireland; marr. Halifax 13 Aug. 1828
Catherine Sullivan (q.v.) (32:
114).

Kirwin, Edward. S. of Michael/Cather-
ine (Sheehy) of Co. Waterford,
Ireland; marr. Halifax 29 Sep.
1841 Mary Goodman (q.v.) (35:140).

Kittey, Sarah. Dau. of John/Margaret
(Hynes) of England; marr. Halifax
19 July 1835 Andrew Myers (q.v.)
(34:136).

Klahold, Caspar. Waldeck Regt.;
mustered at Bear River 11/25 June
1784 (38:260).

Klaupper, Jacob. German Service;
mustered at Bear River 11/25 June
1784 (38:260).

Klingshow, -----. Lieut.; Anspach
Service; plus 1 f.; mustered at
Bear River 11/25 June 1784 (38:
260).

Klington, -----. Quartermaster;
Anspach Service; mustered at Bear
River 11/25 June 1784 (38:260).

Knapp, David. Plus 1 svt.; carpenter;
Port Roseway Associate (6:15).

Knaut, Benjamin. S. of John Philip/
Ann; to (or b.?) Liverpool by 1804
(47:127:277).

Knaut, Phillip Augustus. To Halifax
with Germans who settled Lunenburg. (49:132).

Knight, Mahlon. Plus 1 f./2 ch. 8+;
arr. Annapolis from New York 19
Oct. 1782 (37:125).

Knipchild, Henry. Lieut.; Hessian;

plus 1 f./2 svts.; mustered at
Digby 19 May 1784 (39:123).

Knoweles, Cornelius. S. of Cornelius;
b. Chatham, Mass.; d. Liverpool
bef. 3 Oct. 1769 (50:107).

Knowland, Patrick. S. of James/Marga-
ret; Old Ross, Co. Wexford, Ireland, to Liverpool by 1795 (47:
127:56).

Knowles, Cornelius. Liverpool proprietor (19:101).

Knowles, Cornelius. D. Liverpool 4
July 1794 ae 72nd (49:121).

Knowles, Cornelius. S. of Richard; b.
Chatham, Mass., 10 April 1722;
treasurer of Liverpool 1761 (50:
107).

Knowles, Elizabeth. Dau. of James/
Elizabeth; to (or b.?) Liverpool
by 1801 (47:127:274).

Knowles, Experience. Dau. of Corne-
lius/Mary; to Liverpool by 1768
(47:126:166).

Knowles, Experience. Dau. of Cornelius; b. Chatham, Mass.; d. Liverpool 14 Aug. 1777 (50:107).

Knowles, James. S. of Cornelius/Mary;
to Liverpool by 1779 (47:128:29).

Knowles, James. S. of Cornelius; b.
Chatham, Mass., ca. 1756 (50:107).

Knowles, Martha. Dau. of Cornelius/
Mary; to (or b.?) Liverpool by
1780 (47:126:283).

Knowles, Martha. Dau. of Cornelius;
b. Chatham, Mass., ca. 1748; d.
Liverpool 10 June 1761 (50:107).

Knowles, Mary Hopkins. Wife of Cornelius; b. 12 Mar. 1726 (50:107).

Knowles, Nathaniel. Liverpool proprietor (19:102).

Knowles, Prince. Liverpool proprietor
(19:102).

Knowles, Prince. S. of Samuel; to
Liverpool ca. 1760 (47:126:96).

Knowles, Sophia. Dau. of Prince/

Zerviah; to (or b.?) Liverpool by
1791 (47:127:118).

Knowlton, Daniel. B. ca. 1725; from
Ashford, Conn., and Ware River,
Mass.; plus family; to Onslow (4:
230).

Knowlton, Daniel. Ensign; from Ware
River, Mass.; land grant at Onslow
24 July 1759 (4:222).

Knowlton, Daniel. From Mass.; land
grant at Onslow 21 Feb. 1769 (4:
224).

Knowlton, Daniel. From Mass.; land
grant at Truro 1759 (4:242).

Knowlton, Eleanor. Dau. of Daniel and
Zerviah (Wadkins); married 1774 at
Onslow (4:230).

Knowlton, Mary. From Mass.; land
grant at Onslow 21 Feb. 1769 (4:
225).

Knowlton, Stephen. From Mass.; land
grant at Truro 1759 (4:242).

Knowlton, Zerviah. Wife of Daniel;
dau. of ----- Wadkins; to Onslow
with husband (4:230).

Kraig, -----. Wagon master; see
Kraig, Wagner.

Kraig, Wagner. German Service; mustered at Bear River 11/25 June 1784
(38:260).

Krauss, George. Waldeck Regt.; mustered at Bear River 11/25 June 1784
(38:260).

Kuhn, John. See Ruhn, John.

Kysch. See Kysh.

Kysh, Anthony. Ensign; disbanded
officer, N.J. Vols.; plus 1 f./2
ch./2 svts.; mustered at Digby 19
May 1784 (39:123).

- L -

Labas, Henry. Loyalist; mustered at
Digby 19 May 1784 (39:123).

Laby, Catherine. Dau. of Michael/

Bridget (Conroy) of Co. Cork, Ireland; marr. Halifax 18 Apr. 1830 Edmond Roche (q.v.) (32:118).

Lacy, Edward. S. of Patrick/Catherine (Lee) of Co. Limerick, Ireland; marr. Halifax 21 Jan. 1834 Mary Mullony (q.v.) (33:61).

Lacy, Lawrence. Mariner; not settled; mustered at Digby 19 May 1784 (39:192).

Lacy, Margaret. Dau. of Nicholas/Mary (Kelly) of Co. Wexford, Ireland; marr. Halifax 1 Mar. 1835 Thomas Quigley (q.v.) (34:137).

Ladner, Andrew. Loyalist; mustered at Digby 19 May 1784 (39:123).

Laffan, John. S. of James/Margaret of Co. Kilkenny, Ireland; marr. Halifax 1 May 1815 Elizabeth Maida MacDee (30:107).

Laffin, Edward. S. of Michael/Bridget (Glandon) of Co. Kilkenny, Ireland; marr. Halifax 4 Oct. 1810 Catherine Ros (30:107).

Laffin, Mary. Dau. of Michael/Bridget (Glandon) of Co. Kilkenny, Ireland; widow of William Ryan; marr. Halifax 2 June 1808 William Power (q.v.) (30:109).

Laffin, Peter. S. of Michael/Bridget (Glandon) of Co. Kilkenny, Ireland; marr. Halifax 30 Jan. 1806 Elizabeth Watson (30:107).

Lahey, Bartholomew. S. of James/Eleanor (Nibbett) of Parish Cloyne, Co. Cork, Ireland; marr. Halifax 24 Sep. 1829 Catherine Sullivan (q.v.) (32:114).

Lahey, James. S. of John/Margaret (Magrath) of Co. Cork, Ireland; marr. Halifax 2 June 1831 Ellen Hinessy (q.v.) (33:61).

Lahey, Judith. Dau. of John/Judith (Kelly) of Co. Kilkenny, Ireland; marr. Halifax 10 Oct. 1830 Patrick

Butler (q.v.) (32:106).

Lahey, Thomas. S. of John/Eleanor (McGrath) of Pilltown, Parish Piddown, Kilkenny, Ireland; marr. Halifax 22 Feb. 1826 Elizabeth White (32:114).

Lahy, Bridget. Dau. of John/Joanna (Walsh) of Co. Kilkenny, Ireland; marr. Halifax 24 July 1830 John Walsh (q.v.) (32:120).

Lahy, David. S. of Denis/Catherine (Quinlan) of Co. Cork, Ireland; marr. Halifax 17 Aug. 1834 Mary Ireland (33:61).

Lahy, Honora. Dau. of John/Ellen (McNamara) of Co. Tipperary, Ireland; marr. Halifax 21 Oct. 1833 Martin Kibough (q.v.) (33:61).

Lahy, Joanna. Dau. of Thomas/Mary (Mooney) of Mine?, Co. Tipperary, Ireland; marr. Halifax 10 Jan. 1828 (q.v.) (32:115).

Lahy, John. S. of William/Honora (Simmons) of Co. Kilkenny, Ireland; marr. Halifax 10 Dec. 1833 Mary Carroll widow of John Maney (33:61).

Lahy, Michael. S. of Lawrence/Mary (Talbot) of Co. Tipperary, Ireland; marr. Halifax 3 Feb. 1845 Catherine Scott (q.v.) (35:140).

Lahy, Patrick. S. of Thomas/Judith (Martin) of Co. Kilkenny, Ireland; marr. Halifax 17 May 1833 Marianne Brown (33:61).

Lahy, Patrick. S. of Patrick/Elenor (Gaul) of Co. Tipperary, Ireland; marr. Halifax 14 Sep. 1833 Sarah Gilfoil (q.v.) (33:61).

Lahy, Patrick. Widower of Catherine Beecher; of Co. Cork, Ireland; marr. Halifax 22 Nov. 1833 Margaret Dee (q.v.) (33:61).

Lahy, Roger. S. of John/Elenor (Scully) of Co. Cork, Ireland;

marr. Halifax 11 Feb. 1834 Johanna
Cashman (q.v.) (33:61).

Lake, John. Mariner; not settled;
mustered at Digby 19 May 1784 (39:
192).

Lake, William Robert. S. of William/
Harriot; Sedgeford, Norfolk, England, to Liverpool by 1827 (47:
128:114).

Lally, James. S. of Michael/Margaret
(Fyke) of Parish Kilmore, Co.
Mayo, Ireland; marr. Halifax 10
Jan. 1843 Mary Direns (q.v.)
(35:140).

Lan, James. Pvt., 81st Regt; s. of
John/Mary (Doherty) of Dunmore,
Donegal, Ireland; marr. Halifax 26
Dec. 1823 Charlotte Hall (31:49).

Lamb, Joshua. From Mass.; land grant
at Onslow 21 Feb. 1769 (4:224).

Lamb, Martha. Dau. of William/Mary
(Fitzpatrick) of Nfld.; marr.
Halifax 19 Nov. 1812 William Moran
(q.v.) (30:108).

Lamberson, John. Grantee "Digby New
Grant" 29 Jan. 1801 (5:82).

Lamberson, Teunis. Grantee "Digby New
Grant" 29 Jan. 1801 (5:82).

Laney, Michael. Plus 1 f./2 ch.; carpenter; Port Roseway Associate (6:
15).

Land, Joseph. Loyalist; plus 1 f./2
ch.; mustered at Digby 19 May 1784
(39:192).

Landrigan, Ann. Of Co. Tipperary,
Ireland; widow of Michael Power;
marr. Halifax 22 Sep. 1842 Martin
Calaghan (q.v.) (35:135).

Landrigan, Bridget. Dau. of William/
Margaret (Lary) of Co. Tipperary,
Ireland; marr. Halifax 20 Aug.
1840 Edward Connell (q.v.) (34:
127).

Landrigan, Mary. Dau. of Edmund/
Margaret (Donovan) of Co. Tipper-

ary, Ireland; marr. Halifax 27
Aug. 1843 Michael Shea (q.v.)
(35:144).

Landrikin, Ellen. Spinster; Irish;
21; Liverpool to Nova Scotia June
1864 on INDIAN QUEEN (45:182).

Landy, Joanna. Dau. of Philip/Bridget
(Delany) of Co. Tipperary, Ireland; marr. Halifax 4 Apr. 1842
Pvt. John Stafford (q.v.)
(35:145).

Lane, Juliana. Dau. of William/Mary
(Fitzgibbon) of Churchtown, Co.
Cork, Ireland; marr. Halifax 12
Nov. 1829 Jeremiah Collins (q.v.)
(32:107).

Lange, Jacob. Waldeck Regt.; plus 1
f.; mustered at Bear River 11/25
June 1784 (38:260).

Langford, James. Grantee "Digby New
Grant" 29 Jan. 1801 (5:82).

Langley, Timothy. Arr. Annapolis from
New York 19 Oct. 1782 (37:126).

Langly, Thomas. Loyalist; mustered at
Digby 19 May 1784 (39:192).

Lanigan, Catherine. Dau. of Patrick/
Anne (Jackman) of Callan, Co.
Kilkenny, Ireland; marr. Halifax
15 Feb. 1806 Michael Hickey (q.v.)
(30:106).

Lanigan, Elizabeth. See Kelly, Elizabeth.

Lanigan, John. S. of Thomas/Margaret
(Donelly) of Co. Kilkenny, Ire-
land; marr. Halifax 14 Nov. 1839
Joanna Magrath (q.v.) (34:133).

Lanigan, Margaret. Dau. of Patrick/
Anne (Jackman) of Callan, Kilkenny, Ireland; marr. Halifax 7 Jan.
1804 Michael Tobin (30:111).

Lanigan, Margaret. Dau. of Patrick/
Judith (Dawton) of Co. Kilkenny,
Ireland; marr. Halifax 24 Nov.
1831 Daniel Molony (q.v.) (33:63).

Lannan, Michael. Widower of Catherine

Neill of Co. Kilkenny, Ireland; marr. Halifax 7 Jan. 1833 Joanna Foley (q.v.) (33:61).

Larissy, William. S. of William/ Horora (sic) (Drew) of Co. Kilkenny, Ireland; marr. Halifax 5 Feb. 1831 Mary Anne Cashin (33:61).

Larkin, Joseph. Pvt. 85th King's Light Inf.; of Newry, Co. Down, Ireland; marr. Halifax 14 June 1837 Ann Reardon (q.v.) (34:133).

Larkin, Michael. S. of Patrick/ Bridget (Magher) of Co. Kilkenny, Ireland; marr. Halifax 23 May 1832 Ellen Magrath (q.v.) (33:61).

Larrassy, Catherine. Dau. of Timothy/ Elenor (Moore) of Parish Thomastown, Co. Waterford, Ireland; marr. Halifax 23 Oct. 1825 Edward Burke (q.v.) (31:41).

Larrisey, Anastasia. Dau. of Thomas/ Catherine (Hamilton) of Thomastown, Kilkenny, Ireland; marr. Halifax 13 Feb. 1825 William Skerry (q.v.) (31:53).

Lasage, Minto. Loyalist; mustered at Digby 19 May 1784 (39:123).

Laughlin, Mary. Dau. of John/Joanna (Mulcahy) of Co. Tipperary, Ireland; marr. Halifax 23 July 1832 Roger Kean (q.v.) (33:60).

Laurence, Benjamin. Grantee 'Digby New Grant' 29 Jan. 1801 (5:82).

Laurence, John. S. of Patrick/Bridget (Gibny) of Co. Dublin, Ireland; marr. Halifax 3 July 1835 Mary Daley (q.v.) (34:133).

Lavender, Robert. S. of Robert/Susanah; to (or b.?) Liverpool by 1802 (47:127:274).

Law, Michael. New England to Annapolis on CHARMING MOLLY May 1760 (18:271).

Lawler, Catherine. Dau. of John/Ellen (Magrath) of Ross, Co. Wexford, Ireland; marr. Halifax 26 Sep. 1810 John Naughton (q.v.) (30: 108).

Lawler, James. S. of James/Catherine (Burke) of Queen's Co., Ireland; marr. Halifax 2 Nov. 1820 Mary Anne Scott (q.v.) (31:49).

Lawler, John. S. of Patrick/Honora (Neill) of Co. Waterford, Ireland; marr. Halifax 8 June 1829 Eliza Congrove (q.v.) (32:114).

Lawler, Thomas. S. of Thomas/Mary (Tisdell) of Co. Kilkenny, Ireland; marr. Halifax 4 July 1832 Catherine Riley (q.v.) (33:62).

Lawler, William. S. of James/Joanna (Murphy) of Co. Cork, Ireland; marr. Halifax 17 Oct. 1829 Ann Shortle (q.v.) (32:114).

Lawlor, Catherine. See Riley, Catherine.

Lawlor, Mary Ann. Dau. of William/ Mary (Lamy) of Co. Kilkenny, Ireland; marr. Halifax 8 Feb. 1835 David O'Brien (q.v.) (34:136).

Lawlor, Michael. S. of Patrick/Honora (Macaul) of Co. Roscommon, Ireland; marr. Halifax 7 Oct. 1842 Isabella Quinn (q.v.) (35:140).

Lawlor, Thomas. S. of Patrick/Catherine (Murphy) of Bree, Co. Wexford, Ireland; marr. Halifax 16 Apr. 1822 Susanna Curtin (q.v.) (31: 49).

Lawlor, William. S. of William/Mary (Newman) of Queens Co., Ireland; marr. Halifax 27 Jan. 1814 Elener Shanahan (30:107).

Lawrence, Anne. Dau. of Leget/Mary (Basnes) of New York; marr. Halifax 14 Sep. 1802 Patrick Wallace (q.v.) (30:111).

Lawrence, Benjamin. Loyalist; mustered at Digby 19 May 1784 (39: 123).

Lawrence, Samuel. S. of John/Eliza-
beth (Lee) of Wiltshire, England;
marr. Halifax 30 May 1824 Eleanor
Sullivan (q.v.) (31:49).

Lawson, Jennett. Dau. of James/Isa-
bella (Cruikshank) of Aberdeen,
Scotland; marr. Halifax 27 Nov.
1835 Lawrence Hickey (q.v.)
(34:131).

Lawson, John. Grantee 'Digby New
Grant' 29 Jan. 1801 (5:82).

Lawson, John. Laborer; not settled;
mustered at Digby 19 May 1784
(39:192).

Lawson, John. Plus 1 f./3 ch. 8+/1
ch. -8; arr. Annapolis from New
York 19 Oct. 1782 (37:125).

Layton, Elizabeth. 26; wife of Fran-
cis; Hull, Yorkshire, to Nova
Scotia; on TWO FRIENDS 28 Feb.-7
Mar. 1774 (25:28).

Layton, Francis. 18 mos.; ch. of
Francis; Hull, Yorkshire, to Nova
Scotia; on TWO FRIENDS 28 Feb.-7
Mar. 1774 (25:28).

Layton, Francis. 29; blacksmith;
Hull, Yorkshire, to Nova Scotia;
on TWO FRIENDS 28 Feb.-7 Mar. 1774
(25:28).

Layton, John. 22; husbandman; Hull,
Yorkshire, to Nova Scotia; on TWO
FRIENDS 28 Feb.-7 Mar. 1774 (25:
28).

Lazador, Jacob. Loyalist; plus 1 f./3
ch.; mustered at Digby 19 May 1784
(39:123).

Leach, James. 27; farmer; Hull, Yorkshire, to Nova Scotia; on TWO
FRIENDS 28 Feb.-7 Mar. 1774 (25:
28).

Leacy, Joseph. S. of Martin/Catherine
(Kehoe) of Taghmon, Co. Wexford,
Ireland; marr. Halifax 12 Oct.
1825 Maria Landergan (31:49).

Leahy, Mary. Dau. of Michael/Mary

(Byrnes) of Co. Kilkenny, Ireland;
widow of John Ross; marr. Halifax
6 Nov. 1834 James Barrett (q.v.)
(34:125).

Leahy, William. S. of Dennis/Mary
(Doherty) of Lismore, Co. Waterford, Ireland; marr. Halifax 17
May 1840 Anne Mahar (q.v.) (34:
133).

Lear, Jesse. Plus 1 f./2 ch./2 svts.;
Port Roseway Associate (6:16).

Leary, Edmund. S. of Simon/Johanna
(Keary) of Co. Tipperary, Ireland;
marr. Halifax 23 Feb. 1808 Sarah
Dolby (q.v.) (30:107).

Leary, John. S. of Murtaugh/Catherine
(Kehoe) of Co. Waterford, Ireland;
marr. Halifax 5 Nov. 1814 Anne
Quillinan (30:107).

Leasy, Mary. Dau. of William/Eliza-
beth (Byrne), widow of Thomas
Griffin of Burtonhall, Co. Carlow,
Ireland; marr. Halifax 31 Jan.
1822 James Andrew Creighton (31:
43).

LeBarre, Henry. See Henry LeCarre.

LeCarre, Henry. Arr. Annapolis from
New York 19 Oct. 1782 (37:125).

Leddy, James. S. of Timothy/Mary
(Clarke) of Limerick, Ireland;
marr. Halifax 22 Nov. 1844 Jane
Drummond (q.v.) (35:140).

Lee, Elizabeth. Wife or widow of
Michael; to Liverpool by 1781 (47:
126:282).

Lee, Margaret. Dau. of Peter/Bridget
(Dawson) of Co. Leitrim, Ireland;
marr. Halifax 26 June 1841 John
Fleming (q.v.) (35:138).

Lefurgey, Tunis. Loyalist; mustered
at Digby 19 May 1784 (39:192).

Lefurgy, Henry. Loyalist; plus 1 f./5
ch.; mustered at Digby 19 May 1784
(39:192).

Leigh, Margaret. Dau. of James/Dorothy (Wilson) of England; marr. Halifax 7 Apr. 1818 Robert Phelan *(q.v.)* (31:51).

Leighton, John. Plus 1 f./2 ch.; Port Roseway Associate (6:16).

Leishman, Robert. Master of Transport; mustered at Digby 19 May 1784 (39:123).

Lemas, John. Laborer; English; 35; Liverpool to Nova Scotia June 1864 on INDIAN QUEEN (45:182).

Lemasny, Thomas. S. of Thomas/Mary (Lycet) of Co. Cork, Ireland; marr. Halifax 26 June 1832 Mary Duffy *(q.v.)* (33:62).

Leming, Robert Jr. 17, husbandman; Hull to Fort Cumberland on ALBION 7-14 March 1774 (21:139).

Leming, Robert. 51, husbandman; Hull to Fort Cumberland on ALBION 7-14 March 1774 (21:139).

Lennox, Mary. Dau. of Thomas/Esther of Aughrim, Co. Derry, Ireland; marr. Halifax 9 Oct. 1829 John Morissy *(q.v.)* (32:116).

Lenox, Peter. Plus 1 f./3 ch./2 svts.; Port Roseway Associate (6:16).

Leonard, Daniel. Loyalist; mustered at Digby 19 May 1784 (39:123).

Leonard, James. (Heirs) grantee "Digby New Grant" 29 Jan. 1801 (5:82).

Leonard, James. Loyalist; plus 1 f./3 ch./1 svt.; mustered at Digby 19 May 1784 (39:123).

Leonard, John. Loyalist; mustered at Digby 1y May 1784 (39:192).

Leonard, Margaret. See Condon, Margaret.

Leonard, Michael. S. of Cornelius/Eleanor of Co. Waterford, Ireland; marr. Halifax 27 July 1820 Margaret Condon *(q.v.)* (31:49).

Leonard, Nathaniel. Grandson of Maj.

Shepherd; Stoughton, Mass., to Chester with first settlers (16: 45).

Leonard, Robert. Loyalist; plus 1 f./5 ch/1 svt.; mustered at Digby 19 May 1784 (39:123).

LeRoy, F. P. R. Loyalist; plus 1 f./5 ch.; mustered at Gulliver's Hole/ St. Mary's Bay/Sissiboo 1/6 June 1784; settled at Sissiboo (now Weymouth) (40:262).

LeRoy, Francis P. Grantee "Digby New Grant" 29 Jan. 1801 (5:82).

Leroy, Simon. Plus 1 f./3 ch. 8+; arr. Annapolis from New York 19 Oct. 1782 (37:125).

Lesage, Mentor. Arr. Annapolis from New York 19 Oct. 1782 (37:125).

Letteney, William H. Loyalist; plus 1 f./2 ch./1 svt.; mustered at Digby 19 May 1784 (39:123).

Leuin, Elizebeth. Dau. of John/Sarah; to Liverpool by 20 Oct. 1784 (47: 126:285).

Levenson, Ann. Dau. of John/Isabella (Magregor) of Prince Edward Isl., marr. Halifax 31 Oct. 1841 James Kiley *(q.v.)* (35:140).

Leviday, John. Laborer; English; 40; Liverpool to Nova Scotia May 1864 on EUROCLYDON (45:182).

Lewin, John. Liverpool proprietor (19:102).

Lewin, Rebeccah. Dau. of John/Sarah; to (or b.?) Liverpool by 1779 (47: 127:206).

Lewin, Sarah. Dau. of John/Sarah; to Liverpool by 1776 (47:127:270-271).

Lewis, Elizabeth. Dau. of Charles/ Joanna (Hearn) of Co. Waterford, Ireland; marr. Halifax 16 Oct. 1832 Thomas Kearney *(q.v.)* (33: 60).

Lewis, James. Grantee "Digby New

Grant" 29 Jan. 1801 (5:82).

Lewis, John. Loyalist; mustered at Digby 19 May 1784 (39:123).

Lewis, John. Loyalist; plus 1 f./3 ch.; mustered at Digby 19 May 1784 (39:123).

Lewis, John. To (or b.?) Port Hebert by 1791 (47:127:57).

Licit, Patrick. Grantee "Digby New Grant" 29 Jan. 1801 (5:82).

Lillis, Joanna. Of Co. Cork, Ireland; widow of Thomas Sullivan; marr. Halifax 3 June 1841 James O'Rourke (q.v.) (35:143).

Lincoln, Michael. Loyalist; mustered at Digby 19 May 1784 (39:123).

Lincoln, Phoebe Gould Godfrey. Wife of Thomas; b. Harwich,. Mass., 30 April 1723 (50:108).

Lincoln, Thomas. S. of Thomas; b. Harwich, Mass., 16 Nov. 17835; grantee at Barrington 1759-1769; 1770 census there (50:108).

Linehan, Abigail. Dau. of Patrick/ Mary (Colbert) of Midleton, Co. Cork, Ireland; marr. Halifax 15 May 1833 Edmund Keeffe (q.v.) (33: 60).

Linehan, John. S. of William/Julia (Leary) of Cove of Cork, Ireland; marr. Halifax 28 Sep. 1828 Bridget Shea (q.v.) (32:114).

Linehan, Timothy. Widower of Mary Barrett; of Tralee, Co. Kerry, Ireland; marr. Halifax 10 Feb. 1834 Catherine Walsh (q.v.) (33: 62).

Linerd, Elline. Dau. of Cornelius/ Mary (Power) of Parish Madeliga (sic for Modeligo), Co. Waterford, Ireland; marr. Halifax 17 June 1836 David Harrigan (q.v.) (34: 131).

Lines, Jacob Jr. From Mass.; land grant at Onslow 21 Feb. 1769 (4:

225).

Lines, Jacob. From Mass.; land grant (to heirs) at Onslow 21 Feb. 1769 (4:224).

Lines. See Lynds.

Linnen, James. S. of Edward/Honora (Karney) of Co. Carlow, Ireland; marr. Halifax 11 Oct. 1832 Sarah Neill (q.v.) (33:62).

Linton, John. 28; butcher; Hull, Yorkshire, to Nova Scotia; on TWO FRIENDS 28 Feb.-7 Mar. 1774 (25: 30).

Littany, William H. Grantee "Digby New Grant" 29 Jan. 1801 (5:82).

Little, Ann. 24, wife of Thomas; Hull to Port Cumberland on ALBION 7-14 March 1774 (21:140).

Little, John. Pvt. 64th Regt.; of Co. Leitrim, Ireland; marr. Halifax 15 May 1841 Ellen Walsh (q.v.) (35: 140).

Little, Thomas. 27, tanner; Hull to Port Cumberland on ALBION 7-14 March 1774 (21:140).

Loch, Daniel. From Mass.; land grant at Truro 1759 (4:242).

Loch, Ebenezer. From Mass.; land grant at Truro 1759 (4:242).

Locke, Jonathan. Liverpool proprietor (19:102).

Lockwood, Amos. Plus 1 ch./1 svt.; carpenter; Port Roseway Associate (6:15).

Lodge, James. Plus 1 f./10 ch./2 svts.; Port Roseway Associate (6:16).

Lodge, Mathew. 20; servant/house carpenter; Hull, Yorkshire, to Port Cumberland on JENNY 3-10 April 1775 (22:123).

Loew, Josef. Plus wife/ch./father; Hemmenthal, Canton Schaffhausen, to Halifax 1751 (44:192).

Loew, Michel. Cabinetmaker; plus

wife/ch.; Hemmenthal, Canton
Schaffhausen, to Halifax 1751 (44:
192).

Logan, Bridget. Dau. of Paul/Margaret
(Doherty) of Co. Derry, Ireland;
marr. Halifax 20 July 1838 Patrick
Daly (q.v.) (34:128).

Logan, Jennet. From N.H.; effective
land grant at Truro 31 Oct. 1765
(4:245).

Logan. See Loggan.

Loggan, John. From N.H.; effective
land grant at Truro 31 Oct. 1765
(4:245).

Loggan, William. From N.H.; effective
land grant at Truro 31 Oct. 1765
(4:245).

Lomasny, Garrett. S. of Timothy/Mary
(Fitzgerald) of Co. Cork, Ireland;
marr. Halifax 25 Feb. 1816 Bridget
Fitzgerald (30:107).

Lonan, Frederick. Laborer; English;
25; Liverpool to Nova Scotia May
1864 on EUROCLYDON (45:182).

Londergan, Margaret. Dau. of Thomas/
Mary (McDonnell) of Gammansfield,
Tipperary, Ireland; marr. Halifax
22 June 1805 Timothy Heffernan
(q.v.) (30:106).

Londerghan, Joanna. Dau. of John/
Margaret (Maguire) of Co. Kilkenny, Ireland; marr. Halifax 1 Oct.
1828 Patrick Kenedy (q.v.) (32:
113).

Londrigan, Catherine. Dau. of Pa-
trick/Elenor (Hinessy) of Clonmel,
Tipperary, Ireland; marr. Halifax
23 Feb. 1830 Thomas O'Brien (q.v.)
(32:117).

Londrigan, Catherine. Of Co. Waterford, Ireland; widow of Michael
Morissy; marr. Halifax 21 Nov.
1835 John Cahill (q.v.) (34:127).

Londrigan, John. S. of Thomas/Mary
(Grover) of Clonmel, Co. Tipperary, Ireland; marr. Halifax 7 Feb.
1822 Johanna Ryan (q.v.) (31:49).

Londrigan, Mary. Dau. of Edmond/
Margaret (Donovan) of Co. Tipperary, Ireland; marr. Halifax 7 July
1839 Stephen Brown (q.v.)
(34:126).

Lonergan, Mary. Dau. of Pierce/
Catherine (Condon) of Amberville,
Co. Waterford, Ireland; marr.
Halifax 11 Apr. 1820 John Harney
(q.v.) (31:47).

Lonergan, Patrick. S. of John/Marga-
ret (Magher) of Co. Kilkenny,
Ireland; marr. Halifax 19 Nov.
1837 Catherine Morissy (34:133).

Long, Alexander. Grantee 'Digby New
Grant' 29 Jan. 1801 (5:82).

Long, Jennet. From N.H.; effective
land grant at Truro 31 Oct. 1765
(4:244).

Long, Mary. Dau. of William/Catherine
(Kennedy) of Co. Kilkenny, Ire-
land; marr. Halifax 11 Jan. 1820
Richard Kearn (31:48).

Long, Michael. S. of Patrick/Mary
(Flanigan) of Co. Tipperary,
Ireland; marr. Halifax 31 Oct.
1835 Ann Troy (q.v.) (34:133).

Long, Peter. Grantee 'Digby New
Grant' 29 Jan. 1801 (5:82).

Long, Peter. Loyalist; plus 1 f.;
mustered at Digby 19 May 1784 (39:
192).

Long, William. From Ireland; land
grant at Londonderry 6 Mar. 1775
(4:258).

Long, William. S. of Patrick/Elenor
(Roche) of Co. Kilkenny, Ireland;
marr. Halifax 10 Sep. 1812 Anne
Fitzsimons (30:107).

Longworth, Isaac. Grantee 'Digby New
Grant' 29 Jan. 1801 (5:82).

Longworth, Isaac. Loyalist; plus 1
f./1 ch.; mustered at Digby 19 May

1784 (39:123).

Lonus, John. Lunenburg, Mass., to Chester with first settlers (16: 45).

Lotheride, Robert. From Mass.; land grant at Truro 1759 (4:242).

Lothier, Mary. 21, servant; Hull to Fort Cumberland on ALBION 7-14 March 1774 (21:140).

Loughlin, James. S. of Michael/Ellen (Cummoford) of Co. Kilkenny, Ireland; marr. Halifax 30 Aug. 1836 Anastasia Byrnes (34:133).

Loughran, Walter. Laborer; Irish; 22; Liverpool to Nova Scotia May 1864 on EUROCLYDON (45:182).

Lovell, John. Plus 1 f./1 svt.; farmer; Port Roseway Associate (6:15).

Lovet, Israel. Piscataqua, Mass. (now Me.), to Chester with first settlers (16:45).

Lovett, Ann. Dau. of John/Mary (Moriarty) of Co. Kerry, Ireland; marr. Halifax 10 Jan. 1843 John Murphy (q.v.) (35:142).

Lovett, Phineas. Grantee "Digby New Grant" 29 Jan. 1801 (5:82).

Lovitt, Phineas. Capt.; New England to Annapolis 1760 (18:271).

Lowe, David. Loyalist; plus 1 f./1 ch.; mustered at Digby 19 May 1784 (39:123).

Lowe, George. Plus 1 f./3 svts.; Port Roseway Associate (6:16).

Lowe, John. Grantee "Digby New Grant" 29 Jan. 1801 (5:82).

Lowe, John. Loyalist; plus 1 f./8 ch.; mustered at Gulliver's Hole/ St. Mary's Bay/Sissiboo 1/6 June 1784; settled at Sissiboo (now Weymouth) (40:262).

Lowe, William. Grantee "Digby New Grant" 29 Jan. 1801 (5:82).

Lowe, William. Loyalist; mustered at Gulliver's Hole/St. Mary's Bay/

Sissiboo 1/6 June 1784; settled at Sissiboo (now Weymouth) (40:262).

Lowerson, Mary. 27; to join husband; Hull, Yorkshire, to Port Cumberland on JENNY 3-10 April 1775 (22: 123).

Lowerson, Richard. 32, husbandman; Hull to Fort Cumberland on ALBION 7-14 March 1774 (21:138).

Lowlett, William Loyalist; mustered at Digby 19 May 1784 (39:123).

Lownds, John. Plus 1 f./1 ch./6 svts.; mariner; Port Roseway Associate (6:15).

Lownsberry, Gilbert. Plus 1 f./1 ch. -8; arr. Annapolis from New York 19 Oct. 1782 (37:125).

Lownsberry, Michel. Arr. Annapolis from New York 19 Oct. 1782 (37: 126).

Lowry, Honora. Dau. of John/Catherine (Myers) of Co. Tipperary, Ireland; marr. Halifax 29 Oct. 1833 Philip Purcell (q.v.) (33:66).

Lowry, James. Plus 1 f./1 ch./2 svts.; carpenter; Port Roseway Associate (6:15).

Lowry, Mary. 27; to join husband; Hull, Yorkshire, to Fort Cumberland on JENNY 3-10 April 1775 (22: 123).

Loyd, Margaret. Dau. of William/ Margaret (O'Brien) of Co. Tipperary, Ireland; marr. Halifax 7 Aug. 1832 John Harney (q.v.) (33:59).

Lucas, Thomas. S. of John/Margaret (Wind) of Parish Aglish, Co. Waterford, Ireland; marr. Halifax 9 May 1823 Johanna MacKensy (31:49).

Luce, Ebenezer. From Mass.; land grant at Truro 1759 (4:242).

Ludlam, Jacob. Loyalist; mustered at Digby 19 May 1784 (39:192).

Lull, Benjamin Jr. From Mass.; land grant at Truro 1759 (4:242).

Lull, Benjamin. From Mass.; land
grant at Truro 1759 (4:242).
Lumley, Diana. 14, daughter of Tho-
mas; Hull to Fort Cumberland on
ALBION 7-14 March 1774 (21:137).
Lumley, John. 23; husbandman; Hull,
Yorkshire, to Nova Scotia; on TWO
FRIENDS 28 Feb.-7 Mar. 1774 (25:
29).
Lumley, John. 6, s. of Thomas; Hull
to Fort Cumberland on ALBION 7-14
March 1774 (21:137).
Lumley, Ruth. 44, wife of Thomas;
Hull to Fort Cumberland on ALBION
7-14 March 1774 (21:137).
Lumley, Thomas. 45, farmer; Hull to
Fort Cumberland on ALBION 7-14
March 1774 (21:137).
Lundy, John. Loyalist; mustered at
Digby 19 May 1784 (39:123).
Lunn, William. Loyalist; mustered at
Digby 19 May 1784 (39:192).
Lydiard, Sylvester. S, Peter/Ann
(Ward) of Co. Longford, Ireland;
marr. Halifax 29 Jan. 1834 Cather-
ine Ryan (q.v.) (33:62).
Lynagh, Richard. S. of Michael/Ellen
(Walsh) of Carrick-on-Suir, Co.
Tipperary, Ireland; marr. Halifax
27 Aug. 1829 Margaret Nowlan
(q.v.) (32:114).
Lynch, Catherine. Dau. of James/Honor
(Prendergast) of Co. Cork, Ire-
land; marr. Halifax 25 May 1829
Patrick Mahony (q.v.) (32:115).
Lynch, Catherine. Dau. of John/Marga-
ret (Moran) of Co. Limerick, Ire-
land; marr. Halifax 23 Dec. 1839
James Bennett (q.v.) (34:125).
Lynch, Edward. English; 24; Liverpool
to Nova Scotia June 1864 on INDIAN
QUEEN (45:1.2).
Lynch, Elizabeth. Dau. of Thomas/
Margaret (Savage) of Co. Cork,
Ireland; marr. Halifax 7 Aug. 1844

John Manning (q.v.) (35:141).
Lynch, Fenton. Widower of Mary Con-
nors; of Co. Leix, Ireland; marr.
Halifax 11 Sep. 1832 Elizabeth
Roche (q.v.) (33:62).
Lynch, James. Widower of Honora
Pendergast; of Co. Cork, Ireland;
marr. Halifax 15 Apr. 1833 Mary
Walsh widow of James Lyons (33:
62).
Lynch, John. S. of Denis/Ellen
(Burke) of Co. Waterford, Ireland;
marr. Halifax 4 Oct. 1839 Margaret
Dalton (q.v.) (34:133).
Lynch, John. S. of Denis/Eleanor
(Connell) of Co. Kerry, Ireland;
marr. Halifax 10 May 1843 Joanna
Moore (q.v.) (35:140).
Lynch, Mary. Widow of John Vance of
Co. Galway, Ireland; marr. Halifax
30 May 1841 Pvt. Robert Morrow
(q.v.) (35:142).
Lynch, Michael. S. of William/Marga-
ret (Mullins) of Co. Waterford,
Ireland; marr. Halifax 25 Oct.
1832 Ellen Magrath (q.v.) (33:62).
Lynch, Michael. S. of James/Elenor
(Kinehan) of Co. Kilkenny, Ire-
land; marr. Halifax 31 July 1832
Bridget Smyth (q.v.) (33:62).
Lynch, Patrick. S. of Brian/Catherine
(Owens) of Co. Meath, Ireland;
widower of Margaret Mitchell;
marr. Halifax 21 June 1834 Susanah
McGouvern (33:62).
Lynch, Peter. Plus 1 f./4 ch./8
svts.; hatter; Port Roseway Asso-
ciate (6:15).
Lynch, Philip. S. of Thomas/Catherine
(Dalton) of Co. Cavan, Ireland;
marr. Halifax 2 June 1829 Elleanor
Coile (q.v.) (32:114).
Lynch, Redmond. S. of William/Marga-
ret (Mulgin) of Co. Waterford,
Ireland; marr. Halifax 16 June

1835 Catherine Armon (q.v.) (34: 133).

Lynch, Thomas. S. of Neill/Mary (English) of Co. Mayo, Ireland; marr. Halifax 7 June 1839 Catherine Connelly (q.v.) (34:133).

Lynch, William. S. of John/Ellen (Barry) of Co. Cork, Ireland; marr. Halifax 30 Jan. 1842 Catherine Rahilly (q.v.) (35:140).

Lynds, Bernard. S. of Jacob and Mary (Gould); b. 26 Oct. 1752 Malden, Mass.; to Onslow with parents (4: 230).

Lynds, Jacob. S. of Thomas and Lydia (Green); b. 18 May 1716 Malden, Mass.; antecedents English, not Irish as Miller, Colchester, claims; plus family; Charlestown, Mass., to Onslow (4: 230).

Lynds, Jacob. S. of Jacob and Mary (Gould); b. twin 27 July 1751 Malden, Mass.; to Onslow with parents (4:230).

Lynds, John. S. of Jacob and Mary (Gould); b. 30 Mar. 1757 Malden, Mass.; to Onslow with parents (4: 230).

Lynds, Lydia. Dau. of Jacob and Mary (Gould); b. 25 Mar. 1755 Malden, Mass.; to Onslow with parents (4: 230).

Lynds, Mary, Wife of Jacob; dau. of ----- Gould; to Onslow with husband (4:230).

Lynds, Mary. Dau. of Jacob and Mary (Gould); b. twin 27 July 1751 Malden, Mass.; to Onslow with parents (4:230).

Lynds, Ruth, Dau. of Jacob and Mary (Gould); b. 6 Nov. 1759 Malden, Mass.; to Onslow with parents (4: 230).

Lynds, Thomas. S. of Jacob and Mary (Gould); b. 23 Dec. 1748 Malden,

Mass.; to Onslow with parents (4: 230).

Lyon, Charles. Plus 1 f./1 svt; Port Roseway Associate (6:15).

Lyon, James. From Ireland; land grant at Londonderry 6 Mar. 1775 (4: 258).

Lyon, James. From Mass.; land grant at Onslow 21 Feb. 1769 (4:224).

Lyons, Andrew. S. of Humphrey/Joanna (Dowling) of Bandon, Co. Cork, Ireland; marr. Halifax 5 May 1829 Mary O'Hear (q.v.) (32:114).

Lyons, John. S. of Thomas/Johanna (Hackett) of Cork City, Ireland; marr. Halifax 6 Nov. 1826 Johanna Tobin (32:114).

Lyons, Lawrence. S. of James/Ellen (Quinlan) of Co. Tipperary, Ireland; marr. Halifax 23 Sep. 1833 Joanna Mokler (q.v.) (33:62).

Lyons, Mary. Dau. of William/Catherine (Gorman) of Kilbarry, Co. Cork, Ireland; marr. Halifax 28 July 1823 Pvt. Edmund Sullivan (q.v.) (31:54).

Lyons, Mary. Dau. of Michael/Mary (O'Flaherty) of Co. Mayo, Ireland; marr. Halifax 15 May 1842 (q.v.) (35:135).

Lyons, Michael. S. of Thomas/Mary (Murphy) of Co. Kilkenny, Ireland; marr. Halifax 15 Jan. 1835 Ann Watt (34:133).

Lyons, Thomas. S. of Patrick/Honora (Mullowney) of Newtownhunt, Co. Kilkenny, Ireland; marr. Halifax 21 June 1824 Catherine White widow of Thomas Guinan (31:49).

- M -

MacAnelly, Margaret. Dau. of John/ Hanah (McNamara) of Co. Tyrone, Ireland; marr. Halifax 6 June 1834

(R.C.) (also marr. Parish of St.
Paul's, Halifax (C.of E.) 11 Oct.
1833) Sylvester Keating (q.v.)
(33:60).

Macarthy, James. S. of Cornelius/
Honora (Carey) of Co. Cork, Ire-
land; marr. Halifax 10 Oct. 1829
Eleanor Spence (q.v.) (32:114).

MacAvoy, Catherine. Dau. of William/
Bridger (Elwart) of Co. Kilkenny,
Ireland; marr. Halifax 2 Oct. 1832
Edward Glendon (q.v.) (33:58).

MacCormack, Catherine. Dau. of
Richard/ Bridget (Casey) of Co.
Longford, Ireland; marr. Halifax 4
Nov. 1829 Kenny Goggan (q.v.) (32:
111).

Macculan, Catherine. Of Quebec; marr.
Halifax 28 May 1811 Daniel Egan
(q.v.) (30:105).

MacCulla, Ellen. Dau. of George/
Barbara (Magher) of Co. Kilkenny,
Ireland; marr. Halifax 5 Feb. 1831
Thomas Hinessy (q.v.) (33:59).

MacDodwell, Margaret. Dau. of Owen/
Mary of Co. Fermanagh, Ireland;
marr. Halifax 10 May 1838 William
Gilfoil (q.v.) (34:130).

MacEvoy, John. S. of Patrick/Mary
(Cahill) of Thomastown, Co. Kilkenny, Ireland; marr. Halifax 16
May 1841 Catherine Fitzmaurice
(q.v.) (35:140).

MacFarlane, Ann. Dau. of Ahab/Eliza-
beth (MacCallum) of Glasgow, Scotland; marr. Halifax 10 Aug. 1814
James Kelly (q.v.) (30:106).

MacGilpin, Jane. Dau. of Henry/Jane
(Reed) of Drownmona, Co. Antrim,
Ireland; marr. Halifax 15 June
1825 Daniel McSwiney (q.v.) (31:
54).

MacIver, John. S. of James/Margaret
(Cail) of Co. Donegal, Ireland;
marr. Halifax 28 Apr. 1836 Cather-

ine Walsh (q.v.) (34:134).

MacIvoy, Anastasia. Of Co. Leix,
Ireland; marr. Halifax 21 Aug.
1842 Jeremiah Hobin (q.v.) (35:
138).

Mack, Catherine. Dau. of Henry/
Bridget (Walsh) of Co. Waterford,
Ireland; marr. Halifax 12 Nov.
1835 William Murphy (q.v.) (34:
136).

Mackesy, John. S. of David/Ann
(Murphy) of Co. Carlow, Ireland;
marr. Halifax 13 Oct. 1829 Mary
Kealy (q.v.) (32:115).

Mackey, Bridget. See Weston, Bridget.

Mackey, Bridget. Widow of Richard
Asbel; of Nfld.; marr. Halifax 25
Apr. 1834 David Hinissy (q.v.)
(33: 59).

Mackey, Michael. S. of John/Bridget
(Forrestall) of Co. Kilkenny,
Ireland; marr. Halifax 29 Feb.
1836 Bridget Weston (q.v.) (34:
134).

Maddon, Daniel. Corp., 81st Regt.; s.
of Michael/Catherine (Crotty) of
Co. Tipperary, Ireland; marr.
Halifax 24 Aug. 1822 Jane Anne
Whittingham (31:49).

Maddox, Elizabeth. Dau. of James/Mary
(Murphy) of Placentia, Nfld.;
marr. Halifax 10 Aug. 1802 Michael
Power (q.v.) (30:110).

Madigan, Martin. S. of John/Margaret
(Cusick) of Co. Limerick Ireland;
marr. Halifax 28 Sep. 1841 Mary
Kihoe (q.v.) (35:141).

Madox, Elener. Dau. of James/Mary
(Murphy) of Placentia, Nfld.;
marr. Halifax 27 Oct. 1807 William
Casson (q.v.) (30:103).

Magee, Ellen. Dau. of Francis/Judith
(Murrough) of Co. Armagh, Ireland;
marr. Halifax 2 Mar. 1835 Stephen
Donnelly (q.v.) (34:129).

Magher, Anastasia. Dau, John/Cather-
ine (Power) of Co. Kilkenny,
Ireland; marr. Halifax 4 May 1843
Jeremiah Donohue (q.v.) (35:137).

Magher, Catherine. Dau. of John/Mary
(Douny) of Tramore. Co. Waterford,
Ireland; marr. Halifax 9 Feb. 1834
William Delany; Halifax-Co. Kil-
kenny, Ireland-Halifax ca. 1845
(33:56).

Magher, Daniel. S. of Daniel/Ellen of
Co. Tipperary, Ireland; marr.
Halifax 26 Sep. 1840 Margaret
Magher (q.v.) (34:134).

Magher, Edmund. S. of Philip/Cather-
ine (O'Brien) of Co. Waterford,
Ireland; marr. Halifax 8 Feb. 1842
Mary Power (35:141).

Magher, Ellen. Widow of Michael
Gorman of Co. Tipperary, Ireland;
marr. Halifax 9 Apr. 1839 Thomas
Gully (q.v.) (34:131).

Magher, Honora. Dau. of Timothy/Alice
(Munroney) of Co. Kilkenny, Ire-
land; marr. Halifax 30 Oct. 1832
Edmund Byrnes (q.v.) (33:55).

Magher, James. S. of Timothy/Joanna
(Campion) of Co. Tipperary, Ire-
land; marr. Halifax 7 Dec. 1841
Catherine Walsh (35:141).

Magher, Joanna. Dau. of William/
Honora (Dwyer) of Co. Tipperary,
Ireland; marr. Halifax 29 June
1840 John Duggan (q.v.) (34:129).

Magher, John. S. of Thomas/Catherine
(Donnell) of Co. Tipperary, Ire-
land; marr. Halifax 5 July 1831
Anastasia Walsh (q.v.) (33:63).

Magher, John. S. of Edmund/Mary
(Kavanagh) of Co. Tipperary,
Ireland; marr. Halifax 16 May 1834
Honora McCarthy (q.v.) (33:63).

Magher, John. S. of John/Mary (Cahill) of Co. Tipperary, Ireland;
marr. Halifax 29 Apr. 1843 Ellen

Dudly (q.v.) (35:141).

Magher, John. S. of William/Honora
(Dwyer) of Co. Tipperary, Ireland;
marr. Halifax 10 Aug. 1843 Alice
Oakley (q.v.) (35:141).

Magher, Margaret. Dau. of James/
Catherine (Doyle) of Carlow, Ire-
land; marr. Halifax 20 May 1830
John Madget (32:115).

Magher, Margaret. D, John/Ellen
(Ryan) of Co. Tipperary, Ireland;
marr. Halifax 26 Sep. 1840 Daniel
Magher (q.v.) (34:134).

Magher, Martin. S. of Timothy/Cather-
ine (Kelly) of Waterford City,
Ireland; marr. Halifax 10 June
1833 Joanna O'Brien (q.v.) (33:
63).

Magher, Mary. Dau. of Patrick/Ellen
(Colbert) of Nfld.; marr. Halifax
10 June 1833 Richard Byrnes (q.v.)
(33:55).

Magher, Michael. S. of Andrew/Bridget
(Purcell) of Co. Tipperary, Ire-
land; marr. Halifax 5 Oct. 1833
Catherine Morissy (q.v.) (33:63).

Magher, Michael. S. of John/Joanna
(Hogan) of Co. Tipperary, Ireland;
marr. Halifax 10 Sep. 1844 Ellen
Woods (q.v.) (35:141).

Magher, Nicholas. S. of Nicholas/Mary
(Holleran) of Co. Tipperary, Ire-
land; marr. Halifax 3 Feb. 1845
Joanna O'Brien (q.v.) (35:141).

Magher, Patrick. S. of Philip/Honora
(Magrigor) of Co. Waterford, Ire-
land; marr. Halifax 28 Jan. 1838
Margaret Cashman (q.v.) (34:134).

Magher, Patrick. S. of Nicholas/Mary
(Holleran) of Parish Clonyne, Co.
Tipperary, Ireland; marr. Halifax
30 July 1835 Bridget Gilfoyle
(q.v.) (34:134).

Magher, Richard. S. of Thomas/Mary
(Walsh) of Co. Tipperary, Ireland;

148

marr. Halifax 30 Nov. 1833 Mary
Lambert (33:63).

Magher, Thomas. S. of John/Mary
(Downy) of Co. Waterford, Ireland;
marr. Halifax 23 July 1831 Mary
Elizabeth Bertrim (q.v.) (33:63).

Magher, Thomas. S. of Daniel/Eleanor
of Co. Tipperary, Ireland; marr.
Halifax 14 Oct. 1832 Joanna Quigley (q.v.) (33:63).

Magher, Thomas. S. of Patrick/Mary
(Conrick) of Co. Waterford, Ire-
land; marr. Halifax 3 Jan. 1839
Mary Penlan (q.v.) (34:134).

Magher, Timothy. S. of Nicholas/
Catherine (Hynes) of Co. Tipperary, Ireland; marr. Halifax 21
July 1838 Bridget Freeman (q.v.)
(34:134).

Magee, Samuel. Loyalist; mustered at
Digby 19 May 1784 (39:192).

Magher, William. S. of Michael/Mary
(O'Neill) of Co. Tipperary, Ire-
land; marr. Halifax 10 Sep. 1840
Margaret Davidson (34:134).

Magher, William. S. of Patrick/Mary
(Condon) of Co. Tipperary, Ire-
land; marr. Halifax 9 Apr. 1839
Mary Skihan (q.v.) (34:134).

Magory, Sarah. Dau. of Bernard/Mary
(McIver) of Magherafelt, Co.
Derry, Ireland; widow of Michael
Howard; marr. Halifax 10 June 1833
Pierce Sullivan (q.v.) (33:67).

Magowen, Ann. Dau. of James/Bridget
(MacLown) of Co. Sligo, Ireland;
marr. Halifax 24 Nov. 1831 Michael
Devanny (q.v.) (33:56).

Magown, Mary. Dau. of James/Bridget
(Malon) of Co. Leitrim, Ireland;
marr. Halifax 14 Sep. 1828 William
Gillon (q.v.) (32:111).

Magragh, Bridget. Dau. of John/Mary
(Murphy) of Co. Tipperary, Ireland; marr. Halifax 23 Nov. 1820

David O.Neil (q.v.) (31:51).

Magrah, Mary. Dau. of Luke/Catherine
(Murray) of Ross, Co. Wexford,
Ireland; widow of Thomas Watson;
marr. Halifax 30 June 1803 Edmund
Power (q.v.) (30:109).

Magrath, Andrew. S. of John/Mary
(Mooney) of Parish Stradbally, Co.
Waterford, Ireland; marr. Halifax
28 Aug. 1829 Margaret Whelan
(q.v.) (32:115).

Magrath, Anne. Dau. of Denis/Mary
(Croke) of Co. Tipperary, Ireland;
marr. Halifax 19 Apr. 1841 John
Paine (q.v.) (35:143).

Magrath, Catherine. Of Co. Tipperary,
Ireland; widow of John Connors;
marr. Halifax 9 Oct. 1841 Michael
Coffee (q.v.) (35:136).

Magrath, Edmund. S. of Daniel/Mary
(Furnace) of Co. Kilkenny, Ire-
land; marr. Halifax 28 Nov. 1832
Mary Molony (q.v.) (33:62).

Magrath, Elenor. See McCormack,
Elenor.

Magrath, Ellen. Dau. of Thomas/Mary
(Manning) of Co. Kilkenny, Ire-
land; marr. Halifax 23 May 1832
Michael Larkin (q.v.) (33:61).

Magrath, Ellen. Dau. of Dennis/
Catherine (Daveny) of Co. Tipperary, Ireland; marr. Halifax 25
Oct. 1832 Michael Lynch (q.v.)
(33:62).

Magrath, Ellen. Dau. of James/Cather-
ine (Foley) of Clonmel, Co. Tipperary, Ireland; marr. Halifax 4
May 1841 James Ryan (q.v.) (35:
144).

Magrath, James. 34th Regt.; of Co.
Kildare, Ireland; marr. Halifax 19
Aug. 1837 Mary Irvin (q.v.) (34:
134).

Magrath, Joanna. Dau. of Patrick/
Catherine (Murphy) of Co. Kilken-

ny, Ireland; marr. Halifax 14 Nov. 1839 John Lanigan (q.v.) (34:133).

Magrath, Johanna. Dau. of Silvester/ Ann of Co. Wexford, Ireland; marr. Halifax 17 Aug. 1810 James O'Mely (q.v.) (30:109).

Magrath, Margaret. See Stapleton, Margaret.

Magrath, Maria. Dau. of William/Mary (Milley) of Waterford City, Ireland; marr. Halifax 28 Jan. 1840 Maurice Grady (q.v.) (34:130).

Magrath, Mary. Dau. of James/Elenor (Walsh) of Kilmacow, Co. Kilkenny, Ireland; marr. Halifax 31 July 1829 Patrick O'Connor (q.v.) (32:117).

Magrath, Maurice. S. of Maurice/Madge (Dunn) of Co. Carlow, Ireland; marr. Halifax 15 Apr. 1831 Margaret Griffith (q.v.) (33:62).

Magrath, Patrick. S. of Patrick/Mary (Mirwin) of Waterford City, Ireland; marr. Halifax 1 Oct. 1840 Mary Elizabeth Kelly (34:134).

Magrath, Thomas. S. of Thomas/Ellen (Harrihan) of Co. Waterford, Ireland; marr. Halifax 12 Nov. 1832 Ellen Quinlan (q.v.) (33:62).

Maguire, Hugh. S. of John/Catherine of Parish Gladech, Co. Fermanagh, Ireland; marr. Halifax 22 Sep. 1826 Mary A. Moore (q.v.) (32:115).

Maguire, James. S. of William/Margery (Galliger) of Co. Fermanagh, Ireland; marr. Halifax 20 Feb. 1844 Bridget Higgins (q.v.) (35:141).

Maguire, John. Of Co. Cavan, Ireland; widower of Ann Farrell; marr. Halifax 15 Apr. 1836 Elizabeth Marster (34:134).

Maguire, John. S. of John/Mary (Scully) of Co. Tipperary, Ireland; marr. Halifax 5 Mar. 1831 Bridget Ronan (q.v.) (33:62).

Maguire, Mary. Dau. of John/Bridget (Franklin) of Co. Cavan, Ireland; marr. Halifax 9 Feb. 1833 Michael Syngen (q.v.) (33:67).

Maguire, Rosanne. Dau. of Daniel/ Ellen (McInnis) of Co. Leitrim, Ireland; marr. Halifax 8 Sep. 1842 John Duffy (q.v.) (35:137).

Mahan, John. S. of James/Catherine (Manaher) of Co. Wexford, Ireland; marr. Halifax 24 Jan. 1822 Mary O'Conor (q.v.) (31:49).

Magher, Patrick. Laborer; English; 24; Liverpool to Nova Scotia June 1864 on INDIAN QUEEN (45:182).

Magher, Johanna. English; 11; Liverpool to Nova Scotia June 1864 on INDIAN QUEEN (45:182).

Mahar, Anne. Dau. of Fenton/Elizabeth (Mahan) of Co. Leix, Ireland; marr. Halifax 17 May 1840 William Leahy (q.v.) (34:133).

Mahar, William. S. of James/Mary of Kings Co., Ireland; marr. Halifax 25 June 1814 Mary Whitby (30:107).

Maher, Catherine. Dau. of James/Mary (Morysy) of Clonmel, Co. Tipperary, Ireland; marr. Halifax 2 Feb. 1828 Patrick Fitzpatrick (voided in register) (q.v.) (32:110).

Maher, James. S. of Joseph/Honora (Quinn) of Fethard, Co. Tipperary, Ireland; marr. Halifax 12 Aug. 1826 Mary McGrath (32:115).

Maher, Jane. Dau. of Richard/Jane (Carleton) of Co. Waterford, Ireland; marr. Halifax 7 Feb. 1807 Patrick Gleeson (q.v.) (30:105).

Maher, John. S. of John/Ann (Kelly) of Co. Kilkenny, Ireland; marr. Halifax 12 June 1813 Catherine Mahar (30:107).

Maher, John. S. of Michael/Mary (Walsh) of Ryecash, Gowran, Co.

Kilkenny, Ireland; marr. Halifax 2 Jan. 1822 Bridget Kennedy (31:49).

Maher, Martin. S. of James/Mary of Thurles, Co. Tipperary, Ireland; marr. Halifax 24 Dec. 1812 Mary Watts (30:107).

Maher, Thomas. S. of Thomas/Elinor (Hickey) of Parish Ballyduff, Waterford, Ireland; marr. Halifax 3 June 1822 Nancy Dowd (q.v.) (31:50).

Maher, Thomas. S. of Thomas/Mary (Keily) of Parish Ballyragget, Co. Kilkenny, Ireland; marr. Halifax 24 Jan. 1837 Sarah Fraser (34:134).

Mahon, James. From Ireland; land grant at Londonderry 6 Mar. 1775 (4:258).

Mahon, James. S. of Michael/Catherine (Doran) of Gowran, Co. Kilkenny, Ireland; marr. Halifax 10 Jan. 1828 Joanna Lahy (q.v.) (32:115).

Mahon, Patrick. S. of Michael/Catherine (Doran) of Gowran, Co. Kilkenny, Ireland; marr. Halifax 21 Nov. 1829 Sarah Lawrence (32:115).

Mahone, Timothy. Plus 1 f./2 svts.; Port Roseway Associate (6:16).

Mahony, Bridget. Dau. of John/Mary (Dacy) of Innishannon, Co. Cork, Ireland; marr. Halifax 23 Apr. 1831 John Walsh (q.v.) (33:68).

Mahony, John. Of Co. Cork, Ireland; widower of Catherine Murphy; marr. Halifax 31 Mar. 1845 Martha MacLeherty widow of Timothy Canty (35:141).

Mahony, John. S. of John/Mary (Dacy) of Inishannon, Co. Cork, Ireland; marr. Halifax 4 Oct. 1828 Mary Donagan (q.v.) (32:115).

Mack, Samuel. To Liverpool ca. 1760 (47:126:160).

Mahony, John. S. of Maurice/Mary (Pointze) of Waterford, Ireland; marr. Halifax 4 May 1827 Eleanor Enwright (32:115).

Mahony, John. S. of Maurice/Mary (Pine) of Co. Waterford, Ireland; widower of Ellen Enright; marr. Halifax 28 May 1832 Ann Moran (q.v.) (33:63).

Mahony, John. S. of Morty/Ellen (Sullvan) [sic] of Co. Cork, Ireland; marr. Halifax 31 Jan. 1833 Ellen Caddigan (q.v.) (33:63).

Mahony, John. S. of Charles/Ellen (Chasty) of Dungarvan, Co. Waterford, Ireland; marr. Halifax 27 Apr. 1843 Susanna Peck (35:141).

Mahony, Margaret. Dau. of Daniel/Ellen (Sisk) of Cloyne, Co. Cork, Ireland; marr. Halifax 22 Aug. 1829 Cornelius Desmond (q.v.) (32:108).

Mahony, Patrick. S. of John/Margaret (Slaughtery) of St. John's, Nfld.; marr,. Halifax 3 June 1820 Anne Connell (31:50).

Mahony, Patrick. S. of Daniel/Ann (Price) of Co. Kilkenny, Ireland; marr. Halifax 25 May 1829 Catherine Lynch (q.v.) (32:115).

Mahony, Patrick. S. of James/Catherine (Fitzgerald) of Co. Monaghan, Ireland; marr. Halifax 3 Aug. 1830 Catherine O'Holleran (q.v.) (32:116).

Mahony, Patrick. S. of Lewis/Mary (Dwyer) of Co. Kilkenny, Ireland; marr. Halifax 25 Oct. 1832 Bridget Drea (q.v.) (33:63).

Mahony, Thomas. S. of John/Mary (Dacy) of Inishannon, Co. Cork, Ireland; marr. Halifax 16 Jan. 1830 Ellen Desmond (q.v.) (32:115).

Majoribanks, Thomas. Grantee "Digby New Grant" 29 Jan. 1801 (5:82).

Majoribanks, Thomas. Loyalist; plus 2 f./4 ch.; mustered at Digby 19 May 1784 (39:192).

Makaisie, Lydia. Dau. of Alexander/ Anne (Galagher) of Londonderry, Ireland; marr. Halifax 21 May 1813 John Barclay (q.v.) (30:102).

Mallery, Caleb. Plus 1 f./1 ch./1 svt.; Port Roseway Associate (6: 16).

Mann, Andrew. Grantee "Digby New Grant" 29 Jan. 1801 (5:82).

Mann, John. To Liverpool by 1787 (47:127:54).

Mann, Samuel. Farmer; Port Roseway Associate (6:16).

Manning, Elizabeth. Dau. of William/ Mary (Harrington) of Cloyne, Co. Cork, Ireland; marr. Halifax 22 June 1829 William Bates (q.v.) (32:105).

Manning, James. S. of Bartholomew/ Johana (Alvard) of Glavinan, Kilkenny, Ireland; marr. Halifax 7 Sep. 1820 Elizabeth Murphy widow of John Clark (31:50).

Mack, Samuel. S. of Samuel/Desire; to (or b.?) Liverpool by 1791 (47: 127:118).

Manning, John. S. of John/Catherine (Lester) of Co. Roscommon, Ireland; marr. Halifax 8 Nov. 1814 Madeleine Cloutier (q.v.) (30: 107).

Manning, John. S. of William/Mary (Harrington) of Parish Cloyne, Co. Cork, Ireland; marr. Halifax 22 Nov. 1824 Elenor Lyons (31:50).

Manning, John. S. of Daniel/Mary (Murphy) of Co. Cork, Ireland; marr. Halifax 15 Jan. 1833 Mary Cashman (q.v.) (33:63).

Manning, John. S. of Darby/Margaret (O'Brien) of Co. Cork, Ireland; marr. Halifax 7 Aug. 1844 Eliza-

beth Lynch (q.v.) (35:141).

Mansel, Thomas. Of Co. Tipperary, Ireland; marr. 16 May 1802 Mary Lamb widow of John Fitzmaurice (30:108).

Mansell, Thomas. S. of James/Elenor (Conoher) of Clonmel, Co. Tipperary, Ireland; marr. Halifax 20 July 1811 Lucy Nicholls (q.v.) (30: 108).

Mansfield, Margaret. See Murphy, Margaret.

Mansfield, Peter. S. of Peter/Bridget (Meehan) of Glamore, Co. Kilkenny, Ireland; marr. Halifax 4 Aug. 1822 Isobel Field (31:50).

Manthorn, George. S. of William/ Sally; to (or b.?) Liverpool by 1792 (47:127:125).

Mara, Edmund. S. of John/Johanna (Daly) of Co. Tipperary, Ireland; marr. Halifax 23 Apr. 1812 Elizabeth Williams (30:108).

Mara, Michael. S. of John/Anne (Meran) of Kilbarry, Co. Tipperary, Ireland; marr. Halifax 17 Sep. 1803 Anne Cameron (q.v.) (30:108).

Mara, Michael. S. of John/Margaret (Dullehanty) of Templeorum, Co. Kilkenny, Ireland; marr. Halifax 10 Nov. 1831 Catherine Morissey (q.v.) (33:63).

Mara, Thomas. S. of John/Johanna (Daly) of Co. Tipperary, Ireland; marr. Halifax 9 Dec. 1813 Anne Conlon (30:108).

Mack, William. S. of Samuel/Desire; to (or b.?) Liverpool by 1794 (47: 127:203).

Man, Samuel. B. Elizabethtown, N.J.; s. of David/Sarah; to Liverpool by 1794 (47:127:204).

Marchant, Jesse. Plus 1 f./1 ch.; taylor; Port Roseway Associate

(6:16).

Markley, Denis. S. of James/Mary (Mulcahy) of Dungarvan, Co. Waterford, Ireland; marr. Halifax 10 Sep. 1834 Mary Walsh *(q.v.)* (34: 134).

Marks, Hezekiah. From Mass.; land grant at Truro 1759 (4:242).

Marks, Margaret. Of Three Rivers, Quebec; widow of David Herbert; marr. Halifax 8 June 1842 *(q.v.)* (35:144).

Marks, Robert. Deserted 15 June 1806 from H.M. 98th Regt. of Foot, stationed at Halifax; 5'10", dark complexion, black hair, brown eyes, ca. 32, b. Ireland; advertised *The Weekly Chronicle*, 21 June 1806 (28:34).

Marnell, John. S. of James/Mary (Fintin) of Ballylooby, Co. Tipperary, Ireland; marr. Halifax 20 Apr. 1823 Sarah McCann *(q.v.)* (31: 50).

Mann, Nancy. Dau. of John/Nancy; to (or b.?) Liverpool by 1787 (47: 127:212).

Marple, Richard. Loyalist; plus 4 svts.; mustered at Digby 19 May 1784 (39:192).

Marr, James. Loyalist; plus 1 f./7 ch.; mustered at Digby 19 May 1784 (39:192).

Marsh, Elijah. From Mass.; land grant at Truro 1759 (4:242).

Marsh, Judah. From Mass.; land grant at Truro 1759 (4:242).

MacPherson, Allan. To Liverpool by 1783 (47:127:277).

MacPherson, Hannah. Wife of Allan; to Liverpool by 1783 (47:127:277).

Marsh, Thomas. From Mass.; land grant at Truro 1759 (4:242).

Marshall, Anthony James. Grantee "Digby New Grant" 29 Jan. 1801 (5:

82).

Marshall, Israel. 28, husbandman; Hull to Fort Cumberland on ALBION 7-14 March 1774 (21:138).

Marshall, Joseph. New England to Annapolis on CHARMING MOLLY May 1760 (18:271).

Martin, Ann. Wife of William; b. 1745; bur. Folly Village, Londonderry (4:262).

Martin, Eliza. Dau. of Edward/Elizabeth (Sennett) of Co. Carlow, Ireland; marr. Halifax 20 Jan. 1834 Martin Divine *(q.v.)* (33:56).

Martin, Ellen. See Carleton, Ellen.

Martin, Hugh. S. of Hugh/Bridget (Maguire) of Co. Tyrone, Ireland; marr. Halifax 30 Nov. 1844 Joanna Power (35:141).

Martin, Julia. Spinster; Irish; 19; Liverpool to Nova Scotia June 1864 on INDIAN QUEEN (45:182).

Martin, Michael. S. of Thomas/Elenor (Brennan) of Parish St. Canice, Bonnetstown, Co. Kilkenny, Ireland; marr. Halifax 11 Oct. 1835 Catherine Mullowney *(q.v.)* (34: 135).

Martin, Patrick. S. of John/Margaret (Wallis) of Tullamore, Offaly, Ireland; marr. Halifax 8 Sep. 1822 Mary Davine *(q.v.)* (31:50).

Martin, Patrick. S. of Daniel/Mary (Doyle) of Co. Kilkenny, Ireland; widower of Mary Moran; marr. Halifax 16 Nov. 1830 Margaret Donovan *(q.v.)* (32:116).

Martin, Timothy. S. of Maurice/ Catherine (Devine) of Co. Kerry, Ireland; marr. Halifax 5 Oct. 1844 Mary Shaw *(q.v.)* (35:141).

Martin, William. Born 1741; bur. Folly Village, Londonderry (4: 262).

Martin, William. From Ireland; land

grant at Londonderry 6 Mar. 1775
(4:258).

Mason, Aaron. Plus wife/5 ch.; Marlborough, Mass., to Chester with
first settlers (16:45).

Mason, Aaron. Plus wife/5 ch.; Mass.,
to Chester 30 July 1759 (16:46).

Mason, Abraham. 43; husbandman; Hull,
Yorkshire, to Nova Scotia; on TWO
FRIENDS 28 Feb.-7 Mar. 1774 (25:
29).

Mason, Benjamin. New England to
Annapolis on CHARMING MOLLY May
1760 (18:271).

Mason, Catherine. Dau. of George/
Bridget (Tobin) of Co. Kilkenny,
Ireland; marr. Halifax 18 May 1843
James Troy (q.v.) (35:145).

Mason, John. Lexington, Mass., to
Chester with first settlers (16:
45).

Mathew, Mary. Of Co. Longford, Ireland, a convert to Roman Catholicism; marr. Halifax 6 Dec. 1831
Corp. Jeremiah Murphy (q.v.) (33:
64).

Mathews, Elizabeth. Dau. of John/
Elizabeth (Bradford) of Co. Tipperary, Ireland; marr. Halifax 25
Nov. 1834 Thomas Brown (q.v.) (34:
126).

Mathews, Mary. Dau. of John/Abigail;
to Liverpool ca. 1760 (47:126:96).

Matthew, George. S. of Thomas/Rose
(Meehan) of Thomastown. Co. Kilkenny, Ireland; marr. Halifax 9
Dec. 1813 Anne O'Brien (q.v.)
(30:108).

Matthews, Catherine. Dau. of Michael/
Ann (McMannis) of Co. Meath, Ireland; marr. Halifax 16 May 1830
Thomas Collins (q.v.) (32:107).

Matthews, John. Liverpool proprietor
(19:101).

Matthews, Marjorie. Dau. of Edward/

Catherine (Howard) of Co. Dublin,
Ireland; marr. Halifax 8 Sep. 1816
William Costin (q.v.) (30:104).

Matthews, Thomas. S. of Thomas/Sarah
(Ledurd) of Liverpool, England;
marr. Halifax 3 Apr. 1826 Mary
MacDonald (q.v.) (32:116).

Maturin, Edmund. Rev.; B. Ireland;
settled at Nova Scotia before 1859
(11:309).

Maxey, Bridget. Dau. of David/Margaret (Kenedy) of Clonmel, Co. Tipperary, Ireland; marr. Halifax 16
Feb. 1824 Denis Ryan (q.v.) (31:
53).

Maxfield, Mary. To (or b.?) Liverpool
by 1791 (47:127:57).

Maxwell, David. Plus 1 f./4 ch.; taylor; Port Roseway Associate (6:
16).

Maxwell, William. Mass. to N.S.; to
U.S. 1776; lived 1785 at Mass.
[which then incl. Me.] (36:64).

May, Catherine. Dau. of James/Bridget
(Flood) of Co. Longford, Ireland;
marr. Halifax 9 Jan. 1831 Patrick
Goggin (q.v.) (33:58).

May, Jane. See Donnelly, Jane.

Mayer, John Geo. Plus 3 svts.; farmer; Port Roseway Associate (6:16).

Mayo, Hannah. To Liverpool ca. 1760
(47:126:96).

McAdams, George. Philadelphia, Pa.,
to Liverpool by 1787 (47:127:268).

McAlpine, Donald. Plus 1 f./2 ch.;
Port Roseway Associate (6:16).

McAlpine, John Jr. B. Crown Point,
N. Y., 31 Dec. 1773; to Liverpool
(47:127:52).

McAlpine, John. B. Scotland; s. of
Peter/Christian; to Liverpool by
1784 (47:127:52).

McAlpine, John. Plus 1 f.; carpenter;
Port Roseway Associate (6:16).

McAlpine, John. Plus 1 ch./2 svts.;

farmer; Port Roseway Associate (6:
16).

McArther, Ann. Dau. of Barnaby/Mary
(Mc---) of Omagh, Co. Tyrone, Ire-
land; marr. Halifax 1 May 1842
Denis Murphy (q.v.) (35:142).

McAuliffe, James. S. of Denis/Marga-
ret (Regan) of Co. Cork, Ireland;
marr. Halifax 1 May 1834 Bridget
McDonnell (q.v.) (33:62).

McBride, Alexr. Arr. Annapolis from
New York 19 Oct. 1782 (37:125).

McCabe, Richard. S. of John/Anastatia
(Larkin) of Co. Wexford, Ireland;
marr. Halifax 27 Nov. 1821 Elizabeth Alice Londergan (31:42).

McCain, Thomas. S. of Thomas/Ann
(Hackett) of Co. Westmeath, Ireland; marr. Halifax 30 Apr. 1839
Elizabeth Mitchell (q.v.) (34:
133).

McCallum, Daniel. From Mass.; land
grant at Truro 1759 (4:242).

McCann, Sarah. Dau. of Kirby/Mary
(Carr) of Newtownhamilton, Co.
Armagh, Ireland; marr. Halifax 20
Apr. 1823 John Marnell (q.v.) (31:
50).

McCanniny, Ellen. Dau. of Cormack/
Bridget (Donnelly) of Co. Tyrone,
Ireland; marr. Halifax 16 Jan.
1842 (q.v.) (35:140).

McCarthy, Catherine. Dau. of Lau-
rence/Mary of Co. Cork, Ireland;
marr. Halifax 15 Oct. 1821 John
Nevin (q.v.) (31:51).

McCarthy, Catherine. Dau. of Denis/
Juliana (McSweeny), Killarney, Co.
Kerry, Ireland; marr. Halifax 10
Sep. 1828 John Hope (q.v.) (32:
113).

McCarthy, Catherine. Dau. of Charles/
Ellen (Murry) of Co. Cork, Ire-
land; marr. Halifax 30 July 1833
Jeremiah Murphy (q.v.) (33:64).

McCarthy, Catherine. Dau. of Jere-
miah/Catherine (Driscoll) of Co.
Cork, Ireland; marr. Halifax 7
Apr. 1834 John Ryan (q.v.) (33:
66).

McCarthy, Catherine. Dau. of Flo-
rence/Ann (Kearney) (sic) of Co.
Waterford, Ireland; marr. Halifax
14 Mar. 1839 Charles Moore (q.v.)
(34:135).

McCarthy, Denis. S. of Denis/Abigail
(Fleming) of Co. Waterford, Ire-
land; marr. Halifax 28 Apr. 1830
Mary Walsh (q.v.) (32:114).

McCarthy, Denis. S. of Charles/
Eleanor (Minehan) of Kinsale, Co.
Cork, Ireland; marr. Halifax 5
Sep. 1831 Joanna O'Leary (q.v.)
(33:62).

McCarthy, Ellen. Dau. of John/Honora
(Downey) of Co. Cork, Ireland;
marr. Halifax 28 Feb. 1835 John
Mockler (q.v.) (34:135).

McCarthy, Ellen. Dau. of William/
Margaret (Keeffe) of Co. Cork,
Ireland; marr. Halifax 14 July
1841 Stephen Wooding (q.v.) (35:
146).

McCarthy, Honora. Dau. of Michael/
Mary (Power) of Co. Cork, Ireland;
marr. Halifax 16 May 1834 John
Magher (q.v.) (33:63).

McCarthy, Honora. Dau. of Daniel/
Catherine (Sullivan) of Co. Kerry,
Ireland; marr. Halifax 14 May 1843
Michael Smith (q.v.) (35:144).

McCarthy, John. S. of Colman/Honora
(O'Brien) of Youghal, Co. Cork,
Ireland; marr. Halifax 4 Sep. 1823
Mary Garrett (31:42).

McCarthy, John. S. of Patrick/Bridget
(Murphy) of Kilkenny, Ireland;
marr. Halifax 16 June 1828 Bridget
Foley (q.v.) (32:114).

McCarthy, John. S. of Cornelius/

Honora (Carey) of Co. Cork, Ireland; marr. Halifax 14 Dec. 1830 Catherine Hogarty (q.v.) (32:114).

McCarthy, Mary Ann. Dau. of Daniel/Elenor (Connely) of Co. Cork, Ireland; marr. Halifax 12 Dec. 1820 Daniel Fitzpatrick (q.v.) (31:45).

McCarthy, Mary Anne. Dau. of Denis/Julian (McSweeney) of Killarney, Co. Kerry, Ireland; marr. Halifax 24 June 1825 James Byrne (q.v.) (31:42).

McCarthy, Mary. Dau. of Charles/Margaret (Punch) of Co. Limerick, Ireland; marr. Halifax 4 Feb. 1834 Mathew Kelly (q.v.) (33:60).

McCarthy, Mary. Dau. of Denis/Mary (Byrnes) of Co. Waterford, Ireland; marr. Halifax 18 July 1833 William Shanihan (q.v.) (33:66).

McCarthy, Michael. Pvt. 96th Regt.; s. of John/Honora (Byrne) of Co. Cork, Ireland; marr. Halifax 9 Jan. 1835 Ellen Dalton (q.v.) (34:133).

McCarthy, Michael. Of Doneraile, Co. Cork, Ireland; widower of Johanna Daly; marr. Halifax 25 Oct. 1834 Mary Murphy (q.v.) (34:133).

McCarthy, Patrick. Of Co. Cork, Ireland; marr. Halifax 20 Apr. 1841 Mary Bride (q.v.) (35:140).

McCarthy, Redmond. S. of Coleman/Honor (O'Brien) of Youghal, Co. Cork, Ireland; marr. Halifax 5 Oct. 1816 Margaret Ryan (q.v.) (30: 107).

McCarthy, Thomas. S. of Patrick/Bridget (Murphy) of Co. Kilkenny, Ireland; marr. Halifax 11 Sep. 1828 Mary Nolan (q.v.) (32:114).

McCasline, Dugald. Loyalist; plus 1 f./5 ch.; mustered at Digby 19 May 1784 (39:192).

McCauliff, John. S. of Thomas/Ellen (Doyle) of Co. Cork, Ireland; marr. Halifax 11 Feb. 1836 Joanna Geary (q.v.) (34:133).

McCawley, Patrick. Color Sgt. 34th Regt.; of Co. Donegal, Ireland; marr. Halifax 7 Jan. 1838 Catherine Finn (34:133).

McCay, Charles. From N.H.; effective land grant at Truro 31 Oct. 1765 (4:245).

McClane, Anthony. From Ireland; land grant at Londonderry 6 Mar. 1775 (4:258).

McClane, Samuel. From Ireland; land grant at Londonderry 6 Mar. 1775 (4:258).

McClarn, Isabella. Dau. of James/Isabella; to (or b.?) Liverpool by 1791 (47:127:117).

McClarn, Sarah. Dau. of John/Nancy; to Liverpool by 1787 (47:128:30).

McClelan, John. From Ireland; land grant at Londonderry 6 Mar. 1775 (4:258).

McClelan, Joseph. From Ireland; land grant at Londonderry 6 Mar. 1775 (4:258).

McClelan, Peter. From Ireland; land grant at Londonderry 6 Mar. 1775 (4:258).

McClelan, Robert. From Ireland; land grant at Londonderry 6 Mar. 1775 (4:258).

McClentag, William. From Ireland; land grant at Londonderry 6 Mar. 1775 (4:258).

McClintoch, Thomas. From Mass.; land grant at Truro 1759 (4:242).

McConnell, Benjamin. Grantee "Digby New Grant" 29 Jan. 1801 (5:82).

McConnell, Benjamin. Loyalist; mustered at Gulliver's Hole/St. Mary's Bay/Sissiboo 1/6 June 1784; settled at St. Mary's Bay (Plympton,

Barton, Brighton) (40:262).

McConnell, Joseph. Loyalist; mustered
at Gulliver's Hole/St. Mary's Bay/
Sissiboo 1/6 June 1784; settled at
St. Mary's Bay (Plympton, Barton,
Brighton) (40:262).

McCormack, Elenor. Of Co. Limerick,
Ireland; widow Owen Magrath; marr.
Halifax 27 Apr. 1840 John Troy
(q.v.) (34:139).

McCormack, Philip. S. of Peter/Susan
(MacIlroy) of Co. Tyrone, Ireland;
marr. Halifax 30 Nov. 1839 Honora
Murphy (q.v.) (34:133).

McCormack, Thomas. Corp. 52nd Regt.;
s. John/Catherine (Kennedy) of
Clonmel, Ireland; marr. Halifax 27
Jan. 1830 Elizabeth Turish (q.v.)
(32:114).

McCormic, John. S. of Edward/Margaret
(Gahagan) of Co. Westmeath, Ireland; marr. Halifax 9 Sep. 1813
widow Jane Snowden (q.v.)
(30:107).

McCowan, Andrew. From N.H.; effective
land grant at Truro 31 Oct. 1765
(4:245).

McCree, William. Plus 1 f./2 ch./1
svt.; blacksmith; Port Roseway
Associate (6:16).

McCrummin?, Donald. Plus 1 f./4 ch./4
svts.; farmer; Port Roseway Associate (6:16).

McCulloch, James. Loyalist; mustered
at Gulliver's Hole/St. Mary's Bay/
Sissiboo 1/6 June 1784; settled at
St. Mary's Bay (Plympton, Barton,
Brighton) (40:262).

McCulloch, Robert. Plus 1 f./1 svt.;
Port Roseway Associate (6:16).

McCully, Elizabeth. From Ireland;
land grant at Londonderry 6 Mar.
1775 (4:258).

McCully, William. From Ireland; land
grant at Londonderry 6 Mar. 1775

(4:258).

McCurdy, Alexander. From Ireland;
land grant at Londonderry 6 Mar.
1775 (4:258).

McDaniel, Edmund. S. of Edmund/Jane
(Maher) of Co. Kilkenny, Ireland;
marr. Halifax 27 July 1825 Bridget
widow of Michael Tracy (31:44).

McDead, Edward. Of Co. Donegal,
Ireland; widower of Sarah Duffy;
marr. Halifax 16 Jan. 1842 Ellen
MacCanniny (q.v.) (35:140).

McDonagh, John. S. of Thomas/Ann
(McLaughlin) of Co. Donegal,
Ireland; marr. Halifax 18 May 1833
Eliza Kelly (q.v.) (33:62).

McDonald, -----. Disbanded soldier,
1st N.J. Vols.; mustered at Gulliver's Hole/St. Mary's Bay/Sissi-
boo 1/6 June 1784; settled at St.
Mary's Bay (Plympton, Barton,
Brighton) (40:262).

McDonald, Anne. Dau. of Edward/Elenor
(Croneen) of Co. Kilkenny, Ire-
land; marr. Halifax 20 Dec. 1820
John Ryan (q.v.) (31:53).

McDonald, Anne. Dau. of Thomas/Mary
(Kinnloe) of Thomastown, Co.
Kilkenny, Ireland; marr. Halifax
24 May 1842 Thomas James (q.v.)
(35:139).

McDonald, Brien. S. of William/
Eleanor (Cahill) of Pilltown, Co.
Kilkenny, Ireland; marr. Halifax
12 Sep. 1828 Mary Brawders (q.v.)
(32:115).

McDonald, Christiana. Widow of John
Kily of Scotland; marr. Halifax 10
May 1839 Thomas Dymore (q.v.) (34:
129).

McDonald, David. Waldeck Regt.; mustered at Bear River 11/25 June
1784 (38:260).

McDonald, Donald. Disbanded soldier,
King's American Regt.; mustered at

Gulliver's Hole/St. Mary's Bay/
Sissiboo 1/6 June 1784; settled at
St. Mary's Bay (Plympton, Barton,
Brighton) (40:262).

McDonald, Humphrey. S. of James/
Elespeth; to (or b.?) Liverpool by
1786 (47:127:51).

McDonald, John. S. of John/Mary
(Templeton) of Co. Derry, Ireland;
marr. Halifax 30 Aug. 1831 Catherine Geary (q.v.) (33:62).

McDonald, Margaret. Dau. of John/
Alice (Corcoran) of Nfld.; marr.
Halifax 18 Apr. 1833 James Dowling
(q.v.) (33:57).

McDonald, Mary. Dau. of John/Alice
(Conavan) of Kilkenny, Ireland;
marr. Halifax 3 Apr. 1826 Thomas
Matthews (q.v.) (32:116).

McDonald, Mary. Dau. of Martin/Ann
(Byrne) of Nfld.; marr. Halifax 19
Feb. 1843 John Dillon (q.v.) (35:
136).

McDonald, Michael. Disbanded soldier,
Queen's Rangers; mustered at Digby
19 May 1784 (39:193).

McDonald, Nancy. Dau. of Angus/Mary
of Parish "Avonnod Sheir," Scotland; marr. Halifax 7 Jan. 1827
James Dunn (q.v.) (32:109).

Mcdonald, Soirle. Plus 1 f./1 ch./4
svts.; farmer.; Port Roseway Associate (6:16).

McDonald, William. Grantee "Digby New
Grant" 29 Jan. 1801 (5:82).

McDonnell, Bridget. Dau. of John/
Ellen (Skelly) of Co. Cavan, Ire-
land; marr. Halifax 1 May 1834
James McAuliffe (q.v.) (33:62).

McDonnell, Catherine. Dau. of John/
Ellen (Skelly) of Co. Cavan, Ire-
land; marr. Halifax 18 Aug. 1839
Timothy Sullivan (q.v.) (34: 138).

McDonnell, Ellen. Dau. of Thomas/
Ellen (Kelly) of Co. Kildare, Ire-

land; marr. Halifax 12 Oct. 1842
James Broderick (q.v.) (35: 135).

McDonnell, Margaret. Dau. of Stephen/
Alice (Oats) of Nfld.; marr. Halifax 4 Dec. 1841 William Foley
(q.v.) (35:138).

McDonnell, Mary. Dau. of John/Cather-
ine (Boyle) of Co. Monaghan,
Ireland; marr. Halifax 21 Nov.
1841 Henry Farman (q.v.) (35:137).

McDonnell, Mary. See Kenedy, Mary.

McDormand, Robert. Grantee "Digby New
Grant" 29 Jan. 1801 (5:82).

McDormand, William. Grantee "Digby
New Grant" 29 Jan. 1801 (5:82).

McDougal, John. Loyalist; plus 1 f./1
ch./1 svt.; mustered at Digby 19
May 1784 (39:193).

McDougal, Mary. Dau. of Alexander/
Elizabeth (Campbell) of Argyle-
shire, Scotland; marr. Halifax 8
Jan. 1835 James Tobin (q.v.) (34:
138).

McDuff, Michael. S. of Thomas/Ellen
(Riely) of Cork City, Ireland;
marr. Halifax 30 June 1840 Hannah
Jones (q.v.) (34:133).

McElhinney, Hannah. Wife of Robert;
b. 1758; bur. Folly Village, Londonderry (4:262).

McElhinney, Robert. B. 1747; bur.
Folly Village, Londonderry (4:
262).

McEvoy, Richard. S. of William/
Bridget (Elvard) of Co. Tipperary,
Ireland; marr. Halifax 4 June 1837
Catherine Byrnes (q.v.) (34:133).

McFarlin, Sarah. Dau. of Ahab/Eliza-
beth (Gardner) of Ireland; marr.
Halifax 19 Sep. 1824 Capt. John
Nowland (q.v.) (31:51).

McGary, Margaret. Dau. of Patrick/
Ellen (Bolan) of Co. Sligo, Ire-
land; marr. Halifax 19/21 May 1843
Thomas Trainer (q.v.) (35:145).

McGee, Mary. Dau. of Andrew/Mary (Kelly) of Parish Forgney, Co. Longford, Ireland; marr. Halifax 27 Apr. 1827 Michael Dennan (q.v.) (32:108).

McGee, Thomas. S. of Francis/Julia (Coney) of Co. Armagh, Ireland; marr. Halifax 14 Apr. 1839 Catherine Glazebrook (34:134).

McGee, William. Loyalist; plus 1 f.; mustered at Digby 19 May 1784 (39: 193).

McGennis, Patrick. S. of Luke/Ally (McGuire) of Ballymachugh, Co. Cavan, Ireland; marr. Halifax 28 Oct. 1827 Bridget Byrne (q.v.) (32:115).

McGhee, Samuel. Grantee "Digby New Grant" 29 Jan. 1801 (5:82).

McGibbon, David. Lieut.; disbanded officer; plus 1 svt.; mustered at Digby 19 May 1784 (39:192).

McGiggan, Susanna. Dau. of Robert/Mary of Co. Derry, Ireland; marr. Halifax 31 Oct. 1833 William Mulloy (33:64).

McGinty, Margaret. Dau. of Thomas/Mary (Mulligan) of Co. Monaghan, Ireland; marr. Halifax 1 May 1834 Michael Barton (q.v.) (33:54).

McGora, Sarah. Dau. of Bernard/Mary (MacKiver) of Magherafelt, Derry, Ireland; marr. Halifax 2 Nov. 1820 Michael Howard (31:47).

McGovern, John. S. of Hugh/Margaret of Inniskillen, Co. Fermanagh, Ireland; marr. Halifax 20 Aug. 1813 Mary Flemer/?Fleming (q.v.) (30: 107).

McGovern, Patrick. 64th Regt.; s. of James/Mary (Fousy) of Co. Cavan, Ireland; marr. Halifax 15 Oct. 1841 Catherine Brotherson (35: 140).

McGowen, Catherine. Dau. of Andrew/

Margaret (Coane) of Co. Donegal, Ireland; marr. Halifax 9 Jan. 1835 Thomas Burke (q.v.) (34:126).

McGowen, Michael. B. Ireland; to Liverpool by 1781 (47:127:53).

McGragh, Philip. S. of Philip/Abigail (Connor) of Dungarvan, Co. Waterford, Ireland; marr. Halifax 15 July 1821 Bridget Barron (q.v.) (31:46).

McGrath, Catherine. Liverpool to Nova Scotia April 1864 on KEDAR (45: 182).

McGrath, Dennis. Grantee "Digby New Grant" 29 Jan. 1801 (5:82).

McGrath, Edmund. S. of Michael/Margaret (Clary) of Co. Waterford, Ireland; marr. Halifax 31 Oct. 1835 Elizabeth McGrath, widow of Peter Barron (34:134).

McGrath, Elizabeth. Wife of Edward McGrath; bur. Halifax 7 Feb. 1841 ae. 34 (34:125).

McGrath, Elizabeth. Dau. of William/Bridget (Lannon) of Co. Kilkenny, Ireland; marr. Halifax 21 July 1835 John Walsh (q.v.) (34:139).

McGrath, Ellen. Dau. of Denis/Mary (Croke) of Co. Tipperary, Ireland; marr. Halifax 28 May 1834 James Phelan (q.v.) (33:66).

McGrath, James. Of Clonmel, Co. Tipperary, Ireland; widower of Catherine Foley; marr. Halifax 9 Sep. 1842 Margaret Frider (35: 141).

McGrath, Patrick. Liverpool to Nova Scotia April 1864 on KEDAR (45: 182).

McGrath, William. S. of Denis/Mary (Croke) of Co. Tipperary, Ireland; marr. Halifax 2 June 1834 Ellen Hinessy (q.v.) (33:62).

McGregor, Alexander. Loyalist; mustered at Digby 19 May 1784 (39:

193).

McGuire, John. Loyalist; mustered at
Digby 19 May 1784 (39:192).

McGuire, Patk. Plus 1 f./1 ch. -8;
arr. Annapolis from New York 19
Oct. 1782 (37:125).

McGuire, Patrick. Loyalist; plus 1
f./1 ch.; mustered at Gulliver's
Hole/St. Mary's Bay/Sissiboo 1/6
June 1784; settled at Gulliver's
Hole (a cove and harbor on Digby
Neck) (40:262).

McHenry, Henry. S. of George of Co.
Tipperary, Ireland; marr. Halifax
2 Apr. 1820 Margaret King (q.v.)
(31:47).

McHugo, Patrick. Armourer 74th Regt.;
s. of James/Eleanor (Fahy) of
Lough, Co. Galway, Ireland; marr.
Halifax 28 July 1828 Mary Power
(32:115).

McIntire, John. B. Scotland; to
Liverpool by 1769 (47:126:167).

McIntire, Susannah. See Campbell,
Susannah.

McIntyre, John. B. Scotland; d.
Liverpool 10 Sep. 1771 ae. 31st
(49:125).

McIntyre, John. From Mass.; land
grant at Truro 1759 (4:242).

McIntyre, Thomas. From Mass.; land
grant at Truro 1759 (4:242).

McKabyley, Mathew. S. of Ardal/Susan
(McKaten) of Co. Down, Ireland;
marr. Halifax 21 May 1820 Sally
Kehoe (q.v.) (31:48).

McKay, Donald. Scottish Highlander;
early settler at Shelburne (20:
49).

McKay, John. Loyalist; mustered at
Digby 19 May 1784 (39:193).

McKay, John. Loyalist; mustered at
Gulliver's Hole/St. Mary's Bay/
Sissiboo 1/6 June 1784; settled at
St. Mary's Bay (Plympton, Barton,

Brighton) (40:262).

McKay. See McCay.

McKean, Eliza. Dau. of Joseph/Ann
(Brown) of Co. Tyrone, Ireland;
marr. Halifax 9 Dec. 1835 Richard
Jenkins (q.v.) (34:132).

McKeen, John Jr. From N.H.; effective
land grant at Truro 31 Oct. 1765
(4:245).

McKeen, John. From N.H.; effective
land grant at Truro 31 Oct. 1765
(4:245).

McKeen, William. From N.H.; effective
land grant at Truro 31 Oct. 1765
(4:245).

McKenna, Catherine. Dau. of Charles/
Sarah (Houghry) of Omagh, Co.
Tyrone, Ireland; marr. Halifax 29
June 1834 John Ast (q.v.) (33:54).

McKenna, Daniel. S. of Timothy/Eliza-
beth (Lyons) of Co. Kerry, Ireland; marr. Halifax 2 Feb. 1841
Ellen Horen (q.v.) (35:141).

McKenna, James. S. of Edward/Mary
(Kelly) of Parish Monaghan, Co.
Monaghan, Ireland; marr. Halifax 5
May 1822 Charlotte Munnivan (31:
48).

McKenna, Joseph. S. of Timothy/Alice
(Lyons) of Co. Kerry, Ireland;
marr. Halifax 30 July 1839 Joanna
Horen (q.v.) (34:134).

McKenna, Mary. Dau. of John/Sarah of
Co. Monaghan, Ireland; marr. Halifax 28 Nov. 1833 Thomas McLaughlan
(q.v.) (33:63).

McKenna, Michael. S. of James/Marga-
ret (Blany) of Tralee, Co. Kerry,
Ireland; marr. Halifax 24 Sep.
1829 Abigail Falvey (q.v.) (32:
115).

McKenna, Michael. Widower of Abigail
Falvey; of Co. Kerry, Ireland;
marr. Halifax 23 Nov. 1838 Catherine O'Connell (q.v.) (34:134).

McKenzie, William. Plus 1 f./3 ch./1
svt.; farmer; Port Roseway Associate (6:16).

McKim, Margaret. Wife of William;
born 1755; bur. Folly Village,
Londonderry (4:262).

McKim, William. B. 1735; bur. Folly
Village, Londonderry (4:262).

McKim, William. From Ireland; land
grant at Londonderry 6 Mar. 1775
(4:258).

McKinley, Jasper. From Ireland; land
grant at Londonderry 6 Mar. 1775
(4:258).

McKinney, William. Plus 1 f./2 ch.
8+; arr. Annapolis from New York
19 Oct. 1782 (37:125).

McKinney, William. Loyalist; plus 1
f./3 ch.; mustered at Digby 19 May
1784 (39:192).

McKown, John. Plus 1 f./1 ch. 8+/1
ch. -8; arr. Annapolis from New
York 19 Oct. 1782 (37:125).

McLarn, Robert. S. of James/Isabella;
to (or b.?) Liverpool by 1780 (47:
127:50).

McLarren, Elizabeth. Dau. of James/
Isabella; to (or b.?) Liverpool by
1788 (47:127:125).

McLaughlan, Thomas. S. of William/
Bridget (Kelly) of Co. Donegal,
Ireland; marr. Halifax 28 Nov.
1833 Mary McKenna (q.v.) (33:63).

McLaughlin, Daniel. S. of Henry/Sara
(Boil) of Coleraine, Co. Derry,
Ireland; marr. Halifax 6 Apr. 1818
Catherine Butler (q.v.) (31:49).

McLaughlin, James. Liverpool to Nova
Scotia April 1864 on KEDAR (45:
182).

McLaughlin, Margaret. Dau. of John/
Isabella (McConnal) of Derry,
Ireland; marr. Halifax 8 Dec. 1817
William Holland (30:106).

McLaughlin, Mary. Dau. of Peter/

Susana (Caverly) of Co. Donegal,
Ireland; marr. Halifax 19 Feb.
1833 Edward Smith (q.v.) (33:67).

McLawson, Eliza. 11; dau. of James;
Perthshire; Port Glasgow to Pictou
on COMMERCE 10 Aug. 1803 (51).

McLawson, Isabella. 58; wife of
James; Perthshire; Port Glasgow to
Pictou on COMMERCE 10 Aug. 1803
(51).

McLawson, James. 18; s. of James;
Perthshire; Port Glasgow to Pictou
on COMMERCE 10 Aug. 1803 (51).

McLawson, James. 60; farmer; Perthshire; Port Glasgow to Pictou on
COMMERCE 10 Aug. 1803 (51).

McLawson, John. 21; s. of James;
Perthshire; Port Glasgow to Pictou
on COMMERCE 10 Aug. 1803 (51).

McLean, Bridget. Dau. of Michael/
Bridget (Neill) of Co. Wexford,
Ireland; marr. Halifax 21 Feb.
1830 Walter Spruhan (q.v.) (32:
118).

McLean, John. S. of Keneth/Margaret;
Urrey, Rothshire, No. Britain, to
Cornwallis by 1790 (47:127:279).

McLean, Michael. S. of Patrick/Mary
(Neill) of Parish Machel, Co.
Carlow, Ireland; marr. Halifax 7
Jan. 1828 Catherine Doyle (q.v.)
(32:115).

McLeary, Samuel. Laborer; Irish; 23;
Liverpool to Nova Scotia May 1864
on EUROCLYDON (45:182).

McLeod, Donald. B. Harves, Scotland;
s. of Angus/Margaret; King's
Orange Rangers; to Liverpool by
1781 (47:126:282).

McLeod, Elizabeth. -- of Lieut.
Donald; to (or b.?) Liverpool by
1794 (47:127:204).

McLeod, James. S. of John/Aylse; to
(or b.?) Liverpool by 1793 (47:
127:202).

McLeod, John. Loyalist; mustered at
Digby 19 May 1784 (39:192).

McLeod, William. Plus 1 f./4 ch./1
svt.; carpenter; Port Roseway
Associate (6:16).

McLinden, John. Mariner; Port Roseway
Associate (6:16).

McLinton, Alexr. Plus 1 f./4 ch. 8+;
arr. Annapolis from New York 19
Oct. 1782 (37:125).

McLoughlin, Michael. S. of James/Mary
(Brien) of Co. Wexford, Ireland;
marr. Halifax 13 Nov. 1828 Catherine Perry (q.v.) (32:115).

McMahan, Michael. Widower of Mary
Mooney; of Co. Waterford, Ireland;
marr. Halifax 2 Mar. 1840 Mary
Donnelly (q.v.) (34:134).

McMahon, Francis. Sgt. 98th Regt.; s.
of Arthur/Mary (Canon) of Ireland;
marr. Halifax 22 Jan. 1817 Elizabeth Cann (30:107).

McMahon, Patrick. S. of Michael/Mary
(McCarthy) of Co. Clare, Ireland;
marr. Halifax 29 Jan. 1840 Margaret Thomas (34:134).

McMahon, Thomas. S. of John/Jean
(Britten) of Belfast, Co. Antrim,
Ireland; marr. Halifax 23 Oct.
1831 Jean Ryan (33:63).

McManus, Mary. Dau. of Patrick/Mary
(Wile) of Nfld.; marr. Halifax 6
Feb. 1806 Andrew Coleman (q.v.)
(30: 103).

McMasters, James. Plus 3 svts.;
merchant.; Port Roseway Associate
(6:16).

McMullen, Peter. Grantee "Digby New
Grant" 29 Jan. 1801 (5:82).

McMullen, Peter. Loyalist; plus 1 f.;
mustered at Digby 19 May 1784 (39:
193).

McMullin, Hugh. Plus 1 f./1 ch.;
merchant; Port Roseway Associate
(6:16).

McNall, Joseph. From Mass.; land
grant at Truro 1759 (4:242).

McNamara, Edward. S. of Edward/Mary
(Neill) of Co. Kilkenny, Ireland;
marr. Halifax 26 Nov. 1833 Mary
Dunn (q.v.) (33:63).

McNamara, Hugh. S. of Martin/Mary
(Whelan) of Co. Kilkenny, Ireland;
marr. Halifax 27 Jan. 1834 Bridget
Hickey (q.v.) (33:63).

McNeal, John. Plus 1 f.; carpenter;
Port Roseway Associate (6:16).

McNeil, Neil. Loyalist; plus 1 f./3
ch.; mustered at Digby 19 May 1784
(39:192).

McNelly, Robert. S. of Thomas/Marga-
ret (Graham) of Kent, England;
marr. Halifax 6 Jan. 1834 Eliza
Anderson (q.v.) (33:63).

McNulty, John. 5th Batt. Royal Arty.;
of Dublin, Ireland; marr. Halifax
10 Dec. 1835 Catherine Walsh (34:
134).

McNulty, Patrick. Loyalist; mustered
at Digby 19 May 1784 (39:193).

McNulty, Patrick. S. of John/Polly
(Snee) of Co. Sligo, Ireland;
marr. Halifax 6 Oct. 1842 Margaret
Nolan widow of Richard Lynagh (35:
141).

McNutt, Abner. From Mass.; land grant
at Onslow 21 Feb. 1769 (4:225).

McNutt, Abner. S. of William and
Elizabeth (Thomson); b. 29 Oct.
1756 at Palmer, Mass.; to Onslow
with parents (4:231).

McNutt, Alexander. Esq.; from N.H.;
effective land grant at Truro 31
Oct. 1765 (4:245).

McNutt, Ann. Wife of John; born 1750;
bur. Folly Village, Londonderry
(4:262).

McNutt, Elizabeth. Wife of William;
dau. of ----- Thomps.; to Onslow
with husband (4:231).

McNutt, Eunice. Dau. of William and
Elizabeth (Thomson); b. 21 Oct.
1759 at Palmer, Mass.; to Onslow
with parents (4:231).

McNutt, George. From Ireland; land
grant at Londonderry 6 Mar. 1775
(4:258).

McNutt, James. From Ireland; land
grant at Londonderry 6 Mar. 1775
(4:258).

McNutt, John. B. 1747; bur. Folly
Village, Londonderry (4:262).

McNutt, Margaret. Wife of William; b.
1755; bur. Folly Village, Londonderry (4:262).

McNutt, Sarah. Dau. of William and
Elizabeth (Thomson); b. 30 June
1757 at Palmer, Mass.; to Onslow
with parents (4:231).

McNutt, William. B. 1747; bur. Folly
Village, Londonderry (4: 262).

McNutt, William. From Mass.; land
grant at Onslow 21 Feb. 1769 (4:
224).

McNutt, William. S. of Barnard and
Jane; b. 25 July 1733 Palmer,
Mass.; plus family; to Onslow (4:
231).

McPherson, John. Arr. Annapolis from
New York 19 Oct. 1782 (37:126).

McQueen, John. Loyalist; plus 1 f./1
ch.; mustered at Digby 19 May 1784
(39:193).

McQuire, John. Arr. Annapolis from
New York 19 Oct. 1782 (37:125).

McQuirk, Michael. S. of Edward/
Catherine (Roach) of Co. Wexford,
Ireland; marr. Halifax 11 Jan.
1831 Margaret Finn (q.v.) (33:63).

McSweeny, Eleanor. Widow of James
Hurley, who died at St. John,
N.B.; marr. Halifax 16 July 1828
John Hyde (q.v.) (32:113).

McSwiney, Daniel. S. of Terence of
Tralavis, Co. Cork?, Ireland;

marr. Halifax 15 June 1825 Jane
MacGilpin (q.v.) (31:54).

McVicar, John. Invernesshire, Scotland, to Liverpool by 1791 (47:
127:119).

Mead, Jonas. Grantee 'Digby New
Grant' 29 Jan. 1801 (5:82).

Mead, Jonas. Loyalist; mustered at
Digby 19 May 1784 (39:192).

Meade, Richard. Disbanded soldier,
1st N.J. Vols.; plus 1 f./3 ch.;
mustered at Digby 19 May 1784 (39:
192).

Meads, Stephen. 25, master mariner;
Poole to Nova Scotia on SQUIRREL
Nov. 1775 (24:45).

Meagher, Eleanor. Dau. of John/Mary
(Downey) of Co. Waterford, Ire-
land; marr. Halifax 21 Oct. 1828
Patrick Going (q.v.) (32:111).

Meagher, James. Grantee 'Digby New
Grant' 29 Jan. 1801 (5:82).

Meagher, Patrick. S. of John/Cather-
ine (Power) of Dungarvan, Co. Waterford, Ireland; marr. Halifax 10
June 1834 Catherine Skerry (33:
63).

Mecham, Isaac. From Mass.; land grant
at Truro 1759 (4:242).

Mecham, Jeremiah. From Mass.; land
grant at Truro 1759 (4:242).

Mellin, Rose. Dau. of Francis/Cather-
ine (Boyle) of Co. Antrim, Ireland; marr. Halifax 25 July 1833
John Gamble (q.v.) (33:58).

MELLON, Thomas. Deserted 10th Regiment of Foot at Halifax 2 June
1776 (42:118).

Melvin, Robert. Concord, Mass., to
Chester 30 July 1759 (16:46).

Melvin, Robert. Plus 4 ch.; Concord,
Mass., to Chester with first
settlers (16:45).

Menzies, John. Plus 1 f./3 ch.; taylor; Port Roseway Associate (6:

16).

Merun, Joseph. Loyalist; plus 1 f./1
ch./2 svts.; mustered at Digby 19
May 1784 (39:192).

Mettler, Alzander. Hemmenthal, Canton
Schaffhausen, [Switzerland,] to
Halifax 1751 (44:192).

Mettler, Barbara. Hemmenthal, Canton
Schaffhausen, [Switzerland,] to
Halifax 1751 (44: 192).

Meyer, Jeremiah. Plus 1 f./4 ch.;
farmer; Port Roseway Associate (6:
16).

Meyers, Frederick. Plus 1 f./1 ch./4
svts.; Port Roseway Associate (6:
16).

Mickum, Samuel. B. London, England;
Pa. to Liverpool by 1787 (47:
127:54).

Mihan, Alice. Wife of Sgt. John Ryan;
bur. Halifax 28 June 1839 ae. 24
(34:125).

Mihan, Mary. Dau. of William/Alice
(Morissy) of Co. Kilkenny, Ire-
land; marr. Halifax 21 Nov. 1832
Denis Falvey (q.v.) (33:57).

Mihan, Mary. Dau. of David/Ellen
(Clary) of Nfld.; marr. Halifax 16
Apr. 1842 Patrick Coffee (q.v.)
(35:136).

Mihan, Thomas. S. of William/Alice
(Morrisey) of Co. Kilkenny, Ire-
land; marr. Halifax 28 Apr. 1844
Mary Isles (35:141).

Miler, Catherine. Dau. of James/
Joanna (Brenan) of Co. Kilkenny,
Ireland; marr. Halifax 25 May 1841
Maurice Fleming (q.v.) (35:138).

Miles, John. S. of John/Martha;
Norwich, England, to Liverpool by
1786 (47:127:120).

Millard, Abigail. Dau. of Robert/
Anne; to (or b.?) Liverpool by
1800 (47:127:276).

Millard, Anne. Dau. of Robert/Anne;

to (or b.?) Liverpool by 1796 (47:
127:209).

Millard, Robert Jr. S. of Robert/
Anne; to (or b.?) Liverpool by
1796 (47:127:211).

Millard, Robert. Liverpool proprietor
(19:102).

Millard, Robert. S. of Thomas/Ruth;
to Liverpool by 1768 (47:126:165).

Millard, Ruth. Dau. of Robert/Anne;
to (or b.?) Liverpool by 1792 (47:
127:207).

Millard, Thomas Matthew. S. of Ro-
bert/Anne; to (or b.?) Liverpool
by 1793 (47:127:202).

Miller, Abraham. Grantee "Digby New
Grant" 29 Jan. 1801 (5:82).

Miller, Alexander. From N.H.; effective land grant at Truro 31 Oct.
1765 (4:245).

Miller, David. B. Philadelphia, Pa.;
s. of David/Catherine; to Liverpool by 1797 (47:127:267).

Miller, David. Middlebury, Mass. to
Chester with first settlers (16:
45).

Miller, Ebenezer. From Mass.; land
grant at Truro 1759 (4:242).

Miller, Jeremiah. Loyalist; mustered
at Digby 19 May 1784 (39:192).

Miller, John. Plus 2 svts.; farmer;
Port Roseway Associate (6:16).

Miller, Michael. Disbanded soldier,
84th Regt.; mustered at Digby 19
May 1784 (39:193).

Miller, Thomas. B. Ireland ca. 1767;
Belfast or Greenock to Halifax on
POLLY, spring 1799 (29:83).

Millerick, Daniel. S. of Denis/Mary
(Keliber) of Midleton, Co. Cork,
Ireland; marr. Halifax 31 Jan.
1829 Mary Cushion (q.v.) (32:116).

Millidge, Phineas. Grantee "Digby New
Grant" 29 Jan. 1801 (5:82).

Millidge, Phineas. Ensign; disbanded

officer, 1st N.J. Vols.; mustered
at Digby 19 May 1784 (39:192).

Millidge, Stephen. Plus 1 svt.; farmer; Port Roseway Associate (6:16).

Millidge, Thomas. Grantee "Digby New
Grant" 29 Jan. 1801 (5:82).

Millidge, Thomas. Maj.; disbanded
officer, 1st N.J. Vols.; plus 1
f./3 ch./1 svt.; mustered at Digby
19 May 1784 (39:192).

Milligan, John. Loyalist; mustered at
Digby 19 May 1784 (39:192).

Milligan, Maurice. S. of Michael/Mary
(Power) of Co. Waterford, Ireland;
marr. Halifax 5 Aug. 1840 Ellen
Power (q.v.) (34:135).

Mills, Hope. Grantee "Digby New
Grant" 29 Jan. 1801 (5:82).

Minahan, Darby. S. of Darby/Eliza
(Dunlay) of Ballymacody, Inishan-
non, Co. Cork, Ireland; marr.
Halifax 6 June 1826 Catherine
Dawson (q.v.) (32:116).

Minard, Elijah. To Liverpool by 1767
(47:126:162).

Minard, Levy. S. of Elijah/Mary; to
(or b.?) Liverpool by 1790 (47:
127:268).

Minch, Andrew. Disbanded soldier, 1st
N.J. Vols.; mustered at Digby 19
May 1784 (39:192).

Minehan, Thomas. S. of Daniel/Cather-
ine (Finn) of Co. Kerry, Ireland;
marr. Halifax 1 Oct. 1833 Ellen
Roche (q.v.) (33:63).

Mintur. Slave sold at Windsor 24 Aug.
1779 (46:253).

Mitchel, Hannah. Wife of William; to
Liverpool ca. 1760 (47:126:98).

Mitchel, William. To Liverpool ca.
1760 (47:126:96).

Mitchel, William. To Liverpool ca.
1760 (47:126:98).

Mitchell, -----. Widow; Loyalist;
plus 3 ch.; mustered at Digby 19

May 1784 (39:192).

Mitchell, Elizabeth. Dau. of George/
Elizabeth (Millon) of Co. Tyrone,
Ireland; marr. Halifax 30 Apr.
1839 Thomas McCain (q.v.) (34:
133).

Mitchell, Hannah. Dau. of Elkanah/
Abigail; to (or b.?) Liverpool by
1791 (47:127:123).

Mitchell, J. Waldeck Regt.; mustered
at Bear River 11/25 June 1784 (38:
260).

Mitchell, Lydia. Dau. of James/Lydia
(Kelso) of Co. Tyrone, Ireland;
marr. Halifax 27 Aug. 1839 James
Cullin (q.v.) (34:128).

Mitchell, William. Liverpool proprietor (19:102).

Mitchell, William. S. of William; b.
Chatham, Mass., 30 June 1725;
marr. Liverpool 11 Sept. 1761 (50:
108).

Mockler, John. S. of Patrick/Honora
(Heffernan) of Co. Tipperary, Ire-
land; marr. Halifax 28 Feb. 1835
Ellen McCarthy (q.v.) (34: 135).

Moffatt, James. Plus 1 f./3 ch./2
svts.; merchant; Port Roseway
Associate (6:16).

Mokler, Joanna. Dau. of Richard/Mary
(Cormack) of Co. Tipperary, Ire-
land; marr. Halifax 23 Sep. 1833
Lawrence Lyons (q.v.) (33:62).

Molloy, Bridget. Dau. of George/
Catherine (Grace) of Co. Waterford, Ireland; marr. Halifax 23
Apr. 1825 Thomas O'Neil (q.v.)
(31:51).

Molloy, John. Of Co. Wexford, Ireland; marr. Halifax 2 Nov. 1819
Elizabeth Pinkney (31:50).

Molloy, Mary. Dau. of George/Cather-
ine (Grace) of Parish Whitechurch,
Co. Wexford, Ireland; marr. Halifax 21 May 1826 James Wall (q.v.)

(32:119).

Molony, Ann. Dau. of Andrew/Honora (Doran) of Collumkill, Co. Kilkenny, Ireland; marr. Halifax 30 July 1829 William Flinn (q.v.) (32: 111).

Molony, Bridget. Dau. of David/Mary (Fleming) of Co. Waterford, Ireland; marr. Halifax 1 Oct. 1831 James Kelly (q.v.) (33:60).

Molony, Daniel. S. of John/Mary (Dunn) of Co. Kilkenny, Ireland; marr. Halifax 24 Nov. 1831 Margaret Lanigan (q.v.) (33:63).

Molony, James. S. of William/Esther (Hickey) of Abbeyleix, Queen's Co., Ireland; marr. Halifax 29 July 1829 Bridget Foley (q.v.) (32:116).

Molony, John. Pvt. 30th Regt.; of Limerick, Ireland; marr. Halifax 6 Apr. 1842 Sarah McDonald (35:141).

Molony, John. S. of Michael/Mary (Lacy) of Co. Tipperary, Ireland; marr. Halifax 8 May 1834 Ellen Weston (q.v.) (33:64).

Molony, Mary. Dau. of John/Margaret (Brenan) of Co. Kilkenny, Ireland; marr. Halifax 28 Nov. 1832 Edmund Magrath (q.v.) (33:62).

Molony, Mary. Dau. of David/Mary (Flemming) of Co. Waterford, Ireland; marr. Halifax 6 Nov. 1835 Patrick Walsh (q.v.) (34:139).

Molony, Michael. S. of David/Mary (Flemming) of Co. Waterford, Ireland; marr. Halifax 11 Dec. 1832 Margaret Power (q.v.) (33: 64).

Monaghan, James. S. of Patrick/ Elizabeth (Keilly) of Newtown Forbes, Co. Longford, Ireland; marr. Halifax 15 Feb. 1843 Mary Tallent (q.v.) (35:141).

Monahan, Ann Monk. Dau. of James/Rose

(Levy) of Co. Longford, Ireland; marr. Halifax 3 Nov. 1843 John Tubrid (q.v.) (35:145).

Moody, James. Grantee "Digby New Grant" 29 Jan. 1801 (5:82).

Moody, John. Grantee "Digby New Grant" 29 Jan. 1801 (5:82).

Moolds, William. S. of William/Elizabeth (Latchlea) of Alexandria, USA; marr. Halifax 28 Nov. 1829 Alice Gilfoy (q.v.) (32:116).

Mooney, Mary Anne. Dau. of James/Mary Ann (Solivan) of Newfoundland; marr. Halifax 20 May 1816 Martin Callaghan (q.v.) (30:103).

Mooney, Mathias. S. of Thomas/Alice (Power) of Dungarvan, Co. Waterford, Ireland; marr. Halifax 30 May 1836 Alice Ryan (q.v.) (34: 135).

Moony, Margaret. Dau. of John/Margaret (Magrath) of Co. Waterford, Ireland; marr. Halifax 10 Oct. 1829 Peter Duval (q.v.) (32:109).

Moor, John. S. of Gerard/Alice (Summers) of Bruff, Co. Limerick, Ireland; marr. Halifax 25 Apr. 1808 Ann O'Brien (30:108).

Moor, Mary. See Mullany, Mary.

Moor, Richard. S. of Garrett/Ally (Lomasney) of Parish Knoeley, Tipperary, Ireland; marr. Halifax 9 Sep. 1825 Mary Colder (31:50).

Moore, Charles. S. of William/Joanna of Malta; marr. Halifax 14 Mar. 1839 Catherine McCarthy (q.v.) (34:135).

Moore, Daniel. New England to Annapolis on CHARMING MOLLY May 1760 (18:271).

Moore, David. S. of Daniel/Elizabeth (Drake) of Fox Cove, Nfld.; marr. Halifax 25 Oct. 1812 Hannah Dolan (q.v.) (30:108).

Moore, Garrett. S. of Garrett/Elenor

(Sumners) of Bruff, Co. Limerick, Ireland; marr. Halifax 27 Apr. 1820 Catherine Inglis *(q.v.)* (31:50).

Moore, Hugh. From N.H.; effective land grant at Truro 31 Oct. 1765 (4:245).

Moore, James. From N.H.; effective land grant at Truro 31 Oct. 1765 (4:244).

Moore, Jeremiah. Grantee "Digby New Grant" 29 Jan. 1801 (5:82).

Moore, Jeremiah. Loyalist; plus 1 f./3 ch.; mustered at Digby 19 May 1784 (39:192).

Moore, Joanna. Dau. of William/Bridget (Hanifan) of Co. Kerry, Ireland; marr. Halifax 10 May 1843 John Lynch *(q.v.)* (35:140).

Moore, John B. Loyalist; plus 1 f./3 ch./1 svt.; mustered at Digby 19 May 1784 (39:192).

Moore, Joseph. From N.H.; effective land grant at Truro 31 Oct. 1765 (4:245).

Moore, Joseph. S. of Francis/Bridget (Kelly) of Ross, Co. Wexford, Ireland; marr. Halifax 25 Aug. 1821 Catherine McDonald widow of Patrick Tobin (31:50).

Moore, Margaret. Dau. of Thomas/Mary (Murphy) of Parish Thomastown, Co. Waterford, Ireland; marr. Halifax 13 Sep. 1823 Francis Dunphy *(q.v.)* (31:44).

Moore, Mary A. Dau. of Garrett/Ally (Simons) of Parish Knockany, Co. Limerick, Ireland; marr. Halifax 22 Sep. 1826 Hugh Maguire *(q.v.)* (32:115).

Moore, Mary. See Mullany, Mary.

Moore, Ogle. S. of Lorenzo/Henrietta (Jackson) of Dublin, Ireland; marr. Halifax 24 Aug. 1809 Ellen Ryan *(q.v.)* (30:108).

Moore, Samson. From N.H.; effective land grant at Truro 31 Oct. 1765 (4:244).

Moore, Thomas. Plus 1 f./1 ch.; farmer; Port Roseway Associate (6:16).

Moore, Thomas. S. of Francis/Catherine (Molloy) of Whitechurch, Co. Wexford, Ireland; marr. Halifax 7 May 1825 Anne Grandy widow of John Farrell (31:50).

Moore, William. From N.H.; effective land grant at Truro 31 Oct. 1765 (4:245).

Moore, William. Grantee "Digby New Grant" 29 Jan. 1801 (5:82).

Moorehead, John. Rev.; from Ireland; land grant (to heirs) at Londonderry 6 Mar. 1775 (4:258).

Moran, Ann. Dau. of Thomas/Mary (Neill) of Co. Kilkenny, Ireland; marr. Halifax 28 May 1832 John Mahony *(q.v.)* (33:63).

Moran, Thomas. Of Co. Leix, Ireland; widower of Mary Neill; marr. Halifax 11 Aug. 1840 Ann Haron *(q.v.)* (34:135).

Moran, William. S. of William/Elizabeth (Clerk) of Co. Kilkenny, Ireland; marr. Halifax 19 Nov. 1812 Martha Lamb *(q.v.)* (30:108).

More, Jeremiah. Plus 1 f./3 ch. -8; arr. Annapolis from New York 19 Oct. 1782 (37:125).

More, John. B. Invernesshire, Scotland, 10 May 1767; s. of Alexander/Jane?; to Liverpool by 1794 (47:127;203).

More, John. Grantee "Digby New Grant" 29 Jan. 1801 (5:82).

Morehouse, John. Grantee "Digby New Grant" 29 Jan. 1801 (5:82).

Morehouse, John. Loyalist; plus 1 f.; mustered at Digby 19 May 1784 (39:193).

Morehouse, Jonathan. Grantee "Digby
New Grant" 29 Jan. 1801 (5:82).

Morehouse, Jonathan. Loyalist; plus 1
f./3 ch.; mustered at Gulliver's
Hole/St. Mary's Bay/Sissiboo 1/6
June 1784; settled at Gulliver's
Hole (a cove and harbor on Digby
Neck) (40:262).

Morford, John. Grantee "Digby New
Grant" 29 Jan. 1801 (5:82).

Morford, John. Loyalist; mustered at
Digby 19 May 1784 (39:192).

Morford, Margaret. Grantee "Digby New
Grant" 29 Jan. 1801 (5:82).

Morgan, Anne. Dau. of John/Mary
(Doherty) of Co. Louth, Ireland;
marr. Halifax 13 July 1818 Denis
Inright (q.v.) (31:47).

Morgan, Henry. S. of George/Hannah
(McCarthy) of Co. Down, Ireland;
marr. Halifax 23 Oct. 1811 Mary
Anne Kent (30:108).

Moriarty, Joanna. Dau. of Michael/
Mary (Boland) of Dingle, Co.
Kerry, Ireland; marr. Halifax 9
Nov. 1839 Patrick Kenedy (q.v.)
(34:132).

Moriarty, John. S. of Sylvester/
Bridget (Murphy) of Co. Kerry,
Ireland; marr. Halifax 9 Nov. 1839
Mary Holihan (q.v.) (34:135).

Moriarty, Patrick. S. of Sylvester/
Bridget (Murphy) of Co. Kerry,
Ireland; marr. Halifax 24 Nov.
1838 Elizabeth Kenedy (q.v.) (34:
135).

Morin, Stephen. S. of Stephen/Eliza-
beth; to Liverpool by 1767 (47:
127:119).

Morine, John. S. of Stephen/Susanna;
to (or b.?) Liverpool by 1794 (47:
127:55).

Morissey, Catherine. Dau. of William/
Margaret (Murphy) of Co. Kilkenny,
Ireland; marr. Halifax 10 Nov.

1831 Michael Mara (q.v.) (33:63).

Morissey, Edward. S. of William/Mary
(Keefe) of Co. Waterford, Ireland;
marr. Halifax 15 May 1832 Margaret
Bowes (q.v.) (33:64).

Morissy, Catherine. Dau. of -----/
Joanna (Walsh) of Co. Kilkenny,
Ireland; marr. Halifax 5 Oct. 1833
Michael Magher (q.v.) (33:63).

Morissy, Catherine. See Landrigan,
Catherine.

Morissy, Elizabeth Dau. of John/
Catherine (Fanert) of Co. Cork,
Ireland; marr. Halifax 26 Sep.
1843 James Devlin (q.v.) (35:136).

Morissy, John. S. of Richard/Mary
(Gorman) of Castlehrra?, Kilkenny,
Ireland; marr. Halifax 9 Oct. 1829
Mary Lennox (q.v.) (32:116).

Morissy, Margaret. Dau. of Michael/
Joanna (Walsh) of Co. Kilkenny,
Ireland; marr. Halifax 29 May 1832
Brien Farrell (q.v.) (33:57).

Morissy, Mathew. S. of David/Ellen
(Deasy) of Co. Tipperary, Ireland;
marr. Halifax 21 May 1833 Mary
English (q.v.) (33:64).

Morissy, Patrick. S. of Denis/Mary
(Murphy) of Co. Wexford, Ireland;
marr. Halifax 30 July 1833 Ellen
Griffin (q.v.) (33:64).

Morrice, Ann. Of Limerick, Ireland;
widow of Bartholomew Ast; marr.
Halifax 10 Nov. 1841 Owen Kelly
(q.v.) (35:139).

Morris, David. S. of William/Eliza-
beth (Lewis) of Pembrokesh.,
Wales; marr. Halifax 21 May 1836
Susannah Bradley (q.v.) (34:135).

Morris, Jacob. Loyalist; mustered at
Digby 19 May 1784 (39:192).

Morris, Mary. See Roach, Mary.

Morris, Thomas. S. of John/Catherine
(Sinclair) of Campbelltown West,
Scotland; marr. Halifax 3 Oct.

1841 Mary Keeffe (q.v.) (35:141).

Morrison, John. Esq.; b. 1726 N.H.; bur. Folly Village, Londonderry (4:262).

Morrison, John. From N.H.; effective land grant at Truro 31 Oct. 1765 (4:245).

Morrison, John. From Ireland; land grant at Londonderry 6 Mar. 1775 (4:258).

Morrison, John. S. of John of Londonderry, N.H.; b. 20 Sep. 1726 at N.H.; to Truro 1760 (4:261).

Morrison, Martha. Wife of John; b. 1732; bur. Folly Village, Londonderry (4:262).

Morrison, Mary. See McKown, Mary.

Morrison, Rebecca. Wife of Thomas; b. 1723; bur. Folly Village, Londonderry (4:262).

Morrison, Thomas. B. 1716; bur. Folly Village, Londonderry (4: 262).

Morriss, Lewis. S. of Angelo/Anne (Augustin) of Lisbon, Portugal; marr. Halifax 26 June 1821 Mary Roach (q.v.) (31:50).

Morrissey, Peter. Widower of Bridget Brophy of Co. Kilkenny, Ireland; marr. Halifax 17 Aug. 1817 Catherine Wall widow of Thomas Talbot (30: 108).

Morrissy, Judith. See Dwyer, Judith.

Morrissy, Nicholas. Of Dungarvan, of Co. Waterford, Ireland; widower of Mary Magher; marr. Halifax 8 Feb. 1843 Elizabeth Hartery (q.v.) (35: 141).

Morrissy, Peter. Of Co. Kilkenny, widower of Catherine Wall; marr. Halifax 16 July 1840 Ellen Power (q.v.) (34:135).

Morrissy, Richard. Of Parish Clonmel, Co. Tipperary, Ireland; marr. Halifax 13 Aug. 1825 Johanna Creamer widow of Thomas Holahan

(31:50).

Morrissy, Thomas. S. of Michael/Mary (Managin) of The Bats Ouifors, Kilkenny, Ireland; marr. Halifax 24 Sep. 1822 Mary Fenton (31:50).

Morrisy, Alice. Dau. of Peter/Bridget (Brophy) of Co. Meath, Ireland; marr. Halifax 12 June 1840 William Barron (q.v.) (34:125).

Morrow, Robert. Pvt. 64th Regt.; s. of Charles/Mary (McTyre) of Co. Antrim, Ireland; marr. Halifax 30 May 1841 Mary Lynch (q.v.) (35: 142).

Morse, Abner. New England to Annapolis on CHARMING MOLLY May 1760 (18:271).

Morse, Samuel. New England to Annapolis on CHARMING MOLLY May 1760 (18:271).

Mort, Elener. See Downey, Elener.

Mortaugh. See Mortuagh.

Morton, Abigail. Born Plymouth, Mass., 10 July 1753; dau. of Silvanus; to Liverpool ca. 1760 (47:126:96).

Morton, Abigail. Dau. of Silvanus/Mary; to Liverpool by 1771 (47: 126:281).

Morton, Elijah. To Liverpool ca. 1760 (47:126:100).

Morton, James. S. of Silvanus/Mary; to (or b.?) Liverpool by 1784 (47: 126:283).

Morton, Mary. Wife of Silvanus; to Liverpool ca. 1760 (47:126:96).

Morton, Silvanus Jr. S. of Silvanus/Mary; to Liverpool by 1779 (47: 126:283).

Morton, Silvanus. B. Plymouth, Mass., 5 July 1760; s. of Silvanus; to Liverpool ca. 1760 (47: 126:96).

Morton, Silvanus. To Liverpool ca. 1760 (47:126:96).

Morton, Wire. Liverpool proprietor

(19:102).

Mortuagh, Margaret. Dau. of Benjamin/
Ann (McInnis) of Dublin, Ireland;
marr. Halifax 13 July 1840 William
Horan (q.v.) (34:131).

Moseley, George. Plus 1 f./3 ch.;
sawyer; Port Roseway Associate (6:
16).

Moulthorpe, Enoch. Loyalist; mustered
at Digby 19 May 1784 (39:192).

Mountain, Robert. Of Co. Cork, Ireland; widower of Mary Rutledge;
marr. Halifax 8 Jan. 1835 Mary
Mullany (q.v.) (34:135).

Mudge, Sarah Jessy Henrietta. Wife of
John, Esq.; b. Lancaster, England;
d. 26 Nov. 1818 at Halifax ae 24th
(13:77).

Mulcahy, Bridget. Dau. of John/Sarah
(Leonard) of Dungarvan, Co. Waterford, Ireland; marr. Halifax 2
Nov. 1820 David Condon (q.v.) (31:
43).

Mulcahy, James. S. of James/Honora
(Geary) of Co. Waterford, Ireland;
marr. Halifax 24 Feb. 1838 Mary
Power (34:135).

Mulcahy, James. S. of Mathew/Margaret
(Power) of Co. Waterford, Ireland;
marr. Halifax 13 Oct. 1838 Ellen
Sheehan (q.v.) (34:135).

Mulcahy, Mary. Dau. of Timothy/Marga-
ret (Brenan) of Co. Cork, Ireland;
marr. Halifax 31 Oct. 1833 John
Kanna (q.v.) (33:60).

Mulcahy, Patrick. S. of John/Mary
(Murphy) of Dungarvan, Co. Waterford, Ireland; marr. Halifax 23
Jan. 1845 Elizabeth Oakley (q.v.)
(35:142).

Mulcahy, Thomas. Of Waterford City,
Ireland; marr. Halifax 31 Aug.
1827 Margaret Washington (q.v.)
(32:116).

Mulcahy, Thomas. Of Dungarvan, Co.

Waterford, Ireland; widower of
Margaret Washington of Poortown,
Co. Kilkenny, Ireland; ; marr.
Halifax 12 May 1836 Judith Mullany
(q.v.) (34:135).

Mulcahy, Thomas. Widower of Anastasia; of Co. Waterford, Ireland;
marr. Halifax 9 Jan. 1833 Joanna
Flemming (q.v.) (33:64).

Muldre, Sabrina. Spinster; Irish; 20;
Liverpool to Nova Scotia May 1864
on EUROCLYDON (45:182).

Mulholland, Patrick. S. of Brian/Mary
(Murphy) of Co. Armagh, Ireland;
marr. Halifax 1 Jan. 1840 Eliza
Kenedy (q.v.) (34:135).

Mullaly, John. S. of John/Bridget
(Power) of Co. Tipperary, Ireland;
marr. Halifax 30 July 1833 Mary
Stewart (q.v.) (33:64).

Mullany, Judith. Of Co. Tipperary,
Ireland; marr. Halifax 12 May 1836
Thomas Mulcahy (q.v.) (34:135).

Mullany, Mary. Of Co. Cork, Ireland;
widow of Garret DeCoursey/John
Moore; marr. Halifax 8 Jan. 1835
Robert Mountain (q.v.) (34:135).

Mullany, Mary. Widow of John Moor; of
Co. Cork, Ireland; marr. Halifax
15 Feb. 1831 Garrett DeCourcy
(q.v.) (33:56).

Mullens, Rebecca. Dau. of John/Han-
nah; to (or b.?) Liverpool by 1796
(47:127:209).

Mulligan, Ann. Dau. of Hugh/Sarah
(Byrne) of Co. Wicklow, Ireland;
marr. Halifax 31 Aug. 1837 John
Quinn (q.v.) (34:137).

Mulligan, Esther. Dau. of Hugh/Sarah
(Byrne) of Co. Wicklow, Ireland;
marr. Halifax 22 June 1840 Thomas
Carroll (q.v.) (34:127).

Mullin, Thomas. Plus 1 f./2 ch./2
svts.; blacksmith; Port Roseway
Associate (6:16).

Mullins, John. S. of John/Hannah; to (or b.?) Liverpool by 1798 (47: 127:211).

Mullony, Anastasia. Dau. of Lawrence/ Margaret (Power) of Parish Portlaw, Waterford, Ireland; marr. Halifax 12 Sep. 1829 Edward Walsh (q.v.) (32:120).

Mullony, Mary. Dau. of Richard/ Catherine (Holbran) of Co. Limerick, Ireland; marr. Halifax 21 Jan. 1834 Edward Lacy (q.v.) (33: 61).

Mullowney, Catherine. Dau. of Daniel/ Mary (Dunn) of Co. Kilkenny, Ireland; widow of Kearan Cotton; marr. Halifax 11 Oct. 1835 Michael Martin (q.v.) (34:135).

Mulloy, George. S. of George/Catherine (Grace) of Whitechurch, Co. Wexford, Ireland; marr. Halifax 26 Nov. 1831 Susannah Connelly (q.v.) (33:64).

Mulloy, Valentine. S. of John/Margaret (Cody) of Whitechurh, Co. Wexford, Ireland; marr. Halifax 2 Mar. 1835 Bridget Power (q.v.) (34:135).

Mulloye, Catherine. Dau. of George/ Catherine (Grace) of Whitechurch, Wexford, Ireland; marr. Halifax 23 Oct. 1830 James Fogarty (q.v.) (32:111).

Mullumby, John. S. of Michael/Catherine (Laffan) of Mullinahone, Co. Tipperary, Ireland; marr. Halifax 11 Aug. 1836 Alice Brennan (q.v.) (34:135).

Mulrean, Ann. Of Co. Donegal, Ireland; widow of John Bradley; marr. Halifax 3 Aug. 1837 Henry Williams (q.v.) (34:139).

Mumford, Joseph. Asst. Commissary; plus 4 svts.; mustered at Digby 19 May 1784 (39:193).

Munro, Daniel. Plus 1 f./4 ch.; carpenter; Port Roseway Associate (6:16).

Munro, Nathaniel. Plus 1 f./5 ch.; carpenter; Port Roseway Associate (6:16).

Murchey, William. Plus 1 f./1 ch.; Port Roseway Associate (6:16).

Murdock, Ann. Dau. of James/Maria (Muldoon) of Co. Meath, Ireland; marr. Halifax 17 Jan. 1833 Jeremiah Fling (q.v.) (33:58).

Murphy, Anastasia. Dau. of John/Mary (Casey) of Miramichi, N.B.; marr. Halifax 12 Oct. 1823 John Quan (q.v.) (31:52).

Murphy, Andrew. S. of Bartholomew/ Eleanor (Crane) of Castlelough, Co. Kerry, Ireland; marr. Halifax 7 Jan. 1840 Margaret Ann Ridgeway (34:136).

Murphy, Ann. Dau. of Patrick/Alice (Barron) of Co. Kilkenny, Ireland; marr. Halifax 16 Jan. 1833 Andrew Whelan (q.v.) (33:68).

Murphy, Ann. Dau. of James/Margaret (Cogscrife) of Co. Carlow, Ireland; marr. Halifax 28 Oct. 1839 William Hogan (q.v.) (34:131).

Murphy, Ann. Dau. of Thomas/Mary (Nolan) of Co. Carlow, Ireland; marr. Halifax 8 June 1841 James Sutherland (q.v.) (35:145).

Murphy, Anne. Dau. of Denis/Mary (Whelan) of Co. Kilkenny, Ireland; widow of Tobias Jackman of Nfld.; marr. Halifax 20 Jan. 1803 James Walsh (q.v.) (30:112).

Murphy, Anthony. S. of Anthony/Mary (Moran) of Co. Kilkenny, Ireland; marr. Halifax 7 June 1836 Mary Rino (34:136).

Murphy, Arthur. S. of Arthur/Rebecca (McCarthy) of Killigrew, Co. Wexford, Ireland; marr. Halifax 5

Nov. 1839 Mary Holden (34:135).

Murphy, Bridget. Dau. of John/Bridget (Doyle) of Co. Wexford, Ireland; marr. Halifax 7 May 1831 Daniel Drea (q.v.) (33:57).

Murphy, Bridget. Dau. of John/Honora (Ryan) of Co. Kilkenny, Ireland; marr. Halifax 6 June 1838 Martin Byrne (q.v.) (34:127).

Murphy, Catherine. Dau. of Michael/Mary (Ryan) of Parish Borris, Co. Carlow, Ireland; marr. Halifax 12 Feb. 1822 John Gahen (q.v.) (31:46).

Murphy, Catherine. Dau. of Edmund/Elizabeth (Murry) of Graigue, Co. Carlow, Ireland; marr. Halifax 11 June 1828 James Burns (q.v.) (32:106).

Murphy, Catherine. Dau. of Nicholas/Mary (Daughton) of Co. Tipperary, Ireland; marr. Halifax 8 Sep. 1834 Michael Shanihan (q.v.) (33:66).

Murphy, Cornelius. S. of Denis/Mary (Sulivan) of Co. Cork, Ireland; marr. Halifax 2 Dec. 1820 Judith Downey (q.v.) (31:51).

Murphy, Daniel. Corp. 37th Regt.; of Co. Cork, Ireland; marr. Halifax 8 June 1841 Ann Archibald (35:142).

Murphy, David. S. of Philip/Ellen (Wall) of Co. Tipperary, Ireland; marr. Halifax 28 June 1832 Ann Goggan (q.v.) (33:64).

Murphy, Denis. S. of John/Bridget (Toomy) of Co. Cork, Ireland; marr. Halifax 1 May 1842 Ann McArther (q.v.) (35:142).

Murphy, Edward. S. of John/Elenor (MacDonald) of Co. Tipperary, Ireland; marr. Halifax 20 Apr. 1822 Catherine Nunan (q.v.) (31:51).

Murphy, Edward. S. of Patrick/Catherine (Casy) of Co. Kilkenny, Ireland; marr. Halifax 19 Apr. 1841 Margaret Fily (q.v.) (35:142).

Murphy, Edward. S. of Edward/Mary (Lynch) of Co. Cork, Ireland; marr. Halifax 26 Feb. 1843 Joanna Walsh (q.v.) (35:142).

Murphy, Eleanor. Dau. of John/Mary of Co. Kilkenny, Ireland; marr. Halifax 4 Oct. 1832 John Boyle (q.v.) (33:54).

Murphy, Eliza. Dau. of Arthur/Rebecca (McCarthy) of Parish Killigrew, Wexford, Ireland; marr. Halifax 17 Apr. 1831 John O'Brien (q.v.) (33:65).

Murphy, Ellen. Dau. of Patrick/Catherine (Casey) of Co. Kilkenny, Ireland; marr. Halifax 23 Apr. 1831 Thomas Gorman (q.v.) (33:58).

Murphy, Ellen. Dau. of John/Joanna (McSwiney) of Midleton, Co. Cork, Ireland; marr. Halifax 5 Aug. 1837 John Punch (q.v.) (34:137).

Murphy, Gerald. S. of Patrick/Nancy (Magrah) of Co. Cork, Ireland; marr. Halifax 9 Jan. 1806 Anne Carroll widow of James Bishop (30:108).

Murphy, Honora. Dau. of Edmund/Mary (Lynch) of Co. Cork, Ireland; marr. Halifax 30 Nov. 1839 Philip McCormack (q.v.) (34:133).

Murphy, Jane. Dau. of John/Elizabeth (Morrison) of Co. Waterford, Ireland; marr. Halifax 21 May 1843 George William Ray (q.v.) (35:144).

Murphy, Jeremiah. Corp., 96th Regt; of Dublin, Ireland; marr. Halifax 6 Dec. 1831 Mary Mathew (q.v.) (33:64).

Murphy, Jeremiah. S. of Michael/Ellen (Sullivan) of Co. Cork, Ireland; marr. Halifax 30 July 1833 Catherine McCarthy (q.v.) (33:64).

Murphy, John. S. of Bartholomew/

Margaret (Downey) of New Ross, Wexford, Ireland; marr. Halifax 19 May 1814 Elizabeth Carney (30: 108).

Murphy, John. S. of Daniel/Bridget (Coady) of Rosgarland, Co. Wexford, Ireland; marr. Halifax 25 Nov. 1823 Susanna Bowen (31:51).

Murphy, John. S. of John/Joanna (Mulloy) of Co. Kilkenny, Ireland; marr. Halifax 18 Feb. 1833 Hannah Ryan (q.v.) (33:64).

Murphy, John. S. of Nicholas/Ann (Kearan) of Co. Wexford, Ireland; marr. Halifax 7 Aug. 1837 Bridget Foley (q.v.) (34:135).

Murphy, John. S. of John/Bridget (Doyle) of Co. Wexford, Ireland; marr. Halifax 2 Oct. 1842 Ann Sophia Anderson widow of Patrick Kent (35:142).

Murphy, John. S. of John/Bridget (Toomy) of Co. Cork, Ireland; marr. Halifax 10 Jan. 1843 Ann Lovett (q.v.) (35:142).

Murphy, Juliana. Dau. of John/Juliana (Sweeny) of Co. Cork, Ireland; marr. Halifax 6 Oct. 1831 John Kingston (q.v.) (33:61).

Murphy, Laurence. S. of Laurence/Anne (Farrell) of Queen's Co., Ireland; marr. Halifax 7 Jan. 1820 Elizabeth Miller (31:51).

Murphy, Luke. Plus 1 f./2 svts.; Port Roseway Associate (6:16).

Murphy, Margaret. Dau. of William/Margaret (Simmons) of Myshall, Co. Carlow, Ireland; marr. Halifax 11 June 1828 Thomas Barrett (q.v.) (32:105).

Murphy, Margaret. Dau. of Lawrence/Catherine (Kehoe) of Co. Kilkenny, Ireland; marr. Halifax 16 Nov. 1829 Edward Power (q.v.) (32:117).

Murphy, Margaret. Dau. of Timothy/

Catherine (Sullivan) of Co. Cork, Ireland; marr. Halifax 24 May 1836 Thomas O'Rourke (q.v.) (34:136).

Murphy, Margaret. Dau. of Bernard/Minnie (MacGlown) of Co. Monaghan, Ireland; marr. Halifax 22 July 1842 John Kerns (q.v.) (35:140).

Murphy, Margaret. Of Cork City, Ireland; widow of James Mansfield; marr. Halifax 26 Mar. 1840 Arthur Oakley (q.v.) (34:136).

Murphy, Martha. Dau. of Arthur/Rebecca (McCarthy) of Killigrew, Co. Wexford, Ireland; marr. Halifax 4 May 1837 John Keys (q.v.) (34: 132).

Murphy, Martin. S. of John/Margaret (O'Connor) of Co. Wexford, Ireland; marr. Halifax 3 Jan. 1829 Bridget Quillian (32:116).

Murphy, Martin. S. of Michael/Margaret (Malony), of Co. Kilkenny, Ireland; marr. Halifax 5 June 1832 Mary Dawson (q.v.) (33:64).

Murphy, Martin. S. of Michael/Mary (Quigley) of Co. Kilkenny, Ireland; marr. Halifax 3 Aug. 1843 Bridget Weston (q.v.) (35:142).

Murphy, Mary Ann. Dau. of John/Mary of Co. Wexford, Ireland; marr. Halifax 24 Feb. 1840 Charles Ballard (q.v.) (34:125).

Murphy, Mary. Dau. of Richard/Anne (Moran) of Co. Kilkenny, Ireland; marr. Halifax 2 Oct. 1805 William Dobbin (q.v.) (30:104).

Murphy, Mary. Dau. of Kerns/Catherine (Murphy) of Thomastown, Co. Kilkenny, Ireland; marr. Halifax 20 May 1829 John Prahill (q.v.) (32: 111).

Murphy, Mary. Dau. of Arthur/Rebecca (McCarthy) of Parish Kilnagney, Co. Wexford, Ireland; marr. Halifax 16 Jan. 1826 Philip Holden

(q.v.) (32:113).

Murphy, Mary. Dau. of Peter/Ann
(Cormick) of Co. Wexford, Ireland;
marr. Halifax 27 Oct. 1831 Thomas
Cullerton (q.v.) (33:55).

Murphy, Mary. Dau. of James/Juliana
(Sullivan) of Co. Cork, Ireland;
marr. Halifax 15 Feb. 1831 Thomas
O'Grady (q.v.) (33:65).

Murphy, Mary. Dau. of John/Mary
(McCabe) of Co. Monaghan, Ireland;
marr. Halifax 12 Jan. 1842 John
Henissy (q.v.) (35:138).

Murphy, Mary. Of Co. Carlow, Ireland;
widow of Denis Finlay; marr. Halifax 25 Oct. 1834 Michael McCarthy
(q.v.) (34:133).

Murphy, Michael. S. of Martin/Bridget
(Dollard) of Co. Kilkenny, Ire-
land; marr. Halifax 28 Jan. 1830
Elizabeth Tool (q.v.) (32:116).

Murphy, Michael. S. of Michael/Mary
(Ryan) of Co. Carlow, Ireland;
marr. Halifax 12 May 1831 Eleanor
Jane O'Neill (q.v.) (33:64).

Murphy, Michael. S. of Michael/Julian
(Connell) of Co. Cork, Ireland;
marr. Halifax 24 Oct. 1833 Bridget
Callinan (q.v.) (33:64).

Murphy, Michael. S. of Michael/Mary
(Ryan) of Co. Kilkenny, Ireland;
marr. Halifax 24 Apr. 1843 Ellen
Nolan (q.v.) (35:142).

Murphy, Patrick. S. of Thomas/Mary
(Condon) of Poorstown, Co. Tipperary, Ireland; marr. Halifax 7 Feb.
1827 Anastasia Bulger (q.v.) (32:
116).

Murphy, Patrick. S. of John/Joanna
(Power) of Co. Waterford, Ireland;
marr. Halifax 7 Oct. 1837 Margaret
Connell (q.v.) (34:135).

Murphy, Pierce. Of Ireland; marr.
Halifax 7 Oct. 1819 Frances Hopley
(q.v.) (31:51).

Murphy, Thomas. S. of Thomas/Mary
(Granvell) of Co. Wexford, Ire-
land; marr. Halifax 28 Oct. 1830
Ellen Hogan (q.v.) (32:116).

Murphy, Walter. S. of Stephen/Mary
(Doyle) of Co. Wexford, Ireland;
marr. Halifax 17 Nov. 1820 Mary
Connors (31:50).

Murphy, William. S. of Timothy/Ellen
(Walsh) of Co. Cork, Ireland;
marr. Halifax 7 Nov. 1832 Catherine Conroy (33:64).

Murphy, William. S. of John/Joanna
(Sweeney) of "Parish of the Parish
of Mallow, Co. Cork," Ireland;
marr. Halifax 16 June 1836 Mary
Keane (q.v.) (34:136).

Murphy, William. S. of Patrick/Mary
(Gallavan) of Co. Kilkenny, Ire-
land; marr. Halifax 12 Nov. 1835
Catherine Mack (q.v.) (34:136).

Murray, Abigail. Dau. of William/
Joanna; to (or b.?) Liverpool by
1780 (47:126:281).

Murray, Alex'r. Plus 1 f./1 ch./3
svts.; Port Roseway Associate (6:
16).

Murray, Catherine. Dau. of Nicholas/
Alice (Long) of Co. Wexford, Ire-
land; marr. Halifax 17 Sep. 1813
Patrick Sullivan (q.v.) (30:111).

Murray, Charles. S. of William/Joan-
na; to (or b.?) Liverpool by 1793
(47:127:202).

Murray, Charles. S. of William/Joan-
na; to (or b.?) Liverpool by 1793
(47:127:203).

Murray, James. Plus 1 f./3 ch./1
svt.; harness maker; Port Roseway
Associate (6:16).

Murray, James. S. of James/Ellen
(Meehan) of Co. Kildare, Ireland;
marr. Halifax 14 June 1830 Mary
Heary (q.v.) (32:116).

Murray, John. Loyalist; mustered at

Digby 19 May 1784 (39:192).

Murray, John. S. of Michael/Mary (Walsh) of Kilmacow, Co. Kilkenny, Ireland; marr. Halifax 20 Apr. 1803 Rebecca Hatfield (30:108).

Murray, Mary. Dau. of William/Joanna; to (or b.?) Liverpool by 1793 (47: 127:202).

Murray, Thomas. S. of William/Joanna; to (or b.?) Liverpool by 1786 (47: 127:53).

Murray, William Jr. S. of William/ Joanna; to (or b.?) Liverpool by 1793 (47:127:125).

Murray, William. Liverpool proprietor (19:101).

Murray, William. Plus 1 f./5 ch.; farmer; Port Roseway Associate (6: 16).

Murry, Catherine. Dau. of John/Elizabeth (Dwyer) of Co. Wexford, Ireland; marr. Halifax 14 Sep. 1841 Martin Summers (q.v.) (35: 145).

Murry, Mary. Dau. of Patrick/Annie (Shean) of Co. Tipperary, Ireland; widow of Patrick Ryan; marr. Halifax 26 June 1821 James Peerson (q.v.) (31:51).

Murry, Philip. S. of John of Parish Drumreilly, Co. Leitrim, Ireland; marr. Halifax 1 Oct. 1835 Jane Ramsy (34:136).

Murry, William. To Liverpool ca. 1760 (47:126:98).

Musgrave?, Barthow. Plus 1 f./3 ch.; Port Roseway Associate (6:16).

Mussells, William. King's Pilot; mustered at Digby 19 May 1784 (39: 193).

Mussels, William. Grantee "Digby New Grant" 29 Jan. 1801 (5:83).

Müller, -----. Sgt.; Waldeck Regt.; mustered at Bear River 11/25 June 1784 (38:260).

Müller, George. Waldeck Regt.; plus 1 f./3 ch.; mustered at Bear River 11/25 June 1784 (38:260).

Myers, Andrew. 96th Regt.; of Co. Wicklow, Ireland; marr. Halifax 19 July 1835 Sarah Kittey (q.v.) (34: 136).

Myhan, James. S. of Patrick/Mary (Power) of Carrick-on-Suir, Tipperary, Ireland; marr. Halifax 10 Nov. 1802 (30:108).

- N -

Nagle, Margaret. Dau. of Richard/ Margaret (Keliher) of Cove, Co. Cork, Ireland; marr. Halifax 28 Jan. 1834 Patrick Alexander (q.v.) (33:54).

Nash, George. Loyalist; plus 1 svt.; mustered at Digby 19 May 1784 (39: 193).

Naughton, John. S. of Hugh/Sarah (Faney) of Co. Roscommon, Ireland; marr. Halifax 26 Sep. 1810 Catherine Lawler (q.v.) (30:108).

Neagle, Catherine. Dau. of Henry/Mary (Gleeson) of Co. Offaly, Ireland; marr. Halifax 28 Oct. 1834 Richard Dalton (q.v.) (34:128).

Neagle, Jeremiah. S. of Michael/ Elizabeth (Cooney) of St. Johnswell, Co. Kilkenny, Ireland; marr. Halifax 7 feb. 1829 Bridget White (q.v.) (32:116).

Neal, James. Of Skart, Co. Kilkenny, Ireland; marr. Halifax 15 July 1802 Mary Rourk (q.v.) (30:108).

Neal, Michael James. S. of James/Mary (Rourk) of Waterford, Ireland; marr. Halifax 3 Nov. 1805 Janet McDonald (30:108).

Neiff, Mary. Dau. of Patrick/Mary (Darmody) of Co. Kilkenny, Ireland; marr. Halifax 14 Nov. 1830 Edward Bulger (q.v.) (32:106).

175

Neill, Henry. S. of John/Alice; Co. Kilkinny, Ireland, to Liverpool by 1802 (47:127:275).

Neill, Sarah. Dau. of Mathew/Mary (Mullay) of Co. Carlow, Ireland; marr. Halifax 11 Oct. 1832 James Linnen (q.v.) (33:62).

Neilson, Aron. From Mass.; land grant at Truro 1759 (4:242).

Neilson, Moses. From Mass.; land grant at Truro 1759 (4:242).

Nelson, Alexander. From N.H.; effective land grant at Truro 31 Oct. 1765 (4:244).

Nepath, Anna. Spinster; Irish; 22; Liverpool to Nova Scotia May 1864 on EUROCLYDON (45:182).

Nesbit, -----. Mrs.; Loyalist; plus 2 svts.; mustered at Digby 19 May 1784 (39:193).

Nesbitt, William. Esq.; from N.H.; effective land grant at Truro 31 Oct. 1765 (4:244).

Nesbitt, William. From Ireland; land grant at Londonderry 6 Mar. 1775 (4:258).

Nesham, Ralph. Plus wife/1 ch.; Mass. to Chester with first settlers (16:45).

Nevers, Jonathan. Mass. to N.S.; to U.S. 1776; dead by 1785 (36:64).

Nevers, Phineas. Col.; Mass. to N.S.; to U.S. 1776; lived 1785 at Bangor, Me. (36:64).

Nevill, Thomas. S. of Philip/Mary (Hogan) of Shanakiel, Co. Cork, Ireland; marr. Halifax 6 May 1841 Honora Karigan (q.v.) (35:142).

Nevin, John. 62nd Regt.; s. of Thomas/Mary (Carroll) of Co. Galway, Ireland; marr. Halifax 15 Oct. 1821 Catherine McCarthy (q.v.) (31:51).

Newman, Patrick. S. of John/Mary (Barry) of Castlemartyr, Co. Cork,

Ireland; marr. Halifax 13 Oct. 1825 Mary Porter (31:51).

Newman, Elinor. Dau. of John/Margaret (Flan) of Louisbourg, Cape Breton; marr. Halifax 21 Feb. 1803 Richard Shea (q.v.) (30:110).

Nicholas, Henry. Plus 1 f./2 ch. -8; arr. Annapolis from New York 19 Oct. 1782 (37:126).

Nicholls, John. Grantee "Digby New Grant" 29 Jan. 1801 (5:83).

Nicholls, Lucy. Dau. of Robert/Anne (MacDonald) of Dublin, Ireland; marr. Halifax 20 July 1811 Thomas Mansell (q.v.) (30:108).

Nichols, Henry. Loyalist; plus 1 f./4 ch.; mustered at Digby 19 May 1784 (39:193).

Nichols, Samuel. From Mass.; land grant at Onslow 21 Feb. 1769 (4:224).

Nichols, Sarah. Loyalist; plus 2 ch.; mustered at Digby 19 May 1784 (39:193).

Nicholson, Ebenezer. Liverpool proprietor (19:101).

Nicholson, William. From Ireland; land grant at Londonderry 6 Mar. 1775 (4:258).

Nickerson, -----. Liverpool proprietor (19:101).

Nickerson, Ann. Dau. of Eldad; b. Chatham, Mass. (50:109).

Nickerson, Bathsheba Snow. Wife of Elkanah (50:109).

Nickerson, Bethia. Dau. of Ebenezer; b. Chatham, Mass.; marr. Liverpool 23 Nov. 1769 (2371:108).

Nickerson, Bethiah. Dau. of Ebenezer/Mahitabel; to Liverpool by 1771 (47:126:164).

Nickerson, Caleb. S. of Joshua; b. Chatham, Mass., 22 May 1757 (50:109).

Nickerson, Daniel. S. of Elisha; b.

Chatham, Mass., 2 Mar. 1736; to
Liverpool 1762 (50:108).

Nickerson, Daniel. S. of Elisha; b.
Chatham, Mass., 2 Mar. 1736;
Liverpool proprietor (50:109).

Nickerson, Dorcas. Dau. of Daniel/
Anna; to (or b.?) Liverpool or
Argyle by 1784 (47:127:268).

Nickerson, Ebenezer. S. of Ebenezer;
b. Chatham, Mass.; d. Liverpool
bef. 3 June 1778 (50:108).

Nickerson, Eldad. S. of James/Hannah;
to (or b.?) Liverpool by 1801 (47:
127:272).

Nickerson, Eldad. S. of William; b.
Chatham, Mass., 1723; grantee at
Barrington; d. there ca. 1770 (50:
108).

Nickerson, Eldad. S. of Eldad; b.
Chatham, Mass., 1751 (50:109).

Nickerson, Elisha Jr. Liverpool proprietor (19:102).

Nickerson, Elisha. Liverpool proprietor (19:101).

Nickerson, Elisha. S. of John; b.
Chatham, Mass., 7 Mar. 1706/7;
Harwich to Liverpool (proprietor)
1759-1769 (50:109).

Nickerson, Elizabeth. Dau. of Eldad;
b. Chatham, Mass. (50:109).

Nickerson, Elizebeth. Dau. of Eldad/
Mary; to (or b.?) Liverpool by
1782 (47:127:54).

Nickerson, Elkanah. B. Chatham,
Mass., 14 Feb. 1721/2; Liverpool
proprietor (50:109).

Nickerson, Epiphany. Dau. of James/
Rachel; to (or b.?) Liverpool by
1803 (47:127:271).

Nickerson, Esther Ryder. Wife of
Joshua; b. 4 Mar. 1734/5 (50:109).

Nickerson, Gideon. S. of William; b.
Chatham, Mass.; to Barrington
after 30 Aug. 1764 (50:109).

Nickerson, James. Liverpool proprie-

tor (19:102).

Nickerson, James. S. of Eldad/Mary;
to Liverpool by 1776 (47:126:287).

Nickerson, James. S. ,of Eldad; b.
Chatham, Mass. (50:108).

Nickerson, Jane. Dau. of Ebenezer; to
(or b.?) Liverpool by 1780
(47:127:267).

Nickerson, Jane. Dau. of Ebenezer; b.
Chatham, Mass. (50:108).

Nickerson, Jeremiah. Liverpool proprietor (19:101).

Nickerson, Jesse. S. of Eldad; b.
Chatham, Mass. (50:109).

Nickerson, John. S. of Jeremiah/
Rebecca; to Liverpool by 1771 (47:
127:50).

Nickerson, Joshia. S. of Caleb; b.
Chatham, Mass., 1733; grantee at
Barrington (1761?) (50:109).

Nickerson, Levi. S. of Joshua; b.
Chatham, Mass., 10 Dec. 1759 (50:
109).

Nickerson, Martha. Dau. of William;
b. Chatham, Mass., 4 Sept. 1757
(50:111).

Nickerson, Mary Cahoon. Wife of Eldad
(50:108).

Nickerson, Mary Crowell. Wife of
Prince (50:110).

Nickerson, Mary. Dau. of Eldad; b.
Chatham, Mass. (50:109).

Nickerson, Mehitable Gray. Wife of
Ebenezer; b. Harwich, Mass., 20
Feb. 1726/7; d. Liverpool 12 Nov.
1762 (50:108).

Nickerson, Nathan. S. of Ebenezer; b.
Chatham, Mass., ca. 1728; grantee
at Yarmouth; to Nova Scotia after
8 Oct. 1761 (50:110).

Nickerson, Prince. S. of Thomas; b.
Chatham, Mass., 10 Aug. 1729; to
Barrington betw. 12 Mar. 1761-1
Oct. 1765 (50:110).

Nickerson, Priscilla. Dau. of Elkanah/Bathsheba; to (or b.?) Liverpool by 1781 (47:126:287).

Nickerson, Priscilla. Dau. of Elkanah; b. Chatham, Mass.; marr. at Liverpool 16 Aug. 1781 (50:109).

Nickerson, Rebecca. Dau. of Elkanah; to Liverpool ca. 1760 (47:126:96).

Nickerson, Rebecca. Dau. of Elkanah; b. Chatham, Mass.; marr,. at Liverpool 18 Mar. 1762 (50:109).

Nickerson, Rebeccah. Dau. of Jeremiah/Rebeccah; to Liverpool by 1765 (47:126:168).

Nickerson, Richard. S. of Caleb; b,. Chatham, Mass., 1741; prob marr. Barrington ca. 1766 (50:110).

Nickerson, Salome; Dau. of John/Achsah; to (or b.?) Liverpool by 1795 (47:127:205).

Nickerson, Stephen. Barrington petitioner 19 Oct. 1776 (1:365).

Nickerson, Stephen. S. of William; b. Chatham, Mass., 1 Oct. 1726; grantee at Barrington 1759-1769 (50:111).

Nickerson, Susannah Godfrey Cole. Wife of Nathan (50:110).

Nickerson, Thankful. Dau. of William; b. Chatham, Mass., 27 July 1759 (50:111).

Nickerson, William 3d. S. of William; b. Chatham, Mass., 24 Feb. 1736; Liverpool proprietor (50:111).

Nickols, James. Capt.; Boston, Mass., to Chester 30 July 1759 (16:46).

Nihily, Maurice. Of Co. Kerry, Ireland; widower of Eleanor Calahan; marr. Halifax 10 Feb. 1841 Bridget Creaven (q.v.) (35:142).

Noble, -----. Rev.; Mass. to N.S.; to U.S. 1776; first minister at Bangor, Me. (36:64).

Nolan, Bernard. S. of John/Eleanor (Burns) of Co. Wicklow, Ireland; marr. Halifax 12 Oct. 1828 Eliza-beth Kavanah (q.v.) (32:116).

Nolan, Bridget. of Co. Carlow, Ireland; marr. Halifax 1 July 1841 Patrick Wallace (q.v.) (35:145).

Nolan, Catherine, Dau. of Garrett/Anastasia (Henissy) of Co. Carlow, Ireland; marr. Halifax 28 Feb. 1835 Michael Holland (q.v.) (34:131).

Nolan, Edward. S. of George/Ann (Drugoule?) of Co. Carlow, Ireland; marr. Halifax 22 June 1842 Emilia Kid (q.v.) (35:142).

Nolan, Elizabeth. See Cavanagh, Elizabeth.

Nolan, Ellen. Dau. of Martin/Ellen (Walsh) of Co. Carlow, Ireland; marr. Halifax 24 Apr. 1843 Michael Murphy (q.v.) (35:142).

Nolan, James Charles. Of Dublin, Ireland; widower of Ann Mulloy; marr. Halifax 11 Apr. 1842 Mary Ann O'Sullivan (35:142).

Nolan, John. S. of Maurice/Mary (Kealy) of Co. Kilkenny, Ireland; marr. Halifax 2 Oct. 1832 Mary Wallace (q.v.) (33:64).

Nolan, Mary. Dau. of Daniel/Margaret (Kenny) of Co. Wexford, Ireland; marr. Halifax 11 Sep. 1828 Thomas McCarthy (q.v.) (32:114).

Nolan, Mathew. Widower of Eleanor Power of Waterford, Ireland; of Old Ross, Co. Wexford, Ireland; marr. Halifax 18 Dec. 1832 Honora Burke (q.v.) (33:64).

Nolan, Patrick. S. of Garret/Anastasia (Henissy) of Co. Carlow, Ireland; marr. Halifax 18 June 1834 Ellen Brophy (q.v.) (33:64).

Noonan, James. S. of Patrick/Mary (Cooney) of Co. Cork, Ireland; marr. Halifax 6 Nov. 1804 Catherine Kelly (q.v.) (30:109).

Noonan, James. S. of Maurice/Bridget

(Nevill) of Co. Waterford, Ireland;
marr. Halifax 10 Dec. 1834 Mary
Lawlor (34:136).

Noonan, John Hyacinth. S. of Thomas/
Elizabeth (Robinson) of Co. Galway, Ireland; marr. Halifax 6 Nov.
1815 Frances Duncan (30:109).

Norcross, Samuel. From Mass.; land
grant at Truro 1759 (4:242).

Norris, James. S. of Michael/Margaret
(Marshall) of Co. Kilkenny, Ire-
land; marr. Halifax 16 May 1829
Maria O'Neill (32:116).

Norris, James. S. of Michael/Cather-
ine (Quinlan) of Co. Kilkenny,
Ireland; marr. Halifax 18 Aug.
1836 Isabella Petrie (q.v.) (34:
136).

Northrop, Joseph. Loyalist; plus 1
f./1 ch.; mustered at Gulliver's
Hole/St. Mary's Bay/Sissiboo 1/6
June 1784; settled at Sissiboo
(now Weymouth) (40:262).

Northrop, Joseph. Plus 1 f./1 ch. -8;
arr. Annapolis from New York 19
Oct. 1782 (37:125).

Northrup, Joshua. Grantee "Digby New
Grant" 29 Jan. 1801 (5:83).

Northup, Joshua. Disbanded soldier,
Loyal American Regt.; mustered at
Digby 19 May 1784 (39:193).

Nowlan, Bridget. Dau. of Moses/Mary
(Murry) of Co. Wexford, Ireland;
marr. Halifax 29 Jan. 1822 Samuel
Hawkesworth (q.v.) (31:47).

Nowlan, Catherine. Of Galway, Ireland; widow of Hugh Gordon; marr.
Halifax 26 Sep. 1839 Michael Fo-
gerty (q.v.) (34:130).

Nowlan, Elizabeth. Dau. of John/
Catherine (Connelly) of Galway
Town, Ireland; marr. Halifax 3
feb. 1818 Nicholas Carew (q.v.)
(31:42).

Nowlan, John. S. of John/Catherine
(Connolly) of Galway Town, Ire-
land; marr. Halifax 24 July 1808
Catherine Borgl (30:109).

Nowlan, Margaret. Dau. of Michael/
Eleanor (White) of Co. Waterford,
Ireland; marr. Halifax 27 Aug.
1829 Richard Lynagh (q.v.) (32:
114).

Nowland, John. (Capt.;) s. of John/
Eliza (Power) of Kilmurry, Co.
Kilkenny, Ireland; marr. Halifax
19 Sep. 1824 Sarah McParlin (q.v.)
(31:51).

Nox, Martha. Dau. of Hugh/Mary
(Sweeny) of Co. Longford, Ireland;
marr. Halifax 4 Nov. 1828 John
Ward (q.v.) (32:120).

Nugent, Joanna. Dau. of James/Joanna
(Magher) of Gurtnahoe, Co. Tipperary, Ireland; marr. Halifax 9 Nov.
1838 Michael Connors (q.v.) (34:
128).

Nugent, John. S. of Richard/Rose
(Donnelly) of Co. Meath, Ireland;
marr. Halifax 13 June 1832 Ann
Deer (q.v.) (33:64).

Nugent, Michael. Loyalist; plus 1
f./1 svt.; mustered at Digby 19
May 1784 (39:193).

Nunan, Catherine. Dau. of Thomas/
Margaret (Mahar) of Co. Tipperary,
Ireland; marr. Halifax 20 Apr.
1822 Edward Murphy (q.v.) (31:51).

- O -

O'Brian, Eleanor. Dau. of Thomas/Mary
of Parish Newtown (Shandrum), Co.
Cork, Ireland; marr. Halifax 21
Sep. 1827 Thomas Farrell (q.v.)
(32:109).

O'Brien, Alice. Dau. of Michael/Mary
(Neill) of Co. Kilkenny, Ireland;

marr. Halifax 23 Nov. 1830 Michael
Cody (q.v.) (32:107).

O'Brien, Ann. Dau. of Michael/Alice
(Morisson) of Co. Waterford,
Ireland; marr. Halifax 15 Nov.
1834 William Kenedy (q.v.) (34:
132).

O'Brien, Anne. Dau. of Patrick/Mary
(Anglin) of Cahir, Co. Tipperary,
Ireland; marr. Halifax 9 Dec. 1813
George Matthew (q.v.) (30:108).

O'Brien, Anne. Dau. of Michael/Mary
(Christian) of Waterford, Ireland;
marr. Halifax 29 Sep. 1802 Owen
Scanlon (q.v.) (30:110).

O'Brien, Catherine. Dau. of David/
Bridget (Byrnes) of Co. Carlow,
Ireland; widow of Thomas Hayes
marr. Halifax 5 Feb. 1829 Patrick
Cantfill (q.v.) (32:106).

O'Brien, Catherine. See Coddigan,
Catherine.

O'Brien, Charles. Of Co. Tyrone,
Ireland; marr. Halifax 20 June
1842 Mary Townsend (q.v.) (35:
142).

O'Brien, David. S. of David/Mary
(Kerson) of St. Patrick's, Clashmore, Co. Waterford, Ireland;
marr. Halifax 11 Apr. 1825 Margaret Shanahan widow of Edward Ryan
(31:41).

O'Brien, David. S. of John/Margaret
(White) of Co. Cork, Ireland;
marr. Halifax 8 Feb. 1835 Mary Ann
Lawlor (q.v.) (34:136).

O'Brien, Eleanor. Dau. of Cornelius/
Mary of Co. Waterford, Ireland;
marr. Halifax 8 Feb. 1819 Michael
Pendergast (q.v.) (31:51).

O'Brien, Elenor. Dau. of David/
Bridget (Byrne) of Parish Burrydown,. Co. Carlow, Ireland; marr.
Halifax 28 Aug. 1821 John Ryan
(q.v.) (31:53).

O'Brien, Ellen. Dau. of Michael/
Catherine (Quinn) of Cahir, Co.
Tipperary, Ireland, and widow of
William Frizell; marr. Halifax 16
Sep. 1805 James Dulhanty (q.v.)
(30:105).

O'Brien, Elysia. Dau. of Edward/
Mary(Walsh) of Co. Tipperary, Ire-
land; marr. Halifax 16 Aug. 1815
Dominique, s. of Francis/Blandine
(Gauthier) Alinor, (30:102).

O'Brien, James. S. of John/Eleanor
(Shea) of Castlemartyr, Co. Cork,
Ireland; marr. Halifax 7 Feb. 1829
Ellen Aheron (q.v.) (32:116).

O'Brien, James. S. of Michael/Bridget
(Walker) of Co. Kilkenny, Ireland;
marr. Halifax 7 Jan. 1830 Mary
Anne Murphy (32:117).

O'Brien, James. S. of Michael/Mary
(Evans) of Mullinahone, Co. Tipperary, Ireland; marr. Halifax 30
May 1833 Bridget Cashman (q.v.)
(33:65).

O'Brien, James. S. of Martin/Cather-
ine (Howard) of Co. Kildare, Ireland; marr. Halifax 7 Oct. 1833
Rebecca O'Brien (33:65).

O'Brien, James. Sgt., Rifle Brig.; of
Co. Kildare, Ireland; marr. Halifax 9 May 1833 Anne O'Donnell
(q.v.) (33:65).

O'Brien, Joanna. Dau. of Michael/Mary
(Neill) of Co. Kilkenny, Ireland;
marr. Halifax 17 Nov. 1830 Richard
Henessy (q.v.) (32:112).

O'Brien, Joanna. Dau. of Jeremiah/
Mary (Ward) of Co. Wexford, Ire-
land; marr. Halifax 26 Nov. 1831
Thomas Doyle (q.v.) (33:57).

O'Brien, Joanna. Dau. of Michael/Mary
(Neill) of Co. Kilkenny, Ireland;
widow of Richard Hinissy; marr.
Halifax 10 June 1833 Martin Magher
(q.v.) (33:63).

O'Brien, Joanna. Dau. of Jeremiah/
Mary (Ward) of Co. Wexford, Ireland; widow of Thomas Doyle; marr.
Halifax 26 Sep. 1837 Bernard Kenny
(q.v.) (34:132).

O'Brien, Joanna. Dau. of Thomas/
Joanna (Manaugh) of Co. Tipperary,
Ireland; marr. Halifax 3 Feb. 1845
Nicholas Magher (q.v.) (35:141).

O'Brien, Johanna. See Brown, Johanna.

O'Brien, John. S. of John/Mary
(Evans) of Co. Cork, Ireland; marr.
Halifax 4 July 1813 Grace Ryan
(q.v.) (30:109).

O'Brien, John. S. of John/Maria
(Cottaral) of Co. Cork, Ireland;
marr. Halifax 31 May 1821 Allis
Morrissey (31:41).

O'Brien, John. S. of. Michael/Mary
(Walsh) of Templetrim?, Co. Tipperary, Ireland; marr. Halifax 25
Aug. 1823 Bridget Russell (q.v.)
(31:41).

O'Brien, John. S. of Terence/Cather-
ine (Power) of Co. Waterford, Ireland; marr. Halifax 29 Sep. 1828
Mary Coleman (32:117).

O'Brien, John. S. of Jeremiah/Johanna
(Shallow) of Waterford City, Ire-
land; marr. Halifax 10 Jan. 1827
Jane Farrell (q.v.) (32:117).

O'Brien, John. S. of Timothy/Julia
(Brown), of Parish Youghal, Co.
Cork, Ireland; marr. Halifax 17
Apr. 1831 Eliza Murphy (q.v.) (33:
65).

O'Brien, John. S. of Michael/Mary
(Evans) of Mullinahone, Co. Tip-
perary, Ireland; marr. Halifax 30
Oct. 1832 Ellen Ivers (33:65).

O'Brien, John. S. of John/Mary
(Evans) of Co. Cork, Ireland;
widower of Grace Ryan; marr. Halifax 19 Feb. 1833 Johanna Brown
(q.v.) (33:65).

O'Brien, Lawrence. S. of James/ Bridget (Sinnett) of Co. Kilkenny,
Ireland; marr. Halifax 12 Feb.
1836 Mary Walsh (q.v.) (34:136).

O'Brien, Malachy. S. of Nicholas/
Margaret (Dyer) of Co. Tipperary,
Ireland; marr. Halifax 3 Apr. 1820
Anastatia Drady (q.v.) (31:41).

O'Brien, Margaret. Dau. of Martin/
Catherine (Hardwood) of Rathcoole,
Co. Dublin, Ireland; marr. Halifax
27 Sep. 1829 James Augustus Tallon
(q.v.) (32:119).

O'Brien, Margaret. Dau. of Miles/Mary
(Finn) of Co. Kilkenny, Ireland;
marr. Halifax 21 June 1832 John
Doran (q.v.) (33:56).

O'Brien, Margaret. See Power, Margaret.

O'Brien, Martin. S. of Martin/Joanna
(Whelan) of Parish Kill, Co. Waterford, Ireland; marr. Halifax 11
July 1842 Mary Dullehanty (q.v.)
(35:142).

O'Brien, Mary. Dau. of John/Mary
(McLaver) of Co. Louth, Ireland;
marr. Halifax 14 Dec. 1812 Thomas
Williamson (q.v.) (30:112).

O'Brien, Mary. Dau. of Timothy/Julia-
na (Brown) of Youghal, Co. Cork,
Ireland; marr. Halifax 15 Sep.
1831 Peter Kelly (q.v.) (33:60).

O'Brien, Michael. S. of James/Honora
(MacNamara) of Kilmacthomas, Co.
Waterford, Ireland; marr. Halifax
27 Sep. 1841 Joanna Calnan (q.v.)
(35:142).

O'Brien, Morgan. S. of Thomas/Alice
(Mahony) of Parish Clogheen, Co.
Tipperary, Ireland; marr. Halifax
26 Feb. 1829 Margaret Wall (q.v.)
(32:117).

O'Brien, Robert. S. of Michael/Anas-
tasia (Danihy) of Co. Waterford,
Ireland; marr. Halifax 11 July

1839 Susanah Quinn (34:136).

O'Brien, Terrence. S. of John/Bridget (Gilroy) of Co. Leitrim, Ireland; marr. Halifax 2 July 1833 Margaret Fitzpatrick (q.v.) (33:65).

O'Brien, Thomas. S. of Dominick/ Margaret (O'Donnell) of Clonmel, Tipperary, Ireland; marr. Halifax 23 Feb. 1830 Catherine Londrigan (q.v.) (32:117).

O'Brien, Thomas. S. of John/Ellen (Moore) of Co. Waterford, Ireland; marr. Halifax 22 Nov. 1832 Rachel Sophia Longard (33:65).

O'Brien, Timothy. S. of Patrick/ Judith (Clary) of Co. Tipperary, Ireland; marr. Halifax 15 Feb. 1833 Ellen Burk (q.v.) (33:65).

O'Brien, William. Loyalist; mustered at Digby 19 May 1784 (39:193).

O'Brien, William. S. of John/Catherine (Broaders) of Co. Cork, Ireland; marr. Halifax 24 Jan. 1820 Elizabeth Wooten (31:41).

O'Brien, William. S. of Thomas/ Catherine (Finn) of Co. Cork, Ireland; marr. Halifax 24 Nov. 1835 Margaret Harrigan (q.v.) (34: 136).

O'Brien, William. S. of William/ Bridget (Cusack) of Co. Tipperary, Ireland; marr. Halifax 27 Feb. 1843 Bridget Connors (q.v.) (35: 142).

O'Brien,. Margaret. Dau. of William/ Eleanor (Laffin) of Co. Kilkenny, Ireland; marr. Halifax 20 Mar. 1829 Edmund Fitzgerald (q.v.) (32: 110).

O'Connell, Catherine. Dau. of John/ Honora (Collins) of Mallow, Co. Cork, Ireland; marr. Halifax 23 Nov. 1838 Michael McKenna (q.v.) (34:134).

O'Connell, Hugh. S. of Terrence/Sarah of Co. Armagh, Ireland; marr. Hal-

ifax 18 June 1832 Sophia Smith (33:65).

O'Connell, James. S. of James/Mary (Young) of Parish Glasshouse, Slaiverhue, Kilkenny, Ireland; marr. Halifax 20 Jan. 1830 Sarah Louisa White (32:117).

O'Connell, Jeremiah. S, Darby/Margaret (O'Brien) of Co. Cork, Ireland; marr. Halifax 25 Nov. 1837 Catherine Drowhan (q.v.) (34:136).

O'Connor, Bridget. Dau. of Constantine/Margaret (Cody) of Co. Waterford, Ireland; marr. Halifax 30 May 1803 Lawrence Doyle (q.v.) (30: 104).

O'Connor, Hugh. S. of Timothy/Joanna (Barden) of Co. Kerry, Ireland; widower of Ann O'Connor; marr. Halifax 3 Sep. 1835 Mary Sharp (q.v.) (34:136).

O'Connor, John. S. of John/Ellen (Crotty) of Co. Waterford, Ireland; marr. Halifax 28 Feb. 1832 Mary Ann Dunn (33:65).

O'Connor, John. Widower of Ann Lynch; of Co. Kildare, Ireland; marr. Halifax 5 Oct. 1828 Sarah Hugs, widow of Francis Kelly (q.v.) (32: 117).

O'Connor, Lawrence. S. of Anthony/ Winifred (Murry) of Co. Westmeath, Ireland; marr. Halifax 19 Mar. 1838 Ann Dowling (q.v.) (34:136).

O'Connor, Mary. Dau. of Daniel/Ellen (White) of Co. Waterford, Ireland; marr. Halifax 17 Oct. 1832 Joseph Quinn (q.v.) (33:66).

O'Connor, Patrick. S. of Anthony/ Winefred (Murry) of Parish Durrow, Co. Westmeath, Ireland; marr. Halifax 31 July 1829 Mary Magrath (q.v.) (32:117).

O'Connor, Patrick. S. of Patrick/Mary (Cute) of Co. Kerry, Ireland;

marr. Halifax 12 Nov. 1833 Ellen Scannel (q.v.) (33:65).

O'Connor, Thomas. S. of John/Alice (Elans) of Co. Waterford, Ireland; widower of Mary Ann Parody; marr. Halifax 4 Oct. 1830 Julian Sullivan (q.v.) (32:117).

O'Conor, Mary. Dau. of Patrick/Margaret (Quan) of Clonmel, Co. Tipperary, Ireland; marr. Halifax 24 Jan. 1822 John Mahan (q.v.) (31: 49).

O'Donnell, Ann. Dau. of Richard/ Margaret (Murphy) of Co. Kilkenny, Ireland; marr. Halifax 9 May 1833 Sgt. James O'Brien (q.v.) (33:65).

O'Donnell, Catherine. Dau. of William/Catherine (Walsh) of Co. Waterford, Ireland; marr. Halifax 16 Oct. 1840 William Curtis (q.v.) (34:128).

O'Donnell, Edward. S. of Robert/Mary (Lawrence) of Co. Tipperary, Ireland; marr. Halifax 11 Feb. 1844 Mary Hilchy (35:142).

O'Donnell, Elline. Dau. of John/ Joanna (Crain) of Castlegregory, Co. Kerry, Ireland; marr. Halifax 5 July 1836 Martin Crawley (q.v.) (34:128).

O'Donnell, James. S. of John/Ann (Walsh) of Gammansfield, Co. Tipperary, Ireland; marr. Halifax 2 Oct. 1831 Margaret Cahill (q.v.) (33:65).

O'Donnell, John. S. of Piers/Ann (Langley) of Co. Tipperary, Ireland; marr. Halifax 22 Oct. 1815 Margaret Tobin (q.v.) (30:109).

O'Donnell, Mary. Dau. of William/ Catherine (Walsh) of Co. Waterford, Ireland; marr. Halifax 5 Mar. 1832 Michael Egan (q.v.) (33: 57).

O'Farrell, William. S. of John/Judith

(Molony) of Cloyne, Co. Cork, Ireland; marr. Halifax 9 Nov. 1836 Catherine Walsh (q.v.) (34:136).

O'Flavin, John. S. of John/Honora (Morissy) of Aglish, Co. Waterford, Ireland; marr. Halifax 18 Nov. 1836 Hannah Sullivan (q.v.) (34:136).

O'Gealy, John. S. of Thomas/Catherine (Quan) of Parish Abbeyside, Co. Waterford, Ireland; marr. Halifax 15 Sep. 1835 Mary Dunn (q.v.) (34: 136).

O'Gorman, Richard. S. of Richard/ Margaret (Henessy) of Dromin, Co. Limerick, Ireland; marr. Halifax 19 Dec. 1828 Chritiana Publicover (32:117).

O'Grady, Thomas. S. of James/Margaret (Harigan) of Co. Cork, Ireland; marr. Halifax 15 Feb. 1831 Mary Murphy (q.v.) (33:65).

O'Hara, James. Loyalist; plus 1 f.; mustered at Digby 19 May 1784 (39: 193).

O'Hear, Mary. Dau. of Patrick/Margaret of Co. Down, Ireland; marr. Halifax 5 May 1829 Andrew Lyons (q.v.) (32:114).

O'Holleran, Catherine. Dau. of James/ Catherine (Kennedy) of Co. Tipperary, Ireland; marr. Halifax 3 Aug. 1830 Patrick Mahony (q.v.) (32: 116).

O'Leary, Joanna. Dau. of John/Elenor (Aheran) of Co. Cork, Ireland; marr. Halifax 5 Sep. 1831 Denis McCarthy (q.v.) (33:62).

O'Leary, Mary. Spinster; Irish; 22; Liverpool to Nova Scotia June 1864 on INDIAN QUEEN (45:182).

O'Malley, Patrick. Of Ireland; marr. Halifax 16 Feb. 1843 Elizabeth Jane May (35:143).

O'Mara, Charles. S. of Patrick/Elenor

(Shea) of Co. Tipperary, Ireland;
marr. Halifax 19 Sep. 1833 Joanna
Walsh (33:65).

O'Mara, Joanna. Dau. of Denis/Mary
(Croke) of Callan, Co. Kilkenny,
Ireland; marr. Halifax 5 May 1842
William Ryan (q.v.) (35:144).

O'Mara, Mary. Dau. of Denis/Maria
(Croke) of Callan, Co. Kilkenny,
Ireland; marr. Halifax 27 Apr.
1840 Edward Ryan (q.v.) (34:138).

O'Mara, William. S. of Cormick/ Bridget (Moran) of Co. Leix, Ireland;
marr. Halifax 26 Aug. 1832 Mary
Jane Coleman (33:65).

O'Melia, Lawrence. S. of Francis/Mary
(Kennedy) of Loughrea, Co. Galway,
Ireland; marr. Halifax 19 Jan.
1813 Catherine Cosgrove (q.v.)
(30: 109).

O'Mely, James. S. of Michael/Honora
(O'Hanlon) of Co. Rosscommon, Ire-
land; marr. Halifax 17 Aug. 1810
Johanna Magrath (q.v.) (30:109).

O'Neal, Catherine. Dau. of Michael/
Margaret (Ryan) of Co. Tipperary,
Ireland; marr. Halifax 23 Dec.
1833 Richard Coughlan (q.v.) (33:
55).

O'Neal, Jane. Dau. of Patrick of
Limerick City, Ireland/Janet
(Honery) of Scotland; marr. Halifax 22 Jan. 1818 Thomas Colford
(q.v.) (31:43).

O'Neal, Jane. Dau. of Patrick/Janet
(Honery) of Limerick City, Ireland; widow of Thomas Colford;
marr. Halifax 3 Nov. 1825 Patrick
Leahy (31:49).

O'Neal, Patrick. See O'Neal, Jane.

O'Neil, David. S. of William/Mary
(Havill) of Co. Cork, Ireland;
marr. Halifax 2 May 1820 Margaret
Fallon (q.v.) (31:51).

O'Neil, David. S. of Mark/Bridget

(Walsh) of Co. Carlow, Ireland;
marr. Halifax 23 Nov. 1820 Bridget
Magragh (q.v.) (31:51).

O'Neil, Henry. S. of Lawrence/Marga-
ret (Howlin) of Ferns, Co. Wexford, Ireland; marr. Halifax 10
Oct. 1826 Jean Flood (q.v.) (32:
117).

O'Neil, James. S. of Thomas/Mary
(Walsh) of Co. Kilkenny, Ireland;
marr. Halifax 19 Feb. 1810 Elenor
Stuart (q.v.) (30:109).

O'Neil, Owen. S. of Lawrence/Margaret
(Howlin) of Parish Tintern, Co.
Wexford, Ireland; marr. Halifax 1
Nov. 1825 Mary Cummins (q.v.) (31:
51).

O'Neil, Peter. Of Francis, Co. Tyrone, Ireland; marr. Halifax 8 Oct.
1824 Sarah Russell widow of Richard Dunne (31:51).

O'Neil, Thomas. S. of Denis/Mary
(Carroll) of Parish Tintern, Co.
Wexford, Ireland; marr. Halifax 23
Apr. 1825 Bridget Molloy (q.v.)
(31:51).

O'Neill, Bridget. Dau. of Denis/
Elenor (Morriss) of Cashel, Co.
Tipperary, Ireland; marr. Halifax
5 July 1821 James Fling (31:45).

O'Neill, Denis Jeremiah. S. of Corne-
lius/Elener (Sullivan) of Dunma-
hon, Louth, Ireland; marr. Halifax
6 Feb. 1822 Sophia Boutillier (31:
51).

O'Neill, Eleanor Jane. Dau. of Jo-
seph/Margaret (Parkinson) of England; marr. Halifax 12 May 1831
Michael Murphy (q.v.) (33:64).

O'Neill, Henry. S. of Lawrence/Marga-
ret (Howlin) of Parish Tintern,
Co. Wexford, Ireland; marr. Halifax 17 Sep. 1818 Elizabeth Alice
Butler (q.v.) (31:51).

O'Neill, Margaret. Dau. of John/

Margaret (Doulan) of Machel, Co. Carlow, Ireland; marr. Halifax 24 Sep. 1828 Patrick Holl (Perhaps Hall?) (q.v.) (32:113).

O'Neill, Patrick. S. of Patrick/ Eleanor (Byrne) of Co. Carlow, Ireland; marr. Halifax 1 Feb. 1831 Rebecca Holland (q.v.) (33:65).

O'Neill, Richard. S. of Martin/Margaret (Winn) of Leighlin, Co. Carlow, Ireland; marr. Halifax 14 May 1833 Catherine Blanch (q.v.) (33: 65).

O'Reilly, Dennis. Loyalist; mustered at Digby 19 May 1784 (39:193).

O'Riley, Bernard. Pvt. Royal Can. Regt.; of Co. Armagh, Ireland; marr. Halifax 3 Nov. 1841 Caroline Powell (35:143).

O'Rily, Peter. S. of Philip/Rose (Donohoe) of Co. Cavan, Ireland; marr. Halifax 2 Oct. 1844 Isabella Gains (35:143).

O'Rourke, James. S. of Farrel/Nancy (Doyle) of Dunboyne, Co. Meath, Ireland; marr. Halifax 18 July 1812 Anne Darcy (30:109).

O'Rourke, James. Widower of Catherine Slattery of Herbertstown, Co. Limerick, Ireland; marr. Halifax 3 June 1841 Joanna Lillis (q.v.) (35:143).

O'Rourke, Thomas. S. of John/Catherine (Burke) of Co. Carlow, Ireland; marr. Halifax 24 May 1836 Margaret Murphy (q.v.) (34:136).

O'Rourke, Timothy. S. of William/ Ellen (Canty) of Co. Cork, Ireland; marr. Halifax 14 Jan. 1833 Mary Whelan (q.v.) (33:65).

O'Shaughnasey, Margaret; Spinster; Irish; 20; Liverpool to Nova Scotia June 1864 on INDIAN QUEEN (45:182).

O'Solovan, Cornelius. S. of Timothy/

Elizabeth of Parish Kilmoconoge, Co. Cork, Ireland; marr. Halifax 11 July 1824 Bridget Brown (q.v.) (31:53).

O'Sullivan, Patrick. Widower of Catherine Murray; of Co. Kerry, Ireland; thrice widowed; marr. Halifax 17 Feb. 1828 Mary Snellon (q.v.) (32:117).

O'Brien, Margaret. Dau. of Edward of Co. Tipperary, Ireland; marr. Halifax 7 May 1833 Joseph Bracket (33:54).

Oakes, William. Loyalist; mustered at Digby 19 May 1784 (39:193).

Oakley, Alice. Dau. of Patrick/Margaret (Power) of Co. Waterford, Ireland; marr. Halifax 10 Aug. 1843 John Magher (q.v.) (35:141).

Oakley, Arthur. Of Co. Waterford, Ireland; widower of Catherine Crow; marr. Halifax 26 Mar. 1840 Margaret Murphy (q.v.) (34:136).

Oakley, Elizabeth. Dau. of James/ Catherine (Quan) of Abbeyside, Co. Waterford, Ireland; marr. Halifax 23 Jan. 1845 Patrick Mulcahy (q.v.) (35:142).

Oakly, Ellen. Dau. of Patrick/Margaret (Power) of Co. Waterford, Ireland; marr. Halifax 2 Sep. 1833 Thomas Roche (q.v.) (33:66).

Oaks, Jesse. Grantee 'Digby New Grant' 29 Jan. 1801 (5:83).

Oaks, Phineas. Grantee 'Digby New Grant' 29 Jan. 1801 (5:83).

Offney, William. German Service; mustered at Bear River 11/25 June 1784 (38:260).

Okly, Patrick. Laborer; English; 38; Liverpool to Nova Scotia June 1864 on INDIAN QUEEN (45:182).

Oldfield, William. Of Co. Waterford, Ireland; widower of Mary Hickey; marr. Halifax 11 Nov. 1834 Bridget

Coffee *(q.v.)* (34:136)

Oliver, Ichabod. Disbanded soldier,
1st N.J. Vols.; mustered at Digby
19 May 1784 (39:193).

Olmstead, Moses. From Mass.; land
grant at Truro 1759 (4:242).

Oneal, William. "Yellowman" (i.e.
mulatto?); s. of July/Marolia;
S. C. to Liverpool by 1783 (47:
127:269).

Osborn, Thomas. S. of Thomas/Mary
(Lynagh) of Co. Waterford, Ire-
land; marr. Halifax 26 Nov. 1831
Mary Holly *(q.v.)* (33:65).

Osborne, Jabez. Loyalist; mustered at
Digby 19 May 1784 (39:193).

Osborne, Thomas. Loyalist; plus 1
f./4 ch./2 svts.; mustered at Digby 19 May 1784 (39:193).

Osgood, Abraham. 43, merchant; Poole
to Nova Scotia on SQUIRREL Nov.
1775 (24:45).

Osgood, Thomas B. Liverpool proprietor (19:102).

Ostman, Jacob. German Service; plus 1
f.; mustered at Bear River 11/25
June 1784 (38:260).

Ott, Jabob. Loyalist; plus 1 f./4
ch.; mustered at Digby 19 May 1784
(39:193).

Outhouse, Nicholas. Loyalist; plus 1
f./6 ch.; mustered at Gulliver's
Hole/St. Mary's Bay/Sissiboo 1/6
June 1784; settled at Gulliver's
Hole (a cove and harbor on Digby
Neck) (40:262).

Outhouse, Robert. Loyalist; mustered
at Gulliver's Hole/St. Mary's
Bay/Sissiboo 1/6 June 1784; settled at Gulliver's Hole (a cove
and harbor on Digby Neck) (40:
262).

Owens, Francis. Loyalist; plus 1 f.;
mustered at Digby 19 May 1784 (39:
193).

- P -

Pack, Benjamin. Tailor; Port Roseway
Associate (6:16).

Pack, John. Plus 1 f./4 ch./3 svts.;
tailor; Port Roseway Associate (6:
16).

Padderson, Thomas. Liverpool proprietor (19:101).

Page, John. Loyalist; mustered at
Digby 19 May 1784 (39:193).

Page, Stephen Jr. S. of Stephen/
Priscilla; to (or b.?) Liverpool
by 1791 (47:127:117).

Page, Stephen. To Liverpool by 1766
(47:126:162).

Pain, Christopher. R.I. to N.S.; to
U.S. 1776; dead by 1785 (36:65).

Pain, Mehetabel. Wife of Stephen; to
Liverpool *ca.* 1760 (47:126:95).

Pain, Stephen. To Liverpool *ca.* 1760
(47:126:95).

Paine, John. S. of James/Margaret
(Flanigan) of Tara, Co. Meath ,
Ireland; marr. Halifax 8 Nov. 1835
Catherine Power *(q.v.)* (34:136).

Paine, John. S. of James/Margaret
(Flanigan); of Tara, Co. Meath,
Ireland; widower of Catherine
Power; marr. Halifax 19 Apr. 1841
Anne Magrath *(q.v.)* (35:143).

Paine, Stephen. Liverpool proprietor
(19:102).

Paine, Stephen. S. of Stephen/Mary;
to Liverpool *ca.* 1760 (47:126:96).

Palister, Joseph. 25, labourer; Hull
to Fort Cumberland on ALBION 7-14
March 1774 (21:135).

Palmer, Alphaus. Plus 8 svts.; Port
Roseway Associate (6:17).

Palmer, Benjamin. Plus 1 f./5 ch./3
svts.; farmer; Port Roseway Associate (6:16).

Palmer, John. From Ireland; land

grant at Londonderry 6 Mar. 1775 (4:258).

Palmer, Thomas. 49, master mariner; Poole to Nova Scotia on SQUIRREL Nov. 1775 (24:45).

Park, Elizabeth. Dau. of William/Molly; to (or b.?) Liverpool by 1797 (47:127:273).

Park, Sally. Dau. of William/Molly; to (or b.?) Liverpool by 1801 (47:127:273).

Parke, Mary. Dau. of James/Rebeckah; to Liverpool by 1802 (47:127:275).

Parker, -----. 18 mos.; ch. of William; Hull, Yorkshire, to Nova Scotia; on TWO FRIENDS 28 Feb.-7 Mar. 1774 (25:29).

Parker, Benjamin Jr. S. of Benjamin/Mary; to Liverpool by 1787 (47:127:56).

Parker, Benjamin. Liverpool proprietor (19:101).

Parker, Desire. To Liverpool ca. 1760 (47:126:161).

Parker, Dorothy. Dau. of Richard/Mary (Tallin) of Co. Kilkenny, Ireland; marr. Halifax 29 Nov. 1836 Philip Shipley (q.v.) (34:138).

Parker, Elizabeth. 9; dau.of Mary; Hull, Yorkshire, to Halifax; on JENNY 3-10 April 1775 (22:124).

Parker, Elizabeth. 33; wife of Joseph; Hull, Yorkshire, to Nova Scotia; on TWO FRIENDS 28 Feb.-7 Mar. 1774 (25:30).

Parker, Hannah. Dau. of Benjamin/Mary; to (or b.?) Liverpool by 1778 (47:126:290).

Parker, James. 2; s. of Mary; Hull, Yorkshire, to Halifax; on JENNY 3-10 April 1775 (22:124).

Parker, Jane. Loyalist; mustered at Digby 19 May 1784 (39:193).

Parker, John. 3; s. of William; Hull, Yorkshire, to Nova Scotia; on TWO

FRIENDS 28 Feb.-7 Mar. 1774 (25:29).

Parker, Joseph. 33; rope maker; Hull, Yorkshire, to Nova Scotia; on TWO FRIENDS 28 Feb.-7 Mar. 1774 (25:30).

Parker, Joshua. Plus 2 svts.; carpenter; Port Roseway Associate (6:16).

Parker, Mary. 38; wife of William; Hull, Yorkshire, to Nova Scotia; on TWO FRIENDS 28 Feb.-7 Mar. 1774 (25:29).

Parker, Mary. 40; to join husband; Hull, Yorkshire, to Halifax; on JENNY 3-10 April 1775 (22:124).

Parker, Mary. 74; widow; Hull, Yorkshire, to Nova Scotia; on TWO FRIENDS 28 Feb.-7 Mar. 1774 (25:29).

Parker, Mary. Dau. of Benjamin/Mary; to (or b.?) Liverpool by 1786 (47:127:54).

Parker, Peter. Plus 1 f./4 ch./3 svts.; mariner; Port Roseway Associate (6:16).

Parker, Simeon. Plus 1 f.; arr. Annapolis from New York 19 Oct. 1782 (37:126).

Parker, Simon. Loyalist; plus 1 f.; mustered at Digby 19 May 1784 (39:193).

Parker, Snow. S. of Benjamin/Mary; to (or b.?) Liverpool by 1780 (47:126:283).

Parker, Thomas. S. of Benjamin/Mary; to (or b.?) Liverpool by 1795 (47:127:210).

Parker, William. 2; s. of Joseph; Hull, Yorkshire, to Nova Scotia; on TWO FRIENDS 28 Feb.-7 Mar. 1774 (25:30).

Parker, William. 31; farmer; Hull, Yorkshire, to Nova Scotia; on TWO FRIENDS 28 Feb.-7 Mar. 1774 (25:

29).

Parkes, James. Loyalist; plus 1 f./1 ch.; mustered at Digby 19 May 1784 (39:193).

Parkes, John. Loyalist; mustered at Digby 19 May 1784 (39:193).

Parks, James. Plus 1 f./1 ch -8; arr. Annapolis from New York 19 Oct. 1782 (37:126).

Parle, Mary. Dau. of Thomas/Rebecca; to (or b.?) Liverpool by 1798 (47:127:269).

Parr, John. Loyalist; plus 1 f./1 ch.; mustered at Digby 19 May 1784 (39:194).

Pashley, George. Plus 1 f./1 ch./3 svts.; tailor; Port Roseway Associate (6:16).

Paterson, David. From Mass.; land grant at Truro 1759 (4:242).

Paterson, James Jr. From Mass.; land grant at Truro 1759 (4:242).

Paterson, John. From Mass.; land grant at Truro 1759 (4:242).

Paterson, William. From Mass.; land grant at Truro 1759 (4:242).

Patison, Jonathan. 19, husbandman; Hull to Fort Cumberland on ALBION 7-14 March 1774 (21:134).

Patten, George. Plus 1 f./2 ch./4 svts.; Port Roseway Associate (6:17).

Patterson, -----. Widow; Loyalist; plus 1 ch./1 svt.; mustered at Digby 19 May 1784; settled at Granville (39:193).

Patterson, Alexander. Grantee "Digby New Grant" 29 Jan. 1801 (5:83).

Patterson, John. S. of Thomas/Susannah; to (or b.?) Liverpool by 1793 (47:127:117).

Patterson, Joseph. Arr. Annapolis from New York 19 Oct. 1782 (37:126).

Patterson, Joseph. Loyalist; mustered

at Digby 19 May 1784 (39:193).

Patterson, Susannah. Dau. of Thomas/Susannah; to Liverpool by 1767 (47:127:119).

Patton, Elenor. Dau. of Samuel/Mary (Twiddle) of Co. Antrim, Ireland; marr. 1 May 1823 Patrick Brennan (q.v.) (31:41).

Paul, John. Loyalist; mustered at Digby 19 May 1784 (39:194).

Paulbridge, Frederick. Laborer; English; 22; Liverpool to Nova Scotia May 1864 on EUROCLYDON (45: 182).

Payne, Catherine. See Power, Catherine.

Payzant, Henry. S. of Rev. John/Mary; to (or b.?) Liverpool by 1802 (47:127:272).

Peach, Anna. Dau. of Jacob/Anna; to Liverpool by 1791 (47:128:28).

Peach, James Jr. Loyalist; mustered at Digby 19 May 1784; settled at Granville (39:193).

Peach, John. Liverpool proprietor (19:101).

Peach, Mary. Dau. of John/Elizabeth; to (or b.?) Liverpool by 1796 (47:127:209).

Pearsons, George. S. of Francis/Diana; to (or b.?) Liverpool by 1788 (47:127:125).

Peck, Helen. 15; dau.of Richard; Hull, Yorkshire, to Halifax; on JENNY 3-10 April 1775 (22:125).

Peck, Isaac. 13; s. of Richard; Hull, Yorkshire, to Halifax; on JENNY 3-10 April 1775 (22:125).

Peck, Jane. 17; dau.of Richard; Hull, Yorkshire, to Halifax; on JENNY 3-10 April 1775 (22:125).

Peck, Jane. 42; wife of Richard; Hull, Yorkshire, to Halifax; on JENNY 3-10 April 1775 (22:125).

Peck, Joseph. 2; s. of Richard; Hull, Yorkshire, to Halifax; on JENNY 3-

10 April 1775 (22:125).

Peck, Mary. 20; dau.of Richard; Hull, Yorkshire, to Halifax; on JENNY 3-10 April 1775 (22:125).

Peck, Richard. 46; farmer; Hull, Yorkshire, to Nova Scotia; on TWO FRIENDS 28 Feb.-7 Mar. 1774 (25:28).

Peck, Richard. 47; husbandman; Hull, Yorkshire, to Halifax; on JENNY 3-10 April 1775 (22:125).

Peck, Richard. 5; s. of Richard; Hull, Yorkshire, to Halifax; on JENNY 3-10 April 1775 (22:125).

Peck, Robert. 10; s. of Richard; Hull, Yorkshire, to Halifax; on JENNY 3-10 April 1775 (22:125).

Peck, Rose. 7; dau.of Richard; Hull, Yorkshire, to Halifax; on JENNY 3-10 April 1775 (22:125).

Peckett, Edward. 44, husbandman; Hull to Fort Cumberland on ALBION 7-14 March 1774 (21:136).

Pedan, Margaret. Dau. of John/Margaret (Graham) of Co. Donegal, Ireland; marr. Halifax 27 June 1842 Francis Joice (q.v.) (35:139).

Pedan, Patrick. Pvt. 64th Regt.; of Co. Roscommon, Ireland; marr. Halifax 8 Feb. 1842 Margaret Coony (35:143).

Peek, Rhoda. Dau. of Daniel/Rhoda; to Liverpool by 1771 (47:126:167).

Peerson, James. S. of John/Elizabeth (Fox) of Co. Wexford, Ireland; marr. Halifax 26 June 1821 Mary Murry (q.v.) (31:51).

Pelham, Thomas. S. of Joseph/Sarah of Boston, Mass.; to Liverpool by 3 Oct. 1785 (return dated 1784) (47:126:286).

Pell, Joshua. Plus 1 f./8 ch./4 svts.; farmer; Port Roseway Associate (6:16).

Pemberton, Jeremiah. Plus 2 f./3 ch.

8+; arr. Annapolis from New York 19 Oct. 1782 (37:125).

Pemberton, Thomas. Capt. brig MARS; s. of Thomas/Mary (Kellogg) of Suffield, England; marr. Halifax 10 June 1806 Mary Ryan (q.v.) (30:109).

Pendell, William. To (or b.?) Liverpool by 1791 (47:127:57).

Pender, Mary. Dau. of Patrick/Johana (Burke) of Parish Mickle (Myshall), Co. Carlow, Ireland; marr. Halifax 10 June 1836 James Donoly (q.v.) (34:129).

Pendergast, Michael. S. of Thomas/Alice of Co. Wexford, Ireland; marr. Halifax 8 Feb. 1819 Eleanor O'Brien (q.v.) (31:51).

Pendergast, Patrick. S. of Simon/Catherine (Mulcahy) of Co. Waterford, Ireland; marr. Halifax 7 June 1816 Ruth Pratt widow of John Power (30:109).

Peppard, Laurence. B. 1735 Ireland; bur. Folly Village, Londonderry (4:262).

Perkins, Daniel. Norwich, Conn., to Liverpool by 1793 (47:127:123).

Perkins, John. S. of Simeon/Elizabeth; to (or b.?) Liverpool by 1804 (47:127:273).

Perkins, Judith. Norwich, Conn., to Liverpool by 1793 (47:127:123).

Perkins, Lucy. Dau. of Simeon/Elizabeth; to (or b.?) Liverpool by 1805 (47:127:273).

Perkins, Roger. B. Norwich, Conn., 8 Dec. 1760; s. of Simeon/Abigail; to Liverpool by 1775 (47:126:168).

Perkins, Samuel. New England to Annapolis on CHARMING MOLLY May 1760 (18:271).

Perkins, Simeon. Liverpool proprietor (19:102).

Perkins, Simeon. S. of Jacob; to

Liverpool by 1775 (47:126:168).

Perkins, Zebulon. S. of Daniel/Judith; to (or b.?) Liverpool by 1793 (47:127:123).

Perry, Catherine. Dau. of Thomas/Mary (Steele) of Nfld.; marr. Halifax 13 Nov. 1828 Michael McLoughlin (q.v.) (32:115).

Perry, Ebenezer. New England to Annapolis 1760 (18:271).

Perry, John. S. of Thomas/Mary (Dooly) of Co. Leix, Ireland; marr. Halifax 22 Oct. 1831 Elizabeth Scott (q.v.) (33:65).

Perry, Samuel. Plus 1 f./8 ch.; farmer; Port Roseway Associate (6:16).

Perry, Silas. Plus 1 svt.; farmer; Port Roseway Associate (6:16).

Perry, Thomas. Plus 1 f./3 ch./1 svt.; farmer; Port Roseway Associate (6:16).

Persels, Simon. Arr. Annapolis from New York 19 Oct. 1782 (37:125).

Peterkin, Elizabeth. Dau. of James/Mary (North) of Colchester, England; marr. Halifax 5 May 1811 Patrick Brown (q.v.) (30:102).

Peters, Maurice. Loyalist; plus 1 f./1 ch.; mustered at Digby 19 May 1784 (39:194).

Petil, Silas. Loyalist; mustered at Digby 19 May 1784 (39:193).

Petit, Benjamin. Loyalist; plus 1 f./2 ch.; mustered at Digby 19 May 1784; (39:193).

Petit, Isaac. Loyalist; plus 1 f./2 ch.; mustered at Gulliver's Hole/ St. Mary's Bay/Sissiboo 1/6 June 1784; settled at Sissiboo (now Weymouth) (40:263).

Petrie, Isabella. Dau. of Edmund/ Margaret (Cody) of Sydney, Cape Breton; marr. Halifax 18 Aug. 1836 James Norris (q.v.) (34:136).

Pfitzer, F. Disbanded soldier, Waldeck; mustered at Bear River 11/25 June 1784 (38:260).

Phelan, Anne. Dau. of John/Mary (O'Brien), widow of James Connelly of Co. Tipperary, Ireland; marr. Halifax 11 Jan. 1825 Andrew Cummins (q.v.) (31:43).

Phelan, Bridget. Dau. of Denis/Honora (Cussin) of Parish Ballinakill, Queen's Co., Ireland; marr. Halifax 25 Aug. 1820 Hugh Kenny (q.v.) (31:48).

Phelan, Edmund. S. of John Perry/ Elizabeth (Power) of Co. Kilkenny, Ireland; marr. Halifax 23 Oct. 1831 Mary Brenan (q.v.) (33:65).

Phelan, James. S. of Edward/Johanna (Drohan) of Co. Waterford, Ireland; marr. Halifax 28 May 1834 Ellen McGrath (q.v.) (33:66).

Phelan, James. S. of Luke/Mary (Ragget) of Kells Priory, Co. Kilkenny, Ireland; marr. Halifax 16 Aug. 1842 Mary Fitzgerald (q.v.) (35:143).

Phelan, John. S. of Thomas/Bridget (O'Brien) of Carrick-on-Suir, Tipperary, Ireland; marr. Halifax 22 Apr. 1805 Elenor Bambrick (q.v.) (30:109).

Phelan, Lawrence. S. of John/Honora (Dixon) of Ballytobin, Co. Kilkenny, Ireland; marr. Halifax 2 Dec. 1826 Emilia Philpott (32:117).

Phelan, Michael. S. of James/Honor (Baldie) of Co. Waterford, Ireland; marr. Halifax 8 Oct. 1805 Anne Murray (30:109).

Phelan, Michael. S. of Maurice/Ellen of Co. Kilkenny, Ireland; marr. Halifax 20 Feb. 1841 Jane Nugent (35:143).

Phelan, Michael. S. of Luke/Mary (Ragget) of Kells Priory, Co.

Kilkenny, Ireland; marr. Halifax 7 Sep. 1842 Debora Thompson (q.v.) (35:143).

Phelan, Patrick. S. of John/Johanna (Hickey) of Ballyhail, Co. Kilkenny, Ireland; marr. Halifax 22 Nov. 1823 Margaret O'Brien (31:51).

Phelan, Robert. S. of John/Catherine (Murphy) of Waterford City, Ireland; marr. Halifax 7 Apr. 1818 Margaret Leigh (q.v.) (31:51).

Philip. Black; to Liverpool by 1786 (47:126:163).

Phillips, David. Plus 1 f./2 ch./1 svt.; farmer; Port Roseway Associate (6:16).

Phillips, Doit. Plus 1 f./2 ch. 8+; arr. Annapolis from New York 19 Oct. 1782 (37:125).

Phillips, Fadey. S. of Matthew/Lydia; to (or b.?) Liverpool by 1779 (47: 127:206).

Phillips, Jacob. Loyalist; mustered at Digby 19 May 1784 (39:194).

Phillips, Jesse. S. of Matthew/Lydia; Newark, N. J., to Liverpool by 1787 (47:127:122).

Phillips, Jonathan. S. of David/ Hannah; Newark, N. J., to Liverpool by 1799 (47:127:267).

Phillips, Samuel. Laborer; English; 30; Liverpool to Nova Scotia May 1864 on EUROCLYDON (45:182).

Pickering, Samuel. 23; farmer; Hull, Yorkshire, to Nova Scotia; on TWO FRIENDS 28 Feb.-7 Mar. 1774 (25: 28).

Pickett, Giles. 41, blacksmith; Hull to Fort Cumberland on ALBION 7-14 March 1774 (21:137).

Pickett, James. 16, s. of Giles; Hull to Fort Cumberland on ALBION 7-14 March 1774 (21:137).

Pickett, John. 7, s. of Giles; Hull to Fort Cumberland on ALBION 7-14

March 1774 (21:137).

Pickett, Margaret. 5, daughter of Giles; Hull to Fort Cumberland on ALBION 7-14 March 1774 (21:137).

Pickett, Mary. 38, wife of Giles; Hull to Fort Cumberland on ALBION 7-14 March 1774 (21:137).

Pickett, William. 1, s. of Giles; Hull to Fort Cumberland on ALBION 7-14 March 1774 (21:137).

Pier, Sarah. Dau. of William/Mary (Feild) of Co. Cork, Ireland; marr. Halifax 7 Nov. 1832 John Swiney (q.v.) (33:67).

Pierce, Richard. Loyalist; mustered at Digby 19 May 1784 (39:193).

Pierce, Thomas. S. of Mark/Mary (Brady) of Co. Leix, Ireland; marr. Halifax 28 Jan. 1835 Mary Ann Garner (q.v.) (34:137).

Pierpont, Joseph. From Mass.; land grant at Onslow 21 Feb. 1769 (4: 225).

Pierson, James. Loyalist; plus 1 f.; mustered at Digby 19 May 1784 (39: 193).

Pike, John. S. of William/Sarah (Reynolds) of Exeter, England; marr. Halifax 22 June 1810 Margaret Kelly (q.v.) (30:109).

Pilgrim, Francis. Disbanded soldier, 1st N.J. Vols.; plus 1 f.; mustered at Digby 19 May 1784 (39: 193).

Pinckston, Fleming. Loyalist; plus 1 svt.; mustered at Digby 19 May 1784 (39:194).

Pine, Henry. S. of Stephen/Mary; New York to Liverpool by 1781 (47: 126:287).

Pinkstone, Fleming. Plus 2 svts.; physician; Port Roseway Associate (6:16).

Pipes, Jonathan. 20, husbandman; Hull to Fort Cumberland on ALBION 7-14

March 1774 (21:138).

Pipes, William. 22, husbandman; Hull to Port Cumberland on ALBION 7-14 March 1774 (21:138).

Pipes, William. 49, farmer; Hull to Port Cumberland on ALBION 7-14 March 1774 (21:138).

Pitcher, Moses. Plus 1 f./5 ch./2 svts.; glazier; Port Roseway Associate (6:16).

Pitts, Mary. B. Plymouth, Mass., 15 Oct. 1747; dau. of Thomas/Mary; to Liverpool by 1764 (47:126:164).

Placeway, Robert. Liverpool proprietor (19:102).

Placisceway, Mehebal?. Wife of Robert; to Liverpool ca. 1760 (47:126:96).

Placisceway, Robert. To Liverpool ca. 1760 (47:126:95).

Plaseway, Robert. To Liverpool ca. 1760 (47:126:96).

Plumb, David. Loyalist; mustered at Digby 19 May 1784 (39:193).

Plumb, Jacob. Loyalist; mustered at Digby 19 May 1784 (39:193).

Plunket, Peter. S, Mathew/Catherine (Drugan) of Co. Fermanagh, Ireland; marr. Halifax 13 Aug. 1831 Catherine Farrell (q.v.) (33:66).

Polly, John Jr. From Mass.; land grant at Onslow 21 Feb. 1769 (4:225).

Polly, John. From Mass.; land grant at Onslow 21 Feb. 1769 (4:224).

Pompey. Slave to Capt. Young; mustered at Digby 19 May 1784 (39:194).

Poor, Anne. Dau. of John/Margaret (Knox) of Co. Dublin, Ireland; marr. Halifax 17 May 1803 James Ryan (q.v.) (30:110).

Poore, Catherine. Dau. of Lawrence/Catherine of Kilmacthomas, Co. Waterford, Ireland; marr. Halifax

11 May 1818 Philip Ryan (q.v.) (31:53).

Porter, Asa. Grantee "Digby New Grant" 29 Jan. 1801 (5:83).

Portland, Maria. Dau. of Joseph/Mary (Reil) of Co. Westmeath, Ireland; marr. Halifax 30 Dec. 1839 Martin Fleming (q.v.) (34:130).

Post, David. Grantee "Digby New Grant" 29 Jan. 1801 (5:83).

Post, Gilbert. Grantee "Digby New Grant" 29 Jan. 1801 (5:83).

Post, Gilbert. Loyalist; plus 1 f.; mustered at Digby 19 May 1784 (39:194).

Potter, James. Plus 1 f./6 ch./2 svts.; cutler; Port Roseway Associate (6:16).

Potter, Maria. To (or b.?) Liverpool by 1787 (47:127:55).

Potts, Judge. Black; to (or b.?) Guysborough by 1791 (47:127:57).

Powell, Evan. Grantee "Digby New Grant" 29 Jan. 1801 (5:83).

Power, Ann. See Landrigan, Ann.

Power, Anne. Dau. of Michael/Mary (Bradbury) of St. John's, Nfld.; marr. Halifax 16 June 1805 Thomas Cassidy (q.v.) (30:103).

Power, Anne. Dau. of Joseph/Mary of Co. Waterford, Ireland; marr. Halifax 19 May 1841 Thomas Murphy (35:142).

Power, Bridget. Dau. of Lawrence/Catherine of Kilmacthomas, Co. Waterford, Ireland; marr. Halifax 9 Feb. 1822 Michael Power (q.v.) (31:52).

Power, Bridget. Dau. of William/Mary (Spencer) of Waterford, Ireland; marr. Halifax 12 Nov. 1828 John Condon (q.v.) (32:107).

Power, Bridget. Dau. of Richard/Margaret of Co. Waterford, Ireland; marr. Halifax 2 Mar. 1835

Valentine Mulloy (q.v.) (34:135).

Power, Bridget. Dau. of Thomas/Mary
(Hally) of Co. Waterford, Ireland;
marr. Halifax 27 May 1843 John
Power (q.v.) (35:143).

Power, Bridget. See Purcell, Bridget.

Power, Catherine. Dau. of Thomas/
Elizabeth (Donelly) of Co. Kilkenny, Ireland; marr. Halifax 19 June
1832 Peter Walsh (q.v.) (33:68).

Power, Catherine. Dau. of Thomas/Mary
of Co. Wexford, Ireland; marr.
Halifax 27 Nov. 1835 William
Condon (q.v.) (34:127).

Power, Catherine. Dau. of Richard/
Margaret of Co. Waterford, Ire-
land; marr. Halifax 8 Nov. 1835
John Paine (q.v.) (34:136).

Power, Catherine. Dau. of Lawrence/
Catherine (Power) of Kilmacthomas,
Co. Waterford, Ireland; widow of
Philip Ryan; marr. Halifax 25 Oct.
1834 Thomas Ring (q.v.) (34:137).

Power, Catherine. Dau. of David/
Isabella (Anderson) of Co. Waterford, Ireland; marr. Halifax 20
May 1843 James Wallace (q.v.) (35:
145).

Power, Catherine. Wife of John Payne;
bur. Halifax 29 Oct. 1836 ae. 31
(34:125).

Power, Edmund. S. of Thomas/Margaret
(Larkin) of Shancloon, Waterford,
Ireland; marr. Halifax 30 June
1803 Mary Magrah (q.v.) (30:109).

Power, Edward. S. of Gregory/Judith
(Shea) of Co. Tipperary, Ireland;
marr. Halifax 5 Feb. 1820 Catherine Dulhanty (q.v.) (31:52).

Power, Edward. S. of Thomas/Bridget
(Flinn) of Killbarrymeaden, Co.
Waterford, Ireland; marr. Halifax
9 Aug. 1823 Mary Keating (31:52).

Power, Edward. S. of John/Honora
(Ryan) of Co. Tipperary, Ireland;

marr. Halifax 16 Nov. 1829 Margaret Murphy (q.v.) (32:117).

Power, Edward. S. of Edward/Alice
(Berrigan) of Co. Kilkenny, Ire-
land; marr. Halifax 16 Aug. 1842
Joanna Hogan (q.v.) (35:143).

Power, Eleanor. Dau. of Lawrence/
Catherine of Kilmacthomas, Co.
Waterford, Ireland; marr. Halifax
19 Sep. 1819 Daniel Buckley (q.v.)
(31:41).

Power, Eleanor. See Nolan, Mathew.

Power, Ellen. Dau. of Michael/Eleanor
of Co. Waterford, Ireland; marr.
Halifax 17 May 1832 William Barron
(q.v.) (33:54).

Power, Ellen. Dau. of Nicholas/ Cath-
erine (Clennan) of Co. Waterford,
Ireland; marr. Halifax 5 Aug. 1840
Maurice Milligan (q.v.) (34:135).

Power, Ellen. Dau. of Lawrence/ Catherine (Power) of Kilmacthomas, Co.
Waterford, Ireland; widow of Daniel Buckley; marr. Halifax 16 July
1840 Peter Morrissy (34:135).

Power, Ellen. See Barron, William.

Power, George. S. of John/Anestasia
of Kil St. Lawrence, Co. Waterford, Ireland; marr. Halifax 9 May
1803 Johanna Power (30:110).

Power, Honora. Dau. of John/Honora
(Christopher) of Co. Waterford,
Ireland; marr. Halifax 24 Aug.
1834 Thomas Kiley (q.v.) (33:61).

Power, Joanna. Dau. of Michael/Mary
(Murphy) of Bollens, county?,
Ireland; marr. Halifax 13 Jan.
1824 Nicholas Power (q.v.) (31:
52).

Power, Joanna. Dau. of James/Joanna
(Hynes) of Co. Kilkenny, Ireland;
marr. Halifax 2 Feb. 1829 William
Carey (q.v.) (32:106).

Power, Joanna. Dau. of Richard/Marga-
ret of Co. Waterford, Ireland;

marr. Halifax 3 May 1832 Michael
Callaghan *(q.v.)* (33:55).

Power, Johanna. See Walsh, Joanna.

Power, John. Of Co. Wexford, Ireland;
widower of Mary Murphy; marr. Halifax 20 Feb. 1841 Ellen Phelan
(35:143).

Power, John. Of Thomastown, Co. Kilkenny, Ireland; marr. Halifax 30
Jan. 1842 Bridget Purcell *(q.v.)*
(35:143).

Power, John. S. of Thomas/Bridget
(Kenny) of Parish Passage, Co.
Waterford, Ireland; marr. Halifax
11 May 1824 Mary Farrell (31:52).

Power, John. S. of Pierce/Mary
(Kenny) of Killinaule, Co. Tipperary, Ireland; widower of Margaret
Shelley; marr. Halifax 19 Apr.
1830 Catherine Hackett (32:117).

Power, John. S. of James/Mary (Power)
of Co. Waterford, Ireland; marr.
Halifax 12 Dec. 1837 Mary Dwyer
(q.v.) (34:137).

Power, John. S. of Michael/Joanna
(Reville) of Co. Wexford, Ireland;
marr. Halifax 5 Mar. 1838 Catherine Thompson *(q.v.)* (34:137).

Power, John. S. of James/Mary (Power)
of Co. Waterford, Ireland; widower
of Mary Dwyer; marr. Halifax 30
Sep. 1840 Ann Washington (34:137).

Power, John. S. of Thomas/Bridget
(Kenny) of Parish Passage, Co.
Waterford, Ireland; widower of
Mary Farrell; marr. Halifax 15
Sep. 1842 Mary Kean (35:143).

Power, John. S. of Michael/Ellen
(Power) of Co. Waterford, Ireland;
marr. Halifax 27 May 1843 Bridget
Power *(q.v.)* (35:143).

Power, John. S. of Matthew/Elizabeth;
Waterford, Ireland, to Liverpool
by 1802 (47:127:278).

Power, John. Widower of Catherine

Landergan; of Parish Mothell, Co.
Waterford, Ireland; marr. Halifax
5 Sep. 1825 Catherine Lawler (31:
52).

Power, John. Widower of Anastasia
McNamara; of Co. Waterford, Ire-
land; marr. Halifax 12 May 1841
Bridget Byrne *(q.v.)* (35:143).

Power, Judith. Dau. of Thomas/Mary
(Mackey) of Co. Kilkenny, Ireland;
marr. Halifax 29 Oct. 1831 George
Brennan *(q.v.)* (33:54).

Power, Lawrence. Deserted from H.M.S.
MELAMPOS; 5'5", fair ruddy com-
plexion, short curly hair, 19, b.
Ireland; advertised *The Weekly
Chronicle*, 21 June 1806 (28:34).

Power, Margaret. Dau. of Edmund/Anne
(Griffin) of Co. Waterford, Ire-
land; marr. Halifax 23 July 1821
Patrick Brennan *(q.v.)* (31:41).

Power, Margaret. Dau. of Lawrence/
Catherine of Kilmacthomas, Co.
Waterford, Ireland; marr. Halifax
5 June 1830 William Murphy (32:
116).

Power, Margaret. Dau. of Thomas/Mary
(Holly) of Co. Waterford, Ireland;
marr. Halifax 11 Dec. 1832 Michael
Molony *(q.v.)* (33:64).

Power, Margaret. See Dunphy, Margaret.

Power, Margaret. Widow of Terrence
O'Brien of Co. Waterford, Ireland;
marr. Halifax 31 July 1837 James
Heron *(q.v.)* (34:131).

Power, Mary. Dau. of Edmund/Anastasia
of Waterford, Ireland; marr. Halifax 21 July 1803 Patrick Hunt
(q.v.) (30:106).

Power, Mary. Dau. of Thomas/Eleanor
(Kearney) of St. John's, Nfld.;
marr. Halifax 17 June 1827 Pvt.
Thomas Irwin *(q.v.)* (32:113).

Power, Mary. Of Lawrence, Ballyla-

neen, Co. Waterford, Ireland;
marr. Halifax 3 Sep. 1824 John
Howlett (31:47).

Power, Mary. See Dwyer, Mary.

Power, Maurice. S. of Robert/Mary
(Shea) of Co. Waterford, Ireland;
marr. Halifax 11 June 1842 Margaret Kenny *(q.v.)* (35:143).

Power, Michael. S. of Michael/Elizabeth (Brown) of Co. Derry, Ireland; marr. Halifax 9 Feb. 1822
Bridget Power *(q.v.)* (31:52).

Power, Michael. S. of Edward/Bridget
of Tramore, Co. Waterford, Ireland; marr. Halifax 13 Dec. 1822
Catherine Debay (31:52).

Power, Michael. S. of Michael/Mary
(Walsh) of Co. Waterford, Ireland;
marr. Halifax 18 July 1842 Bridget
Hayden *(q.v.)* (35:143).

Power, Michael. Shipwright; s. of
Michael/ Mary (Barrett) of Youghal, Cork, Ireland; marr. Halifax
10 Aug. 1802 Elizabeth Maddox
(q.v.) (30:109).

Power, Nicholas. Arr. Annapolis from
New York 19 Oct. 1782 (37:126).

Power, Nicholas. Of Parish Abbeyside,
Co. Waterford, Ireland; marr. Halifax 14 Jan. 1836 Bridget Barrett
(q.v.) (34:137).

Power, Nicholas. S. of Michael/Bridget (Roche) of Parish Abbeyside,
Waterford, Ireland; marr. Halifax
13 Jan. 1824 Joanna Power *(q.v.)*
(31:52).

Power, Patrick. S. of Maurice/Catherine (Brophy) of Co. Waterford,
Ireland; marr. Halifax 9 Jan. 1810
Mary Walsh *(q.v.)* (30:110).

Power, Patrick. S. of Lawrence/Catherine (Power) of Kilmacthomas, Co.
Waterford, Ireland; marr. Halifax
10 Oct. 1840 Ellen Gaul *(q.v.)*
(34:137).

Power, Richard. S. of Richard/Mary;
of Co. Waterford, Ireland; marr.
Halifax 28 May 1831 Mary Mandasson
(33:66).

Power, Ruth. See Pratt, Ruth.

Power, Thomas. Plus 1 f./1 ch.; mariner; Port Roseway Associate
(6:16).

Power, Thomas. S. of Thomas/Elenor
(Crow) of Parish Ballygunner, Waterford, Ireland; marr. Halifax 10
Oct. 1821 Elenor Heirs (31:52).

Power, William. Capt.; s. of William/
Bridget (Phelan) of Waterford,
Ireland; marr. Halifax 27 Nov.
1802 Mary Roach *(q.v.)* (30:110).

Power, William. Of Co. Waterford,
Ireland; marr. Halifax 13 July
1802 Elizabeth Haiz (30:109).

Power, William. S. of Peter/Mary
(Monaghan) of Waterford, Ireland;
marr. Halifax 12 Apr. 1806 Elizabeth Hill *(q.v.)* (30:109).

Power, William. S. of Nicholas/Alice
(Flinn) of Co. Waterford, Ireland;
marr. Halifax 2 June 1808 Mary
Laffin *(q.v.)* (30:109).

Powers, Abijah. From Mass.; land
grant at Truro 1759 (4:242).

Powers, Walter. From Mass.; land
grant at Truro 1759 (4:242).

Prendergast, Johanna. Dau. of Patrick/Mary (Cushen) of Parish St.
John, Waterford, Ireland; marr.
Halifax 25 June 1825 Peter Cain
(q.v.) (31:42).

Prendergast, Michael. S. of John/
Elizabeth (O'Connor) of Cork, Ireland; marr. Halifax 1 July 1832
Joanna Aheron *(q.v.)* (33:66).

Prentice, Delight. Dau. of Oliver/
Eunice; to (or b.?) Liverpool by
1799 (47:127;272).

Prescott, Jonathan. S. of Capt. Jonathan; Halifax, Mass., to Chester with first settlers (16:45).

Prescott, Joseph. Glazier; Port Roseway Associate (6:16).

Price, Abijah Jr. From Mass.; land
grant at Truro 1759 (4:242).

Price, Abijah. From Mass.; land grant
at Truro 1759 (4:242).

Price, Asa. From Mass.; land grant at
Truro 1759 (4:242).

Price, Daniel. Of Ireland; marr. Halifax 24 Sep. 1819 Mary Bevin
(q.v.) (31:52).

Pride, William. S. of Ira/Mary; to
(or b.?) Liverpool by 1794 (47:
127:204).

Prime, Michael Jr. Loyalist; mustered
at Digby 19 May 1784 (39:194).

Prime, Michael Sr. Disbanded soldier,
N.Y. Vols.; mustered at Digby 19
May 1784 (39:193).

Pringle, Isaac. S. of Nicholas/Jean
(Maw) of Elderton, Northumberland,
England; marr. Halifax 23 May 1824
Mary Stewart (q.v.) (31:52).

Pringle, Robert. S. of Robert/Mary;
Sunderland, England, to Liverpool
by 1789 (47:127:124).

Pritchard, Gaines. Grantee "Digby New
Grant" 29 Jan. 1801 (5:83).

Procter, Charles. From N.H.; effective land grant at Truro 31 Oct.
1765 (4:244).

Procter, Nathel. Plus 1 f./1 ch. -8;
arr. Annapolis from New York 19
Oct. 1782 (37:126).

Prout, Timothy. Plus 1 f./3 svts.;
Port Roseway Associate (6:17).

Prow, Joseph. From Ireland; land
grant at Londonderry 6 Mar. 1775
(4:258).

Pryor, James. Plus 1 f./1 svt.; mariner; Port Roseway Associate (6:
16).

Pugh, Hugh, Loyalist; mustered at
Digby 19 May 1784 (39:194).

Punch, John. S. of Philip/Mary
(Cottrell) of Midleton, Co. Cork,
Ireland; marr. Halifax 5 Aug. 1837
Ellen Murphy (q.v.) (34:137).

Punt, Catharine. Loyalist; plus 1
ch.; mustered at Digby 19 May 1784
(39:194).

Purcel, Simon. See Simon Persels.

Purcell, Bridget. Of Co. Kilkenny,
Ireland; widow of John Power;
marr. Halifax 15 Apr. 1844 Walter
Dunn (q.v.) (35:137).

Purcell, Bridget. Of Co. Kilkenny,
Ireland; widow of Oliver Cummer-
ford; marr. Halifax 30 Jan. 1842
John Power (q.v.) (35:143).

Purcell, John. S. of Philip/Mary
(Callahan) of Clonmel, Co. Tipperary, Ireland; marr. Halifax 9 Aug.
1803 Catherine Elizabeth Gerhardt
(30:110).

Purcell, Joseph. S. of Richard/Marga-
ret (McCarthy) of Cork City, Ireland; marr. Halifax 8 Nov. 1832
Anne Kelly (33:66).

Purcell, Peretz. Loyalist; plus 1 f.;
mustered at Digby 19 May 1784 (39:
194).

Purcell, Philip. S. of Sylvester/Jo-
anna (Darmody) of Co. Tipperary,
Ireland; marr. Halifax 29 Oct.
1833 Honora Lowry (q.v.) (33:66).

Purcell, Simon. Loyalist; mustered at
Digby 19 May 1784 (39:193).

Purcil, John. S. of Francis/Honor
(Brenan) of Co. Carlow, Ireland;
marr. Halifax 12 July 1821 Sarah
Cammel (31:52).

Purdy, Abraham. Disbanded soldier,
N.Y. Vols.; mustered at Digby 19
May 1784; (39:193).

Purdy, Daniel. Grantee "Digby New
Grant" 29 Jan. 1801 (5:83).

Purdy, Daniel. Or Nathaniel; Loyalist; mustered at Digby 19 May 1784

(39:194).

Purdy, Joseph. Grantee "Digby New Grant" 29 Jan. 1801 (5:83).

Purdy, Joseph. Loyalist; mustered at Digby 19 May 1784 (39:194).

Purdy, Matthew. Loyalist; mustered at Digby 19 May 1784 (39:194).

Purdy, Nathaniel. Grantee "Digby New Grant" 29 Jan. 1801 (5:83).

Purdy, Nathaniel. See Purdy, Daniel.

Putnam, Caleb. S. of ----- and Elizabeth (Nurse widow Putnam) Putnam; bap. Danvers, Mass., 15 June 1750; to Onslow with stepfather Richard Upham (4:231).

Putnam. Caleb. From Mass.; land grant at Onslow 21 Feb. 1769 (4:225).

Pye, Roger. Loyalist; plus 1 f./3 svts.; mustered at Digby 19 May 1784 (39:194).

Pyke, Luke. S. of Edward/Catherine (Walsh) of Co. Kilkenny, Ireland; marr. Halifax 25 Feb. 1816 Sarah Wainwright (30:109).

Pynchon, Joseph. Plus 1 f./2 ch./3 svts.; farmer; Port Roseway Associate (6:16).

- Q -

Quan, John. S. of James of Parish Ballinkerns, Co. Wexford, Ireland; marr. Halifax 12 Oct. 1823 Anastasia Murphy (q.v.) (31:52).

Quann, John. S. of Michael/Alice (Whelan) of Co. Kilkenny, Ireland; marr. Halifax 19 Jan. 1837 Mary O'Brien (34:137).

Queeny, John. S. of Patrick/Helena of Co. Waterford, Ireland; marr. Halifax 10 Feb. 1819 Elizabeth Hart (q.v.) (31:52).

Quigley, David. Disbanded soldier, N.J. Vols.; mustered at Digby 19 May 1784 (39:194).

Quigley, Eleanor. Dau. of Andrew/Bridget (Stapleton) of Co. Kilkenny, Ireland; marr. Halifax 8 Jan. 1835 Richard White (q.v.) (34:139).

Quigley, James. S. of Andrew/Bridget (Stapleton) of St. Johnswell, Kilkenny, Ireland; marr. Halifax 10 June 1824 Margaret Doran (q.v.) (31:52).

Quigley, Joanna. Dau. of Thomas/Margaret (Kelly) of Co. Tipperary, Ireland; marr. Halifax 14 Oct. 1832 Thomas Magher (q.v.) (33:63).

Quigley, Thomas. S. of John/Mary (Forly) of Parish Chapel-Charon, Wexford, Ireland; marr. Halifax 14 Feb. 1825 Mary Lyons (31:52).

Quigley, Thomas. S. of Patrick/Catherine (Nevill) of Co. Wexford, Ireland; marr. Halifax 1 Mar. 1835 Margaret Lacy (q.v.) (34:137).

Quinlan, Ellen. Dau. of John/Margaret (Magher) of Co. Kilkenny, Ireland; marr. Halifax 12 Nov. 1832 Thomas Magrath (q.v.) (33:62).

Quinlan, Joanna. Dau. of John/Margaret (Magher) of Co. Kilkenny, Ireland; marr. Halifax 9 May 1834 William Dowly (q.v.) (33:57).

Quinlan, Michael. S. of John/Honora (White) of Co. Kilkenny, Ireland; marr. Halifax 24 Sep. 1843 Mary Johnson (35:143).

Quinn, Daniel. S. of William/Elizabeth of Co. Leix, Ireland; marr. Halifax 17 May 1842 Ann Haiden (q.v.) (35:143).

Quinn, Isabella. Dau. of Daniel/Mary of Co. Tyrone, Ireland; marr. Halifax 7 Oct. 1842 Michael Lawlor (q.v.) (35:140).

Quinn, John. S. of Daniel/Catherine (Magrath) of Co. Tipperary, Ireland; marr. Halifax 31 Aug. 1837

Ann Mulligan *(q.v.)* (34:137).

Quinn, John. S. of James/Ann (Luby) of Thurles, Co. Tipperary, Ireland; marr. Halifax 20 Apr. 1841 Jean Penny (35:143).

Quinn, Joseph. S. of Thomas/Bridget (White) of Co. Kilkenny, Ireland; marr. Halifax 17 Oct. 1832 Mary O'Connor *(q.v.)* (33:66).

Quinn, Mary. Dau. of Michael/Catherine (Walsh) of Co. Waterford, Ireland; marr. Halifax 10 Feb. 1831 Patrick Ronayne *(q.v.)* (33: 66).

Quinn, Patrick. Ship's cooper; s. of John/Mary (Grady) of Co. Waterford, Ireland; marr. Halifax 27 Oct. 1830 Juliana Cotter *(q.v.)* (32:117).

Quinn, William. S. of Patrick/Mary (Neal) of Carrick-on-Suir, Co. Tipperary, Ireland; marr. Halifax 25 Jan. 1836 Mary Todd *(q.v.)* (34: 137).

Quirk, Eliza. Dau. of Mathew/Mary (Low) of Co. Waterford, Ireland; marr. Halifax 21 May 1839 Thomas Casey *(q.v.)* (34:127).

Quirk, Hannah. Dau. of Thomas/Bridget (Prendergast) of Co. Tipperary, Ireland; marr. Halifax 10 Sep. 1842 Andrew Connors *(q.v.)* (35: 136).

Quirk, Mathew. S. of Mathew/Mary (Loughn) of Co. Waterford, Ireland; marr. Halifax 12 Sep. 1833 Bridget Fleming *(q.v.)* (33:66).

- R -

Rafter, Patrick. S. of William/Winifred (Naughton) of Tulrown-Tyrawly, Co. Mayo, Ireland; marr. Halifax 19 Sep. 1838 Ellen Crowley *(q.v.)* (34:137).

Rafter, William. S. of Edmund/Helena

(Hearley) of Co. Tipperary, Ireland; marr. Halifax 30 Nov. 1816 Mary Cummins *(q.v.)* (30:110).

Raftis, Mary. Dau. of Patrick/Alice (Riley) of Co. Kilkenny, Ireland; marr. Halifax 9 May 1831 Michael Shortal *(q.v.)* (33:67).

Raftis, Mary. Dau. of Patrick/Alice (Riley) of Co. Kilkenny, Ireland; widow of Michael Shortell; marr. Halifax 29 Sep. 1841 Jeremiah Sullivan *(q.v.)* (35:145).

Rahilly, Catherine. Dau. of Thomas/Honora (Walsh) of Co. Kilkenny, Ireland; marr. Halifax 30 Jan. 1842 William Lynch *(q.v.)* (35:140).

Rains, John. From N.H.; effective land grant at Truro 31 Oct. 1765 (4:245).

Rake, John. German Service; mustered at Bear River 11/25 June 1784 (38: 260).

Raleham, John. Loyalist; mustered at Digby 19 May 1784 (39:194).

Ramsay, Philip. Loyalist; mustered at Digby 19 May 1784 (39:194).

Rand, Nathaniel. Plus 1 f./1 ch.; mason; Port Roseway Associate (6: 17).

Randall, Enoch. Liverpool proprietor (19:102).

Randoller, Emanuel. Loyalist; plus 1 f./5 ch.; mustered at Digby 19 May 1784 (39:194).

Rashi, John Philip. Laboring man; not settled; mustered at Digby 19 May 1784 (39:194).

Rattigan, Mary. Dau. of Martin/Margaret (Malone) of Thomond, Co. Wexford, Ireland; marr. Halifax 21 Apr. 1825 David Collins *(q.v.)* (31:43).

Rawson, Nathaniel. New England to Annapolis on CHARMING MOLLY May

1760 (18:271).

Ray, Francis. 60th Regt.; s. of
Peter/Mary (Paris); marr. Halifax
3 Dec. 1817 Mary Roach (q.v.) (30:
110).

Ray, George William. S. of Thomas/
Mary (Brady) of Leeds, England;
marr. Halifax 21 May 1843 Jane
Murphy (q.v.) (35:144).

Ray, Robert. Grantee "Digby New
Grant" 29 Jan. 1801 (5:83).

Ray, Robert. Loyalist; plus 1 f./2
ch./2 svts.; mustered at Digby 19
May 1784 (39:194).

Raymond, Simeon. Grantee "Digby New
Grant" 29 Jan. 1801 (5:83).

Raymond, Simon. Loyalist; plus 1 f./6
ch.; mustered at Gulliver's Hole/
St. Mary's Bay/Sissiboo 1/6 June
1784; settled at Sissiboo (now
Weymouth) (40:263).

Read, Ephraim. Liverpool to Nova
Scotia April 1864 on KEDAR (45:
182).

Ready, Thomas. S. of Thomas/Mary
(O'Brien) of Co. Cork, Ireland;
marr. Halifax 14 Feb. 1831 Margaret Brophy (q.v.) (33:66).

Reagh, John. From Ireland; land grant
at Londonderry 6 Mar. 1775 (4:
258).

Rearden, Mary. Dau. of John/Julia
(Kanty) of Cork City, Ireland;
marr. Halifax 31 Oct. 1826 Jeremiah Donovan (q.v.) (32:108).

Reardon, Ann. Dau. of Daniel/Mary
(Dunagan) of Co. Cork, Ireland;
marr. Halifax 14 June 1837 Pvt.
Joseph Larkin (q.v.) (34:133).

Reath, James. Plus 1 f.; Port Roseway
Associate (6:17).

Records, John. Plus wife/4 ch.; Pembroke, Mass., to Chester with
first settlers (16:45).

Redfield, Elizabeth. 25; servant;

Hull, Yorkshire, to Fort Cumberland on JENNY 3-10 April 1775
(22:123).

Redmond, Daniel. S. of Michael/Anne
(Ryan) of Co. Wexford, Ireland;
marr. Halifax 13 Apr. 1819 Elizabeth Chevery widow of James Allen
(31:52).

Redmond, Edward. S. of Philip/Marga-
ret of Co. Wexford, Ireland; marr.
Halifax 6 June 1834 Bridget Cullerton (q.v.) (33:66).

Redmond, Lawrence. S. of Lawrence/
Mary of Co. Wexford, Ireland;
marr. Halifax 22 Aug. 1812 Margaret Cassidy (q.v.) (30:110).

Reed, Ann. 9, daughter of George;
Hull to Fort Cumberland on ALBION
7-14 Mar. 1774 (21:136).

Reed, Colin. Plus 1 f./1 ch./2 svts.;
Port Roseway Associate (6:17).

Reed, Francis. From Ireland; land
grant at Londonderry 6 Mar. 1775
(4:258).

Reed, George. 1, s. of George; Hull
to Fort Cumberland on ALBION 7-14
Mar. 1774 (21:136).

Reed, George. 33, farmer; Hull to
Fort Cumberland on ALBION 7-14
Mar. 1774 (21:136).

Reed, Hannah. 33, wife of George;
Hull to Fort Cumberland on ALBION
7-14 Mar. 1774 (21:136).

Reed, Isabella. 4, daughter of
George; Hull to Fort Cumberland on
ALBION 7-14 Mar. 1774 (21:136).

Reed, James. Grantee "Digby New
Grant" 29 Jan. 1801 (5:83).

Reed, John. 26, husbandman; Hull to
Fort Cumberland on ALBION 7-14
Mar. 1774 (21:136).

Reed, John. 6, s. of George; Hull to
Fort Cumberland on ALBION 7-14
Mar. 1774 (21:136).

Rees, Thomas. S. of William/Mary; New

Castle Bridge End, Co. Glamorgan, So. Wales, to Liverpool by 1807 (47:128:30).

Regadon, Phebe. Wife or widow of -----; dau. of Zepheniah/Phebe Eldridge; to (or b.?) Liverpool by 1785 (47:127:277).

Reid, Alex'r. Plus 3 svts.; Port Roseway Associate (6:17).

Reid, James. Loyalist; plus 1 f.; mustered at Gulliver's Hole/St. Mary's Bay/Sissiboo 1/6 June 1784; settled at Sissiboo (now Weymouth) (40:263).

Reid, James. Rifle Brig.; s. of James/Eliza (McDonald) of Co. Down, Ireland; marr. Halifax 22 Feb. 1835 Mary Steel (q.v.) (34:137).

Reid, Thomas. Loyalist; plus 1 f./4 ch./3 svts.; mustered at Digby 19 May 1784 (39:194).

Reily, Judith. Of Co. Carlow, Ireland; marr. Halifax 11 Nov. 1819 Patrick Connor (q.v.) (31:43).

Remson, Johannes. Grantee "Digby New Grant" 29 Jan. 1801 (5:83).

Remson, Rem. Grantee "Digby New Grant" 29 Jan. 1801 (5:83).

Renell, John. Disbanded soldier, 57th Regt.; mustered at Digby 19 May 1784 (39:194).

Rey, George. Disbanded soldier, 1st N.J. Vols.; mustered at Digby 19 May 1784 (39:194).

Reynolds, Alice. See Dunphy, Alice.

Reynolds, Christopher. S. of James/Mary (Kean) of Co. Longford, Ireland; marr. Halifax 25 Jan. 1830 Alice Dunphy (q.v.) (32:117).

Reynolds, John. Barrington petitioner 19 Oct. 1776 (1:365).

Reynolds, John. S. of John; b. Chatham, Mass., ca. 1754; marr. at Barrington 1775 (50:111).

Reynolds, Nath. Capt.; Mass. to N.S.; to U.S. 1776; lived 1785 at Mass. [which then incl. Me.] (36:64).

Rhoads, Helen. Loyalist; mustered at Digby 19 May 1784 (39:194).

Rholing, Philip. Waldeck Service; mustered at Bear River 11/25 June 1784 (38:260).

Rice, Ashbel. Grantee "Digby New Grant" 29 Jan. 1801 (5:83).

Rice, Benjamin. New England to Annapolis on CHARMING MOLLY May 1760 (18:271).

Rice, Beriah. New England to Annapolis on CHARMING MOLLY May 1760 (18:271).

Rice, Margaret. Dau. of Martin/Elizabeth (O'Neill) of Co. Kilkenny, Ireland; marr. Halifax 3 Oct. 1829 Michael Byrnes (q.v.) (32:106).

Rice, Rosana. Dau. of late Owen/Mary Ann of Armagh Town, Ireland; b. Limerick; marr. Halifax 16 Jan. 1827 Patrick Walsh (q.v.) (32:120).

Rice, Stephen. New England to Annapolis on CHARMING MOLLY May 1760 (18:271).

Richards, Charles. Plus 1 f./3 ch.; farmer; Port Roseway Associate (6:17).

Richards, Charles. Loyalist; mustered at Digby 19 May 1784 (39:194).

Richards, Iram. Plus 3 svts.; farmer; Port Roseway Associate (6:17).

Richards, James. Loyalist; plus 1 f.; mustered at Digby 19 May 1784 (39:194).

Richards, James. Plus 1 f./1 c, 8+; arr. Annapolis from New York 19 Oct. 1782 (37:125).

Richards, Jesse. Loyalist; mustered at Digby 19 May 1784 (39:194).

Richardson, Ellen. Dau. of John/Ellen (Turnbull) of Edinburgh, Scotland;

marr. Halifax 2 Mar. 1829 George
Dowling *q.v.* (32:109).

Richardson, Margaret. Dau. of John/
Rosana (Morrison) of Dumfries,
Scotland; marr. Halifax 19 Feb.
1833 Patrick Walsh *(q.v.)* (33:68).

Richardson, Peter. From Mass.; land
grant at Onslow 21 Feb. 1769 (4:
224).

Richardson, Philip. From Mass.; land
grant at Truro 1759 (4:242).

Richardson, Reuben. From Mass.; land
grant at Onslow 21 Feb. 1769 (4:
225).

Rickards, Ann. Wife of John; English;
31; Liverpool to Nova Scotia June
1864 on INDIAN QUEEN (45:182).

Rickards, John. Farmer; English; 37;
Liverpool to Nova Scotia June 1864
on INDIAN QUEEN (45:182).

Rieck, John. German Service; mustered
at Bear River 11/25 June 1784 (38:
260).

Riely, John. S. of Michael/Judith
(Purdy) of St. John's, Nfld.;
marr. Halifax 9 July 1808 Jane
Shea *(q.v.)* (30:110).

Rierson, Cornelius. Loyalist; mustered at Digby 19 May 1784 (39:
194).

Riggs, William. S. of Henry/Sindenia;
Eastbourne, nr. Midhurst, Sussex,
England; to Liverpool ca. 1814
(47:128:34).

Riley, Ann. Dau. of James/Norah
(Lahy) of Co. Cavan, Ireland;
marr. Halifax 15 Sep. 1835 Thomas
Cushan *(q.v.)* (34:128).

Riley, Bartholomew. S. of Timothy/
Joanna (Doody) of Co. Cork, Ire-
land; marr. Halifax 26 Sep. 1840
Elizabeth Lively (34: 137).

Riley, Catherine. Dau. of John/Marga-
ret (Whelan) of Co. Kilkenny,
Ireland; marr. Halifax 4 July 1832

Thomas Lawler *(q.v.)* (33:62).

Riley, Catherine. Dau. of John/Marga-
ret (Whelan) of Co. Kilkenny, Ireland; widow of Thomas Lawlor;
marr. Halifax 29 Sep. 1841 Michael
Flinn *(q.v.)* (35:138).

Riley, Margaret. Dau. of David/Mary
(McDonnell) of Parish Kilfane, Co.
Kilkenny, Ireland; marr. Halifax 6
June 1828 Lawrence Ring *(q.v.)*
(32:118).

Riley, Mary. See Croughan, Mary.

Ring, Lawrence. S. of James/Mary
(Byrne) of Parish Gowran, Co. Kilkenny, Ireland; marr. Halifax 6
June 1828 Margaret Riley *(q.v.)*
(32:117).

Ring, Thomas. S. of Patrick/Bridget
(McAvoy) of Ballyragget, Co.
Kilkenny, Ireland; marr. Halifax
25 Oct. 1834 Catherine Power
(q.v.) (34:137).

Ristine, Joseph. Wheelwright; Port
Roseway Associate (6:17).

Ritchie, Andrew. Grantee 'Digby New
Grant' 29 Jan. 1801 (5:83).

Ritchie, John. Grantee 'Digby New
Grant' 29 Jan. 1801 (5:83).

Ritchie, Thomas. Grantee 'Digby New
Grant' 29 Jan. 1801 (5:83).

Rivers, John. Merchant; Port Roseway
Associate (6:17).

Roach, Mary. Dau. of Robert/Margaret
(Doyle) of Youghal. Co. Cork,
Ireland; marr. Halifax 27 Nov.
1802 Capt. William Power *(q.v.)*
(30: 110).

Roach, Mary. Dau. of Morice/Mary of
Co. Wexford, Ireland; marr. Halifax 3 Dec. 1817 Francis Ray *(q.v.)*
(30: 110).

Roach, Mary. Dau. of James/Fanny
(Hays) of Ross, Co. Wexford, Ire-
land; widow of Edward Welsh; marr.
Halifax 26 June 1821 *(q.v.)*

(31:50).

Roach, Mary. Dau. of James/Frances
(Hays) of New Ross, Co. Wexford,
Ireland; widow of Capt. Lewis
Morris; marr. Halifax 5 Feb. 1828
Thomas Flavin (q.v.) (32:110).

Roach, Patrick. S. of James/Catherine
(Farrell) of Parish Lismore,
Waterford, Ireland; marr. Halifax
11 June 1822 Catherine Rafter (31:
52).

Roache, Elizabeth. Dau. of Maurice/
Ann (Cummins) of Co. Cork, Ire-
land; marr. Halifax 25 Apr. 1843
Peter Fleming (q.v.) (35:138).

Roache, Jeremiah. S. of John/Eliza-
beth (Charmont) of Bordeaux,
France; marr. Halifax 14 Nov. 1814
Mary Fitzgibbons (q.v.) (30:110).

Roache, Johanna. Dau. of William/
Elizabeth (Smith) of Cork City,
Ireland; marr. Halifax 29 Nov.
1826 Sgt. John Walker (32:119).

Robard, Margaret. Wife of Robert; to
Liverpool ca. 1760 (47:126:95).

Robard, Robert. To Liverpool ca. 1760
(47:126:95).

Robbinson, Catherine. Dau. of Mi-
chael/Elizabeth (Farrell) of Co.
Carlow, Ireland; marr. Halifax 24
May 1838 Peter Kenny (q.v.) (34:
132).

Robbinson, Eleanor. Dau. of Michael/
Joanna (Byrnes) of Co. Carlow,
Ireland; marr. Halifax 14 Apr.
1831 Thomas Shea (33:66).

Roberts, Henry. Plus 2 f./1 ch. -8;
arr. Annapolis from New York 19
Oct. 1782 (37:125).

Roberts, John. S. of Robert/Margaret;
to (or b.?) Liverpool by 1780 (47:
127:52).

Roberts, Joshua. Loyalist; plus 1
svt.; mustered at Digby 19 May
1784 (39:194).

Roberts, Thomas. S. of Robert/Marga-
ret; to (or b.?) Liverpool by 1794
(47:127:208).

Robertson, Alexander. Plus 1 f./2
ch./2 svts.; farmer; Port Roseway
Associate (6:17).

Robertson, William. Grantee "Digby
New Grant" 29 Jan. 1801 (5:83).

Robertson, William. 15, husbandman;
Hull to Fort Cumberland on ALBION
7-14 Mar. 1774 (21:139).

Robie, Simon Bradstreet. S. of Thomas; born 1770 at Marblehead,
Mass.; to Halifax (17:75).

Robie, Thomas. Loyalist; Boston,
Mass., to Halifax ca. 1775-6 (17:
75).

Robinson, Ann. 15; dau.of John; Hull,
Yorkshire, to Halifax; on JENNY 3-
10 April 1775 (22:124).

Robinson, David. B. ca. 1772; Belfast
or Greenock to Halifax on POLLY,
spring 1799 (29:83).

Robinson, Elizabeth. 30; Hull, Yorkshire, to Halifax; on JENNY 3-10
April 1775 (22:124).

Robinson, Elizabeth. 9; dau.of William; Hull, Yorkshire, to Halifax;
on JENNY 3-10 April 1775 (22:124).

Robinson, Francis. 3; ch. of William;
Hull, Yorkshire, to Halifax; on
JENNY 3-10 April 1775 (22:124).

Robinson, Fred. Loyalist; plus 1 f./4
ch.; mustered at Digby 19 May 1784
(39:194).

Robinson, Fredk. Plus 1 f./1 ch. 8+:
arr. Annapolis from New York 19
Oct. 1782 (37:125).

Robinson, James. Grantee "Digby New
Grant" 29 Jan. 1801 (5:83).

Robinson, James. Loyalist; plus 1
f./6 svts.; mustered at Digby 19
May 1784 (39:194).

Robinson, Jenny. 9; dau.of John;
Hull, Yorkshire, to Halifax; on

JENNY 3-10 April 1775 (22:124).

Robinson, John. 47; husbandman; Hull, Yorkshire, to Halifax; on JENNY 3-10 April 1775 (22:124).

Robinson, John. Grantee 'Digby New Grant' 29 Jan. 1801 (5:83).

Robinson, Jonathan. 5; s. of William; Hull, Yorkshire, to Halifax; on JENNY 3-10 April 1775 (22:124).

Robinson, Peter. Plus 1 f./1 ch./2 svts.; merchant; Port Roseway Associate (6:17).

Robinson, Robert. Grantee 'Digby New Grant' 29 Jan. 1801 (5:83).

Robinson, William. Plus 1 f./2 svts.; Port Roseway Associate (6:17).

Robinson, William. 42; Hull, Yorkshire, to Halifax; on JENNY 3-10 April 1775 (22:124).

Robinson, William. 2; s. of William; Hull, Yorkshire, to Halifax; on JENNY 3-10 April 1775 (22:124).

Roche, Bridget. See Ronan, Bridget.

Roche, Edmond. S. of James/Bridget (Callihan) of Fermoy, Co. Cork, Ireland; marr. Halifax 18 Apr. 1830 Catherine Laby (q.v.) (32:118).

Roche, Elizabeth. Dau. of Thomas/Mary of Co. Wicklow, Ireland; marr. Halifax 11 Sep. 1832 Fenton Lynch (q.v.) (33:62).

Roche, Ellen. Dau. of David/Mary (Sullivan) of Co. Kerry, Ireland; marr. Halifax 1 Oct. 1833 Thomas Minehan (q.v.) (33:63).

Roche, Joanna. Dau. of James/Frances (Hayes) of Ross, Co. Wexford, Ireland; marr. Halifax 12 June 1835 James Towhill (q.v.) (34:139).

Roche, John. S. of Richard/Catherine (Walsh) of Co. Kilkenny, Ireland; marr. Halifax 14 Nov. 1840 (sic for 1830?) Mary Vigours (q.v.) (32:118).

Roche, Thomas. S. of Mathew/Catherine (Shea) of Youghal, Co. Cork, Ireland; marr. Halifax 30 July 1829 Ann Walsh (q.v.) (32:118).

Roche, Thomas. Widower of Ann Nason; of Cloyne, Co. Cork, Ireland; marr. Halifax 2 Sep. 1833 Ellen Oakly (q.v.) (33:66).

Rodden, Charles. S. of Charles/Rose (Coneglan) of Co. Donegal, Ireland; marr. Halifax 6 Oct. 1832 Rose Brown (q.v.) (33:66).

Rodgers, William. From Mass.; land grant at Truro 1759 (4:242).

Rodney, Anne. Dau. of Bartholomew/Grace (Marah) of Derry, Ireland; marr. Halifax 11 July 1820 Michael Kelly (q.v.) (31:48).

Roe, Zebulon. Capt.; Mass. to N.S.; to U.S. 1776; lived 1785 at Eddington, Me. (36:64).

Rogers, Catherine. Dau. of Terence of Parish Inniskillen, Co. Fermanagh, Ireland; marr. clandestine Inniskillen, Ireland, 1821, marr. Halifax 2 Aug. 1824 John Hanlon (q.v.) (31:47).

Rogers, George. R.I. to N.S.; to U.S. 1776; dead by 1785 (36:65).

Rogers, Jeremiah. Plus wife/7 ch.; Hanover, Mass., to Chester with first settlers (16:45).

Rogers, John. From Ireland; land grant at Londonderry 6 Mar. 1775 (4:258).

Rogers, Judith. Dau. of Terrence/Bridget (Corlisk) of Co. Longford, Ireland; marr. Halifax 6 Jan. 1834 Thomas Gunning (q.v.) (33:59).

Rogers, Mary. Dau. of Martin/Ellen (Archer) of Co. Kilkenny, Ireland; marr. Halifax 4 Nov. 1830 Michael Higgins (q.v.) (32:112).

Rogers, Michael. Disbanded soldier, N.J. Vols.; mustered at Digby 19

May 1784 (39:194).

Rogers, Samuel. Capt.; R.I. to N.S.;
to U.S. 1776; lived 1785 at Mass.
[which then included Me.] (36:65).

Rogers, Selome. To (or b.?) Liverpool
by 1791 (47:127:57).

Rogers, Thomas. Hanover, Mass., to
Chester with first settlers (16:
45).

Rohan, Ellen. See Fleming, Martin.

Rollam, Matthew. Loyalist; mustered
at Digby 19 May 1784 (39:194).

Rolligan, John. (Heirs) grantee
"Digby New Grant" 29 Jan. 1801 (5:
83).

Rollo, Robert. Grantee "Digby New
Grant" 29 Jan. 1801 (5:83).

Ronan, Bridget. Dau. of John/Joanna
(Ryan) of Co. Kilkenny, Ireland;
marr. Halifax 10 Nov. 1830 James
Bennett (q.v.) (32:105).

Ronan, Bridget. Widow of John Roche;
d. Michael/Mary (McCarthy) of Co.
Waterford, Ireland; marr. Halifax
5 Mar. 1831 John Maguire (q.v.)
(33:62).

Ronan, David. S. of John/Honora (Lee)
of Cappoquin, Co. Waterford, Ireland; marr. Halifax 13 June 1828
Alice Creedon (q.v.) (32:118).

Ronan, John. Of Youghal, Co. Cork,
Ireland; marr. Halifax 8 June 1842
Margaret Marks (q.v.) (35:144).

Ronan, Margaret. Dau. of Edmund/
Margaret (Carroll) of Co. Limerick, Ireland; marr. Halifax 8 Jan.
1843 Edmund Calaghan (q.v.) (35:
135).

Ronan, Michael. Of Ireland; marr.
Halifax 30 Sep. 1819 Elenor Dinan
(q.v.) (31:52).

Ronan, Patrick. S. of Patrick/Cather-
ine (Mahony) of Youghal, Co. Cork,
Ireland; marr. Halifax 30 Nov.
1822 Sarah Martin widow of Samuel

Gaine (31:52).

Ronan, Patrick. S. of William/Mary
(Drohan) of Co. Waterford, Ire-
land; marr. Halifax 6 July 1835
Mary Skerry (q.v.) (34:137).

Ronan, Thomas. S. of Edmund/Elizabeth
(Power) of Co. Tipperary, Ireland;
marr. Halifax 15 Oct. 1812 Mary
Elizabeth Baker (30:110).

Ronayne, Patrick. Of Youghal, Co.
Cork, Ireland; widower of Sarah
Martin; marr. Halifax 15 Sep. 1842
Christina Sutherland (35:144).

Ronayne, Patrick. S. of Michael/Mary
(McCarthy) of Co. Waterford,
Ireland; marr. Halifax 10 Feb.
1831 Mary Quinn (q.v.) (33:66).

Roney, Hugh. Deserted from H.M.S.
MELAMPOS; 5'7", fair complexion,
short brown hair with grey locks,
26, b. Ireland; advertised The
Weekly Chronicle, 21 June 1806
(28:34).

Rooker, Jael. To (or b.?) Port Hebert
by 1791 (47:127:57).

Roome, John. Loyalist; plus 1 f./6
svts.; mustered at Digby 19 May
1784 (39:194).

Rooney, Anne. Dau. of Lawrence/Maga-
ret (Rooney) of Perce, Lower
Canada; marr. Halifax 27 May 1827
John St. Lawrence Barry (q.v.)
(32:105).

Rooney, Michael. Laborer; Irish; 21;
Liverpool to Nova Scotia May 1864
on EUROCLYDON (45:182).

Roop, Christopher. Loyalist; mustered
at Digby 19 May 1784 (39:194).

Roop, Isaac. Loyalist; plus 1 f./1
svt.; mustered at Digby 19 May
1784 (39:194).

Roop, Jacob. Loyalist; mustered at
Digby 19 May 1784 (39:194).

Roop, John. Loyalist; plus 1 f./1
ch.; mustered at Digby 19 May 1784

(39:194).

Roope, John. Grantee 'Digby New Grant' 29 Jan. 1801 (5:83).

Roost, Eva. See Eva Bollinger (44: 193).

Roost, Hans . Beringen, Canton Schaffhausen, [Switzerland,] to Halifax 1742 (44:193).

Roost, Hans Conrad. Plus wife/ch/; Beringen, Canton Schaffhausen, [Switzerland,] to Halifax 1742 (44:193).

Ropp, George H. German Service; mustered at Bear River 11/25 June 1784 (38:260).

Rose, James. Plus 1 f./4 ch.; farmer; Port Roseway Associate (6:17).

Rose, James. Plus 1 f./1 ch./1 svt.; perriwig maker; Port Roseway Associate (6:17).

Rose, John. Loyalist; mustered at Digby 19 May 1784 (39:194).

Rose, William. Plus 1 f./1 ch./1 svt.; Port Roseway Associate (6: 17).

Rosencrantz, J. German Service; mustered at Bear River 11/25 June 1784 (38:260).

Ross, Alexander. Loyalist; plus 1 f.; mustered at Digby 19 May 1784 (39: 194).

Ross, Anne. Dau. of George/Jean (Beamish) of Co. Cork, Ireland; marr. Halifax 13 Oct. 1831 Thomas Gallivan (q.v.) (33:58).

Ross, Barbara. Dau. of Thomas/Barbara; to (or b.?) Liverpool by 1784 (47:126:289).

Ross, Isabella. Grantee 'Digby New Grant' 29 Jan. 1801 (5:83).

Ross, Jane. Dau. of Alexander/Jane; to (or b.?) Liverpool by 1795 (47:127:268).

Ross, John. Loyalist; plus 1 f.; mustered at Digby 19 May 1784

(39:194).

Ross, Mary. See Leahy, Mary.

Rourk, David. S. of James/Mary (Kelly) of Co. Tipperary, Ireland; marr. Halifax 21 Nov. 1808 Elener Delaney (q.v.) (30:110).

Rourk, John. S. of Owen/Catherine (Arkins) of Parish Castlepollard, Co. Westmeath, Ireland; marr. Halifax 22 Aug. 1836 Catherine Brennan (q.v.) (34:137).

Rourk, Mary. Of City of Waterford, Ireland; marr. Halifax 15 July 1802 James Neal (q.v.) (30:108).

Rourke, Mary. Dau. of Peter/Mary (Power) of Parish St. Mary's, Wexford, Ireland; marr. Halifax 9 Feb. 1828 Joseph Kinselie (q.v.) (32:114).

Routh, John. 22; husbandman; Hull, Yorkshire, to Nova Scotia; on TWO FRIENDS 28 Feb.-7 Mar. 1774 (25: 29).

Routlidge, Diana. 2; dau.of William; Hull, Yorkshire, to Nova Scotia; on TWO FRIENDS 28 Feb.-7 Mar. 1774 (25:30).

Routlidge, Joseph. 18 mos.; s. of William; Hull, Yorkshire, to Nova Scotia; on TWO FRIENDS 28 Feb.-7 Mar. 1774 (25:30).

Routlidge, Sarah. 27; wife of William; Hull, Yorkshire, to Nova Scotia; on TWO FRIENDS 28 Feb.-7 Mar. 1774 (25:30).

Routlidge, William. 30; blacksmith; Hull, Yorkshire, to Nova Scotia; on TWO FRIENDS 28 Feb.-7 Mar. 1774 (25:30).

Row, John Peter. Grantee 'Digby New Grant' 29 Jan. 1801 (5:83).

Rowlands, Esther. Wife of David, M.D.; daughter of Thomas Hassall Esq. of Kilrue, County Pembroke, Wales; died 28 Feb. 1817 at Halifax ae 40 (13:71).

Rowly, William. Pvt., Royal Staff
Corps; s. of John/Margaret (Walsh)
of Dublin, Ireland; marr. Halifax
22 Aug. 1831 Ellen Fahey (q.v.)
(33:66).

Rude, Jabez. From Mass.; land grant
(to heirs) at Onslow 21 Feb. 1769
(4:225).

Ruggles, Jos. Arr. Annapolis from New
York 19 Oct. 1782 (37:126).

Ruggles, Joseph. Loyalist; mustered
at Digby 19 May 1784 (39:194).

Ruhn, John. Or Kuhn; Waldeck Service;
mustered at Bear River 11/25 June
1784 (38:260).

Runyan, Peter. Loyalist; mustered at
Digby 19 May 1784 (39:194).

Rush, Martin. Loyalist; mustered at
Digby 19 May 1784 (39:194).

Russel, Alexr. Plus 1 f.; arr. Annapolis from New York 19 Oct. 1782
(37:125).

Russel, Edmund. Tailor; Port Roseway
Associate (6:17).

Russell, Bridget. Dau. of Philip/
Margaret (Gorman) of Templetrim,
Co. Tipperary, Ireland; marr.
Halifax 25 Aug. 1823 John O'Brien
(q.v.) (31:41).

Russell, Catherine. Dau. of Thomas/
Mary (Walker) of Co. Cork, Ire-
land; marr. Halifax 25 Oct. 1834
John Spencer (q.v.) (34:138).

Russell, John. S. of Thomas/Mary
(Fannon) of Roscrea, Co. Tipperary, Ireland; marr. Halifax 29
July 1821 Mary Burke (q.v.) (31:
52).

Russell, Michael. S. of Philip/Eliza-
beth (Sullivan) of Co. Kilkenny,
Ireland; marr. Halifax 17 Apr.
1811 Catherine Gannon (q.v.)
(30:110).

Rutherford, Henry. Grantee "Digby New

Grant" 29 Jan. 1801 (5:83).

Rutherford, Henry. Loyalist; plus 1
f./2 ch./4 svts.; mustered at
Digby 19 May 1784 (39:194).

Ryan, Alice. Dau. of Richard/Margaret
(Nolan) of Co. Waterford, Ireland;
marr. Halifax 30 May 1836 Mathias
Mooney (q.v.) (34:135).

Ryan, Alice. See Mihan, Alice.

Ryan, Bridget. Dau. of late John/
Margaret of Co. Tipperary, Ire-
land; marr. Halifax 19 July 1817
Richard Bulger (q.v.) (30:103).

Ryan, Bridget. Dau. of John/Mary
(Dwyer) of Nfld.; marr. Halifax 4
July 1818 John Barron (q.v.) (31:
40).

Ryan, Bridget. Dau. of John/Anastasia
of Co. Kilkenny, Ireland; marr.
Halifax 23 Oct. 1831 Lawrence
Connelly (q.v.) (33:55).

Ryan, Bridget. Dau. of Daniel/Cather-
ine (Devereaus) of Co. Waterford,
Ireland; marr. Halifax 10 Sep.
1834 Thomas Killeen (q.v.) (34:
133).

Ryan, Catherine. Dau. of Richard/Mary
of Nfld.; marr. Halifax 19 Oct.
1814 John Sutton (q.v.) (30:111).

Ryan, Catherine. Dau. of Michael/
Eleanor (Butler) of Co. Tipperary,
Ireland; marr. Halifax 29 Jan.
1834 Sylvester Lydiard (q.v.) (33:
62).

Ryan, Catherine. Dau. of James/Brid-
get (O'Donnell) of Co. Tipperary,
Ireland; marr. Halifax 1 Aug. 1842
Jeremiah Sullivan (q.v.) (35:145).

Ryan, Catherine. See Power, Catherine.

Ryan, Cornelius. Plus 1 f./4 svts.;
Port Roseway Associate (6:17).

Ryan, Daniel. 96th Regt.; s. of
David/Sarah (Shaunessy) of Limerick City, Ireland; marr. Halifax

28 Nov. 1828 Honora Gorman (q.v.)
(32:118).

Ryan, Denis. S. of Michael/Bridget of
Thurles, Co. Tipperary, Ireland;
marr. Halifax 16 Feb. 1824 Bridget
Maxey (q.v.) (31:53).

Ryan, Denis. Widower of Catherine
Ryan; of Co. Tipperary, Ireland;
marr. Halifax 19 Feb. 1833 Mary
Divine (q.v.) (33:66).

Ryan, Edward. S. of Martin/Margaret
(Carroll) of Callan, Co. Kilkenny,
Ireland; marr. Halifax 27 Apr.
1840 Mary O'Mara (q.v.) (34:138).

Ryan, Eleanor. See Butler, Eleanor.

Ryan, Eleanora. Dau. of James/Johanna
(Quinn) of Ardmore, Co. Waterford,
Ireland; marr. Halifax 13 Apr.
1820 John Ivory (q.v.) (31:48).

Ryan, Ellen. Dau. of John/Mary of
Clonmel, Co. Tipperary, Ireland;
marr. Halifax 24 Aug. 1809 Ogle
Moore (q.v.) (30:108).

Ryan, Ellen. Dau. of Thomas/Honora
(Looby) of Co. Tipperary, Ireland;
marr. Halifax 2 June 1836 Thomas
Broderick (q.v.) (34:126).

Ryan, Ellen. Dau. of Edward/Margarey
(Hogan) of Callan, Co. Kilkenny,
Ireland; marr. Halifax 26 June
1842 Michael Fitzgerald (q.v.)
(35:137).

Ryan, Grace. Dau. of Robert/Mary
(Sullivan) of Co. Tipperary,
Ireland; marr. Halifax 4 July 1813
John O'Brien (q.v.) (30:109).

Ryan, Hannah. Dau. of Thomas/Mary
(Lyons) of Co. Kilkenny, Ireland;
marr. Halifax 18 Feb. 1833 John
Murphy (q.v.) (33:64).

Ryan, James. S. of Patrick/Margaret
(Wade) of Rush, Co. Dublin, Ire-
land; marr. Halifax 17 May 1803
Anne Poor (q.v.) (30:110).

Ryan, James. S. of John/Ellen (Tow-

hill) of Co. Tipperary, Ireland;
marr. Halifax 4 May 1841 Ellen
Magrath (q.v.) (35:144).

Ryan, Jeremiah. S. of Daniel/Cather-
ine (Linergan) of Ballylooby, Co.
Tipperary, Ireland; marr. Halifax
3 Aug. 1836 Margaret Anderson
(q.v.) (34:137).

Ryan, Joanna. Dau. of Luke/Johanna
(Morrissey) of Carrick, Co. Waterford, Ireland; marr. Halifax 30
Apr. 1826 Daniel Fudge (q.v.) (32:
111).

Ryan, Joanna. Dau. of Thomas/Mary of
Co. Carlow, Ireland; marr. Halifax
9 Jan. 1833 Patrick Deveraux
(q.v.) (33:56).

Ryan, Johanna. Dau. of William/Marga-
ret (Ryan) of Dreen, Co. Tipperary, Ireland; marr. Halifax 7 Feb.
1822 John Londrigan (q.v.) (31:
49).

Ryan, John. S. of Edward/Mary (Martin) of Nfld.; marr. Halifax 20
Dec. 1820 Anne McDonald (q.v.)
(31:53).

Ryan, John. S. of John/Joanna (Hacket) of Co. Tipperary, Ireland;
marr. Halifax 7 Apr. 1834 Catherine McCarthy (q.v.) (33:66).

Ryan, John. S. of Lawrence/Bridget
(Gowan) of Parish Burrydown, Co.
Carlow, Ireland; marr. Halifax 28
Aug. 1821 Elenor O'Brien (q.v.)
(31:53).

Ryan, John. S. of Michael/Margaret
(Eagan) of Parish Ballmikiln, Co.
Kildare, Ireland; marr. Halifax 29
May 1825 Margaret Kinsela (q.v.)
(31:53).

Ryan, John. S. of Thomas/Joanna of
Co. Kilkenny, Ireland; marr. Halifax 19 Sep. 1829 Anastasia Elwart
(q.v.) (32:118).

Ryan, John. Sgt.Maj. 23rd Regt.; of

Ireland; marr. Halifax 19 Jan. 1839 Alice Mihan (34:138).

Ryan, John. Widower of Ann Elwart; of Co. Kilkenny, Ireland; marr. Halifax 4 July 1840 Mary Ann Martin (34:138).

Ryan, Julian. Dau. of William/Julian (Dunn) of Co. Kildare, Ireland; marr. Halifax 1 Nov. 1842 Denis Dunn (q.v.) (35:137).

Ryan, Margaret. Dau. of late Rodger/Mary (Holorahan) of Ireland; marr. Halifax 5 Oct. 1816 Redmond McCarthy (q.v.) (30:107).

Ryan, Mary. Dau. of John/Mary of Waterford, Ireland; marr. Halifax 10 June 1806 Capt. Thomas Pemberton (q.v.) (30:109).

Ryan, Mary. Dau. of Jeremiah/Bridget (Green) of Parish Borris, Co. Carlow, Ireland; marr. Halifax 14 June 1825 Michael Fleming (q.v.) (31:45).

Ryan, Mary. Dau. of Michael/Mary (Hinchin) of Cork, Ireland; marr. Halifax 4 Feb. 1821 James Francis (q.v.) (31:46).

Ryan, Mary. Of Co. Kilkenny, Ireland; widow of John Doyle; marr. Halifax 28 July 1840 Patrick Butler (q.v.) (34:126).

Ryan, Mary. See Laffin, Mary.

Ryan, Mary. See Murry, Mary.

Ryan, Michael. S. of Thomas/Catherine (Keating) of Co. Waterford, Ireland; marr. Halifax 17 Jan. 1843 Catherine Grady (q.v.) (35:144).

Ryan, Moses. Tailor; of Co. Wexford, Ireland; widower of Margaret Hobin; marr. Halifax 27 Aug. 1835 Margaret Sullivan (q.v.) (34:138).

Ryan, Patrick. S. of Edward/Honora of Co. Limerick, Ireland; marr. Halifax 3 Feb. 1810 Mary Doyle (q.v.) (30:110).

Ryan, Patrick. S. of James/Joanna (Hayes) of Co. Waterford, Ireland; marr. Halifax 26 Oct. 1837 Jane Donnelly (q.v.) (34:137).

Ryan, Philip. S. of Thomas/Johanna (Ryan) of Co. Kilkenny, Ireland; marr. Halifax 11 May 1818 Catherine Poore (q.v.) (31:53).

Ryan, Pierce. S. of Michael/Mary (Farrell) of Parish Grange, Co. Kilkenny, Ireland; marr. Halifax 9 Feb. 1823 Mary Cullen (q.v.) (31:53).

Ryan, Pierce. Widower; s. of Michael/Mary (Farrell) of Creagh, Co. Kilkenny, Ireland; marr. Halifax 1 Dec. 1826 Mary Boggy (q.v.) (32:118).

Ryan, Richard. S. of Lawrence/Margaret (Allen) of Co. Tipperary, Ireland; marr. Halifax 16 Dec. 1819 Elizabeth Kennan (31:53).

Ryan, Thomas. S. of Richard/Catherine (Kikan) of Co. Kilkenny, Ireland; marr. Halifax 23 Feb. 1830 Elizabeth Eeds (32:118).

Ryan, William. S. of James/Sarah (O'Daniel) of Co. Tipperary, Ireland; marr. Halifax 7 Sep. 1822 Elizabeth Higgins (31:53).

Ryan, William. S. of Martin/Margaret (Carroll) of Callan, Co. Kilkenny, Ireland; widower of Catherine Magher; marr. Halifax 5 May 1842 Joanna O'Hara (q.v.) (35:144).

Ryder, John. Liverpool proprietor (19:102).

Ryerson, John. Loyalist; mustered at Digby 19 May 1784 (39:194).

- S -

Sackett, ------. Widow; Loyalist; mustered at Digby 19 May 1784 (39:195).

Safford, William. S. of William/
Thankful; Salem, Mass., to Liverpool by 1822 (47:128:113).

Sander, William. Loyalist; plus 1
f./4 ch.; mustered at Digby 19 May
1784 (39:195).

Sander, William. See Sanders, William.

Sanders, Joseph. Loyalist; mustered
at Digby 19 May 1784 (39:195).

Sanders, Samuel. Sailor on PEGGY; not
settled; mustered at Digby 19 May
1784 (39:195).

Sanders, William. Loyalist; plus 1
f./4 ch.; mustered at Digby 19 May
1784 (39:195).

Sanders, William. Plus 1 f./3 ch. 8+;
arr. Annapolis from New York 19
Oct. 1782 (37:126).

Sandford, Elijah. Loyalist; plus 1
f.; mustered at Digby 19 May 1784
(39:195).

Sarsfield, Bridget. Dau. of Patrick/
Ellen (Beresford) of Co. Waterford, Ireland; marr. Halifax 2
Apr. 1839 Edward Walsh (q.v.)
(34:139).

Sarsfield, Patrick. S. of Patrick/
Ellen (Beresford) of Co. Waterford, Ireland; marr. Halifax 10
Nov. 1838 Margaret Goffe (q.v.)
(34:138).

Saul, Andrew. Of Co. Tipperary, widower of Catherine Phelan, marr.
Halifax 8 May 1843 Joanna Kenedy
(q.v.) (35.144).

Saunders, John. Grantee "Digby New
Grant" 29 Jan. 1801 (5:83).

Saunders, Mary. Dau. of James/Joanna
(Evoy) of Nfld.; marr. Halifax 15
July 1836 James Karney (q.v.) (34:
132).

Savage, Anthony. 9, s. of John; Hull
to Fort Cumberland on ALBION 7-14
Mar. 1774 (21:137).

Savage, Edward. From Mass.; land
grant at Truro 1759 (4:242).

Savage, Elizabeth. 55, wife of John;
Hull to Fort Cumberland on ALBION
7-14 Mar. 1774 (21:137). 55 or
35?

Savage, John Jr. From Mass.; land
grant at Truro 1759 (4:242).

Savage, John. 40, labourer; Hull to
Fort Cumberland on ALBION 7-14
Mar. 1774 (21:137).

Savage, John. From Mass.; land grant
at Truro 1759 (4:242).

Savage, John. From N.H.; effective
land grant at Truro 31 Oct. 1765
(4:245).

Savage, Thomas. S. of Timothy/Joanna
(Ryan) of Co. Cork, Ireland; marr.
Halifax 11 June 1836 Mary Walsh
(q.v.) (34:138).

Saxton, George. Grantee "Digby New
Grant" 29 Jan. 1801 (5:83).

Saxton, John. Grantee "Digby New
Grant" 29 Jan. 1801 (5:83).

Saxton, John. Loyalist; mustered at
Gulliver's Hole/St. Mary's
Bay/Sissiboo 1/6 June 1784; set-
tled at St. Mary's Bay (Plympton,
Barton, Brighton) (40:263).

Saxton, Mary. Dau. of Patrick/Johanna
(Ryan) of Nfld.; marr. Halifax 8
Jan. 1820 James Sullivan (q.v.)
(31:54).

Saxton, Timothy. Loyalist; mustered
at Gulliver's Hole/St. Mary's
Bay/Sissiboo 1/6 June 1784; settled at St. Mary's Bay (Plympton,
Barton, Brighton) (40:263).

Saxton, William. Loyalist; plus 1
f./3 ch.; mustered at Gulliver's
Hole/St. Mary's Bay/Sissiboo 1/6
June 1784; settled at St. Mary's
Bay (Plympton, Barton, Brighton)
(40:263).

Scallion, Andrew. S. of Joseph/Margaret (Doyle) of Co. Wexford, Ireland; marr. Halifax 1 Feb. 1821 Elizabeth Edwards (31:53).

Scallion, Michael. S. of John/Joanna (Carbery) of Parish St. Margaret, Co. Wexford, Ireland; marr. Halifax 24 Oct. 1838 Mary Hynes (q.v.) (34:138).

Scanlan, James. S. of William/Marjorie (Molony) of Co. Waterford, Ireland; marr. Halifax 12 Sep. 1816 Mary O'Leary widow of Owen Lannan (30:110).

Scanlan, Stephen. S. of James/Elenor (Keily) of Ross, Co. Wexford, Ireland; marr. Halifax 20 June 1824 Julia Anne Fitzmaurice (q.v.) (31:53).

Scanlon, Honora. Dau. of Edmund/ Catherine (Breen) of Cashel, Co. Tipperary, Ireland; marr. Halifax 14 Sep. 1832 John Clifford (q.v.) (33:55).

Scanlon, John. S. of Hugh/Mary (McCaury) of Co. Fermanagh, Ireland; marr. Halifax 24 Sep. 1806 Catherine Burns (q.v.) (30:110).

Scanlon, Owen. S. of Lawrence/Honor (Kavanah) of Sligo Town, Ireland; marr. Halifax 29 Sep. 1802 Anne O'Brien (q.v.) (30:110).

Scannel, Ellen. Dau. of John/Joanna (O'Connor) of Co. Kerry, Ireland; marr. Halifax 12 Nov. 1833 Patrick O'Connor (q.v.) (33:65).

Schaafer, Caspar. German Service; mustered at Bear River 11/25 June 1784 (38:260).

Schade, I. C. (Or J. C.) German Service; plus 1 f.; mustered at Bear River 11/25 June 1784 (38:260).

Schechan, Frank. Liverpool to Nova Scotia April 1864 on KEDAR (45:182).

Schlauderbeek, M. Waldeck Service; plus 1 f.; mustered at Bear River 11/25 June 1784 (38:261).

Schlaugbaum, Francis. German Service; mustered at Bear River 11/25 June 1784 (38:260).

Schmeisser, Johan Gotllob. B. Mar. 1751 at Weissenfels; minister at Lunenburg 1 May 1782; d. 23 Dec. 1806 (2:297).

Schmidt, J. C. Chaplain; German Service; mustered at Bear River 11/25 June 1784 (38:261).

Schooley, Andrew. Sgt., 1st N.J. Vols.; mustered at Digby 19 May 1784 (39:195).

Schroeder, Thomas. Waldeck Service; mustered at Bear River 11/25 June 1784 (38:260).

Schultze, Gottlieb. German Service; mustered at Bear River 11/25 June 1784 (38:260).

Scidleir, -----. Surgeon; German Service; mustered at Bear River 11/25 June 1784 (38:260).

Scott, Abijah. From Mass.; land grant at Onslow 21 Feb. 1769 (4:224).

Scott, Asa. From Mass.; land grant at Onslow 21 Feb. 1769 (4:225).

Scott, Catharine. 1, daughter of Henry; Hull to Fort Cumberland on ALBION 7-14 Mar. 1774 (21:138).

Scott, Catherine. Of Co. Wexford, Ireland; widow of John Egan; marr. Halifax 3 Feb. 1845 Michael Lahy (q.v.) (35:140).

Scott, Elizabeth. Dau. of Francis/ Winifred (Burke) of Co. Leitrim, Ireland; marr. Halifax 22 Oct. 1831 John Perry (q.v.) (33:65).

Scott, Ephraim. From Mass.; land grant at Onslow 21 Feb. 1769 (4:224).

Scott, George. From N.H.; effective land grant at Truro 31 Oct. 1765

(4:245).

Scott, George. Plus 1 f./1 ch./1 svt.; Port Roseway Associate (6: 17).

Scott, Henry. 27, husbandman; Hull to Fort Cumberland on ALBION 7-14 Mar. 1774 (21:138).

Scott, Henry. 3, s. of Henry; Hull to Fort Cumberland on ALBION 7-14 Mar. 1774 (21:138).

Scott, Joseph. From Mass.; land grant at Onslow 21 Feb. 1769 (4:224).

Scott, Joseph. Lieut.; from Ware River, Mass.; land grant at Onslow 24 July 1759 (4:222).

Scott, Mary Anne. Dau. of George/Mary (MacNamara) of Scotland; marr. Halifax 2 Nov. 1820 James Lawler (q.v.) (31:49).

Scott, Mary. 29, wife of Henry; Hull to Fort Cumberland on ALBION 7-14 Mar. 1774 (21:138).

Scott, Mary. Dau. of Benjamin/Joanna (Mackey) of Co. Tipperary, Ireland; marr. Halifax 15 Apr. 1833 Edward Haney (q.v.) (33:59).

Scott, Mary. See McNamara, Mary.

Scully, Bridget. Dau. of James/ Catherine of Parish Rathcline, Co. Longford, Ireland; marr. Halifax 18 Sep. 1826 Francis Fox (q.v.) (32:111).

Scully, William. S. of John/Ellen (O'Brien) of Co. Tipperary, Ireland; marr. Halifax 13 Nov. 1841 Ellen Dillon (q.v.) (35:144).

Scurr, Alice. 1, daughter of Thomas; Hull to Fort Cumberland on ALBION 7-14 Mar. 1774 (21:134).

Scurr, Charles. 5, s. of Thomas; Hull to Fort Cumberland on ALBION 7-14 Mar. 1774 (21:134).

Scurr, Elizabeth. 39, wife of Thomas; Hull to Fort Cumberland on ALBION 7-14 Mar. 1774 (21:134).

Scurr, Elizabeth. 3, daughter of Thomas; Hull to Fort Cumberland on ALBION 7-14 Mar. 1774 (21:134).

Scurr, Thomas. 34, farmer; Hull to Fort Cumberland on ALBION 7-14 Mar. 1774 (21:134).

Scurr, Thomas. 9, s. of Thomas; Hull to Fort Cumberland on ALBION 7-14 Mar. 1774 (21:134).

Scurr, William. 7, s. of Thomas; Hull to Fort Cumberland on ALBION 7-14 Mar. 1774 (21:134).

Seabury, David. Grantee "Digby New Grant" 29 Jan. 1801 (5:83).

Seahans, Jeremiah. Grantee "Digby New Grant" 29 Jan. 1801 (5:83).

Sears, Alden. Liverpool proprietor (19:102).

Sears, Nathan. Liverpool proprietor (19:102).

Seccombe, John. Rev.; b. Medford, Mass., 25 Apr. 1708; Harvard, Mass., to Chester 1759 (16:44).

Sedel, Bridget. 38; to join husband; Hull, Yorkshire, to Fort Cumberland on JENNY 3-10 April 1775 (22: 123).

Sedel, Francis. 6; ch. of Bridget; Hull, Yorkshire, to Fort Cumberland on JENNY 3-10 April 1775 (22: 123).

Sedel, Mary. 7; dau.of Bridget; Hull, Yorkshire, to Fort Cumberland on JENNY 3-10 April 1775 (22:123).

Sedel, Sarah. 1; dau.of Bridget; Hull, Yorkshire, to Fort Cumberland on JENNY 3-10 April 1775 (22: 123).

Sedgewick, John. 39; farmer; Hull, Yorkshire, to Nova Scotia; on TWO FRIENDS 28 Feb.-7 Mar. 1774 (25: 29).

Seely, Caleb. S. of Ebeneser/Hipsibeth; St. John, N. B., to Liverpool by 1815 (47:128:37).

Semple, Robert. S. of Robert/Mary of Newry, Co. Dublin, Ireland; marr. Halifax 16 Oct. 1842 Mary Spruhan (35:144).

Senuke, E. Waldeck Service; plus 1 f./1 ch.; mustered at Bear River 11/25 June 1784 (38:261).

Sexton, Bridget. Dau. of Mathew/Ellen (McCarthy) of Co. Cork, Ireland; marr. Halifax 1 Oct. 1833 Michael Byrnes (q.v.) (33:55).

Shackford, Josiah. 47, master mariner; Poole to Nova Scotia on SQUIRREL Nov. 1775 (24:45).

Shadden, C. Laborer; English; 21; Liverpool to Nova Scotia May 1864 on EUROCLYDON (45:182).

Shaddock, Ezechiel. S. of Ezechiel/Prudence (Blood) of Boston, Mass.; marr. Halifax 24 Oct. 1830 Catherine Deer (q.v.) (32:118).

Shaddon, Robert. Laborer; English; 26; Liverpool to Nova Scotia May 1864 on EUROCLYDON (45:182).

Shaffner, Ferdinand. Grantee "Digby New Grant" 29 Jan. 1801 (5:83).

Shakespeare, Stephen. Plus 1 f./12 svts.; Port Roseway Associate (6:17).

Shanahan, Simon. S. of Patrick/Winefred (McNamara) of Co. Clare, Ireland; marr. Halifax 27 Feb. 1843 Ellen Sullivan (q.v.) (35:144).

Shanihan, Michael. S. of Martin/Elizabeth (Connelly) of Co. Tipperary, Ireland; widower of Margaret Byrnes; marr. Halifax 8 Sep. 1834 Catherine Murphy. (q.v.) A kinswoman buried in a Catholic cemetery at Hammonds Plains, Halifax Co., N.S. is described as from Driaigloun, Co. Tipperary, Ireland. (33:66).

Shanihan, William. S. of Martin/Elizabeth (Connelly) of Co. Tipperary, Ireland; marr. Halifax 18 July 1833 Mary McCarthy (q.v.). See Michael Shanihan. (33:66).

Sharp, Alexr. Plus 1 f.; arr. Annapolis from New York 19 Oct. 1782 (37:125).

Sharp, Joseph. Pa. to N.S.; to U.S. 1776; lived 1785 at Pa. (36:65).

Sharp, Mary. Dau. of Nicholas/Margaret (O'Connor) of Co. Kerry, Ireland; marr. Halifax 3 Sep. 1835 Hugh O'Connor (q.v.) (34:136).

Sharp, Matthew. Pa. to N.S.; to U.S. 1776; dead by 1785 (36:65).

Sharp, Robert. Pa. to N.S.; to U.S. 1776; lived 1785 at N.S. (36:65).

Sharp, Samuel. Pa. to N.S.; to U.S. 1776; dead by 1785 (36:65).

Sharpe, Joseph. Plus 1 svt.; Port Roseway Associate (6:17).

Sharpe, Samuel. Plus 1 f./4 ch./2 svts.; Port Roseway Associate (6:17).

Shaw, Mary. Dau. of Richard/Mary (Lewis) of Co. Waterford, Ireland; marr. Halifax 5 Oct. 1844 Timothy Martin (q.v.) (35:141).

Shaw, Samuel. From Mass.; land grant at Truro 1759 (4:242).

Shaw, Thomas. Plus 1 f.; Port Roseway Associate (6:17).

Shea, Bridget. Dau. of Patrick/Mary (Vollans) of Parish Kilfinnan, Co. Limerick, Ireland; widow of Jeremiah Shehan; marr. Halifax 28 Sep. 1828 John Linehan (q.v.) (32:114).

Shea, Bridget. Dau. of John/Ellen (Mullony) of Co. Tipperary, Ireland; marr. Halifax 16 June 1842 John Hynes (q.v.) (35:139).

Shea, Catherine. Dau. of David/Mary (Macrate) of Co. Tipperary, Ireland; marr. Halifax 12 Jan. 1840 James Sullivan (q.v.) (34:138).

Shea, Charles William. S. of -----/
Eliza; London, England, to Liverpool by 1813 (47:127:269).

Shea, Elizabeth. Dau. of Richard/
Ellen of Co. Kilkenny, Ireland;
marr. Halifax 4 May 1840 Thomas
Flinn (q.v.) (34:130).

Shea, Jane. Dau. of Philip/Elizabeth
(Blood) of Co. Cork, Ireland;
marr. Halifax 9 July 1808 John
Riely (q.v.) (30:110).

Shea, M. Plus 1 f./1 ch. 8+/2 ch. -8;
arr. Annapolis from New York 19
Oct. 1782 (37:125).

Shea, Mary. Dau. of Cornelius/Marga-
ret (Reacy) of Co. Cork, Ireland;
marr. Halifax 23 Aug. 1821 John
Fitzgerald (q.v.) (31:45).

Shea, Mary. Dau. of Timothy/Eleanor
(Melon) of Co. Cork, Ireland;
marr. Halifax 26 June 1834 William
Wallace (q.v.) (33:68).

Shea, Michael, born Sudeor, Co. Limerick, Ireland; marr. Halifax 20
July 1824 Elizabeth Harrington
(q.v.) (31:53).

Shea, Michael. S. of William/Margaret
(Neiffe) of Co. Kilkenny, Ireland;
marr. Halifax 27 Aug. 1843 Mary
Landrigan (q.v.) (35:144).

Shea, Murtaugh. S. of Denis/Joanna
(Sullivan) of Parish Bunaw, Co.
Kerry, Ireland; marr. Halifax 17
Sep. 1843 Mary Ann English (35:
144).

Shea, Patrick. S. of Denis/Mary
(Flaherty) of Parish Bunaw, Co.
Kerry, Ireland; marr. Halifax 24
May 1845 Elizabeth Smith (q.v.)
(35:144).

Shea, Richard. S. of John/Margaret
(Reily) of John/Mary (Flaw) of Co.
Kilkenny; marr. Halifax 21 Feb.
1803 Elinor Newnan (q.v.)
(30:110).

Shea, Timothy. S. of Timothy/Eleanor
(Whelan) of Co. Cork, Ireland;
marr. Halifax 6 June 1835 Elenor
Kenedy (q.v.) (34:138).

Shea, William. Loyalist; plus 1 f./3
ch.; mustered at Digby 19 May 1784
(39:195).

Shea, William. S. of Richard/Bridget
(Heffernan) of Mullinahone, Tipperary, Ireland; marr. Halifax 31
Oct. 1833 Joanna Walsh (q.v.) (33:
66).

Shea, William. S. of Richard/Bridget
(Heffernan) of Mullinahone, Co.
Tipperary, Ireland; widower of
Joanna Walsh; marr. Halifax 18
Jan. 1843 Bridget Walsh (q.v.)
(35:144).

Sheehan, Anne. Dau. of Rody/Elizabeth
(Heffernan) of Parish St. Mary,
Tipperary, Ireland; marr. Halifax
19 Sep. 1823 James Dunphy (q.v.)
(31:45).

Sheehan, Bridget. Dau. of Patrick/
Mary (Ryan) of Co. Kilkenny, Ire-
land; marr. Halifax 22 May 1832
John Finn (q.v.) (33:57).

Sheehan, Ellen. Dau. of William/
Honora (Power) of Co. Waterford,
Ireland; widow of Michael Dunn;
marr. Halifax 13 Oct. 1838 James
Mulcahy (q.v.) (34:135).

Sheehan, Maurice. S. of James/Bridget
(Grace) of Co. Kilkenny, Ireland;
marr. Halifax 25 July 1842 Ann
Petrie (35:144).

Sheehan, Michael. S. of Thomas/
Eleanor (Ryan) of Parish Caher,
Waterford Diocese, Ireland; marr.
Halifax 9 June 1826 Anne Heslop
(32:118).

Sheehan, William. S. of Michael/Mary
(Bourke) of Cove of Cork, Ireland;
marr. Halifax 5 Sep. 1827 Anne
Janes (q.v.) (32:118).

Shehan, Bridget. See Shea, Bridget.

Shehan, Edward. S. of John/Mary
(Dunn) of Co. Waterford, Ireland;
marr. Halifax 3 Nov. 1828 Catherine Kerwan (q.v.) (32:118).

Shelly, Joanna. Dau. John/Margaret
(Grady) of Co. Tipperary, Ireland;
marr. Halifax 16 Feb. 1830 Nicholas Walsh (q.v.) (32:120).

Shepherd, John. Maj., Stoughton,
Mass., to Chester with first
settlers (16:45).

Shepherd, Stephen. To (or b.?) Liverpool by 1791 (47:127:57).

Sherlock, Andrew. See Charlocke,
Andrew.

Sherman, Robert. Loyalist; mustered
at Digby 19 May 1784 (39:195).

Shiels, Margaret. Dau. of Michael/
Anastasia (Grace) of Kilkenny,
Ireland; marr. Halifax 5 Feb. 1844
Thomas Dillon (q.v.) (35:136).

Shine, Martin. S. of Maurice/Bridget
(Kennedy) of Co. Waterford, Ire-
land; marr. Halifax 12 July 1828
Margaret Connors (q.v.) (32:118).

Shipley, Elizabeth. Wife of Thomas;
Hull to Fort Cumberland on ALBION
7-14 Mar. 1774 (21:137).

Shipley, Philip. Loyalist; plus 1
f./5 ch.; mustered at Digby 19 May
1784 (39:195).

Shipley, Philip. S. of Robert/Anasta-
sia (Collins) of Co. Wexford, Ireland; marr. Halifax 29 Nov. 1836
Dorothy Parker (q.v.) (34:138).

Shipley, Sarah. 3, daughter of Thomas; Hull to Fort Cumberland on
ALBION 7-14 Mar. 1774 (21:137).

Shipley, Thomas. 1, s. of Thomas;
Hull to Fort Cumberland on ALBION
7-14 Mar. 1774 (21:137).

Shipley, Thomas. 31, butcher; Hull to
Fort Cumberland on ALBION 7-14
Mar. 1774 (21:137).

Shook, David. Grantee "Digby New
Grant" 29 Jan. 1801 (5:83).

Shook, David. Loyalist; plus 1 f./2
ch.; mustered at Digby 19 May 1784
(39:195).

Short, Maria Emily. Dau. of William/
Maria (Emerson) of Lowell, Mass.,
marr. Halifax 9 Oct. 1832 James
Walsh (q.v.) (33:68).

Shortal, Michael. S. of James/Elenor
(Crooks) of Co. Leix, Ireland;
marr. Halifax 9 May 1831 Mary
Raftis (q.v.) (33:67).

Shortel, Margaret. Dau. of James/
Eleanor (Crooks) of Queen's Co.,
Ireland; marr. Halifax 14 Nov.
1828 Michael Daley (q.v.) (32:
108).

Shortell, Mary. Of Co. Tipperary,
Ireland; widow of Thomas Croak;
marr. Halifax 21 Nov. 1837 James
Dwyer (q.v.) (34:129).

Shortell, Mary. See Raftis, Mary.

Shortle, Ann. Dau. of James/Ellen
(Crooks) of Queen's Co.,Ireland;
marr. Halifax 17 Oct. 1829 William
Lawler (q.v.) (32:114).

Shortt, Joanna. Dau. of John/Eleanor
(Thompson) of Co. Armagh, Ireland;
marr. Halifax 29 Feb. 1840 Solomon
Brennan (q.v.) (34:126).

Shurtleff, Faith. Dau. of James/
Faith; Plymouth, Mass., to Liverpool by 1761 (47:127:50).

Sibley, David. Grantee "Digby New
Grant" 29 Jan. 1801 (5:83).

Sidell, Ralph. 29, cartwright; Hull
to Fort Cumberland on ALBION 7-14
Mar. 1774 (21:139).

Sinn, David. Plus 1 f./2 ch.; Port
Roseway Associate (6:17).

Simmons, Ebenezer. Liverpool proprietor (19:102).

Simmons, Eleazer. B. Marshfield,
Mass., 15 Mar. 1739; to Liverpool

by 1767 (47:126:169).

Simmons, Eleazer. B. Marshfield,
Mass., 15 Mar. 1739; to Liverpool
betw. 2 April 1767-25 Mar. 1768
(50:111).

Simmons, Judah Mayo. S. of Eleazer/
Priscilla; to (or b.?) Liverpool
by 1792 (47:127:117).

Simmons, Lucy. Dau. of Eleazer/Pris-
cilla; to (or b.?) Liverpool by
1801 (47:127:272).

Simmons, Mary. Dau. of Thomas/Mary
(Kennedy) of Co. Kilkenny, Ire-
land; marr. Halifax 18 July 1830
Denis Tehan (q.v.) (32:119).

Simmons, Priscilla Mayo. Wife of
Eleazer; b. Chatham, Mass., 29
April 1748 (50:111).

Simmons, Priscilla. B. Chatham,
Mass., 29 Apr. 1748; dau. of -----
Mayo; to Liverpool by 1767 (47:
126:169).

Simonds, Joseph. Grantee "Digby New
Grant" 29 Jan. 1801 (5:83).

Simpson, Agnes. Grantee "Digby New
Grant" 29 Jan. 1801 (5:83).

Simpson, Charles. 22, husbandman;
Hull to Fort Cumberland on ALBION
7-14 Mar. 1774 (21:134).

Simpson, Mary. 25, servant; Hull to
Fort Cumberland on ALBION 7-14
Mar. 1774 (21:136).

Simpson, William. Loyalist; mustered
at Digby 19 May 1784 (39:195).

Sinclair, Arthur. Grantee "Digby New
Grant" 29 Jan. 1801 (5:83).

Sinclair, John. Plus 1 f./1 ch.; Port
Roseway Associate (6:17).

Sinclair, Mary. Dau. of George/Marga-
ret (Smyth) of Co. Kilkenny,
Ireland; marr. Halifax 1 Jan. 1839
John Condon (34:127).

Sinclair, Mary. Dau. of George/Marga-
ret (Smythe) of Co. Kilkenny, Ireland; widow of John Condon; marr.

Halifax 24 Oct. 1842 Maurice Bride
(q.v.) (35:135).

Sinton, William. 21, miller; Hull to
Fort Cumberland on ALBION 7-14
Mar. 1774 (21:139).

Sisk, Patrick. S. of Richard/Margaret
(Barret) of Cork Ireland; marr.
Halifax 21 Feb. 1805 Catherine
Hare (30:110).

Sizeland, Solomon. Loyalist; plus 1
f.; mustered at Digby 19 May 1784
(39:195).

Skehen, William. S. of Michael/Marga-
ret (Power) of Co. Tipperary, Ireland; marr. Halifax 1 May 1842
Mary Francis (35:144).

Skelton, Ann. 18, servant; Hull to
Fort Cumberland on ALBION 7-14
Mar. 1774 (21:134).

Skelton, Jane. 36; Hull, Yorkshire,
to Annapolis on JENNY 3-10 April
1775 (22:124).

Skelton, John. 38; servant; Hull,
Yorkshire, to Annapolis on JENNY
3-10 April 1775 (22:124).

Skerry, Eleanor. Dau. of Kearn/Mary
(Walsh) of Ballyhail, Co. Kilkenny, Ireland; marr. Halifax 26 May
1827 Edward Fitzmaurice (32:110).

Skerry, John. Ferryman; s. of Luke/
Mary (Larissy) of Knocktopher,
Kilkenny, Ireland; widower of
Bridget Shea; marr. Halifax 28 May
1807 Maria Meagher (30:111).

Skerry, Mary. Dau. of John/Catherine
(Walsh) of Knocktopher, Co. Kil-
kenny, Ireland; widow of Morris
Kean; marr. Halifax 6 July 1835
Patrick Ronan (q.v.) (34:137).

Skerry, William. S. of Keyrin/Mary
(Walsh) of Ballyhail, Co. Kilkenny, Ireland; marr. Halifax 13 Feb.
1825 Anastasia Larrisey (q.v.)
(31:53).

Skihan, Mary. Dau. of James/Anastasia

(MacDowney) of Co. Tipperary, Ireland; marr. Halifax 9 Apr. 1839
William Magher (q.v.) (34:134).

Skinner, Benjamin. Loyalist; mustered
at Digby 19 May 1784 (39:195).

Skinner, John. Surgeon, Hessian Ser.;
mustered at Digby 19 May 1784 (39:
195).

Skriever, George. Loyalist; mustered
at Digby 19 May 1784 (39:195).

Slattery, Catherine. See O'Rourke,
James.

Slee, John. 22, husbandman; Hull to
Fort Cumberland on ALBION 7-14
Mar. 1774 (21:136).

Slocomb, Robert. Liverpool proprietor
(19:101).

Slocombe, Abigail. Wife or widow of
James; dau. of Nathaniel Freeman;
to (or b.?) Liverpool by 1810 (47:
127:49).

Slocombe, Elizabeth. Dau. of Robert/
Faith; to (or b.?) Liverpool by
1791 (47:127:118).

Slocombe, Hannah. Dau. of Robert/
Faith; to (or b.?) Liverpool by
1787 (47:127:268).

Slocombe, James. S. of Robert/Faith;
to (or b.?) Liverpool by 1797 (47:
127:211).

Slocombe, John. Grantee "Digby New
Grant" 29 Jan. 1801 (5:83).

Slocombe, Polly. Dau. of Robert/
Faith; to (or b.?) Liverpool by
1796 (47:127:211).

Slocombe, Robert. S. of Thomas/Jane;
Taunton, England, to Liverpool by
1761 (47:127:50).

Slocombe, Robert. S. of Robert/Faith;
to (or b.?) Liverpool by 1796 (47:
127:209).

Small, Christian. Disbanded soldier
Hessian Yagers; plus 1 f./1 ch.;
mustered at Digby 19 May 1784 (39:
195).

Smart, John. Plus 1 f./6 ch./5 svts.;
Port Roseway Associate (6:17).

Snellon, Mary. Widow of Richard
Durny; of Co. Wicklow, Ireland;
thrice widowed; marr. Halifax 17
Feb. 1828 Patrick O'Sullivan
(q.v.) (32:117).

Smith, Abner. Loyalist; mustered at
Digby 19 May 1784 (39:195).

Smith, Alexander. Loyalist; plus 1
f./1 ch.; mustered at Digby 19 May
1784 (39:195).

Smith, Archelaus. S. of Stephen; b.
Chatham, Mass., 23 April 1737; to
Barrington 1760 (50:112).

Smith, Austin. Plus 1 f./5 ch. 8+;
arr. Annapolis from New York 19
Oct. 1782 (37:125).

Smith, Barzillai. S. of Solomon; b.
Chatham, Mass. (50:114).

Smith, Benjamin. Plus 1 ch.; farmer;
Port Roseway Associate (6:17).

Smith, Benjamin. S. of John; b. Chatham, Mass., 23 Nov. 1749; to
Barrington 1761 (50:112).

Smith, Betty. Dau. of Stephen/Meheta-
bel; to (or b.?) Liverpool by 1780
(47:127:52).

Smith, Brien. S. of Peter/Mary
(Clarke) of Co. Meath, Ireland; b.
31 Oct. 1811; marr. Halifax 6 July
1833 Elizabeth Doran (q.v.) (33:
67).

Smith, Catherine. Dau. of Thomas/Rose
(MacGahan) of Co. Cavan, Ireland;
marr. Halifax 8 Aug. 1832 John
Warren (q.v.) (33:68).

Smith, Daniel. Legion soldier; to
Liverpool by 1784 (47:127:51).

Smith, David. Rev.; from Ireland;
land grant at Londonderry 6 Mar.
1775 (4:258).

Smith, David. Rev.; born 1732; bur.
Folly Village, Londonderry (4:
262).

Smith, David. S. of David/Catherine;
Va. to Liverpool by 1791 (47:128:
28).

Smith, David. S. of David; b. Chat-
ham, Mass., ca. 1720; grantee at
Barrington 1759-1769; there bef. 7
April 1768 (50:112).

Smith, David. S. of David; b. Chatham, Mass., 30 July 1742 (50:112).

Smith, Desire. Dau. of Solomon; b.
Chatham, Mass. (50:114).

Smith, Dorcas. Dau. of Jonathan/
Elizabeth; to (or b.?) Liverpool
by 1790 (47:127:122).

Smith, Edward. S. of Roger/Catherine
(Mason) of Co. Down, Ireland;
marr. Halifax 19 Feb. 1833 Mary
McLaughlin (q.v.) (33:67).

Smith, Edward. Surgeon; Ireland to
Liverpool by 1787 (47:127:55).

Smith, Elisha. Barrington petitioner
19 Oct. 1776 (1:365).

Smith, Elisha. S. of Solomon; b.
Chatham, Mass., 1749 (50:113).

Smith, Elizabeth Kendrick. Wife of
Elkanah (50:113).

Smith, Elizabeth Nickerson. Wife of
Archelaus; b. Chatham, Mass., ca.
1740 (50:112).

Smith, Elizabeth. 52, wife of Nathaniel; Hull to Fort Cumberland on
ALBION 7-14 Mar. 1774 (21:134).

Smith, Elizabeth. 7, daughter of
Nathaniel; Hull to Fort Cumberland
on ALBION 7-14 Mar. 1774 (21:134).

Smith, Elizabeth. Dau. of Christo-
pher/Mary (Howard) of Co. Kerry,
Ireland; marr. Halifax 24 May 1845
Patrick Shea (q.v.) (35:144).

Smith, Elkanah. Barrington petitioner
19 Oct. 1776 (1:365).

Smith, Elkanah. S. of David; b. Chatham, Mass., ca. 1734; grantee at
Barrington 1759-1769 (50:113).

Smith, Ephraim. Plus 1 f./1 ch./2

svts.; Port Roseway Associate (6:
17).

Smith, Eunice. Dau. of Archelaus; b.
Chatham, Mass. (50:112).

Smith, George. 2; s. of John; Hull,
Yorkshire, to Nova Scotia; on TWO
FRIENDS 28 Feb.-7 Mar. 1774 (25:
28).

Smith, George. Carpenter; Port Roseway Associate (6:17).

Smith, Grace. Dau. of Solomon; b.
Chatham, Mass. (50:114).

Smith, Hannah Shurtleff Bunker. Wife
of Thomas; b. Plymouth, Mass., 11
Jan. 1739/40 (50:114).

Smith, Hannah. Dau. Stephen/Meheta-
bel; to Liverpool by 1769 (47:126:
167).

Smith, Hezekiah. S. of Archelaus; b.
Chatham, Mass., ca. 1755 (50:112).

Smith, Jacob. Grantee "Digby New
Grant" 29 Jan. 1801 (5:83).

Smith, Jacob. Loyalist; plus 1 f./1
ch.; mustered at Digby 19 May 1784
(39:195).

Smith, James. Arr. Annapolis from New
York 19 Oct. 1782 (37:126).

Smith, James. Loyalist; mustered at
Digby 19 May 1784 (39:195).

Smith, Jasper. Grantee "Digby New
Grant" 29 Jan. 1801 (5:83).

Smith, Jasper. Loyalist; mustered at
Digby 19 May 1784 (39:195).

Smith, John Christian. Grantee "Digby
New Grant" 29 Jan. 1801 (5:83).

Smith, John. 18, s. of Nathaniel;
Hull to Fort Cumberland on ALBION
7-14 Mar. 1774 (21:134).

Smith, John. 28, husbandman; Hull to
Fort Cumberland on ALBION 7-14
Mar. 1774 (21:138).

Smith, John. 29; farmer; Hull, Yorkshire, to Nova Scotia; on TWO
FRIENDS 28 Feb.-7 Mar. 1774 (25:
28).

Smith, John. 4; s. of John; Hull, Yorkshire, to Nova Scotia; on TWO FRIENDS 28 Feb.-7 Mar. 1774 (25: 28).

Smith, John. Loyalist; mustered at Digby 19 May 1784 (39:195).

Smith, John. Loyalist; mustered at Digby 19 May 1784 (39:195).

Smith, John. S. of Terrence/Bridget (Corrigan) of Parish Dromore, Co. Tyrone, Ireland; marr. Halifax 30 Jan. 1830 Anne Burdette (q.v.) (32:118).

Smith, John. See Stricht, John.

Smith, Jonathan Aldredge. S. of Stephen; b. Chatham, Mass., 27 Aug. 1747 (50:114).

Smith, Jonathan Jr. Barrington petitioner 19 Oct. 1776 (1:365).

Smith, Jonathan. Barrington petitioner 19 Oct. 1776 (1:365).

Smith, Jonathan. S. of Stephen/Mehetebel; to Liverpool by 1771 (47: 126:289).

Smith, Jonathan. S. of David; b. Chatham, Mass., 9 Nov. 1752; grantee at Barrington; there bef. 24 Sep. 1764 (50:113).

Smith, Jonathan. S. of Solomon; b. Chatham, Mass., 1747 (50:113).

Smith, Joseph. Barrington petitioner 19 Oct. 1776 (1:365).

Smith, Joseph. Loyalist; plus 1 f./3 ch.; mustered at Digby 19 May 1784 (39:195).

Smith, Joshua. Grantee "Digby New Grant" 29 Jan. 1801 (5:83).

Smith, Joshua. Loyalist; plus 1 f.; mustered at Digby 19 May 1784 (39:195).

Smith, Josiah. S. of Stephen Jr./Hannah; to (or b.?) Liverpool by 1797 (47:127:209).

Smith, Lodowick. S. of Stephen/Mehetebel; to (or b.?) Liverpool by

Smith, Lodowick. S. of Stephen; b. Chatham, Mass., 22 Aug. 1756 (50: 114).

Smith, Mahetable. Wife of Stephen; dau. of ----- Eldridge; b. Chatham, Mass.; d. 4 Sep. 1815 ae 86 (49:137).

Smith, Marcy. Dau. of Archelaus; b. Chatham, Mass. (50:112).

Smith, Martin. S. of William/Catherine (Redmond) of Co. Wexford, Ireland; marr. Halifax 23 Oct. 1831 Mary Brophy (q.v.) (33:67).

Smith, Mary. 25; wife of John; Hull, Yorkshire, to Nova Scotia; on TWO FRIENDS 28 Feb.-7 Mar. 1774 (25: 28).

Smith, Mary. 26, servant; Hull to Fort Cumberland on ALBION 7-14 Mar. 1774 (21:138).

Smith, Mary. Dau. of Michael/Ellen (Kelly) of Co. Kilkenny, Ireland; marr. Halifax 16 Feb. 1832 Peter Kelly (q.v.) (33:61).

Smith, Mary. Dau. of David; b. Chatham, Mass., 13 May 1747; marr. at Barrington 8 Nov. 1764 (50: 112).

Smith, Mary. Dau. of Solomon; b. Chatham, Mass. (50:114).

Smith, Mehetable. Dau. of Stephen/Mehetabel; to Liverpool by 1778 (47:126:289).

Smith, Mehitable Eldredge. Wife of Stephen; b. ca. 1729 (50:114).

Smith, Mehiteble. Wife of Stephen; to Liverpool ca. 1760 (47:126:101).

Smith, Michael. S. of Patrick/Ann (Moran) of Co. Kildare, Ireland; marr. Halifax 14 May 1843 Honora McCarthy (q.v.) (35:144).

Smith, Nathaniel. 22, s. of Nathaniel; Hull to Fort Cumberland on ALBION 7-14 Mar. 1774 (21:134).

Smith, Nathaniel. 52, farmer; Hull to

Port Cumberland on ALBION 7-14
Mar. 1774 (21:134).

Smith, Nathaniel. S. of Stephen/
Mehitable; to (or b.?) Liverpool
by 1792 (47:127:207).

Smith, Peter. Disbanded soldier, 3rd
N.J. Vols.; plus 1 f./1 ch.;
mustered at Digby 19 May 1784
(39:195).

Smith, Rachael. 22; Hull to Port Cumberland on ALBION 7-14 Mar. 1774
(21:134).

Smith, Rebecca Hamilton. Wife of Solomon; b. Chatham, Mass., 21 Nov.
1721 (50:113).

Smith, Rebecca. Dau. of William; to
(or b.?) Liverpool by 1792 (47:
127:122).

Smith, Reuben. S. of John; b. Chatham, Mass., ca. 1740; early resident Barrington (1759-1769) (50:
113).

Smith, Robert. 9, s. of Nathaniel;
Hull to Port Cumberland on ALBION
7-14 Mar. 1774 (21:134).

Smith, Samuel. Loyalist; mustered at
Digby 19 May 1784 (39:195).

Smith, Sarah. Black; to (or b.?)
Guysborough by 1791 (47:127:57).

Smith, Sarah. Dau. of Stephen/Meheta-
bel; to Liverpool by 1778 (47:126:
288).

Smith, Shubael. Loyalist; mustered at
Digby 19 May 1784 (39:195).

Smith, Solomon Jr. Barrington petitioner 19 Oct. 1776 (1:365).

Smith, Solomon. Barrington petitioner
19 Oct. 1776 (1:365).

Smith, Solomon. S. of David; b. Chatham, Mass., ca. 1720; at Barrington by 1 July 1762 (50: 113).

Smith, Solomon. S. of Solomon; b.
Chatham, Mass. (50:114).

Smith, Stephen Jr. S. of Stephen/
Mehetabel; to Liverpool by 1772

(47:126:287).

Smith, Stephen Jr. S. of Stephen;
bap. Chatham, Mass., 18 Dec. 1726;
at Liverpool by 1 July 1761
(50:114).

Smith, Stephen. Liverpool proprietor
(19:101).

Smith, Stephen. S. of Stephen; b.
Chatham, Mass.; d. Liverpool 24
June 1827 ae 79 (49:137).

Smith, Stephen. S. of Stephen; b.
Chatham, Mass.; d. 9 Sep. 1807 ae.
81st; Liverpool proprietor (49:
138).

Smith, Stephen. S. of Stephen; b.
Chatham, Mass., 23 May 1749
(50:114).

Smith, Stephen. To Liverpool ca. 1760
(47:126:101).

Smith, Susanna. Dau. of Stephen Jr./
Susanna; to (or b.?) Liverpool by
1799 (47:127:272).

Smith, Susanna. Dau. of Archelaus; b.
Chatham, Mass. (50:112).

Smith, Tabitha. Dau. of Stephen/ Mehetabel; to Liverpool by 1774 (47:
127:53).

Smith, Tabitha. Dau. of Stephen; b.
Chatham, Mass., 20 Mar. 1759 (50:
114).

Smith, Thankful Godfrey Reynolds.
Wife of David (50:112).

Smith, Theodore. Barrington petitioner 19 Oct. 1776 (1:365).

Smith, Theodore. S. of Solomon; b.
Chatham, Mass., 18 Aug. 1751 (50:
114).

Smith, Thomas. Cooper; widower of
Joanna Dobbin; of Co. Tipperary,
Ireland; marr. Halifax 2 May 1830
Mary Jones (q.v.) (32:118).

Smith, Thomas. New England to Annapolis 1760 (18:271).

Smith, Thomas. S. of William/Margaret
(Mara) of Co. Tipperary, Ireland;

arr. Halifax 14 June 1820 Johannah Dobbin (q.v.) (31:53).

Smith, Thomas. S. of John; b. Chatham, Mass., 26 June 1744; grantee
Barrington; marr. there bef. 1770
(50:114).

Smith, Warren. S. of David; b. Chatham, Mass. (50:112).

Smith, Whitford. Plus 2 svts.; Port
Roseway Associate (6:17).

Smith, William. 1; s. of John; Hull,
Yorkshire, to Nova Scotia; on TWO
FRIENDS 28 Feb.-7 Mar. 1774 (25:
28).

Smither, James. Plus 1 f./9 ch./2
svts.; engraver; Port Roseway
Associate (6:17).

Smyth, Bridget. Dau. of Nicholas/
Bridget (Moore) of Co. Kilkenny,
Ireland; marr. Halifax 31 July
1832 Michael Lynch (q.v.) (33:62).

Smyth, Ellen. Dau. of Nicholas/
Bridget (Moore) of Co. Kilkenny,
Ireland; marr. Halifax 25 Sep.
1832 William Waters (q.v.)
(33:68).

Smyth, George. S. of William/Ellen
(Trainer) of New Brunswick; marr.
Halifax 27 Nov. 1841 Mary Donohoe
(q.v.) (35:144).

Smyth, John. S. of Pierce/Elizabeth
(Sweetman?) of Co. Kilkenny, Ire-
land; marr. Halifax 20 Apr. 1830
Catherine Whelan (q.v.) (32:118).

Smyth, John. S. of John/Margaret
(Spillane) of Co. Cork, Ireland;
marr. Halifax 16 Sep. 1841 Joanna
Barry (q.v.) (35:144).

Smyth, Mary. Dau. of John/Bridget
(Doyle) of St. Johns, Nfld.; marr.
Halifax 17 Nov. 1806 Michael De-
loghrey (q.v.) (30:104).

Smyth, Sarah. See Black, Sarah.

Sneedon, Stephen. Grantee "Digby New
Grant" 29 Jan. 1801 (5:83).

Snelling, Henry. Loyalist; mustered
at Digby 19 May 1784 (39:195).

Snodgrass, Andrew. Grantee "Digby New
Grant" 29 Jan. 1801 (5:83).

Snodgrass, Eunice. Grantee "Digby New
Grant" 29 Jan. 1801 (5:83).

Snoograp, Andrew. Loyalist; mustered
at Digby 19 May 1784 (39:195).

Snow, Benjamin. Loyalist; from New
Hampshire; to Annapolis Royal by
1781 (41:14).

Snow, Charlotte. Wife of Prince
William; dau. of Thomas/Hannah
Hart; Cape Breton to Liverpool ca.
1813 (47:128:33).

Snow, Jane. Dau. of Capt. Prince/
Sarah; to (or b.?) Liverpool by
1782 (47:126:282).

Snow, Prince. B. Chatham, Mass., 31
Aug. 1762; s. of Prince; to Liverpool 1762-1763 (47:126:97).

Snow, Prince. Chatham, Mass., to
Liverpool ca. 1762-1763 (47:
126:97).

Snow, Prince. Liverpool proprietor
(19:101).

Snow, Prince. S. of Prince/Sarah; to
(or b.?) Liverpool by 1788 (47:
127:56).

Snow, Prince. S. of Prince; b. Chatham, Mass., 19 Nov. 1738; at
Liverpool bef. July 1760 (50:115).

Snow, Prince. S. of Prince; b. Chatham, Mass., 31 Aug. 1760 (50:115).

Snow, Sarah Atwood. Wife of Prince
(50:115).

Snow, Sarah. Dau. of Prince/Sarah; to
(or b.?) Liverpool by 1794 (47:
127:208).

Snow, Sarah. Wife of Prince; Chatham,
Mass., to Liverpool ca. 1762-1763
(47:126:97).

Snowden, Jane. Widow; dau. Richard/
Jane (Donald) Bell of Durham, England; marr. Halifax 9 Sep. 1813

John McCormic (q.v.) (30:107).

Snowden, Pickering. 22; weaver; Hull, Yorkshire, to Nova Scotia; on TWO FRIENDS 28 Feb.-7 Mar. 1774 (25: 30).

Somner, Thomas. Plus 1 f./ 8 ch.; farmer; Port Roseway Associate (6:17).

Southerland, William. From Ireland; land grant at Londonderry 6 Mar. 1775 (4:258).

Sowles, David. Loyalist; mustered at Digby 19 May 1784 (39:195).

Spalding, Joseph. From Mass.; land grant at Truro 1759 (4:242).

Sparling, Peter. Plus 1 f./6 ch.; Port Roseway Associate (6:17).

Specht, Anthony. Grantee 'Digby New Grant' 29 Jan. 1801 (5:83).

Speed, Paul. Plus 1 f./3 ch./2 svts.; farmer; Port Roseway Associate (6: 17).

Spelman, James. S. of Denis/Mary (O'Neill) of Co. Limerick, Ireland; marr. Halifax 24 Oct. 1842 Margaret Tobin (35:144).

Spence, Eleanor. Dau. of Thomas/Mary (Whelan) of Torbay, Nfld.; marr. Halifax 10 Oct. 1829 James Macarthy (q.v.) (32:114).

Spence, Marianne. Dau. of John/Mary (Cuddy) of Co. Waterford, Ireland; marr. Halifax 10 Apr. 1834 Samuel Charles Adams (q.v.) (33:54).

Spence, Thomas. S. of John/Mary (Cuddy) of Co. Waterford, Ireland; marr. Halifax 4 June 1833 Catherine Kenedy (q.v.) (33:67).

Spencer, James. Laborer; English; 25; Liverpool to Nova Scotia June 1864 on INDIAN QUEEN (45:182).

Spencer, John. Plus 1 f./2 ch.; farmer; Port Roseway Associate (6:17).

Spencer, John. S. of William/Jane (McAvoy) of Co. Tipperary, Ire-

land; marr. Halifax 25 Oct. 1834 Catherine Russell (q.v.) (34:138).

Spencer, Robert. From Ireland; land grant at Londonderry 6 Mar. 1775 (4:258).

Spencer, William. S. of Maurice/ Catherine of Parish Iverk, Co. Kilkenny, Ireland; marr. Halifax 7 Oct. 1824 Bridget Hall widow of Richard Heaney (q.v.) (31:53).

Spring, Catherine. Dau. of Arthur/ Catherine (Lawler) of Co. Kerry, Ireland; marr. Halifax 24 July 1830 Cornelius Falvey (q.v.) (32:109).

Sprinks, James. Plus 1 f./3 ch./1 svt.; Port Roseway Associate (6: 17).

Spruhan, Ann. Dau. of Thomas/Mary (Whelan) of Co. Kilkenny, Ireland; marr. Halifax 24 Apr. 1836 William Tracy (q.v.) (34:139).

Spruhan, Edward. S. of Thomas/Mary (Cody) of Thomastown, Co. Kilkenny, Ireland; marr. Halifax 22 Jan. 1829 Margaret Dunn (q.v.) (32: 118).

Spruhan, Walter. S. of Thomas/Mary (Whelan) of Co. Kilkenny, Ireland; marr. Halifax 21 Feb. 1830 Briget McLean (q.v.) (32:118).

Spulit, Anthony. Hessian officer; plus 1 f./1 ch.; mustered at Digby 19 May 1784 (39:195).

Spurr, Michael. Plus wife/3 sons/3 daus.; New England to Annapolis on CHARMING MOLLY May 1760 (18:271).

Stacey, Mathew. Plus 1 f./1 ch./1 svt.; Port Roseway Associate (6: 17).

Stack, James. S. of Michael/Margaret (Daily) of Tralee, Co. Kerry, Ireland; marr. Halifax 2 June 1813 Ellen Keefe (q.v.) (30:111).

Stackhouse, John. Port Roseway Associate (6:17).

Stafford, John. Pvt., 64th Regt.; s.
of Thomas/Ann (Lynsky) of Co. Roscommon, Ireland; marr. Halifax 4
Apr. 1842 Joanna Landy (q.v.)
(35:145).

Stafford, John. S. of Patrick/Marga-
ret (Evoy) of Duncormuck, Co. Wexford, Ireland; marr. Halifax 14
June 1825 Anne Doherty (31:53).

Stafford, Thomas. S. of John/Julian
(Manning) of Co. Cork, Ireland;
marr. Halifax 30 July 1833 Mary
Ward (q.v.) (33:67).

Stanton, James. Loyalist; plus 1 f.;
mustered at Digby 19 May 1784
(39:195).

Stanton, John. Plus 5 svts.; Port
Roseway Associate (6:17).

Stapleton, Joanna. Dau. of John/
Margaret (Foil) of Co. Leix, Ire-
land; marr. Halifax 8 June 1834
George T. Jones (q.v.) (33:60).

Stapleton, Margaret. Of Co. Tipper-
ary, Ireland; widow of William
Magrath; marr. Halifax 2 Dec. 1837
Thomas Stapleton (34:138).

Stapleton, Michael. S. of Thomas/
Bridget (Ryan) of Co. Tipperary,
Ireland; marr. Halifax 9 Aug. 1811
Anne MacWere (30:111).

Starkin. See Harkin.

Starr, John. Capt.; Conn. to N.S.; to
U.S. 1776; lived 1785 at Groton,
Conn. (36:65).

Starr, William. S. of Edward/Mary
(Hogan) of Kilkeating, Co. Tipperary, Ireland; marr. Halifax 8 Aug.
1826 Mary Anne Young (32:118).

Stavely, Richard. 30; husbandman;
Hull, Yorkshire, to Nova Scotia;
on TWO FRIENDS 28 Feb.-7 Mar. 1774
(25:30).

Stavely, Robert. 26; husbandman;
Hull, Yorkshire, to Nova Scotia;

on TWO FRIENDS 28 Feb.-7 Mar. 1774
(25:30).

Stearns, Benjamin. Loyalist; plus 1
f./1 ch./2 svts.; mustered at Digby 19 May 1784 (39:195).

Steel, John. From Mass.; land grant
at Onslow 21 Feb. 1769 (4:224).

Steel, Mary. Dau. of John/Sarah
(McKinnon) of Cape Breton; marr.
Halifax 22 Feb. 1835 James Reid
(q.v.) (34:137).

Stennager, Henry. Grantee "Digby New
Grant" 29 Jan. 1801 (5:83).

Stennegar, Jane. Grantee "Digby New
Grant" 29 Jan. 1801 (5:82).

Stephans, Anne. Dau. of Thomas/Ele-
nora (Cody) of Ross, Co. Wexford,
Ireland; marr. Halifax 14 May 1820
Richard Haberlin (q.v.) (31:46).

Stephen, John. S. of William/Bridget
(Mantle) of Devonsh., England;
marr. Halifax 20 Nov. 1834 Ellen
Dulhanty (q.v.) (34:138).

Stephen, Phineas. Loyalist; mustered
at Gulliver's Hole/St. Mary's Bay/
Sissiboo 1/6 June 1784; settled at
St. Mary's Bay (Plympton, Barton,
Brighton) (40:263).

Stephens, Enos. Loyalist; mustered at
Gulliver's Hole/St. Mary's Bay/
Sissiboo 1/6 June 1784; settled at
St. Mary's Bay (Plympton, Barton,
Brighton) (40:263).

Stephens, Mary. To Liverpool by 1767
(47:126:162).

Stephens, Priscilla. To Liverpool by
1766 (47:126:162).

Sterriker, Hannah. 12; servant; Hull,
Yorkshire, to Nova Scotia; on TWO
FRIENDS 28 Feb.-7 Mar. 1774 (25:
30).

Stevens, Christopher. From Mass.;
land grant at Onslow 21 Feb. 1769
(4:225).

Stevens, Enos. Loyalist; from New

Hampshire; petitioner at Digby 20
Feb. 1784 (41:18).

Stevens, Enos. Plus 1 f./1 ch. 8+;
arr. Annapolis from New York 19
Oct. 1782 (37:126).

Stevens, Jacob Jr. From Mass.; land
grant at Onslow 21 Feb. 1769 (4:
225).

Stevens, Jacob. From Mass.; land
grant at Onslow 21 Feb. 1769 (4:
224).

Stevens, Phineas. Loyalist; from New
Hampshire; petitioner at Digby 20
Feb. 1784 (41:18).

Stevens, Thomas. From Mass.; land
grant at Onslow 21 Feb. 1769 (4:
224).

Stevenson, Robert. Scotland to Liverpool by 1774 (47:126:287).

Stewart, Charles. 1 1/4; s. of James;
Perthshire; Port Glasgow to Pictou
on COMMERCE 10 Aug. 1803 (51).

Stewart, Donald. 11; s. of James;
Perthshire; Port Glasgow to Pictou
on COMMERCE 10 Aug. 1803 (51).

Stewart, Howes. Liverpool proprietor
(19:101).

Stewart, Isabella. 9; dau. of James;
Perthshire; Port Glasgow to Pictou
on COMMERCE 10 Aug. 1803 (51).

Stewart, James. 37; farmer; Perthshire; Port Glasgow to Pictou on
COMMERCE 10 Aug. 1803 (51).

Stewart, James. Mate of PEGGY; plus 1
svt.; not settled; mustered at
Digby 19 May 1784 (39:195).

Stewart, Janet. 37; wife of James;
Perthshire; Port Glasgow to Pictou
on COMMERCE 10 Aug. 1803 (51).

Stewart, Janet. 7; dau. of James;
Perthshire; Port Glasgow to Pictou
on COMMERCE 10 Aug. 1803 (51).

Stewart, John. Loyalist; plus 1 f./2
ch.; mustered at Digby 19 May 1784
(39:195).

Stewart, John. S. of Alexander/Mary
(McCormack) of Co. Antrim, Ire-
land; marr. Halifax 22 June 1833
Anne Finn (33:67).

Stewart, Mary. Dau. of Alexander/Mary
(McCormic) of Co. Antrim, Ireland;
marr. Halifax 23 May 1824 Isaac
Pringle (q.v.) (31:52).

Stewart, Mary. Dau. of John/Ellen
(Koblin) of Cove, Co. Cork, Ire-
land; marr. Halifax 30 July 1833
John Mullaly (q.v.) (33:64).

Stewart, Nathaniel. Loyalist; plus 1
f.; mustered at Digby 19 May 1784
(39:195).

Stewart, Peter. Plus 1 f.; farmer;
Port Roseway Associate (6:17).

Stockdale, Joseph. 24, husbandman;
Hull to Fort Cumberland on ALBION
7-14 Mar. 1774 (21:137).

Stone, James. S. of Edward/Anne
(Cumer?) of Co. Roscommon, Ire-
land; marr. Halifax 27 Sep. 1813
Elizabeth Cruise (30:111).

Stone, Josiah. Plus 1 f.; arr. Annapolis from New York 19 Oct. 1782
(37:126).

Stone, Patrick. S. of Patrick/Mary
(Kelly) of Creevy, Parish Abbey,
Co. Longford, Ireland; marr. Halifax 17 June 1824 Susan Fleet (31:
53).

Stone, Thomas. S. of Richartd/Cather-
ine (Murphy) of Co. Kilkenny,
Ireland; marr. Halifax 8 Dec. 1833
Ann Beazley (33:67).

Storey, John. From Ireland; land
grant at Londonderry 6 Mar. 1775
(4:258).

Story, Sara. See Witham, Sara.

Straker, Isaac. From Mass.; land
grant at Truro 1759 (4:242).

Stratter, Isaac. See Straker, Isaac.

Stratton, Richard. From Mass.; land
grant at Truro 1759 (4:242).

Street, Ebenezer. Loyalist; plus 1
f./1 svt.; mustered at Digby 19
May 1784 (39:195).

Street, Samuel. Grantee "Digby New
Grant" 29 Jan. 1801 (5:83).

Street, Samuel. Loyalist; plus 1 f.;
mustered at Digby 19 May 1784 (39:
195).

Street, William. Loyalist; mustered
at Digby 19 May 1784 (39:195).

Streeton, Jeremiah. From Mass.; land
grant at Truro 1759 (4:242).

Strembock, Thomas. Farmer; Port Roseway Associate (6:17).

Stricht, John. Loyalist; plus 1 f.;
mustered at Digby 19 May 1784 (39:
195).

Strickland, Frances. Wife or widow;
to (or b.?) Liverpool by 1784 (47:
127:51).

Strickland, Frances. B. Prince Edward
Island 6 June 1792; dau. of John/
Bethiah; to Liverpool by 1800 (47:
127:206).

Strickland, John. B. Great Britain;
to Liverpool by 1774 (47:126:169).

Strickland, Peter. B. Prince Edward
Island 5 Apr. 1789; s. of John/
Bethiah; to Liverpool by 1800 (47:
127:206).

Stuart, Elenor. Dau. of Alexander/
Euphemia of Banff, Scotland; marr.
Halifax 19 Feb. 1810 James O'Neil
(q.v.) (30:109).

Stuart, James. Sir: s. of Rev.Dr.
John: born 2 Mar. 1780 Fort
Hunter, N.Y.; to N.S. before 1798
(7:93).

Stuart, John. Plus 1 f./4 ch./3
svts.; farmer; Port Roseway Associate (6:17).

Stuart, Martha. Wife or widow of
Hower; to Liverpool by 1775 (47:
126:282).

Stuart, Patiance. To Liverpool ca.

1760 (47:126:96).

Stump, John. Loyalist; plus 3 svts.;
mustered at Digby 19 May 1784 (39:
195).

Sudderick, Ichabod. From Mass.; land
grant at Truro 1759 (4:242).

Sudderick, Jesse. From Mass.; land
grant at Truro 1759 (4:242).

Suggett, Ann. 14; dau.of Mary; Hull,
Yorkshire, to Nova Scotia; on TWO
FRIENDS 28 Feb.-7 Mar. 1774 (25:
30).

Suggett, Christopher. 10; s. of Mary;
Hull, Yorkshire, to Nova Scotia;
on TWO FRIENDS 28 Feb.-7 Mar. 1774
(25:30).

Suggett, John. 8; s. of Mary; Hull,
Yorkshire, to Nova Scotia; on TWO
FRIENDS 28 Feb.-7 Mar. 1774 (25:
30).

Suggett, Mary. 12; dau.of Mary; Hull,
Yorkshire, to Nova Scotia; on TWO
FRIENDS 28 Feb.-7 Mar. 1774 (25:
30).

Suggett, Mary. 40; widow; Hull, Yorkshire, to Nova Scotia; on TWO
FRIENDS 28 Feb.-7 Mar. 1774 (25:
30).

Suggett, William. 18; husband [sic];
Hull, Yorkshire, to Nova Scotia;
on TWO FRIENDS 28 Feb.-7 Mar. 1774
(25:30).

Suh, Frederic. Waldeck Service; mustered at Bear River 11/25 June 1784
(38:260).

Sullivan, Ann. See Haiden, Ann.

Sullivan, Catherine. Dau. of Richard/
Joana (Collins) of Co. Cork, Ire-
land; marr. Halifax 13 August 1828
Patrick Kirwen (q.v.) (32:114).

Sullivan, Catherine. Dau. of Daniel/
Margaret (MacCarthy) of Tullogh,
Co. Cork, Ireland; marr. Halifax
24 Sep. 1829 Bartholomew Lahey
(q.v.) (32:114).

Sullivan, Catherine. Dau. of Jere-
miah/Bridget (Murphy) of Co.
Kerry, Ireland; marr. Halifax 9
Oct. 1842 Michael Doyle (q.v.)
(35:137).

Sullivan, Daniel. S. of Thomas/Mary
(Heffernan) of Parish Ballingrana,
Co. Limerick, Ireland; marr. Halifax 18 Apr. 1828 Mary Duffy (q.v.)
(32:119).

Sullivan, Denis. S, Denis/Eleanor of
Berehaven, Co. Cork, Ireland;
marr. Halifax 6 Jan. 1830 Bridget
Sullivan (32:119).

Sullivan, Edmund. Pvt. 60th Regt.; s.
of John/Mary of BallymacCulan,
Kerry, Ireland; marr. Halifax 28
July 1823 Mary Lyons (q.v.) (31:
54).

Sullivan, Eleanor. Dau. of Michael/
Honor (Coughlan) of Parish Buttevant, Cork, Ireland; marr. Halifax
30 May 1824 Samuel Lawrence (q.v.)
(31:49).

Sullivan, Elener. Dau. of James/
Honora (Duggan) of Berehaven, Co.
Cork, Ireland; marr. Halifax 23
June 1823 Michael Bow (q.v.) (31:
41).

Sullivan, Ellen. Dau. of Bartholomew/
Catherine (Donegan) of Co. Cork,
Ireland; marr. Halifax 26 Nov.
1829 Michael Kean (q.v.) (32:113).

Sullivan, Ellen. Dau. of Denis/Marga-
ret of Co. Cork, Ireland; marr.
Halifax 8 Feb. 1831 Edmund Conrick
(q.v.) (33:55).

Sullivan, Ellen. Dau. of Denis/Marga-
ret (Cronan) of Co. Limerick, Ireland; marr. Halifax 27 Feb. 1843
Simon Shanahan (q.v.) (35:144).

Sullivan, Eugene. S. of John/Honora
(Dunlavy) of Co. Kerry, Ireland;
marr. Halifax 14 July 1838 Catherine Harrington (q.v.) (34:138).

Sullivan, Hannah. Dau. of Thomas/Mary
(Riley) of Co. Wicklow, Ireland;
marr. Halifax 18 Nov. 1836 John
O'Flavin (q.v.) (34:136).

Sullivan, Honora. Dau. of William/
Norry (Hayes) of Co. Cork, Ire-
land; marr. Halifax 19 May 1831
Timothy Killeen (q.v.) (33:61).

Sullivan, James. Of Bantry, Co. Cork,
Ireland; marr. Halifax 16 Nov.
1819 Margaret Crofford (q.v.) (31:
54).

Sullivan, James. S. of Patrick/Anne
(Fitzgerald) of Co. Kerry, Ire-
land; marr. Halifax 8 Jan. 1820
Mary Saxton (q.v.) (31:54).

Sullivan, James. S. of Thomas/Mary
(Riley) of Co. Wicklow, Ireland;
marr. Halifax 12 Jan. 1840 Catherine Shea (q.v.) (34:138).

Sullivan, Jeremiah. S. of Cornelius/
Bridget (Falvey) of Co. Kerry,
Ireland; marr. Halifax 29 Sep.
1841 Mary Raftis (q.v.) (35:145).

Sullivan, Jeremiah. S. of Jeremiah/
Abigail (Linehan) of Co. Cork,
Ireland; marr. Halifax 1 Aug. 1842
Catherine Ryan (q.v.) (35:145).

Sullivan, Joanna. Dau. of John J./
Joanna (Connelly); of Co. Cork,
Ireland; marr. Halifax 23 July
1839 Thomas Walsh (q.v.) (34:139).

Sullivan, Joanna. Dau. of William/
Mary (Hayes) of Co. Cork, Ireland;
marr. Halifax 18 Feb. 1841 William
Byrnes (q.v.) (35:135).

Sullivan, Joanna. See Lillis, Joanna.

Sullivan, John. S. of James/Honor
(Duggan) of Co. Cork, Ireland;
marr. Halifax 2 Sep. 1808 Catherine Egan (30:111).

Sullivan, John. S. of Tate/Mary
(Barry) of Co. Waterford, Ireland;
marr. Halifax 25 Sep. 1813 Sarah
Faulkner (30:111).

Sullivan, John. S. of Daniel/Bridget (Hackett) of Thomastown, Kilkenny, Ireland; marr. Halifax 10 June 1813 Elenor Murphy (30:111).

Sullivan, John. S. of John/Margaret (Egan) of Cork City, Ireland; marr. Halifax 26 Apr. 1843 Sarah Duggan (q.v.) (35:145).

Sullivan, Julian. Dau. of Denis/Mary (Harrington) of Co. Cork, Ireland; marr. Halifax 4 Oct. 1830 Thomas O'Connor (q.v.) (32:117).

Sullivan, Margaret. Dau. of John/ Catherine (Bruther) of Kilworth, Cork, Ireland; marr. Halifax 4 July 1820 William Dempsey (q.v.) (31:44).

Sullivan, Margaret. Dau. of John/Mary (Ryan) of Bally-Mountain, Co. Kilkenny, Ireland; marr. Halifax 12 Nov. 1826 Denis Carney (q.v.) (32:106).

Sullivan, Margaret. Dau. of Timothy/ Margaret (Harrington) of Co. Cork, Ireland; marr. Halifax 8 Sep. 1828 Michael Holleban (q.v.) (32:113).

Sullivan, Margaret. Dau. of John/ Joanna (Murphy) of Co. Cork, Ireland; marr. Halifax 24 July 1833 Michael Sullivan (q.v.) (33: 67).

Sullivan, Margaret. Of Co. Kilkenny, Ireland; widow of Denis Karney; marr. Halifax 27 Aug. 1835 Moses Ryan (q.v.) (34:138).

Sullivan, Mary. Dau. of William/Mary (Hayes) of Co. Cork, Ireland; marr. Halifax 27 Oct. 1829 Richard Keefe (q.v.) (32:113).

Sullivan, Mary. Dau. of John/Joanna (Hays) of Co. Kerry, Ireland; marr. Halifax 25 June 1836 Daniel Crowley (q.v.) (34:128).

Sullivan, Michael. S. of Denis/ Catherine (Ryan) of Co. Cork, Ireland; marr. Halifax 24 July 1833 Marga-

ret Sullivan (q.v.) (33:67).

Sullivan, Michael. S. of Darby/Bridget (Murphy) of Co. Kerry, Ireland; marr. Halifax 27 Nov. 1841 Joanna Fitzgerald (q.v.) (35: 145).

Sullivan, Patrick. S. of Denis/ Catherine (Murphy) of Co. Kerry, Ireland; marr. Halifax 17 Sep. 1813 Catherine Murray (q.v.) (30:111).

Sullivan, Patrick. S. of Timothy/ Honora of Co. Cork, Ireland; marr. Halifax 8 Oct. 1828 Honora Harrington (q.v.) (32:119).

Sullivan, Pierce. S. of Pierce/Mary (Magher) of Waterford City, Ireland; marr. Halifax 10 June 1833 Sarah Magory (q.v.) (33:67).

Sullivan, Thomas. S. of John/Joanna (Hayes) of Co,. Kerry, Ireland; marr. Halifax 24 Apr. 1844 Catherine Egar (q.v.) (35:145).

Sullivan, Timothy. S. of Jeremiah/ Ellen (Murphy) of Parish Tuoist, Co. Kerry, Ireland; marr. Halifax 18 Aug. 1839 Catherine McDonnell (q.v.) (34:138).

Sumner, Daniel. New England to Annapolis on CHARMING MOLLY May 1760 (18:271).

Summers, Benjamin. S. of John/Ann (Bell) of Dublin, Ireland; marr. Halifax 22 Apr. 1829 Ellen Casey (q.v.) (32:119).

Summers, Bridget. Dau. of John/Elenor (Shannon) of Parish Templeport, Co. Cavan, Ireland; marr. Halifax 24 Apr. 1821 Thomas Gorman (q.v.) (31:46).

Summers, Martin. S. of Edward/Eleanor (Fardy) of Co. Wexford, Ireland; marr. Halifax 14 Sep. 1841 Catherine Murry (q.v.) (35:145).

Sutherland, James. S. James/Catherine (Butler) of Co. Carlow, Ireland;

aarr. Halifax 8 June 1841 Ann
Murphy (q.v.) (35:145).

Sutherland, Mary. See Terry, Mary.

Sutherland, Patrick. Esq.; Mass., to
Chester with first settlers (16:
45).

Sutherland, William. Plus 1 f.; farmer; Port Roseway Associate (6:17).

Sutton, John. S. of John/Catherine
(Bulger) of Co. Waterford, Ire-
land; marr. Halifax 19 Oct. 1814
Catherine Ryan (q.v.) (30:111).

Sweeney, Ann. Dau. of Robert/Cather-
ine (Doyle) of Co. Longford, Ireland; marr. Halifax 27 Aug. 1833
George Nessel (33:64).

Sweeney, Catherine. Dau. of John/
Joanna (Sweeney) of Co. Cork,
Ireland; marr. Halifax 12 Jan.
1830 John Calihan (q.v.) (32:106).

Sweeney, John. S. of William/Mary
(Burns) of Parish Lismore, Co.
Waterford, Ireland; marr. Halifax
15 Dec. 1826 Allis Lemons (32:
119).

Sweeny, John. Widower of Alice La-
mond; of Co. Waterford, Ireland;
marr. Halifax 22 Apr. 1831 Mary
Rourke (33:67).

Swiney, John. S. of John/Joanna of
Co. Cork, Ireland; marr. Halifax 7
Nov. 1832 Sarah Pier (q.v.) (33:
67).

Syngen, Michael. Widower of Margaret
Connelly; of Co. Tipperary, Ire-
land; marr. Halifax 9 Feb. 1833
Mary Maguire (q.v.) (33:67).

Sypher, Jacob. Grantee "Digby New
Grant" 29 Jan. 1801 (5:83).

Sypher. See Cypher.

- T -

Tackels, Alexander. S. of William/

Jean; b. 15 June 1755 Palmer,
Mass.; to Onslow with parents (4:
231).

Tackels, Christian. Dau. of William/
Jean; b. 28 Feb. 1748 Palmer,
Mass.; to Onslow with parents
(4:231).

Tackels, Elizabeth. Dau. of William/
Jean; b. 21 Mar. 1743 Palmer,
Mass.; to Onslow with parents
(4:231).

Tackels, Hugh Easter. S. of William/
Jean; b. 10 Apr. 1752 Palmer,
Mass.; to Onslow with father
(4:231).

Tackels, James. S. of William/Jean;
b. 11 Feb. 1750 Palmer, Mass.; to
Onslow with father (4:231).

Tackels, Jean. Wife of William, to
Onslow with husband (4:231).

Tackels, Mary Ann. Dau. of William/
Jean; b. 4 June 1744 Palmer,
Mass.; to Onslow with parents
(4:231).

Tackels, Mary. Dau. of William/Jean;
b. 26 May 1741 Palmer, Mass.; to
Onslow with parents (4: 231).

Tackels, William. Palmer, Mass., plus
fam.to Onslow (4:231).

Tackles, Hugh Actor (Easter). From
Mass.; land grant at Onslow 21
Feb. 1769 (4:225).

Tackles, Hugh. From Mass.; land grant
Onslow 21 Feb. 1769 (4:224).

Tacklesat , James. From Mass.; land
grant Onslow 21 Feb. 1769 (4:225).

Tackles, William. From Mass.; land
grant at Onslow 21 Feb. 1769 (4:
224).

Takways, John. Plus 1 f./1 ch./2
svts.; Port Roseway Associate (6:
17).

Talant, Eliza. Dau. of Daniel/Ellen
(Connell) of Co. Waterford, Ire-

land; marr. Halifax 7 May 1839
David Burke (q.v.) (34:126).

Talbot, Catherine. See Wall, Catherine.

Tallant, Bridget. Dau. of Patrick/
Judith (Clary) of Co. Kilkenny,
Ireland; marr. Halifax 19 Nov.
1832 Patrick Deegan (q.v.) (33:
56).

Tallent, Mary. Dau. of Patrick/Julia
of Gowran, Co. Kilkenny, Ireland;
marr. Halifax 15 Feb. 1843 James
Monaghan (q.v.) (35:141).

Tallon, James Augustine. S. of Chris-
topher/Elizabeth (Ashe) of Raheny,
Co. Dublin, Ireland; marr. Halifax
27 Sep. 1829 Margaret O'Brien
(q.v.) (32:119).

Tanner, Hans Jakob. Plus wife/d.-in-
l.; Bargen, Canton Schaffhausen,
to Halifax 1744 (44:194).

Tanner, Hans. Plus wife/ch.; Bargen,
Canton Schaffhausen, [Switzerlan-
d,] allegedly to Carolina but
probably to Halifax 1744 (44:194).

Tanner, Jerg. Bargen, Canton Schaffhausen, [Switzerland,] allegedly
to Carolina but probably to Halifax 1744 (44:194).

Tape, Mark. S. of Mark of Parish
Tallow, Co. Waterford, Ireland;
marr. Halifax 5 Oct. q825 Bridget
Flanagan (q.v.) (31:54).

Tarbell, James. Volunteer; mustered
at Gulliver's Hole/St. Mary's Bay/
Sissiboo 1/6 June 1784; settled at
Sissiboo (now Weymouth) (40:263).

Tarbell, S. Lieut.; disbanded offic-
er, King's American Dragoons; plus
1 f./2 ch./3 svts.; mustered at
Gulliver's Hole/St. Mary's Bay/
Sissiboo 1/6 June 1784; settled at
Sissiboo (now Weymouth) (40:263).

Tarrant, William. Loyalist; mustered
at Digby 19 May 1784 (39:195).

Tatum, Diana. 25, servant; Hull to
Fort Cumberland on ALBION 7-14
March 1774 (21:139).

Taylor, Ann. 26, wife of Michael;
Hull to Fort Cumberland on ALBION
7-14 March 1774 (21:136).

Taylor, Edward. Grantee "Digby New
Grant" 29 Jan. 1801 (5:83).

Taylor, George. 25, farmer; Hull to
Fort Cumberland on ALBION 7-14
March 1774 (21:137).

Taylor, James Augustus. B. Danvers,
Mass., 28 Oct. 1799; s. of
James/Susannah; to Liverpool by
1801 (47:127:123).

Taylor, James. Loyalist; plus 1 f./2
ch.; mustered at Digby 19 May 1784
(39:196).

Taylor, James. S. of William/Ann; to
(or b.?) Shelburne by 1793 (47:
127:123).

Taylor, John. Capt.; disbanded officer, 1st N.J. Vols.; plus 4 svts.;
mustered at Gulliver's Hole/St.
Mary's Bay/Sissiboo 1/6 June 1784;
settled at Sissiboo (now Weymouth)
(40:263).

Taylor, John. From N.H.; effective
land grant at Truro 31 Oct. 1765
(4:245).

Taylor, John. Grantee "Digby New
Grant" 29 Jan. 1801 (5:82).

Taylor, Matthew. From N.H.; effective
land grant at Truro 31 Oct. 1765
(4:245).

Taylor, Michael. 23, farmer; Hull to
Fort Cumberland on ALBION 7-14
March 1774 (21:137).

Taylor, Michael. 45, husbandman; Hull
to Fort Cumberland on ALBION 7-14
March 1774 (21:136).

Taylor William. Grantee "Digby New
Grant" 29 Jan. 1801 (5:83).

Teehan, William. S. of William/Joanna
of Co. Kilkenny, Ireland; marr.

Halifax 7 Aug. 1809 Mary Murphy (30:111).

Tehan, Denis. S. of Thomas/Margaret (O'Donnell) of Fethard, Co. Tipperary, Ireland; marr. Halifax 18 July 1830 Mary Simmons (q.v.) (32:119).

Tench, John. Plus 1 f./1 ch./2 svts.; merchant; Port Roseway Associate (6:17).

Terry, Charles. S. of John/Alicia (Dealy) of Cove of Cork, Ireland; marr. Halifax 23 Aug. 1827 Sarah Pierce (32:119).

Terry, Mary. Dau. of Thomas/Mary (Kelly) of Co. Waterford, Ireland; marr. Halifax 28 Feb. 1843 Thomas Hanigan (q.v.) (35:138).

Terry, Mary. Widow of John Sutherland; of Co. Kildare, Ireland; marr. Halifax 21 Aug. 1832 James Kinsela (q.v.) (33:61).

Thatcher, Abel. Plus 1 svt.; farmer; Port Roseway Associate (6:17).

Thayer, Joseph. New England to Annapolis on CHARMING MOLLY May 1760 (18:271).

Thayer, Moses. New England to Annapolis 1760 (18:271).

Theakston, ----- (Mrs.). Wife of Major; from London; English; 55; Liverpool to Nova Scotia April 1864 on EUROPA (45:182).

Theakston, ----- (Mrs.). Wife of William; from London; English; 20; Liverpool to Nova Scotia April 1864 on EUROPA (45:182).

Theakston, ----- (Mrs.). Wife of Henry; from London; English; 19; Liverpool to Nova Scotia April 1864 on EUROPA (45:182).

Theakston, Eliza. Dau. of Major; from London; English; 12; Liverpool to Nova Scotia April 1864 on EUROPA (45:182).

Theakston, Henry. Painter; from London; English; 20; Liverpool to Nova Scotia April 1864 on EUROPA (45:182).

Theakston, Major. Clerk; from London; English; 55; Liverpool to Nova Scotia April 1864 on EUROPA (45:182).

Theakston, Robert. S. of Major; from London; English; 15; Liverpool to Nova Scotia April 1864 on EUROPA (45:182).

Theakston, Selina. Dau. of Major; from London; English; 18; Liverpool to Nova Scotia April 1864 on EUROPA (45:182).

Theakston, William. Printer's compositor; from London; English; 22; Liverpool to Nova Scotia April 1864 on EUROPA (45:182).

Thibaut, Elenor. Dau. of John/Bridget (Downey) Thibault of Newfoundland; marr. Halifax 22 June 1813 Patrick Ash (q.v.) (30:102).

Thomas, Anna. Wife of John; dau. of Thomas/Mary Mayhew; to Liverpool ca. 1783 (47:127:52).

Thomas, Archibald Jr. From Mass.; land grant at Truro 1759 (4:242).

Thomas, Archibald. From Mass.; land grant at Truro 1759 (4:242).

Thomas, Ebenezer. Liverpool proprietor (19:102).

Thomas, Ebenezer. Loyalist; mustered at Gulliver's Hole/St. Mary's Bay/Sissiboo 1/6 June 1784; settled at St. Mary's Bay (Plympton, Barton, Brighton) (40:263).

Thomas, Elizabeth. Dau. of Mary; English; infant; Liverpool to Nova Scotia June 1864 on INDIAN QUEEN (45:182).

Thomas, Elizabeth. Dau. of John/Anna; to (or b.?) Liverpool by 1804 (47:127:273).

Thomas, Frederick. B. Plymouth, Mass., 20 Dec. 1779; s. of John/Anna; Plymouth, Mass. to Liverpool ca. 1783 (47:127:52).

Thomas, Isaiah. Plus wife/5 ch.; Kingstown, Mass., to Chester with first settlers (16:45).

Thomas, John Jr. B. Plymouth, Mass., 5 Oct. 1775; s. of John/Anna; Plymouth, Mass. to Liverpool ca. 1783 (47:127:52).

Thomas, John. S. of Nathaniel/Elizabeth; Plymouth, Mass., to Liverpool ca. 1783 (47:127:52).

Thomas, Joseph. Loyalist; mustered at Digby 19 May 1784 (39:196).

Thomas, Joseph. Loyalist; plus 1 f./2 ch.; mustered at Digby 19 May 1784 (39:196).

Thomas, Mary (Mrs.). English; 30; Liverpool to Nova Scotia June 1864 on INDIAN QUEEN (45:182).

Thomas, Mary Ann. B. Plymouth, Mass., 14 Jan. 1774; dau. of John/Anna; Plymouth, Mass. to Liverpool ca. 1783 (47:127:52).

Thomas, Mary. Dau of Mary; English; 3; Liverpool to Nova Scotia June 1864 on INDIAN QUEEN (45:182).

Thomas, Nathan'l. Plus 2 svts.; merchant; Port Roseway Associate (6:17).

Thomas, Nathaniel Gardiner. B. Plymouth, Mass., 28 Sep. 1777; s. of John/Anna; Plymouth, Mass. to Liverpool ca. 1783 (47:127:52).

Thomas, Rachel. Dau. of Mary; English; 11; Liverpool to Nova Scotia June 1864 on INDIAN QUEEN (45:182).

Thomas, Richard. Plus 1 f./1 svt.; glazier; Port Roseway Associate (6:17).

Thomas, Stephen. Lancaster, England, to Liverpool by 1784 (47:126:289).

Thomas, Thomas Mayhew. B. Plymouth, Mass., 18 May 1782; s. of John/Anna; Plymouth, Mass. to Liverpool ca. 1783 (47:127:52).

Thomas, William. Capt.; Loyalist; plus 2 ch./3 svts.; mustered at Digby 19 May 1784 (39:195).

Thomas, William. From Mass.; land grant at Truro 1759 (4:242).

Thomas, William. Grantee "Digby New Grant" 29 Jan. 1801 (5:82).

Thomas, William. S. of Mary; English; 9; Liverpool to Nova Scotia June 1864 on INDIAN QUEEN (45:182).

Thompson, -----. Lt.Col.; Loyalist; New York to N.S. 1782 (41:13).

Thompson, Alexander. Grantee "Digby New Grant" 29 Jan. 1801 (5:82).

Thompson, Alexander. Loyalist; plus 1 f./4 ch.; mustered at Digby 19 May 1784 (39:196).

Thompson, Anthony. 20, husbandman; Hull to Fort Cumberland on ALBION 7-14 March 1774 (21:134).

Thompson, Archibald. From Ireland; land grant at Londonderry 6 Mar. 1775 (4:258).

Thompson, Catherine. Widow of Samuel Fleming; of Co. Tyrone, Ireland; marr. Halifax 5 Mar. 1838 John Power (q.v.) (34:137).

Thompson, Debora. Dau. of Robert/Debora (Walsh) of Co. Waterford, Ireland; marr. Halifax 7 Sep. 1842 Michael Phelan (q.v.) (35:143).

Thompson, James. From Mass.; land grant at Truro 1759 (4:242).

Thompson, John. 32, farmer; Hull to Fort Cumberland on ALBION 7-14 March 1774 (21:139).

Thompson, Joseph. 26, farmer; Hull to Fort Cumberland on ALBION 7-14 Mar. 1774 (21:139).

Thompson, Mary. See Walsh, Mary.

Thompson, Richard. 25, farmer; Hull

to Fort Cumberland on ALBION 7-14
March 1774 (21:139).

Thompson, Richard. 30, husbandman;
Hull, Yorkshire, to Nova Scotia;
on TWO FRIENDS 28 Feb.-7 Mar. 1774
(25:30).

Thompson, Robert. Seaman; s. of Rob-
ert/Bridget (Henry) of Dublin,
Ireland; marr. Halifax 20 June
1814 Elizabeth Graham (q.v.)
(30:111).

Thompson, Samuel. Loyalist; mustered
at Digby 19 May 1784 (39:196).

Thompson, Samuel. Loyalist; mustered
at Digby 19 May 1784 (39:196).

Thompson, Thomas. S. of John/Letitia
(Lanigan) of Co. Tipperary, Ireland, and Prince Edward Isl.;
marr. Halifax 3 June 1833 Margaret
Whelan (q.v.) (33:67).

Thomson, Charles. Laborer; English;
45; Liverpool to Nova Scotia May
1864 on EUROCLYDON (45:182).

Thomson, Robert. Plus 1 f.; carpenter; Port Roseway Associate (6:17).

Thorn, Samuel. Dutchess Co., N. Y.,
to Liverpool by 1784 (47:127:56).

Thorne, Edward. Grantee "Digby New
Grant" 29 Jan. 1801 (5:82).

Thornton, Daniel. See Thorrington,
Daniel.

Thornton, Thomas. B. Ireland ca.
1770; Belfast or Greenock to Halifax on POLLY, spring 1799 (29:83).

Thorrington, Daniel. Mass. to N.S.;
to U.S. 1776; dead by 1785 (36:
65).

Threighe, Mary. Dau. of John/Margaret
(McGrath) of Parish Stradbally,
Co. Waterford, Ireland; marr.
Halifax 7 June 1836 John Burke
(q.v.) (34:126).

Throop, Josiah. N.Y. to N.S.; to U.S.
1776; lived 1785 at N.Y. (36:65).

Thursby, William. 28; husbandman;

Hull, Yorkshire, to Nova Scotia;
on TWO FRIENDS 28 Feb.-7 Mar. 1774
(25:30).

Thurston, Lawrence. Loyalist; plus 1
f./2 ch./2 svts.; mustered at Digby 19 May 1784 (39:196).

Tice, Abraham. Loyalist; mustered at
Digby 19 May 1784 (39:196).

Tidd, Samuel. (Heirs) grantee "Digby
New Grant" 29 Jan. 1801 (5:82).

Tidd, Samuel. Loyalist; plus 1 f.;
mustered at Digby 19 May 1784
(39:196).

Tierney, Margaret. Dau. of James/
Bridget (Navan) of Co. Kilkenny,
Ireland; marr. Halifax 18 Feb.
1833 John Washington (q.v.) (33:
68).

Tierney, Patrick. S. of Patrick/
Elizabeth (Connors) of Ballynor-
den, Co. Wexford, Ireland; marr.
Halifax 25 July 1823 Margaret
Polly (31:54).

Tierney, William. S. of John/Ellen
(Mahar) of Co. Kildare, Ireland;
marr. Halifax 11 May 1834 Mary
Curran (q.v.) (33:67).

Tierney, William. S. of John/Ellen
(Mahar) of Co. Kildare, Ireland;
widower of Mary Curren of Co.
Kildare, Ireland; marr. Halifax 26
June 1836 Bridget Keating (34:
138).

Timpany, Robert. Maj.; disbanded
officer; plus 1 f./2 ch./5 svts.;
mustered at Digby 19 May 1784 (39:
195).

Tinan, Michael. S. of Denis/Eleanor
(McGrath) of Parish Portlaw, Co.
Waterford, Ireland; marr. Halifax
27 July 1827 Eleanor Arrigan
(q.v.) (32:119).

Tinan, Michael. S. of Denis/Eleanor
(McGrath) of Co. Waterford, Ireland; widower of Eleanor Arrigan;

marr. Halifax 2 Nov. 1828 Catherine Dunphy (q.v.) (32:119).

Tinehan, John. Of Co. Kilkenny, Ireland; widower of Mary Darcy; marr. Halifax 21 Feb. 1835 Ellen Cain (q.v.) (34:138).

Tinkham, Isaac. Liverpool proprietor (19:102).

Tinkham, Joseph. S. of Joseph/Agness; to Liverpool by 1777 (47:126:283).

Titus, Daniel. Loyalist; mustered at Digby 19 May 1784 (39:196).

Titus, Edmond. Loyalist; plus 1 f.; mustered at Digby 19 May 1784 (39:196).

Titus, Isaac. Grantee "Digby New Grant" 29 Jan. 1801 (5:82).

Titus, Isaac. Loyalist; plus 1 f./5 ch.; mustered at Digby 19 May 1784 (39:196).

Titus, Jacob. Loyalist; mustered at Digby 19 May 1784 (39:196).

Titus, James. Grantee "Digby New Grant" 29 Jan. 1801 (5:82).

Titus, Locey. Loyalist; mustered at Digby 19 May 1784 (39:196).

Tobias, Christian. Grantee "Digby New Grant" 29 Jan. 1801 (5:82).

Tobias, Christian. Loyalist; plus 1 f./4 ch.; mustered at Digby 19 May 1784 (39:196).

Tobias, Christian. Loyalist; to Digby 1783; d. 24 Sep. 1801 (48:304).

Tobias, Daniel. Loyalist; mustered at Digby 19 May 1784 (39:196).

Tobin, Catherine. Dau. of Thomas/Mary (Grace) of Hurlingford, Co. Kilkenny, Ireland; marr. Halifax 17 Sep. 1827 Edward Finn (q.v.) (32:110).

Tobin, Catherine. Dau. of Michael/Mary (Power) of Parish Thomastown, Kilkenny, Ireland; marr. Halifax 7 Aug. 1829 Thomas Walsh (q.v.) (32:120).

Tobin, David. S. of Thomas of Clonmine?, Cashel Diocese, Co. Tipperary, Ireland; marr. Halifax 22 Apr. 1829 Elizabeth Synott widow of Edward Martin (32:119).

Tobin, James. S. of John/Mary of Waterford City, Ireland; marr. Halifax 14 June 1818 Mary Hogan (q.v.) (31:54).

Tobin, James. S. of James/Judith (Carroll) of Roscrea, Co. Tipperary, Ireland; marr. Halifax 8 Jan. 1835 Mary McDougal (q.v.) (34:138).

Tobin, Joanna. Dau. of Thomas/Mary (Grace) of Co. Kilkenny, Ireland; marr. Halifax 27 Jan. 1829 Michael Dooley (q.v.) (32:108).

Tobin, Joanna. Dau. of Michael/Mary (Power) of Co. Kilkenny, Ireland; widow of Patrick Kilfoile; marr. Halifax 29 Sep. 1842 Michael Dillon (q.v.) (35:136).

Tobin, John. Of Co. Kilkenny, Ireland; marr. Halifax 11 July 1816 Catherine Wever (30:111).

Tobin, John. Of Gowran, Co. Kilkenny, Ireland; marr. Halifax 12 Jan. 1841 Catherine Walsh (q.v.) (35:145).

Tobin, John. S. of John/Catherine (Hayes) of Co. Waterford, Ireland; marr. Halifax 5 Feb. 1837 Margaret Tobin (q.v.) (34:138).

Tobin, John. S. of Maurice/Joanna (White) of Co. Tipperary, Ireland; marr. Halifax 10 May 1835 Bridget Walsh (q.v.) (34:138).

Tobin, Judith. Dau. of Michael/Mary (Power) of Co. Kilkenny, Ireland; marr. Halifax 18 Aug. 1828 Patrick Gilfoy (q.v.) (32:111).

Tobin, Margaret. Dau. of James/Margaret (Phelan) of Co. Tipperary, Ireland; marr. Halifax 22 Oct. 1815

John O'Donnell *(q.v.)* (30:109).

Tobin, Margaret. Dau. of John/Honora (Laughlin) of Co. Waterford, Ireland; marr. Halifax 5 Feb. 1837 John Tobin *(q.v.)* (34:138).

Tobin, Nicholas. S. of James/Mary (Birmingham) of Dublin City, Ireland; marr. Halifax 14 Jan. 1804 Harriett Prince (30:111).

Tobin, Patrick. S. of Thomas/Bridget (Murphy) of Parish Mullinahone, Tipperary, Ireland; marr. Halifax 14 Feb. 1830 Catherine Kearns *(q.v.)* (32:119).

Tobin, Sarah. See Whelan, Sarah.

Todd, Mary. Dau. of David/Elizabeth (Connors) of Co. Westmeath, Ireland; marr. Halifax 25 Jan. 1836 William Quinn *(q.v.)* (34:137).

Tolbert, John. Plus 1 svt.; Port Roseway Associate (6:17).

Tong, Elizabeth. Dau. of John/Mercy; to (or b.?) Liverpool by 1794 (47:127:123).

Tonge, Joshua. Loyalist; plus 1 f./1 ch.; mustered at Gulliver's Hole/St. Mary's Bay/Sissiboo 1/6 June 1784; settled at Gulliver's Hole (a cove and harbor on Digby Neck) (40:263).

Tony, Nathaniel. Liverpool proprietor (19:102).

Toohill, Cornelius. Of Parish Cove (Cahir), Co. Tipperary, Ireland; marr. Halifax 10 Sep. 1834 Catherine Dunphy *(q.v.)* (34:139).

Tool, Elizabeth. Dau. of Bernard/Mary (Kinan) of Dublin, Ireland; widow of Michael Farrell; marr. Halifax 28 Jan. 1830 Michael Murphy *(q.v.)* (32:116).

Toole, Patrick. S. of Philip/Catherine (Mackey) of Co. Tipperary, Ireland; marr. Halifax 20 Aug. 1844 Sarah Kline (35:145).

Tooney, Mary. Dau. of James/Margaret (Holihan) of Parish Fermoy, Co. Cork, Ireland; marr. Halifax 15 June 1836 Daniel Buckley *(q.v.)* (34:126).

Toppin, Mary. Dau. of William/Bridget (Headen) of Parish Newton, Co. Waterford, Ireland; marr. Halifax 30 Oct. 1827 John Brian *(q.v.)* (32:106).

Torrens, Ann. See Archibald, Ann.

Torry, Daniel. Liverpool proprietor (19:102).

Totten, James. Loyalist; mustered at Digby 19 May 1784 (39:196).

Totten, Joseph. Loyalist; plus 1 svt.; mustered at Digby 19 May 1784 (39:196).

Totten, William. Loyalist; plus 1 f./1 ch.; mustered at Digby 19 May 1784 (39:196).

Towhill, James. S. of Owen/Elenor (Bennett) of Co. Tipperary, Ireland; widower of Mary Dwyer; marr. Halifax 12 June 1835 Joanna Roche *(q.v.)* (34:139).

Townley. See Townshend.

Townsend, Mary. Dau. of James/Elizabeth (Wheegh) of Prince Edward Isl.; marr. Halifax 20 June 1842 Charles O'Brien *(q.v.)* (35:142).

Townshend, Thomas. Loyalist; plus 1 f.; mustered at Digby 19 May 1784 (39:195).

Tracy, Jedidah. Dau. of Nehemiah; to (or b.?) Liverpool by 1787 (47:127:55).

Tracy, Mary. Of Co. Kilkenny, Ireland; widow of Thomas Dwyer; marr. Halifax 10 May 1835 Timothy Grady *(q.v.)* (34:130).

Tracy, Thomas. S. of William/Margaret (O'Neal) of Co. Carlow, Ireland; marr. Halifax 3 Sep. 1835 Mary Brown *(q.v.)* (34:139).

Tracy, William. S. of Jeremiah/Margaret (Norris) of Mitchelstown, Co. Cork, Ireland; marr. Halifax 24 Apr. 1836 Ann Spruhan (q.v.) (34: 139).

Traen, Robert. From Mass.; land grant at Truro 1759 (4:242).

Trago, Jacob. Legion soldier; to Liverpool by 1784 (47:127:51).

Train, Jonathan. From Mass.; land grant at Truro 1759 (4:242).

Trainer, Thomas. S. of Patrick/Ann (MacManus) of Co. Armagh, Ireland; marr. Halifax 19/21 May 1843 Margaret McGary (q.v.) (35:145).

Trelone, Bennett. Plus 1 f./2 svts.; Port Roseway Associate (6:17).

Tribe, William. Plus 1 f./2 ch./1 svt.; Port Roseway Associate (6: 17).

Triender, James. Loyalist; plus 1 f.; mustered at Digby 19 May 1784 (39: 196).

Trihy, William. S. of John/Bridget (Brown) of Clashmore, Co. Waterford, Ireland; marr. Halifax 23 July 1835 Catherine Bowes (q.v.) (34:139).

Tripp, Acus. Liverpool proprietor (19:101).

Tripp, Acus. S. of Benoni; b. Dartmouth, Mass., 7 Nov. 1731; Chatham, Mass., to Liverpool as proprietor (1759-1769) (50:115).

Tripp, William. Liverpool proprietor (19:102).

Trounier, Mesial. Loyalist; mustered at Digby 19 May 1784 (39:196).

Troy, Ann. Dau. of John/Elenor (Barron) of Rosgroy(?), Co. Leix, Ireland; widow of Edward Walsh; marr. Halifax 31 Oct. 1835 Michael Long (q.v.) (34:133).

Troy, James. S. of Martin/Joanna (Carroll) of Freshport, Co. Kil-

kenny, Ireland; marr. Halifax 18 May 1843 Catherine Mason (q.v.) (35:145).

Troy, John. S. of John/Julia (Magrath) of Kilrossenty, Co. Waterford, Ireland; marr. Halifax 27 Apr. 1840 Elenor McCormack (q.v.) (34:139).

Truman, Ann. 58, wife of William; Hull to Fort Cumberland on ALBION 7-14 March 1774 (21:137).

Truman, William. 22, grocer, s.of William; Hull to Fort Cumberland on ALBION 7-14 March 1774 (21: 137).

Truman, William. 52, miller; Hull to Fort Cumberland on ALBION 7-14 March 1774 (21:137).

Trumbull, George. Grantee "Digby New Grant" 29 Jan. 1801 (5:82).

Trumbull, Robert. Grantee "Digby New Grant" 29 Jan. 1801 (5:82).

Trumbull, William. Grantee "Digby New Grant" 29 Jan. 1801 (5:82).

Trusdell, Alpheus. Arr. Annapolis from New York 19 Oct. 1782 (37: 125).

Trusdell, James. Arr. Annapolis from New York 19 Oct. 1782 (37:125).

Trusdell, John. Plus 2 f./3 ch. 8+/3 ch. -8; arr. Annapolis from New York 19 Oct. 1782 (37:125).

Tubrid, John. S. of Walter/Catherine (Shaughnessy) of Parish Ballybricken, Co. Waterford, Ireland; marr. Halifax 3 Nov. 1843 Ann Monk Monahan (q.v.) (35:145).

Tucker, Dorcas. Dau. of James/Rhoda; to (or b.?) Liverpool by 1793 (47: 127:202).

Tucker, George. Arr. Annapolis from New York 19 Oct. 1782 (37:125).

Tucker, James. To Liverpool ca. 1760 (47:126:96).

Tucker, Mary. Dau. of James/Rhoda; to

(or b.?) Liverpool by 1786 (47:
127:55).

Tucker, Phebe. Dau. of James/Rhoda;
to (or b.?) Liverpool by 1784 (47:
127:49).

Tucker, Reuben. Grantee "Digby New
Grant" 29 Jan. 1801 (5:82).

Tucker, Richard. Liverpool to Nova
Scotia April 1864 on KEDAR (45:
182).

Tullock, Barbary. Dau. of Robert/
Margaret; to (or b.?) Liverpool by
1798 (47:127:211).

Tupper, Abigal. B. New England 20
Mar. 1738; dau. of Deacon Nathan;
to Liverpool 1760 (47:126:162).

Tupper, Elisabeth. B. New England 20
Oct. 1755; dau. of Deacon Nathan;
to Liverpool 1760 (47:126:162).

Tupper, Elizabeth. To Liverpool ca.
1760 (47:126:97).

Tupper, Elizebeth. Dau. of Nathan/
Experience; to Liverpool by 1774
(47:126:167).

Tupper, Experience. Wife of Deacon
Nathan; b. New England; to Liverpool 1760 (47:126:162).

Tupper, Experience. B. New England 11
Feb. 1740; dau. of Deacon Nathan;
to Liverpool 1760 (47:126:162).

Tupper, Experience. Dau. of Medad/
Lois; to (or b.?) Liverpool by
1804 (47:127:278).

Tupper, Hanna. B. New England 8 Mar.
1749; dau. of Deacon Nathan; to
Liverpool 1760 (47:126:162).

Tupper, Hannah. To Liverpool ca. 1760
(47:126:161).

Tupper, Israel. Liverpool proprietor
(19:102).

Tupper, Johanah. B. New England 1
Nov. 1735; dau. of Deacon Nathan;
to Liverpool 1760 (47:126:162).

Tupper, Johannah. To Liverpool ca.
1760 (47:126:98).

Tupper, Martha. B. New England 5 Apr.
1744; dau. of Deacon Nathan; to
Liverpool 1760 (47:126:162).

Tupper, Martha. Dau. of Nathan/Lydia;
to (or b.?) Liverpool by 1799 (47:
128:35).

Tupper, Mary. B. New England 24 Nov.
1753; dau. of Deacon Nathan; to
Liverpool 1760 (47:126:162).

Tupper, Mary. Dau. of Deacon Nathan/
Experience; to Liverpool by 1771
(47:126:164).

Tupper, Medad. B. New England 25 Apr.
1746; s. of Deacon Nathan; to Liv-
rpool 1760 (47:126:162).

Tupper, Nathan, Liverpool proprietor
(19:101).

Tupper, Nathan. B. New England 7 Apr.
1757; s. of Deacon Nathan; to Liverpool 1760 (47:126:162).

Tupper, Nathan. Deacon; b. New England; to Liverpool 1760 (47:126:
162).

Tupper, Nathan. S. of Nathan/Experi-
ence; to (or b.?) Liverpool by
1777 (47:126:284).

Tupper, Nathan. S. of Nathan/Lydia;
to (or b.?) Liverpool by 1799 (47:
127:272).

Tupper, Nathan. S. of Nathan/Experi-
ence (Gibbs); b. Sandwich, Mass.;
d. Liverpool 8 Feb. 1832 ae 74
(49:132).

Tupper, Oliver. S. of Medad/Lois; to
(or b.?) Liverpool by 1803 (47:
127:272).

Tupper, Ward. Liverpool proprietor
(19:102).

Tupper, Ward. To Liverpool by 1766
(47:126:163).

Turger, John. Waldeck Service; plus 1
f./1 ch.; mustered at Bear River
11/25 June 1784 (38:261).

Turish, Elizabeth. Widow of Pvt. Tho-
as Hagarty 52nd Regt. England;

marr. Halifax 27 Jan. 1830 Corp.
Thomas McCormack (q.v.) (32:115).

Turnbull, Robert. Sawyer; Port Roseway Associate (6:17).

Turnbull, Thomas. Plus 1 f.; merchant; Port Roseway Associate (6:
17).

Turner, Alexander Jr. From Mass.;
land grant at Truro 1759 (4:242).

Turner, Andrew. From Mass.; land
grant at Truro 1759 (4:242).

Turner, John. Grantee "Digby New
Grant" 29 Jan. 1801 (5:82).

Turner, John. Plus 1 f./4 ch./2
svts.; Port Roseway Associate (6:
17).

Turner, Joseph. Lancaster, Mass., to
Chester with first settlers (16:
45).

Turner, Nathaniel. Plus wife/2 ch.;
Lancaster, Mass., to Chester with
first settlers (16:45).

Turner, Reuben. From Mass.; land
grant at Truro 1759 (4:242).

Tuttle, Elizabeth. Dau. of Charles/
Mary (Clark) of Co. Fermanagh,
Ireland; marr. Halifax 4 Feb. 1822
Sgt. James Donohoe (q.v.) (31:44).

Twaddle, James. Plus 1 f./5 ch. 8+/2
ch. -8; arr. Annapolis from New
York 19 Oct. 1782 (37:125).

Twitchell, Joseph. From Mass.; land
grant at Onslow 18 Oct. 1759 (4:
223).

Tympany, Robert. Grantee "Digby New
Grant" 29 Jan. 1801 (5:82).

Tynan, Ellen. Dau. of Denis/Ellen
(Magrath) of Portlaw, Co. Waterford, Ireland; marr. Halifax 23
Sep. 1831 Patrick Hickey (q.v.)
(33:59).

Tyrrell, Mary. Dau. of Michael/Mary
(Troy) of Co. Kilkenny, Ireland;
marr. Halifax 24 May 1836 Patrick
Brenan (q.v.) (34:126).

Tyson, Nathan. Loyalist; plus 1 f.;
mustered at Digby 19 May 1784 (39:
195).

- U -

Uhlmann, Johan (Melchior?). Cabinetmaker; Beringen, Canton Schaffhausen, [Switzerland,] to Halifax
1742 (44:195).

Uniacke, Richard John. 4th s. Nor-
man; b. 22 Nov. 1753 at Castletown, Co. Cork, Ireland; settled
at Port Cumberland 1774 (10.238).

Upham, Abigail. From Mass.; land
grant at Onslow 21 Feb. 1769 (4:
225).

Upham, Joshua. Maj.; Loyalist; New
York to N.S. 1782 (41:13).

Upham, Nathan. From Mass.; land
grant at Onslow 21 Feb. 1769 (4:
225).

Upham, Richard Jr. From Mass.; land
grant at Onslow 21 Feb. 1769 (4:
225).

Upham, Richard. B. Malden, Mass.;
bap. there 9 Dec. 1716; plus
family; to Onslow (4:231).

Upham, Richard. From Mass.; land
grant at Onslow 21 Feb. 1769 (4:
224).

Upton, Edward. S. of Charles/Judith
(Seaton) of Nfld.; marr. Halifax
28 Jan. 1813 Mary Dulhanty (q.v.)
(30:111).

- V -

Vail, Nathaniel Jr. Carpenter; Port
Roseway Associate (6:18).

Vail, Nathaniel. Plus 1 f./6 ch.;
millwright; Port Roseway Associate
(6:17).

Vail, Robert. Carpenter; Port Roseway
Associate (6:17).

Valentine, William. Loyalist; mustered at Digby 19 May 1784 (39:196).

Valleau, Peter. Loyalist; mustered at Digby 19 May 1784 (39:196).

VanBuren, Ramaner. Loyalist; mustered at Digby 19 May 1784 (39:196).

VanBuskirk, Thomas. Officer of King's Orange Rangers; plus 2 svts.; mustered at Digby 19 May 1784 (39:118).

Vance, David. B. Ireland 1748; bur. Folly Village, Londonderry (4:262).

Vance, Jane. See Flatcher, Jane.

Vance, Jane. Wife of David; dau. of ----- Hill; b. Ireland 1755; bur. Folly Village, Londonderry (4:262).

Vance, John. From Ireland; land grant at Londonderry 6 Mar. 1775 (4:258).

Vance, Mary. See Lynch, Mary.

VanCleke, Levi. Loyalist; plus 1 f.; mustered at Digby 19 May 1784 (39:196).

VanCleke, Simon. Loyalist; plus 1 f./2 ch.; mustered at Digby 19 May 1784 (39:196).

Vanclick, Simon. Plus 1 f./2 ch.; arr. Annapolis from New York 19 Oct. 1782 (37:126).

VanEmburgh, Gilbert. Grantee "Digby New Grant" 29 Jan. 1801 (5:82).

Vanhorn, Minddert. S. of Richard/Patty; Newark, N. J., to Liverpool by 1788 (47:127:56).

VanTassell, Abraham. Loyalist; plus 1 f./6 ch.; mustered at Digby 19 May 1784 (39:196).

VanTassell, Abraham. Grantee "Digby New Grant" 29 Jan. 1801 (5:82).

VanTassell, William. Grantee "Digby New Grant" 29 Jan. 1801 (5:82).

Vanwelza, David. Grantee "Digby New Grant" 29 Jan. 1801 (5:82).

VanWelza, John. Grantee "Digby New Grant" 29 Jan. 1801 (5:82).

Vassey, Joseph. Plus 1 f.; sawyer; Port Roseway Associate (6:17).

Veckel, Hannah. 20, maid servant; Hull to Fort Cumberland on ALBION 7-14 March 1774 (21:134).

Veckel, Mary. 20, maid servant; Hull to Fort Cumberland on ALBION 7-14 March 1774 (21:134).

Veits, Roger, Grantee "Digby New Grant" 29 Jan. 1801 (5:82).

Velser, Daniel. Loyalist; plus 1 f./5 ch.; mustered at Digby 19 May 1784 (39:196).

Verg, Joseph. S. of Joseph/Mary; to Liverpool by 1779 (47:126:286).

Verg, Joseph. To Port Mouton by 1771 (47:126:286).

Verg, Rebecca. To Liverpool ca. 1760 (47:126:100).

Verge, Mary. Dau. of Joseph/Mary; to (or b.?) Liverpool by 1789 (47:127:208).

Verner, J. D. German Service; plus 1 f./1 ch.; mustered at Bear River 11/25 June 1784 (38:261).

Vigours, Mary. Dau. of Thomas/Mary Anne (Fitzpatrick) of Placentia, Nfld.; marr. Halifax 14 Nov 1840 (sic for 1830?) John Roche (q.v.) (32:118).

Vilot. Slave to William Freeman; to Liverpool by 1786 (47:126:163).

Vitch, Andrew. Plus 2 f./1 ch. 8+; arr. Annapolis from New York 19 Oct. 1782 (37:125).

Vitch, John. Arr. Annapolis from New York 19 Oct. 1782 (37:125).

Vitch, William. Arr. Annapolis from New York 19 Oct. 1782 (37:125).

Vroom, John. Grantee "Digby New Grant" 29 Jan. 1801 (5:82).

Wade, Francis. S. of John/Mary (Ryan)
of Clonmel, Co. Tipperary, Ireland; marr. Halifax 21 July 1802
Mary Hare (30:111).

Wade, Samuel. Plus 1 f./2 ch./4
svts.; blacksmith; Port Roseway
Associate (6:18).

Wady, Humphrey. Loyalist; plus 1 f./4
ch.; mustered at Digby 19 May 1784
(39:196).

Waggner, N. Waldeck Service; mustered
at Bear River 11/25 June 1784 (38:
261).

Waggoner, Richard. Loyalist; mustered
at Digby 19 May 1784 (39:197).

Waid, Richard. S. of Francis/Ellen
(Hasset) of Co. Tipperary, Ire-
land; marr. Halifax 24 Oct. 1833
Mary Deniffe (q.v.) (33:67).

Walker, Adam. Grantee "Digby New
Grant" 29 Jan. 1801 (5:82).

Walker, Adam. Loyalist; plus 1 f./3
ch.; mustered at Digby 19 May 1784
(39:196).

Walker, Adam. Plus 1 f./1 ch. 8+/1
ch. -8; arr. Annapolis from New
York 19 Oct. 1782 (37:126).

Walker, John. Plus 1 f./1 ch.; Port
Roseway Associate (6:18).

Walker, Peter. Disbanded soldier,
N.Y. Vols.; plus 1 f.; mustered at
Digby 19 May 1784 (39:196).

Walker, Peter. Loyalist; plus 1 f.;
mustered at Digby 19 May 1784 (39:
197).

Walker, Tristram. 27, husbandman;
Hull to Port Cumberland on ALBION
7-14 March 1774 (21:139).

Wall, James. S. of Matthew/Johanna
(Dunphy) of Co. Waterford, Ire-
land; marr. Halifax 5 Sep. 1814
Charlotte Hall (30:111).

Wall, James. S. of Matthew/Bridget

(Murphy) of Athy, Co. Kildare,
Ireland; marr. Halifax 21 May 1826
Mary Molloy (q.v.) (32:119).

Wall, John. B. Plymouth, Mass., 26
Apr. 1761; s. of John/Ruth; to
Liverpool ca. 1761 (47:126:99).

Wall, John. Liverpool proprietor (19:
101).

Wall, John. To Liverpool ca. 1761
(47:126:99).

Wall, Margaret. Dau. of John/Eleanor
(Prendergast) of Co. Tipperary,
Ireland; marr. Halifax 26 Feb.
1829 Morgan O'Brien (q.v.) (32:
117).

Wall, Margaret. Dau. of John/Margaret
(Newnan) of Clonmel, Co. Tipperary, Ireland; marr. Halifax 19
Oct. 1834 James Judd (q.v.) (34:
132).

Wall, Mary. B. Plympton, Mass., 13
Nov. 1757?; dau. of John/Ruth; to
Liverpool ca. 1761 (47:126:99).

Wall, Michael. S. of Thomas/Bridget
(Tihiss?) of Co. Kilkenny, Ire-
land; marr. Halifax 10 Dec. 1832
Elizabeth Kingston (q.v.) (33:67).

Wall, Patrick. Of Waterford City,
Ireland; marr. Halifax 26 Aug.
1840 Joanna Kerns (34:139).

Wall, Patrick. S. of John/Elenor
(Prendergast) of Co. Tipperary,
Ireland; marr. Halifax 29 Aug.
1832 Catherine Murphy (33:67).

Wall, Ruth. B. New England 25 July
175-; dau. of John/Ruth; to Liverpool ca. 1761 (47:126:99).

Wall, Ruth. To Liverpool ca. 1761
(47:126:99).

Wall, Thomas. S. of Thomas/Catherine
(McAvoy) of Co. Kilkenny, Ireland;
marr. Halifax 2 July 1829 Mary
Finely (q.v.) (32:119).

Wallace, Catherine. Dau. of Edward/
Mary (Hanrihan) of Thomastown, Co.

Kilkenny, Ireland; marr. Halifax 16 July 1837 George Huson (Hewson) (q.v.) (34:132).

Wallace, Catherine. Dau. of Edward/Mary (Hanrihan) of Columbkill, Thomastown, Co. Kilkenny, Ireland; widow of George Huson; marr. Halifax 20 Jan. 1845 John Barton (q.v.) (35:134).

Wallace, James. S. of Peter/Eleanor (Molloy) of Parish St. James, Co. Wexford, Ireland; marr. Halifax 20 Aug. 1828 Rebecca Elizabeth Smith (32:119).

Wallace, James. S. of Peter/Eleanor (Molloy) of Parish St. John, Co. Wexford, Ireland; marr. Halifax 20 May 1843 Catherine Power (q.v.) (35:145).

Wallace, Mary. Dau. of Thomas/Honora (Nagle) of Co. Cork, Ireland; marr. Halifax 14 Aug. 1831 John Coughlin (q.v.) (33:55).

Wallace, Mary. Dau. of William/Mary (Walsh) of Co. Kilkenny, Ireland; marr. Halifax 2 Oct. 1832 John Nolan (q.v.) (33:64).

Wallace, Patrick. Of Co. Kilkenny, Ireland; marr. Halifax 1 July 1841 Bridget Nolan (q.v.) (35:145).

Wallace, Patrick. S. of James/Honor (Cook) of Callan, Kilkenny, Ireland; marr. Halifax 14 Sep. 1802 Anne Lawrence (q.v.) (30:111).

Wallace, Richard. S. of Richard/Mary (Haley) of Mallow, Co. Cork, Ireland; marr. Halifax 7 Jan. 1834 Bridget Darmody (q.v.) (33:68).

Wallace, Thomas. S. of William/Mary (Walsh) of Co. Kilkenny, Ireland; marr. Halifax 3 Sep. 1832 Elizabeth Galway (q.v.) (33:67).

Wallace, William. S. of Richard/Mary (Haley) of Mallow, Co. Cork, Ireland; marr. Halifax 26 June 1834

Mary Shea (q.v.) (33:68).

Walley, Mehetable. To Liverpool by 1766 (47:126:163).

Walls, George. Plus 1 f./4 ch./1 svt.; Port Roseway Associate (6: 18).

Walsh, Alice. Dau. of John/Mary (Addams); widow of James Fanning; of Co. Tipperary, Ireland; marr. Halifax 11 Jan. 1822 Michael Walsh (q.v.) (31:54).

Walsh, Alice. Dau. of Michael/Frances (Smith) of Co. Kilkenny, Ireland; marr. Halifax 2 July 1838 Richard Walsh (q.v.) (34:139).

Walsh, Anastasia. Dau. of John/Margaret (Keefe) of Co. Kilkenny, Ireland; marr. Halifax 5 July 1831 John Magher (q.v.) (33:63).

Walsh, Ann. Dau. of Maurice/Margaret (Tibis) of Cappoquin, Co. Waterford, Ireland; marr. Halifax 8 Feb. 1829 John Henissy (q.v.) (32: 112).

Walsh, Ann. Dau. of Thomas/Mary of Kilgobinet, Co. Waterford, Ireland; marr. Halifax 30 July 1829 Thomas Roche (q.v.) (32:118).

Walsh, Ann. See Troy, Ann.

Walsh, Bridget. Dau. of Michael/Frances (Smith) of Co. Kilkenny, Ireland; marr. Halifax 10 May 1835 John Tobin (q.v.) (34:138).

Walsh, Bridget. Dau. of Thomas/Bridget (Mihan) of WineGap [sic], Co. Kilkenny, Ireland; marr. Halifax 18 Jan. 1843 William Shea (q.v.) (35:144).

Walsh, Bridget. See Aylward, Bridget.

Walsh, Catherine. Of Gracetown, Co. Tipperary, Ireland; marr. Halifax 10 May 1835 Richard Walsh (q.v.) (34:139).

Walsh, Catherine. Dau. of Edward/Margaret (Mulloye) of Co. Wexford,

Ireland; marr. Halifax 28 Sep. 1829 James Corcoran (q.v.) (32:107).

Walsh, Catherine. Dau. of James/Catherine (Magrath) of Templeoran, Co. Kilkenny, Ireland; marr. Halifax 19 Feb. 1828 Daniel Flinn (q.v.) (32:111).

Walsh, Catherine. Dau. of Martin/Mary (Denison) of Co. Kilkenny, Ireland; marr. Halifax 25 Oct. 1832 Michael Galway (q.v.) (33:58).

Walsh, Catherine. Dau. of Michael/Alice (Walsh) of St. John's, Nfld.; marr. Halifax 10 Feb. 1834 Timothy Linehan (q.v.) (33:62).

Walsh, Catherine. D, James/Mary (Ryan) of Co. Kilkenny, Ireland; marr. Halifax 28 Apr. 1836 John MacIver (q.v.) (34:134).

Walsh, Catherine. Dau. of John/Catherine (Allen) of Nfld.; marr. Halifax 9 Nov. 1836 William O'Farrell (q.v.) (34:136).

Walsh, Catherine. Of Kilmacow, Co. Kilkenny, Ireland; marr. Halifax 12 Jan. 1841 John Tobin (q.v.) (35:145).

Walsh, Edward. S. of Patrick/Ellen (Whelan) of Parish Mooncoyne, Co. Kilkenny, Ireland; marr. Halifax 23 Aug. 1829 Margaret Corcoran (q.v.) (32:120).

Walsh, Edward. S. of Edward/Eleanor (Manning) of Parish Owning, Co. Kilkenny, Ireland; marr. Halifax 12 Sep. 1829 Anastasia Mullony (q.v.) (32:120).

Walsh, Edward. S. of John/Ann (Murphy) of Parish Mooncoyne, Co. Kilkenny, Ireland; marr. Halifax 7 June 1828 Juliana Young (32:120).

Walsh, Edward. S. of Michael/Abigail (O'Mealy) of Co. Tipperary, Ireland; marr. Halifax 2 Apr. 1839 Bridget Sarsfield (q.v.) (34:139).

Walsh, Elizabeth. Dau. of John/Susannah (Costello) of Co. Offaly, Ireland; marr. Halifax 7 Jan. 1836 James Fahy (q.v.) (34:129).

Walsh, Ellen. Dau. of William/Margaret (Fouler) of Co. Waterford, Ireland; marr. Halifax 26 May 1834 Nicholas Deveraux (q.v.) (33:56).

Walsh, Ellen. Of Nfld.; widow of Bartholomew Flinn; marr. Halifax 15 May 1841 Pvt. John Little (q.v.) (35:140).

Walsh, Ellen. See Crowley, Ellen.

Walsh, Ellen. See Daily, Ellen.

Walsh, George. Trader; s. of Patrick/Elizabeth of Co. Wexford, Ireland; marr. Halifax 30 Nov. 1813 Frances Noonan (30:112).

Walsh, Honora. Dau. of John/Catherine (Murphy) of Owning, Co. Kilkenny, Ireland; marr. Halifax 14 May 1828 Thomas Fahy (q.v.) (32:109).

Walsh, Honora. Dau. of William/Mary (Norris) of Co. Waterford, Ireland; marr. Halifax 14 Sep. 1841 William Hanigan (q.v.) (35:138).

Walsh, James. Liverpool to Nova Scotia April 1864 on KEDAR (45: 182).

Walsh, James. S, Richard/Mary (Purcel) of Co. Kilkenny, Ireland; marr. Halifax 21 May 1812 Elener Boyle (q.v.) (30:111).

Walsh, James. S. of Walter/Mary (Shirtty) of Co. Kilkenny, Ireland; marr. Halifax 20 Jan. 1803 Anne Murphy (q.v.) (30:112).

Walsh, James. S. of Patrick/Mary (Corgan) of Dublin, Ireland; marr. Halifax 20 Apr. 1822 Hannah Guy (q.v.) (31:54).

Walsh, James. S. of Philip/Mary (Baker) of Co. Tipperary, Ireland; marr. Halifax 9 Oct. 1832 Maria Emily Short (q.v.) (33:68).

Walsh, James. S. of Patrick/Joanna (Quinn) of Co. Kilkenny, Ireland; marr. Halifax 4 June 1834 Margaret Dee (q.v.) (33:68).

Walsh, James. S. of James/Catherine (Barry) of Co. Cork, Ireland; marr. Halifax 18 Apr. 1839 Catherine Crowly (q.v.) (34:139).

Walsh, Joanna. Dau. of John/Anne (Daley) of Co. Cork, Ireland; marr. Halifax 4 Aug. 1831 Thomas Curtin (q.v.) (33:56).

Walsh, Joanna. Dau. of Richard/Catherine (Delany) of Winegap, Co. Kilkenny, Ireland; widow of Thomas Power; marr. Halifax 31 Oct. 1833 William Shea (q.v.) (33:66).

Walsh, Joanna. Dau. of John/Catherine (Conway) of Co. Tipperary, Ireland; marr. Halifax 26 Feb. 1843 Edward Murphy (q.v.) (35:142).

Walsh, John. S. of John/Mary (Grant) of Parish Caragew, Co. Kilkenny, Ireland; marr. Halifax 14 May 1828 Mary Holy widow of James Gydon (q.v.) (32:120).

Walsh, John. S. of Walter/Alice (Lanegan) Kilkenny City, Ireland; marr. Halifax 2 Nov. 1830 Mary Keefe (q.v.) (32:120).

Walsh, John. S. of Michael/Catherine (Smith) of Parish Mooncoyne, Pollrone, Co. Kilkenny, Ireland; marr. Halifax 24 July 1830 Bridget Lahy (q.v.) (32:120).

Walsh, John. S. of Patrick/Ellen (Whelan) of Co. Kilkenny, Ireland; marr. Halifax 21 July 1835 Elizabeth McGrath (q.v.) (34:139).

Walsh, John. Shipwright; s. of James/Elener (Haiz) of Co. Wexford, Ireland; marr. Halifax 5 Oct. 1807 Johanna Doyle (q.v.) (30: 111).

Walsh, John. Widower of Martha Haley;

s. of John/Mary (Grant) of Co. Kilkenny, Ireland; marr. Halifax 23 Apr. 1831 Bridget Mahony (q.v.) (33:68).

Walsh, Margaret. Dau. of Patrick/Alice (Duncan) of Co. Kilkenny, Ireland; marr. Halifax 30 Nov. 1828 Martin Fitzpatrick (32:110).

Walsh, Margaret. Dau. of Patrick/Mary (Molony) of Cashel, Co. Tipperary, Ireland; marr. Halifax 25 Jan. 1834 Michael Ellis (q.v.) (33:57).

Walsh, Margaret. Dau. of Thomas/Mary (Malony) of Co. Kilkenny, Ireland; marr. Halifax 10 May 1841 Edward Kavanagh (q.v.) (35:139).

Walsh, Margaret. Of Co. Wexford, Ireland; widow of Martin Cullerton; marr. Halifax 17 Sep. 1837 William Dunphy (q.v.) (34:129).

Walsh, Martin. S. of William/Mary (Neal) of Co. Kilkenny, Ireland; marr. Halifax 2 Aug. 1806 Rebecca Jenkins (30:112).

Walsh, Martin. S. of Nicholas/Anastasia (Henneberry) of Co. Kilkenny, Ireland; marr. Halifax 13 Nov. 1813 Johanna Hatfield (30:112).

Walsh, Martin. S. of Thomas/Alice of Co. Kilkenny, Ireland; marr. Halifax 27 Oct. 1831 Ellen Carroll (q.v.) (33:68).

Walsh, Mary. Dau. of Thomas/Margaret (Ryan) of St. Johns, Nfld.; marr. Halifax 9 Jan. 1810 Patrick Power (q.v.) (30:110).

Walsh, Mary. Dau. of James/Catherine (Ryan) of Placentia, Nfld.; marr. Halifax 21 Sep. 1824 Patrick Haily (q.v.) (31:46).

Walsh, Mary. Dau. of James/Anastasia (Mackey) of Co. Kilkenny, Ireland; marr. Halifax 30 Dec. 1828 Patrick Forrestall (q.v.) (32:111).

Walsh, Mary. Dau. of James/Bridget

(Walsh) of Ballygory, Co. Kilkenny, Ireland; marr. Halifax 7 Sep. 1829 Michael Hogan (q.v.) (32: 112).

Walsh, Mary. Dau. of Maurice/Mary (Harrigan) of Co. Cork, Ireland; marr. Halifax 28 Apr. 1830 Denis McCarthy (q.v.) (32:114).

Walsh, Mary. Dau. of Robert/Catherine (Shekly) of Co. Kilkenny, Ireland; marr. Halifax 19 June 1831 Martin Fitzpatrick (q.v.) (33:58).

Walsh, Mary. Dau. of John/Ann (Daley) of Buttevant, Co. Cork, Ireland; marr. Halifax 3 June 1834 James Hayes (q.v.) (33:59).

Walsh, Mary. Dau. of Patrick/Mary (Mullowney) of Parish Camus, Co. Tipperary, Ireland; marr. Halifax 27 Aug. 1836 John Coffil (q.v.) (34:127).

Walsh, Mary. Dau. of Maurice/Mary (Colbert) of Co. Waterford, Ireland; marr. Halifax 10 Sep. 1834 Denis Markley (q.v.) (34:134).

Walsh, Mary. Dau. of Edward/Ellen (Brennan) of Co. Kilkenny, Ireland; marr. Halifax 12 Feb. 1836 Lawrence O'Brien (q.v.) (34:136).

Walsh, Mary. Dau. of Edward/Catherine (Fleming) of Co. Cork, Ireland; marr. Halifax 11 June 1836 Thomas Savage (q.v.) (34:138).

Walsh, Mary. Dau. of Edward/Catherine (Rebby) of Co. Kilkenny, Ireland; marr. Halifax 22 Aug. 1841 James Griffin (q.v.) (35:138).

Walsh, Mary. Of Co. Waterford, Ireland; widow of James Thompson; marr. Halifax 10 July 1838 Thomas Kinna (q.v.) (34:133).

Walsh, Michael. S. of James/Mary (Moore) of Co. Kerry, Ireland; marr. Halifax 11 Jan. 1822 Alice Walsh (q.v.) (31:54).

Walsh, Michael. S. of John/Joanna (Costly) of Co. Offaly, Ireland; marr. Halifax 12 Aug. 1833 Ellen O'Mara (33:68).

Walsh, Michael. S. of Thomas/Ellen (Barry) of Co. Kilkenny, Ireland; marr. Halifax 7 Aug. 1844 Catherine Lively (35:145).

Walsh, Nicholas. S. of Martin/Mary (Denison) of Co. Kilkenny, Ireland; marr. Halifax 16 Feb. 1830 Joanna Shelly (q.v.) (32:120).

Walsh, Patrick. S. of James/Catherine (Eagan) of Parish Holy Cross, Tipperary, Ireland; marr. Halifax 16 Jan. 1827 Rosana Rice (q.v.) (32:120).

Walsh, Patrick. S. of William/Bridget (Roche) of Co. Kilkenny, Ireland; marr. Halifax 22 Jan. 1831 Ellen Kirwen (q.v.) (33:68).

Walsh, Patrick. S. of Patrick/Mary (Moloney) of Cashel, Co. Tipperary, Ireland; marr. Halifax 19 Feb. 1833 Margaret Richardson (q.v.) (33:68).

Walsh, Patrick. S. of William/Bridget (Roche) of Co. Kilkenny, Ireland; widower of Ellen Kirwan of Co. Waterford, Ireland; marr. Halifax 6 Nov. 1835 Mary Molony (q.v.) (34:139).

Walsh, Patrick. S. of Moses/Catherine (Condon) of Adamon, Co. Wexford, Ireland; marr. Halifax 12 Jan. 1843 Ellen Ballard (35:145).

Walsh, Patrick. S. of Thomas/Bridget (Mihan) of Co. Kilkenny, Ireland; marr. Halifax 3 Feb. 1844 Mary Murphy (35:145).

Walsh, Patrick. Widower of Mary Nolan; of Co. Kilkenny, Ireland; marr. Halifax 14 Jan. 1833 Ellen Kennedy (q.v.) (33:68).

Walsh, Peter. S. of Patrick/Alice

(Drenan) of Co. Kilkenny, Ireland; marr. Halifax 19 June 1832 Catherine Power (q.v.) (33:68).

Walsh, Richard. Deserted 15 Aug. 1808 from a Detachment, 1st Bn., 23rd Regt. of Foot or Royal Welsh Fusiliers; 5'8", swarthy complexion, brown hair, grey eyes, 24, b. Ireland; advertised *The Weekly Chronicle*, 26 Aug. 1808 (28:34).

Walsh, Richard. Of Camona, Co. Tipperary, Ireland; marr. Halifax 10 May 1835 Catherine Walsh (q.v.) (34:139).

Walsh, Richard. S. of James/Margaret of Ballingerry, Co. Kilkenny, Ireland; marr. Halifax 4 Feb. 1829 Mary Brawders (q.v.) (32:119).

Walsh, Richard. S. of John/Eleanor (Doulan) of Parish St. John, Kilkenny City, Ireland; marr. Halifax 18 Apr. 1828 Margaret Jones (32:120).

Walsh, Richard. S. of Michael/Elenor (Quirk) of Co. Tipperary, Ireland; marr. Halifax 28 May 1835 Ellen Conway (q.v.) (34:139).

Walsh, Richard. S. of Thomas/Joanna of Co. Kilkenny, Ireland; marr. Halifax 2 July 1838 Alice Walsh (q.v.) (34:139).

Walsh, Thomas. S. of Thomas/Margaret (Ryan) of Carrick-on-Suir, Tipperary, Ireland; marr. Halifax 2 Oct. 1810 Mary Purcell (30:112).

Walsh, Thomas. S. of John/Mary (Grant) of Co. Kilkenny, Ireland; marr. Halifax 6 Feb. 1830 Mary Byrnes (q.v.) (32:120).

Walsh, Thomas. S. of Martin/Bridget (Capel) of Callan, Co. Kilkenny, Ireland; marr. Halifax 8 July 1830 Anne Crook (q.v.) (32:120).

Walsh, Thomas. S. of James/Mary (Grace) of Parish Kilmacow, Co.

Kilkenny, Ireland; marr. Halifax 7 Aug. 1829 Catherine Tobin (q.v.) (32:120).

Walsh, Thomas. S. of Thomas/Honora (Nagle) of Co. Cork, Ireland; marr. Halifax 23 July 1839 Joanna Sullivan (q.v.) (34:139).

Walsh, Thomas. S. of James/Honora (O'Mara) of Co. Tipperary, Ireland; marr. Halifax 16 Apr. 1845 Ann Aheran (q.v.) (35:145).

Walsh, Thomas. Widower of Honora Aheran; of Co. Cork, Ireland; marr. Halifax 11 Jan. 1831 Mary Crowley (q.v.) (33:68).

Walsh, William. S. of Robert/Mary (Ruffe) of Parish Tubbrid, Co. Kilkenny, Ireland; marr. Halifax 26 Oct. 1822 Nancy Feishkence (31:54).

Walsh, William. S. of Thomas/Mary (Murphy) of Co. Wexford, Ireland; marr. Halifax 1 May 1833 Margaret Mahony (33:68).

Walt, Thomas. Loyalist; plus 1 f.; mustered at Digby 19 May 1784 (39:196).

Walters, William. Loyalist; mustered at Digby 19 May 1784 (39:196).

Waltin, Jonathan. Loyalist; plus 1 svt.; mustered at Digby 19 May 1784 (39:197).

Walton, Thomas. 24; husbandman; Hull, Yorkshire, to Halifax; on JENNY 3-10 April 1775 (22:124).

Ward, Ebenezer. Loyalist; plus 1 f./2 ch./1 svt.; mustered at Digby 19 May 1784 (39:196).

Ward, Elizabeth. 22; wife of William; Hull, Yorkshire, to Nova Scotia; on TWO FRIENDS 28 Feb.-7 Mar. 1774 (25:28).

Ward, James. Loyalist; plus 1 f./3 ch.; mustered at Digby 19 May 1784 (39:196).

Ward, John. S. of David/Eleanor (Carthy) of Co. Tipperary, Ireland;
marr. Halifax 4 Nov. 1828 Martha
Nox (q.v.) (32:120).

Ward, Jonah. Loyalist; mustered at
Digby 19 May 1784 (39:196).

Ward, Jonas. Arr. Annapolis from New
York 19 Oct. 1782 (37:125).

Ward, Majr. Plus 1 f./4 ch. 8+/4 ch.
-8; arr. Annapolis from New York
19 Oct. 1782 (37:126).

Ward, Mary. Dau. of Patrick/Joanna
(Power) of Co. Waterford, Ireland;
marr. Halifax 30 July 1833 Thomas
Stafford (q.v.) (33:67).

Ward, Moses. 18 mos.; s. of William;
Hull, Yorkshire, to Nova Scotia;
on TWO FRIENDS 28 Feb.-7 Mar. 1774
(25:28).

Ward, Patrick. S. of Roger/Elizabeth
(Tracey) of King's Co., Ireland;
marr. Halifax 17 Feb. 1829 Mary
Hickey; entire entry ruled out in
register (q.v.) (32:120).

Ward, Thomas. Loyalist; plus 1 f./1
ch./3 svts.; mustered at Digby 19
May 1784 (39:196).

Ward, William. 24; farmer; Hull,
Yorkshire, to Nova Scotia; on TWO
FRIENDS 28 Feb.-7 Mar. 1774 (25:
28).

Warde, Edmund. Farmer; Port Roseway
Associate (6:18).

Warde, Ira. Farmer; Port Roseway
Associate (6:18).

Warl, Thomas. Loyalist; mustered at
Digby 19 May 1784 (39:196).

Warn, Samuel. Loyalist; plus 1 f./2
ch.; mustered at Digby 19 May 1784
(39:197).

Warner, Jessey. Liverpool proprietor
(19:102).

Warregan, Patrick. Loyalist; plus 1
f./1 ch./2 svts.; mustered at Digby 19 May 1784 (39:196).

Warren, Edward. S. of Richard/Susan-
na; widower of Anne Duggan; of Co.
Tipperary, Ireland; marr. Halifax
18 May 1824 Elenor Feader (31:54).

Warren, John. S. of Lawrence/Ann
(Dooly) of Co. Carlow, Ireland;
marr. Halifax 8 Aug. 1832 Catherine Smith (q.v.) (33:68).

Warrengton, James. Loyalist; mustered
at Digby 19 May 1784 (39:197).

Warwick, John. Grantee "Digby New
Grant" 29 Jan. 1801 (5:82).

Washburn, Ebenezer. From Mass.; land
grant at Truro 1759 (4:242).

Washburn, Ebenr. Plus 1 f./3 (5?) ch.
8+/2 ch. -8; arr. Annapolis from
New York 19 Oct. 1782 (37:125).

Washington, Bridget. Dau. of Patrick/
Ann (Ryan) of Poortown, Co. Kilkenny, Ireland; marr. Halifax 16
Sep. 1831 James Whelan (q.v.)
(33:68).

Washington, John. S. of Patrick/Ann
(Ryan) of Poortown, Co. Kilkenny,
Ireland; marr. Halifax 18 Feb.
1833 Margaret Tierney (q.v.) (33:
68).

Washington, John. S. of Patrick/Ann
(Ryan) of Poortown, Co. Kilkenny,
Ireland; widower of Margaret Tier-
ney; marr. Halifax 12 Jan. 1843
Mary Ireland, widow of David Lahy
(35:145).

Washington, Margaret. Dau. of Pa-
trick/Mary (Rine) of Poorstown,
Co. Kilkenny, Ireland; marr. Halifax 31 Aug. 1827 Thomas Mulcahy
(q.v.) (32:116).

Washington, Margaret. See Mulcahy,
Thomas.

Waterman, Elizabeth. B. Plymouth,
Mass., 23 Aug. 1759; dau. of Elkanah; ca. 1760 (47:126:94).

Waterman, Elkanah. Plymouth, Mass.,
to Liverpool ca. 1760 (47:126:94).

Waterman, John. Liverpool proprietor (19:102).

Waterman, Mary. Wife of Elkanah; Plymouth, Mass., to Liverpool ca. 1760 (47:126:94).

Waterman, Mary. Wife or widow; dau. of Silas/Mary West; to Liverpool ca. 1760 (47:126:96).

Waterman, Mercy. B. Plymouth, Mass., 30 July 1757; dau. of Elkanah; ca. 1760 (47:126:94).

Waterman, Mercy. Dau. of Elkanah/Mary; to Liverpool by 1777 (47:126:283).

Waters, Samuel. Plus wife/1 ch.; Mass. to Chester with first settlers (16:45).

Waters, William. S. of William/Ellen (Kelly) of Co. Tipperary, Ireland; marr. Halifax 25 Sep. 1832 Ellen Smyth (q.v.) (33:68).

Watersworth, John. 43; farmer; Hull, Yorkshire, to Nova Scotia; on TWO FRIENDS 28 Feb.-7 Mar. 1774 (25:30).

Watson, Alexander. S. of James/Mary; to (or b.?) Liverpool by 1783 (47:126:285).

Watson, Elizabeth. Dau. of Francis/Sera (Andrews) of Hull, England; marr. Halifax 1 Feb. 1818 John Carroll (q.v.) (31:42).

Watson, Francis. 18; taylor; Hull, Yorkshire, to Annapolis on JENNY 3-10 April 1775 (22:124).

Watson, Isaac. Plus wife/4 ch.; Plympton, Mass., to Chester with first settlers (16:45).

Watson, James Jr. S. of James/Mary; to (or b.?) Liverpool by 1783 (47:126:285).

Watson, John. 33, farmer; Hull to Fort Cumberland on ALBION 7-14 March 1774 (21:138).

Watson, John. Plus 1 f./4 ch./2 svts;

"total 10;" Port Roseway Associate (6:18).

Watson, Mary. See Magrah, Mary.

Watt, Charles. Grantee "Digby New Grant" 29 Jan. 1801 (5:82).

Watt, Thomas. Grantee "Digby New Grant" 29 Jan. 1801 (5:82).

Watters, Samuel. Loyalist; plus 1 ch.; mustered at Digby 19 May 1784 (39:197).

Watts, John. Plus 1 f./2 ch./2 svts.; Port Roseway Associate (6:18).

Watts, R. D. Laborer; English; 20; Liverpool to Nova Scotia June 1864 on INDIAN QUEEN (45:182).

Waymouth, Elizabeth. Dau. of Thomas/Mary (?Gewin) of Devonshire, England; marr. Halifax 20 Nov. 1814 Edward Connolly (q.v.) (30:103).

Weare, Thos. Arr. Annapolis from New York 19 Oct. 1782 (37:125).

Weaver, Michael. Loyalist; to New Edinburgh 21 Jan. 1783; d. 4 June 1797 (48:304).

Webb, Susannah. Dau. of Thomas/Eliza (Spilane) of Co. Cork, Ireland; marr. Halifax 5 Oct. 1831 Jeremiah Conway (q.v.) (33:55).

Webster, Andrew. Dr.; From Orono, Me.; married Liverpool 1811 Anne Barss; remained (19:116).

Webster, Andrew. Dr.; s. of Andrew/Martha; Orono, Mass. (now Me.), to Liverpool by 1811 (47:128:31).

Webster, Andrew. S. of Andrew/Martha; d. Liverpool 10 Aug. 1855 ae 77; from Orono, Me. (49:121).

Webster, John. 25; taylor; Hull, Yorkshire, to Nova Scotia; on TWO FRIENDS 28 Feb.-7 Mar. 1774 (25:29).

Weeks, Simon. Loyalist; plus 4 ch.; mustered at Gulliver's Hole/St. Mary's Bay/Sissiboo 1/6 June 1784; settled at St. Mary's Bay (Plympton, Barton, Brighton) (40:263).

Welch, Morris. Loyalist; plus 1 f./4 ch.; mustered at Digby 19 May 1784 (39:196).

Weld, Morris. Loyalist; plus 1 f./4 ch.; mustered at Digby 19 May 1784 (39:196).

Weldon, Andrew. 12, s. of Ann; Hull to Fort Cumberland on ALBION 7-14 March 1774 (21:140).

Weldon, Ann. 1, daughter of Ann; Hull to Fort Cumberland on ALBION 7-14 March 1774 (21:140).

Weldon, Ann. 38, to join husband; Hull to Fort Cumberland on ALBION 7-14 March 1774 (21:140).

Weldon, Elizabeth. 8, daughter of Ann; Hull to Fort Cumberland on ALBION 7-14 March 1774 (21:140).

Weldon, Thomas. 4, s. of Ann; Hull to Fort Cumberland on ALBION 7-14 March 1774 (21:140).

Wells, Francis. (Heirs) grantee "Digby New Grant" 29 Jan. 1801 (5:82).

Welsh, Mary. See Roach, Mary.

Welsh, Morris. Grantee "Digby New Grant" 29 Jan. 1801 (5:82).

Welton, Bethel. Loyalist; mustered at Digby 19 May 1784 (39:196).

Welton, Ezekiel. Loyalist; plus 1 f./2 ch.; mustered at Digby 19 May 1784 (39:196).

Wentworth, John. Gov.; Loyalist; Portsmouth, N.H., to Boston, Mass., 1775 on CANSO; to Halifax Mar. 1776 (41:4).

West, Bethia. Dau. of Thomas of Liverpool; b. Chatham, Mass., 28 Jan. 1756 (50:115).

West, Bethiah. B. New England 28 Jan. 1756; dau. of Thomas/Sarah; to Liverpool ca. 1760 (47:126:100).

West, Bethiah. Dau. Capt. Thomas/Sarah; to Liverpool by 1774 (47:126:169).

West, Betty. Dau. of John/Phebe; to (or b.?) Liverpool by 1796 (47:127:57).

West, Charles. Liverpool proprietor (19:101).

West, Charles. To Liverpool ca. 1760 (47:126:97).

West, Elizabeth Crowell. Wife of Thomas of Barrington; b. ca. 1738 (50:115).

West, John. Liverpool proprietor (19:101).

West, John. S. of Silas/Mary; to Liverpool ca. 1760 (47:126:96).

West, John. To Liverpool ca. 1760 (47:126:96).

West, Mary. From Plymouth, Mass., to Liverpool ca. 1760 (47:126:94).

West, Mehitabel. Dau. of William/Bethiah; to (or b.?) Liverpool by 1797 (47:127:267).

West, Paul. S. of Thomas/Sarah; to (or b.?) Liverpool by 1791 (47:127:118).

West, Peter. S. of Thomas/Sarah; to (or b.?) Liverpool by 1791 (47:127:117).

West, Phebe. Dau. of John/Phebe; to (or b.?) Liverpool by 1791 (47:127:122).

West, Phebe. Wife of John; to Liverpool ca. 1760 (47:126:96).

West, Sarah Hamilton. Wife of Thomas of Liverpool (50:115).

West, Sarah. B. New England 22 Sep. 1760; dau. of Thomas/Sarah; to Liverpool ca. 1760 (47:126:100).

West, Sarah. Dau. of Thomas/Sarah; to (or b.?) Liverpool by 1780 (47:127:50).

West, Sarah. Dau. of Thomas of Liverpool; b. Chatham, Mass., 22 Sep. 1760 (50:115).

West, Sarah. Wife of Thomas; to Liverpool ca. 1760 (47:126:100).

West, Silas. S. of John/Phoebe; to (or b.?) Liverpool by 1795 (47: 127:206).

West, Thomas. B. ca. 1725; Liverpool proprietor; there bef. 15 Sep. 1762 (50:115).

West, Thomas. B. New England 6 July 1757; s. of Thomas/Sarah; to Liverpool ca. 1760 (47:126:100).

West, Thomas. Grantee at Barrington; d. there bef. 1769 (50:115).

West, Thomas. Liverpool proprietor (19:101).

West, Thomas. S. of Thomas of Liverpool; b. Chatham, Mass., 6 July 1757 (50:115).

West, Thomas. To Liverpool ca. 1760 (47:126:100).

West, William. Liverpool proprietor (19:102).

West, William. S. of Silas/Mary; to Liverpool by 1771 (47:126:164).

Weston, Bridget. Dau. of James/Eliza (Conway) of Parish Kilmacow, Co. Kilkenny, Ireland; marr. Halifax 20 May 1835 Thomas Finley (q.v.) (34:130).

Weston, Bridget. Dau. of James/Elizabeth (Conway) of Parish Kilmacow, Co. Kilkenny, Ireland; widow of Thomas Finlay; marr. Halifax 29 Feb. 1836 Michael Mackey (q.v.) (34:134).

Weston, Bridget. Dau. of James/Elizabeth (Conway) of Kilmacow, Co. Kilkenny, Ireland; widow of John Mackey; marr. Halifax 3 Aug. 1843 Martin Murphy (q.v.) (35:142).

Weston, Ellen. Dau. of James/Honora (Grant) of Co. Kilkenny, Ireland; marr. Halifax 8 May 1834 John Molony (q.v.) (33:64).

Weston, Ellen. Dau. of James/Elizabeth (Conway) of Co. Kilkenny, Ireland; marr. Halifax 29 Apr.

1835 John Kean (q.v.) (34:132).

Weston, Patrick. S. of John/Bridget (Cleary) of Parish Mullinavat, Co. Kilkenny, Ireland; marr. Halifax 25 Oct. 1843 Johanna Carroll (q.v.) (35:145).

Wetton, Richard. Plus 1 f./1 ch./2 svts.; mariner; Port Roseway Associate (6:18).

Wheatley, Thomas. 53; farmer; Hull, Yorkshire, to Port Cumberland on JENNY 3-10 April 1775 (22:123).

Whebby, Edward. S. of Edmund/Ann (Cheany) of Pendover, Somersetsh., England, marr. Halifax 14 June 1833 Bridget Dunn (q.v.) (33:68).

Wheeler, David. From Mass.; land grant at Truro 1759 (4:242).

Wheeler, Deliverance. From Mass.; land grant at Truro 1759 (4:242).

Wheeler, Ephraim. From Mass.; land grant at Truro 1759 (4:242).

Wheeler, George. From Mass.; land grant at Truro 1759 (4:242).

Wheeler, Hezekiah. Loyalist; mustered at Gulliver's Hole/St. Mary's Bay/ Sissiboo 1/6 June 1784; settled at Gulliver's Hole (a cove and harbor on Digby Neck) (40:263).

Wheeler, Mary. Dau. of Raphael/Mary; to (or b.?) Liverpool by 1787 (47: 127:54).

Wheeler, Raphael. Maryland to Liverpool by 1771 (47:126:281).

Wheeler, Samuel. From Mass.; land grant at Truro 1759 (4:242).

Wheeler, William. From Mass.; land grant at Truro 1759 (4:242).

Wheelock, Obediah. New England to Annapolis 1760 (18:271).

Wheely, Catherine. Spinster; English; 26; Liverpool to Nova Scotia June 1864 on INDIAN QUEEN (45:182).

Whelan, Andrew. S. of Edmund/Mary (Power) of Co. Waterford, Ireland;

marr. Halifax 16 Jan. 1833 Ann
Murphy *(q.v.)* (33:68).

Whelan, Catherine. Dau. of Thomas/
Margaret (Delany) of Co. Kilkenny,
Ireland; marr. Halifax 20 Apr.
1830 John Smyth *(q.v.)* (32:118).

Whelan, Catherine. Dau. of John/
Catherine (Scully) of Co. Kilkenny, Ireland; marr. Halifax 28 Jan.
1831 William Clancy *(q.v.)*
(33:55).

Whelan, David. S. of Thomas/Joana
(Heneberry) of Ballyneal, Co. Tipperary, Ireland; marr. Halifax 14
June 1837 Joanna Brophy *(q.v.)*
(34:139).

Whelan, Edward. S. of Maurice/Ellen
(Murphy) of Co. Kilkenny, Ireland;
marr. Halifax 16 Aug. 1832 Mary
widow of Thomas Wall (33:68).

Whelan, James. S. of John/Elizabeth
(Power) of Co. Kilkenny, Ireland;
marr. Halifax 16 Sep. 1831 Bridget
Washington *(q.v.)* (33:68).

Whelan, James. S. of John/Joanna of
Co. Waterford, Ireland; marr.
Halifax 18 June 1832 Elizabeth
Ross (33:68).

Whelan, James. S. of Thomas/Mary
(Egan) of Co. Tipperary, Ireland;
marr. Halifax 27 Aug. 1832 Honora
Clary *(q.v.)* (33:68).

Whelan, Lawrence. S. of Maurice/
Elenor (Murphy) of Co. Kilkenny,
Ireland; marr. Halifax 27 Nov.
1833 Anne Johnston *(q.v.)* (33:69).

Whelan, Margaret. Dau. of Edward/Mary
(Power) of Callan, Co. Kilkenny,
Ireland; marr. Halifax 28 Aug.
1829 Andrew Magrath *(q.v.)* (32:
115).

Whelan, Margaret. Dau. of Mathew/
Alice (Pendergast) of Co. Kilkenny, Ireland; marr. Halifax 3 June
1833 Thomas Thompson *(q.v.)* (33:

67).

Whelan, Margaret. Dau. of Patrick/
Ellen (Dowlin) of Co. Kilkenny,
Ireland; marr. Halifax 16 June
1838 Henry Cooper *(q.v.)* (34:128).

Whelan, Mary. Dau. of Pierce/Margaret
(Roche) of Co. Cork, Ireland;
marr. Halifax 14 Jan. 1833 Timothy
O'Rourke *(q.v.)* (33:65).

Whelan, Mary. Dau. of Walter/Eliza
(Stokes) of Co. Cork, Ireland;
marr. Halifax 3 Mar. 1840 John
Dunn *(q.v.)* (34:129).

Whelan, Patrick. Of Co. Kilkenny,
Ireland; widower of Honora Broth-
ers; marr. Halifax 27 Apr. 1843
Catherine Henebery *(q.v.)* (35:
146).

Whelan, Patrick. Sailor; s. of Pa-
trick/Mary (Burke) of Cove of
Cork, Ireland; marr. Halifax 13
Oct. 1826 Elizabeth Brown (32:
120).

Whelan, Sarah. Dau. of John/Mary
(Moore) of Thurles, Co. Tipperary,
Ireland; widow of John Tobin;
marr. Halifax 25 May 1823 Daniel
Hallaghan *(q.v.)* (31:46).

Wheton?, Richard. See Richard Wetton.

Whidden. See Widden.

Whily, John. S. of John/Ellen (Connors) of Co. Carlow, Ireland;
marr. Halifax 17 July 1835 Catherine Fahey *(q.v.)* (34:139).

Whippey, William. From Mass.; land
grant at Onslow 21 Feb. 1769 (4:
225).

Whippy, Samuel. From Mass.; land
grant (to heirs) at Onslow 21 Feb.
1769 (4:225).

White, Amos. Plus 1 f./4 ch.; tailor;
Port Roseway Associate (6:18).

White, Bridget. Dau. of Michael/
Catherine of St. Johnswell, Co.
Kilkenny, Ireland; marr. Halifax 7

Feb. 1829 Jeremiah Neagle (q.v.)
(32:116).

White, Duncan. Plus 1 f./1 svt.; Port
Roseway Associate (6:18).

White, Gideon. Plus 1 f./3 ch./3
svts.; farmer; Port Roseway Associate (6:18).

White, Gideon. S. of Cornelius of
Marshfield, Mass.; d. Shelburne
1834 (20:46).

White, Henry. From Mass.; land grant
at Truro 1759 (4:242).

White, James. Plus 1 f./3 ch./3
svts.; Port Roseway Associate (6:
18).

White, Richard. Plus 1 f./2 ch./5
svts.; farmer; Port Roseway Associate (6:18).

White, Richard. S. of William/Alice
(Hannan) of Co. Tipperary, Ire-
land; marr. Halifax 8 Jan. 1835
Eleanor Quigley (q.v.) (34:139).

Whitford, Desire. Wife of Joseph; to
Liverpool ca. 1760 (47:126:98).

Whitford, John. Laborer; English; 26;
Liverpool to Nova Scotia May 1864
on EUROCLYDON (45:182).

Whitford, Joseph. Liverpool proprietor (19:102).

Whitford, Joseph. To Liverpool ca.
1760 (47:126:98).

Whitman, John. New England to Annapolis on CHARMING MOLLY May 1760
(18:271).

Whitman, Mercy. Dau. of John/Mercy;
to (or b.?) Liverpool by 1787 (47:
127:55).

Whitmore, Mary. Dau. of Josiah/Mary;
to Liverpool ca. 1760 (47:126:96).

Whittemore, Abigail. B. Plymouth,
Mass., 3 Sep. 1772; dau. of Jo-
siah/Experience; to Liverpool ca.
1784 (47:127:124).

Whittemore, Experience. Wife of
Josiah; dau. of William Sargeant;

to Liverpool ca. 1784 (47:127:
124).

Whittemore, Experience. B. Charlton,
Mass., 15 Apr. 1778; dau. of Jo-
siah/Experience; to Liverpool ca.
1784 (47:127:124).

Whittemore, Experience. Dau. of Jo-
siah/Experience; to (or b.?) Liverpool by 1794 (47:127:204).

Whittemore, Joanna. Dau. of
Josiah/Mary; to Liverpool by 1772
(47:126:165).

Whittemore, Joseph. Plus wife/2 ch.;
Mass., to Chester 30 July 1759
(16:46).

Whittemore, Joseph. Plus wife/2 ch.;
Shrewsbury, Mass., to Chester with
first settlers (16:45).

Whittemore, Josiah Jr. B. Killingsley, Conn., 18 Nov. 1783; s. of
Josiah/Experience; to Liverpool
ca. 1784 (47:127:124).

Whittemore, Josiah. To Liverpool ca.
1760 (47:126:95).

Whittemore, Josiah. S. of Josiah/
Mary; Plymouth, Mass., to Liverpool ca. 1784 (47:127:123-124).

Whittemore, Mary. Wife of Josiah; to
Liverpool ca. 1760 (47:126:95).

Whittemore, Thomas. B. Killingsley,
Conn., 18 Apr. 1780; s. of Josiah/
Experience; to Liverpool ca. 1784
(47:127:124).

Widden, David. From N.H.; effective
land grant at Truro 31 Oct. 1765
(4:245).

Widden James. From N.H.; effective
land grant at Truro 31 Oct. 1765
(4:245).

Wiederholtz, Adolph. Lunenburg,
Mass., to Chester with first
settlers (16:45).

Wiederholtz, Francis. 9; s. of
Adolph; Lunenburg, Mass., to
Chester with first settlers

(16:45).

Wiegman, J. Waldeck Service; mustered at Bear River 11/25 June 1784 (38: 261).

Wiesenborn, J. Waldeck Service; mustered at Bear River 11/25 June 1784 (38:261).

Wigham, John. Arr. Annapolis from New York 19 Oct. 1782 (37:126).

Wilkins, Robert. Plus 1 f./3 ch./3 svts.; grocer; Port Roseway Associate (6:18).

Wilks, John. From Ireland; land grant at Londonderry 6 Mar. 1775 (4: 258).

William, Frederick. Grantee "Digby New Grant" 29 Jan. 1801 (5:82).

William, Thomas. Esq.; grantee "Digby New Grant" 29 Jan. 1801 (5:82).

Williams, Anne. Dau. of Alvin/Phebe (Ryan) of New York; marr. Halifax 19 Oct. 1812 John Crow (q.v.) (30: 104).

Williams, Daniel. Plus 1 f./1 ch.; Port Roseway Associate (6:18).

Williams, Elijah. Esq.; arr. Annapolis from New York 19 Oct. 1782 (37:126).

Williams, Elijah. Loyalist; New York to N.S. 1782 (41:14).

Williams, Ezekiel. From Ireland; land grant at Londonderry 6 Mar. 1775 (4:258).

Williams, Henry. Of Liverpool, England; marr. Halifax 3 Aug. 1837 Ann Mulrean (q.v.) (34:139).

Williams, John Jr. Farmer; Port Roseway Associate (6:18).

Williams, John. Free negro; plus 1 f.; mustered at Digby 19 May 1784 (39:196).

Williams, John. From Ireland; land grant at Londonderry 6 Mar. 1775 (4:258).

Williams, John. Loyalist; mustered at

Gulliver's Hole/St. Mary's Bay/ Sissiboo 1/6 June 1784; settled at Sissiboo (now Weymouth) (40:263).

Williams, John. Plus 1 f./5 ch.; farmer; Port Roseway Associate (6: 18).

Williams, Mary Ann. Dau. of Robert/ Mary (Raredon) of Co. Cork, Ireland; widow of James Culbert 100th Regt.; marr. Halifax 23 June 1825 Leonard Huppert (q.v.) (31:47).

Williams, Richard. Loyalist; plus 1 f./2 svts.; mustered at Digby 19 May 1784 (39:196).

Williams, Samuel. Farmer; Port Roseway Associate (6:18).

Williams, William. New England to Annapolis on CHARMING MOLLY May 1760 (18:271).

Williamson, Thomas. S. of John/Jane (Stuart) of Co. Down, Ireland; marr. Halifax 14 Dec. 1812 Mary O'Brien (q.v.) (30:112).

Willison, John. 36; carpenter; Hull, Yorkshire, to Nova Scotia; on TWO FRIENDS 28 Feb.-7 Mar. 1774 (25: 28).

Willison, William. See Wilson, William.

Wills, Charles. Surgeon; English; 20; Liverpool to Nova Scotia June 1864 on INDIAN QUEEN (45:182).

Wills, Hannah. Loyalist; plus 1 svt.; mustered at Digby 19 May 1784 (39: 197).

Willson, David. Plus 1 f./1 ch. 2 svts.; Port Roseway Associate (6: 18).

Willson, Henry. S. of Henry; b. Chatham, Mass., ca. 1735; sailed own vessel POMPEY DICK to Barrington 1761 (50:115).

Willson, James. Plus 1 f./1 ch.; Port Roseway Associate (6:18).

Willson, Sarah Chase. Wife of Henry

(50:115).

Wilmot, James. Esq.; Loyalist; to Digby 1783; d. 4 Dec. 1804 (48: 305).

Wilmot, James. Grantee "Digby New Grant" 29 Jan. 1801 (5:82).

Wilson, Abraham. Grantee "Digby New Grant" 29 Jan. 1801 (5:82).

Wilson, Abraham. Loyalist; plus 1 f./1 ch.; mustered at Digby 19 May 1784 (39:197).

Wilson, Benjamin. Disbanded officer, 1st N.J. Vols.; mustered at Gulliver's Hole/St. Mary's Bay/Sissiboo 1/6 June 1784; settled at St. Mary's Bay (Plympton, Barton, Brighton) (40:263).

Wilson, Catherine. Dau. of Richard/Mary (Wall) of Co. Waterford, Ireland; marr. Halifax 27 Sep. 1842 David White (35:146).

Wilson, Claud. From Ireland; land grant at Londonderry 6 Mar. 1775 (4:258).

Wilson, James. 19, joiner; Hull to Port Cumberland on ALBION 7-14 March 1774 (21:139).

Wilson, James. From Mass.; land grant at Onslow 21 Feb. 1769 (4:224).

Wilson, James. From Mass.; land grant at Truro 1759 (4:242).

Wilson, James. From Ireland; land grant at Londonderry 6 Mar. 1775 (4:258).

Wilson, James. Laborer; Irish; 19; Liverpool to Nova Scotia May 1864 on EUROCLYDON (45:182).

Wilson, John. 46; farmer; Hull, Yorkshire, to Nova Scotia; on TWO FRIENDS 28 Feb.-7 Mar. 1774 (25: 28).

Wilson, John. Master of Transport; plus 1 svt.; mustered at Digby 19 May 1784 (39:196).

Wilson, John. Plus 1 f./2 ch./1 svt.;

Port Roseway Associate (6:18).

Wilson, Peter. From Mass.; land grant at Onslow 21 Feb. 1769 (4:225).

Wilson, Robert. Loyalist; mustered at Digby 19 May 1784 (39:197).

Wilson, Samuel. From Ireland; land grant at Londonderry 6 Mar. 1775 (4:258).

Wilson, Thomas. 50, joiner; Hull to Port Cumberland on ALBION 7-14 March 1774 (21:139).

Wilson, Thomas. land grant at Londonderry 6 Mar. 1775 (4:258).

Wilson, William. From Ireland; land grant (to heirs) at Londonderry 6 Mar. 1775 (4:258).

Wilson, William. Real name probably Willison; disbanded soldier, 1st N.J. Vols.; carpenter; mustered at Gulliver's Hole/St. Mary's Bay/Sissiboo 1/6 June 1784 (40:263).

Wilton, Ezekiel. See Welton, Ezekiel.

Winchester, Josiah. Grantee "Digby New Grant" 29 Jan. 1801 (5:82).

Winderhold, Joseph. Loyalist; mustered at Digby 19 May 1784 (39: 197).

Windill, -----. Cpl.; German Service; mustered at Bear River 11/25 June 1784 (38:261).

Winn, David. 17, farmer; Hull to Port Cumberland on ALBION 7-14 March 1774 (21:140).

Winn, William. 27, farmer; Hull to Port Cumberland on ALBION 7-14 March 1774 (21:140).

Winslow, Edward. Lt.Col.; Loyalist; New York to N.S. 1782 (41:13).

Winslow, George. To Liverpool ca. 1760 (47:126:96).

Winslow, George. Liverpool proprietor (19:102).

Winslow, John. New England to Annapolis on CHARMING MOLLY May 1760 (18:271).

Winslow, Pelham. Plus 1 f./2 ch./2
svts.; farmer; Port Roseway Associate (6:18).

Winston, Daniel. From Mass.; land
grant at Truro 1759 (4:242).

Wise, Bridget. See Flood, Bridget.

Wise, William. S. of James/Anastasia
(Burke) of Co. Tipperary, Ireland;
marr. Halifax 23 Feb. 1811 Mary
Fitzgerald (q.v.) (30:112).

Wise, William. S. of John/Ann (Downy)
of Co. Tipperary, Ireland; marr.
Halifax 2 July 1833 Ann Croke
(q.v.) (33:69).

Wiswall, Peleg. Grantee "Digby New
Grant" 29 Jan. 1801 (5:82).

Witham, Sara. Widow of John Story; of
Co. Meath, Ireland; marr. Halifax
6 July 1818 Andrew Charlocke
(q.v.) (31:53).

Wolf, Magdalena. Beringen, Canton
Schaffhausen, [Switzerland,] to
Halifax 1742 (44:196).

Woodbury, Nathan. Plus wife/3 ch.;
Mass., to Chester with first settlers (16:45).

Wooding, Stephen. 37th Regt.; s. of
Stephen/Elizabeth (Layton) of
Yorksh., England.; marr. Halifax
14 July 1841 Ellen McCarthy (q.v.)
(35:146).

Woodroffe, Jabez. Grantee "Digby New
Grant" 29 Jan. 1801 (5:82).

Woods, Abigail. Dau. of Joseph/Sarah;
to (or b.?) Liverpool by 1792 (47:
127:117).

Woods, Ellen. Dau. of James/Anastasia
(Mihan) of Clonmel, Co. Tipperary,
Ireland; marr. Halifax 13 July
1843 Lawrence Heffernan (q.v.)
(35:138).

Woods, Ellen. Dau. of Thomas/Maria
(Magher) of Co. Tipperary, Ire-
land; marr. Halifax 10 Sep. 1844
Michael Magher (q.v.) (35:141).

Woods, George. Loyalist; mustered at
Digby 19 May 1784 (39:197).

Woods, John. S. of Patrick/Sally
(McCanagh) of Belfast, Co. Antrim,
Ireland; marr. Halifax 13 Dec.
1822 Sara Gill (31:54).

Woods, Joseph Jr. S. of Joseph/Sarah;
to (or b.?) Liverpool by 1792 (47:
127:275).

Woods, Joseph. Liverpool proprietor
(19:102).

Woods, Joseph. To Liverpool ca. 1760
(47:126:160).

Woods, Mary. Dau. of Joseph/Sarah; to
(or b.?) Liverpool by 1789 (47:
127:125).

Wortman, Philip. Grantee "Digby New
Grant" 29 Jan. 1801 (5:82).

Wortman, Philip. Loyalist; mustered
at Digby 19 May 1784 (39:196).

Wright, Deborah. From Mass.; land
grant at Onslow 21 Feb. 1769 (4:
225).

Wright, James. From N.H.; effective
land grant at Truro 31 Oct. 1765
(4:245).

Wright, John. Grantee "Digby New
Grant" 29 Jan. 1801 (5:82).

Wright, John. Loyalist; mustered at
Digby 19 May 1784 (39:197).

Wrightson, Elizabeth. 20; servant;
Hull, Yorkshire, to Nova Scotia;
on TWO FRIENDS 28 Feb.-7 Mar. 1774
(25:29).

Wriland, H. German Service; plus 1
ch.; mustered at Bear River 11/25
June 1784 (38:261).

Wry, John. 23; weaver; Hull, Yorkshire, to Nova Scotia; on TWO
FRIENDS 28 Feb.-7 Mar. 1774 (25:
30).

Wyse, Alexander. S. of John/Medleton
(McLellan) of London, England;
marr. Halifax 2 Jan. 1837 Bridget
Flood (q.v.) (34:139).

Wyse, Alexander. Ship carpenter; bur. Halifax 29 Apr. 1841 ae. 45 (34: 125).

- Y -

Yandle, Joseph. Laborer; not settled; mustered at Digby 19 May 1784 (39:197).

Yate, Tomas. 22; mason; Hull, Yorkshire, to Nova Scotia; on TWO FRIENDS 28 Feb.-7 Mar. 1774 (25: 29).

Yeomans, John. Pvt., Rifle Brig.; son of Richard/Mary (Jones) of England, marr. Halifax 9 Sep. 1833 Rose Giron (q.v.) (33:69).

Young, Elizebeth. Dau. of Henry/ Elizebeth; to Liverpool by 1762 (47:126:163).

Young, Henry. Liverpool proprietor (19:101).

Young, James. Loyalist; mustered at Digby 19 May 1784 (39:197).

Young, Jane Frances. Wife of George R., Esq.; eldest daughter of Thos. H. Brooking, Esq., of London, England; d. 28 Dec. 1841 at Halifax ae 26 (13:70).

Young, John Jr. S. of John; b. Chatham, Mass., 2 June 1733; d. Liverpool 15 Mar. 1761 (50:116).

Young, Mary Ann. Dau. of William/ Anastasia (Allan) of Kinsale, Co. Cork, Ireland; marr. Halifax 11 Feb. 1834 William Whipples (33: 69).

Young, Mary Doane. Wife of John Jr. (50:116).

Young, Mary. Dau. of -----/Martha; to Liverpool by 1773 (47:126:165).

Young, Solomon. S. of Henry; to Liverpool ca. 1760 (47:126:96).

Young, William. Asst. Sarg. [?Surg.] Gen. Hosp.; plus 1 svt.; mustered at Digby 19 May 1784 (39:197).

Young, Zebulon. From Mass.; land grant at Truro 1759 (4:242).

Yuill, James Jr. From N.H.; effective land grant at Truro 31 Oct. 1765 (4:244).

Yuill, James. From N.H.; effective land grant at Truro 31 Oct. 1765 (4:244).

Yule, Alexander. Seaman; not settled; mustered at Digby 19 May 1784 (39:197).

- Z -

Zeigler, John. Waldeck Service; mustered at Bear River 11/25 June 1784 (38:261).

APPENDIX

IMMIGRANT VESSELS

Name and Source Reference No.

ALBION, 1774 (21)
CANSO, 1775 (41)
CHARMING MOLLY, 1760 (18)
COMMERCE, 1803 (51)
EUROCLYDON, 1864 (45)
EUROPA, 1864 (45)
INDIAN QUEEN, 1864 (45)
JENNY, 1775 (22)
JOSEPH, 1784 (39)
KEDAR, 1864 (45)
MARIANNE (33)
MARS (30)
MELAMPOS, 1806 (28)
PEGGY, 1784 (39)
POLLY, 1799 (29)
POMPEY DICK, 1761 (50)
PROVIDENCE, 1775 (23)
SQUIRREL, 1775 (24)
STAFFORD, 1783 (43)
TWO FRIENDS, 1774 (25)

BIBLIOGRAPHY

PUBLICATIONS SCREENED

Acadiensis, Vols. 1-8 (1901-1908),
all issued.
Family History, New Series, Vol. 9.
The Irish Ancestor, Vols. 6(1974),
7(1975), 8(1976), 9(1977).
Lost in Canada? Vol. 15(1990).
Maine Historical Magazine, Vol.
9(1894).
Mayflower Quarterly, Vol. 52(1986).
National Genealogical Society Quarterly, Vols. 62(1974), 71(1983).
New England Historical and Genealogical Register, Vols. 54(1900),
63(1909), 65(1911), 97(1963),
126(1972), 127 (1973), 128(1974).
New York Genealogical and Biographical Record, Vols. 28(1897),
34(1903).
Ohio State University Bulletin, Vol.
21(1916).
*Pennsylvania German Folklore Society
Yearbook*, Vol. 16(1951).
*Transactions of the Royal Society of
Canada*, 3rd series, Vol. 6(1912).
We Lived, all printed.

ARTICLES ABSTRACTED

(1) Brown, Helen Wright (Mrs.). "A
Barrington, Nova Scotia, Petition,"
New England Historical and Genealogical Register, 60(1906):364-366.

(2) Creighton, Agnes, "An Unforeclosed
Mortgage," *Acadiensis*, 5(1905):4:295-302.

(3) Eaton, Arthur Wentworth Hamilton,
"Bishop Charles Inglis and His Descendants," *Acadiensis*,
8(1908):3:183-202.

(4) Eaton, Arthur Wentworth Hamilton,
"The Settling of Colchester County,
Nova Scotia, by New England Puritans
and Ulster Scotsmen," *Transactions of
the Royal Society of Canada*, 3rd
series, 6(1912):2:221-265.

(5) Edsall, Thomas Henry. "The Digby New
Grant," *New York Genealogical and
Biographical Record*, 28(1897):81-83.

(6) Harding, Anne Borden, "The Port
Roseway Debacle," *New England Historical and Genealogical Register*,
97(1963):3-18.

(7) Jack, David Russell, "Book-Plates,"
Acadiensis, 1(1901):2:90-95.

(8) Jack, David Russell, "Book-Plates,"
Acadiensis, 2(1902):1:43.

(9) Jack, David Russell, "Book-Plates,"
Acadiensis, 3(1903):2:131-133.

(10) Jack, David Russell, "Book-Plates."
Acadiensis, 3(1903):3:236-240.

(11) Jack, David Russell. "Book-Plates,"
Acadiensis, 3(1903):4:310.

(12) Jack, David Russell, "Book-Plates,"
Acadiensis, 4(1904):1:84-86.

(13) Jack, David Russell, "Memorials St.
Paul's Church, Halifax, N.S." *Acadiensis*, 5(1905):1:62-77.

(14) Jack, David Russell, "Old Plate,"

Acadiensis, 4(1904):1:7-9.

(15) Kirkpatrick, Robert F., "Hannah (Gorham) Coop of Queens County, Nova Scotia," The Mayflower Quarterly, 52(1986):165-167.

(16) Leavitt, Emily W. (Miss). "A List of the First Class of Settlers (of Chester, Lunenburg County, N.S.) with Their Families," New England Historical and Genealogical Register, 54(1900):44-46.

(17) Longworth, Israel, "Honorable Judge Robie: A Biographical Sketch," Acadiensis, 1:(1901):2:74.

(18) McLeod, Robert R., "Annapolis," Acadiensis, 4(1904):1:3-4.

(19) McLeod, Robert R., "Old Times in Liverpool, N.S.," Acadiensis, 4(1904):2:96-118.

(20) McLeod, Robert R., "Town of Shelburne," Acadiensis, 8(1908):1:46-49.

(21) Milner, W. C., "Records of Chignecto, Emigrants from England," New England Historical and Genealogical Register, 63(1909):134-140. (ALBION.)

(22) Milner, W. C., "Records of Chignecto, Emigrants from England," New England Historical and Genealogical Register, 65(1911):116,123-125,127. (JENNY.)

(23) Milner, W. C., "Records of Chignecto, Emigrants from England," New England Historical and Genealogical Register, 65(1911):227. (PROVIDENCE.)

(24) Milner, W. C.,"Records of Chignecto, Emigrants from England," New England Historical and Genealogical Register, 65(1911):45. (SQUIRREL.)

(25) Milner, W. C., "Records of Chignecto, Emigrants from England," New England Historical and Genealogical Register, 63(1909):28-31. (TWO FRIENDS.)

(26) "Old Nova Scotia of 1783: Fragments of an Unpublished History," Acadiensis, 2(1902):1:44-45.

(27) Owen, Isabella A., "Charlotte Elizabeth: A Forgotten Authoress, at One Time Resident in Windsor and Annapolis Royal, Nova Scotia," Acadiensis, 1(1901):4:228-235.

(28) Punch, Terrence M., "Irish Deserters at Halifax, Nova Scotia, During the Napoleonic Wars," The Irish Ancestor, 8(1976):1:33-35.

(29) Punch, Terrence M., "The Passengers on the "Polly," The Irish Ancestor, 8(1976):82-85.

(30) Punch, Terrence M., "Some Irish Immigrant Weddings in Nova Scotia 1801-1817," from records at Catholic archdiocese at Halifax, The Irish Ancestor, 6(1974):2:101-112.

(31) Punch, Terrence M., "Some Irish Immigrant Weddings in Nova Scotia 1818-1825," from records at Catholic archdiocese at Halifax, The Irish Ancestor, 7(1975):1:39-54.

(32) Punch, Terrence M., "Some Irish Immigrant Weddings in Nova Scotia 1826-1830," from records at Catholic archdiocese at Halifax, The Irish Ancestor, 7(1975):2:104-120.

(33) Punch, Terrence M., "Some Irish Immigrant Weddings in Nova Scotia 1831-1834," from records at Catholic archdiocese at Halifax, The Irish Ancestor, 8(1976):1:53-69. Some "Halifax" marriages at Dartmouth.

(34) Punch, Terrence M., "Some Irish Immigrant Weddings in Nova Scotia 1834-1840," from records at Catholic archdiocese at Halifax, The Irish Ancestor, 8(1976):2:124-139. Some "Halifax" marriages at Dartmouth.

(35) Punch, Terrence M., "Some Irish Immigrant Weddings in Nova Scotia 1841-1845," from records at Catholic

archdiocese at Halifax, *The Irish Ancestor*, 9(1977):2:132-146. Some "Halifax" marriages at Dartmouth.

(36) "Rebels in Nova Scotia During the Revolutionary War," *The Maine Historical Magazine*, 9(1894):61-70.

(37) "Return of Men, Women & Children arrived at Annapolis from New York 19th Octr. 1782 (360 persons)." *We Lived*, Issue 11(1981):125-126.

(38) Savary, A. W. "Muster Roll of Disbanded Officers, Discharged Soldiers and Loyalists Mustered at Bear River on the 11th and 25th Day of June, 1784," *New York Genealogical and Biographical Record*, 34(1903): 259-261.

(39) Savary, A. W. "Muster Roll of Disbanded Officers, Discharged Soldiers and Loyalists Mustered at Digby, the 19th Day of May, 1784," *New York Genealogical and Biographical Record*, 34(1903):118-123, 192-197.

(40) Savary, A. W. "Muster Roll of the Disbanded Officers, Discharged Soldiers and Loyalists, Taken at Gulliver's Hole, S. Mary's Bay and Sissiboo, 1st and 6th Day of June, 1784." *New York Genealogical and Biographical Record*, 34(1903):261-263.

(41) Siebert, William H., A.M. *The Loyalist Refugees of New Hampshire*, offprint, *The Ohio State University Bulletin*, 21(1916):2:1-23.

(42) Smith, Clifford Neal, "Deserters, Dischargees, and Prisoners of War from the British Tenth Regiment of Foot (North Lincolnshire) during the American Revolution," *National Genealogical Society Quarterly*, 71:114-

120. (Cites Public Record Office, Kew, Surrey, WO-12 Vol. 2750:152.)

(43) Smith, T. Watson. "Loyalist History: John Grant," *Acadiensis*, 1(1901):1:7-18.

(44) Steinemann, Ernst, Dr., ed., "A List of Eighteenth-Century Emigrants from the Canton of Schaffhausen to the American Colonies 1734-1752," *Pennsylvania German Folklore Society Yearbook*, 16(1951):187-196.

(45) Turner, Thomas, "Immigrants from Liverpool to Nova Scotia 1864" (from *Nova Scotia House of Assembly 1865*, Sessional Paper #24, pp. 1-6, Halifax, Immigration Agents Report 25 Feb. 1865), *Lost in Canada?*, 15(1990):4:181-182. (EUROCLYDON.)

(46) Vernon, C. W., "The Deed of a Slave Sold at Windsor, N.S., in 1779,: *Acadiensis*, 3(1903):4:253-254.

(47) "Vital Records of Liverpool, N.S.," *The New England Historical and Genealogical Register*, 126(1972):94-101, 160-169, 281-291; 127(1973):49-57, 117-126, 201-213, 267-280; 128(1974):28-37, 113-118.

(48) Ward, C., "Old-Time Obituaries," *Acadiensis*, 8(1908):4:304-305.

(49) Warman, Charles, transcr, "Epitaphs," *Acadiensis*, 4(1904:2:120-128.

(50) White, Elizabeth Pearson, "Nova Scotia Settlers from Chatham, Mass.," *National Genealogical Society Quarterly*, 62(1974):96-117.

(51) Whyte, Donald, "Scottish Emigrants to New York and Pictou," *Family History* (London: Institute of Heraldic and Genealogical Studies), New Series, 9:51. (COMMERCE)

Nova Scotia
Immigrants

to

1867

Part 2 – From Published Diaries and Journals

Compiled by
Col. Leonard H. Smith Jr.
(A.U.S. Retired)
M.A. (Genealogy), Certified Genealogist

and
Norma H. Smith

Abbott, Abiel. Land grant at Liverpool (55:282).

Abel, Obediah. ?Land grant at Liverpool (55:281).

Adkins, John. Land grant at Liverpool
(55:282).

Adkins, Thomas. Land grant at Liverpool (55:282).

Albree, Obediah. Liverpool proprietor
(56:361).

Allen, Elizabeth. Wife of William; to
Falmouth with husband (56:102).

Allen, Eunice. Wife of Jeremiah; dau.
of ----- Gardner; to Yarmouth with
husband (56:57).

Allen, Jeremiah. Manchester, Mass.,
to Yarmouth 1766 (56:87).

Allen, Jeremiah. S. of Jeremiah/
Eunice (Gardner) of Manchester,
Mass.; b. 6 Apr. 1749; to Yarmouth
1766 (56:57).

Allen, Jeremiah. To Yarmouth 1766
(56:57).

Allen, Jethro. Land grant at Liverpool (55:282).

Allen, Jonas. Land grant at Liverpool
(55:282).

Allen, William. Boston, Mass. to
Shelburne; to Liverpool 1799
(58:62).

Allen, William. Newport, R.I., to
Falmouth ca. 1760 (56:102).

Alline, Henry. S. William/Elizabeth
Allen; b. Newport, R.I., 12 June
1748; to Falmouth with parents ca.
1760 (56:102).

Alline. See Allen.

Annand, William. B. Glasgow, Scotland, 1759; d. Halifax 1820 (58:
324).

Annis, James. S. Thomas/Lydia (Dean)

of Barnstable, Mass.; b. ?1762; to
Liverpool ca. 1785 (56:488).

Ansley, Thomas. Rev.; b. New York
1769; to N.B.; settled at Bridge-
town; d. 1831 (54:184).

Archer, William Gates. S. of John; b.
Cherryfield, Me.; marr. Mary
Mulhall; d. 1861 Pleasant Lake
(59:194).

Arenburg, John Henry. Germany to Halifax 1750 (56:17).

Arenburg, Johann Frederick. Brunsbach
to Halifax 1750 on ANN (58:289)

Arnold, Benjamin. Liverpool proprietor (56:21).

Ashley, Thomas. Land grant at Liverpool (55:282).

Ashley, William. Land grant at Liverpool (55:282).

Ashly, Josiah Jr. Land grant at
Liverpool (55:282).

Atwood, John. Land grant at Liverpool
(55:281).

Atwood, Joshua. Barrington grantee
(58:93).

Atwood, Joshua. Land grant at Barrington (56:16).

Austin, John. Land grant at Liverpool
(55:282).

Mary Mulhall; d. Pleasant Lake 1861
(59:194).

Bain, Alexander. B. Scotland ca.
1754; to Yarmouth 1762; parents
and sister lost at sea enroute
(56:501).

Balets, Nathaniel. ?Land grant at
Liverpool (55:281).

Bamford, Stephen. B. near Nottingham,
England, 1770; to Halifax with
regiment 1802; d. Digby 1848 (59:
181).

Bangs, Joseph. S. Joseph/Thankful
(Hamlin); b. Harwich, Mass., 22
Apr. 1743; admitted Liverpool
proprietor before 2 Dec. 1770
(56:8).

Bangs, Mary. Wife of Joseph; dau. of
Thomas/Mary Pitts; to Liverpool
with husband (56:8).

Barclay, Thomas. Maj.; Loyalist; to
Annapolis (56:419).

Barker, Joseph. Land grant at Liverpool (55:282).

Barnard, Benjamin. S. of Thomas/Mary
(Woodbridge) of Mass.; bap. 1753;
to Yarmouth 1770 (56:114).

Barnard, John. Brother of Benjamin;
to Yarmouth with him (56:114).

Barnes, Seth. Plymouth, Mass., to
Yarmouth before 19 Oct 1775 (56:
114).

Barnes, Seth. S. of Seth/Sarah
(Wooden); Plymouth, Mass., to
Yarmouth 1762 (56:27).

Barns, Seth. Land grant at Liverpool
(55:281).

Barrow, Seth. Land grant at Liverpool
(55:282).

Barrow, Thomas. Land grant at Liverpool (55:282).

Barry, Robert. Loyalist; to Shelburne
(58:339).

Barry, Robert. S. of John; Portsmouth, England, to America pre-
Revolutionary War; to Shelburne
1784 (56:282).

Barss, Benjamin. S. of Benjamin/Sarah
(Cobb) of Barnstable, Mass.; b. 26
Mar. 1710; at Liverpool June 1780
(56:22).

Barss, Jonathan. S. of Benjamin/Jean
(Collins) of Chatham, Mass.;
Liverpool proprietor (56:20).

Barss, Joseph. Capt.; s. of Joseph/
Lydia (Dean); b. 14 Apr. 1754;
Barnstable, Mass., to Liverpool

with mother (56:30).

Barss, Lydia. ?Widow Joseph; dau. of
----- Dean; Barnstable, Mass, to
Liverpool (56:30).

Barss, Ruth. Wife of Jonathan; dau.
of ----- Eldridge of Chatham,
Mass. (56:20).

Bartlet, Benjamin Jr. Land grant at
Liverpool (55:282).

Bartlet, Benjamin. Land grant at
Liverpool (55:281).

Bartlett, Joseph. Liverpool proprietor (56:265).

Bassett, Bachariah. Land grant at
Liverpool (55:282).

Battle, Samuel. B. Plymouth, Mass.;
original proprietor Liverpool;
returned to Plymouth ca. 1767
(56:242).

Baxter, William. Dr.; s. of Capt.
Simon/Prudence (Fox); b. N.H.,
1760; Norton, N.B., to Cornwallis
1782 (58:456).

Bearse. See Barss.

Belfour, Andrew. Scot; set ashore at
Port Joli autumn 1785 (56:312).

Bell, Hugh. S. of Samuel/Ann (Cross);
b. Enniskillen, Ireland, 12 Jan.
1780; marr. Halifax 5 Dec, 1808
Elizabeth Lain (59:226).

Bennet, William. Rev.; b. England,
1770; Manchester, England to
Halifax on SPARROW, 6 Oct. 1800
(58:257).

Berbanks, Timothy Jr. Land grant at
Liverpool (55:282).

Binney, Jonathan. Boston, Mass., to
Halifax 1753 (55:116).

Binney, Jonathan. S. of Thomas/Marga-
ret (Miller); b. Hull, Mass., 7
June 1725; marr. (1) 28 Jan. 1746
Martha Hall; d. Halifax 8 Oct.
1807 (58:363).

Bishop, Samuel. Lisbon, Conn., to
Liverpool by Oct. 1800 (58:256).

Black, John. B. Aberdeen, Scotland;
St. John, [N.B.], to Halifax 1808
(59:155).

Black, William. B. Huddersfield, West
Yorkshire, England, 1760; to N.S.
with parents 1775 (56:188).

Blackden, Ann. B. London, England;
marr. 11 Oct. 1759 Jonathan Prescott; d. Halifax Feb, 1810
(56:437).

Blackwood, Robert. B. Kinross-shire,
Scotland 1786; to N.S. by 1816
(54:187).

Blaney, Stephen. Marblehead, Mass.,
to Yarmouth 25 Apr. 1775 (56:114).

Blowers, Sampson Salter. B. Boston,
Mass., 1743; New York to Halifax
1783 (56:288).

Boggs, Thomas. S. of James/Mary
(Morris); b. Shrewsbury, N.J. 22
May 1771; marr. Halifax 5 Sept.
1800 Sarah DeBlois (59:288).

Bold, John. S. of Thomas/Ann (Howell)
of London, England; at Liverpool
by Jan. 1787 (56:351).

Boomer, Job. S. (twin) of Joshua/
Rebecca (Elsbree); b. Freetown,
Mass., 25 July 1765; to N.S. as
young man (56:115).

Boomer, Joshua. Freetown, Mass., to
Liverpool with granddaughter
Rebecca Macumber (59:110).

Boomer, Joshua. Of Freetown, Mass.;
to Liverpool by Nov. 1786 (56:
343).

Boomer, Joshua. Of Freetown, Mass.;
to Liverpool (56:372).

Boomer, Joshua. S. Caleb/Sarah
(Martin); b. Freetown, Mass., to
N.S. by 1785 (56:115).

Boomer, Joshua. S. (twin) of Joshua/
Rebecca (Elsbree); b. Freetown,
Mass., 25 July 1765; to N.S. as
young man (56:115).

Bourn, Thomas. Land grant at Liver-

pool (55:281).

Boyle, George. Ireland to Liverpool
ca. 1794 (53:122).

Bradford, Barlett. S. of Peleg/Lydia;
b. Kingston, Mass., 14 Apr. 1751;
to Liverpool by 1781 (56:6).

Bradford, Josiah. Land grant at
Liverpool (55:282).

Briggs, George. Liverpool proprietor
(56:65).

Briggs, George. New England to Liverpool, proprietor (56:141).

Briggs, Silus. Land grant at Liverpool (55:282).

Brimhall, Joshua. Land grant at
Liverpool (55:282).

Brown, Andrew. Dr.; Scot; Presbyte-
rian clergyman; Halifax 1787;
Scotland 1795 (56:454).

Brown, Joseph. Rev.; from Cheshire,
England, to Barrington by Mar.
1784 (56:223).

Brown, Nathaniel. Loyalist; Charlestown, Mass., to Grand Pré 1781
(52:42).

Brown, Thomas. Liverpool proprietor
(56:52).

Bruce, James. Member of Council of
West Florida; to Halifax June 1785
(58:228).

Bryant, Timothy. Head of family
(alone) at Liverpool 1787 census
(56:74).

Brymer, Alexander. B. Dundee, Scotland, 1729; Glasgow to Halifax
1759; to London, England 1801
D07:175).

Buchanan, William. From Scotland; at
Liverpool 21 Aug. 1784 (56:242).

Burbank, Betty. Wife of Timothy; to
N.S. with husband (56:1)

Burbank, Elizabeth. Dau. Timothy/
Betty; to N.S. with parents; marr.
Liverpool 26 Nov. 1779 (56:1).

Burbank, Lydia. Wife (2) of Timothy

Burbank; dau. of Elisha/Lydia
(Freeman) Freeman; b. 1730; at
Liverpool Aug. 1798 (58:116).

Burbank, Timothy. Liverpool proprietor (58:116).

Burbank, Timothy. Plymouth, Mass., to
Liverpool (56:1)

Burbank, Timothy. S. of Timothy/Mercy
(Kempton); b. Plymouth, Mass., 9
Feb. 1732; Liverpool proprietor
(56:45).

Burbidge, John. Halifax founder 1749;
d. 1812 ae 95 (59:376).

Burbridge, John. Col.; b. 1717; a
founder of Halifax 1749 (58:30).

Burden, Noah. Land grant at Liverpool
(55:282).

Burden, William. Land grant at Liverpool (55:282).

Burge, Zacheus. Land grant at Liverpool (55:282).

Burnaby, Joseph. S. of Joseph/Lydia;
b. Provincetown, Mass. 14 July
1736; Liverpool proprietor (56:4).

Burnaby, Mercy. Wife of Joseph; dau.
of John/Sarah Gibbs; to N.S. with
husband (56:4).

Burton, John. Rev.; England to Halifax 1792 (54:177).

Buttler, John. Land grant at Liverpool (55:282).

- C -

Caldwell, Jane. Wife of William; dau.
of ----- Jordan; to N.S. with husband (56:29).

Caldwell, William. B. 1736; Stoughton, Mass., to N.S. (56:29).

Cameron, John. Officer in King's
Orange Rangers; b. Fort William,
Scotland; to Liverpool Dec. 1778
(56:10).

Cannon, Jeremiah. Irish; Newfoundland
to Liverpool 1796 (58:1).

Carroll, John. From Ireland; desired
to marry 4 May 1772 at Liverpool
(55:45).

Cheever, Esther. Wife of Rev. Israel;
dau. of ----- Torrey; to Liverpool
with husband (56:8).

Cheever, Israel. Rev.; Mass. to
Liverpool 1761 (56:8).

Cheever, Israel. Rev.; s. of Daniel/
Ruth; Dartmouth, Mass., to Liverpool 1761 (56:11).

Cheever, Israel. S. of Daniel/Ruth
(Meade); b. Concord, Mass., 22
Sep. 1722; to Liverpool 1761 (59:
7).

Chandler, William. Lancaster, England
to N.S. on a warship 1812; settled
at Beach Meadows (59:261).

Cheever, William. S. of Rev. Israel/
Esther (Torrey); b. Dartmouth,
Mass., 18 Oct. 1752; to Liverpool
with parents 1761 (56:8).

Chipman, Handley. R.I. to Horton 1760
(53:111).

Chipman, John. S. of Handley/Jean
(Allen); b. Newport, R.I. 18 Dec.
1744; to Cornwallis by 1778 (58:
184).

Chipman, Thomas Handley. Rev.; b.
R.I. 17 Jan. 1756; to Cornwallis
with parents (56:192).

Chipman, Thomas Handley. S. of Handley; b. R.I., 1756; to N.S. 1760
(53:111).

Chisholm, Angus. B. Scotland; marr.
Liverpool 1 May 1770 Mary Dolliv-
er; drowned 12 Apr. 1779 Port
Medway (56:119).

Chisholm, Angus. B. Scotland; to
Liverpool bef. 18 Oct. 1776
(58:120).

Christie, Angus. Tarleton's Legion;
land grant at Port Mouton bef.
1787 (58:50).

Christie, John. Tarleton's Legion;

land grant at Port Mouton 1784 (56:244).

Christopher, Thomas. S. of William/ Susanna; b. England; at Liverpool by May 1780 (56:17).

Church, Susanna. Wife of Peter; dau. of ----- Tucker; to Falmouth with husband (59:5).

Church, William. Little Compton, R.I.; to Falmouth (59:5).

Churchel, Benj. Land grant at Liverpool (55:281).

Churchel, Jonathan. Land grant at Liverpool (55:282).

Churchel, Zacheus. Land grant at Liverpool (55:282).

Churchill, Josiah. Plymouth, Mass., to Ragged Islands (now Lockeport) by Oct. 1786 (56:340).

Clattenberger, Peter. Darmstadt, [Germany,] to Halifax 1751 on GALE (58:471).

Clements, John. Marblehead, Mass., to Clements' Island, near Yarmouth 1769 (56:108).

Cleveland, Benjamin. Deacon; b. 1733; Windham, Conn., to Horton (53:114).

Cobb, Jabez. Capt.; s. of Elisha/ Lydia (Ryder); Plymouth, Mass., to Liverpool (56:158).

Cobb, Jabez. Land grant at Liverpool (55:281).

Cobb, Jabez. Liverpool proprietor (56:6).

Cobb, Sarah. Wife of Jabez; dau. of ----- Bartlett; to N.S. with husband (56:6).

Cobb, Silvanus. Land grant at Liverpool (55:282).

Cobb, Sylvanus. Capt.; to N.S. after 1749; Liverpool proprietor (56:6).

Cobb, Sylvanus. S. of Jabez/Sarah (Bartlett); b. Plymouth, Mass., 2 Apr. 1754; to N.S. with parents

(56:6).

Cochran, James. S. of Joseph; b. Northern Ireland; to N.S. with father 1761 (58:185).

Cochran, James. S. of Joseph; Ireland to Halifax 1761 (56:1).

Cochran, Joseph. Ireland to Halifax 1761 (56:1).

Cochran, Joseph. Ireland to N.S. 1761 (58:36).

Cochran, Joseph. Northern Ireland to N.S. 1761 (58:185).

Cochran, Thomas. S. of Joseph; Ireland to Halifax 1761 (56:1).

Cochran, William. S. of Joseph; b. Ireland, 1751; to N.S. with father 1761 (58:36).

Cochran, William. S. of Joseph; Ireland to Halifax 1761 (56:1).

Coffee, Barbara. Said to have been slave of Samuel Bartlett at Plymouth, Mass., in 1734; Liverpool proprietor; ?returned to U.S. (56:20).

Coffin, Isaac. B. Boston, Mass., 1759; England to Halifax 16 Oct. 1799 on VENUS (58:212).

Coffin, John. B. 1727; Nantucket to Barrington by July 1789 (56:484).

Coffin, Peter. S. of John/Mary (Davis); b. Nantucket, Mass., 1758; to Barrington bef Apr. 1800 (58:224).

Cohoon, William Jr. S. of William/ Elizabeth (Gallup); b. New England, 20 Sept. 1752; to Port Medway (56:161).

Cohoon, William. S. of William/Sarah, of Chatham, Mass.; b. 23 June 1724; Liverpool proprietor (56:126).

Cole, Benjamin. S. of Benjamin/Desire (Smith); b. Truro, N.E. [Mass.], 15 Sept. 1751; to Liverpool (56:46).

Cole, Benjamin. S. of Israel/Emory;
Liverpool proprietor (56:25).

Cole, Desire. Wife of Benjamin; dau.
of Ebenezer/Desire (Smith) of
Truro, Mass.; to Liverpool with
husband (56:25).

Coll, Benjamin. Land grant at Liverpool (55:282).

Collins, Abigail. Wife of Joseph;
dau. of ----- (Crowell); to Liverpool with husband (56:88).

Collins, Abigail. Wife of Joseph;
dau. ----- Crowell; to N.S. with
husband (56:11).

Collins, Benajah. S. of Joseph/Abi-
gail (Crowell); b. Chatham, Mass.,
29 Oct. 1743; to N.S. with parents
(56:11).

Collins, George. S. of Benajah/Susan-
na (Tracy); b. East Haddam, Conn.,
17 Jan. 1771; at Liverpool Dec.
1789 (56:513).

Collins, Hallet. Plus fam.; b. 1749;
Chatham, Mass., to Liverpool (53:
122).

Collins, Hallet. S. of Joseph/Abigail
[Crowell]; b. Chatham, Mass.,
1749; to Liverpool with parents
ca. 1759 (56:15).

Collins, Joseph Jr. Liverpool proprietor (56:68).

Collins, Joseph. From ?Chatham,
Mass.; to Liverpool (56:88).

Collins, Joseph. From Chatham, Mass.;
a founder of Liverpool (56:11).

Collins, Peter. S. of Joseph/Abigail
(Crowell) of Chatham, Mass.; to
Liverpool with parents; d. 31 July
1788 ae 32nd (56:33).

Collins, Stephen. S. of Joseph/Abi-
gail (Crowell); b. Chatham, Mass.,
31 Oct. 1745; to Liverpool with
parents (56:88).

Connel, Patrick. S. of Morris/Cather-
ine of Lismore, County Waterford,

Ireland; marr. Liverpool 13 Oct.
1796 Mary Peach (58:422).

Cook, Ephraim. To Yarmouth 1762 (56:
71).

Cook, Silvanus. Land grant at Liverpool (55:282).

Copeland, Abraham. Liverpool proprietor (56:434).

Corning, Ebenezer. Beverly, Mass., to
Yarmouth 1764 (56:108).

Corning, Jonathan. S. of David/Pris-
cilla; Beverly, Mass., to Yarmouth
1764 (56:108).

Cotman, Christopher. B. England; to
Liverpool before May 1805 (59:
112).

Cotnam, Christopher. B. England; to
Liverpool; to Ragged Islands by
1787 (56:75).

Coulter, Andrew. Cornet, British
Legion; at Port Mouton 1787 (56:
223).

Coulter, Andrew. Settler at Port
Mouton by July 1787 (56:378).

Courtney, Thomas. Land grant at Shelburne 1784 (56:218).

Craig, John. Rev.; b. Dublin, Ireland, ca. 1750; to N.S. ca. 1784
(58:415).

Craig, John. Rev.; b. Ireland 1759;
to America; to Horton after Revolutionary War (53:123).

Crane, Andrew. B. Ireland, ca. 1764;
marr. Port Medway 22 Dec. 1796
Elizabeth Mack wid. George
Mitchell (58:186).

Crane, John. S. of John/Jane of
Maryland; Liverpool proprietor
(56:249).

Creamer, Michael. B. Ireland; to
Liverpool 1796 (58:25).

Creighton, John. Col.; b. Glaston-
bury, England, 1721; to Halifax
1749 (56:144).

Crosby, Simon. Land grant at Liver-

pool (55:281).

Crosley, Joseph. Land grant at Liverpool (55:282).

Crowell, Archelaus. S. of Judah/Tabitha (Nickerson); b. 20 Aug. 1747; at Port Roseway 1778 (56:22).

Crowell, Jonathan. S. of Jonathan (Liverpool proprietor)/Anne (Collins); b. Chatham, Mass., 6 Apr. 1757; to Liverpool (56:74).

Crowell, Jonathan. S. of Jonathan/Anne (Collins) of Chatham, Mass.; b. 1745; marr. Rochester, Mass., 1772 Joanna Whitmore (58:118).

Crowell, Judah. "Crow Town" (now West Dennis), Mass.; to Barrington (56:22).

Crowell, Tabitha. Wife of Judah; dau. ----- Nickerson; to N.S. with husband (56:22).

Crowell, Thomas Jr. Barrington grantee (56:156).

Crowell, Thomas. S. of Joseph (a N.J. Loyalist who went to N.B.); b. ?New Jersey ca. 1765; d. Shelburne 16 Feb. 1845 (59:75).

Curtis, Zacheus. Land grant at Liverpool (55:282).

- D -

Darling, Jonathan. Land grant at Liverpool (55:282).

Darrow, Edmund. Conn. to Liverpool; drowned 24 Nov. 1784 (56:191).

Darrow, Ichabod. S. of Jonathan/Avis of Stratford and New London, Conn.; early settler at Liverpool (56:272).

Daugherty, Hugh. Loyalist; at Shelburne 1784 (52:41).

Davis, Nicholas. Land grant at Liverpool (55:282).

Day, John. Perhaps of King's Orange

Rangers; at Liverpool by Nov. 1782 (56:167).

Dean, Ephraim. S. of Thomas/Lydia (Cole); b. Barnstable, Mass., 17 Oct. 1734; early settler at Liverpool (56:5).

Dean, Martha. Wife of Ephraim; dau. of ----- Atwood; widow ----- of Young; to N.S. with husband (56:5).

DeBlois, George. B. England 1739; to Boston, Mass., 1761; Salem, Mass., to Halifax 1775 (56:234).

Delong, Simon. Loyalist; land grant at Wilmot 1784 (59:342).

Devereux, William. Land grant at Liverpool (55:282).

DeWolf, Elisha. S. of Nathan/Lydia (Kirtland); b. Saybrook, Conn., 5 May 1756; marr. Horton 1 Sept. 1779 Margaret Ratchford (59:210).

DeWolf, Loran. B. 1754; Saybrook, Conn., to N.S. (53:118).

Dexter, Benjamin. B. Rochester, Mass., 23 Mar. 1758; d. Liverpool 18/19 Apr. 1781 (56:69).

Dexter, Ebenezer. S. Benjamin/Hannah (Barrow); b. Rochester, Mass., 6 Aug. 1728; Liverpool proprietor (56:69).

Dexter, Enoch. S. Benjamin/Hannah (Barrow); b. Rochester, Mass., 6 Mar. 1727; Liverpool proprietor (56:32).

Dexter, Isaac. S. Jonathan/Hannah (Vincent); b. Dartmouth, N.E. [Mass.], 15 Oct. 1751; to Port Roseway ca. 1766 (56:56).

Dexter, Jesse. S. Peleg; b. Rochester, N.E. [Mass.], 18 May 1750; to Liverpool (56:48).

Dexter, Joseph. Land grant at Liverpool (55:282).

Dexter, Joseph. Liverpool proprietor (56:373).

Dexter, Peleg. Land grant at Liverpool (55:282).

Dexter, Peleg. S. of Benjamin/Hannah (Barrow); b. Rochester, Mass., 16 Apr. 1722; to Liverpool ca. 1760 (56:44).

Dimock, Daniel. S. of Shubael; b. Mansfield, Conn., 1736; to Falmouth 1759 (54:7-8).

Dimock, Eunice. Wife of Rev. Shubael; dau. of ----- Marsh; to Newport with husband (59:163).

Dimock, Shubael. B. Mansfield, Conn. 1708; to Falmouth 1759 (54:7-8).

Dimock, Shubael. Rev.; Marshfield, Conn. [sic], to Newport (59:163).

Dimock, Shubael. S. of Rev. Shubael/ Eunice (Marsh); b. Marshfield, Conn., [sic] ca. 1753; to Newport with parents (59:163).

Dimon, Jonathan. Land grant at Liverpool (55:281).

Doane, Eleazer. Mansfield, Conn., to Falmouth 1760 (56:80).

Doane, Hannah. Wife of Eleazer; dau. of ----- Mayo; to N.S. with husband (56:80).

Doane, Jesse. Land grant at Liverpool (55:282).

Doane, Nathan. S. of Eleazer/Hannah (Mayo); b. Mansfield, Conn., 6 Apr. 1751; to N.S. with parents (56:80).

Doane, Thomas. S. of Thomas/Sarah (Barnes) of Chatham, Mass., to Barrington 1764 (56:308).

Doggett, Abigail. Wife of John; dau. of ----- House; to N.S. with husband (56:23).

Doggett, Abner. S. of John/Abigail (House); b. Plymouth, Mass., 16 Aug. 1749; to Liverpool with parents (56:26).

Doggett, Catherine. Dau. of Capt. Samuel/Deborah (Foster); b. Ply-

mouth, Mass., 8 Aug. 1758; at Liverpool June 1787 (56:375).

Doggett, Deborah. Dau. Samuel/Deborah; b. Plymouth, Mass., 8 Aug. 1758; marr. Liverpool by June 1782 ----- Draper (56:140).

Doggett, Ebenezer. Brother of Samuel; to Liverpool by 1760 (56:120).

Doggett, Ebenezer. Land grant at Liverpool (55:282).

Doggett, John. Brother of Samuel; to Liverpool by 1760 (56:120).

Doggett, John. Land grant at Liverpool (55:281).

Doggett, John. Plymouth, Mass., to Liverpool 1754 (56:23).

Doggett, John. S. of John/Abigail (House); b. Plymouth, Mass., 13 Sept. 1759 (sic); to N.S. with parents 1754 [sic] (56:23).

Doggett, John. S. of John/Abigail (House); b. New England, 13 Sept. 1754; marr. Liverpool 1 May 1781 Dorcas Cole (59:168).

Doggett, Samuel. Land grant at Liverpool (55:281).

Doggett, Samuel. S. of Ebenezer/ Elizabeth (Rickard); b. Plymouth, Mass., 20 Jan. 1729; to Liverpool by 1760 (56:120).

Dolliver, Elisha. S. of John/Thankful; b. Maine; to Liverpool with parents (56:91).

Dolliver, John. Gloucester, Mass., and Falmouth, Me.; Liverpool proprietor (56:91).

Dolliver, John. S. of John/Eliza (Wood) of Gloucester, Mass., and Falmouth, Me.; Liverpool proprietor (56:11).

Dolliver, Robert. S. of William/Sarah of Penobscot [Me.]; marr. Liverpool 1 Jan. 1776 Sarah Luin (56:282).

Dolliver, Samuel. Liverpool proprie-

tor (56:3).

Dolliver, Samuel. S. of Samuel/Mary;
Liverpool grantee (58:66).

Dolliver, Thankful. Wife of John; to
Liverpool,with husband (56:91).

Doran, Patrick. From Waterford,
Ireland; b. 6 Nov. 1757; to ?New
Dublin; d. 17 Nov. 1818 (56:163).

Doten, Edward. S. Elisha; b. Plymouth, Mass., 7 Oct. 1716; to
Liverpool 1760 (56:118).

Doten, Phoebe. Wife of Edward; dau.
John/Sarah (Bartlett) Phinney;
Plymouth to Liverpool 1760
(56:118).

Dotey, Edward. Of Plymouth, Mass.;
Liverpool grantee; returned to
Plymouth during Revolutionary War
(56:66).

Dotey, Edward. S. Edward/Phoebe
(Phinney); born Plymouth, Mass.;
to Liverpool with parents (56:66).

Dotey, Elisha. S. Edward/Phoebe
(Phinney); born Plymouth, Mass.;
to Liverpool with parents (56:66).

Dotey, John. S. Edward/Phoebe (Phinney); born Plymouth, Mass.; to
Liverpool with parents (56:66).

Dotey, Lemuel. S. Edward/Phoebe
(Phinney); born Plymouth, Mass.;
to Liverpool with parents (56:66).

Dotey, Phoebe. Wife of Edward, daugh-
ter of John/Sarah (Bartlett)
Phinney; Plymouth, Mass., to
Liverpool with husband (56:66).

Dotey, Thomas. S. Edward/Phoebe
(Phinney); born Plymouth, Mass.;
to Liverpool with parents (56:66).

Doty. See Doten.

Dove, Lemuel. Land grant at Liverpool
(55:282).

Draper, Deborah. Wife of Thomas; dau.
of Samuel/Deborah (Foster) Doggett; b. Plymouth, Mass., 8 Aug.
1758; at Liverpool Nov. 1799

(58:198).

Drew, Lemuel. B. Plymouth, Mass., 18
Jan. 1725; Kingston, Mass., to
Liverpool 1761 (56:248).

Drew, Lemuel. S. Lemuel/Hannah
(Barnes); Kingston, Mass., to
Liverpool 1761 (56:118).

Drew, Seth. S. Lemuel/Hannah
(Barnes); Kingston, Mass., to
Liverpool 1761 (56:118).

Duncan, Henry. Hon.; b. Dundee,
Scotland, 1751; to Halifax by 1788
(58:47).

Dunham, Nathaniel. Land grant at
Liverpool (55:281).

Dunton, John. Land grant at Liverpool
(55:282).

- E -

Eldridge, Elisha. Mansfield, Conn.,
to Yarmouth, grantee (56:123).

Eldridge, Elishama. S. Elisha/Pris-
cilla (Hall); b. Mansfield, Conn.,
9 Sept. 1752; to Yarmouth with
father (56:123).

Eldridge, Zepheniah. Of Chatham,
Mass.; Liverpool proprietor;
returned to U.S. 1783 (56:199).

Ellenwood, Benjamin. Beverly, Mass.,
to Yarmouth 1764 (56:122).

Ellenwood, Benjamin. Beverly, Mass.,
to Yarmouth 1764 (56:13).

Ellenwood, Nathaniel. S. Benjamin/
Susanna (Corning); b. 23 Sep.
1754; to N.S. with parents (56:
13).

Ellenwood, Nathaniel. S. Benjamin/
Susanna (Corning); b. Beverly,
Mass., 23 Sept. 1754; to Yarmouth
with parents 1764 (56:122).

Ellenwood, Susanna. Wife of Benjamin;
dau. ----- Corning; to N.S. with
husband (56:13).

Ellenwood, Susanna. Wife of Benjamin;

dau. ----- Corning; to Yarmouth
with husband (56:122).

Ellis, Ebenezer. Land grant at Liverpool (55:282).

Ernst, Heinrich. Wurttemberg to N.S.
1752 (59:223).

- F -

Falkner, Francis. Land grant at
Liverpool (55:282).

Falt, Joseph. Dr.; surgeon in German
Auxiliary Forces in America;
settled at Petite Riviere (56:
431).

Falt, Joseph. Dr.; German Auxiliary
Forces during Revolutionary War;
to N.S. of (59:375).

Ferguson, Henry. Early Halifax settler (56:125).

Field, Benjamin. Negro; worked for
Simeon Perkins 1787 (58:11).

Fiendel, George Jacob. Deuxponts
[Zweibrucken], Germany, to N.S.,
1752 (56:17).

Fiendel, George Michael. S. of George
Jacob; to N.S. with father (56:
17).

Finley, Francis. Soldier, King's
Orange Rangers; at Liverpool July
1780 (56:30).

Firmage, William. Rev.; England to
N.S. 1783; d. Halifax 28 June 1793
ae 39 (56:198).

Fletcher, Daniel. Land grant at
Liverpool (55:282).

Fletcher, David. Land grant at Liverpool (55:282).

Flint, Thomas. Marblehead, Mass., to
Cape Forchu 1771 (56:124).

Foot, Zachariah. Salem or Beverly,
Mass., to Yarmouth 1769 (56:109).

Foote, Zachariah. Capt.; Beverly,
Mass., to Yarmouth 1769 (56:149).

Forbes, William. Disbanded soldier;

s. of John/Christie; b. Ross-
shire, Scotland; to Shelburne 1783
(58:207).

Ford, Hannah. Dau. of Capt. Theodo-
sius/Hannah (Burbank); widow of
Perez Tinkham; b. Plymouth, N.E.
[Mass.], 17 July 1759; marr. (2)
Liverpool 21 Dec. 1780 Capt. John
Howard (56:60).

Ford, Hannah. Wife of Theodosius;
dau. of ----- Burbank; b. Plymouth, Mass.; to N.S. with husband
(56:12).

Ford, Theodore. Land grant at Liverpool (55:282).

Ford, Theodosius. B. Hanover, New
England; Liverpool proprietor
(56:12).

Ford, Theodosius. B. Hanover, Mass.,
13 Jan. 1735; d. Liverpool 20 Feb.
1777 (56:225).

Foreman, James. B. Coldstream, Ber-
wick-on-Tweed, England, 21 Dec.
1763; to Halifax 1789 (58:186).

Forsyth, William. Rev.; from Sotland;
at Cornwallis ca. 1811 (52:iii).

Foster, Edward. Plymouth, Mass., to
Liverpool (56:151).

Foster, Mary. Wife of Edward; dau.
of ----- Pease; to Liverpool with
husband (56:151).

Foster, Nathaniel. Land grant at
Liverpool (55:281).

Foster, Robert. B. 22 Apr. 1737; to
N.S. of 1775; returned to Kingston
1791 (56:199).

Foster, Thomas Jr. Land grant at
Liverpool (55:281).

Foster, Thomas. S. of John/Hannah
(Stevenson); b. Plymouth, Mass.,
1705; land grant Liverpool 1759
(56:265).

Fowler, Benjamin. King's Orange
Rangers; d. Liverpool May 1784
(56:157).

Fowler, Benjamin. King's Orange Rangers; at Liverpool by Nov. 1782 (56:167).

Francklin, Michael. Lieut. Gov.; b. Devonshire, England, 1720; to N.S. 1752 (56:177).

Fraser, James. B. Farraline, Inverness-shire, Scotland, 1759; to N.S. 1780 (58:128).

Freeman, Barnabas. Land grant at Liverpool (55:282).

Freeman, Barnabas. S. of Elisha/Lydia; b. Rochester, Mass., 21 Jan. 1738; Liverpool proprietor (56:40).

Freeman, Benjam. Land grant at Liverpool (55:282).

Freeman, Benjamin. S. of Samuel/Mary (Doane); b. Bristol, Me., 13 Apr. 1759; to Liverpool with father (56:81).

Freeman, Elisha Jr. Land grant at Liverpool (55:282).

Freeman, Elisha Jr. S. of Elisha; b. Rochester, Mass., 1735; Liverpool proprietor (56:65).

Freeman, Elisha. B. Eastham, Mass. 1701; d. Liverpool 19 May 1777 (56:65).

Freeman, Elisha. B. 1701; from Rochester, Mass.; Queens County pioneer; d. 19 May 1777 (56:176)

Freeman, Elisha. Land grant at Liverpool (55:281).

Freeman, Elisha. Rochester, Mass., to Liverpool ca. 1760 (56:7).

Freeman, Hezekiah. S. of Samuel/Margaret (Smith); b. New England; to Liverpool ca. 1760; to Norwich, Conn., about time of Revolutionary War (56:275).

Freeman, Joseph. S. of Samuel/Margaret (Smith); b. Harwich, Mass., 5 Nov. 1745; Liverpool proprietor (56:12).

Freeman, Josiah. S. of Samuel/Mary (Doane); b. Harwich, Mass., 20 Feb. 1754; marr. Liverpool by July 1781 Mary Young widow John Cobb (56:85).

Freeman, Lathrop. Lieut.; S. of Elisha/Lydia; b. Rochester, Mass.; to Liverpool (56:25).

Freeman, Lydia. Wife of Elisha; to N.S. with husband (56:7).

Freeman, Lydia. Wife of Elisha; dau. of Nathaniel/Mary (Howland) Freeman; b. Eastham, Mass., 1703. (56:176).

Freeman, Margaret. Wife of Samuel; dau. of ----- Smith; to N.S. with husband (56:12).

Freeman, Nathaniel. S. of Elisha/Lydia; Liverpool proprietor (56:7).

Freeman, Patience. Wife of Simeon; dau. of ----- Wood; to Liverpool with husband (56:159).

Freeman, Peleg. S. of Simeon/Patience (Wood); b. Rochester, N.E. [Mass.], 20 Feb. 1758; to Liverpool with father (56:46).

Freeman, Phoebe. Dau. of Elisha/Lydia; b. Rochester, Mass.; marr. Liverpool 25 Mar. 1762 Capt. John West (56:15).

Freeman, Samuel. B. New England, 8 Aug. 1715; to Liverpool ca. 1760, proprietor (56:152).

Freeman, Samuel. From ?Harwich, Mass., to Liverpool 1760 (56:12).

Freeman, Samuel. Liverpool proprietor (56:81).

Freeman, Simeon. From Rochester, Mass.; Liverpool grantee (56:46).

Freeman, Simeon. Liverpool proprietor (56:159).

Freeman, Simon. Land grant at Liverpool (55:282).

Freeman, William. S. of William/

Hannah (Atwood); b. Harwich,
Mass., 22 Mar. 1741; Liverpool
pioneer (56:16).

Frimage, William. B. England; occu-
pied pulpit of "Old Zion" Church
at Liverpool 1783-4; d. Halifax
(54:192).

Fullington, James. Land grant at
Liverpool (55:282).

- G -

Gallond, John. Land grant at Liverpool (55:282).

Gardner, Sarah. Wife of Thomas; dau.
of ----- Wilcox; to Liverpool with
husband (56:90).

Gardner, Sarah. Wife of Thomas; dau.
of ----- Wilcox; to Liverpool with
husband (56:122).

Gardner, Simeon. S. Jonathan/Patience
(Bunker); b. Nantucket, [Mass.,]
1728; perhaps first settler at
Cape Island, Barrington (56:73).

Gardner, Simeon. S. of Jonathan/
Patience (Bunker); b. Nantucket,
[Mass.], 17 Sept. 1728; to Cape
Island near Barrington 1762 (56:
111).

Gardner, Simeon. S. of Jonathan/
Patience (Bunker); b. Nantucket,
Mass., 17 Sept. 1728; Barrington
proprietor (59:208).

Gardner, Thomas. Liverpool grantee
(56:90).

Gardner, Thomas. Liverpool proprietor
(56:122).

Gates, Jonas. S. of Oldham/probably
Mehitabel (Trowbridge); b. Spencer, Mass., 1746; d. N.S. ca. 1823
(58:196).

Gerrish, Benj. B. Boston, Mass. 1717;
to Halifax by 1752 (56:2).

Gerrish, Benjamin. S. Capt. John/
Sarah (Hobbs); b. Boston, Mass.,

19 Oct. 1717; Liverpool proprietor
(59:111).

Gerrish, John. Liverpool proprietor
(59:111).

Gilmore, George. Rev.; Loyalist; to
Grand Pré (52:iii).

Godfree, Joseph. Land grant at Liverpool (55:282).

Godfrey, Alexander. S. Josiah/Eunice;
b. Chatham, Mass.; marr. Liverpool
4 Jan. 1791 Phoebe West; d. Jamaica 1803 (56:279).

Godfrey, Azubah. Wife of Richard;
dau. of Solomon/Eunice (Collins);
to N.S. with husband (56:70).

Godfrey, Benjamin. Chatham, Mass., to
Liverpool, proprietor; returned to
Chatham ca. 1790 (56:4).

Godfrey, Benjamin. Liverpool proprietor (56:128).

Godfrey, Bethiah. Wife of Benjamin;
dau. of Joseph/Deborah (Sears) Atwood; to N.S. with husband (56:4).

Godfrey, John. Early Liverpool settler (56:103).

Godfrey, Lucy. Dau. Benjamin/Bethiah;
b. Chatham, Mass., 1 Jan. 1763; to
Liverpool with father (56:128).

Godfrey, Richard. Liverpool proprietor (56:70).

Godfrey, Ruth. Dau. Joseph; marr.
Liverpool 29 Nov. 1764 Sylvanus
Cobb (56:6).

Godfrey, Warren. S. Richard/Azubah
(Collins); b. Chatham, Mass.; to
N.S. with parents (56:70).

Gogen, Frederick. B. France; to
Halifax 1750; hired by Simeon
Perkins at Liverpool 10 Nov. 1774
(55:85).

Goodering, John. Land grant at Liverpool (55:282).

Goodwin, Henry. Berwick, Me., to
Argyle; land grant 1785 (56:28).

Goodwin, Henry. Berwick, Me., to

Argyle ca. 1771 (56:96).

Goodwin, Nathan. Berwick, Me., to
Argyle ca. 1771 (56:96).

Gorham, Abigail. Wife of David; dau.
of ----- Jackson; to Liverpool
with husband (56:361).

Gorham, David. S. of Jabez/Molly of
Barnstable, Mass.; plus 2 ch.;
Plymouth, Mass., to Liverpool,
proprietor (56:361).

Gorham, Jabez. B. probably at Conn.
ca. 1724; Plymouth, Mass., to
Liverpool ca. 1761 (56:8).

Gorham, Jabez. Land grant at Liverpool (55:282).

Gorham, Jabez. Plymouth, N.E.
[Mass.], to Liverpool before
Revolutionary War (58:491).

Gorham, Jabez. S. of Jabez/Mary
(Burbank); b. Plymouth, N.E.
[Mass.], 14 May 1757; to Liverpool
with parents; to U.S. at time of
Revolutionary War (58::491).

Gorham, James. S. of Jabez/Mary (Burbank); b. Plymouth, Mass., 7 Sept.
1760; to Liverpool with parents
(56:55).

Gorham, Mary. Wife of Jabez; dau. of
Timothy/Mary (Kempton) Burbank; to
N.S. with husband (56:8).

Gorham, Mary. Wife of Jabez; dau. of
----- Burbank; Plymouth, N.E.
[Mass.], to Liverpool with husband
(58:491).

Gould, Thomas. Land grant at Liverpool (55:282).

Gracie, George. Loyalist; b. Scotland; Boston, Mass., to Shelburne
(58:130).

Grandine, Daniel. Loyalist; land
grant at Shelburne 1784 (56:207).

Grandine, William. Rev.; Loyalist;
land grant at Shelburne 1784
(56:207).

Grassie, George. B. Aberdeen, Sco-

tland, ca. 1763; marr. Halifax 21
Mar. 1793 Mary Eliza Shatford
Lawson (59:70).

Gray, Joseph. Esq.; b. Boston, Mass.,
19 July 1729; marr. Halifax 1759
Mary Gerrish (56:9).

Green, James. Loyalist; settled at
Chester (53:113).

- H -

Hadley, Joseph. Liverpool proprietor
(56:3).

Haftham, George, Land grant at Liverpool (55:282).

Hall, Abner. B. 1726; Mansfield,
Conn., to Falmouth (53:114).

Halliburton, Brenton. S. of Dr. John/
Susannah (Brenton); b. Newport,
R.I., 3 Dec. 1775; admitted to
N.S. Bar 1803 (59:330).

Hamilton, Thomas. Land grant at
Liverpool (55:282).

Hammett, George. Tarleton's Legion;
s. of John F., of Culpeper Co.,
Va.; discharged at Port Mouton
1783 (58:227).

Hammond, Elisha. Land grant at Liverpool (55:282).

Hammond, Jedediah. Land grant at
Liverpool (55:282).

Hammond, Rowland. Land grant at
Liverpool (55:282).

Hamond, Benjamin. Land grant at
Liverpool (55:282).

Hargraves, William. Land grant on
Shelburne-Liverpool road 1787
(58:98).

Harley, John. Dr.; b. London, England; to Boston, Mass.; to Lunenburg d. 12 Oct. 1846 (59:222).

Harlow, Bradford. S. of Josiah/Olive
(Hunt); probably b. New England;
to Liverpool with parents (58:42).

Harlow, Jean. Wife of Robert; dau. of

----- West; b. Plymouth, Mass.; to
Liverpool with husband (56:29).

Harlow, Jean. Wife of Robert; dau. of
----- West; to Liverpool with husband (56:72).

Harlow, Josiah. Plymouth, Mass., to
Liverpool ca. 1785 (59:7).

Harlow, Josiah. S. of Samuel/Mary;
?Mass. to Liverpool (56:39).

Harlow, Josiah. Wareham, Mass., to
Liverpool before 1789 (58:42).

Harlow, Mary/Polly. Dau. of
Josiah/Olive (Hunt); b. Plymouth,
Mass.; to Liverpool with parents;
d. (as Mrs. John Locke) Locke's
Island, Shelburne Co. 1855 ae. 74
(59:7).

Harlow, Olive. Wife of Josiah; dau.
of Daniel/Mary (Hunt) of Wareham,
N.E. [Mass.]; to Liverpool
(56:39).

Harlow, Olive. Wife of Josiah; dau.
of ----- Hunt; to Liverpool with
husband (58:42).

Harlow, Olive. Wife of Josiah; dau.
of ----- Hunt; to Liverpool with
husband (59:7).

Harlow, Robert. B. Plymouth, Mass.;
Liverpool proprietor (56:29).

Harlow, Robert. Liverpool proprietor;
from Plymouth, Mass. (56:72).

Harrington, Benjamin. No. Kingston,
R.I., to New Dublin before 1764
(56:122).

Harrington, Ebenezer. R. I. to New
Dublin ca. 1765 (56:13).

Harrington, Ebenezer. To New Dublin
(56:153).

Harrington, Ebenezer. S. of Ebenezer/
Rebecca (Spencer); b. R.I., 11
Apr. 1752; to New Dublin with
parents (56:155).

Harrington, Rebecca. Wife of Ebenezer; dau. of ----- Spencer; to N.S.
with husband (56:13).

Harrington, Rebecca. Wife of Ebenezer; dau. of ----- Spencer; to New
Dublin with husband (56:155).

Harrington, Thomas. S. of Ebenezer/
Rebecca (Spencer); b. R.I., 4 Apr.
1744 (56:13).

Hatch, David. Land grant at Liverpool
(55:282).

Hawkins, Michael H. Liverpool proprietor (56:52).

Hayes, Michael. Tarleton's Legion;
land grant at Port Mouton 1784;
executed 10 July 1786 (56:245).

Headley, Joseph. Liverpool proprietor
(56:33).

Heater, John. S. of John/Susannah,
"of Plymouth and Poole, Great
Britain;" marr. Argyle 29 Apr.
1784 Dorcas Nickerson (56:91).

Hemneon, Philip. Loyalist [sic]; b.
New York, 1788; at Liverpool Mar.
1803 (58:451).

Hewitt, Archelaus. Wells, Me., to
Lockeport (59:212).

Hewitt, John. S. of Archelaus; bap.
Wells, Me., 7 Mar. 1736; to Lockeport (59:212).

Hill, Charles. B. 1747; early Halifax
settler (59:330).

Hinkley, Aaron. Land grant at Liverpool (55:282).

Hoar, John. Land grant at Liverpool
(55:282).

Hoar, Timothy. Land grant at Liverpool (55:282).

Hobbs, Lemuel. Early settler at
Abuptic, Yarmouth Co. (56:132).

Holmes, Benjamin Mulberry. Loyalist;
s. of George/Ann (Mulberry); b.
Boston, Mass., 24 Apr. 1738; to
Halifax 1776 (56:23).

Holmes, Benjamin. B. Plymouth, Mass.;
early settler at Liverpool (56:3).

Holmes, Benjamin. B. Plymouth, Mass.;
Liverpool proprietor (56:80).

Holmes, Rebecca. Wife of Benjamin; to
N.S. with husband (56:80).

Holms, Experiance. Land grant at
Liverpool (55:282).

Holms, James. Land grant at Liverpool
(55:282).

Holms, Jeremy. Land grant at Liverpool (55:282).

Homer, John. S. of Benjamin/Elizabeth
(Crowell); b. Yarmouth, Mass., 28
Sept. 1724; to Barrington (56:57).

Hopkins, Elisha. Barrington grantee
(56:111).

Hopkins, Elisha. Liverpool pioneer
(56:160).

Hopkins, John Jr. B. Chatham, Mass.,
5 Sept. 1750; to Liverpool ca.
1760 (56:9).

Hopkins, John. Eastham and Dartmouth,
Mass., to Liverpool, grantee (56:
5).

Hopkins, John. Land grant at Liverpool (55:282).

Hopkins, John. S. of Elisha/Experi-
ence (Scudder) of Chatham, Mass.;
b. 29 Apr. 1719; to Liverpool ca.
1760 (56:15).

Hopkins, Rebecca. Wife of John; dau.
of ----- Nickerson; to N.S. with
husband (56:5).

Hopkins, Sarah. Wife of Elisha; dau.
----- of Dolliver; to Liverpool
with husband (56:160).

Horton, Levi. Conn. to N.S. 1763
(56:149).

Horton, Nathaniel. Land grant at
Liverpool (55:282).

Hovendon, John. Settler at Port
Mouton by July 1787 (56:378).

Howard, John. Capt., King's Orange
Rangers; to Liverpool Dec. 1778
(56:18).

Hoyt, Jesse. Loyalist; Stamford/
Norwalk, Conn., to Annapolis (58:
352).

Hoyt, Jesse. S. of Jesse/Mary (Redmond); b. 25 Oct. 1767; to Annapolis with parents (58:352).

Hoyt, Mary. Wife of Jesse; dau. of
----- Redmond; to Annapolis with
husband (58:352).

Hunt, Ephraim. S. of Samuel/Lois
(Mayhew); b. Martha's Vineyard,
[Mass.], 28 Sep. 1756; to Liver-
pool with parents (56:114).

Hunt, Lois. Wife of Samuel; dau. of
----- Mayhew; to Liverpool with
husband (56:114).

Hunt, Samuel. Liverpool proprietor
(59:85).

Hunt, Samuel. Martha's Vineyard,
[Mass.,] to Liverpool, proprietor
(56:114).

Hunt, Samuel. S. of William/Jane
(Tilton); Liverpool proprietor;
?from Martha's Vineyard, Mass.
(56:10).

Hunt, Simon. Land grant at Liverpool
(55:282).

Hurd, Jacob. Early Halifax settler
(56:5).

Huston, Robert. Loyalist; to Shelburne (58:23).

Huston, Robert. Loyalist; settled at
Shelburne (59:80).

Hutchinson, Foster. S. of Foster/
Sarah (Mascarene); b. Boston,
Mass., 1761; to Halifax with
father 1776 (58:169).

Hutchinson, Foster. Boston, Mass., to
Halifax 1776 (58:169).

- J -

Jabez, Samuel. Land grant at Liverpool (55:282).

Jackson, James. Of Boston, Mass.;
bought house at Liverpool 1764
(56:270).

James, Edward. B. Southampton, Eng-

land. 1757; served on H.M.S.
DUNKIRK, H.M.S. RESOLUTION, H.M.S.
CENTAUR, H.M.S. ROEBUCK, also
King's Orange Rangers; to Lunen-
burg by Sept. 1780 (56:43).

Janes, Daniel. Loyalist; to Shelburne
(58:113).

Jeans. See Janes.

Jessen, Detlieb Christopher. b. Hol-
stein, Germany, 25 Feb. 1730; to
Halifax 1752 (56:69).

Johnstone, William. B. North Britain
ca. 1713 d. Liverpool 2 Apr. 1800
(56:38).

Joice. See Joyce.

Jones, Henry. Loyalist; land grant at
Guysborough Co. 1785 (56:429).

Jones, Samuel. Land grant at Liverpool (55:282).

Jordan, Edward. From Co. Carlow, Ireland; hanged at Halifax ca. 1809
(59:180).

Joyce, Isaac. S. Seth/Rachael, of
Marshfield, Vt.; Liverpool proprietor (56:124).

- K -

Kelley, James. Manchester, Mass., to
Yarmouth 1765 (56:101).

Kempton, Richard. Liverpool proprietor (56:63).

Kempton, Richard. S. of Thomas/Mary
(Holmes); b. Plymouth, Mass., 28
Oct. 1739; to Cornwallis 1761 (56:
254).

Kendrick, Solomon. S. of Solomon/
Elizabeth (Atkins); from Harwich,
Mass.; Barrington grantee (58:3).

Kenney, Elisha. Land grant at Liverpool (55:282).

Kenney, Heman. Barrington grantee
(56:111).

Kenney, Heman. Cape Cod magistrate;
land grant at Barrington (56:33).

Kenney, Thomas. Land grant at Liverpool (55:282).

Kenny, Elisha. B. Mass.; Liverpool
proprietor (56:503).

Kenny, Elisha. Liverpool proprietor
(56:46).

Kenny, Elisha. Liverpool proprietor
(59:144).

Kenny, Samuel. S. of Elisha/Jane; b.
Sheepscote, N.E. [Sheepscot, Me.],
2 Mar. 1750; to Liverpool with
father (56:46).

Kenny, Samuel. S. of Elisha/Jean/
Jane; b. Shipscut, New England
[Sheepscot, Me.], 22 Mar. 1750; at
Liverpool Mar. 1811 (59:291).

Kimball, Richard. Land grant at
Liverpool (55:282).

Kinton, John. Land grant at Liverpool
(55:281).

Knowlan, James. Probably b. Ireland,
1779; took up residence at Halifax
1834 (59:376).

Knowles, Cornelius. Chatham, Mass; to
Liverpool; proprietor (56:1).

Knowles, Cornelius. S. of Richard/
Martha (Cobb); b. Chatham, Mass.,
10 Apr. 1722; Liverpool proprietor
(56:87).

Knowles, James. Mariner; s. of Corne-
lius/Mary (Hopkins); b. Chatham,
Mass. ca. 1756; marr. Liverpool 26
Nov. 1779 (56:1).

Knowles, Nathaniel. S. of Enos/Sarah
(Sparrow) of Eastham, Mass.;
Liverpool proprietor (56:24).

Knowles, Nathaniel. Chatham, Mass.;
Liverpool proprietor (56:156).

- L -

Lagord, John. Dr.; French; to Liverpool Aug. 1772 (55:47).

Landers, Sealed. Land grant at Liverpool (55:282).

Lavender, Robert. Loyalist; S.C. to Shelburne (59:6).

Lavender, Robert. S. of Robert/Susanna; probably b. S.C.; to Shelburne with parents (59:6).

Lavender, Susanna. Wife of Robert; to Shelburne with husband (59:6).

Law, Stephen. Land grant at Liverpool (55:282).

Leigh, Benjamin. Land grant at Liverpool (55:282).

Leslie, James. Loyalist; settled at Shelburne (59:310).

Leslie, Jasper. Tarleton's Legion; land grant at Port Mouton 1784 (56:478).

Leslie, Jasper. Tarleton's Legion; grant at Port Mouton 1784 (59:222).

Lewin, John. Liverpool proprietor; 1st tavern-keeper (56:37).

Lewin, John. New London, Conn., first tavern-keeper at Liverpool (56:3).

Lewis, John. B. 1765; Eastham, Mass., to Barrington 1786; to Me. ca. 1812 (53:122).

Lewis, Sarah. Wife of Waitstill; dau. of ----- Bliven; to N.S. with husband (56:27).

Lewis, Waitstill Jr. R.I. to Halifax to Yarmouth (56:108).

Lewis, Waitstill Sr. R.I. to Halifax to Liverpool 1775; to Mass. 1776 (56:108).

Lewis, Waitstill. R.I. to Halifax; to Liverpool; ?later returned to Mass. (56:27).

Lewis, Waitstill. S. of Waitstill/Sarah (Bliven); to N.S. with parents (56:27).

Lewyn, John. See Luin, John.

Limau, John. King's Loyal Rangers; d. Liverpool Apr. 1783 (56:181).

Lock, Daniel. Land grant at Liverpool (55:282).

Locke, John. Mrs. See Mary/Polly Harlow.

Locke, Jonathan. B. R.I.; Liverpool proprietor (56:70).

Lovett, Phineas. S. of Phineas; b. Mass., 1745; to N.S. with family ca. 1760 (59:78).

Luin, John. Liverpool proprietor; first tavern-keeper (56:71).

- M -

Macey, Peter. Nantucket whaleman; to Dartmouth 1786; to Milford Haven, Wales ca. 1792 (56:477).

Mack, Samuel. From East Haddam, Conn.; bought property at Liverpool 1765 (56:22).

Macumber, Rebecca. B. ca. 1787; Freetown, Mass., to Liverpool with grandfather, Joshua Boomer (59:110).

Magee, John. Land grant at Liverpool (55:282).

Mahew, Hilyard. Land grant at Liverpool (55:282).

Mahew, Jeremiah Jr. Land grant at Liverpool (55:282).

Mahew, Jeremiah. Land grant at Liverpool (55:282).

Mahew, Nathan. Land grant at Liverpool (55:282).

Mahew, Seth. Land grant at Liverpool (55:282).

Mann, John. Rev.; brother of Rev. James; b. N.Y., 1743; to Shelburne end of Revolutionary War (58:220).

Manning, Edward. B. Ireland 1767; to Wolfville (53:115).

Manning, James. B. Ireland 1763; to Wolfville (53:115).

Manning, Nancy. Wife of Peter; dau. of ----- Carroll; at Falmouth 1770 (59:5).

Manning, Peter. At Falmouth 1770

(59:5).

Manning, Peter. B. Ireland; at Falmouth 1770 (58:110).

Manning, Walter Carroll. S. of Peter/
Nancy (Carroll); b. probably Phil-
adelphia, [Pa.], 15 Feb. 1802; to
Liverpool by July 1798 (58:110).

Manning, Walter Carroll. S. of Peter/
Nancy (Carroll); b. probably at
Philadelphia, [Pa.], 1769-1770; at
Falmouth 1770 (59:5).

Marsden, Joshua. Rev.; Methodist; b.
Warrington, England, 1777; to
Halifax 1800; to Bermuda 1808
(58:391).

Martin, Brotherton. Land grant at
Horton (53:121).

Mathewes, John. Land grant at Liverpool (55:282).

Mathews, John Jr. Land grant at
Liverpool (55:282).

Matthews, John. Liverpool proprietor
(56:110).

McAdam, George. From Philadelphia;
marr. Liverpool 4 Jan. 1787 Hannah
Slocomb (56:510).

McAlpine, John. Loyalist; s. of
Peter/Christian of Scotland;
settled at Shelburne; later to
Liverpool; marr. there 29 Jan.
1784 Rebecca Gannon widow of David
Barss (56:207).

McClearn. See McLearn.

McDonald, Alexander. 42nd Highland-
ers; discharged 1786; settled at
Sandy Bay (58:40).

McDonald, James. Liverpool proprietor
(56:7).

McEwen, James. Loyalist from Boston;
to Liverpool (56:198).

McGill, Andrew. Scot; business in
Halifax; admitted to North British
Society 1780; to Scotland 1790
(56:16).

McGowan, Michael. B. Ireland; marr.

Liverpool 4 May 1781 Mary Dolliver
widow Angus Chisholm (56:119).

McGray, John. Capt.; Marblehead,
Mass., to Yarmouth 1774 (56:38).

McKay, Donald. Loyalist; settled at
Shelburne (56:415).

McKay, John. Loyalist; settled at
Shelburne (56:415).

McKinnon, Ronald. B. Skye, [Scot-
land]; land grant at Argyle 1766
(58:62).

McLannan, James. New York State to
Liverpool by May 1801; d. Pleasant
River 1857 ae 95 (58:307).

McLearn, Isabella. Wife of James; to
N.S. with husband (56:10).

McLearn, James. Scots-Irish; to N.S.
?1760s (56:10).

McLearn, Robert. S. of James/Isabella
b. 14 June 1755; to N.S. with
parents (56:10).

McLearn. See McLarn.

McLeod, Alice. Wife of John; dau. of
----- Harrington; b. R.I.; to N.S.
with husband (56:409).

McLeod, Donald. Lieut., King's Orange
Rangers; s. of Angus/Margaret of
Harris, Western Hebrides; to
Liverpool Dec. 1778 (56:15).

McLeod, John. B. Ireland; had s.
Ebenezer born 1767 Liverpool
(56:409).

McLeod, John. B. Newton, Londonderry
Co., Northern Ireland 1744; land
grant at New Dublin (56:122).

McMaster, Patrick. Boston, Mass., to
Halifax 1776 (58:76).

McPherson, Donald. Capt., British
Legion; settled at Port Mouton
(56:207).

McPherson, Donald. Capt., Tarleton's
Legion; to Port Mouton 1783
(59:110).

Merrick, John. B. England, ca. 1756;
opened painting business Halifax

1789 (58:270).

Mickam, Samuel. B. London, England;
Pa. to Liverpool before 25 May
1787 (56:313).

Miles, John. S. of John/Martha of
Norwich, England; marr. Liverpool
4 June 1786 Thankful Freeman
(56:317).

Millard, Robert. S. of Thomas/Ruth;
R.I. to N.S.; d. 6 Nov. 1808 ae 68
(56:57).

Miller, David. S. of David/Catherine;
b. Philadelphia, [Pa.]; to Liverpool by 11 Aug. 1798 (58:114).

Miller, Garret. Loyalist; b. ?1770;
New York to Halifax (58:31).

Minns, William. Land grant at Shelburne 1784 (56:213).

Mitchell, Jacob. Boston, Mass., to
Halifax 1786 (56:368).

Mitchell, William. Liverpool proprietor (59:250).

Mollison, Robert. Col.; wagonmaster-
general for British Forces at
N.Y.; settled at Port Mouton (56:
211).

Money, Richard. Rev.; England to
Lunenburg 1787; d. 1800 (54:197).

Monk, George Henry. S. of James/Ann
(Dering); b. Norwalk, Conn., 17
Aug. 1748; Member Legislative
Assembly for Hants County 1792
(59:238).

Montagu, Charles Greville. Lord;
Maj.; s. of 3rd Duke of Manchester; b. 29 May 1721; disbanded; to Manchester 1783 (56:217).

Moody, Somersby. Land grant at Liverpool (55:282).

Moore. See More.

Morant. From England; negro preacher
sent out by Lady Huntingdon; at
Birchtown 1786 (56:365).

More, Alexander. Of Rothiemurchus,
Scotland; Clyde River and Liver-

pool by June 1789 (56:479).

More, Janet. Wife of Alexander; to
N.S. with husband (56:479).

Morrill, Levi. Land grant at Liverpool (55:282).

Morris, Alexander. S. of Hon. Char-
les/Mary (Read); b. Hopkinton,
Mass., 21 Mar. 1744; d. Halifax
Jan. 1785 (56:207).

Morris, Charles. Oldest s. of Char-
les/Mary (Read); b. probably at
Boston, Mass. ca. 1732; Hopkinton,
Mass., to Halifax ca. 1761 (56:
45).

Morris, Charles. S. of Charles/Eliza-
beth (Band); b. Hopkinton, Mass.,
18 Nov. 1759; Member Legislative
Assembly for Halifax County 1797
(59:342).

Morris, William. S. of Hon. Charles/
Mary (Read); b. Hopkinton, Mass.,
19 Feb. 1737; at Liverpool Oct.
1783 (56:204).

Morterstock, William. King's Orange
Rangers; head of family at Liverpool 1787 (56:134).

Morton, Elkanah Jr. Land grant at
Liverpool (55:282).

Morton, Joseph. Mass. to Wilmot by
1778 (53:111).

Morton, Mary. Wife of Sylvanus; dau.
of ----- Stephens; to Liverpool
with husband (56:99).

Morton, Sylvanus. Liverpool pioneer
(56:253).

Morton, Sylvanus. S. of Thomas/Abi-
gail (Pratt); b. Plymouth, Mass.,
24 Feb. 1730; to Liverpool ca.
1760 (56:99).

Morton, Sylvanus. S. of Sylvanus/Mary
(Stephens); b. Plymouth, Mass., 5
July 1760; to Liverpool with
parents (56:253).

Mose, David. Land grant at Liverpool
(55:282).

Moser, Anna Maria. Wife of Jacob; b. Switzerland; to Halifax with husband (58:346).

Moser, Jacob. B. Switzerland; to Halifax 1751 on SPEEDWELL (58: 346).

Mullins, John. Liverpool grantee (56:19).

Mulloy, Charles. British Legion; land grant at Port Mouton 1784 (56: 218).

Murdoch, James. Rev.; from Donegal to Grand Pré ca. 1766 (52:ii).

Murray, Joanna. Wife of William; dau. of ----- Tupper; to Liverpool with husband (56:170).

Murray, William. B. Bridgewater, Mass.; Liverpool proprietor (56: 40).

Murray, William. Liverpool proprietor (56:170).

- N -

Neil, Henry. S. of John/Alice of County Kilkenny, Ireland; marr. Lunenburg 2 Nov. 1802 Mary Park (59:54).

Nelson, John. Land grant at Liverpool (55:281).

Nesbitt, William. To Halifax 1749 (56:125).

Nevers, Jabez. Land grant at Liverpool (55:282).

Newell, Henry. S. of Henry/Elizabeth (Grouard) of Boston, Mass.; marr. Barrington 1776 Eunice Smith (56: 73).

Nicholl, Duncan. Loyalist; to Shelburne County (58:339).

Nicholl, Duncan. Loyalist; to Shelburne County (59:91).

Nickerson, Abner. S. of John/Dorcas (Bassett); a first settler at Woods Harbour (56:51).

Nickerson, Daniel. S. of Elisha/ Desire; b. Chatham, Mass., 2 Mar. 1736; to Liverpool ca. 1764; to Litchfield, Me., 1792 (56:27).

Nickerson, Eldad. Barrington grantee (56:83).

Nickerson, Eldad. Eastham, Mass., to Barrington (56:32).

Nickerson, Elisha. S. of John/Mary; Liverpool proprietor; to Argyle, then to U.S. (56:71).

Nickerson, Jeremiah. Harwich, Mass., to Liverpool, proprietor (56:5).

Nickerson, Jesse. S. of Eldad/Mary (Cohoon); b. Chatham, N.E. [Mass.], 1759; to Barrington with father (56:49).

Nickerson, John. S. of John/Dorcas (Bassett); a first settler at Woods Harbour (56:51).

Nickerson, Joshua. Barrington grantee (56:111).

Nickerson, Mary. Wife of Eldad; dau. ----- of Cohoon; to N.S. with husband (56:32).

Nickerson, Mary. Wife of Eldad; dau. of ----- Cohoon; to Barrington with husband (56:83).

Nickerson, Prince. S. of Thomas/Lydia (Covel); b. Chatham, Mass., 10 Aug. 1729; land grant at Barrington (56:22).

Nickerson, Rebecca. Wife of Jeremish; dau. of ----- Hurd; to N.S. with husband (56:5).

Nickerson, Stephen. Barrington grantee (56:111).

Nickleson, Thomas. Eldest s. of John Jeffery, M.P. for Poole, England; b. 1782; to Halifax 1803 (58:387).

Nutter, Valentine. Land grant at Tusket River 1786 (56:288).

Nye, Malatiah. Land grant at Liverpool (55:282).

- O -

O'Brian, Dennis. King's Orange Rangers; at Liverpool June 1783
(56:190).
O'Neal, William. Escaped negro slave
from S.C.; at Shelburne by 8 Oct.
1784; to Liverpool (56:423).
O'Neal, William. Escaped negro slave;
from S.C.; to Liverpool by Dec.
1801 (58:350).
Oliphant. See Olivant.
Olivant, Thomas. Rev.; to Halifax 6
Oct. 1800 on SPARROW; d. 1846 N.B.
(58:258).
Osborn, Samuel. Rev.; Eastham, Mass.
to Barrington 1776 (56:57).

- P -

Panton, George. Rev.; b. America; to
Shelburne 1784; ?returned to U.S.
by 1788 (56:230).
Parker, Benjamin. B. Yarmouth, Mass.;
to Liverpool early (56:6).
Parker, Benjamin. Chatham, Mass., to
Liverpool by July 1776 (58:42).
Parker, Benjamin. New England to
Liverpool 1760 (56:26).
Parker, Mary. Wife of Benjamin; dau.
of ----- Snow; b. Chatham, Mass.;
to N.S. with husband (56:3).
Parker, Mary. Wife of Benjamin; dau.
of ----- Snow; Chatham, Mass., to
Liverpool with husband (58:42).
Parker, Nathaniel. Maj.; b. 1743;
soldier at Quebec 1759; settled in
Annapolis Co. (53:120).
Parker, Nathaniel. S. of William; b.
Dorchester, Mass., 1743; settled
at Annapolis County (58:85).
Parks, James. B. Ireland; settled at
Petite Riviere 1769 (56:46).
Patten, Joseph. Land grant at Liver-
pool (55:281).

Patterson, Thomas. Liverpool proprie-
tor (56:501).
Pattillo, Alexander. B. ?1743; Aber-
deen, Scotland, to Chester 1783
(58:57).
Payzant, John. B. 17 Oct. 1749 (53:
16).
Payzant, John. S. of Louis/Marie; b.
Isle of Jersey 1749; to N.S. pre-
1756; to Quebec; to N.S. 1760
(53:1).
Payzant, Lewis. Huguenot; London,
England, to Halifax 1754 (56:298).
Peach, Jacob. Liverpool grantee
(59:213).
Peach, John. Land grant at Liverpool
(55:282).
Peach, John. Liverpool proprietor
(56:61).
Peach, John. Liverpool proprietor
(58:285).
Peach, John. Liverpool grantee (59:
213).
Pelham, Thomas. S. of Joseph/Sarah;
from Mass.; marr. Liverpool 3 Oct.
1785 Martha Bee; d. there 1 Feb.
1801 (56:236).
Perkins, Abigail. Wife of Simeon;
dau. of Ebenezer Backus; to N.S.
with husband (56:xx).
Perkins, Ebenezer. Norwich, Conn., to
Liverpool Jan. 1773 (55:48).
Perkins, Roger. B. Norwich, Conn., 8
Dec. 1760; to N.S. by June 1780
(56:24).
Perkins, Simeon. S. of Jacob/Jemima
(Leonard); b. Norwich, Conn., 24
Feb. 1735; to Liverpool May 1762
(56:xx).
Pernette, Joseph. B. Strasbourg,
Germany; to N.S. on MURDOCH 1751
(56:59).
Perry, Arthur. Land grant at Liver-
pool (55:281).
Perry, Caleb. Land grant at Liverpool

(55:282).

Perry, Moses. Capt.; Sandwich, Mass., to Cheboque 1761 (56:510).

Perry, Zachariah. Land grant at Liverpool (55:282).

Phillips, Fadey. Sgt., King's Orange Rangers; to Liverpool (56:3).

Phillips, Jonathan. S. of David/ Hannah of Newark, N.J.; b. 25 Oct. 1773; marr. Liverpool 24 Apr. 1799 Mehetabel Jones (58:110).

Phillips, Jonathan. S. of David/ Hannah of Newark, N.J.; b. 25 Oct. 1773; marr. Liverpool 24 Apr. 1799 Mehitabel Jones (58:300).

Pierson, Nicholas. England to Horton; ordained there 1778; to N.B. 1791 (53:110).

Pine, Henry. King's Orange Rangers; at Liverpool May 1782 (56:134).

Plaiseway, Robert. Liverpool proprietor by Sept. 1761; estate appraised 1780 (56:51).

Poole, Samuel Sheldon. S. of Jonathan/Mary (Sheldon); b. Reading, Mass., 25 Mar. 1751; marr. Yarmouth 19 Oct. 1775 Elizabeth Barnes (56:114).

Porter, Josiah. Lexington, Mass., to Overton, near Yarmouth 1783 (56:445).

Power, John. S. of Matthew/Elizabeth of Waterford, Ireland; marr. Liverpool 5 Dec. 1802 Susanna Collins (Mrs. J. R. Taylor) (58:447).

Prescott, Jonathan. Dr.; b. Littleton, Mass., 1725; to Chester 1759 (53.113).

Prescott, Jonathan. S. of Jonathan/ Mary; b. Mass., 24 May 1725; land grant Halifax after 1745 (56:437).

Present, Benjamin. Land grant at Liverpool (55:282).

Present, Peter. Land grant at Liverpool (55:282).

Pride, Ira. S. of William/Margaret (Fales); b. Norwich, Conn., 1741; to Horton with parents (56:61).

Pride, Margaret. Wife of William; dau. of ----- Fales; to Horton with husband (56:61).

Pride, William. Norwich, Conn., to Horton (56:61).

Prince, Christopher. S. of Job/Abigail (Kimball); b. Mass., 1731; from Kingston, Mass., to N.S. prior to Revolutionary War (58:34).

Pringle, Robert. S. of Robert/Mary of Sunderland, England; marr. Liverpool 19 June 1789 Mary Woods (56:479).

Pryor, William. S. of Edward/Jane (Vermilye); b. New York, 3 Jan. 1775; marr. Halifax 19 Mar. 1798 Mary Barbara Voss (59:211).

Puttam, William. Land grant at Liverpool (55:282).

Pyke, Anne. Wife of John; dau. of ----- Scroope; to Halifax with husband 1749 (59:161).

Pyke, John George. S. of John/Anne (Scroope); b. England ca. 1743; to Halifax with parents 1749 (59:161).

Pyke, John. B. England; to Halifax 1749 (59:161).

- R -

Randal, Jacob. Probably a Loyalist; from Va. to Liverpool (59:3).

Randall, Jacob. Loyalist; Va. to Shelburne (58:15).

Randall, Nathan. Loyalist; b. 1763; Va. to Shelburne (58:361).

Reese, Edmund. Rev.; b. France; captured, to Halifax; to N.B. ca. 1814 (59:256).

Reese, Thomas. S. William/Mary; b.
Cardiff, Wales, ca. 1774; marr.
Liverpool 12 Feb. 1807 or 13 June
1815 Margaret Roberts (59:253).
Reichart, Thomas. Palatinate to N.S.
1751 on PEARL (58:297).
Rice, Beriah. Land grant at Annapolis
(53:114).
Rice, Jesse. Dr.; b. Marlboro, Mass.,
25 May 1751; to Yarmouth ca. 1775-
6; to Bakerstown, Me. 1795 (56:
280).
Rice, Timothy. S. of Beriah; b. 1740;
to Annapolis with father (53:114).
Richardson, George. B. Ireland;
ordained at Hammond's Plains Mar.
1822 (54:187).
Ricker, Benjamin. Kittery, Me., to
Argyle ca. 1761 (56:28).
Ricker, Nathaniel. Land grant at
Abuptic, Argyle Township, 1785
(56:8).
Rider, Benjamin. Land grant at Liver-
pool (55:282).
Rider, John. Liverpool proprietor,
probably Halifax to Liverpool 1761
(56:168).
Ring, George. Kingston, Mass., to
Yarmouth 1762 (56:134).
Ripley, Nehemiah. Land grant at
Liverpool (55:282).
Riply, Nehemiah Jr. Land grant at
Liverpool (55:282).
Robens, Joseph. Land grant at Liver-
pool (55:282).
Robens, Nathaniel. Land grant at
Liverpool (55:282).
Roberts, Robert. Liverpool proprietor
(56:11).
Robertson, Margaret. Scot; set ashore
at Port Joli autumn 1785 (56:292).
Robie, Mary. Wife of Thomas; dau. of
----- Bradtreet; to N.S. with hus-
band (58:419).
Robie, Simon Bradstreet. S. of Tho-

mas/Mary (Bradstreet); b. 1775; to
N.S. with parents (58:419).
Robie, Thomas. Loyalist; to N.S. (58:
419).
Ross, Thomas. Capt.; plus fam.; Fal-
mouth, Mass., to Liverpool 1780;
to Grand Manan 1785 (56:14).
Rude, Jacob. ?Newport, R.I., at
Hebron 1787 (59:199).
Rust, John. Land grant at Liverpool
(55:281).

- S -

Salter, Malachy. B. Boston, Mass.
1716; to Halifax (56:1).
Samson, Stephen. Land grant at Liver-
pool (55:281).
Sanford, Daniel. B. 1758; Newport,
R.I., to Cornwallis 1760 (53:110).
Sargent, John. Loyalist; b. Salem,
Mass., 24 Dec. 1749; to Barrington
(56:411).
Schmeisser, Johan Gottlieb. Rev.; b.
Saxony; to Lunenburg 1782
(54:197).
Scott, Thomas. Capt., British Legion;
at Liverpool Oct. 1783 (56:202).
Scott, Thomas. Tarleton's Legion;
land grant at Port Mouton 1784
(56:331).
Seabury, Ann. Dau. of David; to
Annapolis Co. with parents (59:
24).
Seabury, David. Loyalist; s. of
Samuel/Elizabeth (Powell); prob-
ably b. New England; plus wife; to
Annapolis Co. 1783 (59:24).
Seabury, Elizabeth. Dau. of David; to
Annapolis Co. with parents
(59:24).
Seabury, James Lyne. S. of David; to
Annapolis Co. with parents
(59:24).
Seabury, Jane. Dau. of David; to

Annapolis Co. with parents
(59:24).

Seabury, Mary, Dau. of David; to
Annapolis Co. with parents
(59:24).

Seabury, Sarah. Dau. of David; to
Annapolis Co. with parents
(59:24).

Sears, Alden. B. Cape Cod, Mass.;
Liverpool proprietor; returned to
Cape Cod about time of Revolution-
ary War (56:486).

Sears, Josiah. S. of Josiah/Azubah
(Knowles); early settler at Barrington (56:85).

Seccomb, John. Rev.; Boston, Mass.,
to Chester July 1759 (54:143).

Seccombe, John. Rev.; Boston, Mass.,
to Chester 4 Aug. 1759 (54:11).

Sewel, William. Land grant at Liverpool (55:282).

Shaw, Donald. Scot; set ashore at
Port Joli autumn 1785 (56:311).

Shean. See Shion.

Sheheon. See Shion.

Shion, Daniel. Tarleton's Legion;
land grant at Port Mouton 1784
(56:245).

Shurtlif, Abiel. Land grant at Liverpool (55:282).

Shurtlif, Nathaniel. Land grant at
Liverpool (55:282).

Simcocks, James. Born Ireland; d.
Liverpool ae 42 (58:99).

Simmons, Eleazer. B. Marshfield,
Mass., 15 Mar. 1739; Liverpool
proprietor (56:92).

Simmons, Priscilla. Wife of Eleazer;
dau. of ----- Mayo; to Liverpool
with husband (56:92).

Sinclair, Catherine. Land grant at
Port Mouton 1784 (56:374).

Slocomb, Robert. Land grant at Liverpool (55:282).

Slocomb, Robert. Liverpool proprietor

(56:168).

Slocombe. See Slocum.

Slocum, Robert. Early settler at
Liverpool (56:17).

Smith, Archelaus. Cape Cod to Barrington (56:36).

Smith, David Jr. Capt.; s. of David/
Sarah (Hamlin); b. Chatham, Mass.,
30 July 1742; to Barrington with
father (56:36).

Smith, David. Cape Cod to Barrington
1764-1767 (56:36).

Smith, Edward. Dr., Tarleton's Legion; at Liverpool Oct. 1783; land
grant at Port Mouton 1784 (56:
202).

Smith, Elizabeth. Wife of Archelaus;
dau. of ----- Nickerson; to Barrington with husband (56:36).

Smith, John. Land grant at Liverpool
(55:282).

Smith, Jonathan Eldridge. S. of
Stephen/Mehitabel (Eldridge); to
Ragged Harbour, then Liverpool by
Sept. 1787 (56:387).

Smith, Lodowick. S. of Stephen/Mehit-
able (Eldridge); b. Chatham,
Mass., 22 Aug. 1756; to Port Medway (56:93).

Smith, Mehitable. Wife of Stephen;
dau. of ----- Eldridge; to Liverpool with husband (56:148).

Smith, Stephen Jr. S. of Stephen/
Mehitabel (Eldridge); b. Chatham,
Mass., 23 May 1749; to Liverpool
with parents (56:148).

Smith, Stephen. B. 1727; from Chatham, Mass.; deacon at Liverpool
(53:118).

Smith, Stephen. Liverpool proprietor
(56:148).

Smith, Stephen. S. of Archelaus/
Elizabeth (Nickerson); b. probably
at Chatham, Mass. 1764; to Barrington with parents (56:36).

Smith, Thomas Jr. Land grant at
Liverpool (55:282).

Snow, Jabez. Land grant at Liverpool
(55:282).

Snow, Joshua. Land grant at Liverpool
(55:282).

Snow, Martha. Dau. of Cornelius/Mary
(Knowles) Parker; to N.S. with
parents (56:6).

Snow, Nathan. Barrington grantee (56:
89).

Snow, Prince. Liverpool proprietor
(56:14).

Snow, Sarah. Wife of Prince; dau. of
Stephen/Sarah (Collins) Atwood; to
N.S. with husband (56:14).

Snyder, William. Loyalist; from New
York; settled at Shelburne (59:
321).

Sommerville, William. Rev.; from
Ulster by 1833 (52:iii).

Soul, Ebenezer. Land grant at Liverpool (55:282).

Spahrwasser, See Spearwater.

Spearwater, August. Wiesbaden [Ger-
many] to N.S. bef. 1784 (58:203).

Spearwater, Peter. S. of August (also
Spahrwasser); b. Wiesbaden, [Ger-
many]; marr. Liverpool 1788 Magdalena Henrici (58:203).

Spinney, John. B. at sea enroute
England-Marblehead, Mass.; settled
at Port LaTour (56:89).

Sponagle, Ann. Wife of Philip; to
N.S. with husband (59:202).

Sponagle, Anna. Wife of Philip; to
N.S. with husband (58:282).

Sponagle, George. S. of Philip/Anna;
b. (presumably at Palatinate) 25
Dec. 1750; to N.S. with parents
1751 on MURDOCH (58:282).

Sponagle, George. S. of Philip/Ann;
to N.S. with parents (59:202).

Sponagle, Philip. From Palatinate to
Halifax 1751 (59:202).

Sponagle, Philip. Palatinate to N.S.
1751 on MURDOCH (58:282).

Sprott, John. B. Stoneykirke, Wig-
townshire, Scotland 1780; to N.S.
1818 (54:186).

Stanser, Robert. Rev.; s. of Rev.
Robert/Sarah of Harthill, Yorkshire, England; to Halifax 1791
(59:376).

Stephenson, John. Land grant at
Liverpool (55:282).

Stevenson, Robert. Liverpool proprietor (56:12).

Stewart, James. Loyalist; s. of
Anthony; b. Annapolis, Md., 1765;
to Halifax bef. 1798 (58:98).

Stewart, James. S. of Anthony; b.
Annapolis, Md., 1765; marr. Halifax 24 June 1790 Elizabeth Halliburton (59:269).

Stewart, William. Land grant at
Liverpool (55:282).

Stickels, John Frederick. Dr.; b.
Germany; to N.S. 1783 (59:181).

Stimpson, David. Land grant at Liverpool (55:282).

Strickland, John. B. England; marr.
Liverpool 25 Mar. 1774 Bethiah
West (56:65).

Strickland, John. B. England; marr.
Liverpool 28 Mar. 1774 Bertha West
(58:264).

Strickland, Matthew. S. of John/
Bertha (West); b. P.E.I., 14 Feb.
1787; at Liverpool Nov. 1800
(58:264).

Struthers, George. Rev.; from Scotland; at Cornwallis before 1833
(52:iii).

Stuart, Howes. New England to Liverpool by 1764; ?returned to N.E.
(56:26).

Stuart, John. Loyalist; settled at
Shelburne County (58:115).

Stutson, Caleb. Land grant at Liver-

pool (55:281).

Stutson, Elisha. Land grant at Liverpool (55:282).

Sutcliffe, William. Methodist mis-
sionary; plus wife, England to
Halifax Nov. 1804; returned to
England after 1811 (59:77).

Swift, Ephraim. Land grant at Liverpool (55:282).

Swift, Josiah. Land grant at Liverpool (55:282).

Swift, Moses. Land grant at Liverpool
(55:282).

Swift, Samuel. Land grant at Liverpool (55:282).

Swift, Seth. Land grant at Liverpool
(55:282).

- T -

Tapley, Gilbert. Land grant at Liverpool (55:282).

Tapley, John. Land grant at Liverpool
(55:282).

Terry, John. Land grant at Liverpool
(55:281).

Terry, Nathaniel. Land grant at
Liverpool (55:281).

Terry, Thomas Land grant at Liverpool
(55:281).

Thom, James. B. Edinburgh, Scotland,
1751; Leith, Scotland, to Halifax
by 1798 (58:128).

Thomas, Frederick. S. of John/Anne
(Mayhew); b. Plymouth, Mass., 20
Dec. 1779; at Liverpool 25 May
1803 (58:461).

Thomas, Isaac. Land grant at Liverpool (55:281).

Thomas, John. Loyalist; s. of Natha-
niel/Elizabeth (Gardner); b. Plymouth, Mass., 27 Sept. 1745; to
Liverpool 1784 (56:90).

Thomas, John. Loyalist; Plymouth,
Mass., to Liverpool 1784 (56:92).

Thomas, John. Plymouth, Mass., to
Liverpool by Aug. 1773 (55:56).

Thomas, John. Plymouth, Mass., to
Liverpool 6 Sept. 1781 (56:92).

Thomas, John. S. of John; b. Plymouth, Mass., 5 Oct. 1775; at
Liverpool Dec. 1784 (56:256).

Thomas, Mary Ann. Dau. of John/Anna
(Mayhew); b. Plymouth, Mass., 14
Jan. 1774; marr. Liverpool 28 Jan.
1791 Elisha Hopkins; d. 1857 New
York (59:352).

Thomas, Stephen. Dr.; King's Orange
Rangers; from Lancaster, England;
at Liverpool by Oct. 1782 (56:
165).

Thomas, Thomas Mayhew. S. of John/
Anna (Mayhew); b. Plymouth, Mass.,
18 May 1782; at Liverpool 23 Aug.
1798 (58:116).

Thorn, Samuel. Tarleton's Legion;
from Dutchess County, N.Y.; marr.
Liverpool 4 July 1784 Rebecca
Barss (56:236).

Tibbets, Nathaniel. Land grant at
Liverpool (55:282).

Tinkham, Ebenezer. Land grant at
Liverpool (55:282).

Tinkham, Hannah. See Ford, Hannah.

Titcomb, Joshua. Land grant at Liverpool (55:282).

Tonge, Winckworth. 45th Regt., to
Halifax 1749 (56:280).

Torey, Daniel. Liverpool proprietor
(56:21).

Towner, Enoch. Loyalist; Newbury,
Conn., to Lower Granville 1783
(54:191).

Townsend, Gregory. S. of Rev. Jon-
athan/Mary (Sugar); b. Needham,
Mass., 28 Nov. 1732; New York to
N.S. aft. 1783 (58:56).

Trask, Elias. Land grant at Liverpool
(55:281).

Trask, Joseph. Land grant at Liver-

pool (55:282).

Tribble, Joseph. From Plymouth,
Mass.; plus 3 ch.; Liverpool
settler by 1762 (56:337).

Tribble, Sarah. Wife of Joseph; dau.
of ----- Howard; to Liverpool with
husband (56:337).

Tripp, William. Liverpool proprietor
(56:265).

Tulles, John. Scottish immigrant by
1805 (59:96).

Tupper, Experience. Wife of Nathan;
dau. of ----- Gibbs; to Liverpool
with husband (56:25).

Tupper, Israel. Land grant at Liverpool (55:282).

Tupper, Medad. S. of Nathan/Experi-
ence (Gibbs); b. New England, 26
Apr. 1746; to Liverpool with
parents (56:49).

Tupper, Nathan. Land grant at Liverpool (55:282).

Tupper, Nathan. New England to Liverpool 1760 (56:25).

Tupper, Nathan. S. of Medad/Hannah;
b. 6 June 1709; Liverpool proprietor by 1760 (56:4).

Tupper, Nathan. S. of Nathan/Experi-
ence (Gibbs); b. New England 1746;
to Liverpool with parents (56:25).

- U -

Uhlman, Cornelius. From Germany;
lived at Riverport, Lunenburg
County, 1800 (58:209).

Uniacke, Richard John. Esq.; b.
Castletown Roche, County Cork,
Ireland, 22 Nov. 1753; marr. N.S.,
1775 Martha Maria Delesdernier
(56:118).

Utlet, Nathan. Capt.; Conn. to Yarmouth ca. 1770 (56:410).

- V -

VanBuskirk, Jacob. S. of Abraham/
Sophia (VanDam); b. Bergen County,
N.J., 1760-1761; land grant at
Tusket and Shelburne after Revolu-
tionary War (59:357).

VanEmburgh, Abraham. N.J. Loyalist;
to N.S. (59:117).

VanEmburgh, Adoniah. N.J. Loyalist;
to N.S. (59:117).

VanEmburgh, Gideon. N.J. Loyalist; to
N.S. (59:117).

VanEmburgh, Gilbert. N.J. Loyalist;
to N.S. (59:117).

VanEmburgh, James. N.J. Loyalist; to
N.S. (59:117).

VanHorne, Mindert. Loyalist; s. of
Robert/Patty; Newark, N.J., to
Shelburne 1784 ae 23 (58:148).

VanHorne, Patty. Wife of Richard; to
Liverpool with husband (56:506).

VanHorne, Richard. Newark, N.J., to
Liverpool by Dec. 1788 (56:506).

Verge, Joseph. Settled at Liverpool
by June 1780 (56:18).

- W -

Wall, John. Land grant at Liverpool
(55:282).

Wallace, Michael. Loyalist; b. Scotland, 1747; Va. to Halifax
(56:95).

Walsh. See Welsh.

Warden, William. Land grant at Shelburne 1784 (56:396).

Warley, Owen. King's Orange Rangers;
drowned Liverpool 24 June 1783
(56:190).

Washbourn, Ephraim. Land grant at
Liverpool (55:282).

Waterman, Elkanah. S. of John/Hannah
(Cushman) of Plymouth, Mass.;
Liverpool proprietor (56:354).

Waterman, Zenas. S. of Ichabod/Hannah

(Rogers); b. Plymouth, Mass., 29 Dec. 1762; to Liverpool 1785 (56:268).

Watson, Brook. B. England, 1735; Boston, Mass., to Chignecto 1750; to London, England, 1759 (56:262).

Webster, Andrew. S. of Andrew/Martha (Crane); b. Bangor, Me., 1778; to Liverpool via Horton; d. Liverpool 10 Aug. 1855 (58:403).

Weeks, Joshua Wingate. S. of Dr. John/Martha (Wingate); b. Hampton, N.H., 1738; to Annapolis after 1775 (58:504).

Wells, Judah. Capt.; from Colchester, Conn.; land grant at Cornwallis (53:118).

Welsh, Andrew. Tarleton's Legion; land grant at Port Mouton 1784 (56:245).

Wentworth, Benning. S. of Samuel/Elizabeth (Deering); b. Boston, Mass., 16 Mar. 1757; to Halifax by 12 Nov. 1796 (58:402).

Wentworth, Charles Mary. S. of Sir John/Frances (Wentworth Atkinson); b. Portsmouth, N.H., 20 Jan. 1775; member Council of N.S. 16 June 1801; to England 1805 (58:111).

Wentworth, John. Lieut.Gov.; b. N.H., 1737; d. Halifax 8 Apr. 1820 (56:381).

Wernssteed, John. Land grant at Liverpool (55:282).

West, Charles. S. of Silas/Mary of Plymouth, Mass.; Liverpool proprietor (56:361).

West, John. S. of Silas/Mary; b. Plymouth, Mass., 18 Nov. 1739; Liverpool grantee (56:15).

West, Sarah. Dau. of Thomas/Sarah; b. New England, 22 Sept. 1760; marr. 6 Dec. 1780 Liverpool Robert McLarn (56:58).

West, Thomas. From New England;

Liverpool proprietor (56:98).

West, William. S. of Silas/Mary; Liverpool proprietor (56:232).

Wharton, Israel. English origin; lived near Herring Cove (now Brooklyn) by Nov. 1789; d. before 1810 (56:503).

Wheaton, Caleb. S. of Caleb/Mary; marr. Boston, Mass. 6 Nov. 1792 Sally Bryant; d. Guysborough 21 June 1837 (59:228).

Wheaton, John. Lieut., Lt.Col. Timothy Hierlihy's Loyalist Regt.; N.S. Volunteers 1781; s. of Caleb/Mary; b. 1757; settled in N.S. after Revolutionary War (59:228).

Wheeler, Nathan. Land grant at Liverpool (55:282).

Wheeler, Raphael. From Maryland; marr. Liverpool 16 Nov. 1771 Abigail Morton; d. July 1780 (56:29).

Wheelock, Obediah. S. of Obediah/Martha (Sumner); b. Mendon, Mass., 7 July 1738; Capt., Annapolis County Militia 17 July 1770 (58:112).

White, Buchanan V. From Scotland; at Liverpool Sept. 1784; ?to Scotland 1785 (56:244).

White, Gideon. Capt., Montague's Regt.; b. Plymouth, Mass., 1752; to Shelburne 1784 (56:227).

White, William. Scot; at Liverpool Dec. 1786 (56:347).

Whiteman, Jonah. Land grant at Liverpool (55:282).

Whitman, Dorothy. Wife of Edward; dau. Capt. Oldham Gates; to N.S. with husband (59:158).

Whitman, Edward. Mass. to near Lawrencetown, Annapolis Co., bef. Nov. 1805 (59:155).

Whitmore, Josiah. Liverpool proprietor (56:284).

Whitmore. See Whittemore.

Whittemore, Experience. Wife of
Josiah; dau. of ----- Sargent; to
N.S. with husband (58:99).

Whittemore, Josiah. S. of
Joseph/Mehitable (Raymond); b.
Charlestown, Mass., 20 Mar. 1721;
to Liverpool 1760-1761 (56:90).

Whittemore, Josiah. Conn. to N.S.
(58:99).

Whittemore, Mary. Wife of Josiah;
probably dau. of Thomas/Sarah
(Jackson) Hatch; to Liverpool with
husband (56:90).

Whittemore, Thomas. S. of Josiah/
Experience (Sargent); b. Killins-
ley, New England [Killingly,
Conn.], 18 Apr. 1780; to N.S. with
parents (58:99).

Wiggins, Charles. Wiscasset, Me.,
marr. Liverpool Aug. 1800 Maria
McLeod (58:244).

Williams, Isaac. Loyalist; to Liverpool (56:425).

Wist, William. Land grant at Liverpool (55:282).

Wood, Samuel. King's Orange Rangers;
at Liverpool by Nov. 1782
(56:167).

Woodbury, Jonathan. S. of Jonathan;
b. Haverhill, Mass., 1737; to
Yarmouth by 1763 (58:112).

Woodbury, Malachi. S. of Malachi/
Susanna (Larcom); b. 20 Oct. 1752;
Beverly, Mass.; to Liverpool;
later returned to Beverly (56:27).

Woods, Joseph. Liverpool proprietor
(56:84).

Woodworth, Joseph. Land grant at
South Mountain near Bishopville,
1760 (52:40).

Wust, Johann Wendel. Hesse Darmstadt,
[Germany], to Halifax 1751 on
MURDOCH (59:127).

- Y -

Yewell. See Yule.

Young, Henry. Barnstable, Mass., to
Liverpool; proprietor; d. 1792 *ae*
82nd (56:58).

Young, Henry. Land grant at Liverpool
(55:282).

Young, Henry. Liverpool proprietor
(56:37).

Yule, Peter. Land grant Shelburne Co.
1786 (56:280).

APPENDIX

IMMIGRANT VESSELS

Name and Source Reference No.

ALBION, 1772 (57)
ANN, 1750 (58)
GALE. 1751 (58)
MURDOCH, 1751 (56, 58, 59)
PEARL, 1751 (58)
SPARROW, 1800 (58)
SPEEDWELL, 1751 (58)
VENUS, 1799 (58)

OTHER VESSELS

DUNKIRK (56)
RESOLUTION (56)
CENTAUR (56)
ROEBUCK (56)

BIBLIOGRAPHY

PUBLICATIONS SCREENED

(52) Woodworth, Elihu. *The Diary of Deacon Elihu Woodworth, 1835-1836*, Watson Kirkconnell, ed. (Wolfville, N.S.: Wolfville Historical Society, 1972).

(53) Payzant, John. *The Journal of the Reverend John Payzant*, Brian C. Cuthbertson, ed. (Hantsport, N.S.: Lancelot Press for Acadia Divinity College and Baptist Historical Committee, 1981).

(54) Dimock, Joseph. *The Diary and Related Writings of the Reverend Joseph Dimock (1768-1846)*, George E. Levy, D.D., ed. (Hantsport, N.S.: Lancelot Press for Acadia Divinity College and Baptist Historical Committee, 1979).

(55) Perkins, Simeon. *The Diary of Simeon Perkins, 1766-1780*, Harold Innis, ed., facsimile edition (New York: Greenwood Press, 1969; originally published as Champlain Society Publication XIII, Toronto: the society, 1848).

(56) Perkins, Simeon. *The Diary of Simeon Perkins, 1780-1789*, D. C. Harvey, ed., facsimile edition (Toronto: Champlain Society, 1969; originally published as Champlain Society Publication XXXVI, Toronto: the society, 1958).

(57) Perkins, Simeon. *The Diary of Simeon Perkins, 1790-1796*, Charles Bruce Fergusson, ed. (Toronto: Champlain Society, 1961).

(58) Perkins. Simeon. *The Diary of Simeon Perkins, 1797-1803*, Charles Bruce Fergusson, ed. (Toronto: Champlain Society, 1967).

(59) Perkins, Simeon. *The Diary of Simeon Perkins, 1804-1812*, Charles Bruce Fergusson, ed. (Toronto: Champlain Society, 1978).